MW01026246

Envy at Work and in Organizations

Envy at Work and in Organizations

Edited by

RICHARD H. SMITH

UGO MERLONE

MICHELLE K. DUFFY

OXFORD
UNIVERSITY PRESS

Oxford University Press is a department of the University of Oxford. It furthers
the University's objective of excellence in research, scholarship, and education
by publishing worldwide. Oxford is a registered trade mark of Oxford University
Press in the UK and certain other countries.

Published in the United States of America by Oxford University Press
198 Madison Avenue, New York, NY 10016, United States of America.

© Oxford University Press 2017

All rights reserved. No part of this publication may be reproduced, stored in
a retrieval system, or transmitted, in any form or by any means, without the
prior permission in writing of Oxford University Press, or as expressly permitted
by law, by license, or under terms agreed with the appropriate reproduction
rights organization. Inquiries concerning reproduction outside the scope of the
above should be sent to the Rights Department, Oxford University Press, at the
address above.

You must not circulate this work in any other form
and you must impose this same condition on any acquirer.

Library of Congress Cataloging-in-Publication Data
Names: Smith, Richard H., editor. | Merlone, Ugo, editor. | Duffy, Michelle,
1968– editor.
Title: Envy at work and in organizations / edited by Richard H. Smith, Ugo
Merlone, Michelle K. Duffy.
Description: Oxford ; New York : Oxford University Press, [2017]
Identifiers: LCCN 2016004550
Subjects: LCSH: Envy. | Psychology, Industrial.
Classification: LCC BF575.E65 E577 2017 | DDC 152.4/8—dc23
LC record available at http://lccn.loc.gov/2016004550

ISBN 978–0–19–022805–7

9 8 7 6 5 4 3 2 1

Printed by Sheridan Books, Inc., United States of America

CONTENTS

Acknowledgments ix

Contributors xi

Introduction xv

1. What Is the Nature of Envy? 1
   Yochi Cohen-Charash and Elliott Larson

2. A Social-Contextual View of Envy
   in Organizations: From Both Envier
   and Envied Perspectives 39
   Lingtao Yu and Michelle K. Duffy

3. The Two Faces of Envy: Studying Benign
   and Malicious Envy in the Workplace 57
   *Christopher M. Sterling, Niels van de Ven,
   and Richard H. Smith*

4. How Do People Respond to Threatened
   Social Status? Moderators of Benign versus
   Malicious Envy 85
   Jan Crusius and Jens Lange

5. Envy as an Evolving Episode 111
   *Charles E. Hoogland, Stephen Thielke,
   and Richard H. Smith*

6. Competent but Cold: The Stereotype Content
   Model and Envy in Organizations 143
   Elizabeth Baily Wolf and Peter Glick

7. A Social Network Perspective on Envy in Organizations 165
   Theresa Floyd and Christopher M. Sterling

8. Envy, Schadenfreude, and Evaluation: Understanding the Strange Growing of Individual Performance Appraisal 191
   Bénédicte Vidaillet

9. Envy and Its Dynamics in Groups and Organizations 211
   H. Shmuel Erlich

10. The Othello Conundrum: The Inner Contagion of Leadership 225
    Mark Stein

11. Culture and the Elicitation, Experience, and Expression of Envy 243
    Yi Wen Tan, Kenneth Tai, and Cynthia S. Wang

12. Envy and School Bullying in the Japanese Cultural Context 267
    Hidefumi Hitokoto and Masato Sawada

13. "Storms of Slander": Relational Dimensions of "Envy" in Java, Indonesia 297
    Thomas Stodulka

14. The Behavioral Economics of Envy: What Can We Learn From It? 321
    Jérémy Celse

15. Envy and Interpersonal Corruption: Social Comparison Processes and Unethical Behavior in Organizations 347
    Julia J. Lee and Francesca Gino

16. Envy and Injustice: Integration and Ruminations 373
    Paresh Mishra, Steven Whiting, and Robert Folger

17. Disposable Diapers, Envy, and the Kibbutz: What Happens to an Emotion Based on Difference in a Society Based on Equality? 399
    Josh Gressel

18. Envy and Inequality in Romantic
    Relationships   429
    Aaron Ben-Ze'ev

19. The Benefits and Threats from Being Envied
    in Organizations   455
    W. Gerrod Parrott

20. Containing Workplace Envy: A Provisional Map
    of the Ways to Prevent or Channel Envy,
    and Reduce Its Damage   475
    Vittorio Annoni, Susanna Bertini, Mario Perini,
    Andrea Pistone, and Serena Zucchi

    Index   505

ACKNOWLEDGMENTS

The idea for this book came from a 2011 conference on envy in the workplace organized by Il Nodo Group, spearheaded by Mario Perini at the University of Torino in Italy. The initial goal was to produce an edited book based on a subset of talks given by those attending the conference. We ultimately invited other contributors so that we could better survey the extraordinary range of work being done on the topic around the world. We wish to acknowledge the University of Torino and the work done by Mario Perini and Giampiero Divotti to organize the conference, as well as the considerable work Mario did in helping with the initial editorial work for this book.

We also wish to acknowledge the extraordinary editorial team at Oxford University Press. Senior Editor Abby Gross enthusiastically backed the project, even as we shifted to an expanded scope, and then granted us sufficient additional time to complete the project when this was needed. We very much appreciated the wise suggestions she made at various stages. Assistant Editor Courtney McCarroll stewarded the production of the book through to publication. We benefited so much from her expertise, good sense, and patience at every step.

Finally, there were numerous unexpected challenges that hindered a smooth path to completing the book, and each of us wishes to thank our families for their patience as we dealt with these challenges.

CONTRIBUTORS

Vittorio Annoni
Il Nodo Group
Milano, Italy

Elizabeth Baily Wolf
Department of Organizational
  Psychology
Harvard Business School
Boston, Massachusetts

Aaron Ben-Ze'ev
Department of Philosophy
University of Haifa
Haifa, Israel

Susanna Bertini
Il Nodo Group
Torino, Italy

Jérémy Celse
Department of Management,
  Organizations and
  Entrepreneurship
Burgundy School of Business
Dijon, France

Yochi Cohen-Charash
Department of Psychology
The Graduate Center and Baruch
  College
City University of New York

Jan Crusius
Social Cognition Center
University of Cologne
Cologne, Germany

Michelle K. Duffy
Department of Work
  and Organizations
University of Minnesota
Minneapolis, Minnesota

H. Shmuel Erlich
Department of Psychology
The Hebrew University
  of Jerusalem
Jerusalem, Israel

Theresa Floyd
Department of Management
University of Montana School
   of Business Administration
Missoula, Montana

Robert Folger
Department of Management
College of Business
   Administration
University of Central Florida
Orlando, Florida

Francesca Gino
Negotiation, Organizations &
   Markets Unit
Harvard Business School
Harvard University
Boston, Massachusetts

Peter Glick
Department of Psychology
Lawrence University
Appleton, Wisconsin

Josh Gressel
Private Practice
Pleasant Hill, California

Hidefumi Hitokoto
Kokoro Research Center
Kyoto University
Kyoto, Japan

Charles E. Hoogland
Department of Psychology
University of Kentucky
Lexington, Kentucky

Jens Lange
Social Cognition Center
University of Cologne
Cologne, Germany

Elliott Larson
Department of Psychology
The Graduate Center and Baruch
   College, City University
   of New York
New York, New York

Julia J. Lee
Management & Organizations
Stephen M. Ross School
   of Business
University of Michigan
Ann Arbor, Michigan

Ugo Merlone
Department of Psychology
University of Torino
Torino, Italy

Paresh Mishra
Department of Organizational
   Leadership and Supervision
Indiana University—Purdue
   University Fort Wayne
Fort Wayne, Indiana

W. Gerrod Parrott
Department of Psychology
Georgetown University
Washington, D.C.

Mario Perini
Il Nodo Group
Torino, Italy

Andrea Pistone
Il Nodo Group
Roma, Italy

Masato Sawada
Department of Education
Utsunomiya University
Tochigi, Japan

Richard H. Smith
Department of Psychology
University of Kentucky
Lexington, Kentucky

Mark Stein
School of Management
University of Leicester
Leicester, United Kingdom

Christopher M. Sterling
Department of Management
California State
    University, Fresno
Fresno, California

Thomas Stodulka
Institute of Social and Cultural
    Anthropology
Freie Universität Berlin
Berlin, Germany

Kenneth Tai
Department of Organizational
    Behavior and Human Resources
Lee Kong Chian School
    of Business
Singapore Management
    University
Singapore

Stephen Thielke
Department of Psychiatry and
    Behavioral Sciences
University of Washington School
    of Medicine
Seattle, Washington

Niels van de Ven
Department of Social Psychology
Tilburg University
Tilburg, The Netherlands

Bénédicte Vidaillet
Department of Organizational
    Psychology
Institut de Recherche en Gestion
Université Paris Est Créteil
Paris, France

Cynthia S. Wang
Department of Management
Spears School of Business
Oklahoma State University
Stillwater, Oklahoma

Yi Wen Tan
School of Social Sciences
Singapore Management
    University
Singapore

Steven Whiting
College of Business
    Administration
University of Central Florida
Orlando, Florida

Lingtao Yu
Department of Work and
    Organizations
Carlson School of Management
University of Minnesota
Minneapolis, Minnesota

Serena Zucchi
Il Nodo Group
Torino, Italy

INTRODUCTION

About two decades ago, one of us raised the topic of envy with a colleague who taught in a business school. "Oh," he said, in an exaggerated, hushed voice, "we don't use the word *envy* around here."

Why was this? Remarkably, his point, as he went on to explain, was that doing so would immediately trivialize the conversation. For one thing, most economists still favored a view of human decision-making that left little room for emotions that smacked of irrational motivations. Also, if people felt envious, well, that was their problem. Interestingly, even in psychology at the time, only a handful of researchers studied envy. And for people grappling with how to manage envy at work or in organizations, there were precious few resources available for guidance.

Today, the landscape of research and thinking on envy has altered. Even in the field of economics, research trends led by the emerging subdiscipline of behavioral economics incorporate emotion, envy being one example, in efforts to explain decision-making. Psychological research has expanded to examine more deeply a host of previously under-studied emotions. In planning this book, it was easy to find both researchers and practitioners in organizational settings who were engaged in exploring the nature of envy.

What can readers expect to find in this book?

Many contributors tackle definitional questions. All agree that envy is an unpleasant, even painful, emotion that we can often feel when we notice another person's advantage in a domain important to us. All also agree that the pain follows from the impact of being at a disadvantage for self-evaluations and important outcomes in life. This is the easy part of defining envy. Variations in definition arise in what other ingredients might be added to envy beyond this core reaction of painful inferiority. Is envy a hostile emotion, for example? Clearly, the answer to this question has important implications for tracking the role of envy in organizations, as any emotion that brings with it hostile feelings is more likely to lead to negative consequences for both the envier (e.g., dislike from the envied) and the envied (e.g., undermining by the envier)—and generally produce an unpleasant place in which to interact with others.

There is little question that envy often has a hostile nature; after all, so many memorable characterizations of envy in literature highlight hateful feelings. Consider Milton's linking of Satan's motivations with envy, or Shakespeare's portrayal of the disturbingly pitiless Iago. But whether envy, in its elemental, incipient form, is appropriately conceived of as hostile is an open question: at least, judging by the range of views in this book.

Some contributors, such as Sterling, van de Ven, and Smith (Chapter 3), and Crusius and Lange (Chapter 4) suggest that envy is most usefully understood as arising in two important forms, a benign or a hostile form. Early literature on envy acknowledged that laypeople use the term "envy" in the benign, non-hostile sense, but usually assumed this sense as less prototypical, and less useful to study. However, evidence summarized in these and other chapters provides a good case for taking a fresh look at these assumptions. The presence in many languages of separate words denoting benign and hostile forms of envy (though not in English) is an example of evidence that supports this view.

Other contributors, such Cohen-Charash and Larson (Chapter 1), argue for a unitary construct that is neither malicious nor benign. Rather, in their view, envy can have either desirable or undesirable consequences that may or may not include hostility, but this will depend on the context. They bolster their reasoning with a broad sampling of historical and cross-disciplinary views about envy from many sources. Yu and Duffy (Chapter 2) share this view to a degree. They note that the negative consequences of envy have been the typical focus in organizations, but they adopt a more neutral definition of envy as feeling pain at another person's good fortune. They go on to argue that envy can then be expressed and responded to in either a functional or a dysfunctional way, based on a number of contextual factors. Thus, the hostile form or benign form are just two of a number of paths that envy can take. Hoogland, Thielke, and Smith (Chapter 5) provide a model that blends the two perspectives. They view envy as an evolving, dynamic episode, entailing a broad mix of cognitive, affective, and behavioral processes. Although it usually starts with a painful comparison, these contributors see it as quickly differentiating into an experience having largely either a benign or a hostile quality; with both paths representing equally valid episodes of envy.

To an extent, the question of whether envy should be viewed in the unitary sense or as one of two subtypes of envy is not so important in a practical sense. If one backs up a step, the two perspectives are more similar than different. It seems clear that one can zoom in on envy at its initial point, where the pain of inferiority is at least most salient, or zoom out at some later point, when it either has a hostile character or not. As Yu and Duffy suggest, the important point is that there is great benefit in researchers' (and people in organizations') understanding the contextual factors that transform the initial pain of envy once it is triggered. Some of the factors amount to a kind of "poison" that promotes negative outcomes; others serve as an "antidote" that moderates negative outcomes, indeed, sometimes creating positive outcomes for the individual and those around the individual.

The differing views on the question of whether hostility should be considered a basic ingredient of envy can be seen as a broader invitation to examine more specifically the implications of envy in organizations, a challenge that all the contributors in this book embrace. Many chapters emphasize the possible negative outcomes. For example, Lee and Gino (Chapter 15), using the broad theoretical context of social comparison theory, examine the link between envy and unethical behavior in organizations, and suggest that characteristics of an organization's structure, related to performance goals and pay for performance, can aggravate this connection. Erlich (Chapter 9), using psychoanalytic ideas, largely underscores what he suggests are the essentially unavoidable aspects of envy that bring conflict, resentment, and even hatred in group settings. Annoni and his colleagues (Chapter 20), because their main aim is to provide ways for individual and managers organization to cope with envy, largely highlight the negative consequences of envy that would seem to require coping strategies. Vidaillet (Chapter 8) calls attention to the negative consequences of envy in the context of the understanding some of the harmful effects of individual performance-appraisal systems. Wolf and Glick (Chapter 6), in the context of a focus on out-group stereotypes, suggest that envied out-groups appear to be both competent and cold. The envy felt toward such groups, resulting from these stereotypes, often has an undercurrent of resentment, which in turn can cause active harm.

Other contributors take up the challenge while also incorporating the two-subtype theme. Sterling, van de Ven, and Smith (Chapter 3) argue and present evidence that hostile (or malicious) envy can undermine relationships, lead to a range antisocial behaviors, and cause greater turnover. It is also associated with tearing down envied others because their advantage is perceived as unfair. Furthermore, in part because hostile envy is also associated with a sense of frustration and low control, there is little motivation for the envier to improve the self (hence, the tearing down of the envied other). In contrast, benign envy can lead to a self-improvement motivation and enhanced performance in the workplace. This is because it is not only free of hostility (though still painful), but it is also associated with a perception that the other's advantage is achievable over time. Crusius and Lange (Chapter 4) also explore how envy in its benign form can motivate self-improvement, and in its malicious form can motivate tearing down the envied other.

However, despite the common themes across most chapters, readers of this book can expect a range of theoretical and methodological perspectives. Crusius and Lange (Chapter 4) take a social-functional, evolutionary, general approach to envy. They argue that the pathways of envious responding follow from the pursuit of prestige and dominance, and that these alternative ways of achieving social status are linked to benign and malicious envy, respectively. They also expand their analysis by incorporating dispositional moderators, such as dispositional envy and grandiose narcissism, as well emotional expressions of the envied other, such as pride.

Social network researchers Floyd and Sterling (Chapter 7) present a social networks perspective on envy and show how the structure, type, and strength of relationships between individuals in an organization affect individual behavior. This approach provides a unique way of assessing how relative positions among people create a pattern of envy-producing social comparisons that are in turn linked to important organizational outcomes.

Psychoanalytic approaches are well represented. Stein (Chapter 10) uses psychoanalytic tools, and a variety of other traditions, to examine how leadership is often affected by jealousy and envy, felt both by subordinates as well as by leaders. Much of his analysis also uses details from Shakespeare's *Othello* to show how the inner workings of the minds of Iago and Othello reveal common challenges of leadership. He suggests that the contemporary demise of the Gucci family dynasty in Italy reflect similar emotional dynamics. Some of Stein's ideas parallel Erlich's (Chapter 9), noted earlier, as well as those presented by Vidaillet (Chapter 8), also noted earlier.

Researchers focusing on culture are also well represented here. Organizational psychologists Tan, Tai, and Wang (Chapter 11) bring a cross-cultural perspective to studying envy and explore the marked cultural variations in whether envy is felt, how readily it is reduced or transformed into other experiences, and how it is typically displayed or expressed in behaviors. They focus specifically on how two cultural dimensions—individual/collective and horizontal/vertical—affect envy in organizational settings and subsequently appear to influence a host of outcomes, from job satisfaction and performance, citizenship, and counterproductive work behaviors, to group cooperation or competition.

Hitokoto and Sawada (Chapter 12) take a particular culture—the Japanese—and show how strong cultural norms transform the way envy can operate, particularly with regard to bullying in Japanese schools. Envy arises in a distinctive way in Japanese schools, in part because of the value placed on being average and ordinary, rather than superior. Adding to this complexity is that Japanese also differentiate between both benign and malicious subtypes of envy. Bullying often arises in the context of social comparisons that engage both self-improvement motives and concern over the disharmony that deviations from averageness can cause. Hitokoto and Sawada also suggest that envy has implications for the abuse of power that seem to be occurring as Japan goes through cultural changes and technological development.

Stodulka (Chapter 13) outlines an anthropological perspective, which also emphasizes the role of culture in explaining the nature of envy. Using participant observation in a Javanese setting, he analyzes the complex and powerful relational aspects of envy between "enviers" and the "envied." Interestingly, Javanese culture tends to proscribe envy and its private experience and public expression. However, Stodulka shows how younger Javanese are now reacting to conspicuous consumption and the increased desires that result, which then promote an invidious climate despite these proscriptions against envy. Stodulka uses anthropological methods to isolate the often indirect, camouflaged manifestations of the envy—for example, expressions of moral outrage.

Behavioral economist Celse (Chapter 14) first characterizes traditional economic models of behavior that assume that people make rational, self-interested decisions that are unaffected by how their outcomes compare to the outcome of others. He then reviews recent evidence in behavioral economics demonstrating that people do in fact care about relative outcomes and often feel envy when they compare poorly with others. He describes efforts by behavioral economists to integrate envy into their mathematical models of decision-making and give suggestions for how future work might improve these models.

Some chapters, such as those by Mishra, Whiting and Folger (Chapter 16), who come from both the organizational and the social psychology traditions, focus on a particular important challenge to understanding envy. Envy has a complex overlap with feelings of injustice and resentment, yet research on injustice in organizations (e.g., distributive justice, equity theory, procedural justice, and counterfactual thinking) has largely developed separately from research on envy. Using an appraisal theory approach, Mishra, Whiting, and Folger show how these two traditions of research can inform each other, and in so doing, enhance the understanding of each.

Gressel (Chapter 17), a practicing clinical psychologist, examines envy among kibbutzim using semi-structured interviews with current and former kibbutz members. His main focus is on the question of whether the reduction in social and economic inequality in kibbutzim actually brings a reduction or elimination of envy. He finds little evidence for envy being reduced, and some evidence that it is actually stronger than in other contexts in Israel. He explores the possible reasons for these trends, such as the greater visibility of differences, the greater social propinquity in these communities, and the sense that cultural beliefs advocating equality make any differences more acute and painful.

Ben-Ze'ev (Chapter 18) explores how envy operates in romantic relationships. This means a focus on the smallest of groups—two people—and people who share a high level of intimacy. As organizations involve people who have such close relationships, this chapter extends out the range of relevant issues to explore. Ben-Ze'ev emphasizes that envy might seem incompatible with romantic relationships because it implies a negative attitude toward the good fortune of one's partner. However, he suggests that the fact of inequality or inequity in any relationship creates the possibility of envy. And, indeed, intimacy and closeness may sometimes intensify the feeling more than in less intimate relationships, and he shows this in various ways.

Parrott (Chapter 19) examines the multifaceted social and emotional consequences for persons who are the targets of envy in organizations. There is clearly the potential for the envied people to feel ambivalent about their position of superiority. Although another person's envy confirms one's superiority and can produce pride and self-confidence, it can also produce unhappiness in the envied person, an outcome that is especially unwelcome if the envier is a friend. It can also produce hostility and aggression. After all, it may be unclear whether the envy is benign or malicious. Thus, the envy of others is typically a mixed blessing and is something more to be coped with than encouraged. Parrott explores the range of responses that can follow from being envied and reviews studies suggesting the contextual factors predicting these responses.

The final theme in the book concerns how best to cope with envy, mostly from the envier's perspective, but also from the envied person's perspective. We noted Annoni and colleagues' (Chapter 20) full focus on managing envy, but almost every chapter devotes some attention to this broad, challenging territory, sometimes taking advantage of relevant research; other times offering informed speculations. We hope this theme will round out the contents of this book, so that both researchers and those needing to grapple with the actual effects of envy in their workplace or organization will find it useful.

—Richard H. Smith, Ugo Merlone, and Michelle K. Duffy

1 | What Is the Nature of Envy?

YOCHI COHEN-CHARASH AND ELLIOTT LARSON

ALTHOUGH THE EMOTION OF ENVY has been recognized and discussed ever since biblical times, recently there has been a surge in the scientific study of envy by researchers from multiple disciplines. Philosophers, theologians, sociologists, economists, marketing researchers, psychologists, and management researchers all study envy. We see an ever-growing number of empirical and review articles, as well as symposia and talks at international conferences, all dedicated to envy. This trend is indicative of the vast importance of envy in daily life and the quest to understand it. This is good news for all envy researchers and for the consumers of such research. The multidisciplinary study of envy enables scientists and practitioners to understand envy, its causes, its outcomes, and how we can cope with and regulate this unpleasant emotion in the most productive ways. At the same time, reviewing the literature about envy, even within a single discipline such as social psychology, reveals some major challenges. The primary challenge in our opinion is the most basic one—agreeing on the nature of envy.

When reading the extant literature, it is apparent that researchers use a plethora of concepts when referring to envy. For example, envy is considered both benign and malicious (e.g., van de Ven, Zeelenberg, & Pieters, 2009), emulative and admiring (e.g., Rawls, 1971), black and white (e.g., Neu, 1980), or strong and weak (Elster, 1991), to name just a few dyads. Envy is also conceptualized by its context (e.g., workplace, consumer, or neighborhood envy).[1] The question is whether all these conceptualizations refer to the same emotion or to different ones. If to the same emotion, then why use so many adjectives and definitions for it? If to different emotions, why are they all called "envy," and what is the relationship between the different "envy emotions"? For example, what can research findings about one type of envy (e.g., "benign," "consumer") tell us about another type of envy (e.g., "malicious," "workplace")? These diverse conceptualizations of envy have led, in our opinion, to a conceptual ambiguity about the nature of envy. In essence, various researchers examine different "envys" and hence arrive at different and often contradicting conclusions. This leaves the consumers of envy research confused as to the nature of envy and its outcomes.

Of the various conceptualizations of envy, it seems that a major one focuses on envy as leading to either destructive or constructive reactions. This has been the case since ancient biblical writings, through early philosophical texts, and the present day. In modern envy research, the most prevalent terms used are "benign" and "malicious" envy (e.g., van de Ven et al., 2009). In this chapter, we will focus on this particular classification. Our goal is to discuss the roots and outcomes of this classification, and to provide a recommended definition that will help unify research on envy around a singular conceptualization of envy divorced from judgements about its nature (e.g., positive or negative, good or bad).

To this end, we will start with a short historical review of various conceptualizations of envy across eras (e.g., biblical, classical philosophy, and modern times) and disciplines (e.g., psychoanalytical, social-psychological, marketing, and modern philosophy). Following this broad review, we will focus on the classification of envy as "benign" or "malicious," which we refer to as *desirable* and *undesirable* (please see our rationale and definitions below). We critically discuss the ramifications of this classification of envy for the research questions and methodologies characteristic of envy research. Next, we will suggest a conceptualization of envy that we believe will reduce the ambiguity surrounding the construct. We will conclude with a short discussion of the influence our suggested conceptualization of envy may have on future directions of envy research.

Some Terminological Issues

One major challenge with the various classifications of envy is the lack of a clear statement about the basis for any particular classification. That is, envy can be considered either "good" or "bad" (Palaver, 2005), for example, because of the way it is experienced, its outcomes, the motivations of the envious person, and moral convictions, cultural values, or stereotypes held about it. We will revisit this point throughout the chapter, but for now, we establish our viewpoint that this lack of a clear rationale for each conceptualization, inconsistencies between different conceptualizations, and lack of clarity within a particular classification lead to a conceptual ambiguity about the nature of envy. For example, if envy is considered a sin, this implies that the envious person is a sinner. However, if envy is "malicious," can we similarly say that the envious person is malicious? And is that person also a sinner? These classifications imply that the emotion itself is disadvantageous (advantageous) and that envious people are either mean (kind), and/or immoral (moral). Since envy is so ubiquitous, the implication is that people who experience "malicious" envy (that is, most people) are, in the best-case scenario, malicious. Furthermore, implying that envy is a disadvantageous emotion ignores its adaptive and social importance (e.g., Garay & Móri, 2011; Hill & Buss, 2008).

Most researchers of envy agree it is an unpleasant emotion, and many study reactions to and outcomes of envy (e.g., Cohen-Charash, 2009; Duffy, Scott, Shaw, Tepper, & Aquino, 2012; Gino & Pierce, 2010). Therefore, it seems to us that, at least in the majority of current writings about envy in social and organizational psychology, the basis for classifying envy is not its unpleasant experience, but rather its outcomes, or how envious individuals react to their envy. When reactions to envy are undesirable, envy is considered negative, bad, malicious, black, or strong. When reactions to envy are desirable, envy is considered positive, good, benign, white, non-malicious, and weak.[2] Still, as we will show later, many times the basis for a classification is not clearly stated, and it is unclear how many envy constructs exist.

This conceptual ambiguity spills over to the empirical study of envy. That is, researchers' conceptualizations of envy influence the research questions and hypotheses they examine, the measures they use to gauge envy, and, naturally, their findings. Altogether, the theoretical and empirical ambiguities regarding envy *indicate* and *perpetuate* a fundamental disagreement and confusion about the construct of envy.

Of course, since the scientific study of envy is relatively recent, such conceptual ambiguity is expected and can be looked at as part of the processes of understanding envy.[3] However, we believe that progress in the empirical study of envy requires that basic conceptual ambiguities be clarified, and we believe that a good place to start is to separate questions about envy's emotional experience from questions about its outcomes. We hope this chapter initiates this process, by suggesting that the dichotomization of envy as good or benign, or as bad or malicious, even when it is based on the outcomes of envy, is unmerited and results from the lack of differentiation between the experience of envy and its hypothesized outcomes (see also Tai, Narayanan, & Mcallister, 2012). Instead, we suggest that it is best to think of envy as a single construct, which is neither "benign" nor "malicious," and that there are various reactions to envy, some constructive and others destructive.

For the purpose of this chapter, we have chosen to use a different terminology than that of the commonly used terms of "benign" and "malicious." We did this for several reasons. First, the "benign" and "malicious" classification is only one of many used to define envy throughout history and across disciplines. Since we examine envy from a broader perspective, it would be less representative of the literature to use one particular terminology in preference to others. Second, the terms "benign" and "malicious" imply a value judgement of envy and of envious individuals as malicious or kind. We would like to avoid such value judgements. Third, as we will show later, the current benign/malicious terminology mainly relies on defining envy based on the motivations of the envious person rather than on the person's holistic emotional state, such as the person's feelings. Since we believe that an emotion should be defined based on its experience (feelings, cognitions, and action tendencies), we do not want to increase the confusion by presenting additional definitions of benign and malicious envy.

Therefore, for the sake of describing the literature in this chapter, we will discuss envy as a *desirable* or *undesirable* emotion. We define envy as desirable when it is perceived as an emotion leading to constructive reactions (e.g., working harder, reducing the gap with the envied other via self-improvement, improving society). We define envy as undesirable when it is perceived to lead to behaviors that harm the envied other or the desired state or possession. Although desirability is also a value judgement, this one clearly refers to the behavioral outcomes of envy, and not to the emotion itself or to the person experiencing it. Hence, we believe it is less biased than the benign/malicious classification. We do not offer desirability as an alternative conceptualization of envy, though, as we believe envy should be studied as a singular construct with no further judgements about its nature.

Conceptualizations of Envy Across Times and Disciplines

Being of interest to writers and researchers from various disciplines, envy has been conceptualized differently by each. While we discuss the major perspectives, we do not attempt here to provide an exhaustive discussion of each perspective (see other chapters in this volume for more detail on certain perspectives), but rather to present an overview of how the current conceptual ambiguity originated from the multiple conceptualizations of envy that have arisen over the years.

The Theological Perspective

The Old Testament contains many envy-related stories (for a review, see Schimmel, 2008). For example, Cain murdered Abel out of envy, and Joseph's brothers were so envious of him they sold him as a slave to the Egyptians. Envy is considered a sin, rebuked in the Tenth Commandment. This implies that enviers are sinners who will be punished in this and the next life and who are condemned for questioning God's will about the order of things in the world.

At the same time, Judaism sometimes sees envy as a constructive and essential force. It is seen in proverbs like "Scholars' envy increases wisdom," and declarations such as "Be envious for my sake! Were it not for envy the world could not be sustained. No one would plant a vineyard, no one would take a wife, no one would build a house. . .." (Midrash Tehillim [English], 1959). Another example is, "For all of these things result from the fact that man envies his neighbor. If his neighbor builds a home or takes a wife he too will set himself to do so" (Orchot Tzaddikim, 1969). Thus, Judaism recognizes the complex nature of envy and acknowledges the desirable and undesirable ramifications of it.

The Gospel of Mark highlights envy as one of the main causes for Jesus' crucifixion and provides one of the few insights into envy from the New Testament (Hagedorn & Neyrey, 1998; Malina, 2001). Since then, religious leaders, such as priests in the nineteenth century, have condemned envy and emulation because they signify questioning God's creation of various social classes and the social order (Matt, 1998). Emulating the rich out of envy was considered moral dishonesty, a pretense to be what one is not. Therefore, religious leaders called for people to be content with what they have, which is what God has given them. Doing so would mean that people would have better lives in the afterworld while simultaneously protecting the social order of the time, keeping each person at their own status, residence, and abilities. Envy has even been described as a result of imitating Satan (for a review, see Palaver, 2005). Thus, Christianity clearly sees envy as an undesirable emotion.

In Islam, there is a differentiation between two types of envy, *hasad* and *ghibtah*. *Hasad* is seen as an undesirable envy that devours one's faith and destroys the good deeds of a person (Donaldson, 1953). Much like Judaism and Christianity, Islam also considers individuals who experience *hasad* as those who do not respect what Allah has destined for them: "Allah favored some of you over others with wealth and properties; Do they deny the favors of Allah?" (Soorah an-Nahl [16]: 71). In contrast, *ghibtah* refers to the situation in which a person desires to have the same blessings as another, but does not wish to take away the other's blessing. This is seen mostly in two situations: "In [the] case of a man whom Allah has given the Qur'an and who recites it throughout night and day; and a man on whom Allah has bestowed wealth who gives it away throughout night and day" (Saheeh al-Bukharee and Saheeh Muslim) (AHYA.Org, 2014). *Ghibtah* indicates a desirable aspect of envy, leading enviers to work for Allah and to contribute to the larger society (Madelker, 2008).

Buddhism regards envy as one of the five types of poison. It is thought of as a defilement of the mind and is strongly linked to obsession. For Buddhism, envy represents "the strong identity problems of the ego" (De Silva, 2000, p. 141), and Buddha urges his followers to "not overrate what you have received, nor envy others. He who envies others does not obtain peace of mind" (Thinkexist, 2014). Thus, envy is not a sin against God or society, as the monotheistic religions see it, but a sin against the self. While envy is considered an affliction, Buddhism suggests that, through introspection, a person can free him- or herself of such negative emotions by reflecting on their causes and consequences (Ekman, Davidson, Ricard, & Wallace, 2005).

To summarize, among the monotheistic religions, both Judaism and Islam acknowledge some desirable aspects of envy. Whereas Islam recognizes two distinct types of envy, we do not know of such a classification in Judaism. Because there are some acceptable conditions to envy in these religions, specifically Islam's *ghibtah* and Judaism's clear discussions of the motivating power of envy, we believe some of these religions differentiate between the painful experience of envy and its outcomes. However, for Christianity, most of Judaism, and Islam's *hasad*, envy is still seen as a sin and as a sign of questioning God's will, and hence an undesired emotion. Buddhism, on the other hand, emphasizes the *personal* price the envious person pays because of this poisonous emotion and does not acknowledge any desirable aspect of envy.

The Philosophical Perspective

Whereas some early philosophers, such as Aristotle, differentiated emulative, desirable envy from undesirable envy, others, such as Hobbes, viewed envy as a dangerous force leading to the "war of everyone with everyone" (Palaver, 2005, p. 141; see Palavar for a review). Summarizing the writings of the ancient Stoics, D'arms and Kerr (2008) defined envy as "a pain felt toward (or caused by) another's good, good fortune, prosperity, achievements, or favorable circumstances" (p. 40). According to the Stoics, and as described by D'Arms and Kerr, as a competitive emotion, envy functions "to motivate agents in ways that benefit their standing in various kinds of status hierarchies, by improving their comparative position" (p. 40). In line with this conceptualization, the envious person is seen as ambitious and motivated to succeed. Furthermore, when the experience of envy is merited (because the other's advantage harms the envious person's competitive stance), some philosophers see no moral wrong with experiencing it (see also Ben-Ze'ev, 1992; La Caze, 2001, 2002; Rawls, 1971). In fact, to the extent that it motivates the person to improve his or her competitive stance, envy, even if painful, is desirable (D'Arms & Kerr, 2008).

According to D'Arms and Kerr (2008), the goal of the envious person is to reduce the gap with the envied. Although the wish of the envious is to take away the advantage of the rival, it can be done in ways that do not harm the envied or destroy the good. Furthermore, although envy is often accompanied by hostility, hostility is not an essential component of envy; and even if envy is accompanied by hostility, the envious person does not necessarily act on it (Ben-Ze'ev, 1992; D'Arms & Kerr, 2008).

An alternative view is that of Neu (1980), who differentiated between "malicious envy" and "admiring envy." Whereas the goal of the person experiencing "malicious" envy is to lower the other to the level of the envious person or even below it, the goal of the person experiencing "admiring" envy is to raise him- or herself to the level of the envied person. The common denominators between these two types of envy are (a) the understanding that the other person is better off, and (b) the desire to turn this inequality into equality. According to Neu, the invidious comparison turns malicious when the envious person blames the envied for his or her own inferiority. Moreover, Neu believed that the two "types" of envy may have different sources and developmental roots, and that "malicious" envy is always pathological. Like Neu, Elster (1991) differentiated envy from emulation and competition, and saw the former as a destructive force: "The first urge of envy is not 'I, too, must have what he has,' but 'I want him not to have what he has, because it makes me feel that I am less'" (p. 49).

Taylor (1988) suggested a more complicated classification of envy. He first differentiated between envy as an emotion and envy as a disposition. As an emotion, he argued, envy results from a focus on the envied object or from a focus on the envied person. When envy results from a focus on the envied object, it is called "object envy." It can also be called "ideal envy" or "admiring envy" because the other person becomes an ideal and a source for admiration. This envy, according to Taylor, lacks the "defects" that characterize the typically envious person (the one predisposed to experience envy). However, Taylor never clearly explained these "defects." Taylor also identified "state envy," in which the envious person does not care about the object, but rather about the person having it. In this case, the envious person feels deprived and inferior vis-à-vis the envied person and sees the envied as a rival and competitor. When the envied other succeeds, the envious person loses. "State envy," according to Taylor, is unpleasant, and the person's goal is to remove it. The person can do that in one of two ways: wishing to improve his or her own position (called by Taylor "emulative envy"), or wishing to "spoil the other's elevation" (called "malicious" or "destructive" envy; Taylor, 1988, p. 235). Overall, Taylor viewed envy as an aggressive, self-defeating emotion, hence undesirable.

To summarize, the philosophical approach to envy is complex. There is a vast disagreement between various philosophers about the nature and the function of envy, as well as about its outcomes. Whereas philosophers clearly recognize the pain involved in envy, some differentiate between the experience of envy and its outcomes, and show envy as potentially leading to desirable and/or undesirable outcomes. Others differentiate between various types of envy, some considered desirable and others not.

The Sociological, Anthropological, and Cross-Cultural Psychology Perspectives

Sociologists and anthropologists (Foster, 1972; Schoeck, 1969) view envy as a universal, natural, and important emotion. At the same time, while they generally consider envy a hostile, undesirable emotion (e.g., Foster, 1972), there are some researchers from these perspectives who identify desirable features of envy (e.g., Ahier & Beck, 2003; Hughes, 2007). Furthermore, there are major cross-cultural differences regarding envy. Whereas some cultures are tolerant of, and even encourage, envy, other cultures condemn it. In many Western societies, envy is propagated in order to foster economic growth (e.g., Schoeck, 1969), whereas less developed societies seek to avoid envy as a method for maintaining the status quo (for a review, see Salovey & Rothman, 1991). These differences are reflected in cultural norms that influence what people are envious of, whom they envy, how they feel their envy, how they react to it, and their language and vocabulary regarding envy, among others (for reviews, see Lindholm, 2008; Parrott & Rodriguez Mosquera, 2008; Quintanilla & De López, 2013).

For example, Swedes have been shown to be more envious about material objects than are the Javanese, who are more likely to envy others' success in personal development (Adrianson & Ramdhani, 2014). Furthermore, whereas Swedes report experiencing malicious envy, Indonesians report experiencing both benign and malicious envy. Hupka and his colleagues (e.g., Hupka, Zaleski, Otto, & Reidl, 1996, 1997) showed that people in different cultures experience envy differently, talk about it differently, and give different connotations to it. Tan, Tai, and Wang (Chapter 11, this volume) provide a detailed analysis of these types of differences, specifically contrasting collectivistic versus individualistic cultures and horizontal versus vertical cultures. It is important to recognize these types of cross-cultural differences in the way envy is perceived, especially as they may affect how envy is studied across various cultures (Lindholm, 2008).

In addition, cultural norms influence how people experience and perceive being the target of envy. Although most writings emphasize mechanisms designed to avoid envy and protect individuals from being targets of envy (e.g., Foster, 1972), researchers also indicate the benefits of being the target of envy and the fact that in some cultures, being envied is a desired state, reflecting one's status and success (Lindholm, 2008; Parrott & Rodriguez Mosquera, 2008; Rodriguez Mosquera, Parrott, & De Mendoza, 2010). For example, because it enhances and affirms their self-confidence, European Americans attach more positive meaning to being envied than Spaniards do, despite recognizing the negative implications of envy (Rodriguez Mosquera et al., 2010). Thus, all the negativity of envy does not prevent some from wanting to be envied, and this is partially dependent on one's culture.

The sociological, anthropological, and cross-cultural psychology perspectives also emphasize the interplay of envy and egalitarianism; specifically, how envy may promote social justice. Some argue that envy provides insight into the existence of social inequity and exploitation that should be addressed (see Hughes, 2007; Rawls, 1971). From this viewpoint, social envies can be legitimized when there is a group with a significant and enduring sense of injustice relative to other groups (Ahier & Beck, 2003). In such cases, fear of envy in society may drive a third party (e.g., the government) to obviate envy. Elster (1991) uses the example of the Chinese government forcing farmers to cut down their fruit trees so that all were equal. It is these types of acts that speak to envy's impact at more societal and cultural level.

However, for some, even though envy may serve to identify inequality and bring some stability to political and social systems, there are still numerous negative consequences from such actions (e.g., fear of envy hindering innovation) that still make the envy unjustifiable (Schoeck, 1969). Furthermore, some argue that the claim of social inequity may be a tool for disguising one's self-centered feelings of envy (see Gressel, Chapter 17, this volume).

To summarize, envy is a universal emotion, but various cultures treat it differently. Therefore, a key implication of the work from these various perspectives is to avoid an ethnocentric approach to envy. Researchers should approach envy as potentially unique within each setting it is experienced. Similarly, it is important to examine how culture shapes the outcomes and perceptions of envy. In any event, although envy is generally considered undesirable in these literatures, it can also have benefits for individuals and societies alike. Therefore, we can conclude that the sociological, anthropological, and cross-cultural psychology perspectives recognize the difference between the unpleasant experience of envy and the outcomes of envy, seeing it as both a desirable and an undesirable emotion.

The Economic Perspective

For the most part, economists do not advocate any preconceived view of the desirability of envy. That is, envy is not thought of as inherently destructive or constructive, but rather as a state that can lead to constructive and destructive outcomes in terms of their utility to the person and the surroundings (for reviews, see Palaver, 2005; Zizzo, 2008). In fact, many economists do not see envy as an emotion, and refer to it as indicative of a situation where a person prefers another person's allocations to his or her own (Konow, 2003; Podder, 1996; This Saint-Jean, 2009).

Furthermore, some economists think of envy as a motivator of economic growth ("keeping up with the Joneses"), but also as harming such growth (fear equilibrium and destructive equilibrium; Gershman, 2014). According to Gershman, when inequality is low, inequity tolerance is high, and investment opportunities are high, people will respond to their envy by attempting to keep up with the Joneses—that is, they will compete for their relative standing by increasing their efforts. These efforts and competition will improve the economy. However, when inequality is high, inequity tolerance is low, and investment opportunities are scarce, entrepreneurs and affluent people will avoid extra investments because they fear the envy of others. Thus, a *fear equilibrium* will harm economic development. Lastly, when inequality is very high, inequity tolerance is very low, and investment opportunities are very scarce, people will fight each other and will invest in destroying each other, which is the state of *destructive equilibrium.* This state, of course, will harm the economy.

Interestingly, Gershman (2014) differentiated between the reactions of individuals and the long-term influence of envy on the economy. Specifically, individuals may prefer the fear equilibrium to the "keeping up with the Joneses" state because under a fear equilibrium, they do not have to work as hard. When attempting to keep up with the Joneses, which economically is the best situation, people might enter a stressful "rat race" that can take its toll of them.

One challenge for economists studying envy is that the traditional economic assumptions of self-interest and rationality are contradicted by envy (see Celse, Chapter 14, this volume). For example, some studies have demonstrated that envious individuals want to harm the envied so much that they are even willing to harm themselves in the process (e.g., Wobker, 2014; Zizzo & Oswald, 2001). However, Wobker (2014) refers to envy as a problem of finding its optimal level (i.e., a level in which envy motivates constructive reactions), rather than a problem of minimizing envy as much as possible. That is, up to a certain point, envy can lead to constructive reactions. Thus, the level of envy determines the envier's reactions to it. Other researchers point toward environmental conditions and resources as influencing reactions to envy (Gershman, 2014). For example, when property rights are not secure and existing technology enables it, people will destroy others' wealth out of envy. However, when property rights are secured and technology that enables production is readily available, people will use technology to create new wealth by increasing production (Mitsopoulos, 2009).

It seems to us that, out of the various disciplines we have reviewed here, economics is the most neutral one in its treatment of envy. Economists recognize that envy can lead to both desirable and undesirable reactions, and they search for the various conditions that influence these reactions.

The Marketing Perspective

Marketing researchers recognize the existence of two envy types, and most use the terms "benign" and "malicious" envy to denote them. According to Matt (1998), the economic abundance at the end of the nineteenth century led to a culture in which there were enough spoils for everyone, encouraging "aspirational" envy. This has transformed how envy has been viewed since World War I, shifting from a sin to a desirable state that was encouraged by social leaders (see also Palaver, 2005). Envy is a desirable emotion for marketers because it drives consumption, one of the ultimate goals of marketing. Therefore, marketing researchers utilize and encourage "benign" envy to promote the consumption of coveted goods. Specifically, "benign" envy "inspires the envier to purchase the equivalent of this same possession" (Belk, 2011, p. 124), whereas "malicious" envy is "motivated by the desire to cause the other to lose their coveted possessions" (Belk, 2011, p. 124). Because these days coveted goods are by and large plentiful and accessible for those who can afford them, there is no need to harm the envied other. Therefore, modern envy, according to Belk, is mainly "benign."

A major difference between the marketing perspective and other perspectives is the lack of focus on one particular individual as the target of envy, but rather, on creating envy of unknown humans or non-human entities. In Belk's conceptualization, the envied other or others can be anonymous; they can even be virtual others who display or have coveted goods. For example, objects of envy can be clothes on mannequins in luxury stores, members of one's virtual social network (whom one does not necessarily know) who post pictures from their latest trip, or movie characters who have an affluent lifestyle. Thus, the assumption of enviers' similarity to the envied, which exists in most writings about envy, is irrelevant for marketing proponents of "benign" envy.

At the same time, marketing and consumer behavior researchers also recognize "malicious" envy. For example, Sundie, Ward, Beal, Chin, and Geiger-Oneto (2009) demonstrated how envy of the owners of luxury products leads to *schadenfreude* (pleasure at another's misfortune) when these products fail, and van de Ven, Zeelenberg, and Pieters (2011a) showed that, whereas "benign" envy leads people to buy the coveted good, "malicious" envy leads them to select a different product. Overall, however, envy is a tool for marketers and is generally seen to be harmless. Of the various disciplines we have reviewed, marketing seems to be one of the most favorable to envy, in that it sees envy, in general, as a desirable state that promotes consumption and, with it, economic growth.

The Psychological Perspective

Given that psychology is a multidisciplinary field in and of itself, there are several traditions in it, some of which treat envy as a fundamentally undesirable emotion. However, others see envy as an emotion that may be undesirable because of its ramifications for the self and for the envied other, its painful experience, and its immoral intentions, yet believe it can sometimes be beneficial to the envious and the envied other, and hence can be a source of desirable outcomes.

The Psychoanalytical Tradition. Melanie Klein, the psychoanalyst whose views on envy are perhaps most widely known, defined envy as "the angry feeling that another person possesses and enjoys something desirable—the envious impulse being to take it away or to spoil it" (Klein, 1957, p. 181). Klein saw envy as an innate and fundamental state that involves the hatred of all goodness. For her, envy has no constructive value. It spoils all capacity for enjoyment and is a destructive impulse (for more discussion of the Kleinian perspective, see Annoni et al., Chapter 20; Erlich, Chapter 9, this volume). To date, many psychoanalysts still view envy in this way (for reviews, see Stein, 2000a; Vidaillet, 2008).

However, there are other views of envy in psychoanalytical writing. For example, Carl Jung viewed envy as an emotion that can compensate for the envious person's underdog status and hence protect the person's ego and sense of self (for a review, see Anderson, 1997). Furthermore, "through challenging and vying with 'others' that have, or appear to have, superior capacities, envy leads to the development of new skills and capacities" (Anderson, 1997, p. 371). While Jung saw constructive sides to envy, he also identified pathological, destructive envy, which occurs only when the envious person has no other way to protect him- or herself from the threatening, envied other. According to Anderson, envy is not fundamentally evil, but is a developmental necessity that enables people to realize their potential. It becomes pathological when "the urge for individual survival" is exaggerated (Anderson, 1997, p. 380). There are additional perspectives on envy present in the psychoanalytical literature (for examples, see Vidaillet, Chapter 8, this volume, for a discussion of the Lacanian tradition).

Some psychoanalysts, in an interesting recent development, have called for researchers to separate the emotion of envy from its outcomes. For example, Berman (2007, p. 18) views envy as an

> unpleasant emotion (pain, sorrow, anger), resulting from a perception of an adverse difference (gap) between the person's state and that of other. It stems from a comparison between the person and his surroundings and deals with a perception of one's own inferiority as opposed to a perception of the other's superiority (and/or good fortune). The behavioral manifestation of the emotion of envy is subjected to individual differences that are based on personality traits and developmental processes.

This definition recognizes the pain of envy, but also that reactions to it are influenced by various factors, such as one's personality (e.g., self-esteem, the ability to deal with interpersonal tensions, sense of entitlement, being aware of envy and owning it) and the wish for self-actualization.

Furthermore, according to Berman, envy has a component of hope (see also Lazarus, 1991). This is the hope to equalize the lots and achieve the things one wants to have. As such, this hope is another motivating force of envy. Whereas personal and situational variables are external to envy, hope is a part of the emotion itself. Thus, reactions to envy are motivated by both forces unrelated to the emotion (e.g., personality) and forces that are a part of the emotion (e.g., hope).

Evolutionary Psychology. Evolutionary psychologists view envy as a functional emotion essential for survival. Specifically, DelPriore, Hill, and Buss (2012) found that envy helps individuals recognize important areas in their life in which they are in a competitive disadvantage, and motivates them to resolve this disadvantage (for a review, see Hill & Buss, 2008). Because of the scarcity of resources, individuals evaluate their state in relation to others who are likely competitors, rather than in absolute terms (Hill & Buss, 2006). When learning that their relative position is inferior and the object of comparison is essential for adaptation, individuals are motivated to acquire the desired resource.

Moreover, if it is helpful for their own adaptation, people will also strive to take the particular resource away from the other (Hill & Buss, 2006). For example, sometimes survival requires having more of the resource than the rival has (Hill & Buss, 2008). The evolutionary perspective explains some of the characteristics of envy in functional terms. For example, the hostility and ill will typical of envy are designed to help the envious person do whatever he or she needs to do in order to increase his or her adaption and survival chances (Wobker, 2014). Also, hiding the emotion from others is helpful for face-saving purposes and for increasing the possibility that others will help the envious person improve his or her relative position (Hill & Buss, 2008).

Overall, in the evolutionary perspective, the goal of the envious person is to improve his or her competitive position to enable fitness, rather than harm the other person. Although envy can lead to harming the other, this is done in order to enable one's survival and not out of malice. Envy can also lead to societal benefits; for example, by being an impetus for charity (Garay & Móri, 2011).

Social Psychology.[4] Most of the social psychological research on envy is based on social comparison (Miceli & Castelfranchi, 2007; Parrott, 1991; Salovey, 1991; Smith, 2000; Smith & Kim, 2007) and self-evaluation maintenance theories (Salovey & Rothman, 1991; Tesser & Collins, 1988). According to this literature, envy is a result of an upward comparison with a better-off, similar other on a self-relevant domain. Many social psychologists rely on Parrott and Smith's (1993) definition of envy as occurring "when a person lacks another's superior quality, achievement, or possession, and either desires it or wishes that the other lacks it" and as being

> characterized as a constellation of several distinguishable affective elements that ... may include feelings of inferiority, longing, resentment of the circumstances, and ill will toward the envied person, sometimes accompanied by guilt, denial, or awareness of the inappropriateness of the ill will. (p. 906)

In this definition, Parrott and Smith recognize that envy might involve the wish to deprive the other of his or her relative advantage, but at the same time they recognize that envy might lead the envious to desire the envied object without harming the envied. Indeed, as in other disciplines, the dual view of envy as desirable or undesirable exists here also. Moreover, like economists, some social psychologists see envy as neither desirable nor undesirable.

The proponents of envy as an undesirable emotion (often called "malicious" or "hostile" envy) claim that there is no desirable "benign" form of envy (e.g., Silver & Sabini, 1978a, 1978b). Benign envy, in this view, is very similar to inferiority (Castelfranchi & Miceli, 2009; Miceli & Castelfranchi, 2007) or admiration (Smith & Kim, 2007). According to Castelfranchi and Miceli (see also Smith, 2004; Smith & Kim, 2007), envy includes hostility and ill will toward the envied other because of (a) the belief that the envied is the source of the envious' inferiority, and (b) the wish to take the advantage from the envied.

Castelfranchi and Miceli (2009; p. 225) add "helpless inferiority" to the experience of envy—the belief that one will never be able to achieve the envied object and that one will always be inferior to the envied. The envious person, according to Castelfranchi and Miceli, sees him- or herself as generally inferior to the envied. The particular social comparison eliciting envy only makes this inferiority more salient and makes the envied other a convenient target of hostility. Parrott (1991) discussed the negative influence of the social comparison on one's self-concept because it reveals the person's shortcomings and reflects badly on him or her. This is different from Castelfranchi and Miceli's helpless inferiority, as it does not reflect on the person's belief about his or her ability to attain the envied advantage.

The proponents of envy as a desirable emotion (often called "nonmalicious," "benign," "admiring," or "emulative" envy) see it as a painful desire to have what the other has (Crusius & Mussweiler, 2012; Parrott, 1991; van de Ven et al., 2009). Currently, however, there is no clear definition of "benign" envy. For example, Crusius and Mussweiler (2012) define the "benign side of envy" as "an increased motivation to gain the superior good that others have and to improve one's position" (p. 151), and van de Ven, Zeelenberg, and Pieters (2012) define benign envy as "a non-malicious form aimed at improving one's own situation" (p. 195). However, these definitions focus on motives and ignore feelings, which are a major part of any emotion (Ben-Ze'ev, 1997; Lazarus, 1991; Miceli & Castelfranchi, 2007).

Researchers studying benign envy say that, like "malicious" envy, it feels bad (e.g., Belk, 2011; Parrott, 1991; van de Ven et al., 2009). However, it has also been described as "uplifting" (van de Ven et al., 2009, p. 425), inspiring, and less unpleasant than malicious envy (van de Ven et al., 2009). All advocates of the "benign" envy concept agree that it differs from "malicious" envy in that it lacks the hostility and ill will that are the hallmarks of "malicious" envy. Furthermore, according to these researchers, the inherent motivation of "benign" envy is to achieve the envied object, whereas "malicious" envy is characterized by the motivation to take it away from the envied other (e.g., Belk, 2011; Crusius & Mussweiler, 2012; van de Ven et al., 2009). As we will show later, however, research findings are not necessarily in line with these assertions, as they find non-benign envy to lead to constructive reactions as well.

Van de Ven and his colleagues (van de Ven, 2009; van de Ven et al., 2012) found that benign envy is elicited when the envied advantaged is just and deserved, and when the envious feels that he or she has control over changing the envy-provoking situation. Parrott (1991) added the person's own responsibility for the disadvantage as a prerequisite for the experience of benign envy. The relationship between envy and unfairness, however, is one of the major sources of disagreement among envy researchers, and many believe that when the situation is unjust, the resulting emotion is resentment and not envy (e.g., Rawls, 1971).[5] Overall, the difference of "benign" envy from other, closely related emotions such as inferiority, emulation, admiration, and resentment is still unclear (but see van de Ven, Zeelenberg, & Pieters, 2011b).

Other social psychologists view envy as leading to both desirable and undesirable outcomes. These researchers believe that, although envy can be characterized by felt inferiority, hostility, and pain, its outcomes are not necessarily destructive. Rather, depending on various personal and situational factors, reactions to envy can be constructive or destructive (e.g., Cohen-Charash, 2009; Exline & Zell, 2008; Lazarus, 1991; Schaubroeck & Lam, 2004; Tai et al., 2012). In other words, they see envy as a functional, important emotion. Heider (1958), for example, viewed the goal of the envious as reducing the gap with the envied, which can be done in two ways—bringing the other down to the inferior position of the self, or elevating the self to the superior level of the envied person. Clearly, whereas the first way will lead to destructive reactions to envy, the other way might lead to constructive reactions to it.

Leach (2008) views envy as a desire for the specific good and advantage one lacks, combined with anger about this unfulfilled desire. However, and unlike others (e.g., Miceli & Castelfranchi, 2007), Leach believes that ill will is not an essential element in envy but rather a possible result of it. Thus, Leach differentiates between the unpleasant experience of envy and its outcomes.

Recently, some social psychologists have started looking at envy as an evolving episode, suggesting that the experience of envy can change over time (Hoogland et al., Chapter 5, this volume; Parrott, 1991; Smith, 2004). This is a very interesting take on envy and might indicate how appraisal processes influence the experience of envy and reactions to it, which in turn feed back into appraising the new situation that has been created (e.g., Frijda, 1993; Lazarus, 1991). According to Hoogland et al., such temporal changes in the experience of envy allow for both "benign" and "malicious" envy to be experienced at various trajectories of the episode.

However, saying that "because these responses arise from the same conditions and have many similar consequences, they also warrant the label of 'envy'" (Hoogland et al., Chapter 5, this volume) might lead to further confusion. First, the idea that the same circumstance can lead to both "benign" and "malicious" envy further blurs the differences between the two emotions. Second, not all the emotions that are experienced following an envy-provoking event are "envy" (for a general discussion, see Frijda et al., 1991). During an emotion episode, emotions can change (e.g., a particular upward comparison elicits immediate envy, followed by shame, followed by anger, followed by envy) or emotions can remain constant (e.g., envy that lasts weeks but fluctuates in intensity).

We agree with Hoogland et al. that the emotion of envy evolves over time, and call for examinations of the boundaries between envy and other emotions, as well as the start and end of an episode. We also suggest that envy might turn into a *sentiment*, "a disposition to respond emotionally to a certain object" (Frijda, Mesquita, Sonneman, & Van Goozen, 1991, p. 207). When envy is a sentiment, one can experience it toward another person or group by merely seeing them and without any particular social comparison (Fiske, 2015; Fiske, Cuddy, Glick, & Xu, 2002). Therefore, sentiments can last for years (see also Wolf & Glick, Chapter 6, this volume).

Looking at envy as an episode or as sentiment, however, does not solve the question concerning the number of envy types. In fact, it adds additional types of envy to the existing ones. However, looking at envy as an episode or a sentiment is based on the duration of the emotion (e.g., Ekman & Davidson, 1994, pp. 49-96), rather than on outcomes. We are very enthusiastic about this line of thought and hope to see it develop.

Summary

Our brief review reveals differences between various disciplines regarding envy. In some disciplines, envy is considered to be mainly an undesirable emotion; other disciplines recognize both desirable and undesirable aspects of envy; in two disciplines (evolutionary psychology and marketing), envy is mainly considered a desirable emotion. We also showed differences within disciplines. Some researchers of various disciplines see envy as a hostile emotion (Castelfranchi & Miceli, 2009; Cohen-Charash, 2009; Cohen-Charash & Mueller, 2007; Fiske, 2010; Foster, 1972; Hamman, 2013; Klein, 1957; Miceli & Castelfranchi, 2002; Smith & Kim, 2007). Other researchers of various disciplines think that there are two types of envy—benign and malicious (e.g., Belk, 2008; Lange & Crusius, 2015;

Sterling et al., Chapter 3, this volume; van de Ven, 2009). Yet other researchers of various disciplines believe that there is only one kind of envy, and that it leads to different reactions, depending on various factors (e.g., Berman, 2007; Cohen-Charash, 2009; Cohen-Charash & Larson, 2011; D'Arms & Kerr, 2008; Larson, 2013; Tai et al., 2012).

The major point to take from our review is that views of envy as an emotion that is desirable or undesirable are not new, but rather have been presented ever since writing on envy started. However, whereas envy has been perceived to have a dual nature throughout history, with only few exceptions, it has only been in modern envy research that some researchers have explicitly suggested the existence of several types of envy.

The Influence of the Conceptualization of Envy on Current Research and Measurement

We will focus here on the empirical study of envy by social psychologists to discuss the empirical ramifications of the conceptual ambiguity regarding envy. We will show that the conceptualization of envy influences research questions, study designs, and measurement in ways that make it difficult to come up with conclusions about envy.

Research Questions and Study Designs

The view of envy as an undesirable emotion dominated the empirical study of envy until just a few years ago. By and large, social psychologists have been interested in the negative ramifications of envy and have neglected the possible constructive reactions to it. Paradoxically, the recent emergence of the systematic study of "benign" envy has exacerbated this negativity bias, as researchers of "benign" envy have been set to show its constructiveness versus the destructiveness of "malicious" envy.

Relatedly, researchers often look for evidence supporting their favored hypothesis and avoid offering and examining competing hypotheses (the "dominant hypothesis approach," Armstrong, Brodie, & Parsons, 2001). This ultimately can lead to methods and measures designed to confirm the hypothesis, missing potentially interesting findings, and hindering the progress of theory (Cohen-Charash, 2015; Greenwald, Pratkanis, Leippe, & Baumgardner, 1986; Nesse, 2004).

Together, the focus on the negativity of envy, the emergence of the "benign"/"malicious" dichotomy, and the dominant hypothesis approach have led to the perpetuation of perceiving envy as an undesirable emotion, unless it is "benign," in which case it is a desirable emotion that encompasses constructive reactions. The theory and findings showing that non-benign envy can lead to both desirable and undesirable reactions (to be discussed later), although sometimes cited, have been largely ignored when establishing the rationale for studying benign and malicious envy. Research designed to examine the desirable aspects of "malicious" envy and the undesirable aspects of "benign" envy has not been published, to the best of our knowledge.

The Measurement of Envy

The conceptualization of envy directly influences its measurement, as the measure needs to reflect the definition of the construct. Therefore, the meaning of research findings depends on the quality and nature of the measures. Reviewing the empirical literature shows that researchers are using a wide variety of envy measures (for a review, see Cohen-Charash, 2009). Some of these measures reflect specific conceptualiztionts of envy, and others lack a theoretical basis. In addition to the fact that having many measures of envy impairs our ability to understand envy properly, there are additional challenges with existing measures.

Tautology. Starting with the conceptualization of envy as desirable or undesirable, some measures of envy consist of items that represent its alleged outcomes. For example, van de Ven et al. (2012, p. 201) assessed benign envy by asking participants whether they "would be inspired" and "would start to work harder," and assessed malicious envy by asking participants whether they "would secretly wish that their coworker would lose clients" and "would gossip about the coworker to others." These measures operationalize envy by its alleged motivations in a way that does not differentiate the experience of envy from its hypothesized outcomes. In other words, envy is not operationalized as an unpleasant emotional experience, but as a motivation to act in certain ways.

In our opinion, this makes these measures tautological, which leads to nearly inevitable support of hypotheses, keeps the conceptualization of the construct unclear, and makes the internal validity of research questionable (Mackenzie, 2003). That is, it is reasonable to assume that if a person is inspired by the other person and plans to work harder, researchers will find a weak or negative relationship with behaviors intended to harm the other and a positive significant relationship with behaviors such as working harder. However, the meaning of these findings is that motivations lead to behaviors. It is unclear, though, if the emotion of envy is the cause of these behaviors, because envy has been measured as a motivation, not as an emotion.

While we acknowledge the complexity of envy and understand that people identify envy in others based on the other's behavior (Silver & Sabini, 1978a), empirical research implies different methods and measurement. Therefore, we urge envy researchers to ensure they do not operationalize consequences as a part of the emotion and that they avoid tautological issues (Liska, 1969).

Misfit and Vagueness about the Exact Construct Studied. In addition to organizing envy into categories of desirable and undesirable, another classification of envy refers to the relative stability of envy as a (a) *state*, a temporary reaction to a particular upward social comparison with another person (e.g., episodic envy, Cohen-Charash, 2009; Cohen-Charash & Mueller, 2007); (b) *trait*, a relatively stable disposition to react to upward social comparisons with envy (Gold, 1996; Smith, Parrott, Diener, Hoyle, & Kim, 1999); and (c) envy as a *result* of multiple comparisons with multiple others in a given context, such as work or consumerism (e.g., Belk, 2008; Duffy et al., 2012; Duffy & Shaw, 2000; Kim, O'Neill, & Cho, 2010; Matt, 1998; Sterling et al., Chapter 3, this volume).

This last conceptualization of envy has never been discussed in so many words. We call it *chronic envy* for lack of a better term, and see it as a relatively stable state that is limited to a particular context, such as work or leisure (see also Smith, Combs, & Thielke, 2008). As such, it is different from *dispositional envy*, which is not limited to a particular context and is a general tendency to experience envy. It is also different from *episodic envy*, in that its focus is on the better fortune of several others (e.g., many coworkers who have better working conditions) rather than on the better fortune of a particular person (e.g., the one who got the promotion instead of the envious person).

We believe that all three forms of envy (and the newly suggested constructs of episodes of envy and envy as a sentiment) are valid and relevant (but see Salovey, 1991, for a different opinion). However, we urge researchers to use measures that fit the theoretical construct in which they are interested. In other words, if a researcher intends to study episodic envy, it is best if the researcher measures envy as episodic, rather than as chronic or dispositional.

The Need for Theory-Based and Valid Measures. The third issue in the measurement of envy is the tendency of many researchers to measure it using one item ("envy"), two items ("envy" and "jealousy"), or a varied combination of items combined into ad hoc measures that lack a conceptual foundation. Although we recognize some practical advantages of these measures, especially if a study is conducted within an organization and there is a need for short measures, it is important to weigh these benefits against their deficits.

One-item measures, although short and easy to administer, are problematic because, in addition to being of unknown reliability (and hence, validity), they do not reflect the complex nature of envy (Cohen-Charash, 2009; Smith et al., 2008). By not accounting for the full scope of envy, such measures do not allow precise assessment of the experience and, hence, fail to meet major requirements of measurement (Jacoby, 1978; Spector, 1992). One-item measures also have limited predictive validity (Diamantopoulos, Sarstedt, Fuchs, Wilczynski, & Kaiser, 2012).

The two-item measure of envy (i.e., envy and jealousy) is problematic because it is unclear whether research participants perceive it as a measure of envy or of jealousy. Using this two-item measure is probably based on a prevalent confusion between envy and jealousy and the tendency to use them interchangeably. However, envy and jealousy are two different emotions (e.g., Ben-Ze'ev, 1990; East & Watts, 1999; Parrott, 1991) that have some overlap (e.g., Parrott & Smith, 1993; Smith, Kim, & Parrott, 1988; Titelman, 1981). Specifically, whereas envy is concerned with something the person does not have but wants to have, jealousy is concerned with protecting something one already has from others aiming to take it. Thus, envy and jealousy can be seen as two sides of the same coin (for a different view, see Salovey, 1991; Salovey & Rodin, 1986). As they are two different emotions, it is conceptually problematic to use "envy" and "jealousy" as a measure of envy. Moreover, like using one-item measures, two-item measures do not reflect the complexity of envy.

Measures are also deficient when they focus only on one aspect of the emotion. Being a complex emotion, envy, like all emotions, is composed of feelings, cognitions, and action readiness (Cohen-Charash, 2009; Frijda, 1986; Parrott, 1988). Action readiness, however, is not a specific behavior. According to Frijda, the "form or degree of readiness can vary . . . we have the set of programs ready for choosing among them and for execution when circumstances permit" (p. 76). Therefore, emotion definitions and operationalizations should not be too specific regarding behaviors. Each emotion represents a goal, and there are multiple ways to get to that goal. We believe that any definition and operationalization should include both feeling and cognitive components:

An appraisal that someone else has something going well for him or her . . . can result in a positive emotional experience, when one feels happy for the other person's better fortune. . . . In this case, despite the appraisal that another person is doing better than oneself, the person does not feel envy. Similarly, negative, hostile feelings toward another person can occur in the absence of a negative social comparison. For example, anger might occur because of unfair treatment. It is only the specific combination of a negative social comparison and a negative emotional state that is assumed to lead to envy. (Cohen-Charash, 2009, pp. 2130–2131)

The action readiness in envy, in our opinion, is to reduce the envious pain by reducing the gap with the envied other. Therefore, in our opinion, measures that focus only on motivations and wishes, or only on hostile emotions, do not capture the complexity of envy.

Using ad-hoc measures combining several emotion terms with no clear theoretical rationale behind them is another common practice among envy researchers, including those in organizational psychology and organizational behavior. However, the conceptual rationale and the validity of these measures are lacking, as well as their ability to capture the essence of envy. Measurement is only truly valuable when the components of a measure are meaningful, and this meaning can only occur when we utilize theory to develop a measure (Aguinis, Henle, & Ostroff, 2002; Scherbaum & Meade, 2009).

All in all, the lack of a consensus regarding the measurement of envy harms our ability to learn more about it. First, comparing results across studies (for example, in meta-analyses) is virtually impossible, because there are not sufficient studies that examine similar research questions using comparable measures. Second, some envy measures are based on conflicting conceptualizations of envy and lead to conflicting results. Therefore, we hope envy researchers will unite around a very small set of valid measures of envy that will reflect the common denominator for all envy definitions and the exact type of envy studied, which will allow us to better understand envy. We will discuss this more in the last section of this chapter.

Is Envy Desirable or Undesirable?

As Harris and Salovey (2008) pointed out, whether envy is seen as good (desirable) or bad (undesirable) depends on "one's definition of envy . . .

[and] on one's definition of bad" (p. 345). First, whereas envy can be beneficial for one party, it can be detrimental to another. For example, envy can make the envious person suffer but the envied person feel good (Parrott & Rodriguez Mosquera, 2008; Rodriguez Mosquera et al., 2010). Thus, the definition of desirability is not absolute.

Second, once researchers discuss several types of envy, the question arises of why these different emotions are called by the same name. After all, many unpleasant emotions have a dual nature in terms of how beneficial or detrimental their outcomes are. For example, shame is an emotion indicating that a person has committed a moral transgression, and it can lead to self-condemnation, avoidance of others, and blaming others for one's transgressions. At the same time, shame can also lead to appeasing others and restoring social harmony following such transgressions, and it can deter individuals from committing repeated offences (e.g., Keltner & Harker, 1998; Tangney, Stuewig, & Martinez, 2014). Thus, shame can lead to constructive and destructive reactions. Yet, researchers do not talk about "benign" and "malicious" shame, for example. Instead, shame researchers are trying to examine what makes reactions to shame constructive or destructive and are attempting to find a way to funnel reactions to shame in the constructive direction. We believe that envy researchers should adopt a similar model.

Thus far, we have shown that the numerous terms used to describe envy fall into one of two conceptualizations—envy as leading to destructive reactions, or envy as leading to constructive reactions—and that in most disciplines, both conceptualizations exist. Focusing on the empirical investigation of envy in social psychology, one of the disciplines recognizing envy as leading to both destructive or constructive reactions, it is clear that most researchers have examined envy as leading to destructive reactions and unsurprisingly found that envy has negative ramifications. For example, envy was found to lead to unethical behavior (Gino & Pierce, 2009) and deception (Moran & Schweitzer, 2008); to have a negative influence on workgroups (Duffy & Shaw, 2000; Ross, 2007) and leadership (Stein, 1997, 2005); to have a positive relationship with behaviors intended to harm and undermine envied others (Cohen-Charash, 2009; Cohen-Charash & Mueller, 2007; Duffy et al., 2012; Khan, Quratulain, & Bell, 2014), even at the expense of the envious (Wobker, 2014; Zizzo & Oswald, 2001); to impair learning and development (Stein, 2000b), and reduce cognitive resources (Hill, Delpriore, & Vaughan, 2011), among others.

As we have described earlier in this chapter, the recent focus on "benign" envy (e.g., Belk, 2011; van de Ven et al., 2009, 2011a, 2011b) has exacerbated the perception that "malicious" envy only leads to destructive reactions. However, envy researchers not relying on the concept of "benign" envy but rather conceptualizing and measuring envy as a hostile emotion, also found that envy can lead to self-improvement (Cohen-Charash, 2009; Cohen-Charash & Larson, 2011; Larson, 2013; Schaubroeck & Lam, 2004); that envious individuals contribute more to charity (Garay & Móri, 2011; Polman & Ruttan, 2012); that they are less morally hypocritical and judge themselves more harshly than they judge others (Polman & Ruttan, 2012).

Furthermore, there are additional unexplained gaps accompanying the construct of "benign" envy. For example, what happens when there is a gap between motivation and behavior? Natural gifts that someone else has, such as beauty or intelligence, cannot easily be destroyed by an envious person, and sometimes environmental conditions will not allow acting upon one's motivation. Thus, not all action tendencies are acted upon (e.g., Frijda et al., 1991); bad intentions can turn into constructive behaviors (e.g., the person works harder to improve his or her relative status), or envious individuals might opt to do nothing (Berman, 2007). The question is whether envy in such situations of a poor fit between intentions and actions is considered desirable or undesirable. These and other questions currently do not have clear answers.

Our View

We suggest that envy is a painful and unpleasant emotion that can lead to various types of reactions, some of them desirable and others not (Tai et al., 2012). Furthermore, we believe that measures of envy should reflect this pain, but should be devoid of hypothesized predictors of envy, as well as specific motivations and outcomes of envy, in order to avoid tautology. To prevent the confusion of envy with possible rival emotions, such as inferiority, admiration, emulation, and competition (e.g., Belk, 2011; Castelfranchi & Miceli, 2009; Cohen-Charash, 2009), we suggest that definitions of envy be focused on the aspects of envy that are common to all conceptualizations of envy—negative social comparison, feelings of pain, longing for the object of envy, and the goal to eliminate the pain of envy. These elements are seen in all writings about envy, and hence can be the agreed-upon bases of an envy definition.

Note that we differentiate between general motives (reduce the pain) and specific motivations (harm the other or elevate the self). The goal of eliminating or reducing the pain of envy is, in our opinion, the felt action-readiness component of envy, which is an aspect of all emotions (Frijda, 1986; Frijda et al., 1991). However, the execution of action tendencies can be done in several ways and is not a part of the emotion itself (Frijda, 2009; Frijda et al., 1991). For example, Frijda discussed several reactions to fear (withdrawal, flight, freezing, surrender), all "implementing the relational aim of reducing risk" (Frijda, 1986, p. 17). Similarly, envious individuals can reduce the pain by improving themselves, harming the other, cognitively reappraising the situation, or accepting the pain.

Neutral definitions of envy already exist (Berman, 2007; Tai et al., 2012). These definitions do not put a value judgement on envy as desirable or undesirable, malicious or benign. Instead, they reflect the pain inherent in envy and allow the possibility of various ways of dealing with it, some of which are destructive, and others that are constructive. Like Berman, we believe that reactions to envy are determined by personal and situational factors and that one of our goals as envy researchers is to identify these various influences. Therefore, we define envy as a *painful emotion that involves the beliefs that (a) one lacks a desired object that another person has, and (b) the desired object is important to the person's self-concept or competitive position. Envy includes the motivation to reduce the pain it entails and to improve one's relative standing.*

Some Implications for the Future

Whereas we believe that concepts such as malicious, hostile, benign, admiring, and emulating envy are unmerited, we recognize it will take a while before they will lose their cachet, if ever. Given the negative reputation of envy, concepts such as "benign" envy have an intuitive appeal because they do not carry with them the heavy baggage of being a sinful emotion one has to avoid and hide (Parrott, 1991; Silver & Sabini, 1978b). Therefore, people might be willing to admit "benign" envy more than "malicious" envy (Miceli & Castelfranchi, 2007). Benign envy is also recognized in some languages, but not in others (Belk, 2011; van de Ven et al., 2009). Thus, there might also be a cultural component to these terms, and translation issues can complicate things further (e.g., Russell, 1991).

The question is whether, when one tells a friend going on vacation "I envy you so much," one is actually envious, or even "benignly" envious. Researchers doubt this is actually "envy" (e.g., Silver & Sabini,

1978a; Smith & Kim, 2007). We assume that to the extent that vacation-ing (or the ability to go on vacation) is central to one's self-definition, this might indeed be envy. However, in that case, we are doubtful one will confess to it (Elster, 1991; Foster, 1972). Instead, we believe that, because of the negativity related to envy, an envious person will ex-press his or her enviousness in more covert ways and will not admit to experiencing it (Cohen-Charash, Larson, & Fischer, 2013; Fischer & Cohen-Charash, 2009).

We believe researchers will need to offer hypotheses that recognize that no emotion always leads to one type of reaction, to use designs that enable the examination of competing hypotheses, and to use measures that take into account the complete emotional experience, while excluding anteced-ents and outcomes of the emotion, to properly understand what is and is not envy.

What Do We Have Going for Us?

While we have discussed the challenges we face in understanding envy based on past research, we think that envy research has a bright future and an enormous importance in the organizational context. First, we study a construct that is of interest to researchers from multiple disciplines, in-cluding those discussed earlier as well as others, such as neuroscience (Dvash, Gilam, Ben-Ze'ev, Hendler, & Shamay-Tsoory, 2010; Harris, Cikara, & Fiske, 2008; Joseph, Powell, Johnson, & Kedia, 2008; Shamay-Tsoory, 2010a, 2010b; Shamay-Tsoory et al., 2009; Shamay-Tsoory, Tibi-Elhanany, & Aharon-Peretz, 2007). This interdisciplinary study of envy enables us to use the wide knowledge base on envy, borrowing from and contributing to it. Having so many points of view about envy is enriching and enlightening.

Applying Barsade, Brief, and Spataro's (2003) logic to the study of envy, we believe that envy research is heading towards a hybrid para-digm, which consists of presenting and integrating data from as many per-spectives and levels of analysis as possible. For that, we need a common language that facilitates a clear understanding of the implications of our findings. This, of course, will take a great deal of coordination, but we are optimistic that recent symposia and publications such as this volume will help pave the way for this type of interdisciplinary communication.

Second, there is currently a high level of public and professional inter-est in envy. In the past several years, there has been a rise in the popular press's coverage of envy. In fact, recent publications in the *Wall Street*

Journal and *New York Times* reviewed findings we have mentioned in this chapter, providing practical applications of envy research (Aschwanden, 2012; Cohen-Charash, 2014; Tierney, 2011; Wallace, 2014). We believe these types of publications reflect people's desire to understand envy and how they can constructively cope with the emotion. As mentioned earlier, there is a promising presence of envy research in journals and conferences. In a review of some of the biggest journal databases,[6] we found that approximately 19% of articles on envy in peer-reviewed journals have been published since 2010. Similarly, we have seen that envy research is well represented at international conferences. Since 2010, there have been three to eight envy-related presentations and symposia each year at the Academy of Management's annual conference. We are enthusiastic that this type of presence helps increase awareness of our work while also promoting new research in an already burgeoning field.

Third, there are plenty of unanswered questions about envy, in many respects making our work cut out for us. Even if we stay within the scope of this chapter, there is plenty to do, and of course, there are many other areas of envy that are open to exploration. For example, if reactions to envy can be destructive or constructive, the major question is what determines the direction of these reactions. Whereas there is some research on situational and personality variables related to reactions to envy, cognitive and emotional reactions have hardly been investigated. However, it might be that the majority of reactions belong to this covert type of reaction (Berman, 2007). Reappraisals of the situation, the envied object, and the envied other are examples of what we believe are widely used regulation mechanisms, which have not yet been studied. These map nicely onto Hoogland et al.'s (Chapter 5, this volume) model of envy episodes, and our suggestion to examine envy as a sentiment. In fact, these cognitive and emotional variables may prove to be important mechanisms for understanding the link between envy and organizational outcomes. Examining these questions entails changing our research methods and turning to longitudinal designs, multi-source data, and experience-sampling studies, in addition to our current methods.

Having a clear understanding of envy will increase the chances that managers will adopt researchers' insights regarding envy. It should be our aim as a field to ensure that the practicality of our findings is easily accessible to all and, ultimately, accurate and valuable. Therefore, we call for envy researchers to build on our past theories and findings to deepen our understanding of envy.

Earlier in the chapter, we suggested certain guidelines that we believe should be followed when studying envy to help us derive a conceptualization of envy that is built on strong empirical research. We believe this chapter and those that follow in this volume help initiate this conversation and provide the foundation for a coherent voice for envy researchers. To invoke the Jewish proverb, "May envy increase our wisdom."

Notes

1. We will later discuss additional classifications, such as those based on envy's duration (e.g., episodic, dispositional, or chronic envy) and on the nature of its target (e.g., individuals or groups).

2. That being said, we believe that moral convictions, values, and stereotypes are also bases for classifying envy into the "positive" or "negative" clusters. Whereas in some disciplines these are more salient bases (e.g., theology, philosophy), in other disciplines, such as social psychology, these are more implicit bases. This is a question for empirical research.

3. We thank Richard Smith for this comment.

4. We include here also theory and research in organizational behavior and organizational psychology, as these often rely on the same principles as those set forth by social psychologists.

5. Due to space limitations, we will not examine the relationship between envy and injustice in this chapter. See Sterling, van de Ven, and Smith (Chapter 3), and Mishra, Whiting, and Folger (Chapter 16) in this volume for reviews of the topic.

6. Based on a review of online databases, including Communication & Mass Media Complete, EconLit, ERIC, Humanities Source, Philosopher's Index, PsycARTICLES, PsycINFO, Social Sciences, and SOCIndex, conducted in January, 2015.

References

Adrianson, L., & Ramdhani, N. (2014). Why you and not me? Expressions of envy in Indonesia and Sweden. *International Journal of Research Studies in Psychology, 3*, 43–65.

Aguinis, H., Henle, C. A., & Ostroff, C. (2002). Measurement in work and organizational psychology. In N. Anderson, D. S. Ones, H. K. Sinangil, & C. Viswesvaran, Eds., *Handbook of Industrial, Work and Organizational Psychology, Volume 1: Personnel Psychology* (pp. 27–50). Thousand Oaks, CA: Sage Publications Ltd.

Ahier, J., & Beck, J. (2003). Education and the politics of envy. *British Journal of Educational Studies, 51*, 320–343. doi: 10.1046/j.1467-8527.2003.00242.x

AHYA.Org. (2014). Authentic Islamic information and resources. Retrieved May 18, 2014, from http://www.ahya.org/amm/modules.php?name=Sections&op=viewarticle&artid=181.

Anderson, R. W. (1997). The envious will to power. *The Journal of Analytical Psychology, 42*, 363–382. doi: 10.1111/j.1465-5922.1997.00363.x

Armstrong, J., Brodie, R., & Parsons, A. (2001). Hypotheses in marketing science: Literature review and publication audit. *Marketing Letters, 12*, 171–187. doi: 10.1023/A:1011169104290

Aschwanden, C. (2012, July). When envy strikes: How to put jealousy to good use. *O: The Oprah Magazine*. Retrieved on May 18, 2014, from http://www.oprah.com/spirit/Benefits-of-Jealousy-Envying-Friends.

Barsade, S. G., Brief, A. P., & Spataro, S. E. (2003). The affective revolution in organizational behavior: The emergence of a paradigm. In J. Greenberg, Ed., *Organizational Behavior: The State of the Science* (2nd ed., pp. 3–52). Mahwah, NJ: Lawrence Erlbaum Associates, Publishers.

Belk, R. W. (2008). Marketing and envy. In R. H. Smith, Ed., *Envy: Theory and Research* (pp. 211–226). New York: Oxford University Press.

Belk, R. W. (2011). Benign envy. *AMS Review, 1*, 117–134. doi: 10.1007/s13162-011-0018-x

Ben-Ze'ev, A. (1990). Envy and jealousy. *Canadian Journal of Philosophy, 20*, 487–516.

Ben-Ze'ev, A. (1992). Envy and inequality. *Journal of Philosophy, 89*, 551–581.

Ben-Ze'ev, A. (1997). The affective realm. *New Ideas in Psychology, 15*, 247–259.

Berman, A. (2007). Envy at the cross-road between destruction, self-actualization, and avoidance. In L. Navaro & S. L. Schwartzberg, Eds., *Envy, Competition, and Gender: Theory, Clinical Applications and Group Work* (pp. 17–32). New York: Routledge/Taylor & Francis Group.

Castelfranchi, C., & Miceli, M. (2009). The cognitive-motivational compound of emotional experience. *Emotion Review, 1*, 223–231. doi: 10.1177/1754073909103590

Cohen-Charash, Y. (2009). Episodic envy. *Journal of Applied Social Psychology, 39*, 2128–2173.

Cohen-Charash, Y. (2014). How to keep jealousy and envy from ruining your life. Retrieved May 18, 2014, from http://www.huffingtonpost.com/2014/04/24/jealousy-envy_n_5186248.html.

Cohen-Charash, Y. (2015). The value judgment of emotions. Under revision review, *Personality and Social Psychology Review*.

Cohen-Charash, Y., & Larson, E. C. (2011, August). Ability to change a situation and self-esteem as determinants of constructive and destructive reactions to envy. Paper presented at the Annual Meeting of the Academy of Management, San Antonio, TX.

Cohen-Charash, Y., Larson, E. C., & Fischer, A. H. (2013, August). Envious or angry? Self and other reactions to others getting what we want. Paper presented at the Annual Meeting of the Academy of Management, Orlando, FL.

Cohen-Charash, Y., & Mueller, J. S. (2007). Does perceived unfairness exacerbate or mitigate interpersonal counterproductive work behaviors related to envy? *Journal of Applied Psychology, 92*, 666–680.

Crusius, J., & Mussweiler, T. (2012). When people want what others have: The impulsive side of envious desire. *Emotion, 12*, 142–153. doi: 10.1037/a0023523

D'arms, J., & Kerr, A. D. (2008). Envy in the philosophical tradition. In R. H. Smith, Ed., *Envy: Theory and Research* (pp. 39–59). New York: Oxford University Press.

de Silva, P. (2000). *An Introduction to Buddhist Psychology (3rd ed.).* Lanham, MD: Rowman & Littlefield.

Delpriore, D. J., Hill, S. E., & Buss, D. M. (2012). Envy: Functional specificity and sex-differentiated design features. *Personality and Individual Differences, 53,* 317–322. doi: 10.1016/j.paid.2012.03.029

Diamantopoulos, A., Sarstedt, M., Fuchs, C., Wilczynski, P., & Kaiser, S. (2012). Guidelines for choosing between multi-item and single-item scales for construct measurement: A predictive validity perspective. *Journal of the Academy of Marketing Science, 40,* 434–449. doi: 10.1007/s11747-011-0300-3

Donaldson, D. (1953). *Studies in Muslim Ethics.* London: S.P.C.K.

Duffy, M. K., Scott, K. L., Shaw, J. D., Tepper, B. J., & Aquino, K. (2012). A social context model of envy and social undermining. *Academy of Management Journal, 55,* 643–666.

Duffy, M. K., & Shaw, J. D. (2000). The Salieri syndrome: Consequences of envy in groups. *Small Group Research, 31,* 3–23.

Dvash, J., Gilam, G., Ben-Ze'ev, A., Hendler, T., & Shamay-Tsoory, S. G. (2010). The envious brain: The neural basis of social comparison. *Human Brain Mapping, 31,* 1741–1750.

East, M. P., & Watts, F. N. (1999). Jealousy and envy. In T. Dalgleish & M. J. Power, Eds., *Handbook of Cognition and Emotion* (pp. 568–588). New York: John Wiley & Sons.

Ekman, P., & Davidson, R. J. (1994). *The Nature of Emotion: Fundamental Questions.* New York: Oxford University Press.

Ekman, P., Davidson, R. J., Ricard, M., & Wallace, B. A. (2005). Buddhist and psychological perspectives on emotions and well-being. *Current Directions in Psychological Science, 14,* 59–63. doi: 10.1111/j.0963-7214.2005.00335.x

Elster, J. (1991). Envy in social life. In R. J. Zeckhauser, Ed., *Strategy and Choice* (pp. 49–82). Cambridge, MA: MIT Press.

Exline, J. J., & Zell, A. L. (2008). Antidotes to envy: A conceptual framework. In R. H. Smith, Ed., *Envy: Theory and Research* (pp. 315–331). New York: Oxford University Press.

Fischer, A. H., & Cohen-Charash, Y. (2009, July). "No, I'm not at all envious!" Implicit regulation of envy. Paper presented at the Bi-Annual Meeting of the International Society of Research of Emotions, Louven, Belgium.

Fiske, S. T. (2010). Envy up, scorn down: How comparison divides us. *American Psychologist, 65,* 698–706. doi: 10.1037/0003-066x.65.8.698

Fiske, S. T. (2015). Intergroup biases: A focus on stereotype content. *Current Opinion in Behavioral Sciences, 3,* 45–50. doi: http://dx.doi.org/10.1016/j.cobeha.2015.01.010

Fiske, S. T., Cuddy, A. J. C., Glick, P., & Xu, J. (2002). A model of (often mixed) stereotype content: Competence and warmth respectively follow from perceived status and competition. *Journal of Personality and Social Psychology, 82,* 878–902.

Foster, G. M. (1972). The anatomy of envy: A study in symbolic behavior. *Current Anthropology, 13,* 165–186.

Frijda, N. H. (1986). *The Emotions.* Cambridge, MA: Cambridge University Press.

Frijda, N. H. (1993). Moods, emotion episodes, and emotions. In J. M. Haviland & M. Lewis, Eds., *Handbook of Emotions* (pp. 381–403). New York: The Guilford Press.

Frijda, N. H. (2009). Emotion experience and its varieties. *Emotion Review*, *1*, 264–271. doi: 10.1177/1754073909103595

Frijda, N. H., Mesquita, B., Sonneman, N. S., & Van Goozen, S. (1991). The duration of affective phenomena or emotions, sentiments, and passions. *International Review of Studies on Emotion*, *1*, 187–225.

Garay, J., & Móri, T. F. (2011). Is envy one of the possible evolutionary roots of charity? *Biosystems*, *106*, 28–35. doi: 10.1016/j.biosystems.2011.06.004

Gershman, B. (2014). The two sides of envy. *Journal of Economic Growth*, *19*, 407–438. doi: 10.1007/s10887-014-9106-8

Gino, F., & Pierce, L. (2009). The abundance effect: Unethical behavior in the presence of wealth. *Organizational Behavior and Human Decision Processes*, *109*, 142–155. doi: 10.1016/j.obhdp.2009.03.003

Gino, F., & Pierce, L. (2010). Robin Hood under the hood: Wealth-based discrimination in illicit customer help. *Organization Science*, *21*, 1176–1194. doi: 10.1287/orsc.1090.0498

Gold, B. T. (1996). Enviousness and its relationship to maladjustment and psychopathology. *Personality and Individual Differences*, *21*, 311–321.

Greenwald, A. G., Pratkanis, A. R., Leippe, M. R., & Baumgardner, M. H. (1986). Under what conditions does theory obstruct research progress? *Psychological Review*, *93*, 216–229.

Hagedorn, A. C., & Neyrey, J. H. (1998). It was out of envy that they handed Jesus over (Mark 15:10): The anatomy of envy and the Gospel of Mark. *Journal for the Study of the New Testament*, *20*, 15–56. doi: 10.1177/0142064x9802006902

Hamman, J. J. (2013). The memory of feeling: Envy and happiness. *Pastoral Psychology*. doi: 10.1007/s11089-013-0555-3

Harris, C. R., & Salovey, P. (2008). Reflections on envy. In R. H. Smith, Ed., *Envy: Theory and Research* (pp. 335–356). New York: Oxford University Press.

Harris, L. T., Cikara, M., & Fiske, S. T. (2008). Envy, as predicted by the stereotype content model: A volatile ambivalence. In R. H. Smith, Ed., *Envy: Theory and Research* (pp. 133–147). New York: Oxford University Press.

Heider, F. (1958). *The Psychology of Interpersonal Relations*. New York: John Wiley & Sons.

Hill, S. E., & Buss, D. M. (2006). Envy and positional bias in the evolutionary psychology of management. *Managerial and Decision Economics*, *27*, 131–143. doi: 10.1002/mde.1288

Hill, S. E., & Buss, D. M. (2008). The evolutionary psychology of envy. In R. H. Smith, Ed., *Envy: Theory and Research* (pp. 60–70). New York: Oxford University Press.

Hill, S. E., Delpriore, D. J., & Vaughan, P. W. (2011). The cognitive consequences of envy: Attention, memory, and self-regulatory depletion. *Journal of Personality and Social Psychology*, *101*, 653–666. doi: 10.1037/a0023904

Hughes, C. (2007). The equality of social envies. *Sociology*, *41*, 347–363. doi: 10.1177/0038038507074979

Hupka, R. B., Zaleski, Z., Otto, J., & Reidl, L. (1996). Anger, envy, fear, and jealousy as felt in the body: A five-nation study. *Cross-Cultural Research: The Journal of Comparative Social Science*, *30*, 243–264.

Hupka, R. B., Zaleski, Z., Otto, J., & Reidl, L. (1997). The colors of anger, envy, fear, and jealousy: A cross-cultural study. *Journal of Cross-Cultural Psychology, 28*, 156–171.

Jacoby, J. (1978). Consumer research: How valid and useful are all our consumer behavior research findings? A state of the art review. *Journal of Marketing, 42*, 87–96. doi: 10.2307/1249890

Joseph, J. E., Powell, C. A. J., Johnson, N. F., & Kedia, G. (2008). The functional neuroanatomy of envy. In R. H. Smith, Ed., *Envy: Theory and Research* (pp. 245–263). New York: Oxford University Press.

Keltner, D., & Harker, L. (1998). The forms and functions of the nonverbal signal of shame. In P. Gilbert & B. Andrews, Eds., *Shame: Interpersonal Behavior, Psychopathology, and Culture* (pp. 78–98). New York: Oxford University Press.

Khan, A. K., Quratulain, S., & Bell, C. M. (2014). Episodic envy and counterproductive work behaviors: Is more justice always good? *Journal of Organizational Behavior, 35*, 128–144. doi: 10.1002/job.1864

Kim, S., O'Neill, J. W., & Cho, H.-M. (2010). When does an employee not help coworkers? The effect of leader–member exchange on employee envy and organizational citizenship behavior. *International Journal of Hospitality Management, 29*, 530–537.

Klein, M. (1957). *Envy and Gratitude: A Study of Unconscious Sources.* New York: Basic Books.

Konow, J. (2003). Which is the fairest one of all? A positive analysis of justice theories. *Journal of Economic Literature, 41*, 1188–1239. doi: 10.2307/3217459

La Caze, M. (2001). Envy and resentment. *Philosophical Explorations: An International Journal for the Philosophy of Mind and Action, 4*, 31–45.

La Caze, M. (2002). Revaluing envy and resentment. *Philosophical Explorations: An International Journal for the Philosophy of Mind and Action, 5*, 155–158.

Lange, J., & Crusius, J. (2015). The tango of two deadly sins: The social-functional relation of envy and pride. *Journal of Personality and Social Psychology, 109*, 453–472. doi: 10.1037/pspi0000026

Larson, E. C. (2013, August). The sharpened sight of envy: Deservingness and proximity as predictors of constructive and destructive reactions to envy. Paper presented at the Annual Meeting of the Academy of Management, Orlando, FL.

Lazarus, R. S. (1991). *Emotion and Adaptation.* New York: Oxford University Press.

Leach, C. W. (2008). Envy, inferiority, and injustice: Three bases of anger about inequality. In R. H. Smith, Ed., *Envy: Theory and Research* (pp. 94–116). New York: Oxford University Press.

Lindholm, C. (2008). Culture and envy. In R. H. Smith, Ed., *Envy: Theory and Research* (pp. 227–244). New York: Oxford University Press.

Liska, A. E. (1969). Uses and misuses of tautologies in social psychology. *Sociometry, 32*, 444–457.

Mackenzie, S. B. (2003). The dangers of poor construct conceptualization. *Journal of the Academy of Marketing Science, 31*, 323–326.

Madelker, S. (2008). Envy. In *The Encyclopedia of Love in World Religions* (Vol. 1, pp. 184–187). Santa Barbara, CA: ABC-CLIO.

Malina, B. J. (2001). *The New Testament World: Insights from Cultural Anthropology.* Louisville, KY: Westminster John Knox Press.

Matt, S. J. (1998). Frocks, finery, and feelings: Rural and urban women's envy, 1890–1930. In P. N. Stearns & J. Lewis, Eds., *An Emotional History of the United States* (pp. 377–395). New York: New York University Press.

Miceli, M., & Castelfranchi, C. (2002). The mind and the future: The (negative) power of expectations. *Theory and Psychology, 12,* 335–366.

Miceli, M., & Castelfranchi, C. (2007). The envious mind. *Cognition and Emotion, 21,* 449–479.

Midrash Tehillim (English). (1959). *The Midrash on Psalms* (W. G. Braude, Trans.). New Haven: Yale University Press.

Mitsopoulos, M. (2009). Envy, institutions and growth. *Bulletin of Economic Research, 61,* 201–222. doi: 10.1111/j.1467-8586.2009.00313.x

Moran, S., & Schweitzer, M. E. (2008). When better is worse: Envy and the use of deception. *Negotiation and Conflict Management Research, 1,* 3–29.

Nesse, R. M. (2004). Natural selection and the elusiveness of happiness. *Philosophical Transactions of the Royal Society B: Biological Sciences, 359,* 1333–1347.

Neu, J. (1980). Jealous thoughts. In A. Rorty, Ed., *Explaining Emotions* (pp. 425–463). Berkeley, CA: University of California Press.

Orchot Tzaddikim (English). (1969). *Ways of the Righteous.* (S. J. Cohen, Trans.). New York: Feldheim.

Palaver, W. (2005). Envy or emulation: A Christian understanding of economic passions. In W. Palaver & P. Steinmair-Pösel, Eds., *Passions in Economy, Politics, and the Media* (pp. 139–162). Vienna: Lit Verlag.

Parrott, W. G. (1988). The role of cognition in emotional experience. In W. J. Baker, L. P. Mos, H. V. Rappard, & H. J. Stam, Eds., *Recent Trends in Theoretical Psychology* (pp. 327–337). New York: Springer-Verlag.

Parrott, W. G. (1991). The emotional experiences of envy and jealousy. In P. Salovey, Ed., *The Psychology of Jealousy and Envy* (pp. 3–30). New York: The Guilford Press.

Parrott, W. G., & Rodriguez Mosquera, P. M. (2008). On the pleasures and displeasures of being envied. In R. H. Smith, Ed., *Envy: Theory and Research* (pp. 117–132). New York: Oxford University Press.

Parrott, W. G., & Smith, R. H. (1993). Distinguishing the experiences of envy and jealousy. *Journal of Personality and Social Psychology, 64,* 906–920.

Podder, N. (1996). Relative deprivation, envy and economic inequality. *Kyklos, 49,* 353–376. doi: 10.1111/j.1467-6435.1996.tb01401.x

Polman, E., & Ruttan, R. L. (2012). Effects of anger, guilt, and envy on moral hypocrisy. *Personality and Social Psychology Bulletin, 38,* 129–139. doi: 10.1177/0146167211422365

Quintanilla, L., & De López, K. J. (2013). The niche of envy: Conceptualization, coping strategies, and the ontogenesis of envy in cultural psychology. *Culture and Psychology, 19,* 76–94. doi: 10.1177/1354067x12464980

Rawls, J. (1971). *A Theory of Justice.* Cambridge, MA: The Belknap Press of Harvard University Press.

Rodriguez Mosquera, P. M., Parrott, W. G., & De Mendoza, A. H. (2010). I fear your envy, I rejoice in your coveting: On the ambivalent experience of being envied by others. *Journal of Personality and Social Psychology, 99,* 842–854. doi: 10.1037/a0020965

Ross, M. R. (2007). Anti-group as a phenomenon: The destructive aspects of envy, competition, and gender differences in groups, as seen through *The Apprentice*. In L. Navaro & S. L. Schwartzberg, Eds., *Envy, Competition, and Gender: Theory, Clinical Applications and Group Work* (pp. 205–227). New York: Routledge/Taylor & Francis Group.

Russell, J. A. (1991). Culture and the categorization of emotions. *Psychological Bulletin, 110*, 426–450.

Salovey, P. (1991). Social comparison processes in envy and jealousy. In J. Suls & T. A. Wills, Eds., *Social Comparison: Contemporary Theory and Research* (pp. 261–285). Hillsdale, NJ: Lawrence Erlbaum Associates.

Salovey, P., & Rodin, J. (1986). The differentiation of social-comparison jealousy and romantic jealousy. *Journal of Personality and Social Psychology, 50*, 1100–1112.

Salovey, P., & Rothman, A. J. (1991). Envy and jealousy: Self and society. In P. Salovey, Ed., *The Psychology of Jealousy and Envy* (pp. 271–286). New York: The Guilford Press.

Schaubroeck, J., & Lam, S. S. K. (2004). Comparing lots before and after: Promotion rejectees' invidious reactions to promotees. *Organizational Behavior and Human Decision Processes, 94*, 33–47.

Scherbaum, C. A., & Meade, A. W. (2009). Measurement in the organizational sciences: Conceptual and technological advances. In D. A. Buchanan & A. Bryman, Eds., *The Sage Handbook of Organizational Research Methods* (pp. 636–653). Thousand Oaks, CA: Sage Publications Ltd.

Schimmel, S. (2008). Envy in Jewish thought and literature. In R. H. Smith, Ed., *Envy: Theory and Research* (pp. 17–38). New York: Oxford University Press.

Schoeck, H. (1969). *Envy: A Theory of Social Behavior* (M. Glenny & B. Ross, Trans.). New York: Harcourt, Brace & World.

Shamay-Tsoory, S. G. (2010a). One hormonal system for love and envy: A reply to Tops. *Biological Psychiatry, 67*, e5–e6.

Shamay-Tsoory, S. G. (2010b). Oxytocin, social salience, and social approach. *Biological Psychiatry, 67*. doi: 10.1016/j.biopsych.2009.11.020

Shamay-Tsoory, S. G., Fischer, M., Dvash, J., Harari, H., Perach-Bloom, N., & Levkovitz, Y. (2009). Intranasal administration of oxytocin increases envy and schadenfreude (gloating). *Biological Psychiatry, 66*, 864–870.

Shamay-Tsoory, S. G., Tibi-Elhanany, Y., & Aharon-Peretz, J. (2007). The green-eyed monster and malicious joy: The neuroanatomical bases of envy and gloating (schadenfreude). *Brain, 130*, 1663–1678.

Silver, M., & Sabini, J. (1978a). The perception of envy. *Social Psychology, 41*, 105–117.

Silver, M., & Sabini, J. (1978b). The social construction of envy. *Journal for the Theory of Social Behavior, 8*, 313–332.

Smith, R. H. (2000). Assimilative and contrastive emotional reactions to upward and downward social comparisons. In J. Suls & L. Wheeler, Eds., *Handbook of Social Comparison: Theory and Research* (pp. 173–200). New York: Kluger Academics/Plenum Publishers.

Smith, R. H. (2004). Envy and its transmutations. In L. Z. Tiedens & C. W. Leach, Eds., *The Social Life of Emotions* (pp. 43–63). New York: Cambridge University Press.

Smith, R. H., Combs, D. J. Y., & Thielke, S. M. (2008). Envy and the challenges to good health. In R. H. Smith, Ed., *Envy: Theory and Research* (pp. 290–314). New York: Oxford University Press.

Smith, R. H., & Kim, S. H. (2007). Comprehending envy. *Psychological Bulletin, 133*, 46–64.

Smith, R. H., Kim, S. H., & Parrott, W. G. (1988). Envy and jealousy: Semantic problems and experimental distinctions. *Personality and Social Psychology Bulletin, 14*, 401–409.

Smith, R. H., Parrott, W. G., Diener, E. F., Hoyle, R. H., & Kim, S. H. (1999). Dispositional envy. *Personality and Social Psychology Bulletin, 25*, 1007–1020.

Spector, P. E. (1992). *Summated Rating Scale Construction: An Introduction.* Thousand Oaks, CA: Sage Publications.

Stein, M. (1997). Envy and leadership. *European Journal of Work and Organizational Psychology, 6*, 453–465. doi: 10.1080/135943297399033

Stein, M. (2000a). After Eden: Envy and the defences against anxiety paradigm. *Human Relations, 53*, 193–211.

Stein, M. (2000b). "Winners" training and its troubles. *Personnel Review, 29*, 445–459. doi: 10.1108/00483480010296267

Stein, M. (2005). The Othello conundrum: The inner contagion of leadership. *Organization Studies, 26*, 1405–1419. doi: 10.1177/0170840605055339

Sundie, J. M., Ward, J. C., Beal, D. J., Chin, W. W., & Geiger-Oneto, S. (2009). Schadenfreude as a consumption-related emotion: Feeling happiness about the downfall of another's product. *Journal of Consumer Psychology, 19*, 356–373.

Tai, K., Narayanan, J., & Mcallister, D. (2012). Envy as pain: Rethinking the nature of envy and its implications for employees and organizations. *Academy of Management Review, 37*, 107–129.

Tangney, J. P., Stuewig, J., & Martinez, A. G. (2014). Two faces of shame: The roles of shame and guilt in predicting recidivism. *Psychological Science, 25*, 799–805. doi: 10.1177/0956797613508790

Taylor, G. (1988). Envy and jealousy: Emotions and vices. *Midwest Studies in Philosophy, 13*, 233–249.

Tesser, A., & Collins, J. E. (1988). Emotion in social reflection and comparison situations: Intuitive, systematic, and exploratory approaches. *Journal of Personality and Social Psychology, 55*, 695–709.

Thinkexist. (2014). Buddha quotes. Retrieved Dec. 22, 2014, from http://thinkexist.com/quotes/buddha/.

This Saint-Jean, I. (2009). Is *Homo oeconomicus* a "bad guy?" In R. Arena, S. Dow, & M. Klaes, Eds., *Open Economics: Economics in Relation to other Disciplines* (pp. 262–280). New York: Routledge.

Tierney, J. (2011). Envy may bear fruit, but it also has an aftertaste. *The New York Times.* Retrieved May 18, 2014, from http://www.nytimes.com/2011/10/11/science/11tierney.html?_r=0.

Titelman, P. (1981). A phenomenological comparison between envy and jealousy. *Journal of Phenomenological Psychology, 12*, 189–204.

van de Ven, N. (2009). *The Bright Side of a Deadly Sin: The Psychology of Envy.* Dissertatiereeks, Amsterdam: Kurt Lewin Instituut.

van de Ven, N., Zeelenberg, M., & Pieters, R. (2009). Leveling up and down: The experiences of benign and malicious envy. *Emotion*, *9*, 419–429.

van de Ven, N., Zeelenberg, M., & Pieters, R. (2011a). The envy premium in product evaluation. *Journal of Consumer Research*, *37*, 984–998. doi: 10.1086/657239

van de Ven, N., Zeelenberg, M., & Pieters, R. (2011b). Why envy outperforms admiration. *Personality and Social Psychology Bulletin*, *37*, 784–795. doi: 10.1177/0146167211400421

van de Ven, N., Zeelenberg, M., & Pieters, R. (2012). Appraisal patterns of envy and related emotions. *Motivation and Emotion*, *36*, 195–204. doi: 10.1007/s11031-011-9235-8

Vidaillet, B. (2008). Psychoanalytic contributions to understanding envy: Classic and contemporary perspectives. In R. H. Smith, Ed., *Envy: Theory and Research* (pp. 267–289). New York: Oxford University Press.

Wallace, J. B. (2014, April 25). Put your envy to good use. *The Wall Street Journal (Online)*. Retrieved May 15, 2014, from http://www.wsj.com/articles/SB10001424052702304279904579517903705459222

Wobker, I. (2014). The price of envy—an experimental investigation of spiteful behavior. *Managerial and Decision Economics*, *36*, 326–335. doi: 10.1002/mde.2672

Zizzo, D. J. (2008). The cognitive and behavioral economics of envy. In R. H. Smith, Ed., *Envy: Theory and Research* (pp. 190–210). New York: Oxford University Press.

Zizzo, D. J., & Oswald, A. J. (2001). Are people willing to pay to reduce others' incomes? *Annals of Economics and Statistics/Annales d'Économie et de Statistique*, *63/64*, 39–65.

2 | A Social-Contextual View of Envy in Organizations

FROM BOTH ENVIER AND ENVIED PERSPECTIVES

LINGTAO YU AND MICHELLE K. DUFFY

TODAY, UNDER PERHAPS THE SEVEREST global competition we have ever encountered, organizations provide a variety of resources and benefits such as paid vacation, overseas training opportunities, stock bonuses, and other organizational rewards, to attract, motivate, and retain high performers, thus maintaining sustained competitive advantages (Ployhart, Van Iddekinge, & MacKenzie, 2011). However, employees must compete with each other, because these resources and benefits are scarce (Duffy, Shaw, & Schaubroeck, 2008; Tai, Narayanan, & McAllister, 2012). Work-related competitions are likely to elicit social comparisons, and for those who don't fare well in these comparisons and outcome allocations, feelings of envy may be evoked (Duffy et al., 2008). Indeed, a rich and longstanding body of social psychological literature demonstrates that the feeling of envy—a painful emotion that conveys inferiority of self (Smith & Kim, 2007)—stems from unfavorable social comparisons with others who have one's "desired superior quality, achievements, or possessions" (Parrott & Smith, 1993, p. 908). Envy is a natural occurrence in organizations, and employees at all levels are vulnerable to its effects (Menon & Thompson, 2010). Employees may envy a number of others' outcomes such as financial outcomes (i.e., paid vacation, training opportunity, or stock bonus), social standing, or outcomes with more symbolic values (e.g., a luxury office chair), as long as the objects are what people both lack and desire (Tai et al., 2012).

As a result of its prevalence and consequences for organizations and their employees, the study of envy is a dynamic and important field of research for organizational scholars (Cohen-Charash, 2009; Duffy et al.,

2008; Smith & Kim, 2007; Tai et al., 2012). However, the extant organizational envy literature suggests paradoxical reactions to the experience of envy for both enviers and those that are envied. From the perspective of enviers, studies (for reviews, see Lee & Gino, in press; Sterling, van de Ven, & Smith, in press) have linked envy to a variety of deleterious outcomes such as lower self-esteem (Smith & Kim, 2007), social undermining (Duffy, Scott, Shaw, Tepper, & Aquino, 2012) and decreased group performance (Duffy & Shaw, 2000), whereas others have shown that envy is associated with positive outcomes (for reviews, see Sterling et al., in press) such as improved work motivation (Cohen-Charash, 2009), increased job search effort (Dineen, Duffy, Henle, & Lee, in press), and better job performance (Schaubreck & Lam, 2004). Likewise, from the perspective of the envied (for reviews, see Parrott, in press), research results suggest an equally contrasting view—on one hand, being envied is associated with fear of ill will from others (Rodriguez Mosquera, Parrott, & Hurtado de Mendoza, 2010) and lower levels of job performance (Henegan & Bedeian, 2007); on the other hand, being envied is also linked to higher levels of self-confidence (Rodriguez Mosquera et al., 2010) and more pro-social behaviors (van de Ven, Zeelenberg, & Pieters, 2010). It appears, then, that both enviers and the envied may experience and respond to envy in paradoxical ways. Taken together, the current research suggests that envy and being envied can be experienced and responded to in functional or dysfunctional ways (e.g., Hoogland, Thielke, & Smith, in press; Lee & Gino, in press; Smith & Kim, 2007; Sterling et al., in press; Tai et al., 2012; van de Ven, Zeelenberg, & Pieters, 2009). What is less clear, however, is why this is the case. In this chapter, we take steps to address this issue, by asking: *What factors influence the way in which envy is experienced and responded to?*

The aim of this chapter is twofold. First, we provide an up-to-date review of where the literature is on organizational envy, from the perspectives of both enviers and the envied. In doing so, we delineate why the experience of envy and being envied elicit either positive or negative consequences in the workplace. Second, and more important, we examine the role of a variety of social-contextual factors in understanding the way envy is expressed and responded to in the workplace. A central point of our chapter is that the *social context in which the envy is triggered may affect how envy is expressed, when it generates reactions, and in what ways people respond.* By definition, envy could not exist without its social context. Instead of searching for ways to permanently eliminate envy in the workplace, we submit that both researchers and practitioners could benefit from a greater focus on the potential antidotes and/or poisons to envy once it is triggered, particularly the role of social contexts in altering the expression of and response to the feeling of envy. Does a certain social context serve as a *poison* that exacerbates the negative reactions to envy, or does it serve as an *antidote* that mitigates these negative reactions, or even turns them into positive reactions? By emphasizing the differential roles of various social contexts in the expression of and response to envy, we attempt to map out a better way of categorizing various reactions to envy, especially in organizational contexts.

In this chapter, we present foundational work for theory about envy in organizations, with specific attention paid to the role of social context in envy. We first describe what we mean by "the role of social context in envy" (as antidote or poison) and our basic assumptions. We then review the literature to examine how envy is expressed and how people respond to envy from two different perspectives: the *enviers* and the *envied*. Building on this, we propose a theoretical quadrant to map out a variety of reactions to envy (Figure 2.1). In doing so, we also show the necessity for an approach that addresses important boundary conditions in this prior research by paying attention to the role of social context. We then present results from several very recent studies to discuss how enviers and the envied

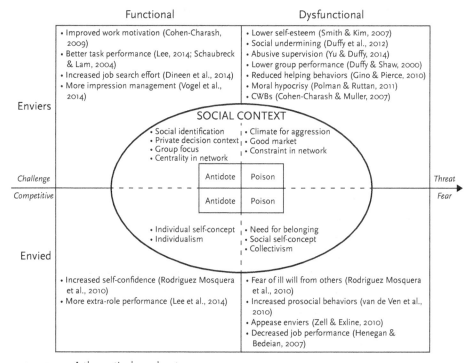

FIGURE 2.1 A theoretical quadrant.

respond to the pain of envy in a variety of social contexts, thus provide a platform for future research on envy in organizations.

A Social-Contextual View of Envy

Emotions influence people's attitudes, relationships, and behaviors in their daily social life (Barsade & Gibson, 2007; Frijda, 1986). Envy is no exception. Importantly, because envy is a painful experience that conveys inferiority of self (Smith & Kim, 2007), envy can be a corrupting force (i.e., can lead to a variety of deleterious outcomes) in the absence of knowledge about how to cope with it appropriately in organizational life. However, every "negative" emotion has its antidote, which can help reduce, or even better, remove potential negative effects; similarly, every "positive" emotion has its poison, which can minimize potential positive effects, and even worse, amplify deleterious influences (Exline & Zell, 2008; Frijda, 1986). Thus, our focus here is on the role of a variety of social contexts as either possible antidotes or poisons to the responses to envy and being envied in the workplace.

For the purposes of this chapter, we have two basic assumptions. First, while envy has long been thought of as an "negative" emotion that leads to a variety of deleterious individual, workgroup/team, and organizational outcomes (for reviews, see Duffy et al., 2008; Smith & Kim, 2007), in this chapter, we stand with Tai and colleagues, adopting a more "neutral" definition of envy as "pain at another person's good fortune" (Tai et al., 2012, p. 107). Second, although envy has been operationalized in three different ways—(1) situational (e.g., Duffy & Shaw, 2000); (2) trait or dispositional (e.g., Smith, Parrott, Diener, Hoyle, & Kim, 1999); and (3) episodic toward a specific target (e.g., Cohen-Charash, 2009; Hoogland et al., in press; Parrott, 1991)—here, we take the first view of considering envy as situational; namely, a general envy of others in a work context, with a particular attention to the social and organizational context of envy. By focusing on the "painful" nature of envy and the role the social context plays, we only claim that envy is a painful experience resulting from unfavorable social comparisons with others in a variety of social organizational contexts, and do not simply construe envy as either a negative or a positive emotion. Indeed, we suggest that it is the nature of various social contexts that helps determine whether envy is expressed and responded to in a functional or dysfunctional way. In other words, *How does social context influence what people do with the pain envy brings?*

The extant organizational literature focuses on envy from two perspectives—that of "the enviers" (i.e., people who lack and desire what others have; Hoogland et al., Chapter 5; Lee & Gino, Chapter 15; Sterling et al., Chapter 3, this volume) and that of "the envied" (i.e., those who are envied for what they have; Parrott, Chapter 19, this volume). In terms of the link between the feeling of envy and responses from enviers, Tai and colleagues (2012) have suggested that enviers are likely to engage in either *threat-based* or *challenge-based* action tendencies. In terms of the link between the feeling of being envied and responses from envied targets, Foster (1972) proposes that a *fear axis* and a *competitive axis* are associated with ambivalent reactions to the experience of being envied. Consistent with this line of reasoning regarding the complexity of the consequences of envy, we propose in this chapter that there are positive and negative reactions to the experience of envy and being envied, depending on a variety of social contexts.

In the following sections, we briefly describe the current envy literature from each perspective (*enviers* and *envied*) and then present some of the most recent empirical studies to demonstrate the role of a variety of social contexts in terms of antidotes and poisons to envy.

Envy in Organizations—Perspective of Enviers

Overview of the Current Literature

Dysfunctional/Negative Reactions of Enviers. Unfavorable upward social comparisons are considered the contexts where the feeling of envy often arises (Gilbert, Giesler, & Morris, 1995; Smith, 2000). In the present of these upward social comparisons, individuals are prone to view comparison others as "rivals," and thus the upward social comparisons elicit more threat-based reactions (Baumeister, Heatherton, & Tice, 1994; MacDonald & Leary, 2005; Tai et al., 2012). This understanding associates envy with negative attitudes and behaviors towards others, especially the target of envy. As an unpleasant discrete emotion, envy has been historically viewed as one of seven deadly sins and is described as a "green-eyed monster" in Shakespeare's writings. In the workplace, the feeling of envy is negatively related to self-esteem (Smith & Kim, 2007), helping behaviors (Gino & Pierce, 2010), and group performance (Duffy & Shaw, 2000), but positively associated with moral hypocrisy (Polman & Ruttan, 2011), reluctance to openly share information with the envied person (Dunn & Schweitzer, 2004), the occurrence of unethical behaviors (Dunn &

Schweitzer, 2006; Gino & Pierce, 2009), and antisocial behaviors toward the envied targets—e.g., counterproductive work behaviors (Cohen-Charash & Mueller, 2007), social undermining (Duffy et al., 2008), abusive supervision (Yu & Duffy, 2014), schadenfreude, aggression, and even crime (see Smith and Kim, 2007, for a review). In general, considerable evidence suggests envy evokes negative attitudinal, relational, and behavioral responses.

Functional/Positive Reactions of Enviers. Recent interest is growing in considering the potentially positive consequences of envy—considering it can evoke functional rather than dysfunctional outcomes (e.g., Crusius & Lang, Chapter 4; Sterling et al., Chapter 3; Stodulka, Chapter 13, this volume; van de Ven et al., 2009). As one fundamental psychological need, people strive to avoid or reduce the painful experience (Gray, 1987; Higgins, 1997). Consistent with the definition of envy as "pain at another's good fortune" (Tai et al., 2012, p. 178), enviers seek different ways to close the gap between the envied target and themselves, and thus reduce their painful experiences. Admittedly, one means people frequently take is to bring the envied target down through a variety of dysfunctional or nega-tive reactions, which we mentioned above. However, this is not the only option. As Mahatma Gandhi noted, "If I have the belief that I can do it, I shall surely acquire the capacity to do it even if I may not have it at the be-ginning." Considering that lacking others' good fortune serves as the basis of envy, scholars suggest that enviers may choose to raise their positions to the level of the envied target (e.g., self-improvement, active learning, or seeking help) to deal with the pain envy brings (Tai et al., 2012; van de Ven et al., 2009). Although not as extensive as the literature regarding dysfunc-tional individual and organizational outcomes, in line with this, emerging research suggests envy is related to improved work motivation (Cohen-Charash, 2009), better task performance (Lee, 2014; Schaubroeck & Lam, 2004), increased job search effort (Dineen et al., in press), more self-improvement (Yu & Duffy, 2014), and more impression management (e.g., exemplification, Vogel, Duffy, Mitchell, & Yu, 2014). By viewing envied others as role models, getting to know more about them, and learn-ing their secrets and new tricks, envious people are likely to reduce the pain envy brings as well.

The Potential Role of Social Contexts

Today's organizations offer many reasons for envious employees not to respond to envy in a dysfunctional manner. It is risky to take such actions, as there are both personal (inner) and social sanctions against it (Duffy et al., 2012). Accordingly, there are two key questions that are interesting and important to ask: first, given the risks of engaging in those dysfunctional actions, *How and why does envy lead enviers to actions such as sabotage and social undermining at work?* And, second, *Can a variety of social contexts serve as an antidote or a poison to envy?* There are some exciting empirical studies that aim to address these questions.

Why do enviers avoid or even ignore the self and social scrutiny to take threat-based actions? This inquiry is important because it helps us clarify possible antidotes or poisons to envy. Duffy and her colleagues (2012) proposed moral disengagement as a mechanism to explain why people take threat-based actions even they are facing self or social sanctions. Specifically, "moral disengagement" (Bandura, Barbaranelli, Caprara, Pastorelli, & Regalia, 2001) refers to a set of cognitive justifications that allow one to overcome one's own and society's sanctions against "bad behaviors." By justifying their unethical behaviors, morally disengaged people tend to perceive that those who are mistreated at work have usually done something to deserve it, and gossiping about colleagues behind their back does not really hurt them. In their first study, Duffy and her colleagues (2012) collected two waves of data separated by eight months from 177 employees at a university hospital, and the results supported their predictions. In order to replicate their findings and extend their theories, they collected data from 408 undergraduate students in 96 teams at a large Southern U.S. university in their second study. Both studies show that envy evokes moral disengagement (e.g., making fun of co-workers "does not really hurt them"; an obnoxious person "does not deserve to be treated well"), which then leads to increased threat-based actions such as socially undermining behaviors toward co-workers in the workplace. Indeed, a recent review (Moore, 2015) pointed out that individuals' discrete negative-valence emotions, such as envy, are reliable predictors of their moral disengagement and subsequent antisocial behaviors.

Are there any possible antidotes or poisons that may mitigate or exacerbate the dysfunctional response to envy? In their empirical work examining the relationship between envy and social undermining, Duffy and colleagues (2012) further proposed that the social context could be considered an "antidote" to envy. Specifically, they identified two contextual factors that moderate the relationship between envy and social undermining at two different stages. First, they draw from social identity theory and argue that "social identification," referring to connections that exist between people or among team members such as personal affiliation, closeness, or similarity, may serve as an antidote to envy. Moral obligation appears to be stronger toward those who "are closer to us" (Opotow, 1990, 1995), whereas the perception of separation from another can generate social differentiation and moral exclusion. As a result, people exclude others outside their scope of justice when they perceive them as different, which implicitly indicates that it is appropriate and perhaps even justified to hurt them. Consistent with this line of reasoning, diversity and team research also suggested that people are more likely to engage in antisocial behaviors towards out-group members than towards in-group members (Halevy, Bornstein, & Sagiv, 2008). Paradoxically, envy is likely to be triggered by social comparisons among individuals who are similar (Smith & Kim, 2007); on the other hand, social identification stops enviers from morally disengaging, which then stops further threat-based action-taking such as social undermining. We argue that one way to resolve or better understand this paradox is that the role of social identification in how envy is triggered and responded to may be different.

Second, scholars argued that the "climate for aggression," defined as the level of acceptance of aggression at work, may also affect the way people choose to respond to envy (Duffy et al., 2012). By encouraging the morally disengaged person to engage in antisocial behaviors, a high climate for aggression (i.e., prevalence of interpersonal aggression in teams, and high levels of tolerance of interpersonal aggression in teams) provides further encouragement or impetus to undermine, whereas a low climate for aggression applies social pressure to "stay in line" despite moral disengagement. Their empirical results demonstrated that high social identification with colleagues and low climate for aggression work as antidotes to envy by stopping moral disengagement (at the first stage) and undermining behaviors (at the second stage) among enviers.

In addition, recent evidence showed that other contextual factors may also change the way envy is expressed and responded to at work. For example, drawing from victim precipitation (i.e., individual characteristics that provoke crime, abuse, and deviance), social comparison, and identity theories, Kim and Glomb (2014) argued that group members' envy is more likely to lead to victimization of the envied targets—high performers, when group members have low work-group identification with high performers. Defined as "shared perceptions among group members of the degree to which people merge their sense of self with the group" (Kim & Glomb, 2014, p. 3), a high level of work-group identification may serve as another antidote to envy, which inhibits group members from victimizing the high performers in the group. In addition, Youn and Goldsmith's (2014) study examined the moderating role of decision context on the relationship between envy and self-improvement. Through three experiments, they found that envy will trigger the desire to self-improve (e.g., hard work, conspicuous consumption, and charitable giving) when the decision context is private (i.e., no worries about signaling negative information about oneself to others); whereas the envy will suppress effort out of a desire to conceal one's envy from others when the decision context is public (i.e., there are social costs associated with demonstrating one's envy). Their findings suggest that a private decision context may serve as another antidote to envy.

So far, we have discussed some recent studies focusing on the antidotal role of a variety of social contexts to envy in the workplace. Taking one step further, *Can social contexts actually turn envy into a "good," not just mitigate the "bad?"* There are some preliminary evidences to support this contention. For example, Duffy, Fang, and Lee's (2011) study examined envy in the context of newcomer socialization, and found that envy among newcomers results in poor socialization outcomes and task performance. However, enviers who maintained a "group focus" had more positive socialization and subsequent job-related outcomes, indicating that "group focus" not only served as an antidote, but actually became a catalyst that turned envy into "good" in the context of newcomer socialization. In addition, Lee (2014) conducted a field study among Korean bank tellers and insurance sales agents to examine the functional role of workplace envy. Drawing insights from counterfactual theory (Coricelli & Rustichini, 2010), he argued that employees who envy co-workers are likely to enhance their task performance through a systematic learning process and work engagement process, especially when the targets of envy are willing to engage in enviers-directed organizational citizenship behaviors (e.g., offering help to enviers). The results supported his argument and implicitly indicated that a friendlier or more supportive relationship with the social referent (i.e., the envied target) may help induce positive outcomes of envy in the workplace.

Besides the antidotal role of social contexts that we discussed above, scholars suggest that certain social contexts may serve as a poison, rather than an antidote, to envy. For example, Cohen-Charash and Mueller (2007) conducted a study to examine the interaction between envy and perceived unfairness in predicting counterproductive work behaviors (CWBs). From a social-exchange perspective, they argued that perceived unfairness, as an indicator of the justice climate in the workplace, may make enviers more likely to engage in CWBs. Across two studies, results supported the poisonous role of perceived unfairness—the interaction of envy and perceived unfairness results in higher levels of interpersonal CWBs. In addition, Dineen and his colleagues (in press) developed a theoretical framework to examine the effects of job-search envy on dysfunctional (e.g., résumé fraud) and functional (e.g., job search effort) job-search behaviors. They theorize that perceived employment opportunity affects situational immutability perceptions and thus predisposes envious job seekers toward either dysfunctional or functional behaviors. In their first study, of 339 unemployed job seekers, results supported their predictions that the labor market could be a poison by which job-search envy leads to increased résumé deviance behaviors when there is a good, rather than a poor, market. In their second two-year study of graduate students, they replicated their previous findings and extended their theories by taking the time factor into account. Results suggested that envious job seekers employ increased efforts in earlier stages of job searching, while engaging in résumé fraud in later stages of a job search, especially when employment opportunities are plentiful. Consistent with research on envy and counterfactual thinking (Coricelli & Rustichini, 2010), a munificent labor market could be a "poison" because the counterfactual reality is easier to imagine and more feasible; as a result, enviers are helpless and hopeless and are thus more likely to engage in dysfunctional behaviors because it is more painful when counterfactuals are mutable and feasible.

We note that the examination of antidotal or poisoning role of various social contexts in envy is still in its infancy, but with a very promising future. Preliminary evidences suggest that social context acts as an antidote or a poison to envy in different ways, such as the following:

1. Identification with others serves as an antidote that mitigates threat-based action tendencies (e.g., undermining; Duffy et al., 2012);
2. Perceptions of labor markets serve as a poison that exacerbates threat-based actions to envy (e.g., résumé deviance) and mitigates challenge-based behaviors (e.g., search effort or jobs applied);
3. Perceived unfairness (for a review on envy and justice, see Mishra, Whiting, & Folger, Chapter 16, this volume) serves as another poison that results in more interpersonal CWBs at work; and

4. Group focus serves as an antidote that even triggers positive, challenge-based behaviors among the enviers (e.g., socialization behaviors).

As noted in the beginning, a limited but growing body of literature has started to investigate the function of envy in the workplace from the perspective of those envied, to which we turn our attention now.

Envy in Organizations—Perspective of the Envied

Overview of the Current Literature

Compared to a large body of research focusing on enviers in organizations, little is known about envied targets and how they react once they perceive they are envied by others. Why is it interesting and important to examine the feeling of being envied in organizations? As we mentioned earlier, many organizational practices and policies encourage social comparisons among employees, which can easily trigger envy at the workplace (Duffy et al., 2008; Tai et al., 2012). More important, envy can induce hostility, sabotage, and social undermining toward envied targets, who are often high performers. Facing with dramatically increased competition in today's global economy, high performers are becoming a key component of organizations' competitive advantages (Ployhart et al., 2011). However, they are also more likely to become the target of envy in organizations (Kim & Glomb, 2014). Therefore, how do envied people perceive themselves as the target of other's envy? How do they respond to the feeling of being envied? What are factors that influence how they perceive and respond to the feeling of being envied? These questions are very critical for both researchers and practitioners.

Dysfunctional/Negative Reactions of the Envied. A limited but growing body of research has started to explore envy from the perspective of *the envied* (e.g., Parrott, Chapter 19, this volume; Rodriguez Mosquera et al., 2010; van de Ven et al., 2010; Zell & Exline, 2010). Similar to the earlier discussion regarding the threat- versus challenge-based reactions of enviers (Tai et al., 2012), extant envied research has also demonstrated that the feeling of being envied is associated with ambivalent experiences (Exline & Lobel, 1999; Foster, 1972). On one hand, being the target of envy may trigger a "fear axis" that elicits unpleasant, anxious, and stressful experiences (Foster, 1972). Consistent with this fear axis, research has shown that envied targets are likely to experience the fear of ill will from others (Rodriguez Mosquera et al., 2010), to increase their prosocial behaviors (van de Ven et al., 2010), and to appease those enviers (i.e., prize sharing or self-deprecating, Zell & Exline, 2010).

Functional/Positive Reactions of Envied. On the other hand, a "competitive axis" may also exist that represents the feeling of pleasure from envied targets. As Mark Twain noted: "Man will do many things to get himself loved, and he will do all things to get himself envied." Recent studies have linked the feeling of being envied to increased self-confidence (Rodriguez Mosquera et al., 2010) and more extra-role performance (Lee, Duffy, & Michaela, 2014). That is to say, the feeling of being envied by others may be associated with increased felt responsibility and obligation to enviers, as well as stronger willingness and commitment to sharing one's knowledge, skills, and resources with enviers. Past research suggests that the difference in responses to being envied may be a function of the characteristics of the enviers (Duffy et al., 2008). For instance, Henegan and Bedeian's (2007) study showed that, when enviers displayed negative attitudes and behaviors, the envied acted in a more modest fashion (e.g., reduced their job performance level) due to the wish to reduce their own discomfort and avoid the further upward social comparisons. Moreover, individual factors such as differences in values, beliefs about success, and dispositional envy may also moderate the ambivalent experiences of being envied (Rodriguez Mosquera et al., 2010). As the experience of being envied is a relatively new area in envy research, unfortunately, little is known about *how, when*, and in *which way* the envied targets tend to choose to respond to the feeling of being envied.

The Potential Role of Social Contexts

Foster (1972) argued all cultures must confront the fact that success is a relational process, which means how well we are doing is always relative to how well others are doing. Therefore, individuals in any cultural contexts need to cope with the potential for envy (for reviews on cultural lens of envy, see Tan, Tai, & Wang, Chapter 11, this volume). In particular, the fear of ill will from others, especially from the enviers, is likely to influence how envied targets respond to the feeling of being envied. As noted in Benjamin Franklin's description of how envied people respond: "A perfect character might be attended with the inconvenience of being envied and hated; and . . . a benevolent man should allow a few faults in himself, to keep his friends in countenance." If Benjamin Franklin is right, what might that mean for organizations? Might envied targets "allow a few faults" at work? If so, under what conditions or contexts, and why might that occur?

Some recent empirical studies provide preliminary evidence. For instance, Lee, Duffy, and Michaela (2014) proposed a theoretical model of being envied at work. Prior research has demonstrated that people react more strongly to their perceptions than to the objective reality; therefore, envy scholars have focused on how people perceive they are envied by others and how they react to such perceptions. According to self-regulation theory (Baumeister & Vohs, 2007), people are using diverse resources (i.e., cognitive, emotional, and relational) for a variety of daily and working tasks. Building on this, Lee and colleagues (2014) argued that the fear of being envied may make envied targets consume more self-regulatory resources in coping with that fear, which will result in fewer resources for task performance at work. Moreover, they proposed that this relationship may depend on the "need for belonging," which refers to a desire to be included by others at work. Specifically, when people having a higher need for belonging perceived they are envied by others, their need for belonging may be a disadvantage due to their fear of losing social relationships. As a result, envied targets with a higher need for belonging might devote more resources to purposely alter their performance (i.e., allow a few faults) to make themselves less competitive than others, so that there is less possibility that they will be excluded by others at work.

Furthermore, based on a cross-cultural sample (Korean and Netherlands), Lee and his colleagues (2014) found that cultural differences in terms of individualism and collectivism differentially affect an envied person's behavioral responses in terms of extra-role performance. Specifically, they found that envied persons working in Korea, because of a social self-concept (i.e., self in connection with or reliance on others; Brewer & Gardner, 1996), tend to lower their extra-role performance. In their second study, they further demonstrated that envied persons working in Korea are more likely to experience ego-depletion due to the fear of being envied, and thus exaggerate the moderating effect of social self-concept on the extra-role performance. From the practical perspective, it is suggested that employees who value social relations are most attractive to organizations on one hand, but they may also be the most affected by envy-inducing organizational practices and policies on the other.

In addition, scholars recently have paid increasing attention to another critical social context—the social network—and examined how the characteristics of a social network (i.e., centrality, constraint, and density) influence people's reaction to the feeling of envy and being envied (for a review on envy and social network, see Floyd & Sterling, Chapter 7, this volume). For example, Sterling, Smith, and van de Ven (2013) conducted a social network analysis of benign envy and malicious envy in the workplace. Results demonstrated that centrality and constraint in the communication network significantly affect people's behavioral reactions to envy. Specifically, they found that centrality (i.e., the number of employees who nominated an individual for a communication relationship) strengthens the positive relationship between benign envy and envier's organizational citizenship behaviors (OCBs) and increased effort, whereas constraint (i.e., the extent to which an individual's ties are concentrated in a single group of interconnected colleagues) strengthens the positive relationship between malicious envy and enviers' turnover intention and deviant behaviors. Furthermore, Lee (2014) proposed that, due to a fear of potentially undermining their workplace social relationships, envied targets are more likely to provide help to enviers when enviers have central positions in friendship networks. In short, recent studies have suggested that the characteristics of social networks play a critical role in shaping people's reactions to the feeling of envy and being envied in the workplace.

In general, the review of extant literature and some recent empirical studies in envy from both perspectives confirms the argument that envy, as one complex social emotion, is not easily aligned with any single mode of attitudes and behavioral tendencies (Frijda, 1986; Frijda, Kuipers, & ter Schure, 1989; Tai et al., 2012). Both enviers and the envied can express and respond to envy in different ways, and a variety of social contexts where envy is triggered may play a critical role in determining how people express and respond to envy. More important, it is particularly worth exploring how to turn the feelings of envy and being envied into some benefits that both enviers and envied people, as well as the organizations, can harvest.

Discussion

The process of reviewing envy literature from two different perspectives—the enviers and the envied, led us to introduce a new theoretical model of envy—a social context model, to better understand how envy is expressed and how people respond in organizations where a plethora of envy-inducing practices and policies exist. The social context model provides a contextual view of envy that helps illuminate the conditions under which envy is perceived and expressed as potentially impactful to employees in workplace. Only within this social context can both enviers and the envied be enabled to perceive and express envy strategically to benefit both individual (i.e., well-being, self-esteem) and organizational outcomes (i.e., job performance). Without considering the social context of envy, existing theory cannot explain why in some situations, envy will be expressed in a dysfunctional form, whereas in others it will be expressed in a functional form; or even more important, why in some situations, both enviers and envied are able to take more positive and challenge-based actions to cope with envy and being envied, while in others, the expression of and responses to envy are more or less negative and threat-based.

This introduction of the social context model of envy helps bring to the fore a clearer understanding of why the feeling of envy or being envied may produce different adaptive expressions and responses for both enviers and envied. We presented some preliminary but exciting results for the role of social contexts in envy, and we also identified, based on existing conceptual and empirical work in the envy literature, a variety of social contexts that are likely to serve as either antidotes or poisons to envy. Our expectation is that the social context of envy matters, as it shapes two important aspects: (1) how the feeling of envy or being envied is expressed; and (2) how enviers and envied respond to feeling envy or being envied. A key insight from this expectation is that these two aspects explicitly explain whether, how and in which ways social contexts "matter" in envy in organizations.

In conclusion, envy can be "within" but also triggered by social context and circumstances. As organizational scholars, we need to know more about the circumstances that not only trigger envy but alter how it is expressed and how people react. Importantly, from the perspective of practice, while many organizations adopt competition-related policies and practices, it is time to know, as any organizations today, how we can encourage benign (vs. malicious) competition that inevitably induces the feeling of envy, but not respond to it through moral exclusion or other threat-based actions. Therefore, we encourage organizational psychology and organizational behavior researchers to take advantage of these two different but related perspectives of enviers and the envied, highlighting the importance of social contexts in understanding envy in organizations.

References

Bandura, A., Barbaranelli, C., Caprara, G., Pastorelli, C., & Regalia, C. (2001). Sociocognitive self-regulatory mechanisms governing transgressive behavior. *Journal of Personality and Social Psychology, 71*, 364–374.

Barsade, S. G., & Gibson, D. E. (2007). Why does affect matter in organizations? *The Academy of Management Perspectives*, *21*(1), 36–59.

Baumeister, R. F., Heatherton, T. F., & Tice, D. M. (1994). *Losing Control: How and Why People Fail at Self-Regulation*. San Diego, CA: Academic Press.

Baumeister, R. F., & Vohs, K, D. (2007). Self-regulation, ego depletion, and motivation. *Social and Personality Psychology Compass*, *1*, 1–14.

Brewer, M. B., & Gardner, W. (1996). Who is this "we?" Levels of collective identity and self-representation. *Journal of Personality and Social Psychology*, *71*, 83–93.

Cohen-Charash, Y. (2009). Episodic envy. *Journal of Applied Social Psychology*, *39*, 2128–2173.

Cohen-Charash, Y., & Mueller, J. S. (2007). Does perceived unfairness exacerbate or mitigate interpersonal counterproductive work behaviors related to envy? *Journal of Applied Psychology*, *92*, 666–680.

Coricelli, G., & Rustichini, A. (2010). Counterfactual thinking and emotions: Regret and envy learning. *Philosophical Transactions of the Royal Society—Biological Sciences*, *365*, 241–247.

Dineen, B. R., Duffy, M. K., Henle, C. A., & Lee, K. (in press). Green by comparison: Deviant and normative transmutations of job search envy in a temporal context. *Academy of Management Journal*.

Duffy, M. K., Fang, R. L., & Lee, K. (2011). Working paper. Envy in newcomer socialization.

Duffy, M. K., Scott, K. L., Shaw, J. D., Tepper, B. J., & Aquino, K. (2012). A social context model of envy and social undermining. *Academy of Management Journal*, *55*, 643–666.

Duffy, M. K., & Shaw, J. D. (2000). The Salieri syndrome: Consequences of envy in groups. *Small Group Research*, *31*, 3–23.

Duffy, M. K., Shaw, J. D., & Schaubroeck, J. M. (2008). Envy in organizational life. In R. Smith, Ed., *Envy: Theory and Research* (pp. 167–189). Oxford, UK: Oxford University Press.

Dunn, J., & Schweitzer, M. (2004). Too good to be trusted? Relative performance, envy, and trust. In R. Weaver, Ed., Proceedings of the Sixty-fourth Annual Meeting of the Academy of Management, New Orleans, Louisiana.

Dunn J., & Schweitzer, M. (2006). Green and mean: Envy and social undermining in organizations. In A. Tenbrunsel, Ed., *Research on Managing Groups and Teams: Ethics in Groups* (pp. 177–197), London: Elsevier Science Press.

Exline, J. J., & Lobel, M. (1999). The perils of outperformance: Sensitivity about being the target of a threatening upward comparison. *Psychological Bulletin*, *125*, 307–337.

Exline, J. J., & Zell, A. L. (2008). Antidotes to envy: A conceptual framework. In R. Smith, Ed., *Envy: Theory and Research*: 315–334. Oxford, UK: Oxford University Press.

Foster, G. (1972). The anatomy of envy: A study of symbolic behavior. *Current Anthropology*, *13*, 165–202.

Frijda, N. H. (1986). *The Emotions*. Cambridge, UK: Cambridge University Press.

Frijda, N. H., Kuipers, P., & ter Schure, E. (1989). Relations among emotions, appraisal, and emotional action tendencies. *Journal of Personality and Social Psychology*, *57*, 212–228.

Gilbert, D. T., Giesler, R. B., & Morris, K. A. (1995). When comparisons arise. *Journal of Personality and Social Psychology*, *69*, 227–236.

Gino, F., & Pierce, L. (2009). Dishonesty in the name of equity. *Psychological Science*, *20*, 1153–1160.

Gino, F., & Pierce, L. (2010). Robin Hood under the hood: Wealth-based discrimination in illicit customer help. *Organization Science*, *21*, 1176–1194.

Halevy, N., Bornstein, G., & Sagiv, L. (2008). "In-group love" and "out-group hate" as motives for individual participation in intergroup conflict: A new paradigm. *Psychological Science*, *19*, 405–411.

Henegan, S., & Bedeian, A. (2007). The perils of workplace performance: Coping with the discomfort of being upward comparison targets. Unpublished manuscript.

Kim, E., & Glomb, T. M. (2014). Victimization of high performers: The roles of envy and work group identification. *Journal of Applied Psychology*, *99*(4), 619–634.

Lee, K. (2014). When and how does workplace envy promote job performance? A study on the conditions and mechanisms for the functional role of envy in workplace behavior. Unpublished dissertation. Minneapolis, MN: University of Minnesota.

Lee, K., Duffy, M. K., & Michaela. S. (2014). Being envied at work. Working paper.

MacDonald, G., & Leary, M. R. (2005). Why does social exclusion hurt? The relationship between social and physical pain. *Psychological Bulletin*, *131*, 202–223.

Menon, T., & Thompson, L. (2010). Envy at work. *Harvard Business Review*, 88 (4), 74–79.

Moore, C. (2015). Moral disengagement. *Current Opinion in Psychology*, *6*, 199–204.

Opotow, S. (1990). Moral exclusion and injustice: An overview. *Journal of Social Issues*, *46*, 1–20.

Opotow, S. (1995). Drawing the line: Social categorization, moral exclusion, and the scope of justice. In B. B. Bunker & J. Z. Rubin, Eds., *Conflict, Cooperation, and Justice: Essays Inspired by the Work of Morton Deutsch* (pp. 347–369). San Francisco, CA: Jossey-Bass.

Parrott, W. G., & Smith, R. H. (1993). Distinguishing the experiences of envy and jealousy. *Journal of Personality and Social Psychology*, *64*, 906–920.

Ployhart, R. E., Van Iddekinge, C. H., & MacKenzie, W. I. (2011). Acquiring and developing human capital in service contexts: The interconnectedness of human capital resources. *Academy of Management Journal*, *54*(2), 353–368.

Polman, E., & Ruttan, R. (2011). Effects of anger, guilt, and envy on moral hypocrisy. *Personality and Social Psychology Bulletin*, 38 (1), 129–139.

Rodriguez Mosquera, P. M., Parrott, W. G., & Hurtado de Mendoza, A. (2010). I fear your envy, I rejoice in your coveting: On the ambivalent experience of being envied by others. *Journal of Personality and Social Psychology*, *99*, 842–854.

Schaubroeck, J., & Lam, S. K. (2004). Comparing lots before and after: Promotion rejectees' invidious reactions to promotees. *Organizational Behavior and Human Decision Processes*, *94*, 33–47.

Smith, R. H. (2000). Assimilative and contrastive emotional reactions to upward and downward social comparisons. In J. Suls & L. Wheeler, Eds., *Handbook of Social Comparison: Theory and Research*. New York: Kluwer Academic/Plenum Publishers.

Smith, R. H., & Kim, S. H. (2007). Comprehending envy. *Psychology Bulletin, 133*, 46–64.

Smith, R. H., Parrott, W. G., Diener, E. F., Hoyle, R. H., & Kim, S. H. (1999). Dispositional envy. *Personality and Social Psychology Bulletin, 25*, 1007–1021.

Sterling, C., Smith, R., & van de Ven, N. (2013). The consequences of benign and malicious envy in the workplace. Paper presented at the Academy of Management 73rd Annual Meeting, Orlando, Florida.

Tai, K., Narayanan, J., & McAllister, D. J. (2012). Envy as pain: Rethinking the nature of envy and its implications for employees and organizations. *Academy of Management Review, 37*, 107–129.

van de Ven, N., Zeelenberg, M., & Pieters, R. (2009). Leveling up and down: The experiences of benign and malicious envy. *Emotion, 9*, 419–429.

van de Ven, N., Zeelenberg, M., & Pieters, R. (2010). Warding off the evil eye: When the fear of being envied increases prosocial behavior. *Psychological Science, 21*, 1671.

Vogel, R., Duffy, M. K., Mitchell, M., & Yu, L. (2014). Two faces of envy: A process model of antecedents and consequences of co-worker's envy. Paper presented at the 74th Annual Meeing of Academy of Management, Philadelphia, PA.

Youn, Y. J., & Goldsmith, K. (2014). At their best when no one is watching: Decision context moderates the effects of envy on the tendency toward self-improvement. Working paper.

Yu, L., & Duffy, M. K. (2014). I abuse you, because I envy you. A self-esteem threat model of envy and abusive supervision. Paper presented at the 74th Academy of Management Annual Meeting, Philadelphia, Pennsylvania.

Zell, A. L., & Exline, J. J. (2010). How does it feel to be outperformed by a "good winner?" Prize sharing and self-deprecating as appeasement strategies. *Basic and Applied Psychology, 32*, 69–85.

3 | The Two Faces of Envy

STUDYING BENIGN AND MALICIOUS ENVY IN THE WORKPLACE

CHRISTOPHER M. STERLING, NIELS VAN DE VEN, AND RICHARD H. SMITH

Introduction

As this book shows, we are starting to understand more about the nature of envy, the content of its emotional experience, and its effects in an organization. Envy is the result of an upward social comparison, one that signals to someone that he or she lacks desired abilities, traits, or rewards enjoyed by another. Organizational scholars recognize that social comparison and envy should be prevalent in organizations as employees are often subject to hierarchical stratification and often compete for scarce organizational rewards, managerial attention, and social status (Vecchio, 1997). Equity theorists and organizational justice theorists have long recognized the importance of comparisons in the workplace, as employees weigh social information obtained from observing and communicating with their peers to make sense of their workplace (Adams, 1965; Greenberg, 1982; Ambrose, Harland, & Kulik, 1991; Folger & Cropanzano, 2001). However, the acknowledgement of social comparison processes is often treated more implicitly in organizational research, and a direct examination of the results of social comparison processes has largely been missing in the organizational literature (Duffy, 2008). This is changing as organizational scholars are realizing the important role that emotions play in motivating organizational behavior (e.g., Lee & Gino, Chapter 15, this volume). A few of the more negative social emotions—those resulting from unfavorable comparisons, such as shame, jealousy, and envy—are related to a wide variety of disruptive and destructive workplace behaviors (Poulson, 2000; Vecchio,

2005). As a result of this association, coupled with a growing interest in workplace deviance, social comparison and social emotions are receiving an increasing amount of attention in organizational scholarship.

Until recently, the outcomes associated with the experience of envy in organizations were thought to be primarily negative, as envy results from an unfavorable, painful comparison to peers. However, research has demonstrated a contradictory pattern at times, showing that envy can generate destructive workplace behaviors and lead to negative organizational outcomes, while other research has shown that envy can lead to more positive and productive workplace behaviors. Gaining a better understanding of how envy leads to specific consequences is important, not only as an exercise of scholarly inquiry, but especially if we are ever to recommend how this emotion can best be managed in our organizations. Should envy be suppressed, as it is a destructive emotion that will harm performance and undermine social relationships? Conversely, can envy be harnessed and used as a motivational tool to increase effort and performance? We argue that the answer to this question lies in conceptualizing and measuring envy, not as a singular emotional experience, but as a complex emotion, subject to appraisal, reappraisal, and reflection. The result of these processes produces an emotion with two distinct manifestations, one malicious and the other benign.

It is interesting to note that some languages actually already have two words for envy. For example, in Dutch, "envy" translates to both *afgunst* and *benijden*. It is striking that in these languages, one word seems to mainly refer to the dark, destructive, and malicious side of envy, while the other word refers to a brighter, constructive, and more benign form of envy. Even in countries where the language has only one word for envy, envy is sometimes referred to as having these two subtypes. For example, in Russia and Brazil, people can refer to "black" and "white" envy, seemingly again referring to envy's destructive and more constructive nature.

The dominant and traditional view of envy in the workplace holds that envy is primarily associated with negative attitudes and behaviors (Duffy, Shaw, & Schaubroeck, 2008; Smith & Kim, 2007). However, recent experimental studies on the social psychology of envy and several findings in organizational psychology suggest that there could be both positive and negative behavioral consequences associated with envy. Indeed, the idea that envy can also motivate people is a recurring theme in the various chapters of this volume (e.g., Annoni, Bertini, Perini, Pistone, & Zucchi, Chapter 20; Cohen-Charash & Larson, Chapter 1; Yu & Duffy, Chapter 2;

Lee & Gino, Chapter 15; Hoogland, Thielke, & Smith, Chapter 5; Vidaillet, Chapter 8; Yiwen, Tai, & Wang, Chapter 11). One explanation for this occurrence considers the existence of two qualitatively different experiences of envy; benign envy and malicious envy (van de Ven, Zeelenberg, & Pieters, 2009). In this chapter, we describe a recently developed measure of both benign and malicious envy and examine its validity by relating it to important organizational outcomes.

Distinguishing Between the Two Types of Envy

Empirical studies focusing on the consequences of workplace envy suggest a primarily destructive pattern (Duffy, Shaw, & Schaubroeck, 2008). Workplace envy has been shown to erode the quality of workplace relationships (Duffy & Shaw, 2000), decrease positive workplace attitudes (Vecchio, 2000), and increase antisocial behavior (Vecchio, 2007; Duffy, Scott, Shaw, & Tepper, 2012; Cohen-Charash & Mueller, 2007). However, some recent work has focused on the positive and adaptive outcomes associated with envy, such as emulation, desire to learn, and increased motivation to succeed (Cohen-Charash, 2009; Schaubroeck & Lam, 2004; van de Ven, Zeelenberg, & Pieters, 2011a, 2011b).

Van de Ven et al. (2009) argue that these different motivations are best understood by seeing envy as containing two subtypes: benign and malicious envy. Malicious envy is the prototypical view of envy (sometimes also referred to as "envy proper," see Smith & Kim, 2007) that leads to a desire to pull down the superior person. Benign envy, on the other hand, is also a painful and frustrating feeling (as it is envy) but it also contains a motivation to improve oneself. The general idea is that envy has a goal to level the difference with the superior other: malicious envy achieves this by pulling down the other, while benign envy does so by moving oneself up. Crusius and Lange (2014) also find that the focus of these envy types is on different aspects of the upward social comparison: whereas the maliciously envious mainly focus on the envied person, the benignly envious mainly focus on the object that makes the other better-off.

Criticism of creating subtypes of envy. There is some debate as to whether it is useful to study envy by using these subtypes (Cohen-Charash & Larson, Chapter 1, this volume; Hoogland, Thielke, & Smith, Chapter 5, this volume; Tai, Narayanan, & McAllister, 2012). One argument is that envy is a singular emotion characterized by pain felt at another's good fortune, and different reactions following envy occur because of the influence of relationships, organizational climate, or beliefs about the self. The distinction between benign and malicious envy is, according to these researchers, based on the motivational outcome of envy and therefore might be tautological. Let us explain why we do think that a distinction between the envy types is useful.

First, the motivational consequences are an essential part of an emotion. We feel emotions because they help us deal with the environment and reach our goals (Cosmides & Tooby, 2000; Zeelenberg, Nelissen, Breugelmans, & Pieters, 2008). According to emotion theory, the motivations an emotion triggers are an integral part of the emotional experience and central to the emotion itself (Frijda, 1988; Roseman, Wiest, & Swartz, 1994). This perspective is based on the work of Arnold (1960), who even defined emotion as a *felt action tendency*. Frijda (1986) followed up on this work and argues that changes in action readiness are the distinguishing feature of emotions. Frijda sees emotions as a response to how a situation affects the interests of a person. Emotions then trigger action tendencies that subsequently serve the person's self-interest by responding to the threat (or opportunity) related to one's interest. Specific emotions arise through specific cognitive appraisals of a situation, but they also elicit specific subsequent motivations in a person. Experiencing an emotion thus provides important information, signaling when something important to an individual's self-interest is happening, and it also readies them for action (Keltner & Haidt, 1999). This occurs on a very basic level; for example, when anger makes the blood move away from internal organs towards the hands and arms to ready those for potential use (Levenson, Ekman, & Friesen, 1990). If emotions are considered without respect to the motivational tendency, shame and guilt might be seen as one emotion (inferior feelings after having done something bad), while the motivational tendencies (withdrawal for shame, repair behavior for guilt) is what largely distinguishes them from each other (De Hooge, Zeelenberg, & Breugelmans, 2007). This theoretical importance of action tendencies in defining emotions is the first reason why we think that making the distinction between benign and malicious envy is useful.

Second, we also think that the fact that many languages have two words for these envy subtypes is a signal that many cultures have found it useful to differentiate these subtypes of envy. The distinction so far was validated in Dutch (van de Ven et al., 2009) and German language (Crusius & Lange, 2014). Additionally, colleagues from various countries have confirmed to us that their language also has two words for the envy subtypes (with Japanese, Polish, and Turkish as examples). Furthermore, in other languages where only one word for envy exists, people have sometimes found other ways to refer to benign and malicious envy. Colleagues from both Brazil and Russia told us that they distinguish between *white* and *black* envy, which seems to map onto the benign and malicious forms of envy as they have been defined.

Words and feelings do not always perfectly overlap. Regarding envy, we do not think that languages (or countries) that use one word are more correct in their definition of envy than those that use two words, or vice versa. We think both are correct, but each focuses on the emotion at a different level. For countries where there is one word for envy (e.g., English, Spanish), the word for envy refers to the pain over the good fortune of others (as Aristotle, in 350 BC, already defined it). Countries that use two words zoom into a more detailed level of this emotion and seem to differentiate benign and malicious envy, as they have been defined by van de Ven et al. (2009). Thus, the second reason why we think that making the distinction between the envy types is useful, is that many languages already make such a distinction.

A third reason why we think that making the distinction between the subtypes of envy is useful is that it allows for novel theoretical insights and predictions. For example, some research found that envy led to *schadenfreude* (the joy over the misfortune of another person), while other research found that it did not (see van Dijk, Ouwerkerk, Goslinga, Nieweg, & Gallucci, 2006). van de Ven, Hoogland, Smith, van Dijk, Breugelmans, and Zeelenberg (2015) found that a distinction in the envy subtypes helped resolve this apparent discrepancy in the literature, as experiencing malicious envy led to schadenfreude, while benign envy did not. Furthermore, and importantly, a manipulation that made the superior position of the envied other undeserved (which is known to elicit malicious envy; van de Ven, Zeelenberg, & Pieters, 2012) increased schadenfreude via its effect on malicious envy. This thus shows that the distinction between envy subtypes helps predict how people will feel and behave next.

This latter effect also fits well with the idea of Tai et al. (2012) that differences in the situation lead to different responses following envy. But where they see envy as a relatively undifferentiated, painful reaction, we think that seeing envy as having two subtypes helps make more precise predictions of organizational behavior, without the need to account for all of the potential individual differences and aspects of organizational context that could affect an individual's appraisal of social comparison events in the workplace. Finally, by using the subtypes, researchers also have to be clear about whether they measure general envy, or one of the subtypes. In the research on the envy–schadenfreude link we discussed before (van de Ven et al., 2015), it was noted that in the scientific debate on whether envy led to schadenfreude or not, those who found effects of envy on schadenfreude included hostility-related questions in their surveys, while those who did not find such an effect used more coveting-related questions as the measure of envy. Both sides of the debate claimed to measure envy, but they did so with very different items, which in turn produced very different results. So the final reason, we think, for making the distinction between the envy types is that doing this forces researchers to clarify whether they define envy as being malicious envy, benign envy, or the combination of the two as general envy.

In this chapter, we describe the development of measures of the experience of both malicious and benign envy for use in the workplace. Employees can experience many events in the workplace that could elicit envy as they compete for scarce resources and promotions, are subject to performance comparisons, and experience different qualities of leader–member exchange. For the purposes of this chapter, we have developed separate measures for benign and malicious envy based on the work of Van de Ven et al. (2009) in order to empirically test how the different subtypes of envy relate to important aspects of organizational behavior.

The Sample

In order to validate our scale, we utilized a sample consisting of employees from a large healthcare organization. These employees represented the main administrative unit and were responsible for several functions, including human resources, marketing, billing and collections, credentialing, and customer service. All data were collected on-site using electronic surveys administered on laptop computers provided by the researchers. The participants completed the survey in small groups of eight in a large boardroom after a short presentation was provided reiterating the Institutional Review Board stipulations, the informed consent process, and detailing how participant confidentiality was protected. To alleviate response burden, electronic surveys were administered in two separate rounds. The first survey contained all sociometric questions, as well as the workplace deviance scale and work effort scale. The second survey contained the remainder of the psychometric questions pertaining to workplace attitudes, perceptions, and emotions. Nearly all of the participants finished the surveys within 15–20 minutes during both administrations. To encourage a high response rate, management allowed all participants to dress casually on the days they completed the surveys, and the research team held several on-site Q&A sessions with potential participants to answer any questions or concerns they might have had.

Out of a total of 142 employees, 124 completed the psychometric surveys, yielding a response rate of 87%. The sample was predominantly female (87%) with an average age of 45 years, and an average tenure of approximately six years within the organization. To the best of our knowledge, we do not believe that one particular gender is more or less predisposed to the experience of envy; it is important to note, however, that higher levels of gender similarity may lead to greater instances of explicit social comparison, resulting in a greater experience of envy (Schaubroeck & Lam, 2004). Similarity to an envied person is equally important for both benign and malicious envy, so we do not expect that this will affect one of the envy subscales more than the other (van de Ven et al., 2009).

The Scale

Based on earlier research on benign and malicious envy, we created items to measure the separate envy types. These items were developed considering the affective, cognitive, and motivational content of each envy subtype (benign and malicious) and were specifically designed to capture the experience of envy in an organizational context. Envy in general can best be described as the pain at the good fortune of others. The experience of benign and malicious envy differ in that benign envy involves more of a focus on the quality, achievement, or object that the self lacks, and on action tendencies of self-improvement or the acquisition of what one lacks. Malicious envy focuses one's attention more on the person who is better-off and activates action tendencies to pull down and degrade the other. Drawing on prior empirical research on the experiential content of both envy subtypes, we developed items (using a 7-point scale ranging from "Never" to "Always") to consider the affective, cognitive, and motivational content of benign and malicious envy (van de Ven et al., 2009). Items created for measuring benign envy included feelings of inspiration, wanting to improve one's own position, and hoping the other would continue their

TABLE 3.1 Factor Loadings

ITEM	ITEM WORDING	FACTOR LOADINGS	
		BENIGN ENVY	MALICIOUS ENVY
1	When I compare myself to successful people at this company it is hard for me to feel resentful.	.591	.063
2	I am motivated to try harder to achieve my own goals when comparing myself with others at this company that are doing well.	.904	.108
3	Even when I am comparing myself to someone at this company that is successful, I hope they continue their success.	.783	−.044
4	When I compare myself with someone successful at this company I feel inspired to do more to get ahead.	.596	−.131
5	Even when I am envious of people I compare myself to, I cannot say I dislike them.	.551	−.160
6	Sometimes people feel envious because they lack the advantages, superior accomplishment and talents enjoyed by others, and secretly wish the other person would lose this advantage, I've felt this way in the past few months.	−.029	.791
7	I feel very frustrated by the success of others at this company when I compare myself to them.	.036	.708
8	At times I may wish that successful people that I compare myself to will experience some kind of setback.	.002	.858
9	I may wish I could do something to take down a notch those successful people I compare myself to at this company, even if I would never actually do that.	−.066	.805
	Eigenvalue	3.950	1.185
	% Variance Explained (unrotated factors)	44	13.17

success. The items used for measuring malicious envy included feelings of intense frustration, negative thoughts about the other, wanting to degrade the other, and hoping the other would fail. Participants were asked to indicate the extent to which they had experienced these various feeling, thoughts, and motivations in the past three months (see Table 3.1 for all the items). For the measure of benign envy, five items were developed. An example scale item is, "I am motivated to try harder to achieve my own goals when comparing myself with others at this company that are doing well." Four items were used for the malicious envy subscale. An example item for the malicious envy scale is, "At times I may wish that successful people that I compare myself to will experience some kind of setback."

An exploratory factor analysis was conducted on the items in both envy subscales to identify the underlying factor structure. Principal components analysis was used with an Oblimin rotation; the resulting scree plot and eigenvalues demonstrate a clear two-factor structure (see Table 3.1). The first factor had an eigenvalue of 3.95, accounting for 43% of the variance. The second factor had an eigenvalue of 1.19, accounting for an additional 13% of the variance. No other factors had an eigenvalue above 1, and together, the two factors accounted for 57% of the variance. The factor loadings of each question on the factor can be found in Table 3.1. Both scales demonstrated sufficient reliability (malicious envy: $\alpha = .82$, benign envy: $\alpha = .73$). The correlation between the two scales was ($r = -.54$, $p < .001$).

A possibility is that the benign and malicious envy scale is capturing an employee's positive or negative attitude about the organization as a whole. In order to test for this, we ran a separate Harman's single-factor test combining the scale items from the benign and malicious envy scales with measures of employee perceptions about their workplace, including job satisfaction, social rewards satisfaction, and perceptions of procedural justice. It is possible that if an employee holds a negative view of their workplace, this dissatisfaction could account for the differences associated with benign and malicious envy. The results of Harman's single-factor test revealed five separate factors with eigenvalues greater than 1, and the first factor accounted for only 35% of total variance. These results suggest that the differences in the benign and malicious envy scale cannot be solely attributed to positive or negative attitudes toward the workplace.

Scale Validity

Scale validity was tested by examining the convergent and discriminant validity of the benign and malicious envy scales. The first step was to analyze the correlation of the envy subscales with several other social comparison–related emotions—those that can result from the performance of others in a domain relevant to the comparer (Tesser, 1991). Social comparison–related emotions have been associated with both positive and negative outcomes. Feelings of hope and pride have primarily

TABLE 3.2 Correlations of Benign Envy and Malicious Envy Scales
with Similar Scales

COMPARISON MEASURE	OBSERVED CORRELATIONS	
	BENIGN ENVY	MALICIOUS ENVY
Experience of Shame Scale (Andrews et al., 2002)	−.207*	.434**
Employee Jealousy (Vecchio, 2000)	−.318**	.556**
Experience of Pride Scale (Tracy & Robins, 2007)	.270*	−.298**
State Hope Scale (Snyder et al., 1996)	.367**	−.428**
Employee Envy Scale (Vecchio, 2000)	−.361**	.446**
Dispositional Envy Scale (Smith et al., 1999)	−.262**	.585**

NOTE: $N = 124$
*$p < .05$. **$p < .01$.

been associated with positive organizational outcomes, and feelings of shame and jealousy have primarily been associated with negative organizational outcomes (Andrews, Qian, & Valentinel, 2002; Youssef & Luthans, 2007; Fisher & Ashkanasy, 2000; Vecchio, 2000; Tracy & Robbins, 2007; Grandey, Tam, & Brauburger, 2002). Thus we would expect benign envy to be positively correlated with hope and pride, and malicious envy to be positively correlated with shame and jealousy. In order for the envy subscales to discriminate from these social comparison–related emotion measures, the association should be low to moderate in strength.

Table 3.2 shows the relationships between the various measures. As expected, the Malicious Envy Scale demonstrated low to moderate positive correlations with the Experience of Shame Scale (Andrews et al., 2002) ($r = .43$, $p < .001$), the Employee Jealousy Scale (Vecchio, 2000) ($r = .56$, $p < .001$) and demonstrated low to moderate negative correlations with the Experience of Pride Scale (Tracy & Robins, 2007) ($r = −.30$, $p = .001$), and the State Hope Scale (Snyder et al., 1996) ($r = −.43$, $p < .001$).

The Benign Envy Scale showed an opposite pattern of results (see Table 3.2) demonstrating low to moderate negative correlations with the Experience of Shame Scale ($r = −.21$, $p = .021$), the Employee Jealousy Scale ($r = −.32$, $p < .001$) and demonstrating low to moderate positive correlations with the Experience of Pride Scale ($r = −.27$, $p = .002$), and the State Hope Scale ($r = .37$, $p < .001$). Overall, the pattern of results suggests that the envy subscales are related to other validated measures of social comparison–related emotions, but the strength of these correlations is not high enough to suggest that they are redundant.

Next, the association between the envy subscales and previously used measures of envy was investigated. Traditionally used measures of envy (Smith, Parrott, Hoyle, & Kim, 1999; Vecchio, 2000) tend to emphasize the destructive and hostile component of envy, thus emphasizing malicious envy (Smith & Kim, 2007). For this reason, we expected these measures to be positively correlated with the malicious envy subscale. We expected that these measures would be more strongly correlated with the malicious envy subscale than the other social comparison–based emotion measures. Correlations can be found in Table 3.2. The malicious envy scale was moderately correlated with the Employee Envy Scale ($r = .45$, $p < .001$) and was also moderately correlated with the Dispositional Envy Scale ($r = .59$, $p < .001$). The benign envy scale demonstrated a low to moderate negative correlation with the Employee Envy Scale ($r = -.36$, $p < .001$) and the Dispositional Envy Scale ($r = -.26$, $p = .003$). As expected, malicious envy is more strongly related to traditional measures of envy than other social comparison–related emotions. The one exception to this is the correlation between malicious envy and the Employee Jealousy Scale. The reason for the strong positive correlation between the Malicious Envy Scale and the Employee Jealousy Scale is probably due to the close association between the concepts of jealousy and envy and the frequent interchangeability of the two terms in the English language. The traditional measures of envy are also more strongly correlated to the Malicious Envy Scale than to the Benign Envy Scale; this is expected, as the Benign Envy Scale focuses on a separate component of envy. This is perhaps also one reason why envy has so often been linked to negative behavior in the workplace, as the measures have only tapped into malicious envy.

Predictive Validity

In order to test the predictive validity of the envy subscales in an organizational setting, we ran several ordinary least-squares (OLS) regression analyses to test the relationship between benign and malicious envy with organizational outcomes. As noted earlier, malicious envy has most often been associated with a focus on the envied other and a desire to even the score by pulling that person down. Benign envy, on the other hand, has most often been associated with a focus on one's goals and self-improvement. Based on these empirical findings, we generally expected that benign envy would be positively related to work effort and organizational citizenship behavior, and malicious envy would be positively related to workplace deviance and turnover intentions.

Control variables. In the subsequent analyses, we controlled for gender to account for potential gender differences in the dependent variables, as scholars have shown that women are less likely to engage in deviant behavior toward their peers (Pearson & Porath, 2004). We also controlled for rank, as higher-status members of the organization are more likely to engage in incivility toward their lower-status colleagues (Pearson & Porath, 2004). We also controlled for organizational tenure (measured as months in the organization), as scholars have found that those who behave uncivilly toward others tend to have spent two or more years longer in the organization than their targets have (Pearson & Porath, 2004).

To make sure our scales for benign envy and malicious envy have predictive value, we also controlled for two other important organizational factors: procedural justice and job satisfaction. Procedural justice was measured using the procedural justice dimension of the Organizational Justice Scale (Colquitt, 2001). Procedural justice was included in the model to capture employees' sense of the fairness of the policies and procedures used to distribute organizational rewards. As such, this measure was used as a proxy for an employee's perception of goal attainability, their idea of whether or not the organization is a "level playing field." If employees perceive high levels of procedural justice, they should be more likely to believe that high levels of performance and greater organizational rewards are attainable. Procedural justice was measured using self-reports on a 7-item, 7-point Likert scale, with responses ranging from "Completely Disagree" to "Completely Agree." Sample items include: "My work procedures are free from bias," and "I have been able to express my views and feelings regarding work procedures." This scale demonstrated a high level of reliability ($\alpha = .82$).

Finally, we controlled for an employee's satisfaction with their job and their co-workers. Job satisfaction was measured using the three-item overall job satisfaction index of the Michigan Organizational Assessment Scale (Cammann, Fichman, Jenkins, & Klesh, 1979). Items were: "In general, I like working here," "In general, I don't like my job (reverse coded), and "All in all, I am satisfied with my job." This scale demonstrated high reliability (α = .84). Satisfaction with co-workers was measured using the 3-item Social Rewards Scale (Seashore, Lawler, Mirvis, & Cammann, 1982). Items were: "I am satisfied with the respect I receive from the people I work with," "I am satisfied with the way I am treated by the people I work with," and "I am satisfied with the friendliness of the people I work with." This scale demonstrated high reliability (α = .89). Job satisfaction has been shown to relate strongly to workplace deviance (Bennett & Robinson, 2003; Judge, Scott, & Ilies, 2006). Correlations between all variables used for testing the predictive validity of the envy subtypes are shown in Table 3.3.

Benign envy and positive work behavior. Some empirical results from lab studies show that benign envy is associated with motivational gain and a desire for self-improvement (van de Ven et al., 2011a,b). However benign envy differs from other positive social comparison based emotions such as admiration. Both admiration and benign envy can independently lead to a motivation to do better (van de Ven, 2015). Benign envy likely does this to resolve the frustration of the upward social comparison (van de Ven et al., 2011b), while admiration does because it makes people internalize the ideals of the admired person (Schindler, Zink, Windrich, & Menninghaus, 2013). Benign envy seems to result in an increased focus on the desired object or trait the envied person has, as opposed to a focus on the other that occurs with malicious envy (Crusius & Lange, 2014).

Based on these findings, our benign envy scale should also be related to positive motivations in the work setting. Because of the upward motivation and desire for self-improvement that benign envy produces, we expected employees to engage in positive, voluntary workplace behavior. Although we did not explicitly measure the domain of envy in the organization, we assume that experienced envy results from a social comparison alerting the employee to their relative standing within the organization. Several scholars have shown that work performance is a critical focus for comparison in organizations, and that information concerning performance is often available and relevant, whether it be through the posting of objective performance milestones or via third-party gossip (Barr & Conlon, 1994; Molleman, Nauta, & Buunk, 2007; Lam et al., 2011). We believe that individuals can improve their relative standing by increasing both in-role and extra-role performance, measured with work effort and organizational citizenship behavior, respectively. An employee can "close the gap" by working harder or becoming a more helpful corporate citizen.

TABLE 3.3 Bivariate Correlations

	N	M	SD	1	2	3	4	5	6
1 Malicious Envy	124	2.25	1.02	—					
2 Benign Envy	124	5.14	0.85	−.517**	-				
3 Gender	124	0.87	0.34	−.007	−.019	—			
4 Tenure	124	77.65	76.97	−.090	−.074	.036	—		
5 Rank	124	0.11	0.32	−.150	.085	−.243**	−.049	—	
6 Job Satisfaction	124	5.33	1.11	−.222*	.371**	−.112	−.127	.080	—
7 Procedural Justice	124	4.77	1.09	−.263**	.267**	−.148	−.034	.129	.653**
8 Social Rewards Satisfaction	124	5.07	1.20	−.293**	.426**	−.111	.046	.099	.681**
9 Effort	124	5.87	1.05	−.192	.318**	−.007	.043	.105	.227*
10 Organizational Citizenship Behavior	124	5.41	0.76	−.245**	.244**	.040	.047	.234**	.088
11 Deviant Behavior	124	1.72	0.47	.372**	−.190*	−.057	−.070	−.104	−.357**
12 Turnover Intentions	124	3.39	1.26	.217*	−.204*	.024	−.067	.025	−.700**

	7	8	9	10	11	12
1 Malicious Envy						
2 Benign Envy						
3 Gender						
4 Tenure						
5 Rank						
6 Job Satisfaction						
7 Procedural Justice	—					
8 Social Rewards Satisfaction	.563**	—				
9 Effort	.175	.200*	—			
10 Organizational Citizenship Behavior	.164	.180*	.284**	—		
11 Deviant Behavior	−.256**	−.299**	−.279**	−.282**	—	
12 Turnover Intentions	−.288**	−.549**	−.081	−.082	.342**	—

* Correlation significant at .05 level (2-tailed).
** Correlation significant at .01 level (2-tailed).

To measure work effort, we used the Work Effort Scale (Wright, Kacmar, McMahan, & DeLeeuw, 1995; Kacmar, Zivnuska, & White, 2007). The original scale included eight items, and we used a sub-scale of four items that dealt only with "self-initiated effort." Participants were asked to indicate on a 7-point Likert scale ranging from "Completely Disagree" to "Completely Agree" the extent to which they engaged in the following behaviors in the last few months: "Tried to do things better at work than I have in the past," "Tried to do more than was asked of me," "Tried to work harder," and "Tried to get more things done on time." This scale demonstrated very high reliability (α = .94). Table 3.4 contains the regression analyses testing the relationship between, especially, the Benign Envy Scale and work effort. The full model with all controls as predictors of work effort was not significant—$F(6,118) = 1.19$, $p = .318$—and explained 5.7% of the variance. Adding the benign and malicious envy scales explained another 6.6% of the variance, and the model was significant: $F(8,116) = 2.02$, $p = .050$. The Benign Envy Scale significantly predicted work effort: (β = .27, p = .015) when controlling for other relevant controls.

To measure organizational citizenship, we used a nine-item scale based on the work of Turnley, Bolino, Lester, and Bloodgood (2003). Example items include, "I adhere to informal organizational rules devised to maintain order," and "I generally help others who have been absent" (α = .68). For organizational citizenship behavior, we did not find an effect of the envy scales as we had predicted (see Table 3.4). The original model was significant, $F(6,118) = 2.33$, $p = .037$, and explained 10.7% of the variance. Adding the scales for benign and malicious envy did allow improvement of the model by another 3.7%, $F(8,116) = 2.42$, $p = .019$, but benign envy did not significantly predict organizational citizenship behavior (β = .14, p = .208).

Malicious envy and negative work behavior. Malicious envy differs from benign envy by producing a pulling-down motivation rather than a moving-up motivation (van de Ven et al., 2009). Malicious envy most closely resembles envy proper, the subject of traditional envy studies, and is thus associated with feelings of hostility and ill-will (Smith & Kim, 2007). Malicious envy is a much more frustrating and negative experience than benign envy, although the desire to close the gap between self and envied target is still present. While benign envy is associated with an increased focus on the self, malicious envy tends to sharpen the focus on

TABLE 3.4 Regression Results

VARIABLE	EFFORT		OCB		DEVIANT BEHAVIOR		TURNOVER INTENTIONS	
	MODEL 1	MODEL 2	MODEL 1	MODEL 2	MODEL 1	MODEL 2	MODEL 1	MODEL 2
Gender	.043	.029	.123	.108	-.124	-.102	-.020	-.013
Tenure	.051	.075	.035	.039	-.088	-.048	-.107	-.084
Rank	.092	.077	.241	.221	-.101	-.057	.062	.079
Job Satisfaction	.063	.071	-.124	-.114	-.174	-.040	-.528*	-.537**
Procedural Justice	.055	.042	.156	.148	-.041	-.195	.315*	-.423**
Social Rewards	.128	.005	.150	.057	-.179	-.103	-.433*	.313**
Malicious Envy		-.024		-.106		.365*		.165*
Benign Envy		.274*		.139		.110		.105
R-Square	.057	.123	.107	.144	.137	.231	.433	.452
ΔR-Square	.057	.066*	.107	.037	.137*	.094*	.433**	.019
Adjusted R-Square	.009	.062	.061	0.084†	.093	.177	.404	.414

NOTE: Standardized coefficients are reported. ΔR-Square report changes from the previous model.
* p < .05.
** p < .01.
† p < .1.

the envied other. This other-focus has been demonstrated in a series of experiments that show that envious individuals tend to more accurately recall information about their envied peers than a control group does (Hill, DelPriore, & Vaughan, 2011). These studies also showed that this redirection of attention to the envied other can deplete self-regulatory resources, making it harder for individuals to control their subsequent behavior. In addition to possible self-regulatory depletion, the experience of malicious envy is associated with feelings of dislike toward the envied target, increased perceptions of injustice and unfairness, and a desire to take away from the envied individual (van de Ven et al., 2009). These feelings of dislike and sense of injustice coupled with a decrease in self-regulatory resources enable individuals experiencing malicious envy to morally disengage, increasing the probability that these individuals can engage in harmful actions such as social undermining (Duffy et al., 2012). Employees experiencing malicious envy will thus be motivated to "even the score" through undermining, hindering, or embarrassing envied others. A few studies have shown that envy can result in behavior specifically targeted at the envied other, such as interpersonal harming and social undermining (Lam et al., 2011; Duffy et al., 2012). Malicious envy not only results in feelings of dislike and increased attention on the envied other but also results in thoughts of injustice and undeservedness. Thus the organization may also be a target of malicious envy's retribution. Employees typically expect a fair workplace, one that is free of bias when it comes to handing out organizational rewards, and this constitutes a major dimension in an employee's psychological contract (Coyle-Shapiro, 2002). However when an employee perceives organizational unfairness, as is the case with malicious envy, employees may also be motivated to punish the organization for psychological contract violation. Therefore, the scale developed for malicious envy should be related to workplace deviance, a measure of deviant behavior that includes both interpersonal and organizationally directed deviance (Robinson & Bennett, 2000).

Workplace deviance was measured using the Workplace Deviance Scale (Robinson & Bennett, 2000). Adopting the approach used in previous research (Lee & Allen, 2002), we used 27 items from the original workplace deviance scale. Items were self-reported using a 7-point Likert scale ranging from "Never" to "Always." Like Lee and Allen, we dropped items that had too little variance, with more than 90% responding "Never" to the item (the following items were dropped from the analysis: "Falsified a receipt to get reimbursed for more money than you spent on business expenses," "Use an illegal drug or consume alcohol on the job," "Drag out work in order to get overtime," "Played a mean prank on someone at work," and "Publicly embarrassed someone at work"). This approach resulted in a 22-item scale with high reliability ($\alpha = .90$). Sample items include, "Made fun of someone at work," "Said something hurtful at work," and "Acted rudely to someone at work."

Table 3.4 contains the regression analyses testing the relationship between our envy scales and workplace deviance. The model with all controls as predictors of workplace deviance was significant, $F(6,118) = 3.09$, $p = .008$, and explained 13.7% of the variance. Adding the scales for benign and malicious envy explained another 9.4% of the variance, $F(8,116) = 4.31$, $p < .001$. The Malicious Envy Scale indeed predicted workplace deviance ($\beta = .37$, $p < .001$), when controlling for other relevant factors such as job satisfaction, perceptions of justice, and satisfaction with one's co-workers.

While an employee who experiences malicious envy may be motivated to engage in workplace deviance, they may be unable to do so. Organizational researchers have demonstrated that employees need both motivation and discretion to engage in behavior that deviates from norms (Scott, Colquitt, & Paddock, 2009). Individuals who engage in workplace deviance may be subject to sanctions or punishment from their peers and the organization, and thus may not be able to act upon their motivations. These individuals are still subject to the experience of malicious envy, which is both unpleasant and threatening to an individual's identity and sense of self-worth. Thus faced with ego-threatening upward comparisons, individuals may choose to withdraw physically or psychologically from the workplace in order to limit the amount of upward comparisons they are subject to. Vecchio (2000) found that individuals experiencing envy in the workplace had higher propensities to quit. Therefore, we predicted that our scale for malicious envy should be related to turnover intentions, measured using the Turnover Intentions Scale from the Michigan Organizational Assessment Questionnaire (Cammann, Fichman, Jenkins, & Klesh, 1979; $\alpha = .94$).

Table 3.4 contains the regression analyses testing the relationship between malicious envy and turnover intentions. The model with all controls as predictors of turnover intentions was significant, $F(6,118) = 14.9$, $p < .001$, and explained 43% of the variance. Adding the scales for benign and malicious envy explained another 1.9% of the variance, $F(8,116) = 11.85$, $p < .001$. Malicious Envy did indeed predict turnover intentions ($\beta = .165$, $p = .052$), when controlling for other relevant controls.

General Discussion

In order to understand the complex, sometimes contradictory, effects of workplace envy, we argue that a useful way to conceptualize and measure envy is to differentiate between benign and malicious envy. The existence of these two qualitatively different envy subtypes is supported both by empirical studies (Crusius & Lange, 2014; van de Ven et al., 2011) and by common language usage, as many languages have distinct terms to identify these envy subtypes (van de Ven et al., 2009). In this study, we tested and validated a set of scales that we believe can be usefully and practically employed to further understand and evaluate workplace envy.

Our envy subscales exhibited good reliability, and the factor structure and item loadings displayed two underlying factors, as expected. Both benign and malicious envy scales were significantly correlated with other social comparison–related emotions, but the strength of this correlation was low to moderate, showing expected similarity but also establishing discriminant validity. Also as expected, malicious envy was more strongly related to traditional measures of envy, including dispositional envy (Smith, 1999) and employee envy (Vecchio, 2000), which was also expected, given the emphasis on the destructive component of envy in these measures. However, these correlations were moderate in strength, suggesting that the Malicious Envy Scale is neither redundant nor interchangeable with the other two.

Benign and malicious envy had a negative, moderate correlation with each other. We ran several tests to explore whether or not benign envy was simply the absence or inverse of feeling envy. The fact that when the items for these two scales are combined they nonetheless display a distinct two-factor structure, and the fact that the correlation between the two factors is moderate in strength, provide evidence that these two envy subtypes are not simply the inverse of each other. Additionally, the results for turnover intentions revealed an interesting pattern. Malicious envy had a significant and positive relationship with turnover intentions. Benign envy also had a positive, but not significant, relationship with turnover intentions. Although these results were not significant and should be interpreted with caution, it appears that both benign and malicious envy are positively related to turnover intentions. This probably follows because both benign and malicious envy are unpleasant emotional experiences, and one potential way for alleviating this pain is to withdraw from the workplace.

Predictive validity was established using OLS regressions to test the association between benign and malicious envy with several voluntary workplace behavior measures. These models controlled for an individual's job satisfaction, satisfaction with co-workers, and perceptions of organizational fairness. Generally speaking, malicious envy was more strongly related to counterproductive behaviors, including increased workplace deviance and greater turnover intentions. Benign envy was significantly related with higher levels of work-related effort but did not demonstrate a significant relationship with organizational citizenship behavior. Although we did expect that employees might try to even the gap by engaging in extra-role behavior, this did not appear to be the case in this sample. Empirical studies have shown that the experience of benign envy is associated with an increased focus on the self and especially one's own goals (van de Ven et al., 2009; Crusius & Lange, 2014). It may be that increasing one's effort is believed to be the most direct route to improving one's performance in an organization.

In sum, we conclude that our measures of benign and malicious envy demonstrate adequate reliability and validity and can be used to help understand the causes and consequences of workplace envy.

Limitations

One potential criticism of the scales and their validation procedures is that they were based on employee self-reports. Employees rated their own experience of benign and malicious envy, workplace attitudes, and several other emotion items. We did take several steps to ameliorate the problem of relying on self-report measures. First, we tested for common method using Harman's one-factor test. The results showed several underlying factors, which makes it unlikely that the differences in our envy subscales can be attributed to negative attitudes about the workplace or negative affectivity.

Our approach for exploring workplace envy by differentiating and measuring the benign and malicious components of envy might be criticized for being tautological because our conceptualization and measurement of the envy subtypes also include a motivational component (Cohen-Charash & Larson, Chapter 1, this volume). It has been suggested that a better approach is to focus on measuring the initial pain and feelings of inadequacy that accompany initial envious reactions. The different outcomes associated with envy, according to this approach, can then later be attributed to individual differences and the situational context in which the social comparison is being made.

We have two points to make on this criticism. The first deals with a question of measurement. In order to appropriately measure envy this way (i.e., focusing on each individual's unique experience), it would be necessary to use event-sampling methodology. While this technique can yield many useful and nuanced findings, it is unfortunately seen as invasive and cumbersome, and it is very difficult to employ in a workplace setting (McWilliams & Siegel, 1997). The purpose of our scales is to create a tool that is reliable and valid, that usefully approximates the experience of workplace envy, and that allows researchers to explore how envy affects workplace behavior. We argue that a measure that captures only the affective experience of an emotion will not have predictive value in itself. Appraisal theorists have argued that it would be very difficult to separate the affective component of an emotion and the motivation it produces (Stein & Hernandez, 2007). Specific situations give rise to a combination of specific feelings and specific motivations, and an emotion is actually the combination of these feelings and motivational tendencies. Appraisal theorists also argue that emotions are more like feedback systems that include arousal and an individual's appraisal of the situation, as well as past and future actions (Baumeister, Vohs, Dewall, & Zhang, 2007). Similarly, Stein, Hernandez, and Trabasso (2010) argued that "emotional responses include affective responses, but they occur because of the appraisal of personally meaningful goals. They also encode a plan of action" (p. 584).

An additional argument related to the possible tautological nature of our measures is that envy is a specific painful experience, and the different outcomes it produces actually stem from individual and situational differences. While we wholeheartedly agree that the context of social comparisons in the workplace is likely to have profound effects on emotional experience and organization behavior, we argue that this approach creates a relatively undifferentiated notion of envy, making it possibly more difficult to separate and study the antecedents and consequences of envy in the workplace. In our validation studies, we included situational measures of the justice and collaborative climate of the organization and still found significant effects for both benign and malicious envy on important workplace behaviors. We argue that our envy scales can be used to understand both the antecedents and consequences of workplace envy and serve as an important diagnostic tool concerning emotional experience in the workplace. In preliminary work on the antecedents of benign and malicious envy, organizational justice was an important predictor differentiating between an individual's experience of benign and malicious envy. When the workplace was perceived as fair and just, individuals were more likely to experience benign envy, with the inverse being true for the experience of malicious envy (Sterling, 2013).

Future Directions and Managerial Implications

We very much agree with the other scholars in this volume that the context of social comparison should be given more attention. We believe that the two-subtype approach is a useful way of observing both the antecedents and the consequences of workplace envy. Research on envy in organizations should thus progress by looking at potential contextual moderators of the experience and expression of envy (Crusius & Lange, Chapter 4, this volume). We strongly suspect that organizational policies and practices (Yu & Duffy, this volume), cross-cultural differences (Tan, Tai, & Wang, Chapter 11, this volume), and social network structure and position (Floyd & Sterling, Chapter 7, this volume) will influence whether or not the experience of envy is malicious or benign.

The question remains of how the emotional experience of envy is best handled or managed in the workplace. The answer probably does not lie in the elimination of envy. Research in the field of clinical psychology has argued that envy is deeply rooted in our childhood development and is probably an inevitable experience (Erlich, Chapter 9, this volume). Furthermore, organizational scholars have recognized that two fundamental aspects of organizational life contribute to the pervasiveness of envy, hierarchy, and competition (Vecchio, 2007). Additionally, the more people think "*it could have been me*" when they see someone who is better off than they are, the stronger their envy is (Van de Ven & Zeelenberg, 2015). But an organization would not want to eliminate this feeling, as that can probably only be done by preventing people from feeling they could obtain that better position. Organizations can vary by their hierarchical divisions and the amount of internal competition, so it is unlikely that envy can be completely removed from organizational life. Perhaps a better approach to managing envy in organizations is to ensure that the experience of envy is benign rather than malicious (Sterling & Labianca, 2015). Future research should focus on the factors that differentiate the experience of benign envy from the experience of malicious envy.

Both benign and malicious envy result from social comparison. Employees come to make sense of their identity and their place within an organization by comparing their abilities, rewards, and performance to that of their peers. Whether or not this comparison results in benign or malicious envy depends in part on how the individual appraises the situation: Are the results obtainable, and do the referent others deserve their success? These appraisals are partly driven by the context in which these comparisons are made: Whom, specifically, do individuals compare themselves to? How similar is the individual to the referent other? What is the relationship between the individual and the referent other? A recent study has demonstrated that context plays an important role in the social comparison process: when comparisons were made within the context of a competitive workgroup, upward comparisons typically resulted in harming behavior, but when comparisons were made within the context of a more collaborative workgroup, these negative effects were muted (Lam, van der Vegt, Waller, & Huang, 2011). Similarly, research in social psychology has demonstrated that characteristics of the relationship between comparer and referent, such as the amount of relative deprivation, perceptions of similarity, and psychological closeness to the social referent, all have a significant impact on the emotional outcomes of the social comparison process (Lockwood & Kunda, 1997; Mussweiler et al., 2004). Studies examining the consequences of both benign and malicious envy have typically focused on a single episodic occurrence of envy either through guided recall or scenario-based questionnaires. While this approach has been vital to understanding the affective, cognitive, and motivational processes associated with benign and malicious envy, these approaches often neglect the organizational context in which these social comparisons are made. Individuals in organizations often have more than one referent other, and these referent relationships are relatively stable over time (Kulik & Ambrose, 1992). Considering comparison events in isolation may give us an incomplete picture of what drives behavior in the workplace. In order to better understand how the experience of benign and malicious envy relates to broader patterns of individual behavior in organizations, an approach that is able to incorporate multiple referent others may help us better understand the antecedents to experiencing benign or malicious envy.

Studies in both social psychology and management have recognized the importance of identifying referent others. Lawrence (2006) and Shah (1998) have both recognized that employees have specific individuals with whom they compare themselves, an organizational reference group that is used to make sense of their standing in the workplace. Zell and Alicke (2010) demonstrated that individuals are disproportionately affected by the social comparison outcomes of a relatively small group of individuals that are proximate and assessable to the comparer. Therefore, we expect that, in addition to individual differences and organizational context, the comparison context will also have an impact on the experience of benign and malicious envy and subsequent behavioral outcomes. A previous study adopting a social network perspective demonstrated that the number of referent others and the relationships between these referent others had a significant impact on whether or not an employee experienced benign or malicious envy, and these envy subtypes mediated several behavioral outcomes (Sterling, 2013; for a discussion of how social networks can influence envy, see Floyd & Sterling, Chapter 7, this volume).

We thus believe that our benign and malicious envy subscales are a reliable and valid method for studying the antecedents and consequences of envy in the workplace, and further research using these instruments can help us better understand how workplace envy can be managed. It is unlikely that we can completely eradicate envy in the workplace, as other scholars have remarked. Instead, perhaps managerial interventions should focus on creating an environment that supports employee perceptions that high levels of performance are obtainable, and the procedures with which employees are rewarded and promoted are transparent, fair, and just. Because of the importance of these two appraisal aspects, we argue that further research should focus on the relationship between envy and managerial actions to improve leader member exchange (LMX), training, and organizational justice (Sterling & Labianca, 2015). Preliminary evidence also points to the fact that whom we compare ourselves to matters, and more research is needed to better understand how referent selection occurs in the workplace. If we can reliably distinguish between the experience of benign and malicious envy for employees in a workplace and better understand the influence that context has on the comparison process, we should be better able to determine what organizational actions lead to feelings of benign envy while minimizing feelings of malicious envy. This focus should help inform managerial decisions on processes such as team assignments, mentorship programs, employee recognition programs, and feedback and appraisal systems. It is our assertion that future research directed in this way can help minimize the destructive influence of envy in our organizations while preserving the motivational potential.

References

Adams, J. S. (1965). Inequity in social exchange. In L. Berkowitz, Ed., *Advances in Experimental Social Psychology,* 2(267–299). New York: Academic Press.
Ambrose, M. L., Harland, L. K., & Kulik, C. T. (1991). Influence of social comparisons on perceptions of organizational fairness. *Journal of Applied Psychology*, 76(2), 239–246.

Andrews, B., Qian, M., & Valentine, J. D. (2002). Predicting depressive symptoms with a new measure of shame: The Experience of Shame Scale. *British Journal of Clinical Psychology, 41*(1), 29–42.

Aristotle. (350 BC/1954). *The Rhetoric and the Poetics of Aristotle* (W. R. Roberts, Trans.). New York: Modern Library.

Arnold, M. B. (1960). *Emotion and Personality.* New York: Columbia University Press.

Barr, S. H., & Conlon, E. J. (1994). Effects of distribution of feedback in work groups. *Academy of Management Journal, 37*(3), 641–655.

Baumeister, R. F., Vohs, K. D., DeWall, C. N., & Zhang, L. (2007). How emotion shapes behavior: Feedback, anticipation, and reflection, rather than direct causation. *Personality and Social Psychology Review, 11*(2), 167–203.

Bennett, R. J., & Robinson, S. L. (2003). The past, present, and future of workplace deviance research. In J. Greenberg, Ed., *Organizational Behavior: The State of the Science* (pp. 247–281). Mahwah, NJ: Lawrence Erlbaum Associates.

Cammann, C., Fichman, M., Jenkins, D., & Klesh, J. (1979). The Michigan organizational assessment questionnaire. Unpublished manuscript, University of Michigan, Ann Arbor.

Clanton, G. (2007). Jealousy and envy. In J. E. Stets & J. H. Turner, Eds., *Handbook of the Sociology of Emotions* (pp. 410–442). New York: Springer.

Cohen-Charash, Y., & Mueller, J. S. (2007). Does perceived unfairness exacerbate or mitigate interpersonal counterproductive work behaviors related to envy? *Journal of Applied Psychology, 92*(3), 666–680.

Cohen-Charash, Y. (2009). Episodic envy. *Journal of Applied Social Psychology, 39*(9), 2128–2173.

Colquitt, J. A. (2001). On the dimensionality of organizational justice: A construct validation of a measure. *Journal of Applied Psychology, 86*(3), 386.

Cosmides, L., & Tooby, J. (2000). Evolutionary psychology and the emotions. *Handbook of Emotions, 2*, 91–115.

Coyle-Shapiro, J. A. M. (2002). A psychological contract perspective on organizational citizenship behavior. *Journal of Organizational Behavior, 23*(8), 927–946.

Crusius, J., & Lange, J. (2014). What catches the envious eye? Attentional biases within malicious and benign envy. *Journal of Experimental Social Psychology, 55*, 1–11.

De Hooge, I. E., Zeelenberg, M., & Breugelmans, S. M. (2007). Moral sentiments and co-operation: Differential influences of shame and guilt. *Cognition and Emotion, 21*(5), 1025–1042.

Duffy, M. K., & Shaw, J. D. (2000). The Salieri syndrome: Consequences of envy in groups. *Small group research, 31*(1), 3–23.

Duffy, M. K., Shaw, J. D., & Schaubroeck, J. M. (2008). Envy in organizational life. In R. H. Smith, Ed., *Envy: Theory and Research* (pp. 167–189). Oxford, UK: Oxford University Press.

Duffy, M. K., Scott, K. L., Shaw, J. D., Tepper, B. J., & Aquino, K. (2012). A social context model of envy and social undermining. *Academy of Management Journal, 55*(3), 643–666.

Fisher, C. D., & Ashkanasy, N. M. (2000). The emerging role of emotions in work life: An introduction. *Journal of Organizational Behavior, 21*(2), 123–129.

Folger, R., & Cropanzano, R. (2001). Fairness theory: Justice as accountability. In J. Greenberg and R. Cropanzano, Eds., *Advances in Organizational Justice* (vol. 1, pp. 1–55). Stanford, CA: Stanford University Press.

Frijda, N. H. (1986). *The Emotions*. Cambridge, UK: Cambridge University Press.

Frijda, N. H. (1988). The laws of emotion. *American Psychologist*, *43*(5), 349.

Grandey, A. A., Tam, A. P., & Brauburger, A. L. (2002). Affective states and traits in the workplace: Diary and survey data from young workers. *Motivation and Emotion*, *26*(1), 31–55.

Greenberg, J. (1982). *Equity and Justice in Social Behavior*. New York: Academic Press.

Hill, S. E., DelPriore, D. J., & Vaughan, P. W. (2011). The cognitive consequences of envy: Attention, memory, and self-regulatory depletion. *Journal of Personality and Social Psychology*, *101*(4), 653.

Judge, T. A., Scott, B. A., & Ilies, R. (2006). Hostility, job attitudes, and workplace deviance: Test of a multilevel model. *Journal of Applied Psychology*, *91*(1), 126.

Kacmar, K. M., Zivnuska, S., & White, C. D. (2007). Control and exchange: The impact of work environment on the work effort of low relationship quality employees. *The Leadership Quarterly*, *18*(1), 69–84.

Keltner, D., & Buswell, B. N. (1996). Evidence for the distinctness of embarrassment, shame, and guilt: A study of recalled antecedents and facial expressions of emotion. *Cognition and Emotion*, *10*, 155–171.

Keltner, D., & Haidt, J. (1999). Social functions of emotions at four levels of analysis. *Cognition and Emotion*, *13*, 505–521.

Kulik, C. T., & Ambrose, M. L. (1992). Personal and situational determinants of referent choice. *Academy of Management Review*, *17*(2), 212–237.

Lam, C. K., Van der Vegt, G. S., Walter, F., & Huang, X. (2011). Harming high performers: A social comparison perspective on interpersonal harming in work teams. *Journal of Applied Psychology*, *96*(3), 588–601.

Lawrence, B. S. (2006). Organizational reference groups: A missing perspective on social context. *Organization Science*, *17*(1), 80–100.

Lee, K., & Allen, N. J. (2002). Organizational citizenship behavior and workplace deviance: The role of affect and cognitions. *Journal of Applied Psychology*, *87*(1), 131.

Levenson, R. W., Ekman, P., & Friesen, W. V. (1990). Voluntary facial action generates emotion-specific autonomic nervous system activity. *Psychophysiology*, *27*, 363–384.

Lockwood, P., & Kunda, Z. (1997). Superstars and me: Predicting the impact of role models on the self. *Journal of Personality and Social Psychology*, *73*(1), 91.

McWilliams, A., & Siegel, D. (1997). Event studies in management research: Theoretical and empirical issues. *Academy of Management Journal*, *40*(3), 626–657.

Molleman, E., Nauta, A., & Buunk, B. P. (2007). Social comparison-based thoughts in groups: Their associations with interpersonal trust and learning outcomes. *Journal of Applied Social Psychology*, *37*(6), 1163–1180.

Pearson, C. M., & Porath, C. L. (2004). On incivility, its impact, and directions for future research. In R. W. Griffin & A. M. O'Leary-Kelly, Eds., *The Dark Side of Organizational Behavior* (pp. 403–425). San Francisco, CA: John Wiley & Sons.

Poulson, C. F., III. (2000). Shame and work. In N. M. Ashkanasy, C. E. J. Hartel, & W. J. Zerbe, Eds., *Emotions in the Workplace: Research, Theory, and Practice* (pp. 250–271). Westport, CT: Quorum Books.

Roseman, I. J., Wiest, C., & Swartz, T. S. (1994). Phenomenology, behaviors, and goals differentiate discrete emotions. *Journal of Personality and Social Psychology*, *67*(2), 206.

Schaubroeck, J., & Lam, S. S. (2004). Comparing lots before and after: Promotion rejectees' invidious reactions to promotees. *Organizational Behavior and Human Decision Processes*, *94*(1), 33–47.

Schindler, I., Zink, V., Windrich, J., & Menninghaus, W. (2013). Admiration and adoration: Their different ways of showing and shaping who we are. *Cognition & Emotion*, *27*(1), 85–118.

Scott, B. A., Colquitt, J. A., & Paddock, E. L. (2009). An actor-focused model of justice rule adherence and violation: The role of managerial motives and discretion. *Journal of Applied Psychology*, *94*(3), 756.

Seashore, S. E., Lawler, E. E., Mirvis, P., & Cammann, C. (1982). *Observing and Measuring Organizational Change: A Guide to Field Practice*. New York: Wiley.

Shah, P. P. (1998). Who are employees' social referents? Using a network perspective to determine referent others. *Academy of Management Journal*, *41*(3), 249–268.

Smith, R. H., & Kim, S. H. (2007). Comprehending envy. *Psychological Bulletin*, *133*(1), 46.

Smith, R. H., Parrott, W. G., Diener, E. F., Hoyle, R. H., & Kim, S. H. (1999). Dispositional envy. *Personality and Social Psychology Bulletin*, *25*(8), 1007–1020.

Snyder, C. R., Sympson, S. C., Ybasco, F. C., Borders, T. F., Babyak, M. A., & Higgins, R. L. (1996). Development and validation of the State Hope Scale. *Journal of Personality and Social Psychology*, *70*(2), 321.

Stein, N. L., & Hernandez, M. W. (2007). Assessing emotional understanding in narrative on-line interviews: The use of the NarCoder. In J. A. Coan & J. J. B. Allen, Eds., *Handbook of Emotion Elicitation and Assessment* (pp. 298–317). New York: Oxford University Press.

Stein, N. L., Hernandez, M. W., & Trabasso T. (2010). Advances in modeling emotion and thought: The importance of developmental, online, and multilevel analyses. In M. Lewis, J. M. Haviland-Jones & L. F. Barrett, Eds., *Handbook of Emotions* (pp. 574–586). New York: The Guilford Press.

Sterling, C. M. (2013). A tale of two envys: A social network perspective on the consequences of workplace social comparison. (Doctoral dissertation). Lexington, KY: University of Kentucky.

Sterling, C. M., & Labianca, G.J. (2015). Costly comparisons: Managing envy in the workplace. *Organizational Dynamics*, *44*(4), 296–305.

Tai, K., Narayanan, J., & McAllister, D. J. (2012). Envy as pain: Rethinking the nature of envy and its implications for employees and organizations. *Academy of Management Review*, *37*(1), 107–129.

Tesser, A. (1991). Emotion in social comparison and reflection processes. In J. Suls & T. A. Walls, Eds., *Social Comparison: Contemporary Theory and Research* (pp. 115–145). Hillsdale, NJ: Lawrence Erlbaum Associates.

Tracy, J. L., & Robins, R. W. (2007). The psychological structure of pride: A tale of two facets. *Journal of Personality and Social Psychology*, *92*(3), 506.

Turnley, W. H., Bolino, M. C., Lester, S. W., & Bloodgood, J. M. (2003). The impact of psychological contract fulfillment on the performance of in-role and organizational citizenship behaviors. *Journal of Management*, *29*(2), 187–206.

van de Ven, N. (2016). Envy and admiration: Emotion and motivation following upward social comparison. *Cognition and Emotion*. Manuscript in press.

van de Ven, N., Hoogland, C., Smith, R. H., van Dijk, W. W., Breugelmans, S. M., & Zeelenberg, M. (2015). When envy leads to schadenfreude. *Cognition and Emotion*, *29*(6), 1007–1025.

van de Ven, N., & Zeelenberg, M. (2015). The counterfactual nature of envy: "It could have been me." *Cognition and Emotion*, *29*(6), 954–971.

van de Ven, N., Zeelenberg, M., & Pieters, R. (2009). Leveling up and down: The experiences of benign and malicious envy. *Emotion*, *9*(3), 419.

van de Ven, N., Zeelenberg, M., & Pieters, R. (2011a). The envy premium in product evaluation. *Journal of Consumer Research*, *37*(6), 984–998.

van de Ven, N., Zeelenberg, M., & Pieters, R. (2011b). Why envy outperforms admiration. *Personality and Social Psychology Bulletin*, *37*(6), 784–795.

van de Ven, N., Zeelenberg, M., & Pieters, R. (2012). Appraisal patterns of envy and related emotions. *Motivation and Emotion*, *36*(2), 195–204.

van Dijk, W. W., Ouwerkerk, J. W., Goslinga, S., Nieweg, M., & Gallucci, M. (2006). When people fall from grace: Reconsidering the role of envy in schadenfreude. *Emotion*, *6*(1), 156.

Vecchio, R. P. (1997). It's not easy being green: Jealousy and envy in the workplace. In R. P. Vecchio, Ed., *Leadership: Understanding the Dynamics of Power and Influence in Organizations* (pp. 542–562). Notre Dame, IN: University of Notre Dame Press.

Vecchio, R. P. (2000). Negative emotion in the workplace: Employee jealousy and envy. *International Journal of Stress Management*, *7*(3), 161–179.

Wright, P. M., Kacmar, K. M., McMahan, G. C., & Deleeuw, K. (1995). P= f (MXA): Cognitive ability as a moderator of the relationship between personality and job performance. *Journal of Management*, *21*(6), 1129–1139.

Youssef, C. M., & Luthans, F. (2007). Positive organizational behavior in the workplace; The impact of hope, optimism, and resilience. *Journal of Management*, *33*(5), 774–800.

Zeelenberg, M., Nelissen, R. M., Breugelmans, S. M., & Pieters, R. (2008). On emotion specificity in decision making: Why feeling is for doing. *Judgment and Decision Making*, *3*(1), 18–27.

4 | How Do People Respond to Threatened Social Status?

MODERATORS OF BENIGN VERSUS MALICIOUS ENVY

JAN CRUSIUS AND JENS LANGE[*]

Introduction

It is uncontroversial that people can react in strong ways when they fall short of the superior standards set by others. Indeed, envy—the painful emotion that may result in such situations—is often considered to be a primary motivator for human behavior (Foster, 1972; Rawls, 1971; Schoeck, 1969; Smith & Kim, 2007; Tocqueville, 1840). The socially harmful consequences of envy may be a reason why it is such a detested and socially controlled emotion (Clanton, 2006). Nevertheless, the behavioral outcomes of envy are far from uniform. Even though envy may drive people to antagonize and aggress against superior others, it may also intensify their efforts for higher performance in ways that are directed at improving one's own outcome without hostility.

Recent research (Crusius & Lange, 2014; Falcon, 2015; Lange & Crusius, 2015a, 2015b; van de Ven, Zeelenberg, & Pieters, 2009, 2011a, 2011b) has tied these diverging manifestations to two qualitatively distinct forms of envious responding: malicious and benign envy. A crucial question concerns the factors that determine whether one type or the other dominates invidious responses. What predicts whether people will feel and act with benign or with malicious envy? Here, we examine possible moderators at the personal and social levels of analysis. Our premise in doing so is that benign and malicious envy are fundamental reactions to status threat. We posit that, in order to understand envy, it is important to investigate how people deal with situations in which upward social comparisons call into question their social status.

[*] The authors contributed equally to this chapter.

Benign and Malicious Envy as Distinct
Emotional Reactions to Status Threat

People have a universal tendency to think about and evaluate their own outcomes relative to those of others (Corcoran, Crusius, & Mussweiler, 2011). By definition, such social comparisons—if they point to one's own shortcomings—are the outset of every episode of envy. Even so, some dimensions of social comparisons seem to have a particularly strong potential to evoke envy. For example, when DelPriore, Hill, and Buss (2012) asked American university students to describe situations in which they envied someone, they reported several common themes. Large proportions of them felt envy because their counterparts were more attractive, had greater access to financial resources, owned luxury products, or had achieved greater success in their careers as students, athletes, or professionals. Highly similar results have been found for younger adolescents (Poelker, Gibbons, Hughes, & Powlishta, 2015) and German university students (Crusius & Lange, 2014; Rentzsch & Gross, 2015). The content of these incidents of envy is in line with research showing that envy occurs for comparison dimensions that are self-relevant (e.g., Salovey & Rodin, 1984; Silver & Sabini, 1978; for a review, see Smith & Kim, 2007).

In what way are these comparison dimensions so highly self-relevant? Arguably, a common denominator of them is that they reflect value, importance, and influence in society—in the envier's eyes, but also, and maybe even more importantly, in the eyes of others. In fact, it has been shown that individuals' feelings of self-worth with respect to certain attributes more strongly relate to how others value these attributes than to how individuals themselves do (Santor & Walker, 1999). In another study, envy was particularly likely and led to more hostile tendencies when the comparison domain was particularly competitive, and thus, possibly more status-relevant (Rentzsch, Schröder-Abé, & Schütz, 2015). Therefore, envy seems especially likely for attributes that observers respect, admire, and perceive as allowing a person control over important resources, or—put more abstractly—attributes that define and confer social status.[1] Notably, such a view bears a resemblance to a Lacanian concept of envy. According to this psychoanalytic approach, envy takes place in and is shaped by a triangle of the envier, the envied, and the gaze of the omnipresent "Big Other," who constantly needs to be impressed so that the envier becomes validated (Vidaillet, 2007; Vidaillet, Chapter 8, this volume).

Here we argue that, from an evolutionary point of view, envy's purpose may be to regulate status. Being superior in status-relevant domains such as those mentioned above yields important social benefits. These benefits should have contributed to survival and reproduction throughout our evolutionary past (for a review, see Anderson, Hildreth, & Howland, 2015). For instance, physical attractiveness promotes mating success; talent and achievements accrue admiration; and financial resources bring power. Hence, superiority in these domains gives rise to respect and influence—two key dimension of social status (Cheng, Tracy, Foulsham, Kingstone, & Henrich, 2013; Henrich & Gil-White, 2001; Magee & Galinsky, 2008). Social status itself is associated with a wide range of positive consequences. For example, high status leads to increased well-being (Anderson, Kraus, Galinsky, & Keltner, 2012b) and ascriptions of competence even in the absence of objective criteria for skills and knowledge (Anderson & Kilduff, 2009). For these reasons, people should not only have a fundamental motive to achieve status (Anderson et al., 2015), they should also be equipped with emotions that help them in attaining this goal (Steckler & Tracy, 2014). In this sense, envy may be adaptive because it alerts the individual to personal shortcomings in status-relevant domains and spurs corrective action (Hill & Buss, 2008; Hill, DelPriore, & Vaughan, 2011; Steckler & Tracy, 2014).

In addition to being an alarm signal, envy may—in essence—achieve its purported motivational function in two ways. Enviers can either try to attain (or surpass) the status of the superior other, or they can try to reduce it, either by inflicting actual harm on the envied person, or by (at least mentally) derogating the other. Recent research suggests that these diverging pathways of responses to being outperformed reflect two qualitatively distinct forms of envy.[2] Both are marked by high levels of frustration (Crusius & Lange, 2014; Lange & Crusius, 2015b) but contain different motivational elements: *benign envy* entails the motivation to move upwards, whereas *malicious envy* entails hostility and the motivation to harm or disparage the other (see also Sterling, van de Ven, & Richard Smith, Chapter 3, this volume, and Hoogland, Thielke, & Smith, Chapter 5, this volume). In several languages (such as Dutch, German, Arabic, or Russian), these forms of envy are marked by distinct words that connote their differences (Crusius & Lange, 2014; van de Ven et al., 2009). However, they can also be reliably distinguished as two different taxa of emotional experiences in languages that have only one word for envy (such as English or Spanish; Falcon, 2015; van de Ven et al., 2009). Furthermore, in line with a functional account of benign and malicious envy, the two forms are associated with divergent patterns of early attention-allocation, either on means for improvement for benign envy, or on the envied person (rather than their superior attribute or outcome) for malicious envy (Crusius & Lange, 2014).

Finally, this dual conceptualization of envy maps onto two diverging strands of motivational and behavioral correlates of envy. On one hand, envy has been associated with a range of outcomes characterizing benign envy, such as increased desire and approach motivation (Crusius & Mussweiler, 2012), higher effort, and improved performance (Lange & Crusius, 2015a, 2015b; Schaubroeck & Lam, 2004; van de Ven et al., 2011a). On the other hand, envy has been associated with outcomes indicating malicious tendencies, such as hostility toward and derogation of superior others (Salovey & Rodin, 1984), uncooperative behavior and social undermining tendencies (Duffy, Scott, Shaw, Tepper, & Aquino, 2012; Parks, Rumble, & Posey, 2002), or *schadenfreude*—pleasure at the misfortune of others (Smith et al., 1996; van de Ven et al., 2015).

A crucial question remains; namely, what are the determinants of benign and malicious envy? (For research regarding moderators that intensify a particular envy form once it has evolved, see Yu & Duffy, Chapter 2, this volume; for the moderating role of culture on envy in general, see Tan, Tai, & Wang, Chapter 11, this volume.) Based on our conceptualization of benign and malicious envy as functional responses whose pivotal aim is to deal with status threat, we will make several predictions about potential moderators at the dispositional and social levels of analysis. As research about the elicitation of benign versus malicious envy is still in its infancy, many of these predictions still await empirical scrutiny. (For a detailed model about the more immediate factors that influence how benign and malicious envy episodes may unfold in time, refer to Hoogland, Thielke, and Smith, Chapter 5, this volume.)

The Role of Control and Deservingness Appraisals

What may determine whether one type of envy or the other is evoked in a given situation? A crucial starting point is the differing appraisals that underlie benign and malicious envy. Even though both forms of envy share several features in that they are based on upward social comparisons with similar others, occur in domains of high-self relevance, and result in high levels of frustration (Crusius & Lange, 2014; Lange & Crusius, 2015b), benign and malicious envy are associated with markedly different appraisal patterns. One important difference concerns *personal control*; that is, the perceived ability to improve one's own lot relative to the other person's in the future. Appraisals of high personal control increase the likelihood of benign envy relative to malicious envy. A second important difference between benign and malicious envy concerns the perceived *deservingness* of the superior outcome of the envied. Appraisals of low deservingness increase the likelihood of malicious relative to benign envy (Crusius & Lange, 2014; Lange & Crusius, 2015a; Lange, Crusius, & Hagemeyer, 2015; van de Ven et al., 2009, 2011b; van de Ven, Zeelenberg, & Pieters, 2012).[3]

Consequently, variables affecting subjective appraisals of personal control and deservingness during threatening social comparisons should influence whether benign or malicious envy determine behavior. On a broader level, the notion that envy is fundamentally about how people deal with status disadvantages suggests that these appraisals and their ensuing emotional reactions should be related to how people construe and interpret status differences and the ways in which they aim to attain status.

Benign and Malicious Envy as Emotional Underpinnings of the Pursuit of Prestige and Dominance

According to a prominent model of the evolution of social rank, status rests on two coexisting pillars: prestige and dominance (Cheng et al., 2013; Cheng, Tracy, & Henrich, 2010; Henrich & Gil-White, 2001). This model posits that status based on *prestige* is conferred to people who are perceived to be competent, skilled, and successful in achieving their goals. Status based on *dominance* is achieved by coercive tactics such as inducing fear and intimidation or engaging in aggressive behavior.

Most important for the present purposes, the model holds that a prestige-based strategy should be most beneficial to confident individuals who have the skills and the capacity to climb to a higher level. In contrast, a dominance-based strategy should be most beneficial to individuals who have more to gain from coercion because they possess the physical ability to control others. Furthermore, the pursuit of prestige has been theorized to be adaptive in environments in which gains can be reached via rank-based emulation of superior others. In such environments, emulative effort is an effective means to move upwards in the hierarchy, which is perceived to be based on merit, legitimacy, and principles of fairness, and which rewards sharing information about how people can climb the social ladder. In contrast, dominance is thought to be adaptive in environments in which rank is based on zero-sum type social conflict about valuable resources, but not on merit and the sharing of information (Cheng et al., 2013, 2010; Henrich & Gil-White, 2001).

We argue that the factors that determine whether pursuing status via prestige or dominance is more beneficial correspond to benign and malicious envy's diverging appraisal patterns. A perception of high personal control and high deservingness of others' successes should indicate a situation in which status can be best attained via prestige. A perception of low personal control and low deservingness should, in contrast, indicate a situation in which status can be best attained via dominance. From this perspective, we speculate that benign envy and malicious envy may be emotional processes whose purpose is to contribute to the regulation of social status based on prestige versus dominance, respectively.

Given this reasoning, we can try to identify moderating variables that shift people's tendency to react with benign or malicious envy to status threats by pinpointing factors that influence their diverging appraisals of personal control and the perceived deservingness of the other person's outcome. To put it differently, we can examine factors that alter people's construal of status differences and how they therefore attempt to attain and defend their own status.

Dispositional Moderators of Benign versus Malicious Envy

One strategy to identify moderators of benign versus malicious envy as responses to status threats is to apply a research approach to inter-individual differences. Even though envy is usually understood as a universal, culturally shared emotion that everyone may experience at least occasionally (Smith & Kim, 2007), some people appear to be more prone to experiencing envy than others. In line with this hypothesis, several lines of research have shown that people have a stable tendency to react to superior others with envy. The most widely used scale to measure such a proneness for envy is the Dispositional Envy Scale (DES; Smith, Parrott, Diener, Hoyle, & Kim, 1999). Along with other scales such as the York Enviousness Scale (Gold, 1996) or the Envy subscale of Veselka, Giammarco, and Vernon's (2014) Vices and Virtues Scale, DES conceptualizes dispositional envy as a unidimensional trait. Its rationale and its correlates make it clear that the DES taps into hostile elements of envious responding. Specifically, as it was aimed at measuring the antisocial "envy proper" (Smith & Kim, 2007), it contains items that measure perceptions of injustice and resentment. In a similar vein, Gold's and Veselka et al.'s envy scales entail items that involve begrudging feelings against superior others. Furthermore, all these scales correlate with anger and hostile tendencies. Thus, these envy scales have focused on the malicious side of the envious personality.

Furthermore, another recently developed envy scale focuses on individuals' inclination to engage in frustrating upward comparisons, explicitly excluding envy's motivational component (Rentzsch & Gross, 2015). Given this unitary conceptualization, this scale may tap into the benign as well as the malicious variants of envious dispositions, without, however, differentially predicting them.

Measuring Dispositional Benign and Malicious Envy

Given that state envy can be disentangled into two forms that are highly similar in some respects but bear strikingly diverging outcomes, such a distinction may be fruitful in investigating dispositional envy as well. To aid in this undertaking, we developed the Benign and Malicious Envy Scale (BeMaS) with the aim to assess stable inclinations to react with benign or malicious envy to upward social comparisons (Lange & Crusius, 2015b; for a similar approach to measuring inter-individual differences in benign and malicious envy in organizations, see Sterling, van de Ven, & Smith, Chapter 3, this volume), thereby complementing the previous scales.

To do so, we constructed a set of items with the intention to tap only into the distinguishing characteristics of both forms of envy—the thoughts, feelings, and motivational tendencies that should be unique emotional components of each form. For example, for the malicious envy subscale, participants indicate their agreement to items such as, "Envious feelings cause me to dislike the other person," or "Seeing other people's achievements makes me resent them." The benign envy subscale includes items such as "Envying others motivates me to accomplish my goals," or "When I envy others, I focus on how I can become equally successful in the future."

We conducted several studies to establish the psychometric quality and the validity of the BeMaS. In particular, the subscales have good reliability, confirmatory factor analyses confirmed that a two-dimensional model had a better fit to the data than a unidimensional model, and a retest study showed that responses to the subscales were stable (Lange & Crusius, 2015b, Study 1 and Supplementary Materials). Several findings suggest that the subscales have convergent and discriminant validity. Specifically, the benign and malicious envy scales are only slightly positively correlated with each other across studies. Nevertheless, social comparison orientation (Gibbons, & Buunk, 1999) predicted both benign and malicious envy. As expected, the more people were inclined to compare themselves with others, the more prone they were to react with benign and malicious envy (Lange & Crusius, 2015b, Study 3). In line with their respective conceptualizations, only the malicious, but not the benign, subscale of the BeMaS correlated with the DES.

Finally, we investigated whether the BeMaS predicts benign and malicious envy at the episodic level. To do so, we exposed participants to a highly successful comparison standard (Lange & Crusius, 2015b, Study 2). The comparison standard was presented by means of an interview in which several informational cues kept it ambiguous whether this success was controllable and deserved (because it resulted from effort) or not (because there were lucky circumstances). Confirming their shared affective core, both dispositional benign and malicious envy (inconspicuously measured in a previous session several weeks before) predicted frustration in response to the upward comparison standard. Furthermore, and most crucially, dispositional benign envy predicted state benign envy (but not state malicious envy) in reaction to the upward comparison standard. In contrast, dispositional malicious envy predicted state malicious envy (but not state benign envy). Taken together, these data suggest that people differ in their proneness to experience benign as well as malicious envy, and that the BeMaS may be a useful tool for examining both common and diverging moderators of these traits and their behavioral outcomes.

Motivational Predictors of Benign and Malicious Envy at the Trait Level

As suggested above, treating benign and malicious envy as diverging emotional pathways toward status mediated by appraisals of personal control and perceived deservingness allows us to examine several moderating variables affecting these processes. One important class of variables relates to motivational dispositions about achievements. At its core, the achievement motive is concerned with the attainment of important goals set by certain standards of excellence (McClelland, Atkinson, Clark, & Lowell, 1953). For status-relevant domains, these standards are intrinsically defined in a social way—for example, by the higher achievements set by other people.

Importantly, people can strive for achievements in distinct ways, and they differ chronically in their inclination to do so (Atkinson, 1957).

Dispositional *hope for success* results in the motivation to approach upward goals. In contrast, dispositional *fear of failure* results in the motivation to avoid failures in order to reach these goals. These motivational tendencies fit the diverging appraisals of benign and malicious envy. In particular, the more optimistic hope for success should be related to appraisals of control, which lead to benign envy (van de Ven et al., 2012). In contrast, fear of failure should be related to appraisals of low control, which lead to malicious envy (van de Ven et al., 2012). In line with this reasoning, we found that chronic hope for success was linked to dispositional benign envy, and chronic fear of failure was linked to dispositional malicious envy (Lange & Crusius, 2015b, Study 3).

Such relationships can also be investigated on a domain-specific level. To do so, we asked a sample of professionals to complete measures of the chronic goal-orientation they have with regard to work-related achievement goals (Baranik, Barron, & Finney, 2007). Work-related approach goals as well as avoidance goals were positively linked with a measure (Gibbons & Buunk, 1999) of participants' inclination to compare with others. However, having approach goals uniquely predicted dispositional benign envy, whereas avoidance goals uniquely predicted dispositional malicious envy (Crusius, Lange, & Corcoran, 2015). In another study, we again measured work-related achievement goals, but asked participants to report a recent episode of envy they had experienced at work. In line with the evidence on the dispositional level, work-related approach goals uniquely predicted envy episodes that were rated to be more benign, whereas work-related approach goals uniquely predicted envy episodes that were rated to be more malicious by the participants (Crusius et al., 2015).

Finally, we collected data on how dispositional benign and malicious envy are related to goal-setting by athletes (Lange & Crusius, 2015b). We approached marathon and half-marathon runners a day before they entered the competition and asked them to complete the BeMaS and to indicate their goal for their race (i.e., the time intended to finish). Recording their race number allowed us to download their actual finishing time after the race. During marathon training, most athletes should be confronted with faster runners. We hypothesized that the hope for success that characterizes benign envy should lead to higher approach goals. In line with this reasoning, dispositional benign envy was associated with higher goals for the race. These higher goals mediated the positive relationship of dispositional benign envy and race performance. In contrast, and also in line with our reasoning, dispositional malicious envy was associated with a reduced likelihood to report any goal for the race, which may be indicative of goal avoidance.

Taken together, these findings suggest that broad motivational inclinations as well as domain-specific motivational tendencies predict the proneness to experience benign or malicious envy. Having a more optimistic, approach focus to goal attainment is associated with an increased likelihood to experience benign envy, whereas a more pessimistic, avoidant focus on goal attainment is associated with an increased likelihood to experience malicious envy. These findings dovetail with evidence that optimism moderates the effects of social comparison on performance (Gibbons, Blanton, Gerrard, Buunk, & Eggleston, 2000). Furthermore, they are in line with the finding that activating an *incremental* framework of personality (implying that traits can change; see Dweck, 1999) as opposed to activating an *entity* framework of personality (implying that traits do not change) increases benign envy (van de Ven et al., 2011a).

In addition, these findings invite speculation about closely related beliefs and core self-evaluative tendencies that influence the way people interpret and pursue personal goals (e.g., Judge, Erez, Bono, & Thoresen, 2002). For example, whether people chronically attribute their own (and also others') failures and successes in goal pursuit to internal or external reasons, as well as their generalized beliefs in self-efficacy, should affect whether people tend to respond with benign or malicious envy to superiors' comparison standards. This should happen to the extent that these variables determine how people appraise their own personal control and the perceived deservingness of the superior outcomes of others. As a further example, depression, which predicts both dispositional (Smith et al., 1999) as well as episodic envy (Appel, Crusius, & Gerlach, 2015), may be expected to foster malicious rather than benign envy, as it involves perceptions of low personal control (for a discussion, see Appel, Gerlach, & Crusius, 2016).

Chronic Need for Status: The Case of Grandiose Narcissism

If envy is an emotion whose purpose is to regulate social status, another way to shed light on the dispositional moderators of envious responding is to consider people with an enhanced desire for status. This desire is particularly strong in people characterized by high levels of grandiose narcissism. Narcissists not only have a firm belief in their own superiority, they are also strongly preoccupied with their own successes and feel entitled to better treatment than others (Morf & Rhodewalt, 2001). Thus, high status may be their greatest concern.

Such an excessive concern for superior status implies that narcissists should be particularly sensitive to social comparison information, because superiority is dependent on comparisons with others. Indeed, narcissism is associated with a stronger inclination for social comparison (Bogart, Benotsch, & Pavlovic, 2004). Furthermore, narcissists are particularly concerned with praise that informs them about their superiority, more strongly than with factual performance feedback (Morf & Rhodewalt, 2001; Morf, Torchetti, & Schürch, 2012), which is in line with their constant concern with self-validation and status maintenance (Back et al., 2013; Morf & Rhodewalt, 2001).

Even though narcissists believe that they are superior to others, life does not prevent those others from outperforming them from time to time. In addition, narcissists' concern for comparative information should render such upward social comparisons particularly salient to them. Given their need for status, such threatening comparisons should be particularly motivating for narcissists. This envious dynamic has often been assumed to contribute to narcissists' tendency to lash out against others (Kernberg, 1975). Indeed, when rivals outperform them, narcissists engage in hostility against them and derogate them (Morf & Rhodewalt, 1993; South, Oltmanns, & Turkheimer, 2003). These antisocial behaviors come with severe social costs by causing ascriptions of aggressiveness and low trustworthiness to narcissists by their peers (Back et al., 2013; Paulhus, 1998). However, narcissists not only try to maintain and gain status by antagonizing others, they also engage in assertive self-enhancement strategies that lead to high social attractiveness, admiration by others, popularity (Back, Schmukle, & Egloff, 2010; Vazire, Naumann, Rentfrow, & Gosling, 2008), and the ascription of competence by their peers (Back et al., 2013; Paulhus, 1998). Back and colleagues (Back et al., 2013) have tied these paradoxical outcomes to two correlated but distinct facets characterizing grandiose narcissism at the trait level. *Narcissistic admiration* involves grandiose fantasies, striving for uniqueness, and charming behaviors, which are connected to the ascription of social potency by others. In contrast, *narcissistic rivalry* involves striving for supremacy, active devaluation, and aggressiveness towards others, which are connected to a proneness for social conflict.

These diverging strategies to achieve social status match the distinct motivational outcomes of benign and malicious envy. The self-enhancement strategies of narcissistic admiration are similar to the upward-directed motivational tendencies of benign envy. In contrast, the antisocial strategies of narcissistic rivalry are similar to the hostility of malicious envy. Furthermore, the facets of benign and malicious envy appear to share chronic motivational foundations. Back et al. (2013) posit that hope for success fuels narcissistic admiration, and that fear of failure fuels narcissistic rivalry. Based on this model of narcissism, we theorize that benign and malicious envy are distinct emotional pathways that can elucidate the complex behavioral and social outcomes of narcissism.

In addition, disentangling these processes may explain why there has been no empirical evidence for the connection of envy and grandiose narcissism. Even though it is widely believed that envy is a crucial part of narcissism (e.g., Kernberg, 1975; Pincus et al., 2009), this relationship could not be shown in previous research. If anything, only vulnerable narcissism has been linked to envy (e.g., Krizan & Johar, 2012). The surprising absence of this relationship may be due to the fact that the most frequently used measure of narcissism, the Narcissistic Personality Inventory (Raskin & Terry, 1988), taps into narcissistic admiration more strongly than into narcissistic rivalry (Back et al., 2013). However, the DES, the most widely used measure of dispositional envy, reflects only dispositional malicious envy (Lange & Crusius, 2015b). If, as we hypothesize, narcissistic admiration is linked specifically to benign envy, and narcissistic rivalry is linked to malicious envy, previous research could not identify these links.

We tested these hypotheses in a series of studies (Lange et al., 2015), whose results suggest that the specific forms of narcissism and envy are part of related yet distinct personality patterns. In particular, one study showed that narcissistic admiration and rivalry as well as dispositional benign and malicious envy relate to the propensity to compare oneself with others. Narcissists were more prone to engage in social comparisons, which is the precondition for envy. Furthermore, narcissistic admiration and dispositional benign envy shared hope for success as a motivational impetus. In contrast, narcissistic rivalry and dispositional malicious envy shared fear of failure as a motivational impetus. In another study, narcissistic admiration predicted episodic benign envy in response to a superior comparison standard, whereas narcissistic rivalry predicted malicious envy toward this standard. In line with a social-functional account of envy, these relationships were explained by corresponding appraisals of personal control (which were positively related to narcissistic admiration) and deservingness (which were negatively related to narcissistic rivalry).

A final study supported the notion that the behavioral outcomes of benign and malicious envy may mediate the contradicting social effects of envy. In particular, this study again showed evidence for the distinct pathways from narcissistic admiration to dispositional benign envy and from narcissistic rivalry to dispositional malicious envy. Most importantly, these pathways predicted the peer-reported frequency of corresponding behavioral outcomes. Peers observed that individuals characterized by narcissistic admiration would more often yield prestige-related social outcomes, such as being complimented by others and being perceived as ambitious. In contrast, according to peer perceptions, individuals characterized by narcissistic rivalry more frequently expressed schadenfreude and engaged in gossip. In other words, their peers perceived them to be more prone to derogate others. Benign versus malicious envy mediated these links, respectively. Taken together, this evidence suggests that the specific forms of the narcissistic personality (which match prestige- and dominance-based routes to status) predict whether these people will respond with benign or malicious envy to threatening comparisons. In addition, these envious responses seem to carry important social outcomes.

Other Forms of Chronic Status Threat

In addition to shedding light on the role of envy in how narcissists strive to fulfill their insatiable need for status, these findings imply that benign or malicious envy may also result from other forms of chronic status threat. For example, chronically low socio-economic status has been associated with *cultures of honor*, cultures in which people are inclined to use violent strategies to defend their reputation when it is threatened (Cohen, Nisbett, Bowdle, & Schwarz, 1996; Henry, 2009). The more stable and essentialist view of identity, the belief in honor seems to entail, should undermine appraisals of personal control. That is why cultures of honor should foster malicious envy. Chronic status threats may also produce specific forms of envy in interaction with situational variables. For example, recent evidence suggests that the fear of downward mobility of high-status individuals can increase subjective appraisals of unfairness when an authority introduces objectively fair measures to reduce inequality (Burleigh & Meegan, 2013). According to the present analysis, such a situation should also increase the likelihood of malicious envy upon encountering upward social comparison standards.

In summary, these findings highlight that conceptualizing envy as a response to a status threat allows us to identify dispositional moderators of benign and malicious envy. We now turn to the social variables that may shift envious responding to either of the two forms.

Social Level of Analysis

Envy is essentially a social emotion. By definition, it follows from unflattering comparisons in a dyad of an envier and an envied person (Heider, 1958; Parrott & Smith, 1993; Smith & Kim, 2007). In addition to being defined by a social relationship, social variables have been hypothesized and shown to shape envious responses in several ways on inter-individual, group, and societal levels. For example, much evidence suggests that interpersonal similarity contributes to the intensity of envy (e.g., Salovey & Rodin, 1984; Schaubroeck & Lam, 2004; for a review, see Smith & Kim, 2007). Furthermore, intergroup competitiveness and status differences decrease an outgroup's warmth and increase their competence, thereby fostering envy (Caprariello, Cuddy, & Fiske, 2009). Social identification with one's group dampens envy-driven social undermining against ingroup members (Duffy et al., 2012). Finally, diverging self-construals in Eastern and Western cultures shape envious inclinations (Tan, Tai, & Wang, Chapter 11, this volume). Thus, the social nature of envy can hardly be underestimated. However, little is known about the social variables affecting whether envy is modulated toward its benign or malicious form. To investigate this question, we outline a social-functional approach to envy that allows us to derive several specific hypotheses.

A Social-Functional Approach to Envy

As described above, we conceptualize envy as a functional emotion signaling the need to address perceived differences in social status conferred to the self and others. A high position in the social hierarchy is associated with respect, admiration, and intimidation on the side of observers, leading to important evolutionary benefits. Benign envy may serve the goal to reach a similar status in the future, whereas malicious envy would serve the goal of harming the status of competitors. Hence, envy's function might be the maintenance and establishment of hierarchical structures, a central *social function* of emotions (Fischer & Manstead, 2008; Keltner & Haidt, 1999; Manstead & Fischer, 2001; Parkinson & Manstead, 2015).

Social-functional approaches see emotions as responses to social signals. Furthermore, they analyze emotions as elicitors of corresponding functional reactions in observers (van Kleef, 2009; van Kleef, van Doorn, Heerdink, & Koning, 2011). For instance, embarrassment displays convey commitment and a propensity for prosociality, fostering trust and affiliation in observers (Feinberg, Willer, & Keltner, 2012). If envy is indeed a social-functional response to status differences, any emotional display of high status or a social variable distinctively affecting the emotional ramifications of status hierarchies should evoke and affect envy more strongly than the mere information of having a worse outcome than another person has. Based on this notion, we discuss social, status-related variables that may modulate envy toward its benign or malicious manifestation.

The Envied Person's Pride

The envied person is an essential social element in every envy episode. A social-functional approach predicts that a status display by the envied person should enhance envious responses above and beyond superior outcomes per se. A status signal to observers is pride (Martens, Tracy, & Shariff, 2012; Shariff & Tracy, 2009; Tracy, Shariff, Zhao, & Henrich, 2013). In fact, pride and status are so intrinsically linked that pride displays convey status even when contextual information contradicts this assessment (e.g., when pride is displayed by a homeless person; Shariff, Tracy, & Markusoff, 2012). Therefore, superior individuals' pride displays should spur envy. We investigated this prediction in a series of studies (Lange & Crusius, 2015a) in which we exposed participants to proud counterparts in ostensible or scenario-based competitions. Pride displays increased envy compared to emotionally neutral displays or embarrassment (an emotion that conveys low status; Shariff & Tracy, 2009). Crucially, in all cases, the objective achievement of the superior person was equally outstanding. Thus pride—as a social signal of status—additively fosters envy.

Moreover, pride also has two forms (Tracy & Robins, 2007) that relate to the distinct pathways to social status outlined above. In *authentic pride*, the person attributes success to effort, whereas in *hubristic pride*, the person attributes success to talent. The pride forms differ in the information they convey to observers (Cheng et al., 2013, 2010). Authentic pride is likable and conveys prestige. Liking fosters appraisals of high deservingness (Feather, 1999) and prestige suggests that the individual is willing to share skill and know-how (Cheng et al., 2013), arguably increasing perceptions of personal control. For these reasons, we predicted that authentic pride spurs benign envy. Hubristic pride is less likable and conveys dominance. Disliking fosters appraisals of low deservingness (Feather, 1999) and dominance suggests that the individual aggressively defends a fixed status hierarchy (Cheng et al., 2013), arguably undermining perceptions of personal control. Therefore, we predicted that hubristic pride increases malicious envy. In a series of studies, we either measured perceived authentic and hubristic pride in recalled envy episodes, or manipulated the pride forms via videos, pictures with disambiguating attribution information, or verbally. These studies indeed showed the hypothesized distinct effects of authentic and hubristic pride on benign and malicious envy. These relations were mediated by differences in liking and perceptions of prestige and dominance and manifested in corresponding benign and malicious motivational inclinations and actual envy-driven behavior (Lange & Crusius, 2015a).

Even though these data show that authentic pride increases effort and that hubristic pride increases malicious behavior, it would be interesting to investigate whether and how enviers achieve their social goals in the long term. For instance, dominance displays like hubristic pride foster schadenfreude in the maliciously envious person if the dominant competitor suffers (Boecker & Lange, 2015). When enviers express this happiness publicly, it might serve as a social signal to others that the superior person has lost dominance. In fact, in scenario studies, schadenfreude expressions in front of a superior person and others reduced the conferral of dominance to the hubristically proud person. However, when schadenfreude was expressed in front of others but not to the superior person, dominance conferral was unaffected (Boecker & Lange, 2015). Schadenfreude displays themselves may thus convey that an inferior individual no longer fears the superior person, thereby leveling status differences in an expression of dominance.

We argue that benign envy should translate into observable performance benefits (Lange & Crusius, 2015a, 2015b; van de Ven et al., 2011a), ultimately increasing status. However, recent research also suggests that benignly envious individuals may sometimes conceal their self-improvement tendencies in public. This is the case because they fear social devaluation for acting on a norm-diverging emotion (Youn & Goldsmith, 2015). As status is conferred only by observers, benignly envious behavior could sometimes fail to enhance the envier's status, at least in the short term. If that is correct, benign envy might instead increase status, particularly in the long term, when signals of prestige become consolidated and apparent outside of the immediate emotional context. Thus, future research should investigate the effectiveness of envy-driven behavior in response to pride displays over time.

The effect of pride displays on the modulation of envy toward its benign and malicious form is the only social variable that has been investigated so far. Other implications of a social-functional account of envy still await empirical scrutiny.

Power Hierarchies

One area of research that may inform the search for moderators of benign and malicious envy is research on power in social hierarchies (Magee & Galinsky, 2008). *Power* is defined as asymmetrical control over resources (which may—in the current conceptualization—be seen as an instrument to exert dominance). Power leads to a stronger focus on the self and increased distance from other people in the hierarchy. This stabilizes power differences between group members (for a review, see Smith & Magee, 2015). In contrast, status in the form of prestige relates to an other-focus when securing a higher position in the social hierarchy. As long as observers confer prestige, they can also take it away. Thus, hierarchies based on power or prestige differ crucially with respect to the mutability they convey. Perceptions of mutability in prestige-based hierarchies propel upward mobility—competitive behavior directed at increasing personal status (Hays & Bendersky, 2015). These efforts might be an effect of benign envy, as mutability should enhance appraisals of personal control (van de Ven et al., 2012). Furthermore, power hierarchies should increase malicious envy as powerful individuals treat others more unjustly (Blader & Chen, 2012). In summary, everything else being equal, we predict that power hierarchies promote malicious envy.

Non-Emotional Status Cues

As alluded to above, a social-functional approach predicts that status cues communicated by others should affect the intensity and the form of envy. Research has applied a social-perceptual approach (Brunswik, 1956) to identify such cues. This research has investigated how prestigious or dominant individuals convey their status, and which cues observers utilize to infer either prestige or dominance in others. For instance, prestigious individuals speak with higher vocal pitch, greater loudness, and greater loudness variability, and observers use these cues to infer high prestige (Ko, Sadler, & Galinsky, 2015). In addition, people infer prestige when others show extreme confidence (Anderson, Brion, Moore, & Kennedy, 2012a), are extraverted (Anderson, John, Keltner, & Kring, 2001), use a socially attractive verbal style (e.g., seeking approval, appearing self-deprecating, or using humor), or demonstrate confident bodily displays (Cheng, 2013). Dominant individuals speak more frequently and give input in group discussions early on (Anderson & Kilduff, 2009). In addition, observers infer dominance when others use an intimidating and entitled verbal style (e.g., appearing overbearing, humiliating others, or forcefully pushing their ideas), expansive and aggressive bodily displays, or lower vocal pitch (Cheng, 2013). Thus, certain cues in status hierarchies shape their structure by signaling prestige or dominance. These should modulate envious inclinations towards their benign or malicious manifestations.

Group-Based Pride and Envy

A social-functional approach suggests that envy can also be elicited at the group level (see Mackie, Silver, & Smith, 2004, for a review of group-based emotions). In parallel to the relationship of pride and envy on the personal level, the specific form of group-based pride should also determine group-based envy. An important example may be national pride in the form of nationalism or patriotism. Although the two are positively correlated to a moderate extent, people differ over whether they endorse *patriotism*— the love for one's country and close attachment to it—or *nationalism*— perceptions of a country's superiority and supremacy (Kosterman & Feshbach, 1989). Crucially, patriotic beliefs are fostered through intragroup comparisons with the goal to improve one's own standing (Mummendey, Klink, & Brown, 2001). In contrast, nationalistic beliefs are fostered through intergroup comparisons with the goal to outperform other nations (Mummendey et al., 2001). They increase outgroup derogation strategies such as infrahumanization—the belief that the members of a different group are less human than the members of one's own group (Viki & Calitri, 2008). Moreover, emphasizing the naturalistic origin of a country (essentialism) after an identity threat increases nationalistic tendencies and diminishes the acceptance of cultural diversity (Li & Brewer, 2004). This pattern of results suggests that patriotism entails self-promotional concerns that resemble the pursuit of prestige-based status. On the contrary, nationalism seems to entail self-protective concerns with the goal of supremacy over other countries, resembling the pursuit of dominance-based status. Therefore, applying a social-functional model of envy and pride as status-regulating emotions, we predict that perceiving patriotism fosters benign envy and that perceiving nationalism fosters malicious envy on the group level.

Conclusion

In this chapter, we have applied a social-functional approach to envy. We have conceptualized envy as being fundamentally an emotion driving people to respond to a status threat. In the form of benign envy, it may prompt behavior in pursuit of status based on prestige. In the form of malicious envy, it may prompt behavior in the pursuit of status based on dominance. In our view, such a concept may help us answer the crucial question of what determines whether people will react with benign or malicious envy when they are confronted with a superior comparison standard. We have reviewed initial evidence for such factors on the dispositional as well as the social level, but many questions remain to be explored. We are optimistic that focusing on how envy can be adaptive in how people regulate social hierarchies can yield many insights in future research.

Notes

1. In this chapter, we use the term *status* in an inclusive sense, referring to differences in people's rank in the social hierarchy (Cheng, Tracy, Foulsham, Kingstone, & Henrich, 2013; Steckler & Tracy, 2014).

2. This dual account of envy follows the idea that emotions can be distinguished via differences in appraisal patterns, feelings, motivations, action tendencies, and behavioral outcomes (Roseman, Spindel, & Jose, 1990; van de Ven, Zeelenberg, & Pieters, 2009; for a more detailed discussion, see Sterling, van de Ven, & Smith, Chapter 3, this volume). In the case of envy, some researchers (Cohen-Charash & Larson, Chapter 1, this volume; Tai, Narayanan, & McAllister, 2012) exclude motivational and behavioral aspects from the definition of envy, preferring a more outcome-agnostic conceptualization. Note that the focal question of this chapter ("Which moderating variables determine benign and malicious envy and their respective outcomes?") is, at least in part, independent from this debate.

3. See Hoogland et al., Chapter 5, this volume, for a more complete description of the appraisals of benign and malicious envy and how they can be distinguished from the positive emotion of admiration and from resentment (also see Leach, 2008; Smith, Parrott, Ozer, & Moniz, 1994; van de Ven, Zeelenberg, & Pieters, 2012).

References

Anderson, C., Brion, S., Moore, D. A., & Kennedy, J. A. (2012a). A status-enhancement account of overconfidence. *Journal of Personality and Social Psychology, 103*, 718–735. doi:10.1037/a0029395

Anderson, C., Hildreth, J. A. D., & Howland, L. (2015). Is the desire for status a fundamental human motive? A review of the empirical literature. *Psychological Bulletin, 141*, 574–601. doi:10.1037/a0038781

Anderson, C., John, O. P., Keltner, D., & Kring, A. M. (2001). Who attains social status? Effects of personality and physical attractiveness in social groups. *Journal of Personality and Social Psychology*, *81*, 116–132. doi:10.1037//0022-3514.81.1.116

Anderson, C., & Kilduff, G. J. (2009). Why do dominant personalities attain influence in face-to-face groups? The competence-signaling effects of trait dominance. *Journal of Personality and Social Psychology*, *96*, 491–503. doi:10.1037/a0014201

Anderson, C., Kraus, M. W., Galinsky, A. D., & Keltner, D. (2012b). The local-ladder effect: Social status and subjective well-being. *Psychological Science*, *23*, 764–771. doi:10.1177/0956797611434537

Appel, H., Crusius, J., & Gerlach, A. L. (2015). Social comparison, envy, and depression on Facebook: A study looking at the effects of high comparison standards on depressed individuals. *Journal of Social and Clinical Psychology*, *34*, 277–289. doi:10.1521/jscp.2015.34.4.277

Appel, H., Gerlach, A. L., & Crusius, J. (2016). The interplay between Facebook use, social comparison, envy, and depression. *Current Opinion in Psychology*, *9*, 44–49. doi:10.1016/j.copsyc.2015.10.006

Atkinson, J. W. (1957). Motivational determinants of risk-taking behavior. *Psychological Review*, *64*, 359–372. doi:10.1037/h0043445

Back, M. D., Küfner, A. C. P., Dufner, M., Gerlach, T. M., Rauthmann, J. F., & Denissen, J. J. A. (2013). Narcissistic admiration and rivalry: Disentangling the bright and dark sides of narcissism. *Journal of Personality and Social Psychology*, *105*, 1013–1037.

Back, M. D., Schmukle, S. C., & Egloff, B. (2010). Why are narcissists so charming at first sight? Decoding the narcissism–popularity link at zero acquaintance. *Journal of Personality and Social Psychology*, *98*, 132–145. doi:10.1037/a0016338

Baranik, L. E., Barron, K. E., & Finney, S. J. (2007). Measuring goal orientation in a work domain construct validity: Evidence for the 2 × 2 framework. *Educational and Psychological Measurement*, *67*, 697–718. doi:10.1177/0013164406292090

Blader, S. L., & Chen, Y.-R. (2012). Differentiating the effects of status and power: A justice perspective. *Journal of Personality and Social Psychology*, *102*, 994–1014. doi:10.1037/a0026651

Boecker, L., & Lange, J. (2015). Dominance Displays and Schadenfreude (unpublished raw data). Cologne, Germany: University of Cologne.

Bogart, L. M., Benotsch, E. G., & Pavlovic, J. D. P. (2004). Feeling superior but threatened: The relation of narcissism to social comparison. *Basic and Applied Social Psychology*, *26*, 35–44. doi:10.1207/s15324834basp2601_4

Brunswik, E. (1956). *Perception and the representative design of experiments.* Berkeley, CA: University of California Press.

Burleigh, T. J., & Meegan, D. V. (2013). Keeping up with the Joneses affects perceptions of distributive justice. *Social Justice Research*, *26*, 120–131. doi:10.1007/s11211-013-0181-3

Caprariello, P. A., Cuddy, A. J. C., & Fiske, S. T. (2009). Social structure shapes cultural stereotypes and emotions: A causal test of the Stereotype Content Model. *Group Processes & Intergroup Relations*, *12*, 147–155. doi:10.1177/1368430208101053

Cheng, J. T. (2013). Two Ways to the Top: Evidence That Dominance and Prestige Are Distinct yet Viable Avenues to Social Rank. (Unpublished doctoral dissertation.) Vancouver: University of British Columbia.

Cheng, J. T., Tracy, J. L., Foulsham, T., Kingstone, A., & Henrich, J. (2013). Two ways to the top: Evidence that dominance and prestige are distinct yet viable avenues to social rank and influence. *Journal of Personality and Social Psychology*, *104*, 103–125. doi:10.1037/a0030398

Cheng, J. T., Tracy, J. L., & Henrich, J. (2010). Pride, personality, and the evolutionary foundations of human social status. *Evolution and Human Behavior*, *31*, 334–347. doi:10.1016/j.evolhumbehav.2010.02.004

Clanton, G. (2006). Jealousy and envy. In J. E. Stets & J. H. Turner, Eds., *Handbook of the Sociology of Emotions* (pp. 410–442). New York: Springer.

Cohen, D., Nisbett, R. E., Bowdle, B. F., & Schwarz, N. (1996). Insult, aggression, and the southern culture of honor: An "experimental ethnography." *Journal of Personality and Social Psychology*, *70*, 945–959.

Corcoran, K., Crusius, J., & Mussweiler, T. (2011). Social comparison: Motives, standards, and mechanisms. In D. Chadee, Ed., *Theories in Social Psychology* (pp. 119–139). Oxford, UK: Wiley-Blackwell.

Crusius, J., & Lange, J. (2014). What catches the envious eye? Attentional biases within malicious and benign envy. *Journal of Experimental Social Psychology*, *55*, 1–11. doi:10.1016/j.jesp.2014.05.007

Crusius, J., Lange, J., & Corcoran, K. (2015). How Approach and Avoidance Goals Relate to Benign and Malicious Envy (unpublished raw data). Cologne, Germany: University of Cologne.

Crusius, J., & Mussweiler, T. (2012). When people want what others have: The impulsive side of envious desire. *Emotion*, *12*, 142–153. doi:10.1037/a0023523

DelPriore, D. J., Hill, S. E., & Buss, D. M. (2012). Envy: Functional specificity and sex-differentiated design features. *Personality and Individual Differences*, *53*, 317–322. doi:10.1016/j.paid.2012.03.029

Duffy, M. K., Scott, K. L., Shaw, J. D., Tepper, B. J., & Aquino, K. (2012). A social context model of envy and social undermining. *Academy of Management Journal*, *55*, 643–666. doi:10.5465/amj.2009.0804

Dweck, C. S. (1999). *Self-theories: Their Role in Motivation, Personality, and Development. Essays in Social Psychology*. New York: Psychology Press.

Falcon, R. G. (2015). Is envy categorical or dimensional? An empirical investigation using taxometric analysis. *Emotion*, *15*, 694–698. doi:10.1037/emo0000102

Feather, N. T. (1999). Judgments of deservingness: Studies in the psychology of justice and achievement. *Personality and Social Psychology Review*, *3*, 86–107. doi:10.1207/s15327957pspr0302_1

Feinberg, M., Willer, R., & Keltner, D. (2012). Flustered and faithful: Embarrassment as a signal of prosociality. *Journal of Personality and Social Psychology*, *102*, 81–97. doi:10.1037/a0025403

Fischer, A. H., & Manstead, A. S. R. (2008). Social functions of emotion. In M. Lewis, J. Haviland, & L. Feldman Barrett, Eds., *Handbook of Emotion* (pp. 456–470). New York: Guilford Press.

Foster, G. M. (1972). The anatomy of envy: A study in symbolic behavior. *Current Anthropology*, *13*, 165–202. doi:10.1086/201267

Gibbons, F. X., Blanton, H., Gerrard, M., Buunk, B., & Eggleston, T. (2000). Does social comparison make a difference? Optimism as a moderator of the relation between comparison level and academic performance. *Personality and Social Psychology Bulletin, 26*, 637–648. doi:10.1177/0146167200267011

Gibbons, F. X., & Buunk, B. P. (1999). Individual differences in social comparison: Development of a scale of social comparison orientation. *Journal of Personality and Social Psychology, 76*, 129–142.

Gold, B. T. (1996). Enviousness and its relationship to maladjustment and psychopathology. *Personality and Individual Differences, 21*, 311–321. doi:10.1016/0191-8869(96)00081-5

Hays, N. A., & Bendersky, C. (2015). Not all inequality is created equal: Effects of status versus power hierarchies on competition for upward mobility. *Journal of Personality and Social Psychology, 108*, 867–882. doi:10.1037/pspi0000017

Heider, F. (1958). *The Psychology of Interpersonal Relations.* Hillsdale, NJ: Lawrence Erlbaum Associates.

Henrich, J., & Gil-White, F. J. (2001). The evolution of prestige: Freely conferred deference as a mechanism for enhancing the benefits of cultural transmission. *Evolution and Human Behavior, 22*, 165–196. doi:10.1016/S1090-5138(00)00071-4

Henry, P. J. (2009). Low-status compensation: A theory for understanding the role of status in cultures of honor. *Journal of Personality and Social Psychology, 97*, 451–466. doi:10.1037/a0015476

Hill, S. E., & Buss, D. M. (2008). The evolutionary psychology of envy. In R. H. Smith, Ed., *Envy: Theory and Research* (pp. 60–70). New York: Oxford University Press.

Hill, S. E., DelPriore, D. J., & Vaughan, P. W. (2011). The cognitive consequences of envy: Attention, memory, and self-regulatory depletion. *Journal of Personality and Social Psychology, 101*, 653–666. doi:10.1037/a0023904

Judge, T. A., Erez, A., Bono, J. E., & Thoresen, C. J. (2002). Are measures of self-esteem, neuroticism, locus of control, and generalized self-efficacy indicators of a common core construct? *Journal of Personality and Social Psychology, 83*, 693–710. doi:10.1037//0022-3514.83.3.693

Keltner, D., & Haidt, J. (1999). Social functions of emotions at four levels of analysis. *Cognition & Emotion, 13*, 505–521. doi:10.1080/026999399379168

Kernberg, O. F. (1975). *Borderline Conditions and Pathological Narcissism.* New York: J. Aronson.

Ko, S. J., Sadler, M. S., & Galinsky, A. D. (2015). The sound of power: Conveying and detecting hierarchical rank through voice. *Psychological Science, 26*, 3–14. doi:10.1177/0956797614553009

Kosterman, R., & Feshbach, S. (1989). Toward a measure of patriotic and nationalistic attitudes. *Political Psychology, 10*, 257–274. doi:10.2307/3791647

Krizan, Z., & Johar, O. (2012). Envy divides the two faces of narcissism. *Journal of Personality, 80*, 1415–1451. doi:10.1111/j.1467-6494.2012.00767.x

Lange, J., & Crusius, J. (2015a). The tango of two deadly sins: The social-functional relation of envy and pride. *Journal of Personality and Social Psychology, 109*, 453–472. doi:10.1037/pspi0000026

Lange, J., & Crusius, J. (2015b). Dispositional envy revisited: Unraveling the motivational dynamics of benign and malicious envy. *Personality and Social Psychology Bulletin, 41*, 284–294. doi:10.1177/0146167214564959

Lange, J., Crusius, J., & Hagemeyer, B. (2016). The Evil Queen's dilemma: Linking narcissistic admiration and rivalry to benign and malicious envy. *European Journal of Personality*, *30*, 168–188. doi:10.1002/per.2047

Leach, C. W. (2008). Envy, inferiority, and injustice: Three bases of anger about inequality. In R. H. Smith, Ed., *Envy: Theory and Research* (pp. 94–116). New York: Oxford University Press.

Li, Q., & Brewer, M. B. (2004). What does it mean to be an American? Patriotism, nationalism, and American identity after 9/11. *Political Psychology*, *25*, 727–739. doi:10.1111/j.1467-9221.2004.00395.x

Mackie, D. M., Silver, L. A., & Smith, E. R. (2004). Intergroup emotions: Emotion as an intergroup phenomenon. In L. Z. Tiedens & C. W. Leach, Eds., *The Social Life of Emotions* (pp. 227–245). New York: Cambridge University Press.

Magee, J. C., & Galinsky, A. D. (2008). Social hierarchy: The self-reinforcing nature of power and status. *The Academy of Management Annals*, *2*, 351–398. doi:10.1080/19416520802211628

Manstead, A. S. R., & Fischer, A. H. (2001). Social appraisal: The social world as object of and influence on appraisal processes. In K. R. Scherer, A. Schorr, & T. Johnstone, Eds., *Appraisal Processes in Emotion: Theory, Research, Application* (pp. 221–232). New York: Oxford University Press.

Martens, J. P., Tracy, J. L., & Shariff, A. F. (2012). Status signals: Adaptive benefits of displaying and observing the nonverbal expressions of pride and shame. *Cognition & Emotion*, *26*, 390–406. doi:10.1080/02699931.2011.645281

McClelland, D. C., Atkinson, J. W., Clark, R. A., & Lowell, E. L. (1953). *The Achievement Motive. Century Psychology Series* (Vol. XXII). East Norwalk, CT: Appleton-Century-Crofts.

Morf, C. C., & Rhodewalt, F. (1993). Narcissism and self-evaluation maintenance: Explorations in object relations. *Personality and Social Psychology Bulletin*, *19*, 668–676. doi:10.1177/0146167293196001

Morf, C. C., & Rhodewalt, F. (2001). Unraveling the paradoxes of narcissism: A dynamic self-regulatory processing model. *Psychological Inquiry*, *12*, 177–196. doi:10.1207/S15327965PLI1204_1

Morf, C. C., Torchetti, L., & Schürch, E. (2012). Narcissism from the perspective of the dynamic self-regulatory processing model. In W. K. Campbell & J. D. Miller, Eds., *The Handbook of Narcissism and Narcissistic Personality Disorder* (pp. 56–70). Hoboken, NJ: John Wiley & Sons.

Mummendey, A., Klink, A., & Brown, R. (2001). Nationalism and patriotism: National identification and out-group rejection. *British Journal of Social Psychology*, *40*, 159–172. doi:10.1348/014466601164740

Parkinson, B., & Manstead, A. S. R. (2015). Current emotion research in social psychology: Thinking about emotions and other people. *Emotion Review*, *7*, 371–380. doi:10.1177/1754073915590624

Parks, C. D., Rumble, A. C., & Posey, D. C. (2002). The effects of envy on reciprocation in a social dilemma. *Personality and Social Psychology Bulletin*, *28*, 509–520. doi:10.1177/0146167202287008

Parrott, W. G., & Smith, R. H. (1993). Distinguishing the experiences of envy and jealousy. *Journal of Personality and Social Psychology*, *64*, 906–920. doi:10.1037/0022-3514.64.6.906

Paulhus, D. L. (1998). Interpersonal and intrapsychic adaptiveness of trait self-enhancement: A mixed blessing? *Journal of Personality and Social Psychology, 74,* 1197–1208. doi:10.1037/0022-3514.74.5.1197

Pincus, A. L., Ansell, E. B., Pimentel, C. A., Cain, N. M., Wright, A. G. C., & Levy, K. N. (2009). Initial construction and validation of the Pathological Narcissism Inventory. *Psychological Assessment, 21,* 365–379. doi:10.1037/a0016530

Poelker, K. E., Gibbons, J. L., Hughes, H. M., & Powlishta, K. K. (2015). Feeling grateful and envious: Adolescents' narratives of social emotions in identity and social development. *International Journal of Adolescence and Youth,* 1–15. doi:10.1080/02673843.2015.1067895

Raskin, R., & Terry, H. (1988). A principal-components analysis of the Narcissistic Personality Inventory and further evidence of its construct validity. *Journal of Personality and Social Psychology, 54,* 890–902. doi:10.1037/0022-3514.54.5.890

Rawls, J. (1971). *A Theory of Justice* (rev. ed.). Cambridge, MA: Harvard University Press.

Rentzsch, K., & Gross, J. J. (2015). Who turns green with envy? Conceptual and empirical perspectives on dispositional envy: dispositional envy. *European Journal of Personality, 29,* 530–547. doi:10.1002/per.2012

Rentzsch, K., Schröder-Abé, M., & Schütz, A. (2015). Envy mediates the relation between low academic self-esteem and hostile tendencies. *Journal of Research in Personality, 58,* 143–153. doi:10.1016/j.jrp.2015.08.001

Roseman, I. J., Spindel, M. S., & Jose, P. E. (1990). Appraisals of emotion-eliciting events: Testing a theory of discrete emotions. *Journal of Personality and Social Psychology, 59,* 899–915. doi:10.1037/0022-3514.59.5.899

Salovey, P., & Rodin, J. (1984). Some antecedents and consequences of social-comparison jealousy. *Journal of Personality and Social Psychology, 47,* 780–792. doi:10.1037/0022-3514.47.4.780

Santor, D. A., & Walker, J. (1999). Garnering the interest of others: Mediating the effects among physical attractiveness, self-worth and dominance. *British Journal of Social Psychology, 38,* 461–477. doi:10.1348/014466699164275

Schaubroeck, J., & Lam, S. S. K. (2004). Comparing lots before and after: Promotion rejectees' invidious reactions to promotees. *Organizational Behavior and Human Decision Processes, 94,* 33–47. doi:10.1016/j.obhdp.2004.01.001

Schoeck, H. (1969). *Envy: A Theory of Social Behavior.* New York: Harcourt, Brace & World.

Shariff, A. F., & Tracy, J. L. (2009). Knowing who's boss: Implicit perceptions of status from the nonverbal expression of pride. *Emotion, 9,* 631–639. doi:10.1037/a0017089

Shariff, A. F., Tracy, J. L., & Markusoff, J. L. (2012). (Implicitly) judging a book by its cover: The power of pride and shame expressions in shaping judgments of social status. *Personality and Social Psychology Bulletin, 38,* 1178–1193. doi:10.1177/0146167212446834

Silver, M., & Sabini, J. (1978). The social construction of envy. *Journal for the Theory of Social Behaviour, 8,* 313–332. doi:10.1111/j.1468-5914.1978.tb00406.x

Smith, P. K., & Magee, J. C. (2015). The interpersonal nature of power and status. *Current Opinion in Behavioral Sciences, 3,* 152–156. doi:10.1016/j.cobeha.2015.04.007

Smith, R. H., & Kim, S. H. (2007). Comprehending envy. *Psychological Bulletin, 133,* 46–64. doi:10.1037/0033-2909.133.1.46

Smith, R. H., Parrott, W. G., Diener, E. F., Hoyle, R. H., & Kim, S. H. (1999). Dispositional envy. *Personality and Social Psychology Bulletin, 25*, 1007–1020. doi:10.1177/01461672992511008

Smith, R. H., Parrott, W. G., Ozer, D., & Moniz, A. (1994). Subjective injustice and inferiority as predictors of hostile and depressive feelings in envy. *Personality and Social Psychology Bulletin, 20*, 705–711. doi:10.1177/0146167294206008

Smith, R. H., Turner, T. J., Garonzik, R., Leach, C. W., Urch-Druskat, V., & Weston, C. M. (1996). Envy and schadenfreude. *Personality and Social Psychology Bulletin, 22*, 158–168. doi:10.1177/0146167296222005

South, S. C., Oltmanns, T. F., & Turkheimer, E. (2003). Personality and the derogation of others: Descriptions based on self- and peer report. *Journal of Research in Personality, 37*, 16–33. doi:10.1016/S0092-6566(02)00526-3

Steckler, C. M., & Tracy, J. L. (2014). The emotional underpinnings of social status. In J. T. Cheng, J. L. Tracy, & C. Anderson, Eds., *The Psychology of Social Status* (pp. 201–224). New York: Springer.

Tai, K., Narayanan, J., & McAllister, D. J. (2012). Envy as pain: Rethinking the nature of envy and its implications for employees and organizations. *Academy of Management Review, 37*, 107–129. doi:10.5465/amr.2009.0484

Tocqueville, A. de. (1840). *Democracy in America* (Harvey C. Mansfield and Delba Winthrop, Trans.). Chicago: University of Chicago Press.

Tracy, J. L., & Robins, R. W. (2007). The psychological structure of pride: A tale of two facets. *Journal of Personality and Social Psychology, 92*, 506–525. doi:10.1037/0022-3514.92.3.506

Tracy, J. L., Shariff, A. F., Zhao, W., & Henrich, J. (2013). Cross-cultural evidence that the nonverbal expression of pride is an automatic status signal. *Journal of Experimental Psychology: General, 142*, 163–180. doi:10.1037/a0028412

Van Kleef, G. A. (2009). How emotions regulate social life: The emotions as social information (EASI) model. *Current Directions in Psychological Science, 18*, 184–188. doi:10.1111/j.1467-8721.2009.01633.x

Van Kleef, G. A., Van Doorn, E. A., Heerdink, M. W., & Koning, L. F. (2011). Emotion is for influence. *European Review of Social Psychology, 22*, 114–163. doi:10.1080/10463283.2011.627192

Vazire, S., Naumann, L. P., Rentfrow, P. J., & Gosling, S. D. (2008). Portrait of a narcissist: Manifestations of narcissism in physical appearance. *Journal of Research in Personality, 42*, 1439–1447. doi:10.1016/j.jrp.2008.06.007

Van de Ven, N., Hoogland, C. E., Smith, R. H., van Dijk, W. W., Breugelmans, S. M., & Zeelenberg, M. (2015). When envy leads to schadenfreude. *Cognition and Emotion, 29*, 1007–1025. doi:10.1080/02699931.2014.961903

Van de Ven, N., Zeelenberg, M., & Pieters, R. (2009). Leveling up and down: The experience of benign and malicious envy. *Emotion, 3*, 419–429. doi:10.1037/a0015669

Van de Ven, N., Zeelenberg, M., & Pieters, R. (2011a). Why envy outperforms admiration. *Personality and Social Psychology Bulletin, 37*, 784–795. doi:10.1177/0146167211400421

Van de Ven, N., Zeelenberg, M., & Pieters, R. (2011b). The envy premium in product evaluation. *The Journal of Consumer Research, 37*, 984–998. doi:10.1086/657239

Van de Ven, N., Zeelenberg, M., & Pieters, R. (2012). Appraisal patterns of envy and related emotions. *Motivation and Emotion, 36*, 195–204. doi:10.1007/s11031-011-9235-8

Veselka, L., Giammarco, E. A., & Vernon, P. A. (2014). The Dark Triad and the seven deadly sins. *Personality and Individual Differences, 67*, 75–80. doi:10.1016/j.paid.2014.01.055

Vidaillet, B. (2007). Lacanian theory's contribution to the study of workplace envy. *Human Relations, 60*, 1669–1700. doi:10.1177/0018726707084304

Viki, G. T., & Calitri, R. (2008). Infrahuman outgroup or suprahuman ingroup: The role of nationalism and patriotism in the infrahumanization of outgroups. *European Journal of Social Psychology, 38*, 1054–1061. doi:10.1002/ejsp.495

Youn, Y. J., & Goldsmith, K. (2015). At Their Best When No One Is Watching: Decision Context Moderates the Effect of Envy on the Tendency Toward Self-improvement (unpublished manuscript). Evanston, IL: Northwestern University.

5 | Envy as an Evolving Episode

**CHARLES E. HOOGLAND, STEPHEN THIELKE,
AND RICHARD H. SMITH**

Introduction

In this chapter, we propose that some of the key problems with defining
and characterizing envy derive from neglecting the dynamic nature of the
experience. In particular, collapsing the early, middle, and late experiences
and responses leads to confusion about benign (non-hostile) and malicious
(hostile) envy, the necessary elements in envy generally, and the relationship between envy and other emotions. We define an "episode" of envy as
an unfolding, blended experience, including the appreciation of a situation
that triggers envy; the feelings felt initially and over time; the thoughts occurring during the process; and the behaviors manifested (Parrott, 1991).
Although this typology is necessarily complex because of its focus on
envy as an evolving experience, we will argue that it can integrate findings
that otherwise seem contradictory, explain observed differences between
benign and malicious envy, and give direction to future research on envy
generally, and in organizations specifically.

The Envy Episode

The proposed structure of an envy episode is shown in Figure 5.1. The episode is not a fixed program, but rather develops in various directions depending on individual and contextual factors. From the starting point of a
perception of an invidious advantage, several paths may be taken, entailing
diverse affective states, cognitions, and actions. Some of these are considered essential elements in certain definitions of envy, and some are typically associated with other emotions. Instead of seeking to carve up the
figure into "real envy" and "other experience," we will suggest that all of

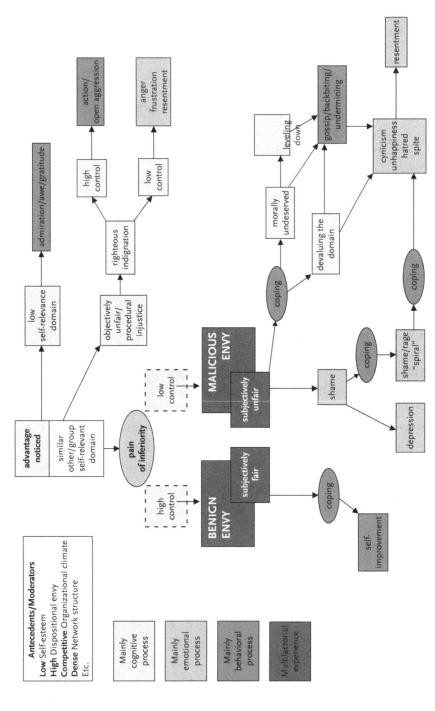

FIGURE 5.1 Model of envy as an evolving episode.

the elements shown are relevant to understanding the varied experiences in envy episodes. We propose that setting a firm boundary where envy ends and another emotional state begins is not particularly useful for understanding the full nature of envy. In order to sustain an inclusive focus, we will first consider the starting point of the perception of another's advantage and will then discuss each of the break-points in an episode, relating them to debates about what envy is and is not.

In exploring episodes of envy, we suggest that there is much heterogeneity in experiences that can be given the label of "envy." The framework covers the processes most commonly addressed in theory and research. We recognize that there might be other emotional, cognitive, and behavioral processes at each of the stages of an episode. Figure 5.1 should not imply that every person would, under the same circumstances, have the same reactions (e.g., Sterling, van de Ven, & Smith, Chapter 3, this volume), or even that the same individual would have the same experience at different times (e.g., Cohen-Charash & Larson, Chapter 1; Yu & Duffy, Chapter 2; Tan, Tai, & Wang, Chapter 11, this volume). Also, multiple responses may occur simultaneously, and the use of break-points does not imply that only one path may be taken at any time. For example, one may well intensify one's efforts toward improvement while simultaneously seeking to cut an envied competitor down to size in an attempt to reduce a disadvantage. This approach emphasizes the broad repertoire available to those experiencing envy. By considering how people play out envy, we thus expand its definition and emphasize the range of experiences that it can entail.

It is worth noting that a long historical tradition has formulated envy as a dynamic process. For example, a categorical description for envy dating back at least to Kant's *The Metaphysics of Morals* used the term *passion* rather than *emotion* (Kant, 1797/1996). This is more than an anachronism, since "passion" connotes an especially complex, intense, and lengthy experience, not a homogeneous state. The progression is toward a resolution of the passion, as people attempt to cope with it in any of a virtually limitless number of ways. Building on Kant's categorization, our approach considers theory and research on the personal and contextual factors affecting envy in order to outline explicitly the course that this "passion" can take.

We emphasize that the progression of envy need not follow an unvarying course. An episode of envy may be short, but many people will experience prolonged episodes of envy that vary in tenor and severity based on the current situation. Recent organizational research has supported this notion. For instance, a study of bank tellers conducted before and after they were denied a promotion indicated that perceived similarity to the future promotee, coupled with high hopes for promotion,[1] bolstered promotion envy upon being passed over, increased perceptions that one's work was unjustly (under)rewarded, and decreased the perceived likability of the successful promotee. This occurred both directly and over time, via distributive injustice perceptions (Schaubroeck & Lam, 2004). Nonetheless, envy was positively related to job performance, perhaps in part because there seemed to be a future possibility of promotion in the organization. In this case, the course of envy was determined by expectations, the individual's sense of justice, and contextual factors.

Other organizational research has illustrated how envy's consequences can shift dramatically, and in the process, evolve. In a study of job-seekers, Dineen, Duffy, Henle, and Lee (2015) found that, early in the search, envy of those more successful in their job searching was associated with increased job-seeking effort. Months later, however, envy often assumed a more destructive quality and was associated with unethical behaviors such as résumé fraud (for a review, see Yu & Duffy, Chapter 2, this volume). As Dineen and colleagues concluded, prolonged failure to obtain a job may have shifted job-seekers' framing of the situation from one of challenge to one of threat. Such a transition would lead to dysfunctional behaviors, as one's sense of personal control fades and the undesirable situation seems increasingly unchangeable. Exacerbating matters, self-regulatory resources may also be depleted as a job search wears on, making it more difficult to resist engaging in the deviant behaviors that envy sometimes motivates (Dineen et al., 2015; see also Cohen-Charash & Mueller, 2007). Moral identity may therefore play an increasingly important role in determining whether one will continue to resist the temptation to violate ethical standards in order to close the painful gap between the self and more successful others (Dineen et al., 2015). However, the exact amount of time that has passed since the genesis of envious feelings will matter less than one's ongoing interpretation of the situation, regardless of the timeframe. In order to account for this variability, our model of envy as an evolving episode does not specify a time-limited "program," but rather suggests a number of factors, including subjective judgements of the situation, that influence the evolution of reactions to perceiving another's advantage.

A Basic Ingredient of Envy—Painful Perceived Inferiority—Differentiates Envy from Other Emotions

Although construing envy as an evolving episode expands the range of experiences that can be placed in the category of "envy," it is important to avoid unnecessary blurring with other emotions. As reflected in Figure 5.1, at the core of all characterizations of envy is a painful feeling of inferiority caused by perceiving that another person (or group) possesses something that we lack. All definitions of envy posit an initial painful condition, a perception about another individual's advantage, which precedes and is the primary spur for the other evolving experiences. Why might the perception of another's advantage be painful? This is largely because the inferiority is often perceived to negatively impact us in some way: there are direct or indirect undesirable *implications* for our self-feelings or the achievement of our goals. Thus, pain would seem to be a straightforward, predictable, and indeed adaptive (e.g., Hill & Buss, 2007), response.

The pain and inferiority inherent in envy differentiate envy from *admiration* or *awe*, as shown at the first break-point in Figure 5.1. Perceiving that another person (or group) possesses something we lack does not necessarily produce a painful feeling. With admiration and awe, there can be a disadvantageous discrepancy between the self and the other, but the experience is essentially a positive rather than a negative one (Algoe & Haidt, 2009; Keltner & Haidt, 2003; Schurtz, Blincoe, Smith, Powell, Combs, & Kim, 2012; Shiota, Keltner, & Mossman, 2007). The attribute may not have been self-relevant in the first place (e.g., Salovey & Rodin, 1984). Or an attribute that was initially self-relevant may quickly become devalued as a way of coping with the painful experience (e.g., Tesser, 1988), sometimes causing envy to be transmuted straight away into admiration or awe (e.g., van de Ven, Zeelenberg, & Pieters, 2009). Completely downplaying the attribute may encourage an apparent absence of any strong emotion. Thus, even as the painful feeling of inferiority arises, a variety of responses can be set in motion that transmute this initial reaction and propel it in different directions.

This characterization of envy, emphasizing painful feelings of inferiority, also differentiates it from *greed*, which involves the desire for more and more of something (but without regard to whether another person happens to have it). Greed is perhaps an unpleasant state involving a sense of lack or deprivation, but despite a starting condition that shares some similarity with envy (i.e., a desire for something), it takes a different initial form and probably evolves differently (Seuntjens, Zeelenberg, Breugelmans, & van de Ven, 2015).

The fact that the unpleasantness of envy involves *another person* possessing the attribute—that is, it is a social comparison—importantly differentiates envy from other discontented states, bad moods (e.g., Smith, Parrott, Diener, Hoyle, & Kim, 1999), and other negative experiences that do not originate, at their core, from the experience of a *social* discrepancy. The social nature of the experience is also integral to the later responses to it.

Finally, that envy involves the lack of a thing possessed by another (a two-person situation) (but see Vidaillet, Chapter 8, this volume, regarding a Lacanian view emphasizing the role of the Other in envy) differentiates it from *jealousy*, which involves the threat of losing something one *already has* (usually a special relationship with another person) to a rival (a triangle situation). The rival might possess enviable traits, and, indeed, once the rival obtains the affections of the significant other, this might create a kind of envy, but the emotion evolving from a recognition of these advantages can be distinguished from the anger, the sense of betrayal, and the general distress characteristic of jealousy (Parrott & Smith, 1993).

Main Evolving Paths of Envy Episodes: Benign or Malicious

So far, the generic and static definition of envy would read: Envy is the painful feeling of inferiority caused by perceiving that another person has something we desire but lack. This bare-bones definition incorporates a considerable amount of theoretical and empirical work on envy, but it does not resolve many of the key questions about how envy is experienced. For example, does envy require a perception of limited control over the domain of comparison? Does envy always have a hostile character (as most chapters in this volume assume), or can it evolve in a benign direction? Must envy contain a component of injustice, and, if so, how should envy be differentiated from resentment? In what circumstances do responses such as aggression, resentment, and self-improvement appear, and how are they related to the core experience of envy? Such questions can encourage unresolvable debates about what "real envy" is or is not. We propose that attending to the evolving consequences of that initial condition, and identifying how different cognitions and feelings develop from it, can clarify how different types of experiences arise, each worthy of bearing the label of "envy,"—whether relatively malicious or benign in character.

The Role of Hostility in Envy and Evolving Episodes of Envy

Considering envy as an episode helps situate the relationship between envy and hostility. Some perspectives deemphasize the importance of hostility in envy. For example, much traditional research in the field of economics posits that envy arises when a person prefers what someone else has to his or her own state (Celse, Chapter 14, this volume). Such a definition does not include any necessary emotional response, much less a hostile one. For instance, Tai, Narayanan, and McAllister's (2012) theoretical paper on envy in organizations argues that envy is best characterized as "pain" in reaction to another's advantage. Although Tai et al. (2012) leave intentionally vague how severe and debilitating this pain could be in a typical case of envy, and they do identify conditions that shape subsequent and distinctive reactions in a hostile direction (Tan et al., Chapter 11, this volume), they suggest that a sufficient measure of envy would focus on tapping this initial pain—which is not necessarily hostile—in reaction to a perceived disadvantage (Cohen-Charash & Larson, Chapter 1, this volume).

Some research in social psychology is consistent with a definition limited to a perception of another's advantage and a feeling of painful inferiority (e.g., Feather & Sherman, 2002; Hareli & Weiner, 2002; Leach & Spears, 2008). For example, a set of studies by Leach and Spears (2008) examined various factors linked to intergroup schadenfreude (pleasure at another group's misfortune), envy being one possible cause. Envy was measured using items such as: "I would like us to be like the Free University team" and "I want us to have what the Free University team has." (The Free University team was the main competitor.) It is unclear whether these items assessed a clearly painful experience, but to the extent that they did, they would appear to fit the basic, two-feature definition. Another example is research by Hareli and Weiner (2002), also examining schadenfreude, but in the interpersonal rather than the intergroup context. The items used in one of their studies were "envy, jealousy, desire to have something the other has, and wishing to be like the other." These approaches to envy generally limit the experience to one perception (another's advantage) and one feeling (inferiority, though not necessarily painful), without considering how the perceptions or feelings might initially be more elaborate (e.g., contain hostility) or evolve (e.g., develop into hostility), or what the later responses might be. We will see that restricting the definition in this way neglects some of the most common cognitions, feelings, and behaviors that are foremost when considering envy as an evolving episode.

One might wonder why hostility is absent from these conceptions of envy just noted. If one considers cultural exemplars of individuals in the throes of envy, hostility is a salient ingredient. Literary creations such as Shakespeare's Cassius and Iago, Sergeant Claggart in Melville's *Billy Budd*, and, more recently, Salieri in Shaffer's (1979) *Amadeus*, are all openly hostile, and eventually murderous, as a result of their envy. We have many biblical stories, starting with Cain and Abel (Schimmel, 1997), to suggest the hostile aspects of envy as well. Many dictionary definitions of envy contain a hostile component. A good, standard-setting example is the *Oxford English Dictionary*'s definition of "to envy":

> To feel displeasure and ill-will at the superiority of (another person) in happiness, success, reputation, or, the possession of anything desirable; to regard with discontent at another's possession of (some superior advantage which one would like to have for himself). (Envy, v.1, 2014)

Early psychoanalytic and social science treatments of envy also empha-sized hostility as a core feature (e.g., Bonovitz, 2010; Duffy, Shaw, & Schaubroeck, 2008; Foster, 1972; Klein, 1957; Silver & Sabini, 1978; Smith & Kim, 2007; Vecchio, 2007; and see most chapters, this volume), though other types of envy have also been noted. For example, Klein (1957), taking a psychoanalytical perspective, argued that envy is an angry feeling that is frequently accompanied by a wish to destroy or take away the object of desire. Foster (1972), from an anthropological perspective, argued that because envy usually implies ill will, it is an emotion to be feared.

There is some suggestion that laypeople include hostility in their defini-tions of envy. In the first empirical study of envy, Silver and Sabini (1978) asked participants to watch videotaped interactions between two indi-viduals. One was significantly advantaged over the other. Viewers were most likely to attribute envy to the disadvantaged person when this person made inappropriate, hostile statements behind the back of the advantaged person. Expressed discontent alone, without hostility, was much less likely to seem generated by envy. As another example, Smith and colleagues provided evidence that manipulating envy produced greater schadenfreude (an outcome implying ill-will) if the envied person suffered, and reported envy (containing items suggesting hostility) mediated this effect (Smith, Turner, Garonzik, Leach, Urch-Druskat, & Weston, 1996).

Most empirical studies focusing on the consequences of workplace envy suggest a primarily destructive pattern (e.g., Duffy et al., 2008; Duffy, Scott, Shaw, Tepper, & Aquino, 2012; Duffy & Shaw, 2000; Vecchio, 2005; Vecchio, 2007). An example would be a pair of longitudinal studies by Duffy and colleagues (2012) in which social-contextual determinants of the effects of envy on social undermining (e.g., covertly badmouthing team members) were examined. Among both hospital workers (Study 1) and teams of upper-level undergraduate business students (Study 2), envy was associated with later social undermining when identification with one's team or workgroup was low, an effect mediated via moral disengagement (i.e., justifications that one invents for antisocial, immoral behaviors, such as the target's "deserving" ill-treatment). However, in the second study, it was also observed that even when a person low in identification with his or her workgroup was experiencing a great deal of envy, such envy had no effects via moral disengagement when team-undermining norms were low. That is, when it was apparent that team-undermining behaviors were rare rather than common in one's group, the envy→moral disengagement→social undermining process was disrupted. This research illustrated not only damaging effects of envy in the workplace, but also the crucial importance of the social context to whether envy evolves to have destructive effects. In a similar vein, Sterling (2013) found that a densely interconnected network structure (in which social monitoring was likely) served as a protective factor against malicious envy and against hostile, counterproductive work behaviors.

These examples seem to indicate that hostility necessarily or predictably evolves from the starting conditions of envy, and, indeed, that hostility may be inherent in the starting conditions. An early review of scientific research on envy labeled "envy proper" as having hostility as a signature feature (Smith & Kim, 2007), and, until very recently, this has been the dominant view. Yet this stance may fail to allow for some common alternate experiences that can occur in response to the initial conditions described above (the perception of another's advantage and a feeling of painful inferiority). Because these responses arise from the same conditions and have many similar consequences, they also warrant the label of "envy." When envy is considered as an evolving episode, hostility becomes one common, but not predetermined, trajectory. As seen in Figure 5.1, and described further below, hostility is most likely to occur in competitive settings conducive to perceived low control and unfairness (e.g., Smith, Parrot, Ozer, & Moniz, 1994; van de Ven et al., 2009), or when self-esteem is low (Feather, 2014; Tai et al., 2012) and dispositional envy is high (Smith et al., 1999). Other conditions, such as cooperative settings conducive to perceived high control and fairness perceptions, can produce a more benign response, especially when self-esteem is high and dispositional envy is low. These responses are not fixed: an initially benign response may take on a more hostile character over time as perceptions of the situation change (e.g., Dineen et al., 2015), or vice versa. We propose a framework, as seen in Figure 5.1, for how benign and malicious experiences can arise or evolve from similar, basic starting conditions of painful perceived inferiority.

The Evolution of Benign and Malicious Envy

Some theories of envy, even while emphasizing hostility, have acknowledged that there is another, more benign, form of envy (Foster, 1972; Silver & Sabini, 1978; Smith & Kim, 2007). For example, Silver and Sabini (1978), in their conceptual analysis of envy noted earlier, described the "two ways" that the term *envy* can be used. The negative, hostile form is "the kind of envy that we would not like to see ourselves harboring" and is a form of "transgression" (p. 106). They suggested that the milder, positive form is different from the hostile form, insofar as it is an emotion that one would not mind admitting to. Indeed, to say you envy someone in this sense can be a "compliment."

In the early research and speculation about envy, the benign form was generally deemphasized, sometimes because it was seen as less consequential. Thus, Foster (1972, p. 168), despite discussing envy in the mild sense as well, wrote:

> To me, real envy of another implies, if not the wish to change places
> with the person envied, at least the willingness to make a real effort
> to achieve what is desired or, if this goal is impossible, to deprive the
> envied person of the object of envy. The kind of envy that interests me is
> that which has a major impact on the mental state and personality of the
> envier, perhaps warping judgement and producing irrational fantasies,
> and which arouses in the person envied real feelings of fear, discomfort,
> or guilt.

Some recent theoretical and empirical work supports the theory that the benign form is just as much "real envy" as its malicious variant (e.g., Belk, 2011; Sterling et al., Chapter 3, this volume; van de Ven, Hoogland, Smith, van Dijk, Breugelmans, & Zeelenberg, 2015; van de Ven et al., 2009). Belk (2011), for example, makes a strong case that the contemporary "consumption landscape" with its "branding, advertising, mass media, [and] consumer credit," along with increases in discretionary income and the relaxing of social hierarchies, means that "contemporary consumption is driven far more by benign envy involving the desire to 'level up' through consumption emulation rather than 'level down' by harming others" (p. 117). Many languages (e.g., Dutch, German, Polish, Russian, Thai, and Turkish) have separate words for benign envy and hostile envy (or "malicious envy"), suggesting that many cultures have found it functional to distinguish between two types of envy. English, with a single term for both, is a notable exception. But this does not mean that the English word "envy" connotes only one of them: research using American participants has shown that, when they report feeling envy, the distribution of experiences that are benign and malicious (based on content coding) is approximately 50/50 (van de Ven et al., 2009). Even if one could make a theoretical argument that envy should best be considered in the narrow "pain plus inferiority" sense described above, the experience of envy, in its typically reported and evolving forms, may quickly coalesce into a different form. The cultural differences in the definitions of envy testify to the variety of ways it can be described, or which features of it are emphasized (or possibly which "stage" of envy is most salient), rather than to different underlying constructs.[2]

Thinking of envy in terms of two primary subtypes that evolve out of the same starting condition helps make sense of the seemingly inconsistent ways that people conceive of envy. This approach also resolves some inconsistencies in the empirical literature on envy and explains why envy sometimes predicts destructive behavior and sometimes does not (for reviews, see "Discussion," van de Ven et al., 2015; Sterling et al., Chapter 3, this volume). For example, some research (cited above) fails to show that envy leads to schadenfreude (e.g., Feather & Sherman, 2002; Leach & Spears, 2008), while other research suggests that it does (e.g., Smith et al., 1996; Sundie, Ward, Beal, Chin, & Geiger-Oneto, 2009; van Dijk et al., 2006). However, recent studies show that when both types of envy are manipulated and measured, envy does lead to schadenfreude, but only when it is malicious in subtype (van de Ven et al., 2015). Also, although some empirical studies focusing on the consequences of workplace envy suggest a primarily destructive pattern (Duffy & Shaw, 2000; Duffy et al., 2008; Vecchio, 2000, 2007), some other work has focused on the positive and adaptive outcomes linked with envy, such as emulation, motivation to learn, and general enhanced motivation (Cohen-Charash, 2009; Schaubroeck & Lam, 2004; van de Ven, Zeelenberg, & Pieters, 2011a, 2011b). Rather than having to argue that envy is either basically a hostile or a non-hostile emotion, or that there is a "real envy" (Foster, 1972) or "envy proper" (Cohen-Charash, 2009; Smith & Kim, 2007) contrasted with more benign experiences, positing that two types of envy evolve in response to different conditions resolves the apparent contradictions (Floyd & Sterling, Chapter 7, this volume).

Defining envy through its benign or malicious aspects might seem circular, since the motivations toward the individual with a perceived advantage (implying a subsequent behavior) then appear to be equivalent to how one feels about that advantage (Cohen-Charash & Larson, Chapter 1, this volume; Tai et al., 2012; but see Sterling et al., Chapter 3, this volume). Yet, returning to our model, delineating the temporal sequence in an envy episode resolves the circularity. The critical issue is to ascertain how benign or malicious envy (and their implied, evolving motivations and be-havioral intentions) could arise *in various circumstances*. The focus then becomes more on the factors that guide this process rather than on an inherent type of envy. Two important factors identified in Figure 5.1 are perceived control and perceived fairness of the envied person's advantage. As noted above, perceived high control and fairness encourage benign envy, and perceived low control and unfairness encourage malicious envy (Sterling et al., Chapter 3, this volume; van de Ven et al., 2009). Also as noted, other factors are likely to be important, such as self-esteem (Tai et al., 2012) or a competitive climate versus a cooperative climate (e.g., Yu & Duffy, Chapter 2; Sterling et al., Chapter 3, this volume). Each of these factors can play a role at any of the stages of the evolving experience of envy, as indicated by the "Antecedents/Moderators" box in Figure 5.1.

What the Definition of Envy Means to Organizations

Whether envy (or an episode of envy) includes a hostile component is no trivial matter. If envy is defined in a non-hostile sense, and indeed if it trends toward being a mild emotional state that motivates people to work harder, then it may be an emotion to foster in organizations rather than to minimize (e.g., Cohen-Charash, 2009; Schaubroeck & Lam, 2004; Sterling et al., Chapter 3, this volume). In the Hareli and Weiner (2002) study, for instance, not only was envy uncorrelated with schadenfreude, but it was also *positively* correlated with a desire to help an advantaged person. This sort of outcome would also have important implications for organizational settings. Fostering envy would not only increase motivation to work hard, but it might also increase the desirable outcome of people helping others, even those doing better (but see Sterling et al., Chapter 3, this volume, and Sterling, 2013, for evidence that both malicious and benign envy may encourage organizational turnover).

In contrast, if envy requires an element of hostility, it is a disruptive, destructive emotion to be feared and prevented. For example, top perform-ers might fear public recognition of their success and even reduce their personal performance when they perceive that others are threatened by their success (Yu & Duffy, Chapter 2, this volume; Exline & Lobel, 1999;

Exline, Single, Lobel, & Geyer, 2004). Such fear might not be baseless, given that, for example, envy causes also-rans to have less positive feelings toward successful promotees (Schaubroeck & Lam, 2004). Such envy might also reduce group identification, group cohesion, and satisfaction with the group, and even group productivity (Duffy & Shaw, 2000; Duffy et al., 2012). Even deviant behaviors, such as acting rudely toward or belittling a coworker, could also increase due to envy, and, not surprisingly, such incivility may encourage turnover intentions (Sterling, 2013). Thus, some well-intended organizational procedures that stoke envy, including ranking, "Employee of the Month," and public rewards for performance, might have serious unintended negative consequences (as many chapters in this book emphasize; see Vidaillet, Chapter 8, this volume, for an example).

Further Evolution of the Envy Episode: Reactions and Responses to Malicious or Benign Envy

So far we have described how envy can evolve in a benign or malicious way, some of the factors that influence this process, and how different paths produce divergent effects in organizations. Yet this is only the beginning or surface of the process, and a more complete discussion requires considering both the individual's motivations and her or his responses to the experience of benign or malicious envy.

Formulating motivational features of emotions raises fundamental questions about how "emotion" itself should be defined. For instance, it could be argued that the motivational consequences are actually critical features of emotions, since emotions arise because they reflect concerns over achieving important goals (Cosmides Frijda, 1986; & Tooby, 2000; Roseman, Wiest, & Swartz, 1994; Sterling et al., Chapter 3, this volume; Zeelenberg, Nelissen, Breugelmans, & Pieters, 2008). Emotion theorists such as Frijda (1987; Frijda, Kuipers, & ter Schure, 1989) argue that action tendencies and appraisals cannot be separated. Emotions (following cognitive appraisals) thus involve both feelings and motivations.

In an attempt to systematically determine the commonalities among several theories of emotion, Barrett (2012) performed a factor-analysis suggesting that most affective theories map onto two basic dimensions of high/low arousal and positive/negative valence. At the most fundamental level, an emotion thus seems to be an automatic evaluative reaction to a stimulus that identifies the stimulus as good or bad. Theorists such as

Russell (2003) and Scherer (2005), however, postulate that emotion contains a number of components, such as feelings, thoughts, and action tendencies (e.g., behavioral approach or avoidance).

In our view, an episode of envy may start as a quick, painful, negatively valenced reaction to an upward comparison, but it quickly becomes overlaid with unconscious and conscious appraisals of the situation, and then the varied action tendencies inherent to complex social emotions (Frijda et al., 1989). The "envy-as-pain" perspective (Tai et al., 2012) is only the first part of this process (envy as pain due to an appraisal of inferiority). But to understand the full experience of envy, we must incorporate the context and the appraisals throughout the evolving episode. It is possible that the initial pain of envy may occur before other appraisals of the advantage are made. Part of the appraisal process is a simple judgement that one's disadvantage is "bad." But the additional appraisals are crucial to the process of envy's evolving into malicious or benign forms, and the behaviors that attend such an experience. Such appraisals will continue being updated as an episode of envy continues, leading envy to take a turn for the worse or the better, or to dissipate altogether. At this level, benign and malicious envy meet the criteria of (1) being emotions and (2) being separate emotions, as they involve different antecedents, thoughts, and action tendencies, although both entail an unpleasant awareness of one's inferior outcome.

This perspective is consistent with envy as a "homeostatic emotion," which, while painful, motivates people to narrow the invidious gap in one way or another (Tai et al., 2012). "Basic" envy, benign envy, and malicious envy share this motivation (e.g., Cohen-Charash & Larson, Chapter 1, this volume). Modern conceptions of evolutionary psychology emphasize that people have evolved to react *flexibly* to environmental conditions in ways that ultimately maximize their reproductive fitness (Neuberg, Kenrick, & Schaller, 2010; see also Buss & Schmitt, 1993). These conceptions maintain that the psychological "ABCs" (affect, behavior, and cognition) arise through the interaction of the current context and the individual's personality. As such, emotion-driven responses are not monotonic, proceeding predictably every time that emotion appears.

Furthermore, Crusius and Lange (2014) found that benign envy and malicious envy bias attentional processing in starkly different ways, and that the differences are reflected in their motivational functions. Attentional bias is directed toward the means through which one can better one's own outcome during benign envy, whereas malicious envy shifts attention toward the envied person. These attentional biases aid in the narrowing of the self–other gap, while reflecting the basic motivational difference between benign and malicious envy—building oneself up vs. tearing another down (van de Ven et al., 2009; van de Ven et al., 2015). Looking backwards to much earlier theories of envy, this concept of envy as an adaptive response fits with envy's status as a passion, as distinguished from a discrete emotional reaction, a sentiment, or an affection (see Dixon, 2003). Envy subsumes various emotions, but the whole experience is not a unitary or homogeneous one, or one that happens all at once. Instead, it is a process of being acted on and reacting. As with other passions (such as romantic jealousy), envy does not simply "come and go," but rather the passion *demands* that a reaction occur, be it cognitive, behavioral, or both.

Given that reactions of benign and malicious envy are triggered by different evaluations of one's current context, they are both "functional" in the sense that they lead to different motivations and behaviors that nevertheless serve the common goal of reducing an invidious gap between self and other, resolving the demands of the passion (or homeostatic impulse) that is envy, and allowing it to dissipate. In either case, appreciating that motivational factors serve as a break-point in the evolution of benign or malicious envy obviates the problem of circular logic, and allows for the identification of specific factors that determine which type of envy will occur.

Envy is painful, and coping with a painful experience is crucial to how envy unfolds. Figure 5.1 identifies various break-points at which different types of coping occur. The appraisal process is critical to coping during and following the experience of stressful situations, including the recognition that another enjoys a superior position (Lazarus & Folkman, 1984). Primary appraisals involve interpreting what a situation means and determining whether it is a threat. Therefore, when another's advantage is perceived as being of little personal consequence, admiration, not envy, is likely to occur (van de Ven et al., 2011a). This would be expected to involve minimal pain. After defining the degree of relevance, secondary appraisals of what can be done about the situation occur. ("Secondary" implies that the initial appraisals determine which path is taken, not necessarily that these are entirely separate processes. They may occur simultaneously.) This can entail gathering more information and reappraising the situation itself, thereby making it less threatening, but it may also include deciding to deal with either the problem or the emotion itself (Gross, 2002).

A comprehensive treatment of the many ways one might cope with envy in organizational settings is beyond the scope of this chapter, but considering examples of how people might cope with envy may help resolve some seeming inconsistencies in the literature. For instance, Schaubroeck and Lam (2004) found that bank tellers who were denied a promotion often envied the promotee and liked him or her less, yet that envy was linked with increased job performance. Thus, it would appear that the envy was relatively malicious, given that it coincided with less liking of the promotee, yet it motivated a positive response, which should be related to benign envy. This does not mean that malicious envy was absent; rather, given the circumstances, people decided to cope with their inferior position by redoubling their efforts in order to merit a promotion the next time around. Whether the envy had a less hostile character at that later time is unclear, although that would seem likely. Put another way, malicious envy need not always have negative interpersonal consequences, and, perhaps, benign envy need not have positive ones (cf. Cohen-Charash, 2009). Indeed, benign envy may take on a more hostile edge if one feels little possibility of self-improvement, as the primary appraisal of one's disadvantage being a threat will remain without the "safety valve" of potential self-improvement (van de Ven et al., 2011a).

Evolution of a Justice Component

The benign versus malicious envy distinction often subsumes another thorny definitional question that has important implications for models of envy. This concerns the question of whether appraisals of fairness and justice should be considered as constituent elements of envy, and, if so, how they affect the feelings found in envy. Research on benign and malicious envy indicates that perceiving the envied person's advantage as unfair predicts malicious envy (and its hostile quality) (Sterling et al., Chapter 3, this volume; van de Ven, et al., 2012). Such appraisals are not found with benign envy, which, by the same logic, suggests why benign envy seems free of hostility. Yet, if we return once again to our initial definition of envy, it includes nothing about whether the envying person believes the disadvantage to be unfair.

Including a justice component in envy can create obvious conceptual blurring between envy and emotions resulting from more clear-cut cases of unfairness. If an advantage is perceived to be truly unfair, then the emotion might no longer be described as envy; rather, it is resentment or indignation. The phrase "righteous indignation" excludes envy by suggesting that the emotion is motivated by moral precepts. This interpretation seems to shift the domain from that of emotion theory to that of equity theory or procedural justice (Folger & Martin, 1986; Mark & Folger, 1984; see also Feather & Naim, 2005; Feather & Sherman, 2002). With procedural justice, for example, we feel resentment if another's advantage appears caused by a violation of culturally sanctioned rules, or is "objectively" unfair. As indicated in Figure 5.1, we might redress that injustice via open aggression if we feel empowered to take such corrective action (Johar, 2011; Križan & Smith, 2014; Smith et al., 1994). Justice-based experiences might thus seem separate from envy.

Nevertheless, there is a long literary and scholarly tradition of including a justice component in envy, sometimes even preceding the distinction between malicious and benign envy. Cultural exemplars of envy generally "resent" or "begrudge" the envied person's advantage and believe that advantage to be unfair (e.g., Shaffer's [1979] Salieri). There is little difference between the injustice suffered by the individual ("I am wronged") and that suffered by society ("the world is wronged"). In these cases, it is exactly this perceived global injustice that motivates hostile actions. The inclusion of unfairness in the definition fits with malicious but not benign envy, and the traditional focus on malicious envy has encouraged attention to this feature.

Resentment is a cognitive reaction to an apparently unjust situation. Most dictionary definitions suggest the presence of a resentful component in envy. The *Webster's New World Dictionary* (1982) entry on envy reads: "a feeling of discontent and ill will because of another's advantages, possessions, etc.; *resentful* dislike of another who has something that one desires." The *Random House Webster's Unabridged Dictionary* (2nd ed., 2005) suggests that: "To envy is to feel *resentful* and unhappy because someone else possesses, or has achieved, what one wishes oneself to possess, or to have achieved." Although these definitions do not spell out the context of resentment (such as whether an expectation of fairness or justice is a requirement for envy), they clearly suggest that the person who feels envy thinks that something is not right. Importantly, the "something that is not right" need not have been caused by the envied other's personal wrongdoing. Remarkably, Johar (2011) found that people who lost in a competition experienced invidious hostility toward the victor, even when the victory happened entirely by chance (i.e., there was no violation of a standard of fairness). Although participants were angry with the external actor who created the beneficiary's unjust advantage, participants apparently displaced some of their hostility toward that actor in the form of malicious envy toward the innocent (but apparently unfairly advantaged) beneficiary.

We propose that the perceived justness of one's own and the envied other's deserts will determine how an envy episode evolves, and that all the alternate paths can be considered "real envy." First, as noted above, there is some evidence that, unless the envying person feels at least a sense of injustice when confronting the advantaged person, malicious envy will fail to have its characteristic hostile edge. Second, the recent work on understanding what distinguishes benign from malicious envy highlights the role of justice appraisals. Perceived undeserved advantages (over and above clear-cut procedural injustice) predict and cause malicious envy (Duffy et al., 2012; Sterling et al., Chapter 3, this volume; van de Ven et al., 2011a). Third, evolutionary psychologists (e.g., DelPriore, Hill, & Buss, 2012; Hill & Buss, 2006) argue that envy functions primarily to spur actions that reduce the discrepancy between the self and the advantaged person. Being disposed to perceive the advantage as subjectively unfair would mean that action is also more likely to ensue. Thus, an outside observer might not agree that an envying person's resentment is warranted, and, indeed may label the resentful person as "envious"; however, the subjective experience of the envying person is as much based on a general outrage that "things are not right" as it is on a personal failure implying that "I am not adequate." This subjective, blended experience might best begin to capture what the experience of malicious envy is like.

We suggest that a key factor in these appraisals is, once again, the perception of control (Major, Testa, & Bylsma, 1991; Smith, 2000). As illustrated in Figure 5.1, perceived control, or lack thereof, after noticing another's self-relevant advantage provides a main break-point in an evolving episode of envy. The sense of unfairness can arise because many of the attributes that produce invidious advantages are, or seem to be, beyond the control of the disadvantaged person (e.g., natural abilities or inherited wealth) (Križan & Smith, 2014; Smith, 1991; Smith et al., 1996). Thus, the people enjoying the advantages will not seem to deserve them, nor will the envying person feel deserving of his or her disadvantage. Normally, people do not feel blame for outcomes over which they have no control. Thus, if they compare poorly with others on dimensions in which control is low, a sense of "unfairness" might easily arise. In Figure 5.1, this sense of control is integral to whether envy evolves to become benign or malicious.

The role of perceptions of control also illustrates the complex ways that deservingness and fairness appraisals influence reactions to another person's advantage. Research about how appraisals lead to benign envy versus malicious envy suggests that benign envy, although a frustrating experience, is associated with much greater perceived control than malicious envy (van de Ven et al., 2009). This pattern probably helps explain why malicious envy is also more associated than benign envy is with beliefs that the envied person's advantage is undeserved. Perceptions of fairness and one's sense of control thus seem to be overlapping conditions that together influence how envy evolves.

As suggested by Figure 5.1, feeling little personal control over one's disadvantage is likely to make that disadvantage seem less fair in a subjective sense, even if one's culture endorses that disadvantage as "objectively" fair (Križan & Smith, 2014; Smith & Kim, 2007). This may well lead to private shame, devaluing the domain of comparison, or convincing oneself that the other is morally undeserving of the advantage, each of which has a number of possible negative sequelae. On the other hand, if one feels a sense of control over the situation, that advantage is more likely to be seen as fair and to lead to coping through self-improvement efforts.

The Role of Shame in the Evolving Episode of Envy

Some theorists, especially those approaching envy from a psychodynamic or psychoanalytical viewpoint (e.g., Gilbert, 1998; Kaufman, 1989; Morrison & Lansky, 2008; Vidaillet, Chapter 8, this volume) have claimed that shame is an essential component of, or at least antecedent to, envy (see also Leach & Spears, 2008, for a social psychological perspective). Shame itself is a complex emotion that often includes, but does not necessitate, consideration of social factors (Keltner & Buswell, 1997). For instance, one may feel shame because one's actions or thoughts violate personal standards or social standards (Keltner & Buswell, 1997; Wolf, Cohen, Panter, & Insko, 2010). Envy-related hostility may itself be considered socially inappropriate, since most social discourse encourages respect or admiration for people who succeed (Vidaillet, Chapter 8, this volume). The shame associated with inferiority might thus be related to individual or social expectations of success and social standing, as well as to the direct pain of inferiority. Regardless of its cause, the shame related to inferiority is assumed to lead to a kind of lashing out as a way of coping with the shame, sometimes called the *shame-rage spiral* (Poulson, 2000; Retzinger, 1991) or *ressentiment,* anger resulting from the pain of inferiority (Nietzsche, 1887/1967, cited in Leach & Spears, 2008, p. 1383).

The processes involved are difficult to isolate and measure, but are probably integral to the evolving experience of envy in some situations. For example, an individual may be especially prone to hostile envy across a gamut of possible situations if she or he has deep-seated shame, a global feeling of "badness" or inferiority. Any acute feelings of inferiority could trigger this shame and its destructive consequences. Other individuals, without this backdrop of shame, would be less likely to appraise situations as unfair, or to have a low sense of control. Disentangling what aspects of envy may be due to inferiority and what aspects are related to coping responses (including inappropriate hostility) is very difficult, largely because people are not forthcoming about discussing shameful feelings or actions (see Montaldi, 1999, for further discussion of this and other important issues). In point of fact, people may not even be fully aware of that shame or its effects (Morrison & Lansky, 2008). It might seem alluring to try to research envy in only a "pure" form by ignoring feelings of shame attendant to it, yet excluding shame from experiences of envy may, in many cases, result in a failure to appreciate an essential feature of how it can be experienced. We propose that, as with the break-point between malicious and benign envy, the presence of shame influences how malicious envy further evolves. While shame probably exists on a continuum, in Figure 5.1 we suggest that high or low levels of shame influence the response to subjective unfairness.

The issue of how shame relates to envy demands consideration of the role of unconscious processes in envy (e.g., Annoni et al., Chapter 20, this volume), a topic very much neglected in social science treatments of envy, but a key feature of psychodynamic and psychoanalytic models. Exactly because envy (or at least malicious envy) is so shameful, it is likely that the person experiencing it does not even acknowledge it, and measuring behavioral or cognitive consequences of it seems impossible. It is quite possible that envy-driven behavior is most potent in these circumstances—when, for example, the envying person may be most motivated, unawares, to justify hostility and to manufacture reasons to find another person's advantage unfair (e.g., Smith & Kim, 2007; Smith, Combs, & Thielke, 2008). There is at least some indirect empirical evidence of this as well. Specifically, Leach, Spears, Branscombe, and Doosje (2003) found that more casual fans of Dutch soccer who nonetheless felt the pain of inferiority following a Dutch loss were less likely to feel schadenfreude after the legitimately superior Italian team lost a game, as long as norms emphasizing open, honest expression of feelings were made salient. Shame-reducing contexts might thus diminish hostile sentiments.

Considering envy as an episode posits that shame is a reactive process related to coping with malicious envy. Other ways of coping involve devaluing the domain in question ("sour grapes"), finding other domains of comparison ("at least my hair looks good, even if he has great teeth and a fancy car"), or behaviors to bring down the one with the advantage (as through gossip or backbiting) (see Gross, 2002, for a review of emotion-regulation strategies such as reappraisal and suppression). The deeper motivations for these actions are complex and might be thought of as ways to prevent or protect against the shame that would be required if one honestly confronted one's inferiority. Shame also has behavioral consequences such as aggression, and showing aggression would in many circumstances be detrimental and less adaptive than coping with the emotion. Despite some uncertainty about the psychological processes, we propose that shame may be an important part of the evolution of an episode of envy.

Key Break-points in Envy Episodes

Our review of how an episode of envy evolves has suggested two ways to resolve conflicts in defining and characterizing envy. The first is to clarify how malicious and benign envy arise. We have already noted that these subtypes conform to the two main ways that people think about envy. It is unfortunate that English has only one word for envy. However, this does not prevent the average person from thinking in terms of either the benign or malicious subtype. Furthermore, most researchers who write in English, when laying out their conceptions of envy, have not been able to ignore the two ways that the term *envy* is used. By considering that these two forms of envy arise in different circumstances, the model of envy as an evolving episode resolves inconsistencies in the empirical literature. For instance, an empirical question such as whether envy causes schadenfreude only makes sense if one considers the subtype of envy that is being considered (van de Ven et al., 2015). In an organizational context such as the workplace, there may be a number of people feeling inferior and desiring a coveted raise received by someone else. Recognizing the dynamic processes leading the initial pang of envy toward more productive benign envy or destructive malicious envy could be a key to understanding which employees will be more inclined to help or hinder the envied person once she suffers a setback (Floyd, Hoogland, & Smith, 2016).

Second, formulating envy as an episode resolves when and how a sense of unfairness influences the experience of envy. The presence of injustice-appraisals in malicious envy helps explain its hostile nature; the relative absence of injustice-appraisals in benign envy helps explain its benign nature. This distinction would not be apparent if envy were conceived of in a static form, or if the debate focused entirely on whether "real envy" requires a perception of fairness. We propose that perceived unfairness develops from an initial envy experience (involving the pain of inferiority at the recognition of another's advantage), and that it usually occurs in settings of low personal control. Under different circumstances, benign envy arises, usually without a perception of unfairness and generally with a higher sense of personal control.

Although the empirical literature has not yet adequately addressed the temporal aspects of envy, considering it as an episode with various trajectories helps explain why different envy-related experiences can have such different durations and characters. Both benign envy and malicious envy involve the frustrating of a goal (represented by the envied other), but with benign envy there is a belief that the frustration will be temporary, or that the envier's actions can remediate the situation. With malicious envy, however, the frustration seems as if it will be more chronic and sustained, persisting despite any efforts. As with the justice appraisals, formulating two subtypes of low and high control identifies key break-points in an evolving envy episode. Nor is control static: it may initially be perceived as high, but eventually, given repeated failures to narrow the invidious gap, the goal of (greater) parity with the envied other may seem impossible (e.g., Dineen et al., 2015). This, coupled with the subjective injustice of the failure to improve one's position despite redoubled effort, can lead to perceiving that the other's superiority is unfair and undeserved. As a homeostatic "passion" that must be resolved, one's initial motivation to move oneself up may then give way to a malicious motivation to tear the other down, assuming one has not neutralized the envy by devaluing the domain of inferiority.

Shame seems to be integral to some experiences of envy, especially in the development of malicious envy. Because it is hard to formulate unconscious processes, the exact role of shame is somewhat nebulous; shame could be a response to certain envy-provoking situations, or inherent in the individual, or both. It is also unclear whether shame is a requirement for certain types of behavioral reactions, such as aggression.

Different Episodes of Envy

We have highlighted ways that envy can be understood as an episode rather than a static state, and how it evolves over time. This is not a new idea (Parrott, 1991), but it seems to have been largely forgotten in debates about how to define and characterize envy. We have argued that focusing on envy's dynamic nature resolves some of these definitional challenges. Consideration of the evolving nature of the experience seems especially important when the emotion is intensely unpleasant, threatening to the person's self-views, or shameful. All these factors promote hostility and malicious envy, and it is this pathway that involves the most intense emotions. In these cases, perhaps at even its incipient stage, envy may already be shaped by quick, unconscious efforts to cope with its unpleasant, painful nature. Ways of coping may range from repressing aspects of the emotion to externalizing the cause of the emotion, or relabeling the emotion.

Conceived in this way, any experience following from the initial conditions we described (painful inferiority following the perception of another's advantage) might be considered envy, although the exact boundaries of an episode are hard to define. It is likewise unclear at what point during an episode one can reliably say that the person is no longer feeling envy, or how many of the resultant emotions, cognitions, and behaviors should be considered to be part of envy. For example, after experiencing the painful consequences of envy, one might engage in efforts to fend off future envy, such as by undermining the object of envy or preventing exposure to her or his advantage, and there is no simple algorithm to identify whether these should be subsumed in the original experience. Based on our model, these reactions could be considered potential paths that are part of the evolution of a complex and dynamic emotional reaction.

Studying Parts of Envy Episodes

While there may be advantages to narrowing the definition of envy in order to allow more focused research, the limited sense of envy usually represents the first, often fleeting stage in an episode of envy. We conceive of the typical "experience" of envy as the *range* of feelings, cognitions, and behaviors between this initial state and an end point in which a coping process plays itself out. This initial state will develop a benign or malicious character, depending on various moderating factors, especially fairness and a sense of control. In order to capture most broadly yet specifically the essential aspects of the experience of envy, it makes the most sense to measure and formulate envy-related variables at the point at which envy assumes either a benign or malicious character, seen in Figure 5.1 as the primary break-point. This does not preclude the possibility, however, that an episode of envy will take on a wholly different character, depending on external and internal events. Additional research might focus on other break-points, such as that related to shame.

A Model of Envy as an Evolving Episode

As we have described in this chapter, our model conveys a relatively holistic, comprehensive view of how envy evolves. In the interest of parsimony, however, our model and the figure that represents it (Figure 5.1) may oversimplify some aspects of episodic envy. For example, there are undoubtedly bidirectional relationships between many of the constructs shown (e.g., disliking of another should affect whether the other is perceived as undeserving of an advantage, but perceiving the other as undeserving could very well increase disliking of him or her). Also, the model omits pathways indicating that, depending on their results, coping efforts can lead to envy's dissipation or to its transmutation. Moreover, core self-evaluations, such as self-esteem and self-efficacy, are important determinants of the course of envy and are likely to affect many of the constructs within the model, but they cannot easily be placed within it (Tai et al., 2012; van Dijk, Ouwerkerk, Wesseling, & van Koningsbruggen, 2011). The role of shame as a response to and driver of envy is not clear. Because there is not much empirical research about the evolution of envy, we note such factors but do not specify their roles at the various points in an envy episode. Alternate responses are possible at all of the break-points, although we have endeavored to describe the most likely and most fully investigated in prior thinking on envy.

   To summarize, the model begins with the noticing of another person's (or group's) advantage, someone who shares similarities on attributes that engender social comparisons (Festinger, 1954; Tesser, 1988; Tesser, Millar, & Moore, 1988). This core experience is in all definitions of envy. Based on the social comparison literature, we assume that "positive" emotions such as admiration and awe will result if the domain of comparison is low in self-relevance and if the advantage is perceived to be fairly obtained. If the advantage is unfairly obtained (by some objective standard), righteous indignation will arise, with corrective action ensuing if the means are present; if the advantage is fairly obtained (as in a fair fight), deep frustration, anger, and resentment could result for the loser.

Envy can arise if the domain of comparison is self-relevant (e.g., Salovey & Rodin, 1984). At this stage, envy may assume either a benign or malicious character, and the distinction derives from a perception of fairness and a sense of control. Categories straddle the "pain of inferiority" construct to suggest that there is some ambiguity about when control appraisals occur in the process of recognizing the advantage.

Perceptions of control are very important in defining how envy evolves. Generally, if control is high, then perceptions of fairness will also be present, which will further promote the path of benign envy. If perceptions of control are low, a coping process will often lead to a subjective sense that the advantage enjoyed by the envied other is unfair, making malicious envy more likely.

Malicious envy can evolve in a number of different ways. If factors encourage shame, then the reaction is more internal and depressive, or more externalizing as part of a "shame/rage spiral." Malicious envy can also provoke a more immediate rebuke of the envied person's moral worth, providing a basis for believing their advantage more clearly undeserved, thus warranting leveling actions. Yet another course is to devalue the domain of comparison.

Concluding Remarks: Envy Episodes in Organizations

This chapter has attempted to tackle some definitional and methodological challenges by emphasizing envy's episodic nature and recognizing its place within a larger framework of related thoughts, feelings, and behaviors. In doing so, we have also tried to reconcile apparent discrepancies in the empirical literature and reduce conceptual confusion surrounding this complex social emotion. By examining envy as an evolving episode with a series of break-points, one can begin to appreciate when and why different members of organizations would respond more constructively or destructively to a painful awareness of another person or group's superior fortune or quality. In an organizational context, it is possible to extrapolate about the kinds of judgements employees make at various break-points. For example, if an employee decides at one break-point that he is unable to control his relative inferiority, he may be more likely at another break-point to decide that the other's advantage is unfair or undeserved, setting the stage for initially unvalenced envy to take on a malicious character.

Given the frequency of social comparison and promotion events, organizational leadership might profit from interventions designed to favorably influence these judgements and possibly to obviate the destruction wreaked by malicious envy and resentment (Floyd et al., 2016). Maintaining a non-judgemental, shame-free, "open door" policy might facilitate the ability to learn of these potentially damaging feelings (Dogan & Vecchio, 2001), which understandably are hidden most of the time from co-workers and supervisors. Based on this example alone, one might argue that there is merit in distinguishing between benign and malicious envy, because that recognition would help leaders choose the best course of action for the individual and the organization, promoting more prosocial and less anti-social behavior.

Although we believe there are sound theoretical bases for our model of envy as an unfolding episode, and sound historical bases for considering it a dynamic passion rather than a homogeneous or static emotion, such a model remains to be empirically supported beyond the specific conceptual links we have outlined. To help address this, one fruitful avenue for future research on envy might be to conduct longitudinal "diary" studies where, for example, the time-course of reactions to important events, such as another's winning a desired job promotion, can be studied in real-time and correlated with physiological measures such as heart rate (for a review, see Bolger, Davis, & Rafaeli, 2003). The advantage of the physiological measures could be that they help predict negative outcomes following another's good fortune above and beyond self-reported emotions, which are often subject to limitations imposed by participants' limited willingness and ability to respond accurately. This problem applies particularly to recognizing and reporting shame.

Adapting more traditional, cross-sectional methods might allow a simultaneous assessment of a number of thoughts and feelings as new information on a target of envy becomes available. For example, how might one's envious feelings toward an enviable person change after one hears him make an arrogant versus a humble statement? One might devise a multi-stage experiment to find out in a carefully controlled manner. Using such an approach, researchers might, over time, test multiple "chunks" of this or other models of envy as an episode.

It is worth reiterating that this model of envy is neither fully comprehensive nor the last word on the matter. Nonetheless, we believe that organizational leadership and social emotion scholars alike can benefit from viewing envy as an emotion, or more broadly, a passion, that develops over time.

Acknowledgments

The authors thank Edward G. Brown for his helpful comments on a version of the chapter.

Notes

1. Similarly, a series of studies by van de Ven and Zeelenberg (2015) indicated that counterfactual thoughts suggesting one *almost* obtained a desired end-state will increase envy toward those who have achieved it.

2. Although frequently used to identify hostility-tinged envy in the literature (e.g., Parrott, 1991; Bedeian, 1995; van de Ven, Zeelenberg, & Pieters, 2010), the word "malicious" may be too strong. While a thorough treatment of envy and culture is beyond the scope of this chapter, it should be noted that fundamental differences between cultures may play a major role in whether and which kind of envy is experienced in a given situation (Adrianson & Ramdhani, 2014). Triandis and Gelfand (1998; cf. Oyserman, Coon, & Kemmelmeier, 2002) place cultures along two continua, the first being individualistic–collectivistic (emphasizing personal independence vs. interdependence), and the other being vertical–horizontal (stressing social hierarchy vs. equality). By crossing these two continua, cultures can be categorized into any of four distinct categories. The "vertical–horizontal" dimension may be particularly relevant to envy. Vertical-individualistic cultures such as the United States emphasize personal achievement; thus it seems likely that envy in response to another's superior attributes, especially in its more malicious forms, may be more likely in such cultures. In the context of intergroup competition, however, people in vertical-collectivistic cultures might be particularly prone to envy when another group or even an entire culture appears to outcompete them. These speculations await empirical testing, as much cross-cultural work remains to be done on envy and related emotions.

References

Adrianson, L., & Ramdhani, N. (2014). Why you and not me? Expressions of envy in Sweden and Indonesia. *International Journal of Research Studies in Psychology*, *3*(3), 43–65.

Algoe, S. B., & Haidt, J. (2009). Witnessing excellence in action: The "other-praising" emotions of elevation, gratitude, and admiration. *Journal of Positive Psychology*, *4*(2), 105–127.

Barrett, L. F. (2012). Emotions are real. *Emotion*, *12*(3), 413–429.

Bedeian, A. G. (1995). Workplace envy. *Organizational Dynamics*, *23*(4), 49–56.

Belk, R. (2011). Benign envy. *Academy of Marketing Science Review*, *1*(3–4), 117–134.

Bolger, N., Davis, A., & Rafaeli, E. (2003). Diary methods: Capturing life as it is lived. *Annual Review of Psychology*, *54*(1), 579–616.

Bonovitz, C. (2010). Comparative perspectives on envy: A reconsideration of its developmental origins. *Contemporary Psychoanalysis*, *46*(3), 423–438.

Buss, D. M., & Schmitt, D. P. (1993). Sexual strategies theory: An evolutionary perspective on human mating. *Psychological Review*, *100*(2), 204–232.

Cohen-Charash, Y. (2009). Episodic envy. *Journal of Applied Social Psychology*, *39*(9), 2128–2170.

Cohen-Charash, Y., & Mueller, J. S. (2007). Does perceived unfairness exacerbate or mitigate interpersonal counterproductive work behaviors related to envy? *Journal of Applied Psychology*, *92*(3), 666–680.

Cosmides, L., & Tooby, J. (2000). Evolutionary psychology and the emotions. In M. Lewis & J. M. Haviland-Jones, Eds., *Handbook of Emotions* (pp. 91–115). New York: Guilford Press.

Crusius, J., & Lange, J. (2014). What catches the envious eye? Attentional biases within malicious and benign envy. *Journal of Experimental Social Psychology*, *55*(Nov. 2014), 1–11.

Dixon, T. M. (2003). *From Passions to Emotions*. Cambridge, UK: Cambridge University Press.

DelPriore, D. J., Hill, S. E., & Buss, D. M. (2012). Envy: Functional specificity and sex-differentiated design features. *Personality and Individual Differences*, *53*(3), 317–322.

Dineen, B. N., Duffy, M. K., Henle, C. A., & Lee, K. (2015). Green by comparison: Deviant and normative transmutations of job search envy in a temporal context. *Academy of Management Journal*. Advance online publication. doi: 10.5465/amj.2014.0767

Dogan, K., & Vecchio, R. P. (2001). Managing envy and jealousy in the workplace. *Compensation and Benefits Review*, *33*(2), 57–64.

Duffy, M. K., Scott, K. L., Shaw, J. D., Tepper, B. J., & Aquino, K. (2012). A social context model of envy and social undermining. *Academy of Management Journal*, *55*(3), 643–666.

Duffy, M. K., & Shaw, J. D. (2000). The Salieri syndrome: Consequences of envy in groups. *Small Group Research*, *31*(1), 3–23.

Duffy, M. K., Shaw, J. D., & Schaubroeck, J. M. (2008). Envy in organizational life. In R. H. Smith, Ed., *Envy: Theory and Research* (pp. 167–189). New York: Oxford University Press.

Envy. (1982). *Webster's New World Dictionary (2nd College Edition)*. New York: Simon & Schuster.

Envy. (2005). *The Random House Webster's Unabridged Dictionary* (2nd ed.). New York: Random House.

Envy, v.1. (June 2014). In *Oxford English Dictionary Online*. Retrieved 17 June 2014 from www.oed.com.

Exline, J. J., & Lobel, M. (1999). The perils of outperformance: Sensitivity about being the target of a threatening upward comparison. *Psychological Bulletin*, *125*(3), 307–337.

Exline, J. J., Single, P. B., Lobel, M., & Geyer, A. L. (2004). Glowing praise and the envious gaze: Social dilemmas surrounding the public recognition of achievement. *Basic and Applied Social Psychology*, *26*(2–3), 119–130.

Feather, N. T. (2014). Deservingness and schadenfreude. In W. W. van Dijk & J. W. Ouwerkerk, Eds., *Schadenfreude: Understanding Pleasure at the Misfortune of Others* (pp. 29–57). New York: Oxford University Press.

Feather, N. T., & Naim, K. (2005). Resentment, envy, schadenfreude, and sympathy: Effects of own and other's deserved or undeserved status. *Australian Journal of Psychology*, *57*(2), 87–102.

Feather, N. T., & Sherman, R. (2002). Envy, resentment, schadenfreude, and sympathy: Reactions to deserved and undeserved achievement and subsequent failure. *Personality and Social Psychology Bulletin*, *28*(7), 953–961.

Festinger, L. (1954). A theory of social comparison processes. *Human Relations*, *7*(2), 117–140.

Floyd, T. M., Hoogland, C. E., & Smith, R. H. (2016). The role of leaders in managing envy and its consequences for competition in organizations. In S. Braun, C. Peus, & B. Schyns, Eds., *Leadership Lessons from Compelling Contexts* (*Monographs in Leadership and Management*, vol. 8, pp. 129-156). Bradford, UK: Emerald Group Publishing.

Folger, R., & Martin, C. (1986). Relative deprivation and referent cognitions: Distributive and procedural justice effects. *Journal of Experimental Social Psychology*, *22*(6), 531–546.

Foster, G. M. (1972). The anatomy of envy: A study in symbolic behavior. *Current Anthropology*, *13*(2), 165–202.

Frijda, N. H. (1986). *The Emotions*. Cambridge, UK: Cambridge University Press.

Frijda, N. H. (1987). Emotion, cognitive structure, and action tendency. *Cognition and Emotion*, *1*(2), 115–143.

Frijda, N. H., Kuipers, P., & ter Schure, E. (1989). Relations among emotion, appraisal, and emotional action readiness. *Journal of Personality and Social Psychology*, *57*(2), 212–228.

Gilbert, P. (1998). What is shame? Some core issues and controversies. In P. Gilbert & B. Andrews, Eds., *Shame: Interpersonal Behavior, Psychopathology, and Culture* (pp. 3–38). New York: Oxford University Press.

Gross, J. J. (2002). Emotion regulation: Affective, cognitive, and social consequences. *Psychophysiology*, *39*(3), 281–291.

Hareli, S., & Weiner, B. (2002). Dislike and envy as antecedents of pleasure at another's misfortune. *Motivation and Emotion*, *26*(4), 257–277.

Hill, S. E., & Buss, D. M. (2006). Envy and positional bias in the evolutionary psychology of management. *Managerial and Decision Economics*, *27*(2–3), 131–143.

Johar, O. (2011). What Makes Envy Hostile: Perceived Injustice, or a Frustrated Search for an Explanation? (Master's thesis.) Retrieved from Digital Repository @ Iowa State University. URL: http://lib.dr.iastate.edu/cgi/viewcontent.cgi?article=3162&context=etd

Kant, I. (1797/1996). The metaphysics of morals. In M. Gregor, Ed. and Trans., *The Cambridge Edition of the Works of Immanuel Kant: Practical Philosophy* (pp. 353–604). New York: Cambridge University Press.

Kaufman, G. (1989). *The Psychology of Shame: Theory and Treatment of Shame-Based Syndromes*. New York: Springer.

Keltner, D., & Buswell, B. N. (1997). Embarrassment: Its distinct form and appeasement functions. *Psychological Bulletin*, *122*(3), 250–270.

Keltner, D., & Haidt, J. (2003). Approaching awe, a moral, spiritual, and aesthetic emotion. *Cognition and Emotion*, *17*(2), 297–314.

Klein, M. (1957). Envy and gratitude. *Psyche*, *11*(5), 241–255.

Križan, Z., & Smith, R. H. (2014). When comparisons divide. In Z. Križan & F. X. Gibbons, Eds., *Communal Functions of Social Comparison* (pp. 60–91). New York: Cambridge University Press.

Lazarus, R. S., & Folkman, S. (1984). *Stress, Appraisal, and Coping*. New York: Springer Publishing.

Leach, C. W., & Spears, R. (2008). "A vengefulness of the impotent": The pain of in-group inferiority and schadenfreude toward successful out-groups. *Journal of Personality and Social Psychology*, *95*(6), 1383–1396.

Leach, C. W., Spears, R., Branscombe, N. R., & Doosje, B. (2003). Malicious pleasure: Schadenfreude at the suffering of another group. *Journal of Personality and Social Psychology*, *84*(5), 932–943.

Major, B., Testa, M., & Bylsma, W. (1991). Responses to upward vs. downward comparisons: The impact of esteem-relevance and perceived control. In J. Suls & T. A. Wills, Eds., *Social Comparison: Contemporary Theory and Research* (pp. 237–260). Hillsdale, NJ: Erlbaum.

Mark, M. M., & Folger, R. (1984). Responses to relative deprivation: A conceptual framework. In P. Shaver, Ed., *Review of Personality and Social Psychology*, (vol. 5, pp. 192–218). Beverly Hills, CA: Sage.

Morrison, A. P., & Lansky, M. R. (2008). Shame and envy. In L. Wurmser & H. Jarass, Eds., *Jealousy and Envy: New Views about Two Powerful Feelings* (pp. 179–187). New York: The Analytic Press.

Neuberg, S. L., Kenrick, D. T., & Schaller, M. (2010). Evolutionary social psychology. In S. T. Fiske, D. T. Gilbert, & G. Lindzey, Eds., *Handbook of Social Psychology* (5th ed., vol. 2, pp. 761–796). Hoboken, NJ: John Wiley & Sons.

Oyserman, D., Coon, H. M., & Kemmelmeier, M. (2002). Rethinking individualism and collectivism: Evaluation of theoretical assumptions and meta-analyses. *Psychological Bulletin*, *128*(1), 3–72.

Parrott, W. G. (1991). The emotional experiences of envy and jealousy. In P. Salovey, Ed., *The Psychology of Jealousy and Envy* (pp. 3–30). New York: Guilford.

Parrott, W. G., & Smith, R. H. (1993). Distinguishing the experiences of envy and jealousy. *Journal of Personality and Social Psychology*, *64*(6), 906–920.

Poulson, C. (2000). Shame and work. In N. Ashkanazy, C. Hartel, & W. Zerbe, Eds., *Emotions in Organizational Life* (pp. 250–271). Westport, CT: Quorum Books.

Retzinger, S. (1991). *Violent Emotions: Shame and Rage in Marital Quarrels*. Newbury Park, CA: Sage.

Roseman, I. J., Wiest, C., & Swartz, T. S. (1994). Phenomenology, behaviors, and goals differentiate discrete emotions. *Journal of Personality and Social Psychology*, *67*(2), 206–221.

Russell, J. A. (2003). Core affect and the psychological construction of emotion. *Psychological Review*, *110*(1), 145–172.

Salovey, P., & Rodin, J. (1984). Some antecedents and consequences of social-comparison jealousy. *Journal of Personality and Social Psychology*, *47*(4), 780–792.

Scherer, K. R. (2005). What are emotions? And how can they be measured? *Social Science Information*, *44*(4), 695–729.

Schimmel, S. (1997). *The Seven Deadly Sins: Jewish, Christian, and Classical Reflections on Human Nature*. New York: The Free Press.

Schurtz, D. R., Blincoe, S., Smith, R. H., Powell, C. A. J., Combs, D. J. Y., & Kim, S. H. (2012). Exploring the social aspects of goosebumps and their role in awe and envy. *Motivation and Emotion*, *36*(2), 205–217.

Seuntjens, T. G., Zeelenberg, M., Breugelmans, S. M., & van de Ven, N. (2015). Defining greed. *British Journal of Social Psychology*, *106*(3), 505–525.

Shaffer, P. (1979). *Amadeus*. London: Royal National Theatre.

Shiota, M. N., Keltner, D., & Mossman, A. (2007). The nature of awe: Elicitors, appraisals, and effects on self-concept. *Cognition and Emotion*, *21*(5), 944–963.

Silver, M., & Sabini, J. (1978). The perception of envy. *Social Psychology*, *41*(2), 105–117.

Smith, R. H. (1991). Envy and the sense of injustice. In P. Salovey, Ed., *The Psychology of Jealousy and Envy* (pp. 79–99). New York: Guilford Press.

Smith, R. H. (2000) Assimilative and contrastive emotional reactions to upward and downward social comparisons. In J. Suls & L. Wheeler, Eds., *Handbook of Social Comparison: Theory and Research* (pp. 173–200). New York: Plenum.

Smith, R. H., Combs, D. J. Y., & Thielke, S. M. (2008). Envy and the challenges to good health. In R. H. Smith, Ed., *Envy: Theory and Research* (pp. 290–314). New York: Oxford University Press.

Smith, R. H., & Kim, S. H. (2007). Comprehending envy. *Psychological Bulletin*, *133*(1), 46–64.

Smith, R. H., Parrott, W. G., Diener, E., Hoyle, R. H., & Kim, S. H. (1999). Dispositional envy. *Personality and Social Psychology Bulletin*, *25*(8), 1007–1020.

Smith, R. H., Parrott, W. G., Ozer, D., & Moniz, A. (1994). Subjective injustice and inferiority as predictors of hostile and depressive feelings in envy. *Personality and Social Psychology Bulletin*, *20*(6), 705–711.

Smith, R., Turner, T., Garonzik, R., Leach, C., Urch-Druskat, V., & Weston, C. (1996). Envy and schadenfreude. *Personality and Social Psychology Bulletin*, *22*(2), 158–168.

Sterling, C. M. (2013). A Tale of Two Envys: A Social Network Perspective on the Consequences of Workplace Social Comparison. (Doctoral dissertation.) Retrieved 30 July 2014 from uknowledge.uky.edu.

Sundie, J. M., Ward, J. C., Beal, D. J., Chin, W. W., & Geiger-Oneto, S. (2009). Schadenfreude as a consumption-related emotion: Feeling happiness about the downfall of another's product. *Journal of Consumer Psychology*, *19*(3), 356–373.

Tai, K., Narayanan, J., & McAllister, D. J. (2012). Envy as pain: Rethinking the nature of envy and its implications for employees and organizations. *Academy of Management Review*, *37*(1), 107–129.

Tesser, A. (1988). Toward a self-evaluation maintenance model of social behavior. In L. Berkowitz, Ed., *Advances in Experimental Social Psychology* (vol. 21, pp. 181–227). New York: Academic Press.

Tesser, A., Millar, M., & Moore, J. (1988). Some affective consequences of social comparison and reflection processes: The pain and pleasure of being close. *Journal of Personality and Social Psychology*, *54*(1), 49–61.

Triandis, H. C., & Gelfand, M. J. (1998). Converging measurement of horizontal and vertical individualism and collectivism. *Journal of Personality and Social Psychology*, *74*(1), 118–128.

van de Ven, N., Hoogland, C. E., Smith, R. H., van Dijk, W. W., Breugelmans, S. M., & Zeelenberg, M. (2015). When envy leads to schadenfreude. *Cognition and Emotion*, *29*(6), 1007–1025.

van de Ven, N., & Zeelenberg, M. (2015). On the counterfactual nature of envy: "It could have been me." *Cognition and Emotion*, *29*(6), 954–971.

van de Ven, N., Zeelenberg, M., & Pieters, R. (2009). Leveling up and down: The experiences of benign and malicious envy. *Emotion*, *9*(3), 419–429.

van de Ven, N., Zeelenberg, M., & Pieters, R. (2010). Warding off the evil eye: When the fear of being envied increases prosocial behavior. *Psychological Science*, *21*(11), 1671–1677.

van de Ven, N., Zeelenberg, M., & Pieters, R. (2011a). Why envy outperforms admiration. *Personality and Social Psychology Bulletin*, *37*(6), 784–795.

van de Ven, N., Zeelenberg, M., & Pieters, R. (2011b). The envy premium in product evaluation. *Journal of Consumer Research*, *37*(6), 984–998.

van de Ven, N., Zeelenberg, M., & Pieters, R. (2012). Appraisal patterns of envy and related emotions. *Motivation and Emotion*, *36*(2), 195–204.

van Dijk, W. W., Ouwerkerk, J. W., Wesseling, Y. M., & van Koningsbruggen, G. M. (2011). Towards understanding pleasure at the misfortunes of others: The impact of self-evaluation threat on schadenfreude. *Cognition and Emotion*, *25*(2), 360–368.

Vecchio, R. P. (2000). Negative emotion in the workplace: Employee jealousy and envy. *International Journal of Stress Management*, *7*(3), 161–179.

Vecchio, R. P. (2005). Explorations in employee envy: Feeling envious and feeling envied. *Cognition and Emotion*, *19*(1) 69–81.

Vecchio, R. P. (2007). Cinderella and Salieri in the workplace. In S. Gilliland, D. D. Steiner, & D. Skarlicki, Eds., *Managing Social and Ethical Issues in Organizations* (pp. 109–134). Charlotte, NC: Information Age Publishing.

Wolf, S. A., Cohen, T. R., Panter, A. T., & Insko, C. A. (2010). Shame proneness and guilt proneness: Toward the further understanding of reactions to public and private transgressions. *Self and Identity*, *9*(4), 337–362.

Zeelenberg, M., Nelissen, R. M., Breugelmans, S. M., & Pieters, R. (2008). On emotion specificity in decision making: Why feeling is for doing. *Judgment and Decision Making*, *3*(1), 18–27.

6 | Competent but Cold

THE STEREOTYPE CONTENT MODEL
AND ENVY IN ORGANIZATIONS

ELIZABETH BAILY WOLF AND PETER GLICK

PEOPLE INEVITABLY JUDGE OTHERS THEY ENCOUNTER. The Stereotype Content Model (SCM; e.g., Cuddy, Fiske, & Glick, 2008) suggests that, intentionally or not, perceivers ask two fundamental questions about unfamiliar others they meet: First, what are this person's intentions—does this person wish to help or hurt me? Second, how well can this person enact these intentions to help or hurt me? In sum, when judging others, perceivers do not simply evaluate targets globally as all good or all bad, but instead evaluate (a) how good versus bad the person's intentions are, and (b) how good versus bad the person will be at enacting those intentions (e.g., Fiske, Cuddy, & Glick, 2007).

The SCM proposes that the answers to these two questions inform perceptions on two fundamental trait dimensions: *warmth* and *competence*. The more people seem to have good intentions toward others, the warmer they are judged, and the more people seem able to enact these intentions, the more competent they seem. The warmth dimension consists of traits that indicate concern for others, such as friendly, helpful, trustworthy, and moral, whereas the competence dimension consists of ability-related traits, such as intelligent, powerful, skillful, and efficient. Although these dimensions are sometimes referred to by other names (e.g., *communion* and *agency*), an impressive body of evidence collected over many decades, using many thousands of participants from all over the world, concludes that they are both fundamental and universal to how humans evaluate each other (e.g., Abele & Wojciszke, 2007; Fiske, Cuddy, & Glick, 2007).

Warmth and competence perceptions not only influence how people perceive individuals' traits, but also how they categorize social groups (e.g., Fiske, Cuddy, Glick, & Xu, 2002). The SCM posits that all groups in society can be sorted along the warmth and competence dimensions and are often stereotyped as high on one dimension, but low on the other. For example, mentally disabled people tend to be stereotyped as warm but incompetent, whereas the rich tend to be stereotyped as competent but cold. The particular warmth-competence combination applied to a group determines how people in a society view and feel about that group. Specifically, people tend to admire groups stereotyped as high in both competence and warmth, but feel contempt for groups low in both competence and warmth. Groups that are high on one dimension but low on the other evoke ambivalent feelings: groups stereotyped as low in competence but high in warmth are pitied (which combines sympathy and assumptions of the pitied group's inferiority), whereas groups stereotyped as high on competence but low in warmth are envied (which combines admiration with resentment).

This chapter focuses on the stereotypes about and typical behavior toward envied groups. First we summarize the theoretical principles of the SCM and an extension of the theory known as the Behaviors from Intergroup Affect and Stereotypes (BIAS) map (Cuddy, Fiske, & Glick, 2007). We then show how the theory relates to research on intergroup envy. Finally, we apply the theory and related findings to how intergroup envy manifests in organizations.

The Stereotype Content Model

The SCM provides a model for understanding the systematic principles that underlie how different groups are stereotyped in society (e.g., Fiske, Cuddy, Glick, & Xu, 2002). Figure 6.1 illustrates how the model's two dimensions, warmth and competence, apply to various groups that were nominated by participants as "important groups in American society."

The SCM challenged previous paradigms for studying stereotyping. Prior to the SCM, most stereotyping research had focused on the cognitive processes of stereotyping (e.g., Macrae & Bodenhausen, 2000). The cognitive approach tends to view stereotype content (the particular traits attributed to a group) as a given and focuses solely on the cognitive and behavioral consequences that follow from the stereotypes. In other words, cognitive theorists asked: Once stereotypes of groups exist, how do these stereotypes bias perceptions of members of those groups? The cognitive perspective (e.g., Hamilton & Troiler, 1986) illuminated

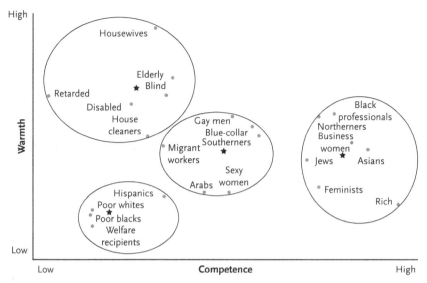

FIGURE 6.1 Scatter pot and cluster analyses of competence and warmth ratings for American groups. Each group's competence and warmth scores are plotted along the x- and y-axes, respectively. Stars indicate cluster centers.

Reproduced from Fiske, Cuddy, Glick, & Xu (2002).

how perceivers are biased toward seeking confirmation for their initial stereotype-based perceptions by seeking out information that fits, rather than challenges, their stereotypes (e.g., Snyder & Swann, 1978), interpreting ambiguous information as stereotype-consistent (e.g., Darley & Gross, 1983), and remembering stereotype-consistent information better (e.g., Bodenhausen, 1988). Cognitive theorists seemed to assume that stereotype content was not itself predictable or not the proper subject for social psychological theories (see Fiske & Neuberg, 1990, for a review).

Prior motivational theories of prejudice addressed stereotype content in a broad sense. Typically, these theories assumed that disadvantaged groups or societal "out-groups" are stereotyped negatively across a host of traits. The in-group's desire to create and maintain a positive self-image (e.g., social identity theory; Tajfel, 1981) and to justify the exploitation and subordination of other groups (e.g., social dominance theory; Sidanius & Pratto, 1999), theoretically leads the in-group to characterize out-groups as inferior in every way. Social identity theorists assumed that disadvantaged groups would themselves attempt to construct a positive image of their group, but that they could only do so by appropriating positive, but generally less socially valued, traits (Tajfel, 1981). Thus, research from prior motivational perspectives tended to focus on uniformly unflattering stereotypes toward disadvantaged groups.

By contrast, the SCM proposed, not only that the content of stereotypes toward different groups was (a) predictable—following from structural relations between the groups—but also (b) often mixed—flattering in some ways (even assigning valued traits toward societal out-groups) but unflattering in others. Specifically, many groups are disliked but respected (viewed as low on warmth but high on competence) or liked but disrespected (viewed as high on warmth, but low on competence). Furthermore, the SCM suggests that which groups fall into which category can be predicted by knowing two key aspects concerning the group's structural position within a society.

The two structural factors that the SCM proposes to determine stereotype content are *group status* and *competition with societal referent groups* (e.g., the middle class, U.S. citizens). Groups that have higher status and more power are seen as more competent than groups that have lower status and less power. Perceiving high-status groups as more competent justifies the existing system (e.g., Jost & Banaji, 1994) because people supposedly get what they deserve (e.g., Lerner & Miller, 1978). Furthermore, groups perceived as not being competitive with other groups—either because they are perceived as lacking the ability to compete or as having goals similar to those of other social groups—are seen as warmer than competitive groups. Competition can be perceived or can be structurally embedded due to, for example, limited resources that each group needs or desires (e.g., a water crisis that creates competition for this necessary resource). Groups that are not viewed as a threat to the in-group's resources are rewarded with perceptions of high warmth (e.g., Glick & Fiske, 2001). By contrast, because competitive out-groups frustrate and threaten the in-group's goals, competing groups are perceived as having negative intent (e.g., Fiske & Ruscher, 1993).

Although being perceived as warm has advantages (such as inhibiting attacks and promoting friendliness), warmth often represents a low-status attribute in individualistic cultures (though not consistently in collectivistic cultures; Cuddy et al., 2015; Torelli, Leslie, Stoner, & Puente, 2014). People who are warm are viewed as other-focused, prioritizing others' needs over their own, which implies deference to others (e.g., Ridgeway, 2001). Therefore, perceiving an individual (e.g., a bumbling but nice neighbor) or a group (e.g., the elderly) as warm but incompetent does not evoke cognitive dissonance (e.g., Eagly & Mladinic, 1994; Glick & Fiske, 2001). In fact, perceiving lower status groups as warm has distinct advantages for dominant groups, encouraging the subordinated group to defer and suggesting that, despite the status hierarchy, intergroup relations can remain pleasant. Jackman (1994) suggests that such paternalistic relations represent dominant groups' preferred way to stabilize the hierarchy, creating several benefits for dominants: pleasant relations promote ideological influence over subordinated groups, paternalism reinforces a positive group image for dominants as benefactors rather than exploiters, and the patina of cooperation between the groups helps avoid the costs of open conflict.

The SCM proposes that where a group falls on the warmth and competence dimensions predicts emotional reactions to its members, aided by social comparisons and outcome attributions. Because shared versus competing goals promote warmth perceptions, warm groups are viewed as being on the "same team," whereas cold groups are viewed as the competition. Thus, warmth perceptions are related to whether group-based social comparisons are assimilative (i.e., seeking to associate oneself and one's group with the other group) or contrastive (i.e., seeking to disassociate or differentiate oneself and one's group from the other group). The status differences that underpin competence stereotypes determine whether social comparisons are downward (i.e., we are better than they are) or upward (i.e., they are better than we are). The specific warmth-competence combination, in turn, determines the precise quality of intergroup comparisons that generate emotional and behavioral consequences (e.g., Fiske, Cuddy, Glick, & Xu, 2002).

Specifically, SCM theorists propose that warm and competent groups elicit upward, assimilative social comparisons (i.e., wanting to be associated with a group that is viewed as better than one's own), which in turn produce admiration. Incompetent and cold groups elicit downward, contrastive social comparisons (i.e., wanting to distance oneself from the other group, which is viewed as inferior to one's own), which evoke contempt. Warm but incompetent groups elicit downward, assimilative comparisons (i.e., willingness to associate with or include the group, but nevertheless seeing the group as inferior to one's own), which lead to pity. Cold but competent groups elicit upward, contrastive comparisons (i.e., desire to distance oneself from the group along with a grudging admiration for their perceived skills and status), which spark envy (for more on the connection between social comparisons and emotional reactions, see Smith, 2000). It is this painful, upward contrastive comparison (and the feeling of inferiority it elicits) that defines envy and differentiates it from other emotions (e.g., Hoogland, Thielke, & Smith, Chapter 5, this volume).

Admiration (toward competent and warm groups) and contempt (toward incompetent and cold groups) are linked to dispositional attributions for success or its lack, respectively (Weiner, 2005). These groups are believed to deserve their relatively higher or lower position in the social hierarchy: warm and competent groups are seen as having earned their higher social position, whereas cold and incompetent groups are viewed as having caused their own fall from grace. By contrast, envied (competent but cold) and pitied (incompetent but warm) groups receive more situational attributions concerning their social positions: they are believed not to fully deserve the positive or negative outcomes they have received (Rozin, Lowery, Imada, & Haidt, 1999; Smith, Parrott, Ozer, & Moniz, 1994; Weiner, 2005). Pity toward incompetent but warm groups evokes compassionate concern about these groups' lower status and outcomes, which can elicit support for paternalistic (e.g., protective) policies or behaviors aimed at helping these groups (Nadler & Halabi, 2006). Envy evokes resentment toward the status and resources competent but cold groups possess, often accompanied by viewing the group as not deserving its success and a desire to cut the group "down to size" (Feather, 1994).

The SCM has been validated in a variety of nations (e.g., Cuddy et al., 2009). Across ten countries, Cuddy and colleagues (2009) found, not only that social groups can reliably be categorized on the SCM's warmth and competence dimensions, but also that groups' perceived status and competition predicted perceptions of warmth and competence. However, one major difference, moderated by cultural values, emerged: collectivistic cultures did not display in-group or reference-group favoritism. That is, in collectivistic cultures, unlike in individualistic cultures, societal reference groups and in-groups were not placed in the high-warmth, high-competence cluster. Collectivistic cultures' desire for harmony and consequent modesty norms (i.e., proscriptions against appearing to elevate oneself above others) may explain this difference. However, although these studies supported the SCM's predictions that status positively predicts competence perceptions, and competition negatively predicts warmth perceptions, they did not assess individuals' emotional reactions to groups. Therefore, it is unknown whether individuals in collectivistic cultures would report feeling envy toward members of high-competence, low-warmth groups (for information on differences in the elicitation, experience, and expression of envy in different cultures, see Tan, Tai, & Wang, Chapter 11, this volume).

The Behaviors from Intergroup Affect and Stereotypes Map

An expansion of the SCM, the BIAS map (Cuddy et al., 2007) addresses how warmth and competence stereotypes determine behavioral tendencies toward a group. The BIAS map extends the SCM by (a) proposing how the emotions evoked by each warmth-competence combination mediate behavioral consequences (i.e., the types of actions likely to be exhibited toward groups), and (b) classifying behavioral tendencies along two dimensions: facilitative versus harmful, and active versus passive. See Figure 6.2 for a depiction of how the BIAS map relates to the SCM.

Affect is a better predictor of both discrimination and intent to discriminate than cognition is (e.g., Dovidio, Brigham, Johnson, & Gaertner, 1996; Schutz & Six, 1996; Talaska, Fiske, & Chaiken, 2008; Zajonc, 1998). Because affective reactions better predict behavior, Cuddy, Fiske, and Glick (2007) theorized that the emotions that follow from the various SCM stereotype categories—admiration, contempt, pity, and envy—meditate the relationship between the stereotype contents (i.e., cognition) and behavioral tendencies toward members of different groups. These behavioral tendencies may be positive or negative: groups may be facilitated

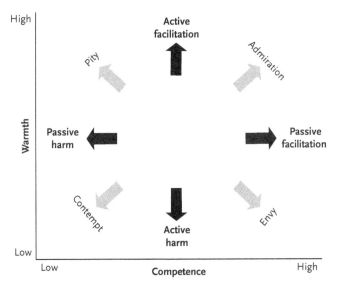

FIGURE 6.2 The Behaviors from Intergroup Affect and Stereotypes (BIAS) map. Competence and warmth are represented on the x- and y- axes. Gray arrows represent emotions, black arrows represent behavioral tendencies.

Reproduced with permission from Cuddy, Fiske, and Glick (2007).

or harmed. Facilitative behavior leads to favorable outcomes or gains for the target group, whereas harmful behavior leads to detrimental outcomes or losses for the group. Furthermore, behaviors may be active (e.g., attack) or passive (e.g., neglect). The BIAS map specifies the chain from stereotypes, to emotions, to different behavioral tendencies toward groups.

Overall, the warmth (compared to competence) dimension exerts a stronger influence on behavioral tendencies (Wojciske et al., 1998). Warmth may take precedence because it relates to others' perceived intent (are they friend or foe?), a concern that logically precedes the question of whether another person is capable of enacting his or her intentions. As a result, warmth better predicts overall evaluations than competence. Furthermore, probably because evolution selected people to be especially wary of foes, negative warmth information (e.g., someone behaving unkindly) is weighted more heavily than negative competence information (e.g., someone behaving unintelligently) when forming impressions of others (Wojciske et al., 1998; Wojciszke, Brycz, & Borkenau, 1993).

Because warmth influences perceptions more strongly than competence, Cuddy, Fiske, and Glick (2007) theorized—and found—that warmth perceptions play a central role in active behaviors toward members of stereotyped groups. Active behaviors are those conducted with direct and overt intentions to affect the target group. Examples would include initiating interaction and offering help (on the positive side) or overtly segregating or attacking (on the negative side). Cuddy et al. also theorized and found that, because competence is secondary to warmth and only reflects an ability to enact intentions (rather than the valence of intentions), competence perceptions predict passive behavioral tendencies. Passive behaviors are less deliberate than active behaviors, generally reflecting less intensity, effort, engagement, and obvious intention to affect the target group. Examples include allowing oneself to be associated with another group or tolerating proximity without seeking it out (on the positive side) and neglect or passive exclusion (on the negative side).

Stereotypes about a group's warmth determine active behaviors (i.e., whether a group is actively harmed or facilitated), and stereotypes about a group's competence determine passive behaviors (i.e., whether a group is passively harmed or facilitated). Groups low in both competence and warmth (i.e., hated groups) are either actively harmed (e.g., attacked) or passively harmed (e.g., excluded and neglected). Groups that are high in both competence and warmth (i.e., admired groups) are either actively facilitated (e.g., helped, sought out) or passively facilitated (e.g., associated with when circumstances dictate). Ambivalently stereotyped groups can receive more mixed behaviors, depending on whether the positive or negative side of the ambivalence toward the group is activated. For example, groups stereotyped as low in competence but high in warmth (i.e., pitied groups) may be actively facilitated (e.g., helped) when their perceived warmth is made salient, but receive passive harm (e.g., neglect) when their perceived lack of competence is salient. Groups high in competence but low in warmth (i.e., envied groups) may be passively facilitated (e.g., tolerated) when their competence is salient or actively harmed (e.g., attacked) when their lack of warmth is made salient. We elaborate more below on the behaviors toward envied groups predicted by the BIAS map.

Understanding the SCM and BIAS map helps explain the often-conflicting emotions and behavioral tendencies that envied, in comparison to other, groups elicit. The following section details how envied groups are perceived and treated, providing examples of specific groups that tend to receive this pattern of ratings in the United States.

Intergroup Envy

Groups perceived as high in competence but low in warmth (i.e., high social status and in competition with the social referent groups) elicit envy. In American samples, envied groups include feminists, businesswomen, Asians, Jews, and the rich (Fiske et al., 2002). In South Korea, employers, the rich, and intellectuals fall into the envied category (Cuddy et al., 2009). In Western Germany, it is career women, the rich, and feminists (Asbrock, 2010); however, unlike in American samples, Germans currently rate Jews as equivalently warm and competent to Germans, perhaps due to sensitivities about the Holocaust (for a psychoanalytical perspective on contemporary Germans' tendency to see Jews as an admirable group, see Erlich, Chapter 9, this volume). In various European samples that rated European Union (EU) nations, Germany and the United Kingdom (both relatively wealthy and influential) represent envied nations (Cuddy et al., 2009). Similarly, students in 11 nations rated the United States as high in competence but low in warmth (Glick et al., 2006). Members of envied groups are usually seen as extremely competent (perhaps "too competent"), but also as lacking humanity: they are rated as less emotionally complex, less experienced with adversity, less self-aware, and less moral than members of other groups (e.g., Harris, Cikara, & Fiske, 2008).

Envy implies both respect and resentment (e.g., Feather, 1994), which can elicit two different behavioral tendencies, depending on the context: passive facilitation or active harm (Cuddy, Fiske, & Glick, 2007). People often engage in passive facilitation: they associate with envied groups to take advantage of their resources and competence. For example, participants indicated that they would be more likely to cooperate with, unite with, and associate with a fictitious immigrant group that was described as envied by other groups in their society, than with an immigrant group that was described as hated or pitied (Cuddy, Fiske, & Glick, 2007). However, envy may also lead people to engage in active harm by dehumanizing, attacking, ridiculing, and sabotaging members of envied groups (e.g., Harris, Cikara, & Fiske, 2008). For example, Cikara and Fiske (2012) found that people smile more when negative events happen to people from envied groups than when they happen to pitied, admired, or hated groups. Furthermore, this tendency was affected by changes to the social structural factors underlying the SCM: smiling at envied group members' misfortunes decreased when either their status decreased or their cooperation increased.

When do people actively harm versus passively facilitate envied groups? Becker and Asbrock (2012) had participants evaluate a member of a competent-but-cold group of young professionals gentrifying a neighborhood. The tendency to passively facilitate versus actively harm this envied group depended on the manipulated salience of an individual group member's (lack of) warmth versus competence. When a young professional target made his competence salient (by mentioning that he had to work late at the office), participants were more likely to tolerate, respect, and establish contact with the young professionals in the neighborhood (compared to when he made his lack of warmth salient, or did nothing). However, when the young professional made his lack of warmth salient (by mentioning that he was not interested in meeting people from the neighborhood), participants were more likely to want to vandalize the properties bought by members of the group and petition against their moving into the neighborhood (compared to when he made his competence salient or did nothing). Across conditions, however, participants were more likely to report intentions to passively facilitate than to actively harm. Several chapters in this volume similarly explore moderators that affect when envy elicits positive versus negative behaviors (see Crusius & Lange, Chapter 4; Wu & Duffy, Chapter 2; Hoogland, Thielke, & Smith, Chapter 5; and Sterling, van de Ven, & Smith, Chapter 3, this volume).

People may also be especially likely to actively harm envied groups when their own group experiences a drop in their standard of living, which can activate ingrained suspicions about envied groups. Specifically, Glick

(2002; see also Glick, 2005, 2008) proposed that envied groups face a particular risk of being scapegoated when difficult life circumstances occur (see Staub, 1989). Exaggerated views of envied groups' competence combined with extreme coldness render them culturally plausible culprits for large-scale negative events (e.g., an economic depression) that generate a strong need for explanation and solution. People desperately seek to understand why negative events occur so that they may solve the problem that caused the negative events. When events have no clear, well-understood cause, people may seek a human agent to blame, and stereotypes guide this process. What kind of individual or group could both want, and have the capability, to cause large-scale negative events? The answer: groups perceived as cold (i.e., intent on causing harm) but competent (i.e., capable of causing harm).

Historical examples show abundant scapegoating of envied minorities when nations experience a decline. Anti-Semitism in Europe may represent the most enduring example. Arguably, two thousand years of anti-Semitism, first rooted in religious differences and then the Jews' socioeconomic position in Europe, can be explained through the envious prejudice lens. Specifically, because Christianity started as a break-away Jewish sect, like a child rejected by its more established and powerful parent, early Christians experienced threat when most Jews failed to agree that Jesus was the Messiah (Sandmel, 1978). Judaism was therefore an important early competitor to Christianity, and, in Christianity's first few centuries, a more "dominant" religion. Furthermore, Judaism could not be dismissed as unimportant to Christianity, given that Jesus himself was Jewish and the Hebrew Bible (Old Testament) justified considering Jesus to be the Messiah. Hence, as the original "people of the Bible," the Jews necessarily retained an outsized importance to later European converts to Christianity, who resented Jews' continued rejection of Christianity (Sandmel, 1978). Jews' perceived resistance to God led to the conclusion that Jews must be allied with the Devil, a powerful (competent) but evil (cold) entity.

Further exacerbating these dynamics, Christian prohibitions against usury led to Jews' occupying a money-lending role. The shift from a feudal to a mercantile economy created the need for credit, and some Jewish banking families (e.g., the Rothschilds) became incredibly wealthy, fostering increased envious resentment and stereotypes of Jews as exploiting Christians by controlling the money supply (Brustein, 2003). Jewish success in new occupations in a changing economy—e.g., as merchants, doctors, and later in the media—reinforced their position as high-status and competitive with the Christian in-group.

Because Jews served an important economic role (e.g., providing credit), they were often tolerated and passively facilitated. Yet the Jews were scapegoated and actively harmed when difficult events occurred. For example, lacking medical theories to explain the bubonic plague, medieval Europeans scapegoated the Jews (and witches), who were perceived as allies of the Devil, and therefore as having the supernatural capabilities and evil intent to spread disease (Cohn, 2007). The Nazis' secular version of scapegoating blamed Jewish industrialists as having caused Germany's unexpected defeat in the Great War: only powerful industrialists could pull off such sabotage, and only Jewish industrialists had the perceived intent to undermine Germany from within. Consistent with this reasoning, fascist writings in Germany and Italy characterized the Jews as both cold and incompetent (e.g., Durante, Volpato, & Fiske, 2010), as did older anti-Semitic conspiracy theories such as *The Protocols of the Elders of Zion*.

Glick (2008) suggested that similar dynamics were evident in geno-cidal attacks on Armenian Christians (who occupied a similar middle-man position in the Ottoman Empire as the Jews did in Europe), intellectu-als in Cambodia (seen as highly competent, but competing with and ex-ploiting the rural population) during Pol Pot's genocidal regime, and in the Rwandan genocide against the Tutsis (a socioeconomically success-ful and traditionally privileged minority). Each genocidal attack occurred during difficult times (e.g., economic collapse, loss of territory, political upheaval) that demanded explanation and action. In each case, successful minorities who were previously passively facilitated (at least periodically) during better times, but who were stereotyped as competent but cold, were attacked. Thus, under certain circumstances, intergroup envy can turn es-pecially ugly, motivating exclusion and even extermination, justified by its perpetrators as "self-defense," necessary to save the in-group from a cold-hearted and dangerously competent "enemy."

Intergroup Envy in Organizations

Although competence is highly valued in workplace settings, and physical attacks against organizational groups are not tolerated, groups perceived as highly competent but lacking in warmth nevertheless face challenges at work. Individuals from envied groups may be stereotyped as unsuitable for specific professions, roles, or tasks requiring warmth and sociability and offered those exclusively requiring cold technical competence instead. For example, because Asian Americans are stereotyped as intelligent, hard-working, nerdy, and socially awkward (e.g., Lin, Kwan, Cheung, & Fiske, 2005), an Asian American team member may be asked to analyze data and create graphs for a presentation instead of delivering the presentation or socializing with the client. Supporting this idea, Waytz and Norton (2014) found that Americans are more comfortable outsourcing jobs that involved "feeling" (as opposed to "thinking") to Irish, Australian, and Spanish workers than to British, Chinese, and German workers. Workers from these high-competence, low-warmth cultures were deemed more "robotic," and therefore less capable of doing "feeling" jobs, than individuals from high-warmth, low-competence cultures (see Cuddy et al., 2009, for the warmth and competence ratings of each culture).

Furthermore, high-quality leadership is now believed to require both warmth and competence, which may disadvantage members of envied groups. Historically, different leadership styles tended to exclusively emphasize one dimension or the other. For example, authoritarian or autocratic leadership emphasized the need for dominance and competence, whereas democratic or participative leadership emphasized the need for warmth (Chemers, 1997). However, over time, stereotypes about leadership have shifted to include both dimensions (e.g., Koenig, Eagly, Mitchell, & Ristikari, 2011). Given that good leadership is now seen as requiring excellent social skills and a focus on others in addition to competence, leaders are often explicitly evaluated on their ability to demonstrate warmth as well as competence (e.g., Eagly & Carli, 2007). This may be especially true in organizations that emphasize learning and/or continuous quality improvement, where effective communication, participation, and psychological safety are highly valued (e.g., Eagly & Karau, 2002). Given that members of envied groups are often seen as lacking warmth, members of these groups may face discrimination that presents obstacles to reaching the highest levels of their organizations.

For example, extensive research has demonstrated that businesswomen suffer at work from the stereotype that they lack warmth (for a review, see Rudman, Moss-Racusin, Glick, & Phelan, 2012). Although women in general, especially women in "traditional" roles, tend to be stereotyped as highly warm but lacking competence, childless businesswomen and women in powerful roles tend to be stereotyped as competent but cold (e.g., Fiske et al., 2002; Cuddy, Fiske, & Glick, 2004). In contrast to stereotypical expectations for women to be communal and warm, businesswomen who demonstrate competence tend to be perceived as aggressive and hostile (e.g., Heilman, 2001; Rudman, 1998). In addition to these social costs, women also receive economic penalties such as lower pay, discrimination in hiring and promotion, and inferior negotiation outcomes (e.g., Rudman et al., 2012). These social and economic penalties are often referred to as "backlash" (e.g., Rudman, 1998).

Consistent with the SCM, backlash effects are particularly strong when women advocate for themselves and/or compete with social referent group members for resources (Rudman, Moss-Racusin, Glick, & Phelan, 2012; Rudman, 1998). Consistent with the BIAS map, women in these positions are often passively facilitated (i.e., associated with, and hired into, low-level positions); however, they may also be actively harmed (i.e., discriminated against and harassed). For example, Berdahl (2007) found that women who had assertive, dominant, and independent personalities and/or worked in more masculine professions were significantly more likely to be sexually harassed than women who had less assertive personalities and/or worked in traditionally feminine occupations.

Envied Organizations

A limited number of studies have examined how the SCM and BIAS map may be relevant, not only for individuals from different groups within organizations, but also for understanding how perceivers react and relate to organizations as a whole. Like individuals, organizations also may have envied identities. For example, Aaker, Vohs, and Mogilner (2010) examined how consumers react to nonprofit and for-profit organizations by manipulating whether a product was sold on a ".com" or ".org" website. Presumably, nonprofits are viewed as warmer (i.e., more cooperative in their goals) but perhaps less competent than for-profit organizations (which, by definition, seek to maximize their resources). Participants evaluated a website selling a messenger bag, and indicated their interest in purchasing it. Participants perceived the for-profit company (.com website) as more competent, but less warm, than the nonprofit company (.org website). Furthermore, the greater perceived competence of the for-profit translated into greater interest in buying the messenger bag from the for-profit than from the non-profit. However, when the non-profits increased their status and credibility, they were perceived as both warm *and* competent, which translated into greater purchasing intent for the credible non-profit than the cold for-profit.

Extending this work, Kervyn, Fiske, and Malone (2012) found that specific brands can be sorted along the SCM's dimensions. A hypothetical brand's intentions toward "ordinary people" (positive or negative) predicted participants' ratings of its warmth and perceptions of the brand's ability to achieve its goals (i.e., to enact intentions) predicted ratings of its competence. Warmth and competence ratings, in turn, predicted emotions in the SCM's predicted patterns. In a second study, participants evaluated 16 well-known brands on the positivity of the brand's intentions (i.e., whether it has good intentions toward ordinary people and acts in the public's best interests) and abilities (i.e., whether the brand has the ability, skill, and effectiveness to implement its intentions and goals). Participants rated luxury brands such as Mercedes, Porsche, Rolex, and Rolls-Royce as having negative intentions and high ability (i.e., competent but cold). These brands elicited more envy than brands that were warmer or less competent. Ratings of warm intentions and ability both positively and independently predicted participants' purchasing intent and loyalty to the brand. However, the authors point out that this may be related to the focus in the items on intentions toward "ordinary people"/"the public" and suggest that perceived envy among "ordinary people" may in fact help brands sell their products to high-end customers. Future research should test this assertion.

In sum, being envied has both positive and negative consequences for individuals within organizations and for organizations themselves. Individuals respect, but do not like, envied groups or organizations. Respect brings benefits such as perceptions of extreme competence and desire to purchase products when things go well. However, dislike creates drawbacks, such as sabotage, suspicion, perceptions of social ineptitude, backlash, and schadenfreude (i.e., perceivers feel pleasure at envied group members' pain).

Future Directions

Given the importance of collaborative work teams involving people from different nations, an important area for future research is to examine how envy may affect cross-cultural collaboration. For example, do individuals from envied cultures (e.g., British or German citizens) get assigned different tasks than individuals from pitied cultures (e.g., Portuguese or Greek citizens) in global teams? Do individuals take perceptions of different countries into account when making decisions about which global assignments to take? Similarly, future research could examine perceptions of the warmth and competence of different occupations, organizational units within companies, and/or industries. For example, are organizational units that are stereotyped as more competent but less warm denied resources or help when they request it because people feel envy towards them? Similarly, are people who are from groups that are stereotyped as competent but not warm disproportionately allocated to these organizational units or industries?

Furthermore, future investigations could examine whether stereotypes about how an employee's perceptions of his or her organization's (or organizational unit's or supervisor's) warmth and competence influence engagement in prosocial/organizational citizenship versus deviant/counterproductive work behaviors. Robinson and Bennett (1995) developed a typology of deviant workplace behaviors, which includes a serious versus minor dimension that mirrors the BIAS map's focus on active versus passive behaviors. The distinction between prosocial and deviant similarly mirrors the BIAS map's facilitation versus harm dimension. Future work could integrate these perspectives by examining whether perceptions of an organization's warmth and competence (e.g., comparing a for-profit with a non-profit), similar to perceptions of justice (e.g., Cropanzano & Byrne, 2000), influence employees' engagement in and loyalty to their organizations. Possibly organizations or organizational units that are perceived as highly competent but as lacking warmth receive more passive facilitation and passive prosocial/organizational citizenship behaviors (e.g., attending more work functions) but also experience greater incidents of serious/active deviant behaviors by their employees (e.g., sabotaging equipment, stealing).

Finally, if an envied organization suffers a scandal, it may face a severe backlash from customers and have a difficult time overcoming suspicions that the scandal was due to callousness or intentional manipulation. For example, an envied oil company, as compared to a non-profit utility, that accidentally produces an environmental disaster may be more likely to be suspected to have cut corners and not to care as much about the cleanup. Future work should explore how individuals judge the behaviors and decisions of competent but cold organizations when these organizations encounter setbacks or scandals.

Conclusion

People perceive both individuals and groups along two dimensions: competence and warmth. Competence is predicted by status, whereas warmth is predicted by perceived competition for valued resources. Groups or individuals who are seen as highly competent, but lacking warmth, tend to be envied. Envy, in turn, often elicits passive facilitation (e.g., tolerating interaction or business exchange), but has an undercurrent of resentment and suspicion. Therefore, when times become difficult or competition between groups increases, envy may elicit active harm (e.g., attacking, harassing, looting, etc.). Envious stereotypes that combine perceived lack of warmth and an abundance of competence can influence perceptions of individuals within organizations (e.g., Asian American or female professionals) and of organizations themselves (e.g., for-profits, luxury brands). These stereotypes may sometimes have advantages when competence is highly valued, but can translate into worse consequences for individuals from envied groups when their perceived lack of warmth characterizes them as unfit for organizational tasks, including leadership. Moreover, because the envied are resented and viewed as self-interested, people are particularly likely to turn against them when they stumble, or to blame them for negative outcomes.

References

Aaker, J., Vohs, K. D., & Mogilner, C. (2010). Nonprofits are seen as warm and for-profits as competent: Firm stereotypes matter. *Journal of Consumer Research*, *37*(2), 224–237. http://doi.org/10.1086/651566

Abele, A. E., & Wojciszke, B. (2007). Agency and communion from the perspective of self versus others. *Journal of Personality and Social Psychology*, *93*(5), 751–763. http://doi.org/10.1037/0022-3514.93.5.751

Asbrock, F. (2010). Stereotypes of social groups in Germany in terms of warmth and competence. *Social Psychology*, *41*(2), 76–81. http://doi.org/10.1027/1864-9335/a000011

Becker, J. C., & Asbrock, F. (2012). What triggers helping versus harming of ambivalent groups? Effects of the relative salience of warmth versus competence. *Journal of Experimental Social Psychology*, *48*(1), 19–27. http://doi.org/10.1016/j.jesp.2011.06.015

Berdahl, J. L. (2007). The sexual harassment of uppity women. *The Journal of Applied Psychology*, *92*(2), 425–437. http://doi.org/10.1037/0021-9010.92.2.425

Bodenhausen, G. V. (1988). Stereotypic biases in social decision making and memory: Testing process models of stereotype use. *Journal of Personality and Social Psychology*, *55*, 726–737. http://dx.doi.org/10.1037/0022-3514.55.5.726

Brustein, W. (2003). *Roots of Hate: Anti-Semitism in Europe Before the Holocaust*. New York: Cambridge University Press.

Cikara, M., & Fiske, S. T. (2012). Stereotypes and schadenfreude: Affective and physiological markers of pleasure at outgroup misfortunes. *Social Psychological and Personality Science*, *3*(1), 63–71.

Chemers, M. M. (1997). *An Integrative Theory of Leadership.* Mahwah, NJ: Lawrence Erlbaum Associates.

Cohn, S. K. (2007). The Black Death and the burning of Jews. *Past and Present, 196*(1), 3–36.

Cropanzano, Russell & Byrne, Zinta S. (2000). Workplace justice and the dilemma of organizational citizenship. In Mark Van Vugt, Mark Snyder, Tom R. Tyler, Anders Biel, (Eds), *Cooperation in modern society: Promoting the welfare of communities, states and organizations. Routledge studies in social and political* (pp. 142–161). New York, NY: Routledge, xiv, 245.

Cuddy, A. J. C., Fiske, S. T., Kwan, V., Glick, P., Demoulin, S., Leyens, J., et al. (2009). Stereotype content model across cultures: Towards universal similarities and some differences. *The British Journal of Social Psychology, 48*(1), 1–33. http://doi.org/10.1348/014466608X314935.

Cuddy, A., Fiske, S., & Glick, P. (2004). When professionals become mothers, warmth doesn't cut the ice. *Journal of Social Issues, 60*(4), 701–718. Retrieved from http://onlinelibrary.wiley.com/doi/10.1111/j.0022-4537.2004.00381.x/full

Cuddy, A. J. C., Fiske, S. T., & Glick, P. (2007). The BIAS map: Behaviors from intergroup affect and stereotypes. *Journal of Personality and Social Psychology, 92*(4), 631–648. http://dx.doi.org/10.1037/0022-3514.92.4.631

Cuddy, A. J. C., Fiske, S. T., & Glick, P. (2008). Warmth and competence as universal dimensions of social perception: The Stereotype Content Model and the BIAS Map. In M. P. Zanna, Ed., *Advances in Experimental Social Psychology* (vol. 40, pp. 61–149). New York: Academic Press.

Cuddy, A. J., Wolf, E. B., Glick, P., Crotty, S., Chong, J., & Norton, M. I. (2015). Men as cultural ideals: Cultural values moderate gender stereotype content. *Journal of Personality and Social Psychology, 109*(4), 622–635. http://dx.doi.org.ezp-prod1.hul.harvard.edu/10.1037/pspi0000027

Darley, J. M., & Gross, P. H. (1983). A hypothesis-confirming bias in labeling effects. *Journal of Personality and Social Psychology, 44*, 20–33. http://dx.doi.org/10.1037/0022-3514.44.1.20.

Dovidio, J. F., Brigham, J. C., Johnson, B. T., & Gaertner, S. L. (1996). Stereotyping, prejudice, and discrimination: Another look. In C. N. Macrae, C. Stangor, & M. Hewstone, Eds., *Stereotypes and Stereotyping* (pp. 276–319). New York: Guilford Press.

Durante, F., Volpato, C., & Fiske, S. T. (2010). Using the Stereotype Content Model to examine group depictions in fascism: An archival approach. *European Journal of Social Psychology, 40*(3), 465–483.

Eagly, A. H., & Carli, L. L. (2007). *Through the Labyrinth: The Truth about How Women Become Leaders.* Boston: Harvard Business School Press.

Eagly, A. H., & Karau, S. J. (2002). Role congruity theory of prejudice toward female leaders. *Psychological Review, 109*, 573–598.

Eagly, A. H., & Mladinic, A. (1994). Are people prejudiced against women? Some answers from research on attitudes, gender stereotypes, and judgements of competence. *European Review of Social Psychology, 5*, 1–35. http://dx.doi.org/10.1080/14792779543000002

Feather, N. T. (1994). Attitudes toward high achievers and reactions to their fall: Theory and research concerning tall poppies. *Advances in Experimental Social Psychology, 26*, 1–73.

Fiske, S. T., Cuddy, A. J. C., & Glick, P. (2007). Universal dimensions of social cognition: Warmth and competence. *Trends in Cognitive Sciences*, *11*(2), 77–83. http://doi.org/10.1016/j.tics.2006.11.005

Fiske, S. T., Cuddy, A. J. C., Glick, P., & Xu, J. (2002). A model of (often mixed) stereotype content: Competence and warmth respectively follow from perceived status and competition. *Journal of Personality and Social Psychology*, *82*(6), 878–902. http://doi.org/10.1037//0022-3514.82.6.878

Fiske, S. T., & Neuberg, S. L. (1990). A continuum of impression formation, from category-based to individuating processes: Influences of information and motivation on attention and interpretation. *Advances in Experimental Social Psychology*, *23*, 1–74. http://doi.org/10.1016/S0065-2601(08)60317-2

Fiske, S. T., & Ruscher, J. B. (1993). Negative interdependence and prejudice: Whence the affect? In D. M. Mackie & D. L. Hamilton, Eds., *Affect, Cognition, and Stereotyping: Interactive Processes in Group Perception* (pp. 239–268). San Diego, CA: Academic Press.

Glick, P. (2002). Sacrificial lambs dressed in wolves' clothing: Envious prejudice, ideology, and the scapegoating of Jews. In L. S. Newman & R. Erber, Eds., *Understanding Genocide: The Social Psychology of the Holocaust* (pp. 113–142). Oxford, UK: Oxford University Press.

Glick, P. (2005). Choice of scapegoats. In J. F. Dovidio, P. Glick, & L. A. Rudman, Eds., *On the Nature of Prejudice: 50 Years After Allport* (pp. 244–261). Malden, MA: Blackwell.

Glick, P. (2008). When neighbors blame neighbors: Scapegoating and the breakdown of ethnic relations. In V. M. Esses & R. A. Vernon, Eds., *Explaining the Breakdown of Ethnic Relations: Why Neighbors Kill* (pp. 123–146). Malden, MA: Blackwell.

Glick, P., & Fiske, S. T. (2001). An ambivalent alliance: Hostile and benevolent sexism as complementary justifications for gender inequality. *American Psychologist*, *56*(2), 109–118.

Hamilton, D. L., & Trolier, T. K. (1986). Stereotypes and stereotyping: An overview of the cognitive approach. In J. F. Dovidio & S. L. Gaertner, Eds., *Prejudice, Discrimination, and Racism* (pp. 127–163). San Diego, CA, US: Academic Press.

Dovidio, J. F., & Gaertner, S. L., Eds. (1986). *Prejudice, Discrimination, and Racism* (pp. xiii, 127–163). San Diego, CA: Academic Press.

Harris, L. T., Cikara, M., & Fiske, S. T. (2008). Envy as predicted by the stereotype content model: Volatile ambivalence. In *Envy: Theory and Research* (pp. 133–147). New York: Oxford University Press.

Heilman, M. E. (2001). Description and prescription: How gender stereotypes prevent women's ascent up the organizational ladder. *Journal of Social Issues*, *57*(4), 657–674. http://doi.org/10.1111/0022-4537.00234

Jackman, M. R. (1994). *The Velvet Glove: Paternalism and Conflict in Gender, Class, and Race Relations*. Berkeley and Los Angeles: University of California Press.

Jost, J. T., & Banaji, M. R. (1994). The role of stereotyping in system-justification and the production of false consciousness. *British Journal of Social Psychology*, *33*, 1–27.

Kervyn, N., Fiske, S., & Malone, C. (2012). Brands as intentional agents framework: How perceived intentions and ability map brand perception. *Journal of Consumer Psychology*, *22*(2), 166–176. http://doi.org/10.1016/j.jcps.2011.09.006.Brands

Koenig, A. M., Eagly, A. H., Mitchell, A. A., & Ristikari, T. (2011). Are leader stereotypes masculine? A meta-analysis of three research paradigms. *Psychological Bulletin, 137*(4), 616–642. http://doi.org/10.1037/a0023557

Lerner, M. J., & Miller, D. T. (1978). Just world research and the attribution process: Looking back and ahead. *Psychological Bulletin, 85*(5), 1030–1051.

Lin, M. H., Kwan, V. S. Y., Cheung, A., & Fiske, S. T. (2005). Stereotype content model explains prejudice for an envied outgroup: Scale of anti-Asian American stereotypes. *Personality and Social Psychology Bulletin, 31*(1), 34–47. http://doi.org/10.1177/0146167204271320

Macrae, C. N., & Bodenhausen, G. V. (2000). Social cognition: Thinking categorically about others. *Annual Review of Psychology, 51*, 93–120.

Nadler, A., & Halabi, S. (2006). Intergroup helping as status relations: Effects of status stability, identification, and type of help on receptivity to high-status group's help. *Journal of Personality and Social Psychology, 91*(1), 97–110.

Ridgeway, C. L. (2001). Gender, status, and leadership. *Journal of Social Issues, 57*(4), 637–655.

Robinson, S. L., & Bennett, R. J. (1995). A typology of deviant workplace behaviors: A multidimensional scaling study. *Academy of Management Journal, 38*(2), 555–572. http://doi.org/10.2307/256693

Rozin, P., Lowery, L., Imada, S., & Haidt, J. (1999). The CAD triad hypothesis: A mapping between three moral emotions (contempt, anger, disgust) and three moral codes (community, autonomy, divinity). *Journal of Personality and Social Psychology, 76*, 574–586.

Rudman, L. A. (1998). Self-promotion as a risk factor for women: The costs and benefits of counterstereotypical impression management. *Journal of Personality and Social Psychology, 74*(3), 629–645.

Rudman, L. A., Moss-Racusin, C. A., Glick, P., & Phelan, J. E. (2012). Reactions to vanguards: Advances in backlash theory. In P. Devine & A. Plant, Eds., *Advances in Experimental Social Psychology* (vol. 45, pp. 167–228). San Diego, CA: Academic Press.

Sandmel, S. (1978). *Anti-Semitism in the New Testament?* Augsburg Fortress Publishing.

Schutz, H., & Six, B. (1996). How strong is the relationship between prejudice and discrimination? A meta-analytic answer. *International Journal of Intercultural Relations, 20*, 441–462.

Sidanius, J., & Pratto, F. (1999). *Social Dominance: An Intergroup Theory of Social Hierarchy and Oppression.* New York: Cambridge University Press.

Smith, R. H. (2000) Assimilative and contrastive emotional reactions to upward and downward social comparisons. In J. Suls & L. Wheeler, Eds., *Handbook of Social Comparison: Theory and Research* (pp. 173–200). New York: Plenum.

Smith, R. H., Parrott, W. G., Ozer, D., & Moniz, A. (1994). Subjective injustice and inferiority as predictors of hostile and depressive feelings of envy. *Personality and Social Psychology Bulletin, 20*, 705–711.

Snyder, M., & Swann, W. B. (1978) Hypothesis-testing processes in social interaction. *Journal of Personality and Social Psychology, 36*, 1202–1212. http://dx.doi.org/10.1037/0022-3514.36.11.1202

Staub, E. (1989). *The Roots of Evil: The Origins of Genocide and Other Group Violence*. New York: Cambridge University Press.

Tajfel, H. (1981). Social stereotypes and social groups. In J. C. Turner & H. Giles, Eds., *Intergroup Behavior* (pp. 144–162). Oxford, UK: Basil Blackwell.

Talaska, C. A., Fiske, S. T., & Chaiken, S. (2008). Legitimating Racial Discrimination: Emotions, Not Beliefs, Best Predict Discrimination in a Meta-Analysis. *Social Justice Research*, *21*(3), 263–396. http://doi.org/10.1007/s11211-008-0071-2

Torelli, C. J., Leslie, L. M., Stoner, J. L., & Puente, R. (2014). Cultural determinants of status: Implications for workplace evaluations and behaviors. *Organizational Behavior and Human Decision Processes*, *123*(1), 34–48. http://doi.org/10.1016/j.obhdp.2013.11.001

Waytz, A., & Norton, M. I. (2014). Botsourcing and outsourcing: Robot, British, Chinese, and German workers are for thinking—not feeling—jobs. *Emotion*, *14*(2), 434–444. http://doi.org/http://dx.doi.org/10.1037/a0036054

Weiner, B. (2005). *Social Motivation, Justice, and the Moral Emotions: An Attributional Approach*. Mahwah, NJ: Erlbaum.

Wojciszke, B. (2005). Affective concomitants of information on morality and competence. *European Psychologist*, *10*, 60–70.

Wojciszke, B., Brycz, H., & Borkenau, P. (1993). Effects of information content and evaluative extremity on positivity and negativity biases. *Journal of Personality and Social Psychology*, *64*, 327–336.

Zajonc, R. B. (1998). Emotions. In D. T. Gilbert, S. T. Fiske, & G. Lindzey, Eds., *Handbook of Social Psychology* (4th ed., vol. 1, pp. 591–634). Boston: McGraw-Hill.

7 | A Social Network Perspective on Envy in Organizations

THERESA FLOYD AND CHRISTOPHER M. STERLING

Introduction

This chapter seeks to examine the development and consequences of envy, using a social networks perspective. The social network perspective considers that individuals are embedded in a web of relationships that significantly influence individual behavior (Borgatti, Mehra, Brass, & Labianca, 2009). Much of the activity that takes place inside an organization occurs within a structure of informal relationships. These relationships, although informal, often involve key communication-based interactions that allow employees to do their jobs. People often compare their levels of performance and awards attained to those of their coworkers. They gather this social comparison information through direct inquiry and third-party gossip. We argue that the content and structure of informal relationships will affect people's access to and interpretation of social comparison information, ultimately shaping an individual's experience of envy and their resultant behavioral reactions.

In effect, this chapter contributes a more contextualized examination of envy by considering how an important aspect of social context, the composition and structure of relationships, influences envy. Although envy has often been described as a universal emotion, envy scholars have increasingly turned their attention to the role that social, cultural, and organizational contexts play in shaping the different experiences, expressions, and reactions associated with envy. (For research regarding envy and relational characteristics such as referent cognitions, see in this volume: Wolf & Glick, this Chapter 6, Mishra, Whiting, & Folger, Chapter 16; for research regarding envy and cultural differences, see Hitokoto & Sawada,

Chapter 12; for research regarding envy and organizational context, see Yu & Duffy, Chapter 2, this volume).

We begin by examining dyadic implications of social networks for the development and consequences of envy, such as the bonds that exist between potential enviers and the targets of their envy, the type and strength of the relationships, and the frequency of interactions between the dyads. We also explore implications beyond the dyad—which can only be understood by considering the overall network structure in which employees are embedded—such as how the overall network structure creates a context within which interactions take place, how the relative positions of a potential envier and the target of envy within the network structure and their respective individual network characteristics affect the likelihood of comparison and the development of envy, and how the cognitions that employees have about workplace networks affect social comparison and the development of envy. Our goal is to open up a discussion about how social networks within organizations influence (1) social comparison processes, (2) the development of envy and the form it takes, and (3) the consequences of envy, with a specific focus on the behavior of the envier. Our hope is to inspire both envy researchers and social network researchers to consider conducting empirical research at the intersection of social networks and envy, with the goal of improving our understanding of both.

First, we will provide a list of definitions important to the social network perspective. Second, we will explain the common theoretical mechanisms that explain how social networks affect individual and group outcomes. Third, we will review the work done to date that incorporates the social context into the study of social comparisons and envy. Finally, we will discuss the opportunities afforded by applying the theoretical mechanisms of social networks to the study of envy in organizations.

The Social Network Perspective

Individual employees in organizations experience widely varying challenges and enjoy equally widely varying opportunities and outcomes. One explanation for the differences in experiences and outcomes is the unique talents, abilities, and traits of each employee, often called their *human capital*. Research on individual differences in human capital explains a great deal about the different outcomes achieved by different employees in organizations (Barrick & Mount, 1991; Cote & Miners, 2006; Judge & Bono, 2001). However, research using this approach tends to consider each individual in a vacuum and fails to take fully into account the social context within which individual employees operate. Social network research considers both the content of individuals' relationships and their embeddedness in the overall social structure as important aspects of social context that influence individual behavior (Brass, 2012). For an example of how the social network perspective complements the human capital perspective, we consider the following question: How could we understand the potential consequences of one employee being promoted over another? Without a deeper understanding of the social context, we would probably predict that this particular situation could evoke a fair amount of envy in the passed-over employee. Could we then predict whether the particular employee will react positively and be motivated to work harder in order to gain the next promotion, or, conversely, react in a retaliatory manner aimed at undermining the other successful individual? In order to answer this question, we require a deeper understanding of the social context. For example, what type of relationship did the envier have with the envied? Was it a collaborative and supportive one, or one marked by rivalry and competition? How does their dyadic relationship fit within the broader social structure? Suppose that the envier has other referents who have also recently received promotions. This latest promotion could then remind the employee of his inferiority within his reference group. This type of social context may affect the focal employee's experience of envy, potentially leading to subsequent deviant behaviors. This example illustrates that research on social networks has a natural fit with research on envy, and opens up a new realm of possibilities for research in both areas.

Network Definitions

A social network is made up of actors—who can be individuals, groups, organizations, or industries—and the connections between the actors, which can be defined in a number of different ways (e.g., who communicates with whom, advice-seeking, friendship). For the purposes of this chapter, we will focus on networks of individuals defined by their relationships with each other, but it is important to note that networks can be studied at multiple levels of analysis (Brass, Galaskiewicz, Greve, & Tsai, 2004).

Researchers often depict social networks using network graphs, within which the actors are symbolized by dots, or *nodes*; and the connections, or *ties*, between the actors are symbolized by lines (Borgatti, Everett, & Johnson, 2013, p. 100). The type of tie defines the network (i.e., a network of friendship ties between individuals within an organization is defined as the *friendship network* of the organization). There are infinite possibilities for the types of ties that can be used to define networks. Some examples include advice-seeking, information-sharing, or liking. Many of these kinds of relationships may be relevant for examining the development and consequences of envy. Past research has also examined networks defined by ties of *social comparison*, where respondents indicated the people to whom they compared themselves within their organizations (Shah, 1998; Sterling, 2013).

An actor's position within the network can provide opportunities and benefits. For example, actors who are more central in communication networks have better and faster access to information flowing through the network than actors who are on the periphery of the network (Brass, 1984). In Figure 7.1, Actor C is central and Actor I is peripheral.

The overall *structure* of the network, defined by the interconnections between the actors, can be described in terms of its *density*, or the relationships that exist between all actors. Density is simply the number of existing ties divided by the number of possible ties (Borgatti et al., 2013). Granovetter (2005, p. 34) noted that in dense networks, norms for appropriate behavior are "clearer, more firmly held, and easier to enforce." Accordingly, dense networks are often associated with a high level of trust between the actors, agreed-upon norms for behavior, and sanctions against behavior that goes against the norms (Coleman, 1988). It is also possible to describe the structure of individual networks, which are made up of the ties between a focal individual, or *ego*, and her contacts, or *alters,* and the

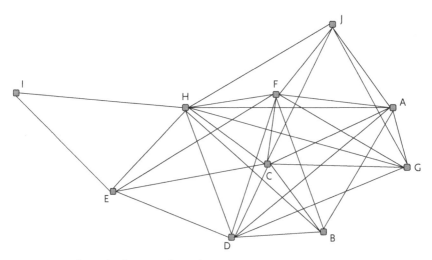

FIGURE 7.1 Example of a network graph.

ties between her alters. Ego networks that are dense have been found to be efficient in the sharing of tacit information (Hansen, 1999) and can also provide higher levels of social support (Coleman, 1988). However, dense ego networks also exercise constraints upon ego's behavior, due to the ability of their members to monitor and sanction other members for violating group norms (Burt, 1992). In dense networks, the importance of maintaining status and a favorable reputation within the group is increased, often creating competitive pressures within the group (Burt, 2010). We will explore more fully later in the chapter how the level of density in individual networks can influence the development and consequences of envy.

In contrast, ego networks that are *sparse* and include connections to people in other groups can provide benefits in the form of early access to non-redundant information, the opportunity to control the flow of information between groups, and the ability to combine ideas from diverse sources (Burt, 1992; Burt, Kilduff, & Tasselli, 2013). In illustration, Figure 7.2 shows two ego networks. Both individuals have five contacts. Paul's contacts, in Network A, in addition to being connected to Paul, are also mostly connected to each other, making Paul's network dense. Natalie's contacts, in Network B, are mostly unconnected to each other. The lack of connection between many of Natalie's contacts, or *structural holes*, means that Natalie is connected to more diverse groups of people, providing her with access to unique information and ideas.

Network research has a long history of examining the consequences of networks for individuals and groups. A more recent stream of research examines the *antecedents* of networks: factors that influence the formation of networks (Brass, 2012). Although we acknowledge that envy can affect the formation of networks, for the purpose of this chapter, we focus on the impact that networks have on envy, thus examining how envy can

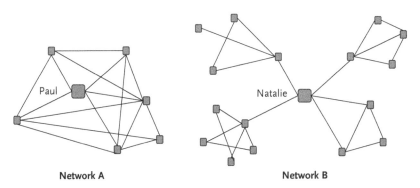

Network A   Network B

FIGURE 7.2 Examples of ego network graphs.

be a consequence of networks, or how networks influence whether envy develops, the form that it takes, and its consequences.

Social Network Theory

Research on the consequences of networks can be understood as focusing on two broad goals: (1) explaining differences between actors in performance and outcomes, and (2) explaining similarities between actors in attitudes and behavior (Borgatti & Foster, 2003; Brass, 2012). In general, differences between actors can be explained by variations in the opportunities for action by the actor provided by the network. Similarities between actors can be thought of as a result of the network's acting on individuals—through the influence of direct contacts or through similarities in experiences afforded by the network (Borgatti & Foster, 2003). Two mechanisms explain how networks provide opportunities and impose constraints on actors: the *flow* mechanism and the *bond* mechanism. The "flow" mechanism conceives of the underlying network as a series of pipes through which things like information, resources, and support can flow (Borgatti & Halgin, 2011). Actors who occupy favorable positions in the network are more likely to have access to timely and unique information and resources, based on the increased flow opportunities provided by their network connections. The "bond," or coordination, mechanism conceives of network ties as bonds that can enable actors to act as one for the benefit of both (Borgatti & Halgin, 2011). The actors in the bond network benefit due to the greater capabilities associated with the two actors essentially combining into one node and acting in concert.

A typology developed by Borgatti and Foster (2003) and further refined by Borgatti and Halgin (2011) is helpful for understanding how the explanatory goals and the explanatory mechanisms of networks fit together. In the two-by-two table shown in Table 7.1 (Borgatti & Halgin, 2011), the

TABLE 7.1 Network Goals and Mechanisms

	EXPLANATION FOR: MECHANISM	
	DIFFERENCES IN SUCCESS	SIMILARITIES IN CHOICE
Flow-based	Capitalization	Contagion
Bond-based	Cooperation	Convergence

Adapted from Borgatti & Halgin, 2011.

goals of networks are listed across the top, and the explanatory mechanisms are listed down the left side. Differences in performance and outcomes afforded by the network have been called *social capital* and *network advantage* in past research, and can be more simply defined as variation in *success* between actors in the network. Similarity in attitudes and behaviors has also been called *homogeneity* in past research, and can be more simply defined as similarity in *choice* between actors in the network.

Flow-based mechanisms for explaining differences in success are called "*capitalization.*" Capitalization occurs when the network provides unique opportunities for more frequent, timelier, and more diverse flows of information, resources, or support (Borgatti & Halgin, 2011). A number of network theories use a flow-based explanation for variation in achievement: Granovetter (1973) notes that actors' weak ties provide more help in getting a job because they connect the actor to diverse groups and thus provide non-redundant information about job opportunities. Lin (1999) argues that ties to contacts who are high in resources or status can help an individual achieve her own status, through the resources, information, legitimacy, and support that her contacts provide. Burt asserts that actors who have sparse networks, characterized by structural holes, not only have access to non-redundant information, but also have early access to information and opportunities to be the one to introduce new information to one's group (Burt, 1992; Burt et al., 2013).

Capitalization processes could affect both the development of envy and the form that envy takes, as well as the potential consequences of envy. An individual with access to a number of opportunities due to his position within the workplace network is a potential object of envy to others. In addition, the frequency of contacts or the relationship between a potential envier and the target of his envy may mitigate or aggravate the development of envy and affect the form envy may take. Also, the access to resources that the envier may enjoy can greatly affect the consequences of envy. Enviers with control over resources are more formidable because of the possibility that they may withhold those resources. Conversely, enviers with access to resources may be more likely to believe that they have opportunities for similar successes and may experience a more benign form of envy, motivating self-improvement behaviors rather than undermining behaviors aimed at tearing down others (van de Ven, Zeelenberg, & Pieters, 2011).

Flow-based mechanisms for explaining similarity between actors are called "*contagion.*" Contagion explains similarities in beliefs, attitudes, and behavior as the result of social influence processes that occur between actors who are directly connected to each other (Borgatti & Halgin, 2011). Researchers have used contagion to explain why actors have similar attitudes and beliefs (Erickson, 1988; Friedkin & Johnsen, 1999; Umphress, Labianca, Brass, Kass, & Scholten, 2003), engage in similar behaviors (Bamberger & Biron, 2007), and adopt innovations previously adopted by their friends (Coleman, Katz, & Menzel, 1966; Valente, 1995). In a classic study, Coleman, Katz, and Menzel (1966) found that doctors began to prescribe the new drug tetracycline not solely based upon their rational decision-making processes, but also because of the influence of their friends who were already prescribing it.

Contagion processes could affect the spread of the potential consequences of envy, especially if the envier has numerous opportunities to influence others due to his position within the network, number of contacts, frequency of interactions, lack of relationship constraints, or individual network structure.

In contrast to the contagion explanation proposed in the first tetracycline study (Coleman et al., 1966), later re-analysis of the data suggested an alternative explanation: that doctors adopted the new drug *not* because of the influence of their direct contacts, but rather because they mimicked the actions of doctors who were *structurally equivalent*—those who occupied similar positions within the network (Burt, 1987). Structurally equivalent individuals may not have ties with each other, but they have similar patterns of ties to others. The authors argued that doctors monitored the action of others with whom they were structurally equivalent, and adopted the innovation so as not to be outstripped by others with whom they were in competition. It can be argued that the doctors were adapting in similar ways to the similar structural environment in which they found themselves (Borgatti et al., 2009). This process is called "*convergence.*" Convergence uses a bond-based mechanism to explain why actors are similar (Borgatti & Halgin, 2011).

Convergence processes could affect the development of envy and the form it may take. First, since convergence helps explain similarities between actors within a network, it can lead to the identification of referent others for social comparison. Actors who are similar on a number of dimensions are more likely to compare themselves against each other (Festinger, 1954), leading to increased chances for the development of envy. However, actors who are more similar are also more likely to identify with each other, perhaps mitigating the development of envy (Duffy, Scott, Shaw, Tepper, & Aquino, 2012) and/or influencing the form it may take.

Bond-based explanations for differences in achievement are called "*cooperation*." Cooperation occurs when actors act in concert, exclude others, or exploit divisions (Borgatti & Halgin, 2011). Coleman's (1988) concept of social capital existing as the result of closed networks that enable trust through providing norms for and enforcing sanctions on behavior is a bond-based explanation. In a different vein, the concept of the *arbitrage opportunities* provided by sparse network is also an example of a bond-based explanation for variation in success. Arbitrage opportunities include opportunities to bring diverse groups together, present ideas to different groups differently, and translate and detect unique information in order to develop new opportunities (Burt et al., 2013).

Cooperation processes could influence the consequences of envy in a number of ways. The overall network structure of the organization and the individual network structure of the envier's ego network each provide a context within which actors interact. If the network structure is very dense, with a large number of interconnections between the actors, then there are likely to be accepted norms for appropriate behavior and sanctions against inappropriate behavior (Coleman, 1988), which would limit an envier's opportunities to act out against the target of her envy. On the other hand, dense networks are also likely to lead to inescapable comparison information, again because of the large number of interconnections between the actors, increasing the likelihood of the development of envy (Sterling, 2013). Future research would do well to disentangle those structural factors that affect both the elicitation of envy and the behavioral consequences of the emotion.

Types of Ties

Networks are defined by the types of ties that connect the actors within them. There are as many possible networks as there are possible questions we can ask about the ways that people interact with each other. The type of tie that defines the network plays a huge part in determining the things that can flow within the network. For example, friendship can support flows of many different types, including social support, gossip, and money. In contrast, ties defined strictly by a work relationship will support more limited kinds of flows, such as business information and resources. And some ties can be *multiplex* (Borgatti et al., 2013), in which the actors may see each other as friends, work colleagues, *and* softball teammates.

Ties can be divided into two main types: *events* and *states* (Borgatti & Halgin, 2011). Events are discrete occurrences: they happen once and then are over. Events can be further divided into *interactions* and *flows*. In a conversation by the water cooler (interaction), two colleagues could exchange gossip (flow) about a third colleague. This interaction and the flow associated with it are both examples of events (Borgatti & Halgin, 2011). It is possible to measure the frequency of events over time; recurring events can become good sources for flows of information, and repeated interaction may result in the formation of a relationship.

A relationship is an example of a state that is continuous while it exists. In other words, as long as two people are friends, their friendship is continuously in effect until one or the other of them decides to end the friendship. In addition to *social relationships*, other examples of states include *similarities*, like co-memberships, co-participation, geographic proximity, and shared attributes (Borgatti et al., 2009). These different types of ties can be thought of as pipes through which different things can flow. Therefore, type of tie is most important to consider when using a flow-based mechanism to explain phenomena. For example, some network studies have identified social referent relationships as a type of network tie. Shah (1998) demonstrated that employees vary in terms of whom they choose as social referents when trying to understand their own level of performance. Sterling, Shah, and Labianca (2015) demonstrated that characteristics of these referent networks were differentially related to the experience of two forms of envy: benign and malicious.

Network Cognitions

A third network mechanism that doesn't fit neatly into Table 7.1 is the concept of networks as *prisms*. In this concept, an actor's network ties act as signals of the actor's quality or status. A story about the financier Baron de Rothschild aptly illustrates the concept: An acquaintance petitioned him for a loan, which he refused. Instead, he made the following offer: "I will walk arm-in-arm with you across the floor of the Stock Exchange, and you soon shall have willing lenders to spare" (Cialdini & De Nicholas, 1989, p. 45). In the story, the apparent friendship between de Rothschild and his acquaintance was a signal to observers that was strong enough to ensure that the acquaintance would be able to secure the needed funds. In other words, the acquaintance's network acted as a prism that signaled his quality to observers. Research in this vein has shown that an individual's reputation as a good performer is enhanced by being seen as having a prominent friend in the organization (Kilduff & Krackhardt, 1994), and that in cases of market uncertainty where reputation is key, being seen as having high-status contacts is a signal of quality to potential exchange partners (Podolny, 2001). Cognitions about networks, regardless of their accuracy, can affect the development and form of envy.

We have briefly described some of the ways that an understanding of the social networks of organizations may help shed light on the processes underlying the development, form, and consequences of envy. This attention to the social context has until recently been under-explored in envy research. However, there are a few recent examples of research that take into account the social context in ways that are helpful in improving our understanding of envy. We briefly review this research next.

Envy and the Social Context

In a two-study project including hospital employees and student teams, Duffy and colleagues (2012) developed a social context model of envy and social undermining. In the development of their theory, the authors considered how social identification and social norms moderated the relationships between envy and moral disengagement; and between moral disengagement and social undermining, a potential consequence of envy. They found that moral disengagement mediated the relationship between envy and social undermining; that social identification mitigated the positive relationship between envy and moral disengagement; and that team norms for undermining augmented the positive relationship between moral disengagement and social undermining (Duffy et al., 2012). This research is a good first step in considering the overall social context's effect on the development and consequences of envy. Taking a social network approach could compliment and extend this important work. First, a social network approach would allow future researchers to make direct, specific links between the targets of envy and consequences to those targets, rather than measuring envy and its consequences at the aggregate level. Second, it would help account for interdependence between actors, which could greatly affect the likelihood of an individual's acting on feelings of envy. Third, it would enable future researchers to take into account the overall network structure, which provides strong clues to the possibility of norms for behavior and sanctions for bad behavior.

Social Networks and Social Comparisons

One theoretical piece and one empirical study focus more directly on how the network perspective can contribute to our understanding of social comparison processes. Erickson (1988), in her theoretical discussion on the relational basis of attitudes, proposed that our understanding of social comparison processes can be greatly enhanced by the social network perspective. She argued that individuals form their attitudes primarily through interpersonal processes. Additionally, she argued that the formation of attitudes is influenced both by the nature of the relationships between individuals and by the overall structure of the network within which they interact. Based on these suppositions, she proposed a number of propositions about the nature of social comparison as influenced by network dyads, cliques, and overall social space (Erickson, 1988).

Shah (1998) used a network perspective to empirically determine whom employees select as social referents. Selection of social referents has a significant impact on the development of envy, since individuals compare themselves to their social referents, and social referents who are perceived by the focal individual as achieving superior outcomes may be potential targets of envy. In her study, Shah tested whether cohesion (close friendships) or similarity (occupying similar positions in the overall network, also called *structural equivalence*; Burt, 1987) was a better predictor of whom an individual will select as a social referent. She acknowledged that the referent choice is limited by the awareness of the actor and the proximity of and actor's access to social comparison information, and is thus constrained by the actor's social network (Burkhardt & Brass, 1990). The actor cannot compare himself to someone of whom he is not aware. Considering three factors likely to be important in the selection of social referents: similarity, availability, and relevance (Festinger, 1954), Shah proposed that friends are likely to fulfill the similarity and availability requirements, while structurally equivalent others are likely to fulfill the similarity and relevance requirements. She found that when it comes to questions about job-related information, people are more likely to choose structurally equivalent others, and that friends are chosen as referents for social comparison and for general information about the organization. This is an interesting result because comparisons between close friends could potentially be detrimental to the relationship, especially in cases where one friend has noticeably better achievement or success. Shah proposed that people might avoid comparisons in instances where there was likely to be a great differential (Shah, 1998). Conversely Tai and colleagues (2012), in a theoretical piece, propose that referent cognitions—specifically, the belief that one's referent other is warm and/or competent—could lead to positive behavioral responses to envy. This leads to a research question: how relational multiplexity affects the experience of envy, which we explore more fully later in the chapter.

Social Networks and Envy

So far, we have described research that has touched on envy developing within an overall social context, and research that specifically examines social comparison processes within the context of social networks. We are aware of only one project that specifically and directly examines the development, form, and consequences of envy within the context of social networks in an organization. Sterling (2013), in his study of a large healthcare organization, used a motivation-opportunity framework to understand the consequences of workplace social comparisons on the development and form of envy and its associated extra-role behaviors. He examined two potential forms that envy can take: benign envy and malicious envy, and argued that the social structure of an individual's reference *group*—the set of referent others indicated by the focal actor (Lawrence, 2006)—affects the form that envy may take. Informed by previous research that suggested that benign envy and malicious envy inspire very different behavioral responses (van de Ven et al., 2011), Sterling specifically measured the differential in achievement between individuals and the people within their reference groups and related it to feelings of benign and malicious envy and resulting extra-role behaviors like work effort, organizational citizenship behavior, and deviant behavior. He found that benign envy is related to the positive outcome of greater work effort, while malicious envy is related to deviant behavior and turnover intentions. Additionally, he found that the performance difference between an individual and his reference group is positively related to malicious envy and negatively related to benign envy. He found that reference group size and density—which is the extent to which each actor within an individual's reference group also compares to the others—are related to the form that envy takes, with reference group size negatively related to malicious envy and positively related to benign envy, and reference group closure positively related to malicious envy. This research argues that the network structure of reference groups shapes the exposure that individuals have to potentially damaging upward comparisons. In dense reference groups, the importance of relative standing is increased and social comparison information is broadcast widely, quickly saturating the network through third-party gossip. Although not a network study, the "Disposable Diapers, Envy, and the Kibbutz" author (Gressel,

Chapter 17, this volume) makes a similar argument. In explaining why the kibbutz life led to increased envy, Gressel argues that its arrangement and distribution of relationships greatly increases levels of social propinquity, allowing individuals to more easily compare themselves with others, resulting in greater envy. Finally, Sterling found that individual network constraint in the communication network mitigates the positive relationship between malicious envy and deviant behavior, due to the norms and sanctions imposed on behavior by closed networks.

In summary, Sterling's research showed that:

1. Individuals have reference groups rather that single referent others, and that the structure of the network of the reference group has an impact on the form that envy takes;
2. The two forms of envy are related to different behavioral reactions—with benign envy related to greater work effort and malicious envy related to turnover intentions and deviant behavior; and
3. The structure of the individual's communication network affects his ability to behave as motivated by malicious envy.

Because envy and its resulting behaviors were measured at the general level, opportunities exist to examine specifically the target of envy and the target of resulting deviant or citizenship behavior. In addition, future research could examine other domains for comparison beyond performance, such as popularity, attitudes, and rewards—with the added possibility of examining how the multiplexity of comparison relationships affects the development and consequences of envy (Sterling, 2013). And an opportunity exists to examine how the *composition* of the network of the reference group—the characteristics of the individuals—affects the development of envy (Sterling, 2013).

Applying the Social Network Perspective to the Study of Envy

The relative dearth of research using a social network perspective to study the development and consequences of envy affords a number of opportunities for future researchers. Perhaps the first, most obvious, opportunities are methodological. We will briefly describe some methodological opportunities afforded by the social network perspective, and then move on to discuss the perhaps more interesting theoretical opportunities that exist.

Methodological Opportunities

The first methodological opportunity has been partially explored by Shah (1998) and Sterling (2013) in their studies described above: to use a social network method to measure whom employees name as their social referents. However, additional opportunities remain. Although Shah asked her participants to name referents for social comparison, and answer questions about job-related information and questions about general information about the organization, we are unaware of any study that has used social network methods to measure social referents for different dimensions of comparisons, such as popularity, rewards, or status. It is likely that employees use different referents when comparing themselves to their peers on the dimension of job performance than the ones they use for the dimension of rewards. It may make more sense to compare oneself to a peer who has similar work responsibilities for the first, while anyone who is at a similar hierarchical level within the organization is a relevant referent for the second. This opens up possibilities suggested by Sterling (2013) for examining the impact of potentially multiplex comparison relationships, such as examining which types of comparisons have stronger effects on the development of envy, perhaps identifying specific comparison antecedents for the two forms of envy, or examining whether multiplex referent relationships have larger impact on the develop of envy and its consequences.

Another methodological opportunity is to use social network methods to specifically identify the targets of envy and targets of prosocial or antisocial behavior, as suggested by Duffy and colleagues (2012). Asking employees to name the specific people for whom they feel envy, and also perhaps asking them to rate the extent of their envy or to name the comparison dimension that led to the feelings of envy, opens up numerous opportunities to go deeper in understanding how felt envy relates to resulting behavior and possible repercussions beyond the dyad of envier and target. Naturally, these types of questions are sensitive, and are likely to be difficult to collect. However, network researchers have a history of finding ways to encourage candid responses from their participants. Research on negative network ties is a good example (Labianca & Brass, 2006; Labianca, Brass, & Gray, 1998). One possible alternative is to ask employees to name whoever has engaged in deviant behavior against them.

Theoretical Opportunities

While the methodological opportunities outlined above provide the opportunity for a deeper understanding of envy within the confines of the theoretical framework that already exists, we believe that the possible theoretical opportunities hold even more promise. For the remainder of the chapter, we propose to apply what we know about the mechanisms by which social networks affect individual and group outcomes—namely, the flow mechanism and the bond mechanism—to:

1. Explore more fully how networks might affect the social comparison processes that lead to envy;
2. Explore the impact networks might have on the development of envy into one of its forms: benign or malicious; and
3. Explore the impact that networks might have on the likelihood and severity of deviant behavior by those who feel malicious envy.

While Sterling (2013) focused for the most part on the size and structure of the network made up by the reference group of an individual, we focus instead on the other networks employees are likely to be embedded within: friendship networks, advice networks, and workflow networks.

Our goals for this section are threefold. To propose possibilities for future research that:

1. Examine the influence that social networks have on the social comparison processes that lead to envy, including the selection of referents and the likelihood and frequency of comparison;
2. Examine the moderating effect that networks have on the relationship between social comparison and the development of the two forms of envy: benign and malicious; and
3. Examine the moderating effect that networks have on the likelihood and severity of deviant behavior on the part of the envier.

Figure 7.3 shows the model that guides our discussion and propositions. In Figure 7.3, "network cohesion" refers to *flow* mechanisms that explain how the direct connections between people affect both differential opportunities for success (*Capitalization* in Table 7.1) and similarity between actors (*Contagion* in Table 7.1). "Network homogeneity" refers to the *bond* mechanism that explains similarity between actors (*Convergence* in Table 7.1). "Network position" refers to the *flow* mechanism that explains differential opportunities for success (*Capitalization* in Table 7.1); and "network structure" refers to the *bond* mechanism that explains differential opportunities for success (*Cooperation* in Table 7.1).

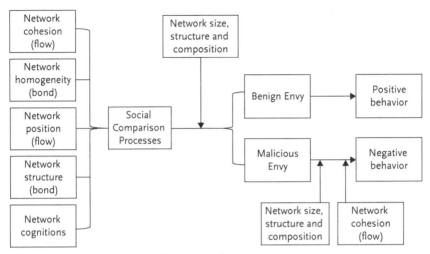

FIGURE 7.3 Social networks and envy model.

Social Networks' Influence on Social Comparison Processes That Lead to Envy

Network cohesion and network homogeneity. Shah (1998) explored how *network cohesion* and *homogeneity* affected people's choices for referent others within their organization, and found that employees more often chose as social referents (on the dimension of job performance) those with whom they had a strong cohesive relationship (friendship). Since social referent choice directly affects the development of envy, it is important to fully explore the network characteristics that those choices.

While cohesion can be understood as a close, strong relationship, as described by Shah, it can also be understood simply as the presence of a direct tie between two actors (Borgatti & Halgin, 2011). This tie does not necessarily have to be one of friendship. It can be a strictly professional relationship, like some relationships between supervisors and subordinates; it can be a workflow relationship, in which one person relies upon another for inputs necessary to their job tasks; or it can be a relationship wherein one person seeks advice from another. It can even be a tie that signifies the dislike that one person feels for another. The different kinds of possible ties that directly link one person to another have very different repercussions for the individuals involved in the relationship—not all will act like the strong friendship ties that Shah studied (Labianca & Brass, 2006). Therefore, opportunities exist to examine how the type of relationship, strength of relationship, and frequency of interaction affect the choice of social referents Similarly, homogeneity, as defined by structural equivalence (occupying similar positions within a network; Burt, 1987) can be measured in many different kinds of networks. It seems likely that structural equivalence within the friendship network is very different from structural equivalence in the workflow network—the structurally equivalent individuals are competing for very different kinds of rewards, resources, and information. Therefore, it is important to examine how structural equivalence in different kinds of social networks affects social comparison and the development of envy.

In addition to the capitalization and convergence processes described above, contagion processes can also have an effect on the choice of social referents. Individuals are exposed to different opinions and attitudes, depending upon the people to whom they are connected. Referent choices may be influenced by contagion processes in densely connected workgroups, since their members are likely to look to each other to confirm their opinions and attitudes (Erickson, 1988).

Network position. The employee's position within the overall network can also have an effect on the size and composition of their reference group. Employees who are central in the organizational network may have a larger pool of possible referents, since they are often connected to a larger number of people. However, they may feel less compelled to compare themselves to others if they have achieved a certain level of success within the organization. People on the periphery of the network may feel more motivation to compare themselves to others, because they realize they are out of the loop and have a desire to fit in. On the other hand, people on the periphery may be happy to be where they are and lack the ambition to move up within the organization—and thus have little motivation for engaging in social comparison.

In addition to individual employees' positions within the overall network, the respective network positions of an employee and his potential referents will affect the choice of social referents. Research has shown that the choice of social referents is limited by the network within which employees are embedded (Burkhardt & Brass, 1990), which suggests that people who are connected only by long paths of indirect ties are less likely to choose each other as social referents. In addition, it seems reasonable that individuals who occupy very different positions within the social network would be less likely to select each other as social referents, even if a direct tie exists, since people often choose social referents who are relatively similar to themselves (Festinger, 1954). Imagine a highly popular employee who occupies a central place within the network and who is friends with another employee who is on the periphery. It seems unlikely that either one would choose the other as a social referent, but that is a question to be resolved empirically.

Network structure. The overall structure of the network of the organization, department, or workgroup, as well as the structure of an employee's individual network, can each have influence over the employee's choice of social referents. A *core-periphery structure* is a relatively common type of organizational network structure. It is characterized by a core group of individuals who occupy central positions within the network and have many ties to each other, and by actors on the periphery who have many ties into the core but very few among themselves (Borgatti et al., 2013). In this kind of structure, those on the periphery are perhaps more likely to choose core individuals as social referents, both because they have more direct ties with those individuals and also because the overall structure of the network tends to focus attention on the core individuals (Borgatti et al., 2013). In contrast, in organizational networks that are characterized by a *clumpy structure*—one in which there exist numerous clusters with many ties within clusters but very few ties between clusters—choices of social referents are more likely to occur within rather than between the clumps in the network.

Individual network structure is likely to influence referent choice, based upon availability of options and perceived appropriateness of choice. Individuals whose networks are more interconnected, or dense, may have fewer options in choosing their social referents, because their social worlds are constrained by the limited contact they have outside their immediate group (Burt et al., 2013). In addition, they may feel constrained in their choice by the strong norms associated with closed networks (Burt, 2005; Coleman, 1988)—they may feel compelled to compare themselves to people who are approved by the group. In contrast, individuals in sparse networks have relatively more freedom to choose and also have more visibility to numerous choice options (Burt et al., 2013).

Network cognitions. One aspect of network research that cannot be ignored is how employees perceive and evaluate the networks around them. Work done to study the accuracy of employees in perceiving social networks has found that, on the whole, people are not very accurate, often over-perceiving their own centrality, over-perceiving the reciprocity of their own ties (Krackhardt, 1987; Kumbasar, Rommey, & Batchelder, 1994), and over-perceiving the extent of clustering, or clumping, in friendship networks (Kilduff, Crossland, Tsai, & Krackhardt, 2008). Given the often-inaccurate perceptions of networks, it seems possible that employees may not be very good at recognizing structurally equivalent others—those who occupy similar positions within the network—which casts doubt upon the assumed competition between structurally equivalent people and also the perceived relevance of a structurally equivalent other as a social referent. However, employees who are highly central in the network have been found to be more accurate in perceiving the overall network structure (Krackhardt, 1987), which may influence their choice of social referents—they may be better at selecting people who are relevant referents.

Next, we will explore how social networks might influence the development and form of envy.

Social Networks' Influence on the development and form of envy

Network size, structure, and composition. "Network size" refers to the size of employees' individual, or *ego*, networks. Employees with small ego networks are likely to experience more exposure to potentially envy-inspiring comparisons, since they have fewer communication options than employees with larger ego networks. Because they have fewer sources for comparison, the importance of surpassing each referent is heightened, which can result in increased competition and rivalry (Sterling, 2013).

Ego network structure can also be a factor. In dense, or closed, ego networks, employees may experience lower feelings of control because of norms and sanctions imposed by closed networks (Coleman, 1988; Granovetter, 2005). Low feelings of control have been found to be related to malicious envy (Buunk, Collins, Taylor, VanYperen, & Dakof, 1990), which suggests that employees with dense ego networks may be more likely to feel malicious envy than employees in sparse networks, who are more likely to have more options of social referents (Sterling, 2013) and less likely to feel "trapped" by their network.

Ego network composition should also have an impact on the development of envy. "Network composition" refers to the characteristics of the individuals' contacts, or *alters*, within her network. These characteristics include demographic characteristics like gender, race, age, and education; work-related characteristics like functional area, rank, title, and experience; attitudes and opinions; and networks characteristics like network position (centrality). Potential enviers might benefit from having a wise mentor within their network, who can coach them through experiences with upward comparisons and encourage the development of benign envy and its attendant positive behavioral reactions. In addition, individuals whose ego networks are characterized by variability in performance enjoy more options for the choice of referent others that may provide opportunities for downward comparisons, lessoning the likelihood of feelings of malicious envy. Finally, Wolf and Glick (Chapter 6, this volume) have discussed how the perceived warmth and competence of referents could affect the experience of envy. Examining the composition of reference groups in terms of their perceived warmth or competence could help explain different reactions to envy.

Social Networks' Influence on deviant behavior resulting from malicious envy

Network size, structure, and composition. We propose that the size of the envier's ego network affects the magnitude of impact of any deviant behavior. Individuals with large ego networks necessarily have contact with a larger number of people, so their deviant behavior towards a target of envy has the potential to have a bigger negative impact on the target. However, we also propose that if the target of the envy has a large network, their network's size provides them with some protection against deviant behavior, by providing them with more opportunities for social support.

Ego network structure is also important. As we've mentioned a number of times, dense networks often impose norms for behavior and sanctions against poor behavior (Coleman, 1988; Granovetter, 2005), which suggests that individuals with dense ego networks will have fewer opportunities to engage in deviant behavior. On the other hand, individuals with sparse ego networks enjoy relatively more freedom in their behavior. As Burt and his colleagues suggest, sparse, open network structures provide few opportunities for reputation to form (Burt et al., 2013)—people are simply not monitoring each other that closely in sparse networks. Therefore, there is more opportunity for deviant behavior on the part of an envier. Earlier we pointed out that individuals in sparse networks are *less likely* to feel malicious envy, yet they enjoy *more opportunities* for engaging in deviant behavior. On the flip side, those in dense networks are *more likely* to feel malicious envy, yet they have *fewer opportunities* for engaging in deviant behavior. This conundrum raises a question that can only be resolved empirically: Are dense or sparse ego networks better for preventing the negative outcomes associated with malicious envy? The content of ties is also a factor. Sterling (2013) found that dense referent networks motivated malicious envy, but dense communication networks mitigated the relationship between malicious envy and deviant behavior.

Individuals' ego network composition can also affect the potential impact of deviant behavior on the target. If the envier has a network characterized by many connections to powerful others, then any deviant behavior is likely to be more damaging to the target. On the other hand, if the target of envy has many connections to powerful others, they provide protection from the deviant behavior.

Network cohesion. We have discussed the constraints that can be imposed upon behavior by the structure of an individual's ego network. Under the heading of "network cohesion" (direct ties), we group the potential constraints that *relationships* can impose upon behavior. The type and strength of the relationships may affect the likelihood of deviant behavior: it seems unlikely that an individual would engage in deviant behavior towards a close friend, but that is a question to be resolved empirically. There are opportunities to test how a number of potential relational constraints like strength of tie, type of relationship, multiplexity of the relationship, and asymmetry of the relationship affect the likelihood or severity of deviant behavior (Brass, 2012). It seems possible that relational constraints may act to prevent deviant behavior in the absence of organizational or network constraints.

In addition to possible relational constraints, the dependence relationship within the envier/target dyad will influence the likelihood and severity of deviant behavior. If the envier depends on the target of envy for resources or information, the envier should be less likely to engage in deviant behavior towards the target. On the other hand, if the target depends on the envier for resources or information, then any deviant behavior is likely to be much more harmful to the target.

Conclusion

Envy in organizations is an inherently social issue. Envy occurs within dyadic relationships and also within a broader social context. We propose that the social network perspective provides unique methodological and theoretical opportunities for deeper understanding of the impact of the social context within which envy and its consequences occur. There is a relative dearth of research that uses the social network perspective to examine the processes related to envy. We described a number of ways in which the social network perspective can aid in the study of social comparison processes, the development and form of envy, and the likelihood and severity of deviant behavior associated with malicious envy, with the hope of inspiring additional research on the intersection of social networks and envy in organizations.

References

Bamberger, P., & Biron, M. (2007). Group norms and excessive absenteeism: The role of peer referent others. *Organizational Behavior and Human Decision Processes, 103*(2), 179–196.

Barrick, M. R., & Mount, M. K. (1991). The big five personality dimensions and job performance: a meta-analysis. *Personnel Psychology, 44*(1), 1–26.

Borgatti, S. P., Everett, M. G., & Johnson, J. C. (2013). *Analyzing Social Networks.* SAGE Publications Limited.

Borgatti, S. P., & Foster, P. C. (2003). The network paradigm in organizational research: A review and typology. *Journal of Management, 29*(6), 991–1013.

Borgatti, S. P., & Halgin, D. S. (2011). On network theory. *Organization Science, 22*(5), 1168–1181.

Borgatti, S. P., Mehra, A., Brass, D. J., & Labianca, G. (2009). Network analysis in the social sciences. *Science, 323*(5916), 892–895.

Brass, D. (2012). A social network perspective on organizational psychology. In S. Kozlowski, Ed., *The Oxford Handbook of Organizational Psychology* (pp. 107–117). Oxford, UK: Oxford University Press. Forthcoming

Brass, D. (1984). Being in the right place: A structural analysis of individual influence in an organization. *Administrative Science Quarterly, 29*(4), 518–539.

Brass, D. J., Galaskiewicz, J., Greve, H. R., & Tsai, W. (2004). Taking stock of networks and organizations: A multilevel perspective. *Academy of Management Journal, 47*(6), 795–817.

Burkhardt, M. E., & Brass, D. J. (1990). Changing patterns or patterns of change: The effects of a change in technology on social network structure and power. *Administrative Science Quarterly, 35*(1), 104–127.

Burt, R. S. (1987). Social contagion and innovation: Cohesion versus structural equivalence. *American Journal of Sociology, 92*(6), 1287–1335.

Burt, R. S. (1992). *Structural Holes: The Social Structure of Competition.* Cambridge, MA: Harvard University Press.

Burt, R. S. (2005). *Brokerage and Closure: An Introduction to Social Capital.* Oxford: Oxford University Press.

Burt, R. S. (2010). *Neighbor Networks: Competitive Advantage Local and Personal.* Oxford: Oxford University Press.

Burt, R. S., Kilduff, M., & Tasselli, S. (2013). Social network analysis: Foundations and frontiers on advantage. *Annual Review of Psychology, 64*, 527–547.

Buunk, B. P., Collins, R. L., Taylor, S. E., VanYperen, N. W., & Dakof, G. A. (1990). The affective consequences of social comparison: Either direction has its ups and downs. *Journal of Personality and Social Psychology, 59*(6), 1238.

Cialdini, R. B., & De Nicholas, M. E. (1989). Self-presentation by association. *Journal of Personality and Social Psychology, 57*(4), 626.

Coleman, J. S. (1988). Social capital in the creation of human capital. *American Journal of Sociology*, *94*, S95–S120.

Coleman, J. S., Katz, E., & Menzel, H. (1966). *Medical Innovation: A Diffusion Study.* Indianapolis, IN: Bobbs-Merrill.

Cote, S., & Miners, C. T. (2006). Emotional intelligence, cognitive intelligence, and job performance. *Administrative Science Quarterly*, *51*(1), 1–28.

Duffy, M. K., Scott, K. L., Shaw, J. D., Tepper, B. J., & Aquino, K. (2012). A social context model of envy and social undermining. *Academy of Management Journal*, *55*(3), 643–666.

Erickson, B. H. (1988). The relational basis of attitudes. *Social Structures: A Network Approach*, *99*, 121.

Festinger, L. (1954). A theory of social comparison processes. *Human Relations*, *7*(2), 117–140.

Friedkin, N. E., & Johnsen, E. C. (1999). Social influence networks and opinion change. *Advances in Group Processes*, *16*, 1–29.

Granovetter, M. (2005). The impact of social structure on economic outcomes. *Journal of Economic Perspectives*, *19*(1), 33–50.

Granovetter, M. S. (1973). The strength of weak ties. *American Journal of Sociology*, *78*(6), 1360–1380.

Hansen, M. T. (1999). The search-transfer problem: The role of weak ties in sharing knowledge across organization subunits. *Administrative Science Quarterly*, *44*(1), 82–111.

Judge, T. A., & Bono, J. E. (2001). Relationship of core self-evaluations traits—self-esteem, generalized self-efficacy, locus of control, and emotional stability—with job satisfaction and job performance: A meta-analysis. *Journal of Applied Psychology*, *86*(1), 80.

Kilduff, M., Crossland, C., Tsai, W., & Krackhardt, D. (2008). Organizational network perceptions versus reality: A small world after all? *Organizational Behavior and Human Decision Processes*, *107*(1), 15–28.

Kilduff, M., & Krackhardt, D. (1994). Bringing the individual back in: A structural analysis of the internal market for reputation in organizations. *Academy of Management Journal*, *37*(1), 87–108.

Krackhardt, D. (1987). Cognitive social structures. *Social Networks*, *9*(2), 109–134.

Kumbasar, E., Rommey, A. K., & Batchelder, W. H. (1994). Systematic biases in social perception. *American Journal of Sociology*, *100*(2), 477–505.

Labianca, G., & Brass, D. J. (2006). Exploring the social ledger: Negative relationships and negative asymmetry in social networks in organizations. *Academy of Management Review*, *31*(3), 596–614.

Labianca, G., Brass, D. J., & Gray, B. (1998). Social networks and perceptions of intergroup conflict: The role of negative relationships and third parties. *Academy of Management Journal*, *41*(1), 55–67.

Lawrence, B. S. (2006). Organizational reference groups: A missing perspective on social context. *Organization Science*, *17*(1), 80–100.

Lin, N. (1999). Social networks and status attainment. *Annual Review of Sociology*, *25*, 467–487.

Podolny, J. M. (2001). Networks as the pipes and prisms of the market. *American Journal of Sociology, 107*(1), 33–60.

Shah, P. P. (1998). Who are employees' social referents? Using a network perspective to determine referent others. *Academy of Management Journal, 41*(3), 249–268.

Sterling, C. M. (2013). A Tale of Two Envys: A Social Network Perspective on the Consequences of Workplace Social Comparison. *Theses and Dissertations–Management.* Paper 5.

Sterling, C. M., Shah, P. P., & Labianca, G. (2015). *Keeping Up with Jones and the Rest of the Neighborhood: Social Networks and Workplace Envy.* Paper presented at the XXXV Sunbelt Social Networks Conference, June 2015, Brighton, England.

Tai, K., Narayanan, J., & McAllister, D. J. (2012). Envy as pain: Rethinking the nature of envy and its implications for employees and organizations. *Academy of Management Review, 37*(1), 107–129.

Umphress, E. E., Labianca, G., Brass, D. J., Kass, E., & Scholten, L. (2003). The role of instrumental and expressive social ties in employees' perceptions of organizational justice. *Organization Science, 14*(6), 738–753.

Valente, T. W. (1995). *Network Models of the Diffusion of Innovations.* Cresskill, NJ: Hampton Press.

van de Ven, N., Zeelenberg, M., & Pieters, R. (2011). The envy premium in product evaluation. *Journal of Consumer Research, 37*(6), 984–998.

8 | Envy, Schadenfreude, and Evaluation

UNDERSTANDING THE STRANGE GROWING
OF INDIVIDUAL PERFORMANCE APPRAISAL

BÉNÉDICTE VIDAILLET

Introduction

Some studies on workplace envy have explored the consequences of specific managerial and organizational practices, tools, and systems on the development of this emotion (Duffy, Shaw, & Schaubroeck, 2008; Nickerson & Zenger, 2008; Schaubroeck & Lam, 2004). In particular, some researchers have looked at the effects of contemporary systems of performance evaluation (Stein, 2000; Vidaillet, 2008a) based on the definition of key performance indicators, the formulation of individual objectives, performance measurement, "rewards" or "sanctions," generally accompanied by a staged comparison of employees that often leads to a ranking in which everyone is assigned a position. In such a performance appraisal system, the evaluation process is no longer just an aspect of the profession but the pivotal element supposed to structure certain aspects that, until now, were relatively independent to it. The relationship between a working individual and his/her activity on one hand (i.e., the very definition of the activity, the conception of the tasks, the organization of labor), and the institution s/he works for, on the other (i.e., what one gains from one's occupation—recognition, remuneration, etc.—in return for what one contributes) become here entirely dependent on evaluation. Conventional thought about individual performance appraisal has addressed it as a process intended to provide a rational basis for managerial decision-making about people—for instance, to determine whether employees require further training and exposure; or whether they qualify for additional pay, promotion, or some other related benefit. However, it has also been shown how harmful these practices could be to organizations, by reinforcing envy among team workers (Vidaillet, 2008a) and, as a consequence, by preventing workers from functioning collectively, by generating tension and conflicts (Stein, 2000), and by preventing bonding.

The harmful consequences of appraisal systems

The development of envy is not the only problem resulting from this type of system. First, in spite of the widespread practice of performance appraisal, its effectiveness is frequently questioned (Taylor et al., 1995): Conflicting purposes often undermine attempts at evaluation, and the flaws of the procedures used—including the use of vague qualities, irrelevant measurement criteria, superficial checklists, lack of rater training, low levels of supervisory motivation—lead to unfair evaluations (Baron & Kreps, 1999; Nurse, 2005; Rice, 1996). More importantly, "behind a mask of objectivity and rationality, executives [may] engage in much manipulation in an intentional and systematic manner" (Longnecker et al., 1996, p. 183) because "the formal appraisal process is indeed a political process, and . . . few ratings are determined without some political consideration." Hence, managerial discretion and effectiveness, not accuracy, may be the primary concern of the practicing executive in appraising subordinates. In this approach, organizations are arenas in which negotiations, networking, and the development of political strategies play an important role in determining who gets what, and within what context. What matters might very well "turn out to be not . . . how well one performs, but whom one knows" (Nurse, 2005, p. 1179). The strategies aiming at influencing the judgement of one's manager can be extremely diverse: Self-staging, flattery, self-promotion, over-zealousness, or Information Manipulation (Gardner & Martinko, 1988; Prendergast, 1993).

Second, these evaluation methods, like any management tool, can negatively affect workers' behavior and undermine their performance (Adler & Harzing, 2008; Anderson et al., 1993; Courty & Marschke, 1997). Thus, economist Maya Beauvallet (2009) compiled an inventory of the research studies showing the absurdity of many performance evaluation and incentive systems. For example, finding that a certain type of patient died regularly on the operating table, a hospital fixed a maximum quota of "losses" per surgeon; as a result of this, none of the surgeons were willing to operate on this type of patient when that fatal quota was almost reached. In the United States, a research study in the field of educational sciences (Linn, 2000) examined the States in which there existed a system whereby teachers and schools were remunerated or penalized according to the performance of their students on their tests. It appeared that in those schools, the teachers focused on teaching their students how to correctly answer the questions in the tests, rather than on teaching them fundamental knowledge and skills.

Third, although the advocates of such evaluation methods insist on their "fairness," Castilla and Benard (Castilla, 2008; Castilla & Benard, 2010) show that the opposite is often true: When an organizational culture promotes meritocracy (compared with when it does not), managers in that organization may ironically show greater bias in favor of men over equally performing women in translating employee performance evaluations into rewards and other key career outcomes. They call this the "paradox of meritocracy": "an organizational culture that prides itself on meritocracy may encourage bias by convincing managers that they themselves are unbiased, which in turn may discourage them from closely examining their own behaviors for signs of prejudice" (Castilla & Benard, 2010, p. 567).

Fourth, researchers in the field of work psychology have shown that individual performance evaluation practices and the associated series of indicators, means of standardization, contractualization, and individualization have contributed to the deterioration of people's health at work (Clot, 2010; Dejours, 2006; Dujarier, 2006): By intensifying work, by constantly raising production targets and tracking and eliminating "downtimes," which were actually periods of physical rest, of information exchange or knowledge sharing between colleagues; by reinforcing one's impression of coping alone with the increasingly testing physical and mental demands of work; and finally, by generating the discouraging feeling, among employees, of not being able to "do one's work well" because the targets to be reached are more and more constrained, standardized, and monitored.

Finally, if one looks at the situation from Foucault's perspective, one can denounce these evaluation systems as a particularly disturbing form of the "liberal art of governing" (Foucault, 2004):

> We have engaged in a society in which the power of law is not diminishing but is being integrated into a far more general type of power: That of normalization. Which implies a completely different supervision and control mechanism. Permanent visibility and classification of individuals, hierarchisation, qualification, the establishment of limits, diagnosis. (Foucault, 1994, p. 77)

Under the guise of evaluating, the aim is actually to normalize, control, and impose behaviors. In this perspective, evaluation tools pertain to new techniques used in a society in which supervision is generalized (Gori & Del Volgo, 2009).

The number of highlighted issues and criticism should in theory lead to the decline of such evaluation methods. Quite the opposite happens, in fact. A study of the human resources management practices of more than 800 American companies shows that more than 95% used individual performance assessment methods in 2002, versus 45% in 1971 (Dobbin et al., 2008). In France, a recent study of a representative sample of 1,000 staff working in private companies of more than 50 people shows that, in 2010, 73% of the staff were evaluated by such methods (Methis/IFOP, 2011). From a small initial number of American private companies such as General Electric, IBM, Rank Xerox or McDonald's, they have spread across countries to all sorts of organizations: Private, public organizations, associations; German, French, Danish. Originally restricted to specific jobs (sales) or specific functions (CEOs of publicly listed companies), they can now apply to everyone, from layman to management.

A key question is therefore to understand why, paradoxically, despite the harmful effects of the evaluation systems and the complaints they generate, most people are favorable to their development. What are their reasons? Why would people support practices that end up affecting them negatively? In this chapter, we will make the case that envy is one trigger that explains the growing demand for individual performance appraisal. Such a statement leads us to look with new eyes into the link between envy and contemporary evaluation systems: Envy is not only a consequence of those systems, but also may be partly at the root of their development.

A Brief Detour via Lacan

I base our reasoning in this chapter on the conception of envy developed by French psychoanalyst, Jacques Lacan. This conception helps analyses very precisely one's double relation to "the other," a relationship that plays a role in envy and is very useful for understanding envy in organizational contexts (Vidaillet, 2007, 2008a, 2008b): According to Lacan, envy puts into play the envious, an almost identical other, which Lacan calls the "little other," and an Other which Lacan calls the Big Other and whose gaze is captured by the little other because the latter is supposed to possess something that the envious lacks and needs in order to capture the Other's gaze and hence exist in His eyes.

Lacan addressed the question of envy by commenting on a statement by Saint Augustine (Confessions, 1, chapter 7): "I have myself observed a baby to be jealous, though it could not speak; it was livid as it watched bitterly another infant at the breast" (Lacan, 1962, session of March 14th). For Lacan, the child in this scene is not jealous, but envious. He points out that the very young child who is watching his or her infant sibling has been weaned for a long time and does not need the maternal breast any longer. It is the sight of the non-weaned brother that creates envy because this sight reminds the child of his/her own weaning; i.e., of the first severance. It is when he can see that another is usurping his own place in the relationship with the mother that the child apprehends for the first time what he is deprived of and experiences an unbearable loss. The envious child cannot find the support he needs to be able to separate from his mother, to bear the omnipresent anxiety resulting from his separation from her, and from the fact that he no longer knows what he is in her desire (or in "the Other's desire") (Lacan, 1986, 2004). In the case described by Saint Augustine, the envious child suffers from understanding for the first time that s/he has been separated from the mother and from losing what s/he was in her desire. This approach emphasizes that envy is deeply related to the gaze and that it is a three-part play (Vidaillet, 2007) involving the envious, the envied, and the third one who gazes at the envied while the envious himself gazes at this gaze. Envy must not be mistaken for jealousy, which also involves a triangle of three people. From a psychoanalytical perspective, jealousy is an emotion that is more "mature" than envy: It requires that the child be already separated from his/her mother for him/her to accept that she has relations of love with other people. Whereas in envy, the child suffers from understanding for the first time that he/she has been separated from the mother.

This approach also insists on the fact that the envious does not envy the other's possession of the prized object as such, but rather the way the other is able to enjoy this object, which is why it is not enough for him simply to steal and thus gain possession of the object. His true aim is to destroy the other's ability to enjoy the object. As Lacan-inspired philosopher Slavoj Žižek (2009) underlines,

Envy must be placed within the triad of envy, thrift, and melancholy, the three forms of not being able to enjoy the object. ... In contrast to the subject of envy, who envies the other's possession and/or *jouissance* of the object, the miser possesses the object, but cannot enjoy/consume it. ... As for the melancholic subject, like the miser he possesses the object, but he loses the reason that made him desire it. (p. 77)

Let us now talk about the demand for evaluation: Our hypothesis is that the latter is partly motivated by envy. We must therefore closely examine what, in the demand for evaluation, is at play in one's relation to the little other and to the Big Other, to the gaze, and to enjoyment.

Envy, Feeling of Injustice, and Undue Enjoyment

What is really remarkable about contemporary evaluation practices is the wish for "transparency." Of course, who would be against transparency? But if one looks a little closer, one realizes that the wish for transparency is not necessarily motivated by a noble sentiment towards others.

What facet of the other is shown to us in contemporary evaluation? Evaluation, such as we know it today, almost always goes hand in hand with open comparison; the results of the evaluation are visible, displayed in the name of transparency. One's relationship to the other is largely simplified here: It is an other that is comparable to oneself, an other whose singularity is eradicated; of this other, one only keeps what can serve as a benchmark for comparison. The aim is to differentiate oneself from this other, using well-defined criteria, thanks to which we can be openly compared, measured; to show that we can "distinguish ourselves from the rest." The aim is not so much to find out what marks we have obtained, as to compare our marks with others; it is less to get gratification for oneself than to find out exactly which gratification the others could obtain. Evaluation, in this sense, is of no interest if its results are kept secret; it is a means of situating oneself in relation to, of comparing oneself to, the other, to watch the other. Why such a desire to watch the other, to know exactly what he does and what he gets? This, according to us, is where envy may come into play.

Envy is strongly related to the supposed enjoyment of the other. What the infant desires is what he/she believes the other possesses: The total and absolute enjoyment of what he/she is deprived of. The child is all the more frustrated as he/she imagines that the other enjoys all possible satisfactions. This enjoyment cannot be shared: It is not available to the child precisely because the other has "stolen" it from him.

This is in keeping with the hypothesis according to which envy contains resentment (Heider, 1958; Parrott, 1991; Schoeck, 1969; Smith, 1991):

The people who feel envy tend to compare themselves unfavorably to other persons and to feel that the envied person is underserving of his or her advantage (Heider, 1958), or, that they, themselves are undeserving of disadvantage (Ben-Ze'ev, 2000). According to van de Ven et al. (2009), perceptions of injustice and unfairness are typically associated with the experience of malicious envy (see also Sterling, van de Ven, & Smith, Chapter 3, this volume). Envious people may also feel that the person they envy has taken away what they deserved for themselves (Schimmel, 2008). The envied advantage is perceived and felt, subjectively, as undeserved. This is very much different from pure cases of resentment proper, which has more "objective" validity (e.g., Smith, 1991; Leach, 2008). In this case, the natural anger resulting from unfair treatment can be expressed more openly, because of its objective quality. In contrast, envious resentment, being more subjective and lacking in consensual legitimacy, cannot be expressed directly.

In the context of work, one is quick to imagine that the other gets more enjoyment than oneself, does less, and gets more. She may fantasize the other as one who enjoys himself more than she, and cannot bear this idea of the other getting more if he doesn't deserve it. The performance appraisal might very well take away some of this undeserved enjoyment. The aim of appraisal systems is precisely to "lay everything on the table": To measure accurately and show openly what each one is supposed to contribute and receive, in sake of a socially acceptable cause—justice and fairness. One can imagine that evaluation will put things straight. Because the subject assumes that the other gets more enjoyment than she herself does, and undeservedly so, the demand for evaluation may hence be considered as a way of controlling the enjoyment of the other and removing his undue enjoyment (or "*surplus jouissance*" in Lacanian terms). She is prepared to be evaluated so that the other can also be; and even if the price to pay for the subject may be high, the other is fantasized as certainly losing more than she. The subject is ready to make a sacrifice if she can deprive the other from some enjoyment. This is in line with findings in experimental economics, which suggest that envy can push individuals to make efforts or to pay to alter others' position or reduce others' income, and that an envious mindset will cause people to accept less-than-optimal monetary reward as long as another participant's advantage is reduced (Zizzo, 2008; see also Celse, Chapter 14, this volume). Ironically, the result is that envy can motivate people to act in way that reduces the absolute level of their possible outcomes. If envy leads them to introduce individual performance appraisal systems, the loss may be high if we consider all the problems described at the beginning of this chapter: Loss of autonomy, increased control, inappropriate targets, impossibility to work as a team, loss of motivation, and so on.

In a study of the opinion of workers from several companies about individual performance appraisal systems recently introduced (Vidaillet, 2013), the results show that after first complaining about increased pressure and loss of autonomy, they ended up justifying the new system by stating a specific case: The case of "Mr. Do-Nothing" who spoiled the motivation of all the staff in the department, because he did nothing, was paid like everybody else, and no one said anything. Evaluation was supposed to eliminate the Do-Nothings by getting them back on the straight and narrow. Or the case of that "Mrs. Goody-Two-Shoes," who took all the credit, and was always pretending that everything happened thanks to her! Individualized evaluation would for sure put things and the Mrs. Goody-Two-Shoes back in their place.

Our point here is not to suggest that Mr. Do-Nothing and Mrs. Goody-Two-Shoes don't exist, but to highlight that the systematic appearance of these cases, whatever the company and the work context, leads us to believe that it refers to the fantasy of an other imagined to be an "enjoyment robber" (or *"jouissance* robber" in more Lacanian terms) (Žižek, 2009), which is a key mechanism of envy. According to Lacan, fantasy is a narrative structure whose content can vary greatly, which rests on the imaginary promise of recapturing lost enjoyment, but also on a key element: The obstacle that explains the loss of enjoyment (Žižek, 2009). In the cases described above, the obstacle manifests itself in the form of the people accused of taking and receiving more than they should, and hence, of provoking lack of motivation and discouragement among their colleagues. Evaluation thus leaves the impression that such feelings could be overcome as the lost enjoyment could be recaptured.

Envy and the Secretive Side of Work

This fantasy of an other being an "enjoyment robber" can be supplemented by an element specific to the workplace. Researchers in work psychology have demonstrated something that may seem strange or counterintuitive: In order to do one's work properly, one must also be able to conceal certain things (Clot, 2010; Dejours, 2003; Molinier, 2008). Indeed, while working consists of filling the gap that constantly occurs between what is prescribed and the reality of the situation, "doing one's work properly" requires, most of the time, that one break some rule. For instance, it is impossible to comply with all the rules and requirements at the same time; indeed, some rules inevitably contradict others, and one has to choose which one to comply with in such a situation. To some degree, therefore, working implies playing with the rules, which is often necessary in order to be able to work properly. This play sometimes becomes part of the "tricks of the trade," (i.e., used on a regular basis). This behavior, by revealing the contradictions inherent in ordinary work,

> makes it perfectly understandable that s/he who has not given up doing her/
> his work properly, therefore zealously, showing initiative and originality,
> quickly learns that s/he will have to exercise his/her intelligence away from
> the eyes of the hierarchy, sometimes of her/his peers or even of her/his sub-
> ordinates, or s/he will have to ensure their complicity and loyalty, which is
> not that simple. Being able to exercise intelligence at work requires discre-
> tion. (Dejours, 2003, p. 17)

Each individual will have developed her/his own tricks, will have learned to hide these tricks and to keep the secret.

But the secret can become intolerable. Knowing that everything is not exposed can soon lead a subject to fantasize about this secret inherent to the other, to the person one works with or who works in the office or department next door. The other may be suspected to use his secrets, not in order to do his job properly, but on the contrary, to "take advantage of the system," to misuse it to his advantage, to do less work, to clear off, etc. The problem with this secretive dimension, which is normally part of ordinary work, lies in the fact that it may excite the fantasy that the other uses this gray area to enjoy more than us. This certainly explains the success of the idea of "transparency" that comes with evaluation: The promise of evaluation is that everything everyone does, what everyone gets up to on the sly, how they take advantage of the system, will be revealed, brought into the open.

Let us also note that envy is associated with a sense of scarcity (Foster, 1972; Lindholm, 2008): What is given to one is necessarily taken away from the other, and there cannot be enough of it for everyone. This is the reason why envy can intensify when resources have to be shared, particularly when they are scarce and/or diminishing. In contemporary evaluation practices, this notion of scarcity and of the necessity to distribute resources thriftily is central. The discourse used to justify the implementation of these practices underlines the necessity to economize and to tighten budgets, reserves, and pools of productivity to be exploited, etc. The overall budget will not increase; it might even be cut; but in any case, those who get good results have nothing to fear, and they will be rewarded according to their merit. This discourse about the growing scarcity of resources may foster envy, which in turn may activate the demand for evaluation: "Put in place individual performance evaluation procedures to ensure that what's left of the cake is shared fairly! We can no longer afford to waste and to give to those who do not deserve to get." And therefore "transparency" is highlighted as a way to avoid waste and injustice.

Stealing the Other's Tricks

As presented previously, the secretive side of work may encourage the subject to imagine that their colleagues use their secrets to misuse the system to their advantage and get undeserved enjoyment. Another consequence is that the person would really like to uncover the little secrets, the ropes, the tricks of the trade, which the other has learned. So it's no longer about imagining that the other is better off than oneself; it's about stealing his/her secret so as to benefit from it.

Evaluation often goes hand in hand with showing models and with benchmarking. This involves identifying existing "best practices" in order to implement them and use them as the referent model on the basis of which evaluation will be performed. This generally implies that the following questions are answered: Who are the best employees? What do they do in order to be the best? What in their practices can be used and transmitted to other workers? In an extract of a documentary on work that was very successful in France (Viallet, 2009), a consultant paid by a company (Fenwick) goes with a "top salesman," a "referent," to clients; the consultant observes and then interviews this salesman so that the latter explains the reasons why he has behaved in such and such a manner with the client: The objective then being to teach the other salesmen the practices thus revealed and formalized and to raise the performance level expected from the employees—who are now supposed to have become excellent. Isn't it wonderful to be able to appropriate the know-how of this excellent salesman, to be able to capture this "extra something" he is supposed to possess, that secret which at the moment he alone enjoys? All of a sudden, every salesman can now appropriate, equip himself with the know-how that top salesman has built, more or less tacitly, over years of practice; every employee can now become excellent. Isn't that what one dreams of—stealing from the other the secret of his success, obtaining the magic ring one dreams of having for oneself? That "extra something" that the other is supposed to possess: That is what is involved in envy (Vidaillet, 2008b). One always believes that the other, the one one envies, holds the secret of success. And this is what is promised to the employees with evaluation: Evaluation procedures are implemented to "help them improve themselves"; everyone will be able to benefit from those good practices, to put them into place, and it is on this basis that they will be evaluated. It is out of the question that only a few workers possess them. So our hypothesis here is that one may ask for evaluation so that one can capture that "extra something" the other is supposed to possess and that makes him better than oneself.

Envy and Instability of Places

Before contemporary evaluation practices were developed, there were still grading, ranking, or comparison practices, involving evaluation at some stage—for instance, under the form of competitive examinations, which people belonging to well-defined hierarchies underwent in order to move from one category to another. In those cases, comparison and evaluation result in permanent changes in position; they are changes in the symbolic order: They are controlled, there are rites of passage; the conditions of passage are very demanding, and when one moves up a category, one cannot move back down again. These distinctions are often a necessary step to get more distinctions or marks of recognition. And one cannot change categories whenever one wants to; there are specific times for this; and generally these moments are relatively rare: For example, French school children are evaluated—with the baccalaureate examination—on the knowledge they have acquired at the end of secondary-school. All this creates symbolic borders and separations. But this isn't fun. We know that one needs time to change categories. We know that if the other is in one place and we are not, it might be difficult to change this hierarchical order. We have to tolerate the difference and the gaps.

What Do Contemporary Evaluation Practices in Organizations Offer Us?

By breaking up time into very short periods, and by organizing, within these periods, competitions in which, supposedly, everything can be replayed, contemporary evaluation practices tend to make work feel like huge, endless gambling matches or like video game sessions that follow one after another indefinitely. They have the characteristic of assigning a highly fluid position, which is—unlike the status that is linked with a position within a career—*not* long-term oriented. No stable expectations of recognition can be deduced from this position, as the performance appraisal and the ranking that generally follows always refer to a certain point in time and are therefore tagged as temporary, short-lived, reversible. The only thing that counts seems to be your results at time t. An individual may be bad one day, but could become the best the day after if he puts in the necessary effort. Or he might do well today, but this does not mean anything in the future because what he will have achieved before will not be taken into account when he is evaluated.

Hence, when introduced, contemporary evaluation systems can have a radical impact on existing work positions. Sociologist Nicolas Belorgey (2010) uses the case of hospital emergency services: An evaluation system has been introduced, aiming to increase the staff productivity through quantitative and measurable targets, supported by financial rewards. The main performance indicator is the patient's waiting time, which must be reduced as much as possible (ironically, using pre-existing data, Belorgey shows that shorter waiting times statistically increase the chance one will have to come back later). The staff from one hospital are ranked according to this indicator, as are the chief doctors nationwide. Belorgey reports a meeting of the chief doctors: Professor Dumont, a renowned 50-year-old university professor, who is a high-ranking member of the institution, ends up being lectured for "bad behavior." He is advised to follow the example of 30-year-old Dr. Dupre, a low-ranking doctor in a small-town hospital, who gets much better results according to this indicator (but whose return rate is also much higher, which is not taken into account in the evaluation method). While traditional ranking systems give us clearly defined positions and define mandatory steps to achieve higher positions, the new evaluation systems can magically lift such constraints, disturb the old order, blur the positions. When young Dr. Dupre should normally have waited years, passed many exams, changed hospitals in order to slowly climb the ladder, he suddenly becomes a star thanks to the new performance evaluation system.

The evaluation system provides a supposedly neutral ranking that suddenly questions the position of the one who was previously enjoying a dominating position and whose fame and skills get challenged. The evaluation systems can apparently trigger the fall of the powerful, whose position previously seemed unquestionable. It can supposedly highlight the true value, expose the truth. And the happy ones are not only the beneficiaries of the systems, like Dr. Dupre, but also the ones that attend the show, enjoying the humiliation and the fall of the powerful, already waiting for the next ranking, when today's winner will inevitably also hit the ground.

Behind the support for contemporary evaluation systems and its apparent quest for fairness, one may see the sign of a more shadowy and counter-intuitive feeling: *Schadenfreude*. This is the feeling of hoping for and enjoying the other's misfortune, when the other had an attribute that one does not have and then loses it or is deprived of what he seemed to enjoy. The key benefit of such evaluation systems is that the other cannot acquire anything stable, that no position can be maintained forever. Powell et al. (2008) explain why envy is so closely linked to schadenfreude:

> Envy is a painful emotion derived from the presence of a desired attribute in another person, and, therefore, the pain is relieved, pleasantly, by something that harms the possessor of this attribute. . . . In fact, the more one considers the nature of envy, the more fitting it seems that an envied person's misfortune should be pleasing. . . . The social comparison foundations of envy mean that misfortunes befalling an envied person should alter the social comparison matrix in the envying person's favor. Sometimes the reversal of fortunes is complete and may turn advantage to disadvantage. (p. 150)

Furthermore, the hostility associated with dominance that one finds in envy may sometimes come about because one's early upbringing fosters an extravagant view of the self that ultimately failed to be confirmed by actual achievement and social evaluations (Sullivan, 1956; Powell et al., 2008). The implementation of an individual performance appraisal system can create the hope for a person to finally get adequately recognized. This may also be a conclusion from Nicolas Belorgey's study that looks into the reasons why the evaluation system in the emergency services may be approved or rejected: The opponents to the system are usually the ones with the highest professional or social recognition, the "Established" ones, as defined by Elias and Scotson (1994); the ones who approve of the evaluation system are normally less recognized and can be classified as the "Outsiders." Interviews with the Outsiders show a certain bitterness or lack of satisfaction with their position, and highlight their hopes that things will change thanks to the new system.

Finally, another possible mechanism by which envious considerations could motivate the request for such evaluation systems has to do with the desire for instant gratification. Watkins (2004) claims that those predisposed to gratitude may, since they are predisposed to a thankful mindset, be more willing to wait for gratification, while those less disposed to gratitude may be less able to control their urges. As highlighted above, contemporary evaluation systems split work processes into a chain of competitive sessions amongst workers, with the promise of quick and calibrated rewards whereby everyone could know precisely what they will gain; while traditional hierarchical systems are based on longer-term evaluation and less frequent rewards.

Being Under the Permanent Gaze of the Other

Another potential link between envy and the demand for evaluation systems may be related to the central place of the Other's gaze in envy. To understand this link, let's return to the crucial moment in childhood when the child will separate himself from his mother (the first Other). According to Lacan, this occurs when the child understands that he exists also outside of the image of himself his mother's gaze is sending to him. What he will definitively lose at this moment is what he was in her desire. The fact of not knowing what one is in the Other's desire is accompanied by an omnipresent anxiety (Lacan, 1973, 1986). The kernel of this anxiety is the absolute uncertainty as regards what he is now for the Other: He doesn't know who he is, as he doesn't know what he is for the Other, what he is in the Other's desire. But this questioning is also precisely what will cause the child's own desire.

What characterizes the envious is the fact that he cannot do without the Other's gaze. What the envious desires is to capture the gaze of the Other who is the only one who can give him the illusion of being "complete" (lacking nothing), and the feeling of existing (Vidaillet, 2008b). Imagining that the Other turns her gaze away from him to look at an other leaves him with a horrible feeling of being erased, eradicated. His uncertainty about his identity is then too strong, and, instead of making space for his own desire, generates unbearable and extremely painful anxiety.

With contemporary evaluation mechanisms, the person gets to be under the constant gaze of this "big Other." This gaze can materialize under the form of very sophisticated tools and information systems that are able to capture a huge number of data concerning the evaluated person, hence making visible things that no human eyes could ever detect. This omnipresent gaze can also appear under the form of the "mystery shopper" in charge of gathering and analyzing specific information about products and services; or of the "normal" client whose opinion is permanently sought.

The Other is not only watching what workers are doing and what they produce; "He" gives an appreciation, assigns precise values, which can then be translated into incentives, promotions, etc. This feedback may come from managers. Hence, the chief executive officer (CEO) of Carglass, talking about the firm's employees, explains in a documentary that *"for them (the 'co-workers') to be happy, . . . they need a boss who's capable of helping them develop, of pushing, coaching them, that is to say to tell them when they're doing well and when they're not."* Further on, a human resources manager—who trains the managers of Carglass centers—says: *"The notion of acknowledgement of the people we work with, implies that one . . . tells them when things are fine but also when they're not. 'There are things we're happy with . . . well done' (he claps his hands); and then 'there are things we're not happy about, so . . . it's not well done'"* (Viallet, 2009).

It also frequently happens that this feedback does not come from a "real" Other. For instance, in a restaurant chain, all restaurants are evaluated monthly; many performance indicators are used, and at the end of each appraisal session, the computer gives marks from one to ten according to how successful the restaurant has been in achieving its objectives. When they are interviewed, the employees say: *"It's very inspiring, because once you've put the data into the computer, you have to wait for the answer and then you know if you're doing well or not! What is ok and what isn't ok. That's the only motivating thing in this job"* (Montchatre, 2011).

The link between evaluation and gaze has been widely commented on by researchers who use the thought of Michel Foucault to denounce how disciplinary and normative power is exercised through evaluation systems (Gori & Del Vogo, 2009). But this conception does not allow us to understand why people may seek this gaze, and why they are waiting for this feedback on what they are supposed to be. From what does the subject feel he can escape by entrusting the Other with defining "what is ok" and "what isn't ok" about him? From the anxiety that comes with his desire; from this part of himself that makes him move but escapes him. It is difficult to cope with the anxiety of not knowing what we are in the Other's desire, and at the same time to be affected by this desire. The illusion brought about by contemporary evaluation practices is to believe that it might be possible to escape this anxiety. And as the envious are particularly prone to feel that anxiety, our hypothesis is therefore that envy may prompt the subject to ask to be evaluated, so as to feel that he is always under the Other's gaze and to hope that he can avoid the anxiety of never knowing exactly "who he is."

An Other to Give Enjoyment

The envious wants to capture the Other's gaze, so as to feel that he exists, but also to ensure that the Other takes enjoyment in seeing him. What the envious would like is to completely fulfil the Other's desire, so that the Other then has no need to look anywhere else. The envious believes that the condition for him to stop feeling the lack, for him to feel whole, is to enable the Other himself to not lack anything. In the scene described by Saint Augustine and commented on by Lacan, the envious child suffers from seeing his mother look with such pleasure at his younger brother whom she is breastfeeding. The issue here is not that the older child is not given the breast (he was weaned a long time ago), but that he has lost his mother's gaze and with it the illusion of entirely fulfilling her, of being his mother's unique object of desire.

In this story, as Lacan puts it, "there is a big Other to give pleasure [*jouissance*] to." Thus, our hypothesis here is that the fantasy of being the one who gives the Other enjoyment, which is at play in envy, is where the demand for evaluation comes from. Who, in evaluation, is this big Other to give enjoyment? It may be the manager. It may also be the client. He is the One whom one must ultimately answer to, the One one wants to please completely and fully. That's Him, the Other who wants His money's worth and Whom the subject has to please whatever the cost. The figure of the king-client (Dujarier, 2006) justifies the whole evaluation chain. It is in order to satisfy Him that the subject is evaluated and that the latter accepts being evaluated. Thus, in Carglass (Viallet, 2009), during a training seminar for new employees, the trainer explains: *"We want every single client who contacts Carglass to say 'Wow, that was an exceptional experience! I really didn't expect, when I contacted a place like Carglass, to experience this level of proximity, of service quality.' The way you answer the phone—don't we often say that it is the first impression that counts—well, you're the one who's going to create this first impression. This is why we say that your role is crucial."*

And when it comes to activities that do not have to do with objects, but directly with people, when the activities are about caring, educating, protecting, searching, when they involve public money, the trap works even better. Thus, there is a Society, a Citizen, supposedly crouching in the shadows, obsessed about being "accounted to," able to infallibly judge one's results, judge what is produced for Him, assess the usefulness of what is done by those who conceive of themselves as great tools serving the Other's enjoyment.

Conclusions

In this chapter we have tried to understand a very strange fact: Contemporary evaluation systems have spread across countries to all sorts of organizations despite the complaints and criticism they generate. We have assumed that the growing demand for individual performance appraisal may be partly motivated by envious feelings that develop at the workplace. Evaluation systems may then be regarded as a very interesting social phenomenon: Partly motivated by envy, a taboo and unavowable emotion, they cannot be justified as such; hence their development is in general supported by noble and rational statements such as the quest for fairness or transparency.

However, we should not forget another very important link between envy and individual performance appraisal systems: As mentioned in the introduction, they can also trigger envy. Which then creates a vicious circle: Envy being potentially at the root of systems that will then strengthen it. This confirms that envy is an emotion that no society can claim to get rid of, especially when the way to cope with it underestimates its destructive potential and misjudges its functioning.

References

Adler, N., & Harzing, A.-W. (2008). When knowledge wins: Transcending the sense and nonsense of academic rankings. *Academy of Management Learning & Education*, *8*(1), 72–95.

Anderson, K., Burkhauser, R., & Raymond, J. (1993). The effect of creaming on placement rates under the Job Training Partnership Act. *Industrial and Labor Relations Review*, *46*(4), 613–624.

Baron, J. M., & Kreps, D. M. (1999). *Strategic Human Resources: Frameworks for General Managers*. New York: Wiley.

Beauvallet, M. (2009). *Les stratégies absurdes: Comment faire pire en croyant faire mieux*. Paris: Seuil.

Belorgey, N. (2010). *L'hôpital sous pression: Enquête sur le nouveau management public*. Paris: La Découverte.

Castilla, E. J. (2008). Gender, race, and meritocracy in organizational careers. *American Journal of Sociology*, *113*, 1479–1526.

Castilla, E. J., & Benard, S. (2010). The paradox of meritocracy in organizations. *Administrative Science Quarterly*, *55*, 543–576.

Clot, Y. (2010). *Le travail à cœur*. Paris: La Découverte.

Courty, P., & Marschke, G. (1997). Measuring government performance: Lessons from a federal job-training program. *The American Economic Review*, *87*(2), 383–388.

Dejours, C. (2003). *L'évaluation du travail à l'épreuve du reel*. Paris: INRA éditions.

Dobbin, F., Schrage, D., & Kalev, A. (2008). Someone to Watch Over Me: Coupling, Decoupling, and Unintended Consequences in Corporate Equal Opportunity. Paper presented at the American Sociological Association Meeting, Boston, MA.

Dujarier, M. A. (2006). *L'idéal au travail*. Paris: P.U.F.

Duffy, M. K., Shaw, J. D., & Schaubroeck, J. M. (2008). Envy in organizational life. In R. H. Smith, Ed., *Envy: Theory and Research* (pp. 167–189). Oxford University Press.

Elias, N., & Scotson, J. L. (1994). *The Established and the Outsiders*. London: Sage.

Foster, G. M. (1972). The anatomy of envy: a study in symbolic behaviour. *Current Anthropology*, *13*(2), 165–201.

Foucault, M. (1994). L'extension sociale de la norme. *Dits et écrits. t. III* (pp. 74–79). Paris, Gallimard.

Foucault, M. (2004). *Naissance de la biopolitique. Cours au Collège de France, 1978–1979*. Paris, Gallimard.

Gardner, W. L., & Martinko, M. J. (1988). Impression management in organizations. *Journal of Management*, *14*(2), 321–338.

Gori, R., & Del Volgo, M. J. (2009). L'idéologie de l'évaluation: un nouveau dispositif de servitude volontaire? *Nouvelle Revue de psychosociologie*, *2*(8), 11–26.

Heider, F. (1958). *The Psychology of Interpersonal Relations*. New York: John Wiley.

Lacan, J. (1962). L'identification. Le séminaire. Livre IX (unpublished).

Lacan, J. (1986). *L'éthique de la psychanalyse. Le séminaire. Livre VII. 1959–1960*. Paris: Seuil.

Lacan, J. (2004). *L'angoisse. Le séminaire. Livre X. 1962–1963*. Paris: Seuil.

Leach, C. W. (2008). Envy, inferiority, and injustice: Three bases for anger about inequality. In R. H. Smith, Ed., *Envy: Theory and Research* (pp. 94–116). New York: Oxford University Press.

Lindholm, C. (2008). Culture and envy. In R. H. Smith, Ed., *Envy: Theory and Research* (pp. 227–244). New York: Oxford University Press.

Linn, R. (2000). Assessments and accountability. *Educational Researcher*, *29*(2), 4–16.

Longnecker, C. O., Sims, H. P., & Gioia, D. A. (1996). Behind the mask: The politics of employee appraisal. In G. R. Ferris & M. R. Buckley, Eds., *Human Resources Management: Perspectives. Context. Functions and Outcomes* (3rd ed., pp. 183–195. Englewood Cliffs, NJ: Prentice Hall.

Methys/IFOP (2011). Les salariés et la performance après la crise. Available at http://www.methys.com/docs/PresentationMETHYS.pdf

Molinier, P. (2008). *Les enjeux psychiques du travail. Introduction à la psychodynamique de travail*. Paris: Payot.

Montchatre, M. (2011). Ce que l'évaluation fait au travail—Normalisation du client et mobilisation différentielle des collectifs dans des chaînes hôtelières. *Actes de la recherche en sciences sociales*, *189*(September), 42–57.

Nickerson, J., & Zenger, T. (2008). Envy, comparison costs, and the economic theory of the firm. *Strategic Management Journal, 29*(13), 1429–1449

Nurse, L. (2005). Performance appraisal, employee development and organizational justice: Exploring the linkages. *International Journal of Human Resource Management, 16*(7), 1176–1194.

Parrott, W. G. (1991). The emotional experiences of envy and jealousy. In P. Salovey, Ed., *The Psychology of Jealousy and Envy* (pp. 3–30). New York: Guilford.

Powell, C. A. J., Smith, R. H., & Schurtz, D. R. (2008). *Schadenfreude* caused by an envied person's pain. In R. H. Smith, Ed., *Envy: Theory and Research* (pp. 148–164). New York: Oxford University Press.

Prendergast, C. (1993). A theory of "yes men." *The American Economic Review, 83*(4), 757–771.

Rice, B. (1996). Performance review: The job nobody likes. In G. R. Ferris & M. R. Buckley, Eds., *Human Resources Management: Perspectives. Context. Functions and Outcomes* (3rd ed., pp. 213–232). Englewood Cliffs, NJ: Prentice Hall.

Schaubroeck, J., & Lam, S. S. K. (2004). Comparing lots before and after: Promotion rejectees' invidious reactions to promotes. *Organizational Behavior and Human Decision Processes, 94*, 33–47.

Schimmel, S. (2008). Envy in Jewish thought and literature. In R. H. Smith, Ed., *Envy: Theory and Research* (pp. 17–38). New York: Oxford University Press.

Schoeck, H. (1969). *Envy: A Theory of Social Behavior.* New York: Harcourt, Brace, & World.

Smith, R. H. (1991). Envy and the sense of injustice. In P. Salovey, Ed., *Psychological Perspectives on Jealousy and Envy* (pp. 79–99). New York: Guilford.

Stein, M. (2000). "Winners" training and its trouble. *Personnel Review, 29*(4), 445–460.

Sullivan, H. S. (1956). *Clinical Studies in Psychiatry.* New York: W.W. Norton.

Taylor, M. S., Tracy, K. B., Renard, M. K., Harrison, J. K., & Carroll, S. J. (1995). Due process in performance appraisal: A quasi-experiment in procedural justice. *Administrative Science Quarterly, 40*, 495–523.

Van de Ven, N., Zeelenberg, M., & Pieters, R. (2009). Leveling up and down: The experiences of benign and malicious envy. *Emotion, 9*(3), 419–429.

Viallet, J. R. (2009). *La mise à mort du travail.* Yami 2 Productions.

Vidaillet, B. (2007). A Lacanian theory's contribution to the study of workplace envy: A case study. *Human Relations, 60*(11), 1669–1700.

Vidaillet, B. (2008a). *Workplace Envy.* London: Palgrave McMillan.

Vidaillet, B. (2008b). Psychoanalytic contributions to understanding envy: Classic and contemporary contributions. In R. H. Smith, Ed., *Envy: Theory and Research* (pp. 267–89). New York: Oxford University Press.

Vidaillet, B. (2013). *Evaluez-moi! Evaluation au travail: les ressorts d'une fascination.* Paris: Seuil.

Watkins, P. C. (2004). Gratitude and subjective well-being. In R. A. Emmons & M. E. McCullough, Eds., *The Psychology of Gratitude* (pp. 167–192). New York: Oxford University Press.

Žižek, S. (2009). *Violence.* London: Profile Books.

Zizzo, D. J. (2008). The cognitive and behavioral economics of envy. In R. H. Smith, Ed., *Envy: Theory and Research* (pp. 190–210). New York: Oxford University Press.

9 | Envy and Its Dynamics in Groups and Organizations

H. SHMUEL ERLICH*

> Envy is more irreconcilable than hatred.
>
> *—François de la Rochefoucauld (1613–1680)*
>
> Envy is the tax which all distinction must pay.
>
> *—Ralph Waldo Emerson (1909)*

I N THIS CHAPTER, I SET MYSELF the task of looking at the phenomenon of envy as it pertains to and occurs in groups, institutions, and organizations from a psychoanalytic perspective, informed by group relations methodology and experience. I will focus on such questions as: Can we meaningfully speak of envy of groups and organizations (i.e., large numbers of people) beyond the envious individual? And if so, what might be the manifestations and the underlying dynamics of such envy? Finally, what ways and means are available to us if we wish to combat or to minimize such envy? Would such a project be feasible at all, or should we give it up before we get started?

One of the difficulties we immediately face concerns the term "envy" itself. Envy is certainly one of the oldest and most universally known feelings. If, as la Rochefoucauld suggests, it is more resistant to reconciliation than hate, then it is even earlier to develop and more primitive than hate (it is interesting to note that Freud had indeed suggested that hate was earlier than love). And if, as Emerson (1909) says, "envy is the tax that all distinction must pay," then envy is the inevitable accompaniment of the awareness of differences. It must therefore be true that perceived developmental

* Sigmund Freud Professor of Psychoanalysis (Emeritus), The Hebrew University of Jerusalem; Training and Supervising Analyst, Israel Psychoanalytic Society; Board Representative, IPA; founding member of OFEK, Israel Association for the Study of Group and Organizational Processes.

advances that lead towards greater differentiation (in and from others) also contribute to the creation and inflation of envy.

There is no question that when we speak of envy we are in the sphere of the purest, probably most primitive and deeply rooted, emotionality. I would not be surprised if in the future we discover that this emotional upheaval has a primordial evolutionary and neuropsychological basis (Dvash et al., 2010) and that we share certain forms of envy with other animals (Range et al., 2009).

This mammalian rock-bottom emotional root out of which envy differentiates is in some measure also reflected in linguistic usage. In biblical Hebrew, the same root (KANO) denotes envy, jealousy, and zealousness; such as, for instance, in God being El KANA, translated as a "jealous God," but probably more appropriately as a "zealous" one. In English there is a linguistic overlap, as well as differentiation, between *envy* and *jealousy*, and a verbal affinity between "*jealous*" and "*zealous*." This seems to parallel the German overlapping meanings of *Neid* with the various forms and connotations of *Eifer, Eiferer, eifern,* and *Eifersucht.* All these linguistic terms imply or suggest, in addition to envy, great agitation and a rising fury that might spill over into action, but also be expressed in pain and withholding. These linguistic relationships must reflect a common psychological (and perhaps psychophysical) root for the experience of agitation, arousal, and pain.

Melanie Klein, in her groundbreaking work *Envy and Gratitude* (1957), was aware of these close yet different linguistic meanings, and dealt with them by making a distinction between envy, as the more primitive, pre-Oedipal and pernicious feeling, and jealousy as the more advanced Oedipal state.

We have to note, however, that all these different meanings of envy refer to the *individual*, his psyche and his inner world and emotional feeling tones. We cannot escape the observation that, like other emotions, envy belongs to the individual level. How, then, is it possible to speak of "envy" in the sphere of groups, institutions, and organizations? What might be the meaning of such an attribution? These are difficult questions that may require a certain shifting and refocusing of our thinking.

The first notable issue has to do with what is meant by a "group": Is it simply the aggregate of the individuals who make it up, or some new entity or level? If we have the first meaning in mind—that is, the group as a collection of the individuals who constitute it—then we can speak of a given state or emotion only insofar as it pertains to particular individuals in the group. We cannot speak of the *group* as being envious, unless, of course, we may by some ingenious way either assume and ascertain that all, or at least the vast majority of, the individuals in the group actually feel envious. This approach to the understanding of the group was taken by Freud in his pioneering psychoanalytic discourse on group processes, *Group Psychology and the Analysis of the Ego* (1921). I have described this approach as "summation" (Erlich, 1996), since it focuses on the individual psyche and regards group events and states as "summed up" across the numerous individuals that contribute to it.

A rather different understanding of the group as entity was suggested by Bion (1961), who treated it as a new unity and an emergent phenomenon. Employing Kleinian concepts, he saw the meaning of what transpires in the group as reflected in the transference of the *group as a whole* to the analyst or leader, analogous to the individual patient's relatedness to the analyst or the infant to its mother. This enabled Bion to speak of a "group mind" and of the "group-as-a-whole" phenomenon, observable in the transference. The crucial difference and advance this implies is that it enables us to understand what an individual group member does or says as, not merely representing his/her particular and unique self, but also as reflecting an underlying group feeling or position; namely, the *basic assumption* (unconscious) of the group at the moment. Bion (1961) described three such basic group assumptions: BA Dependency, BA Pairing, and BA Fight-Flight. All three labels refer to what the group is unconsciously engaged in. The unconscious basic assumption behavior describes what is actually going on in the group mind, which differs from its declared adaptive and rational task, referred to as the *Work Group*. I described this new emergent level as "*organismic*," since it regards the group as a new organism and a living entity in its own right (Erlich, 1996).

As many other chapters in this book exemplify, there is already a notable body of research in social and organizational psychology that deals with envy at the organizational and group level. These researches are based on studies conducted from what I referred to above as the "summative" perspective; that is, with envy as a manifestation of the envy of *individuals* within an organization. These studies suggest that envy stems from what are essentially well-known sources, such as competition, lack of adequate resources and supplies, feelings of being shortchanged and overlooked, or being the object of unequal treatment within the organization. The remedies offered for these manifestations of envy are equally straightforward: they call for greater transparency of organizational structure and bureaucracy, more evenhandedness in allocating responsibilities and rewards, increasing democratization by leveling organizational authority and structure, and more openness and impartiality in handling individual ambitions for advancement. Since envy is seen to stem from understandable and justified social causes and to express the individual's reaction to such deprivations, the legitimate and understandable solution is in the direction of removing and ameliorating the causes of frustration, anger, and envy as much as possible. Perhaps the suggestion, which has become a trend in the current organizational world, to level and flatten the organizational structure and hierarchy (e.g., Rajan & Wulf, 2006) is one illustration of a solution that carries within it the danger of exacerbating the inherent problems, a theme I will come back to.

The approach described rests, not only upon a conception of the group as consisting of the sum of the individuals in it, but also upon a deeper conception, and possibly a misconception, about human nature. Yet this point of view is prevalent in academic circles and among both professionals and the public. In many ways it represents a pre-Freudian or early-Freudian (that is, a pre-psychoanalytic) point of view that extols and relies heavily on the rational and enlightened sides of human beings. Envy in this view represents a reactive emotional response to frustration and lack, to absence and shortage, and generally to unfavorable comparisons. It follows that if these underlying causes would be eliminated, or at least ameliorated, these powerful feelings would also diminish and perhaps even disappear. Therefore, a better, more impartial, egalitarian, and evenhanded distribution of supplies and means would significantly contribute to such rectification.

Taking Melanie Klein's view, as an example of one who was opposed to this stance, we can say that, as far as the individual human being and his psyche are concerned, the above-described stance falls sadly short of the truth in terms of what we actually meet in people. In Klein's view, envy is not only fundamental and primary, but *inevitable*. The major thrust of Klein's discovery about envy is that it does not stem merely from loss, lack, and deprivation of love and love-supplies, but, far more fundamentally, from its opposite—from the very fulfillment and satisfaction of desire. In this far-reaching conception of envy (as distinguished from jealousy!) the infant's envy is aroused by the very fullness and abundance of the breast that he is offered and receives. It is not a matter of "not having," but of "having." It is what the breast *contains* and *offers* that arouses the greed and insatiability of the infant, along with the powerful wish to possess it and extract from it, forcefully and agitatedly, that which he desires and it has to offer. The breast arouses his zeal and *Eifer* (i.e., his agitated and aroused desire), as much as his *Eifersucht* (i.e., his envy and greed). It is a powerful motive force, born of the drives that are inherent in the infant as human being that sweep him along a course of destructive, possessive, eviscerating desire, at the very same time that it leads to fulfillment and satiation. Actual maternal behavior may soften and alleviate this thrust of envy to some extent, or contribute to making it worse; but it *cannot* entirely prevent or preempt it. The solution takes place internally (and not externally) when the child, in the depressive position, becomes more capable of combining and integrating his love and his hate, developing a new way of relating to the object of desire in less intentionally harmful ways. Yet once again, even at this stage, everything is far from paradisiacal, since envy has now been supplanted by guilt about the aggressive wishes previously directed at the object.

Broadly speaking, therefore, psychoanalysis, certainly in its "classical," i.e., Freudian, Kleinian, and Bionian formulations, tells us that envy in its early, primitive sense is essentially unavoidable. It is the corollary of desire and drive, rather than of external circumstances. The question is not *whether* it will happen, but *how* powerful, pernicious, and destructive it will be, and *what* may, to some extent, alleviate it. There seems to be little question that this is true at the level of the individual. But can we observe the same phenomenon at the group and organizational levels?

A pertinent example comes to mind, which may help throw some light on this question: the belief that envy, as well as other ill feelings and emotional problems, is the product of social circumstances, led to the utopian idea of communal life, best exemplified by the kibbutz movement (see Gressel, Chapter 17, this volume). The kibbutz was designed, among other aims, to overcome and uproot the various maladies of human nature, which were ideologically attributed to the ills of "bourgeois society." It represented a social movement and an organization of group life in which communal ideals were to replace and heal individual neurotic shortcomings, such as possessiveness and envy, but also sexual inhibition, Oedipal rivalries, and incestuous longings (Rosner & Tannenbaum, 1987; Sosis & Ruffle, 2004). In brief, everything that stems from instinctual strivings that were seen as leading to psychopathology on both the individual and group levels was to be uprooted and replaced by a newly created ego-ideal of devotion to the group and its ideals, such as Zionism, shared labor and responsibilities, and the building of a new, freer, and better society. It is noteworthy that the early kibbutz ideology was psychoanalytically quite aware and well informed (i.e., of psychoanalysis at its early, 1920s state; Golan, 1959). It aimed to demonstrate that a better social system—that is, a new and enlightened organization of family and group life—would literally lead to the disappearance of known forms of (neurotic) psychopathology and to an improved way of life.

Without going into the details, it is by now well established that this experiment failed miserably. It appeared to hold up very well during the pre-state and initial period of Israel's existence, when war and economic shortage rendered it attractive in many ways. Even then, however, if one looked below the surface, one of the first indications that this grand experiment would eventually fail was the extent and power of envy. Not only did the new system not do away with it, but in many ways it magnified and amplified it. Living in close quarters, without the anonymity that characterizes urban and ordinary rural life, magnified the awareness of what others did or did not have, and with it came envy and the "narcissism of minor differences" (Freud, 1918). Questions like who owns a private electric kettle or a wardrobe became major causes of envious splits, of hatred and persecution. The phenomenon extended to all areas of activity, such as: Who does privileged work? or Who is granted permission to study at the university at the kibbutz's expense? The first serious manifestation of the collapse of the system appeared when the majority of kibbutz children, upon reaching adulthood, abandoned it for life in the city, many of them emigrating from the country. As society as a whole became much more prosperous, the kibbutz organization simply folded and went into bankruptcy. In the last decade, almost all the kibbutzim, with few exceptions, have been economically privatized, instituting private ownership and income, often with severe effects of hardship and poverty to individuals.

The kibbutz movement is a prime example of two aspects of envy at the social and organizational level: On one hand, it was a concerted attempt to minimize or eliminate envy and its destructive influence by means of a specially organized mode of group living. On the other hand, it offered a convincing demonstration of the almost complete failure to overcome the fundamentals of human nature by organizational means or through social engineering.

The case of the kibbutz represents the failed attempt by a social organization to overcome individual human nature. The following two examples represent different manifestations of cases in which envy characterizes and colors the group as a whole. The first example comes from the organizational life of psychoanalysis; the second derives from my experience in a series of working conferences focused on the relationship between Germans and Jews.

The institutional life of psychoanalysis is marked by the highly specific and problematic issue of the training analysis, or, more correctly put, of the training *analyst*. All the different schools of psychoanalysis have the same requirement: the candidate, i.e., the analyst-to-be, needs to undergo a personal analysis as part of his or her analytic training. There are various ideas about when this should take place, its desirable frequency, duration, and timing, and so on. But every psychoanalytic institute requires its candidates to have a personal analysis. The personal analysis is perhaps the most important learning experience of the future analyst, and it is often said to be the most significant factor in shaping his future analytical stance and technique and serve as a model for later practice, even more than the supervised cases and didactic courses and seminars, the two additional and complementary components of psycho-analytic training.

There are very few, if any, other professions in which such an important role is played by the requirement to undergo a deeply emotional, intimate, and prolonged experience with a member of the profession. Even if such an example exists, it does not carry the additional burden associated with the fact that this highly personal experience leads to becoming a member of the same social institution as the person with whom one shared this experience; i.e., with one's analyst. It is perhaps comparable to growing up and becoming a member of the same family as one's father and mother. In the case of the family, however, growth eventually leads to parting from it in order to start a new family. In the case of the future analyst, on the contrary, growth is what makes him forever a part of the "parental" family. A move towards leaving is usually regarded as a destructive attempt to split and undermine the psychoanalytic institute.

Obviously this is an extremely sensitive and potentially volatile issue. It is not the aim of the personal analysis to make the candidate dependent, subservient, or lacking in autonomy. Quite the contrary: the de-idealization of the analyst and the profession is thought to be an important outcome of the candidate's analysis, along with other achievements. However, even if this is not expressed aloud, it is still regarded as what will forge and seal the analysand's connectedness with psychoanalysis forever. It constitutes a significant link in what the French prefer to call the "transmission" of psychoanalysis or the "formation" of the psychoanalyst, and in this sense it has a decidedly intergenerational character.

From this perspective, which is the prevalent one within the predomi-nant Eitingon model[1] of training, it is understandable why it was felt that such a delicate and important function should be entrusted to the very best analysts in the community. These selected members are bestowed with the title of "Training Analyst," with the formal connotation that they are empowered to perform the analysis of candidates on behalf of their psy-choanalytic institute and society.

It should be equally clear that the introduction of this differentiation or gradation into the psychoanalytic society, regardless of the validity of the rationale supporting it, has become a major source of envy within institutionalized psychoanalysis. To quote Emerson again, *"Envy is the tax that all distinction must pay."* Introducing a gradient of distinction into a social group may well lead to envious attacks, to splitting and projection. Indeed, one of the major characteristics of psychoanalytic societies is their tendency to split into splinter groups. This often takes on an ideological cast, behind which there are typically two reasons: sexual boundary violations (often by training analysts), and issues around being or becoming a training analyst. Reflecting on these two issues, it is striking that both motives are closely related to incest problems: sexual boundary violations are obviously of an incestuous nature; but so is the issue of becoming a training analyst, since it derives from the wish to attain parental status and recognition. Both issues therefore involve the intergenerational boundary, and the social prohibition or sanction of crossing it. It is an incestuous dynamic, which reveals the extent of its intrinsic relatedness to unconscious wish fulfillment.

The envy we observe in this case is the envy inherent in the Oedipal situation, involving competition and narcissistic defeat. From a psychoanalytical point of view, there can be no organizational or group solution to this envy. Instead of a *solution,* there must be a *resolution* of the issue, and this depends entirely on how each individual resolves his intergenerational conflicts.

There appears to be no good structural solution for the problem of the training analyst. The training analysis may, of course, be removed from the "training" period and put on an entirely personal and free basis, so that (almost) any analyst can perform it, as is the case in the French model. However, putting together bits and pieces of different models that have their deep and specific rationales is both counter-indicated and violates the internal consistency and integrity of each model. Moreover, even in the French model,[2] the problem has merely been shifted to the next level—of supervision—where again there is selection as to who is entitled to perform it. Other solutions, such as enabling everyone who meets certain administrative criteria to become a training analyst, have the seeming advantage of allaying or circumventing the envy about being appointed or not. In effect, however, it shifts the burden of selection to the candidates: they effectively "appoint" training analysts by choosing to work with them, doing so according to their own criteria, which may not always be the best. Most important, it certainly does not eliminate envy—it merely makes it even more difficult to bring it in the open.

The case of psychoanalysis and the training analysts' status is instructive in several ways. It represents an institutional enactment of an intergenerational issue: it takes a specific individual psychodynamic issue and enacts it at the institutional level.

The individual dynamics of oedipal and pre-oedipal transferences that find expression in organizational settings are, of course, ubiquitous. Most, if not all, social institutions develop and set up internal gradients of status, hierarchy, authority, and responsibility—e.g., the school system, the university, the army, the church, a bank, or a supermarket. Why, then, is this problem of envy so uniquely destructive in psychoanalytic institutions? The answer seems to be related to the particular nature of this organization: In ordinary social systems, the gradient of social distinction and intergenerational differentiation is inherent, and whatever problems the individual has with it are referred back to him and must be taken up by him individually. There are, of course, instances in which the intergenerational issue is enacted in an ideological crusade or social revolution, but as soon as the revolution has taken hold, the issue persists and returns (as in the example of the kibbutz). The psychoanalytic institution, on the other hand, is unique in that it represents the idea of dealing with the intergenerational (oedipal and pre-oedipal) issue and "curing" the individual of it. I suggest that what happens in psychoanalytic institutes and societies is that the problem that was, hopefully or supposedly, resolved individually is displaced into the organizational realm, where it is vigorously acted out. In other words, while individual psychoanalysts have dealt with their oedipal issues, psychoanalytic institutes and societies have become the container into which these issues and their associated envy are projected and are directed at the organizational structure where they exert their pernicious destructive influence.

The last example is based on my experience in what are known as the "Nazareth Conferences."[3] These are a series of working conferences focused on the shadow cast by the Holocaust on Germans and Jews, as well as on others. The conferences were begun at the initiative of a group of German and Israeli analysts and were aimed at the difficulties in analytic and therapeutic work encountered on both sides of the perpetrator–victim divide. The premise for this continuing effort is that each group needs the actual presence of the other (in social reality and not only in internal fantasy) in order to be able to carry out its own work. A specially adapted version of a Tavistock group relations conference method[4] was designed and employed. Seven such conferences took place from 1994 to 2010—in Nazareth, Bad Segeberg, and Cyprus.[5]

The proposition of providing a container for mutual exploration by Germans and Israeli Jews aroused great anxiety in all those involved. One indication of this anxiety was the original intention to limit attendance to psychoanalysts. Aside from the fact that the initial initiative came from psychoanalysts and was addressed to fellow analysts, it was thought that the latters' professional capacity for dealing with emotional and unconscious processes would provide a suitable container for the dreaded explosiveness. This defensive posture was gradually and cautiously given up, and the conferences are now open to psychoanalysts, psychotherapists, and "others from similar or different organizations and professions who have a particular interest in working at the topic of the conference."

There are certain prominent features that were observed to repeat over different conferences and changing memberships. One of them was a theme of emotional deprivation, which seems to reveal a fundamental aspect of the parent–child relationship in wartime German families and in the following decades. One can only wonder and speculate about the essential truth revealed here about the finer and darker parts of the early object relations experienced by German infants and children, and the possible effects this has had on German society and history. The conclusion that such early object relations exist may be far-reaching. At the immediately observable level, however, one could certainly observe several characteristic traits of German members that seem directly related to this difficulty.

let me illustrate some of these manifestations—for instance, how aggression was handled and expressed, or the pain of loneliness and emotional isolation—are beyond the scope of this chapter. They involved both individual and interpersonal ways of coping with the experience of external care and handling that were "correct" and adequate, yet coupled with emotional distance. But there are further observations that become evident *only at the group level*. The German *group* in the conferences often seemed to lose its bearings among several possible modes of action and reaction. They were imprisoned by the fear of open confrontation, struggle, and strife, and preferred a course of endless polite and "civilized" discussion and debate, conducted in the most orderly and democratic way, but in effect becoming completely paralyzed and unable to act in timely fashion, thus becoming gradually irrelevant. Another manifestation was being extremely efficient and task-oriented, but becoming oblivious of or cruelly disregarding the feelings and concerns of others.

Another observable difficulty was the feeling of shame the German group struggled with. This was evident especially in the large group settings, where Germans often felt tongue-tied, shy, and ashamed of their poor command of English (the language used in such multinational settings). Although most non-Germans were just as inarticulate, they were much less hampered by this disadvantage. In actuality, the often quite superior capacities of the Germans for thinking and reflection were not realized by them. They consistently saw themselves as stupid, imperceptive, and inferior to the Israelis and Jews. They were clearly hampered by shame and guilt.

But it was not only shame and guilt. One of the striking features was the *envy* the Germans openly expressed toward the Israeli-Jewish members. Although the Germans were clearly and in many ways the majority group, they perceived the relatively small group of Israelis as the strong ones, and readily idealized them as powerful, united, and with a clear sense of group and individual identity. The most precious quality for which the Germans envied the Israelis was their seeming vitality, which seemed to be in stark contrast to their own more isolated experience. It also explained another surprising finding: the extent to which the Germans mourned the absence and disappearance of "their" Jews. It is as if the deeply rooted German ambivalence succeeded in getting rid of a beloved as well as hated object, and it was sorely missed and longed for.

Envy in this case was not an individual but definitely a group phenomenon, and its implications are to be sought and observed at the group level. One underlying dynamic of this envy is the idealization of the Jews and Israelis: They were perceived as smart, intelligent, sure of themselves, courageous, unified, and cohesive, and above all—possessing a well-defined identity with which they were at ease and at peace. It is not necessary to point out that these were, quite literally, projections, or more precisely, projective identifications. The German group projected their own difficult parts—an embattled and beleaguered identity, fears and anxieties around aggression, feelings of not being at-one with their inner self and with the world outside. They ascribed to the Jews these wished-for idealized qualities, and in turn felt themselves impoverished and lacking in all these wonderful attributes.

Envy in this case is the product of *a group process of projective identification.* It is important to note that, at the same time, this primitive defense serves as a link between the individual and group dynamics. The role played by projective identification at the individual level, especially in those who suffer from severe psychopathology, such as severe borderline disorders, is ubiquitous and well known. It is easy to overlook the fact that projective identification, among its multiple other functions, also represents an essential mechanism of group formation, group spirit, and group action. This was already discovered and described by Freud, although he did not use the term "projective identification" and contented himself with speaking about "substitution" and identification. Freud regarded the *substitution* by each group member of the leader's ego ideal for his own, and his *identification* with the other group members on the basis of this common substitution, as the basis of group formation and mass behavior. Using Kleinian terminology, we may say that what holds the group together is this glue of projective identification—i.e., projecting idealized parts of oneself into the group, especially onto the leader, and identifying with them.

The group, as Bion put it, is a fantasy, shared and maintained by its members. It is a dangerous fantasy, because it can lead one to feel and act in ways that as an individual one might not wish and would not condone. Yet it is also a necessary fantasy, because without it one would feel all alone, isolated, and without a larger entity to belong to. This "binocular vision" (Bion, 1961) needs to be maintained in order to deal with the essentially dualistic nature of the human being: on one hand, possessing a sense of individuality and being an autonomous subject, and on the other, a deep-seated herd mentality of belonging to and being part of a group or a collective. As an inevitable corollary of this dual nature, deep feelings of envy develop toward others—for what they have, what they are, and what is desired.

This chapter represents an attempt to trace the vicissitudes of envy as it occurs in groups and organizations, using psychoanalytic tools and concepts. From a psychoanalytic point of view, attempts to minimize or eliminate envy through social engineering and modification, which may feed ideological causes and political strivings, are doomed to failure. A major component of envy is unavoidable, since it stems from indispensable intergenerational conflicts. Some of these issues represent the projection of envy into social and organizational structures; others are limited to the individual's difficulties in coping with it. The most dangerous aspect of envy in groups occurs when, through the dynamics of idealization and denigration, "the Other" becomes the representative of all that is wanted and desired, which was projected into him. It is this last that we must be most on guard against.

Notes

1. For an up-to-date schematic description of the three models of training approved by the International Psychoanalytic Association, see Appendices A and B of the IPA Procedural Code:

http://www.ipa.world/IPA/en/IPA1/Procedural_Code/Requirements_for_qualifica-tion_and_admission_to_membership.aspx

2. See note ii.

3. Erlich, H. S., et al, (2009).

4. Colman and Bexton (1975), Colman and Geller (1985).

5. The focus has since shifted to an all-European perspective, "European Victims and Perpetrators, Now and Then," which took place in Poland in 2012 and 2014.

References

Bion, W. R. (1961). *Experiences in Groups.* New York: Basic Books.

Colman, A. D., and Bexton, W. H. (Eds.). (1975). *Group Relations Reader.* Sausalito, CA GREX.

Colman, A. D., and Geller, M. H. (Eds.). (1985). *Group Relations Reader 2.* Washington, DC: A.K. Rice Institute.

Dvash, J., Gilam, G., Ben-Ze'ev, A., Hendler, T., and Shamay-Tsoory, S. G. (2010). The envious brain: The neural basis of social comparison. *Human Brain Mapping*, 31, 1741–1750.

Emerson, R. W. (1909). *Journals of Ralph Waldo Emerson.* Boston: Houghton Mifflin.

Erlich, H. S. (1996). Ego and self in the group. *Group Analysis*, *29*, 229–243.

Erlich, H. S., Erlich-Ginor, M., and Beland, H. (2009). *Fed with Tears—Poisoned with Milk. Germans and Israelis: The Past in the Present. The Nazareth Group-Relations Conferences.* Giessen, Germany: Psychosozial Verlag.

Freud, S. (1918). The taboo of virginity. *Standard Edition of the Complete Psychological Works of Sigmund Freud* (vol. 11, pp. 191–208). London: Hogarth Press.

Freud, S. (1921). Group psychology and the analysis of the ego. *Standard Edition of the Complete Psychological Works of Sigmund Freud* (vol. 18, pp. 69–143). London: Hogarth Press.

Golan, S. (1959). Collective education in the kibbutz. *Psychiatry*, *22*, 167–177.

Rajan, R. G., and Wulf, J. (2006). The flattening firm: Evidence from panel data on the changing nature of corporate hierarchies. *Review of Economics and Statistics*, *88*(4), 759–773.

Range, F., Horn, L., Viranyi, Z., and Huber, L. (2009). The absence of reward induces inequity aversion in dogs. *Proceedings of the National Academy of Sciences*, *106*, 340–345.

Rosner, M., and Tannenbaum, A. S. (1987). Organizational efficiency and egalitarian democracy in an intentional communal society: The kibbutz. *British Journal of Sociology*, *38*, 521–545.

Sosis, R., and Ruffle, B. J. (2004). Ideology, religion, and the evolution of cooperation: Field experiments on Israeli kibbutzim. In Michael Alvard, Ed., *Socioeconomic Aspects of Human Behavioral Ecology (Research in Economic Anthropology)* (vol. 23, pp. 89–117). Bingley, England: Emerald Group Publishing Limited.

10 | The Othello Conundrum

THE INNER CONTAGION OF LEADERSHIP

MARK STEIN

Introduction*

The past few decades have been witness to a burgeoning interest in the study of emotions and their relevance to leadership. From Peters and Waterman's writings (Peters & Waterman, 1982; Peters, 1987) on passion and commitment, through to Goleman's (1996, 2004) work on emotional intelligence, numerous views have been formulated arguing that understanding the emotions is a *sine qua non* of understanding leadership and of leading effectively. Works inspired by psychoanalytic ideas constitute an important part of this literature. Authors such as Hirschhorn (1988, 1998), Gabriel (1997, 1999), Kernberg (1998), Obholzer (1994), and Kets de Vries (1995) have used psychoanalytic concepts to unravel certain of the complex emotions and dynamics associated with leadership.

In another, related, area of work authors have used the classics of literature as a means of accessing certain of the more subtle, intractable, and complex themes of emotions and leadership: the mythology of ancient Greece as well as the tragedies and comedies of Shakespeare, in particular, have been used. Winstanley (2004), for example, uses Ovid's epic tale of Phaethon to explore issues of power, ambition, and rites of passage, while Corrigan—quoting the immortal lines "Once more unto the breach, dear friends, once more" (Henry V: III.i.1, in Corrigan, 1999: 11)— draws on Shakespeare to address issues of leadership and commitment. Psychoanalytically inspired authors, too, have borrowed substantially

* This article was originally published in *Organization Studies* and has been reprinted with permission from SAGE Publications.

from such traditions: drawing on Greek mythology, Sievers's (1996) paper uses the story of Zeus and Athena to explore issues of leadership and succession, while Kets de Vries uses Shakespeare's *King Lear* to illustrate similar themes (Kets de Vries, 1995), as well as the role of the "organizational fool" in using humor to provide honest feedback to the leader (Coutu, 2004). Greek and Shakespearean classics are valuable because experiences that many of us share but cannot easily articulate are given shape and meaning by them. These texts explore such issues by personifying human dilemmas and then providing eloquent, precise expressions of them. They are particularly helpful in articulating some of the more complex, painful, and seemingly intractable aspects of the dilemmas associated with leadership. Clearly, with different objectives, more traditional scientific discourses are less likely to succeed in doing this.

This paper seeks to contribute to these discourses by bringing some of the above strands together in a psychoanalytic study of leadership and emotions in Shakespeare's *Othello*[1]; while there are many aspects to the play, the issue of leadership has been selected here. Although Othello was once great and heroic, he is now an ageing and vulnerable military leader, unable to protect himself from the malign influence of another person. This "other" person—the subordinate Iago—is understood here not only to be an individual character in the external world, but to be an internal part of the leader's mind that is dominated by feelings of jealousy and envy. This part of the leader's mind, under outside influence, is capable of destroying all that is essential for the survival of the leader and the organization. Although such forces exist in extreme form in the drama of *Othello*, it is suggested in this chapter that they are of considerable concern to all leaders. These forces—it is argued—need to be examined, struggled with, and learnt from. When they are not appropriately dealt with, they may become malignant and capable of wreaking considerable havoc and destruction.

Such are the broad themes that occupy our focus here. The structure of the chapter is as follows: First, a brief précis of the play is presented. After this, we examine the central character of Iago and his relationship with Othello. They are examined initially from sociopolitical and organizational points of view; following this, Iago is seen as representing part of Othello's mind, expressing primitive feelings of jealousy and envy. On this basis, the idea of "Othello's conundrum" is formulated. Finally, we will turn to the present and examine the demise of the Gucci family dynasty as a contemporary example, following which there is a consideration of the implications and a conclusion.

Outline of *Othello*

Othello, a black Moor, known to be a great military general serving in the Venetian army, has eloped with and secretly married Desdemona, the beautiful daughter of a Venetian senator. On account of his foreignness in the Venetian setting, Othello is regarded with suspicion, and is accused of having forced Desdemona into marriage. It is only after the couple have defended their decision in the presence of the Doge (Duke) that their marriage is accepted. It is at this point that Othello is authorized by the Doge to lead a Venetian army to defend the island of Cyprus against an anticipated attack by the Turks. He and Desdemona, their marriage as yet unconsummated, leave with the Venetian army for Cyprus that night.

Although their arrival in Cyprus coincides with news that the Turkish fleet has apparently been destroyed in a storm, the dangers for Othello now emerge from a different source. Iago, a relatively lowly ensign, or standard bearer, cannot bear the fact that Othello has acquired Desdemona as his young and beautiful wife. He is also filled with hatred and vengeance because Othello overlooked him in favor of Cassio for the post of lieutenant. Iago hatches a terrible and destructive plot, aimed at his rival Cassio and at the relationship between Othello and Desdemona. He begins by persuading Roderigo, who is also in love with Desdemona, that Cassio is having an affair with Desdemona, and that he should attempt to kill Cassio. He also manages to get Cassio drunk while on duty, a serious misdemeanor for a lieutenant. Following a drunken brawl, Cassio is removed from the post of lieutenant and replaced by Iago. Iago then engages in a variety of activities—including goading Othello and providing fabricated "evidence"—designed to persuade him that Desdemona is having an affair with Cassio. Although Othello was a great and highly experienced military leader, he is now aging, and his eyesight is poor. Consequently, he is dependent on Iago—his trusted subordinate and confidant—in order to see. He is strongly swayed by Iago, especially in the famous and fateful "temptation scene" (Act 3, Scene 3). Iago's persuasion and fabricated "evidence" strengthen Othello's anxieties that—like others in Venetian society—Desdemona, too, may have grounds to reject him. Finally, Othello succumbs fully to the view Iago intends him to have. Humiliated and filled with rage, he murders his wife by smothering her. He then learns that Iago had invented the story of Desdemona's infidelity and fabricated the evidence. Tortured by self-hate, Othello kills himself. Thus, Iago's evil influence is destructive both at the organizational and the personal level:

by the end of the play, much of the Venetian military leadership in Cyprus is in ruins, without so much as a shot being fired by the Turks, and both Othello and Desdemona lie dead in their wedding chamber, their marriage unconsummated.

Iago and Othello

We now turn to examine the roles and characters of Iago and Othello, and the relationship between them; the importance in the drama of this relationship is reflected by a long history of scholarship. As Bradley has argued, "[e]vil has nowhere else been portrayed with such mastery as in the character of Iago" (Bradley, 1992: 178). Iago always manages to construe events in the worst possible way, suggesting to people that they have been duped or are under attack from others; he preys on their minds until they are persuaded of the view he wants them to have. In doing so, he acts in a duplicitous, Machiavellian way by trying to convey the impression that he is operating from a very helpful and a highly moral position, "all faithfulness [and] all integrity" (Machiavelli, 1997: 63). Indeed, it is remarkable that virtually everyone turns to Iago for advice and support, including those who die as a result of his actions.

Iago also obscures or destroys any evidence that may contradict his view of the world, using other apparent "evidence" built on deception and lies. With perfect timing, he always arrives at the crucial point, ready to persuade others at their most exposed moments; he then uses arguments—constructed with perverse logic—that are grounded in a profound knowledge of these people's vulnerabilities. He is able at will to evoke either extreme anxiety or confusion in his victims, giving him the power to enjoin people to do things that run counter to their better nature.

Most markedly, Othello is infected by Iago's destructiveness. Othello's position as a leader is a major factor that promotes his vulnerability. Othello is in a highly dependent position: as a leader, he is unable to gather information, make decisions, or engage in action without the help of others on whom he depends. This problem is exacerbated by his foreignness: he is a black Moor and not a Venetian, serving in the Venetian army. The context of a potential war also promotes a situation of considerable anxiety for Othello, reinforcing a dependence on Iago that is both practical and emotional. Furthermore, he also relies on Iago to see for him on account of his age and poor eyesight. So, despite Iago's relatively lowly status as a standard bearer in the military, Othello is very strongly under his influence.

The "External Iago"

The Sociopolitical Level

The character and role of Iago—as well as his tragic relationship with Othello—may be explored at a variety of different levels. Beginning with the sociopolitical level, Iago represents an extreme conservatism that seeks to protect a relatively homogenous society from being penetrated and influenced by an outsider: in several different ways, Iago insinuates that Othello's foreignness and blackness are a cause for suspicion. This tone is created at the outset when Iago tells Desdemona's father (a Venetian senator) that he has been robbed of his daughter by "an old black ram . . . [who is] tupping your white ewe" (I.i.87–88). The sexual nature of this innuendo is significant because it is not unusual for the mixing of races—then as now—to be tolerated up until there is a suggestion of sexual relations, marriage, and progeny. Through these kinds of statements, Iago succeeds in creating an ugly, vengeful mood, with Desdemona's father requesting that Othello be apprehended and that the marriage—a "treason of the blood!" (I.i.167)—be nullified.

The apparent theft of Desdemona is an issue serious enough to require the intervention and judgement of the highest authority in Venice, the Doge, in whose presence Othello is forced to defend himself against the accusation of "thieving" Desdemona, drugging her, and forcing her into marriage. Despite being found to be innocent, the very fact of this trial—with the full *gravitas* of the Doge's presence—lends weight to the perception that Othello is an outsider and a proper target for suspicion. As Green (1992) points out, the play begins and ends with trials, the first of which concerns Othello's purported "theft" of Desdemona, and the second, her murder. A sense is conveyed that Othello is a "subject between two trials" (Green, 1992: 324), and thus he is always external to—and under the scrutiny of—the Venetian authorities and conservative Venetian society, represented in different ways by the Doge and Iago. Moreover, being immediately dispatched to Cyprus suggests that—insofar as he is accepted into the society—he is only granted a place at the periphery.

The Organizational Level

These events also need to be understood at an organizational level: society's prejudices almost invariably permeate the organization, especially as experienced by the "outsider" himself. From the outset, Othello feels that he does not have full "authority from above" (Obholzer, 1994) because, as a foreign Moor, he feels he does not have the full sanction of the Venetian establishment, on whose behalf he is working. Neither does Othello feel he has "authority from below" (Obholzer, 1994) or effective "followership" (Barnard, 1948; Hersey & Blanchard, 1993), the importance of which can hardly be overestimated (Offermann, 2004). This lack of sanctioning by his subordinates leads Othello to become very suspicious of them.

As a consequence of feeling so undermined, and in the absence of any understanding of Iago's motives, Othello turns to him for support. This is of significance organizationally because—having bypassed the hierarchy that is intended to support him—Othello has invested all his trust in Iago, a relatively low-ranking ensign.

There are two problems here. First, Iago is intensely jealous of Othello's marriage to the beautiful Desdemona and is engaged in a plot to destroy it. From an organizational point of view, the attack on Othello's sexual relationship with his spouse is simultaneously an undercutting of his authority as a leader, attacking his most personal and vulnerable weakness; as is implied by Strati (1999), corporeality, sexuality, and intimacy are not somehow "left behind" when we enter work, but are interwoven with the world of work in profound ways.

Second, having been denied promotion, Iago is engaged in a deadly struggle for succession: he has his eye on the post of lieutenant, and (perhaps unsurprisingly) has directed his accusations against Cassio, the current incumbent in that post. Interestingly, Iago's ambitions for the lieutenant post also have a deeper significance: it is intriguing to note that the term lieutenant or *lieu*-tenant—as we are reminded by Green (1992)—signifies one who takes the place of another, and is brimming with implicit meaning: Cassio is Othello's lieutenant and heir apparent. In other words, Iago's ambitions are not just to replace Cassio as lieutenant, but to replace Othello himself, the military leader.

The "Inner Iago"

The *Malin Genie* and the Othello Conundrum

We now shift focus to examine Iago, not as an external character, but as representing the jealous and envious part of the mind of Othello, the leader. According to this reading, the tortuous interchange between Iago and Othello during the play refers to a terrible dialogue that goes on within

Othello's own mind, and the increasing power of Iago signifies the ever-more-powerful influence of the part of Othello's mind that is dominated by feelings of jealousy and envy.

One reason for advocating the above view is that Iago's nature corresponds closely to the kind of "inner demon" that has been the subject of clinical psychoanalytic study in recent years. The psychoanalyst Melanie Klein (1975a, 1975b) proposed that we unconsciously experience ourselves as being inhabited by a number of internal mental objects or characters, and that these may influence and shape many of our most important struggles in the world outside. Conversely, what goes on in the outside world also has an influence on the nature and shape of the inner theater of our internal world. Most significantly, Iago's nature is remarkably similar to an internal mental object (Klein, 1975a; 1975b) of a particular kind. This is one that inhabits the mind and—filling it with jealousy and envy—attacks all that seems "good," including all meaningful connections between the person and the outside world (Bion, 1967; Rosenfeld, 1987). Such a creature is committed to the destruction not only of love and affection, but, in the organizational context, of leadership, authority, meaning, and learning. In a sense, Othello is suffering from being inhabited by a "parasitic" creature akin to Descartes's *malin genie*, the "malicious genie" whose contagious presence deceives the "host" at every point (Descartes, 1912). Othello's conundrum is therefore whether he should tolerate these feelings of jealousy and envy and live with his uncertainty about Desdemona's purported infidelity, or, following the *malin genie's* advice, try to rid himself of these feelings by killing her and Cassio.

In the "temptation scene"—"perhaps the most breath-taking scene in the whole of Shakespeare" (Honigmann, 1997: 37)—Iago invades Othello's mind by casting aspersions on the integrity and character of Othello's lieutenant, Cassio, causing Othello to become increasingly anxious. It is in this scene that Othello's dilemma opens up as a gaping chasm in front of him: his conundrum is at its most frightening. Early on in the "temptation scene," Iago stirs up Othello's curiosity by implicitly criticizing Cassio's behavior. When Othello asks him what he has said, he replies *"Nothing, my lord; or if – I know not what"* (III.iii.36; my italics). This response provides the kindling that reignites ever-increasing anxiety within Othello's mind: as Eagleton argues, into this "nothing"—a "temptingly blank text" (Eagleton, 1986: 65)—Othello will read "something" of a very persecutory nature. This "nothing" therefore becomes a haunting presence that inhabits and terrifies the subject; Othello is unable to rid his mind of it.

The innuendo in the temptation scene continues unabated. Othello then feels driven to find out more about Cassio. Othello: "Is he honest?" Iago: "Honest, my lord?" Othello: "Honest? Ay, honest." Iago: "My lord, for aught I know." Othello: "What dost thou think?" Iago: "Think, my lord?" (III.iii.103–108). Finally, exasperated, Othello responds: "Think, my lord! By heaven, thou *echo*'st me / As if there were some *monster* in thy thought / Too hideous to be shown" (III.iii.109–111; my italics). In effect, through his coldness and his echoing technique, and by implying that there is something too awful to be spoken about, Iago has established himself as a haunting, monster-like presence invading Othello's mind.

Jealousy

Having established himself as a haunting, inner demon in Othello's mind, Iago continues his quest by evoking strong feelings of jealousy in Othello. Jealousy, as Klein (1975b) argues, is an emotion that involves intolerance or hatred of the relationship between two other parties; one feels jealous because someone—to whom one is attached or for whom one feels love—shows more affection, interest, or love towards the third party. It is thus important to note that an attack motivated by jealousy is usually directed against this third party. "Delusional jealousy" (Meltzer, 1967) is a clinical condition in which the subject feels excluded by others who he falsely believes to have close or even intimate relations with each other.

Jealousy can be particularly problematic for leaders, for various reasons. One concerns the fact that, in front of their teams, leaders are always alone—and often feel alone—in their roles; they have no peers. As a consequence, leaders may be more likely to feel jealous of other relationships from which they feel excluded. While subordinates seem to have the time and opportunity to develop relationships with others, leaders may feel themselves to be too busy and too isolated, and may also feel that they should not compromise their unique position by fraternizing with those lower in the hierarchy. Another reason is that latent feelings of jealousy in the leader may be ignited by contagion emerging from their subordinates: the leader is thus vulnerable because subordinates may try—consciously or unconsciously—to evoke their jealousy and set them against other, rival, subordinates. In the *Othello* story, Othello's jealousy of Desdemona and Cassio, in part, is a result of contagion that emerges from Iago's inhabitation of Othello's mind.

During the course of the temptation scene, Othello is less and less able to bear his feelings of jealousy about the purported relationship between

Desdemona and Cassio, with the conundrum in which he finds himself feeling more and more intolerable. His reaction is to turn to a desperate search for the "truth": following a moment of despair, his mood suddenly changes, and he feels driven to seize Iago, demanding: "Villain, be sure thou prove my love a whore / Be sure of it, give me the *ocular proof*" (III.iii.362–363; my italics).

Othello's demand for ocular (i.e., visual) proof occupies a pivotal moment in the play. The implication of the requirement for ocular proof is that, through observation, such data can be witnessed and therefore verified; it embodies, as Grady (1996) argues, a nascent scientific approach. However, the demand for such scientific proof constitutes a paradox at the center of the drama: as Othello's thinking and perceptual apparatus are "inhabited" by Iago, such "verification" can draw only on illusory evidence. As Parker argues, implicit in the concept of ocular proof is the notion of *evidentia*, or "counterfeit representation" (Parker, 1996). Furthermore, once inhabited by the "demon" Iago, not only does Othello "see" things that do not occur, but even his speech becomes infected, his fluid prose style changing to short, staccato-like sentences. His mind and its judgements, too, are corrupted: he has entirely lost his mental capacity to examine and explore issues without immediately engaging in unthinking action. Therefore, just as the Cartesian *malin genie*, the "malicious genie," destroys all perceptual judgements, so with Othello: the distorting "inner demon," firmly lodged in Othello's mind leads him to become insanely jealous of the relationship between Desdemona and Cassio and be incapable of examining evidence properly and thinking for himself. The demand for ocular or scientific proof—a *leitmotif* for the play—thus signifies the inevitability of Othello's downfall.

Envy

Together with strong feelings of jealousy, the "inner demon" also infects Othello with intense feelings of envy. In contrast with jealousy, envy concerns only two parties, namely the self and another (Klein, 1975b; Joseph, 1986; Rosenfeld, 1987). Born of the pain of knowing that someone has something one would like and does not have, envy fundamentally involves the self's desire to damage this other whom it perceives to be better off. Thus, envy is also different from jealousy insofar as it is—in its extreme form—an exclusively destructive emotion: it is accompanied by *Schadenfreude*, the satisfaction or pleasure derived from witnessing someone else's misfortune. Being grounded in hatred, envy appears meaningless, often operating in a silent, insidious way. Moreover, and in contrast with jealousy, envious attacks can be made against someone one loves and depends on; this makes it a particularly damaging emotion.

Like jealousy, envy may be a particular problem for the leader because it can be contagiously communicated into the mind of the leader by a subordinate: consciously or unconsciously, the subordinate may be inclined to stoke the leader's envy. Partly as a result of contagion from Iago, Othello harbored—as well as jealousy—more specific feelings of envy towards the young, vivacious, and beautiful Desdemona, who had many of the attributes that Iago and Othello lacked. But another factor is that others may be felt to be free of some of the responsibilities that burden the leader: leaders may feel that their subordinates, their spouses, and others around them have easier lives, leaving them envious of the apparent freedom of these others.

Returning to Othello, it is noteworthy that Iago's envious declaration about Desdemona that he will "turn her virtue into pitch" (II.iii.355) is enacted by Othello. If, as is argued by some, Othello's problem is entirely one of jealousy, he would have been more likely to spare Desdemona and focus his attention exclusively on damaging or getting rid of Cassio: one who is consumed with jealousy attacks the person who is seen to be associated with the desired person, rather than the desired person him/herself. The murder of Desdemona, however, suggests a much more malign envious attack on her beauty, femininity, and virtuousness. The killing of Desdemona thus completes the destruction by envy of Othello's most important and intimate association with another.

Tragically, Othello's relentless pursuit does finally yield the "truth," but not the one he expected: this is the terrible twist in the tail of his quest. Having murdered his wife and arranged for the killing of Cassio, Othello is finally made aware of the magnitude of his blindness to Iago. At this moment, he becomes aware that Iago has become so firmly lodged within his mind that he feels he must kill himself to destroy the demon within. So, in the end, the terrible curse of the inner demon has destroyed leadership, camaraderie, love, and the leader himself.

Gucci—a Contemporary Reference

Like all of Shakespeare's plays, *Othello* was a reworking of earlier stories by other authors; written around 1601, *Othello* was principally inspired by an Italian short story published a few decades earlier in Venice by Italian author Giraldo Cinthio. Some three centuries after *Othello*, elsewhere in Italy a factual reworking of these themes began: this is the story of the Gucci family dynasty. Despite the obvious external differences between these stories—insofar as they are both about jealousy and envy and their destructiveness within an organization—they share some remarkably similar strands.

A small, family concern founded in Florence at the turn of the twentieth century, Gucci developed into one of the world's most successful global fashion and leather goods businesses. At the peak of its success, however, it descended into a hateful, ever-renewing series of battles and court cases within the ranks of its leadership.

Some of Gucci's biggest problems emerged in the 1970s in a multi-way struggle between brothers Aldo and Rodolpho Gucci, the controlling shareholders of the company, and their sons. The brothers were particularly unhappy that Aldo's son, Paolo, could not be dissuaded from developing his own independent brand of "Paolo Gucci" products. Paolo was summarily dismissed from his post, following which he retaliated by initiating a series of court cases against his father and the company: no fewer than ten such court cases took place over the next few years (Forden, 2000: 79), the defense of which cost Gucci tens of millions of dollars in legal fees. In 1982, the Gucci company sued for peace and Paolo was allowed back into the company, only to be sacked again a few months later. Still a shareholder, Paolo attended a board meeting in Florence shortly thereafter. A scuffle ensued, with Paolo emerging with blood streaming from his cheek, shouting that "[t]hey tried to kill me" (Forden, 2000: 85) and demanding that the police be called. The massive international press coverage of this incident substantially damaged Gucci's reputation.

Over the next few years, Maurizio Gucci, Rodolpho's son, made peace with his cousin Paolo: the two struck a deal and formed a new company with Maurizio as president, forcing Aldo to step down from the role (Rodolpho had died in 1983). A short while later, the deal collapsed amidst considerable acrimony. In the meantime, Aldo, who had not wanted to stand down, retaliated by publicly accusing Maurizio of tax evasion and receiving his inheritance by fraud (McKnight, 1989: 186). But Aldo's court evidence against Maurizio gave him only little respite from his own problems because, finally, his own son Paolo succeeded in getting him, at 86 years of age, sentenced to a year in prison on grounds of tax evasion. Later, Paolo's wife divorced him and subsequently had him jailed for failing to pay alimony and child support. He died, plagued with debt, in London in 1995 (Forden, 2000: 90).

As for Maurizio, the accusation of tax evasion was only one difficulty among many. Having initially been disowned by his father because his fiancée was felt to be a social climber and not of his class, Maurizio felt himself to be under the scrutiny of a harsh, critical gaze; throughout his life, this feeling never abated. Then, following reconciliation and moving to the United States to join Gucci New York (and ultimately becoming head of Gucci worldwide), Maurizio found his uncle and cousins trying to get him arrested for the illegal export of capital. He returned to Italy and was then forced to flee to Switzerland, living there for a year in order to avoid the Italian authorities; he was only allowed back into Italy following a deal with the Italian judges (Forden, 2000). During this time, he had an acrimonious separation from his wife and began a number of other relationships. In 1995, in the denouement of the plot, Maurizio's wife paid contract killers to murder him, a crime for which she subsequently began a long prison sentence. By this time, the entire Gucci family was in complete disarray and had sold its shares of the business; to this day, they have nothing further to do with it.

In spite of the external differences between *Othello* and the Gucci story, they share some remarkable parallels. As if infected by several inner Iagos, members of the Gucci family seemed more concerned to destroy each other's lives than they were to enjoy their own: had they been able to contain their intense jealousy and envy, they could have led lives—at least in material terms—that others only dream of. The Gucci story is perhaps best summed up by Judge William C. Conner of the New York District Court, who compared the family to Cain and Abel, the biblical story of jealousy and envy; the decades of legal dispute, added Judge Conner, had been "at enormous cost" (Forden, 2000: 88) to the family. As in *Othello*, the difficulties were exacerbated by questions of who truly "belonged" and deserved to be a leader, as opposed to those who were felt to be intruders or imposters.

Implications and Conclusion

We now turn to examine the implications of the *Othello* study. First, *Othello* focuses our attention on the importance of understanding the emotions of others in the organization, a theme familiar from other parts of the literature (Fineman, 1993; Kets de Vries, 1995, 1999; Gabriel, 1999). As suggested by Bion (1961), it is essential for the leader to make emotional contact with the life of the group, as well as make sense of their interpersonal relations; such emotional intelligence (Coutu, 2004; Goleman, 1996) is a prerequisite for leadership. As is clear from *Othello*, it is particularly important that the leader is able to understand some of the jealousy, envy, and interpersonal rivalry—exacerbated by powerful interdependencies—that are often present in organizations (Kernberg, 1998; Halton, 1994; Obholzer, 1994; Stein, 1997, 2000). Othello's difficulty in understanding such feelings, and especially his inability to consider that Iago's activities might be grounded in jealousy and envy, constituted a fundamental blind spot in his thinking, and led to catastrophic consequences.

Second, notwithstanding the above, *Othello* draws our attention to the importance of the leader's understanding what goes on within his/her own mind. In this context, the central question therefore focuses on the identity of an individual leader as well as of the organization per se (Brown, 2001), of a single *dramatis persona* within a broader context of *dramatis personae*. It is thus important here that Iago should not be considered exclusively as an overpowering follower—an *éminence grise*—exercising influence over Othello. The fundamental point is that the enemy, represented here by Iago, is essentially an interior one: it lies not only within our own ranks, but most problematically within our own minds. Even if in real life the issue of "the enemy within" is usually not as extreme as in *Othello*, the broad themes of the play will be familiar to many: as has been argued by Obholzer, it is not unusual for leaders to be subjected to psychological jeering or "barracking by inner world figures" (Obholzer, 1994: 41), as Othello so clearly felt. Thus, to the traditional leadership concerns about people and production (Blake and Mouton, 1964), or about individual, team, and task needs (Adair, 1979), should be added a concern for the inner self—"the workplace within" (Hirschhorn, 1988)—if we are to avoid being corrupted or destroyed by what goes on within our own minds.

Third, the focus on the inner world of jealousy and envy has important implications for theory. When we read Iago to be an inner character within the leader's mind, we posit jealousy and envy as "drivers" or internal causal agents of the destruction of leadership. *Othello* is particularly helpful to us in this regard, because, not only have jealousy and envy been little studied in the organizational literature (Stein, 1997; 2000), but the play also helps us focus on the more specific idea of these emotions as internal, destructive causal agents within the leader's psyche.

Fourth, of particular relevance to contemporary organizations, *Othello* focuses our gaze on the central problem of uncertainty. If much of the executive leadership process involves performing off the cuff (*a bracchia*) against a variety of canvasses (*canovacci*) (Mangham, 1986), the true test of leadership must surely come when these canvasses are rather less known, or even unknown, before the scene, and this is increasingly true in the turbulent environments facing today's leaders. Othello's feelings of jealousy and envy are intensified by the uncertainties and sense of the unknown that drive him to act in rash ways. This points to the fundamental importance of leaders' understanding how uncertainty may interrelate with the complex emotions explored in this paper.

Fifth, the globalizing tendencies of modern organizations make leaders more prone to the issues faced by Othello: in organizations that work across national, racial, and linguistic boundaries, many leaders, at certain points and in some contexts, become "outsiders." As "outsiders" lacking local awareness, such leaders are more likely to depend on "insider" employees or confidants, and are therefore more likely to be exposed to the contagion of jealousy and envy witnessed in the play.

Sixth, and finally, the increasing critical scrutiny of leaders in contemporary organizations makes such leaders prone to the phenomena identified in this chapter. One aspect of this is "the audit society" (Power, 1997), whose programmatic ambition—premised on a desire for a kind of universal "ocular proof"—is to allow auditors to invade every interstice of organizational life; as a consequence, there is a considerable undermining of trust and increase of suspicion and anxiety. While this affects people at every level within the organization, it is likely, especially when things go wrong, that leaders will be especially vulnerable: as the familiar phrase goes, "the buck stops with them." Another aspect of this scrutiny is the increasing media attention focused on chief executive officers, board members, and other leaders: whatever justification there may be for this, one unfortunate consequence is that these leaders may be more inclined to feelings of isolation and vulnerability. Adding to this is the use of "360-degree feedback," now almost universally used among leaders at senior levels within Fortune 500 companies (Ghorpade, 2000). Helpful though 360-degree feedback may sometimes be, on other occasions it produces suspicion, distrust, and an intense desire for "ocular proof" that links the (anonymous) feedback to particular people. In one case, Federal Privacy Act requests were filed in order to discover the sources of certain feedback (Ghorpade, 2000). These circumstances may thus increase hostile feelings—including jealousy and envy—in relation to the leader, causing spiraling destructiveness in organizations. For these reasons, the themes of *Othello* have considerable relevance for organizations today.

Note

1. Unless otherwise stated, all references to *Othello* are to the Arden version (E. A. J. Honigmann, editor, *The Arden Shakespeare: Othello*. Walton-on-Thames: Thomas Nelson, 1997). Citations are made using the convention of the form: (II.ii.351) (Act Two, Scene Two, Line 351).

References

Adair, J. (1979). *Action-Centred Leadership*. Aldershot, UK: Gower.

Barnard, C. (1948). *Organization and Management*. Cambridge, MA: Harvard University Press.

Bion, W. (1961). *Experiences in Groups and Other Papers*. London: Tavistock.

Bion, W. (1967). *Second Thoughts: Selected Papers on Psycho-analysis*. London: William Heinemann.

Blake, R. R., & Mouton, J. (1964). *The Managerial Grid*. Houston: Gulf.

Bradley, A.C. (1992). *Shakespearean Tragedy*. London: Macmillan.

Brown, A. (2001). Organization studies and identity: Towards a research agenda. *Human Relations, 54*(1), 113–121.

Corrigan, P. (1999). *Shakespeare on Management: Leadership Lessons for Today's Managers*. London: Kogan Page.

Coutu, Diane L. (2004). Putting leaders on the couch: An interview with Manfred Kets de Vries. *Harvard Business Review, 82*(1), 64–72.

Descartes, R. (1912). *A Discourse on Method: Meditations on the First Philosophy; Principals of Philosophy*. London: Dent.

Eagleton, T. (1986). *William Shakespeare*. Oxford, UK: Blackwell.

Fineman, S. (1993). *Emotions in Organizations*. London: Sage.

Forden, S. G. (2000). *The House of Gucci*. New York: William Morrow.

Gabriel, Y. (1997). Meeting God: When organizational members come face to face with the supreme leader. *Human Relations, 50*(4), 315–342.

Gabriel, Y. (1999). *Organizations in Depth: The Psychoanalysis of Organizations*. London: Sage.

Ghorpade, J. (2000). Managing the five paradoxes of 360-degree feedback. *Academy of Management Executive, 14*(1), 140–150.

Goleman, D. (1996). *Emotional Intelligence: Why It Can Matter More than IQ*. London: Bloomsbury.

Goleman, D. (2004). What makes a leader? *Harvard Business Review, 82*(1), 82–92.

Grady, H. (1996). *Shakespeare's Universal Wolf: Studies in Early Modern Reification*. Oxford, UK: Clarendon Press.

Green, A. (1992). Othello: A tragedy of conversion: Black and white magic. In J. Drakakis (ed.), *Shakespearean Tragedy* (pp. 316–353). London: Longman.

Halton, W. (1994). Some unconscious aspects of organizational life: Contributions from psychoanalysis. In A. Obholzer and V. Z. Roberts (eds.), *The Unconscious at Work: Individual and Organizational Stress in the Human Services* (pp. 11–18). London: Routledge.

Hersey, P., & Blanchard, K. (1993). *Management of Organizational Behaviour: Utilizing Human Resources* (6th ed.). Upper Saddle River, NJ: Prentice Hall.

Hirschhorn, L. (1988). *The Workplace Within: Psychodynamics of Organizational Life*. Cambridge, MA: MIT Press.

Hirschhorn, L. (1998). *Reworking Authority: Leading and Following in the Post-modern Organization*. Cambridge, MA: MIT Press.

Honigmann, E. A. J. (ed.). (1997). *The Arden Shakespeare: Othello*. Walton-on-Thames, UK: Thomas Nelson.

Joseph, B. (1986). Envy in everyday life. *Psycho-analytic Psychotherapy, 2*, 13–30.

Kernberg, O. (1998). *Ideology, Conflict and Leadership in Groups and Organizations*. New Haven, CT: Yale University Press.

Kets de Vries, M. (1995). *Organizational Paradoxes: Clinical Approaches to Management*. London: Routledge.

Kets de Vries, M. (1999). Navigating between "live volcanoes" and "dead fish." *European Management Journal, 17*(1), 8–19.

Klein, M. (1975a). *Love, Guilt and Reparation, and Other Works 1921–1945*. London: The Hogarth Press and the Institute of Psychoanalysis.

Klein, M. (1975b). *Envy and Gratitude and Other Works 1946–1963*. London: The Hogarth Press and the Institute of Psychoanalysis.

Machiavelli, N. (1532). The Prince. In K. Grint (ed.), *Leadership: Classical, Contemporary and Critical Approaches* (pp. 55–69). Oxford, UK: Oxford University Press.

Mangham, I. (1986). *Power and Performance in Organizations: An Exploration of Executive Process*. Oxford, UK: Blackwell.

McKnight, G. (1989). *Gucci: A House Divided*. London: Pan.

Meltzer, D. (1967). *The Psychoanalytical Process*. Perthshire, UK: Clunie Press.

Obholzer, A. (1994). Authority, power and leadership: Contributions from group relations training. In A. Obholzer & V. Z. Roberts (eds.), *The Unconscious at Work: Individual and Organizational Stress in the Human Services* (pp. 39–47). London: Routledge.

Offerman, L. R. (2004). When followers become toxic. *Harvard Business Review, 82*(1), 54–60.

Parker, P. (1996). Shakespeare and rhetoric: "Dilation" and "delation" in *Othello*. In P. Parker and G. Hartman (eds.), *Shakespeare and the Question of Theory* (pp. 54–74). New York: Routledge.

Peters, T. (1987). *Thriving on Chaos: Handbook for a Management Revolution*. London: Pan.

Peters, T. J., & Waterman, R. H. (1982). *In Search of Excellence: Lessons from America's Best-Run Companies*. London: Harper and Row.

Power, M. (1997). *The Audit Society: Rituals of Verification*. Oxford, UK: Oxford University Press.

Rosenfeld, H. (1987). *Impasse and Interpretation: Therapeutic and Anti-therapeutic Factors in the Psychoanalytic Treatment of Psychotic, Borderline, and Neurotic Patients*. London: Tavistock and the Institute of Psycho-Analysis.

Sievers, B. (1996). Greek mythology as means of organizational analysis: The battle of Larkfield. *Leadership and Organization Development Journal, 17*(6), 32–40.

Stein, M. (1997). Envy and leadership. *European Journal of Work and Organizational Psychology, 6*(4), 435–465.

Stein, M. (2000). After Eden: Envy and the defences against anxiety paradigm. *Human Relations*, *53*(2), 193–211.

Strati, A. (1999). *Organizations and Aesthetics*. London: Sage.

Winstanley, D. (2004). Phaethon: Seizing the reins of power. In Y. Gabriel (ed.), *Myths, Stories, and Organizations: Premodern Narratives for Our Times* (pp. 176–191). Oxford, UK: Oxford University Press.

11 | Culture and the Elicitation, Experience, and Expression of Envy

YI WEN TAN, KENNETH TAI, AND CYNTHIA S. WANG

Introduction

Envy, an intense and painful emotion, is experienced when another individual possesses an attribute or quality that one views as personally relevant but does not possess (Schimmel, 2008; Smith & Kim, 2007). The negative arousal arising from envy has been historically documented by philosophers. Plato, for example, defined envy as pain experienced as a result of other's good fortune (Plato, 2007/360 B.C.), whereas Immanuel Kant described envy as averseness in witnessing others' superior outcomes (Kant, 1797). The roots of envy (*invidia* in Latin), along with its discouragement, can also be traced back to the Ten Commandments from the Bible, which state that "Thou shalt not covet thy neighbor's house, . . . , neighbor's wife, [etc.]," and that "the avoidance of envious feelings and that one should not have the desire to possess what is not his" (Deuteronomy 5:21; Cohen-Charash & Larson, Chapter 1, this volume).

These conceptions of envy suggest that it has been prevalent throughout time and across cultures. From an evolutionary standpoint, envy is proposed as a universal and adaptive emotion (Brown, 1991) that aids in survival and reproduction (Anderson, Hildreth, & Howland, 2015; Hill & Buss, 2006). As competition is inherent in the fight for survival, individuals compare themselves socially with others to determine their relative standing in society (Smith, 1991). When people engage in upward social comparisons, it often elicits envy (Smith & Kim, 2007). These envious feelings may serve as a signal to people that there is strategic interference from their competitors and that they are facing a competitive disadvantage (Hill & Buss, 2006). In contrast, when people perceive themselves as

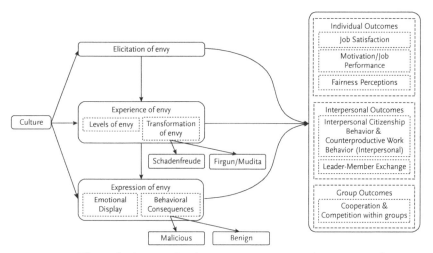

FIGURE 11.1 Effects of culture on the elicitation, experience, and expression of envy, and their impact on organizational outcomes.

envied targets, feelings of superiority may motivate them to maintain their competitive advantage (Festinger, 1954; Taylor & Brown, 1988).

Although the experience of envy may be universal, it may be more complex in some cultures than in others (Adrianson & Ramdhani, 2014). In this chapter, we first document literature that outlines the cultural differences in the elicitation of envy, experience and feelings of envy, as well as in the expression of envy in terms of emotional or behavioral displays. We then discuss why these cultural differences may exist, provide an organizational lens, and discuss implications for future research. We summarize our theoretical model in Figure 11.1.

Elicitation of Envy

As mentioned earlier, people may feel envious after engaging in upward social comparisons. Differences in likelihood of engaging in upward social comparisons across cultures will hence cause differences in the likelihood that people will feel envious across cultures. In the following section, we review literature that suggests that the likelihood that envy is elicited may differ across cultures and then propose how it may differ for cultures that vary on the individualistic–collectivistic and horizontal–vertical dimensions.

Individualistic vs. Collectivistic Cultures. We suggest that the likelihood of eliciting envy differs between individualistic and collectivistic cultures. In individualistic cultures, people are likely to construe others as separate from one another and from their social memberships. In contrast, in collectivistic cultures, people are likely to construe others in relation to one another and as extensions of their social groups (Hofstede, 1980). Whereas individualistic cultures tend to emphasize competition, collectivistic cultures tend to emphasize cooperation (Gardner, Gabriel, & Hochschild, 2002). As such, we can expect that people in individualistic cultures may engage in more upward social comparisons with others than do people in collectivistic cultures, and therefore are more likely to feel envious.

However, the effect of individualistic versus collectivistic cultures on the elicitation of envy is likely to depend on the group membership of the envied target. For example, in collectivistic cultures, a superior target who is perceived to be an in-group member may be less likely to elicit envy than one who perceived as an out-group member. This is because people in collectivistic cultures tend to focus more on group goals than on individual goals (Gudykunst et al., 1992), and the superior achievements of an in-group member are more likely to be seen as a group achievement than as an individual achievement (Brewer & Weber, 1994; Oyserman & Lee, 2008). As a result, the envious person can bask in the glow of the envied target's glory if the envied target is an in-group member. In contrast, people in collectivistic cultures may be biased against out-group members (Yamagishi, Jin, & Miller, 1998) and are more likely to perceive an out-group member's superior achievements as an individual achievement that competes with their in-group. Thus, those from collectivistic cultures may be more likely than those from individualistic cultures to feel envious toward a superior out-group target.

Horizontal versus Vertical Cultures. In addition to the effect individualism–collectivism may have, differences in the elicitation of envy may also emerge between horizontal and vertical cultures. Members of a kibbutz community who value equality among members have been observed to feel envious more easily, as well as with greater intensity, than people who are not on a kibbutz (see Erlich, Chapter 9; Gressel, Chapter 17, this volume). People in horizontal cultures perceive greater similarity with others than do people in vertical cultures (Triandis & Gelfand, 1998). As such, they may feel more envious because they are more likely to view the achievements of the envied target as obtainable. Indeed, Sawada (2006) asserted that envious persons who view envied targets as similar are more likely to appraise the envied targets' achievements as obtainable and they feel more envious as a result. This is also in line with the observation that people choose others who are similar to them to be their referent targets for social comparisons (e.g., Darley & Aronson, 1966; Festinger, 1954; Gordon, 1966; Hakmiller, 1966; Wheeler, 1966).

Horizontal cultures, compared to vertical cultures, are also more likely to value equality and less likely to emphasize hierarchy (Triandis & Gelfand, 1998). Horizontal cultures are therefore more egalitarian, with their members expecting to garner the same outcomes as others. This expectation of equality, however, increases their sensitivity towards inequality (Gressel, Chapter 17, this volume). As such, perceivers will feel envious of a target if their outcomes are not as good as those of the target's. Together, these observations suggest that in horizontal cultures, when people stand out from norms of equality, envy is elicited.

Recent examinations of certain cultures support this proposition that individuals in horizontal cultures may be more likely to feel envious than individuals in vertical cultures. For example, members of kibbutz communities, who tend to value equality among members, are more likely to feel envious and feel it with greater intensity (see Erlich, Chapter 9; Gressel, Chapter 17, this volume). The exhibition of envy is also prevalent in, e.g., the Swat of Northern Pakistan and in the United States—cultures that value egalitarianism (Lindholm, 2008). These findings suggest that individuals from cultures such as Japan, India, and China, which tend to be more vertical, may display a lower prevalence of envy than those from more horizontal cultures, like the United States.

In situations where the envious person is of a higher status than the envied target, the prediction that those from horizontal cultures will exhibit more envy than those from vertical cultures may reverse, especially for those from cultures that are also individualistic in nature. Specifically, we expect that such envied targets in vertical–individualistic (hereafter, VI) cultures will be more likely to feel envious than those in horizontal–individualistic (hereafter, HI) cultures. As people in VI cultures, compared to HI cultures, care more about status and are more likely to compete with others to acquire it (Triandis & Gelfand, 1998), it can be expected that, in a VI culture, when a lower-status individual attains an achievement, a higher-status individual may feel threatened and as a result be envious of the lower-status individual.

Encapsulated Cultures. Thus far, we have discussed how the elicitation of envy may differ between cultures. However, within a particular culture, there may be subcultures that have different egalitarian beliefs. Specifically, cultures with an encapsulated system are unique in that they have subcultures, which are marked off from each other by boundaries and have egalitarian beliefs within each subculture (i.e., members in each subculture have identical access to things considered good in life; Foster, 1972). An example of such a culture is the caste system in India. People in these cultures may be more likely to feel envious of a superior target within the same subculture or caste due to the egalitarian beliefs. However, they may be less likely to feel envious of a superior target with higher-caste status, as they may not think about how they can achieve more to be on the same level with those who have a competitive advantage. Hence, for cultures with encapsulated subcultures, envy is less likely to be elicited when the envious person and the envied target are of different statuses. Interestingly, observations about the Javanese suggest that encapsulation may be useful to avoid eliciting envy in others, specifically, others of lower status (see Stodulka, Chapter 13, this volume).

In summary, we propose that there are cultural differences in the likelihood of eliciting envy. Specifically, individualistic cultures, which tend to be competitively oriented, should elicit more envy than collectivistic cultures, which tend to be more cooperatively oriented. Furthermore, in collectivistic cultures, envy is more likely to emerge when the envious target is perceived to be an out-group member than when the envious target is perceived to be an in-group member. We also suggest that horizontal cultures elicit more envy than vertical cultures due to perceptions of similarity and equality with others. In addition, it is important to consider whether cultures have encapsulated systems, as the likelihood of eliciting envy may differ depending on whether the envious person and the envied target are within the same subculture or are of different subcultures.

Experience of Envy

After envy is elicited, its form may be altered due to its unpleasant nature. Specifically, envy may be altered in two ways—it is either reduced or transformed into other emotions. We propose how the reduction or transformation of envy may vary for cultures that differ on the dimensions of individualism–collectivism and horizontalism–verticalism.

Reducing Feelings of Envy. When people experience envy, they may be motivated to alter their envious feelings, as they may perceive that the expression of envy is undesirable. Social or cultural norms may influence perceptions of acceptability of expressing envy (Crusius & Mussweiler, 2012; Eid & Diener, 2001; Exline, Single, Lobel, & Geyer, 2004; Rodriguez Mosquera, Parrott, & Hurtado, 2010). For example, the Javanese have prescriptive norms, and one salient norm is that people must not envy (*iri*) others' achievements (see Stodulka, Chapter 13, this volume). In addition, the acceptability of expressing other negatively valenced emotions, such as guilt, also differs across cultures; whereas people from collectivistic cultures report that expressing guilt is desirable because it signals a concern for relational harmony, people from individualistic cultures report that expressing guilt signals a negative evaluation of the self and therefore is less desirable (Eid & Diener, 2001).

In individualistic cultures, which emphasize autonomy and independence (Bochner, 1994; Kashima & Callan, 1994), envy is thought to motivate economic and social competition; therefore, the expression of envy may be more acceptable (Salovey, 1991; Schoeck, 1969). In contrast, in collectivistic cultures, which emphasize the values of connectedness, harmony, and cooperation (Triandis, 1995), the expression of envy may be less desirable because it may disturb the social equilibrium (Salovey & Rothman, 1991). To align themselves with the level of perceived social or cultural acceptability, people from collectivistic cultures may alter their feelings of envy through emotional regulation.

Emotional regulation is defined as the process by which we "influence which emotions we have, when we have them, and how we experience and express these emotions" (Gross, 1998, p. 271). People may regulate their emotions, such as envy, in different ways. One way is through "deep acting," whereby people modify their envious feelings to match the required displays (Grandey, 2003). An alternative method is through reappraisal, whereby people cognitively re-evaluate the emotion-eliciting situation (Gross, 2001). Therefore, members of collectivistic cultures, in which it is probably less acceptable to express envy, may regulate and thereby reduce their envy through deep acting or reappraisals.

Consistent with this theorizing, research documents cultural differences in emotion-regulation strategies such as reappraisals (Morling, Kitayama, & Miyamoto, 2003; Taylor, Sherman, Kim, Jarcho, & Takagi, 2004). For example, compared to members in individualistic cultures, members in collectivistic cultures (e.g., Bangladesh, Israel, Hong Kong) are more likely to adopt reappraisal strategies to regulate their emotions, particularly negative emotions (Matsumoto et al., 2008). However, contrary to the predictions above, there are observations from collectivistic cultures like Japan and Java that find that people experience envy and even express their envy behaviorally through bullying (see Hitokoto & Sawada, Chapter 12; Stodulka, Chapter 13, this volume). One possibility is that the envied targets are perceived as out-group members. Hence, people in collectivistic cultures may be more likely to regulate their envy toward in-group members through deep acting or reappraisals, especially since envy is thought to be a socially disapproved emotion in collectivistic cultures (Salovey & Rothman, 1991); but when it comes to out-group members, envy may be viewed as more acceptable and therefore experienced to a greater extent.

Transforming Feelings of Envy. The experience of envy may not only be reduced but may also be transformed into other emotions. In the following sections, we will discuss how envy can be transformed into *firgun/mudita* or schadenfreude and how this may differ across cultures.

Transforming Feelings of Envy into Firgun *or* Mudita. A close examination of the languages in different cultures reveals words that suggest that envy may be emotionally regulated to become a positive emotional experience despite its unpleasant nature. For example, in the Israeli society, there is a term, *firgun*, which is used to describe "happiness at another's success" (Cohen-Charash, Erez, & Scherbaum, 2008). Similarly, in Pali, an ancient language used in India used especially by Buddhists, the term *mudita* is understood as "rejoicing in the good fortune of others" (Menon & Thompson, 2010). Envy may be transformed into *firgun* or *mudita* because of the culturally embedded norms about the perceived desirability of expressing envy (Tai, Narayanan, & McAllister, 2012). However, it remains unclear what are the psychological mechanisms that may underlie the transformation of envy into positive emotional experiences (i.e., *firgun* or *mudita*).

Past research on emotional regulation may provide some insight into how envy can transform into a positive emotional experience. For example, the envious person may reappraise the envious episode and transform their feelings of envy into positive emotions. In particular, one may reappraise the envious episode and perceive that the envied target is deserving of the competitive advantage over him/her, and thereafter reduce the feelings of envy and even possibly increase feelings of joy for the envious person. Consistent with this argument, past research suggests that reappraising the situation may indeed both decrease negative emotions and increase positive emotions (Gross, 2002; Wang, Sivanathan, Narayanan, et al., 2011).

Taking together our arguments, we suggest that the transformation of envy into *firgun* or *mudita* may be contingent upon cultural differences in the engagement of emotional regulation strategies, especially the reappraisal or deep-acting strategy. Specifically, we can expect that members in collectivistic cultures will be more likely to emotionally regulate the pain associated with envy into joy associated with *firgun* or *mudita* than those in individualistic cultures. Future research can investigate whether there are cultural differences in the transformation of envy into *firgun* or *mudita*.

Transforming Feelings of Envy into Schadenfreude. Besides being transformed into *firgun* or *mudita,* envy may be transformed into schadenfreude. Indeed, past studies find that when an envied target experiences a misfortune, the feelings of envy may transform into schadenfreude (Brigham, Kelso, Jackson, & Smith, 1997; Smith, Turner, Garonzik, Leach, Urch-Druskat, & Weston, 1996), which is defined as taking pleasure in another person's misfortune (Heider, 1958).

There may be cultural differences in the likelihood of transforming envy into schadenfreude. Research has shown that some people feel more pleased when "tall poppies" or high achievers (i.e., envied targets) fall from grace than others (Feather, 2012). Specifically, individuals who favor the fall of tall poppies tend to be lower in power and achievement values, and those who feel that the tall poppies were more deserving of the misfortune also tend to value equality more (Feather, 2012). This suggests that individuals in cultures who are less achievement-oriented and value equality are more likely to transform their envy into schadenfreude.

Since horizontal cultures value equality (Triandis & Gelfand, 1998) and individualistic cultures value achievement (McClelland, 1961), we suggest that people in these cultures are more likely to feel schadenfreude when an envied target suffers a misfortune. If we consider the combination of these two cultural dimensions, we may expect people from horizontal–individualistic cultures (HI) to be the most likely to transform their feelings to envy to schadenfreude when the envied target suffers a misfortune. Future research can examine whether these cultural dimensions indeed predict people's feelings of schadenfreude towards an envied target who falls from grace.

Expression of Envy

Since the perceived desirability of expressing envy may differ across cultures, the actual expression of envy may also differ across cultures. In addition, the experience of envy can manifest behaviorally in different ways. In the following section, we review the literature on how culture may influence people's expression of envy. We then discuss how the emotional and behavioral expressions of envy may differ across cultures along the dimensions of individualism–collectivism and horizontalism–verticalism.

Emotional Display of Envy. Other than aligning the experience of envy with the cultural norms through emotional regulation strategies, individuals may alternatively alter the emotional display that feelings of envy will elicit. This can be achieved through surface acting, which refers to modifying the emotional display without changing the experience or feelings (Grandey, 2003). One way to surface act is to suppress the emotional display (Grandey, 2003). The presence of different cultural norms for emotional expression suggests that cultural differences in the expression of envy will emerge through surface acting to reduce its emotional display (Ekman & Friesen, 1971). For instance, some cultures have norms that require their members to regulate their emotions to adhere to institutional roles and standards, while other cultures have norms that encourage their members to express unregulated emotions (Gordon, 1989).

In the context of envy, members in collectivistic cultures may be more likely to engage in emotional regulation through surface acting and as a result, be less likely to express envy than people in individualistic cultures. For example, recent research shows that Japanese students are more efficient than European American students at suppressing a negative emotion (Murata, Moser, & Kitayama, 2013). Furthermore, the Japanese are less comfortable expressing their negative emotions (Stephan, Stephan, & De Vargas, 1996; Stephan, Stephan, Saito, & Barnett, 1998). In contrast, people in individualistic cultures are more comfortable expressing their emotions (Stephan et al., 1996, 1998), and because they believe that envy can motivate economic and social development (see Salovey, 1991; Schoeck, 1969), they may be more willing to express it.

Behavioral Expressions of Envy. Given that the feeling of envy is adaptive in that it serves as a signal to envious people that they are facing a competitive disadvantage, it should drive them to react in ways that can reduce the competitive disadvantage. Beyond the cultural differences in the expression of envy along the dimension of individualism–collectivism, behavioral differences may also emerge within this cultural dimension. Specifically, because people in VI cultures (versus HI cultures) care about and compete with others for status (Triandis & Gelfand, 1998), they may be more likely to act on their envy by competing with others to rectify their perceived competitive disadvantage. Hence, even though people in individualistic cultures may experience envy as a result of social comparisons, if their individualism is more horizontal in nature, they may not express these feelings of envy behaviorally.

Benign and Malicious Envy. The recent psychological research that distinguishes benign from malicious envy may reveal other insights about potential cultural differences in the behavioral expressions of envy (e.g., Bedeian, 1995; Belk, 2011; Polman & Ruttan, 2012; van de Ven, Zeelenberg, & Pieters, 2009; van de Ven, Zeelenberg, & Pieters, 2012). Whereas "benign envy" refers to envy without hostility and is associated with a moving-up motivation targeted at improving the envious person's position, "malicious envy" refers to envy with hostility and is associated with a pulling-down motivation targeted at undermining the envied target's position (see Crusius & Lange, Chapter 4, this volume, for a review; van de Ven et al., 2009). Thus, the major difference between benign and malicious envy is the type of behavioral expression that results from feelings of envy.

Culture may be an important factor that influences the relationship between the experience of envy and its benign or malicious behavioral expression. We suggest that collectivistic cultures that emphasize interpersonal harmony are imbued with social norms that encourage envious parties to engage in behaviors aligned with the benign form of envy (see Hitokoto & Sawada, Chapter 12, this volume; Singelis, 1994). This is consistent with recent research that shows that Javanese individuals provide behavioral descriptions that are related to benign form of envy (e.g., improving oneself) (Adrianson & Ramdhani, 2014). In addition, while the Japanese have expressions for both benign envy (*urayami*) and malicious envy (*netami*), there are differences in the understanding of the two expressions for seven-year-olds, who have better understanding of the word *urayami* than the word *netami* (Hitokoto & Sawada, Chapter 12 of this book; Sawada, 2006).

In contrast, members from individualistic cultures, who are less likely to emphasize interpersonal harmony, may be more likely to engage in behaviors aligned with the malicious form of envy. For example, Swedish individuals are more likely to provide free word associations that are associated with the malicious form of envy (Adrianson & Ramdhani, 2014). Hence, people in collectivistic cultures may be more likely to engage in benign envy, whereas people in individualistic cultures may be more likely to engage in malicious envy.

Although people in collectivistic cultures may be more likely to experience benign envy, their motivation to improve may be more pronounced when the envied target is an in-group member. This is because the envious person is better able to associate with the envied target and will be more likely to emulate the desired achievements. In addition, people in collectivistic cultures are also less likely to engage in malicious envy with an envied in-group target as they are concerned about in-group harmony (Leung, 1988). With out-group members, however, people in collectivistic cultures may engage in malicious envy because of a greater in-group/out-group distinction and bias (Tajfel, 1974). For example, an envied out-group target may be seen as unique and one who disrupts interpersonal harmony, which results in that target being maliciously bullied (see Hitokoto & Sawada, Chapter 12, this volume, for a review). Hence, even though people in collectivistic cultures are more likely to engage in benign envy and less likely to engage in malicious envy, the group membership of the envied target may also need to be considered.

Summary

Envy is defined as pain experienced due to another person's good fortune. Although envy may be universally experienced, cultures may influence people's elicitation (i.e., whether envy is experienced), experience (i.e., feelings of envy), and expression (i.e., displays or behaviors) of envy. In terms of the elicitation of envy, we suggest that cultures may differ in their emphasis on competition, perceptions of similarity to others, and extent of egalitarianism. In addition, cultural differences in the perceived desirability of expressing envy may affect people's motivation to reduce the experience of envy through emotional regulation strategies, such as reappraisals or deep acting. Furthermore, cultural differences in engagement of emotion regulation strategies may also transform the experience of envy into positive emotional experiences such as *firgun* or *mudita*. Cultural differences in the degree to which equality and achievement are valued also may have an impact on the experience of envy, as envy may also be transformed into schadenfreude.

   In terms of the expression of envy, cultural differences in the perceived desirability of expressing envy may again play an important role, as they may affect people's emotional display of envy by motivating them to engage in emotion regulation, such as surface acting or suppression. Moreover, different cultural norms, such as those concerning interpersonal harmony, may also affect behavioral expressions of envy. Specifically, people may alter their behaviors in reaction to envy so as to adhere to the cultural norms. Some cultures may be more likely to engage in the malicious form of envy, while other cultures may be more likely to engage in the benign form of envy.

Cultural Differences in Envy
in Organizational Settings

We now apply the earlier reviewed research on cultural differences in
envy to organizational settings. For example, our proposition that those
from collectivistic cultures will be less likely to feel and express envy than
those from individualistic cultures suggests that the effects of envy on organizational outcomes may be less prominent in collectivistic cultures. In
particular, in this section, we discuss how culture may affect employees'
experiences and expressions of envy and lead to different individual, interpersonal, and group outcomes in the organizational context. At the individual level, we examine how culture may influence the effects of envy on
job-related attitudes and outcomes, such as satisfaction, motivation, performance, and fairness perceptions. At the interpersonal level, we explore
how culture may influence the relationship between envy and interpersonal outcomes such as leader–member exchange, interpersonal citizenship behaviors, and interpersonal counterproductive work behaviors. At
the group level, we discuss how culture may affect the effects of envy on
group outcomes, such as cooperation and competition within groups.

Individual Level

Job Satisfaction. Past research finds that employees who experience
greater envy towards others in the organization report lower levels of job
satisfaction (Vecchio, 2005). Cultural differences in the elicitation and experience of envy can result in different levels of job satisfaction across
cultures. For example, as individualistic cultures emphasize competition
more than collectivistic cultures do (Gardner et al., 2002), members in
individualistic cultures may be more likely to feel envious and hence exhibit less job satisfaction than the members in collectivistic cultures. In
horizontal cultures, people who stand out in terms of job achievement will
be seen as violating the norms of equality (Triandis & Gelfand, 1998),
which may elicit feelings of envy in others and subsequently lower their
job satisfaction.

After envy is elicited, employees in different cultures may adopt different emotional regulation strategies as a response, which may in turn
affect their levels of job satisfaction. For instance, as we proposed that
individuals from collectivistic cultures are more likely to transform their
feelings of envy into *firgun* or *mudita* than are individuals from individualistic cultures, it is likely that the former will experience higher levels

of job satisfaction after an envious episode. Future research can examine whether culture influences the effects of envy on job satisfaction.

Motivation and Job Performance. Culture may also modulate the effects of envy on job performance. The cultural variations in the endorsements of benign or malicious envy may lead to different motivations to improve job performance. Given that recent research finds that when people feel benign envy as opposed to malicious envy, they are more motivated to increase their performance (Crusius & Mussweiler, 2012; van de Ven et al., 2009), it can be expected that collectivistic cultures will be more likely to improve their job performance than individualistic cultures, as collectivistic cultures emphasize interpersonal harmony and will express envy in a benign way. The purported relationship between benign envy and performance is supported by the finding that benign envy is more likely than admiration to motivate people to improve their performance because the feelings of frustration following benign envy provide the impetus to improve (van de Ven, Zeelenberg, & Pieters, 2011).

However, within collectivistic cultures, perceived group membership of an envied co-worker may influence the effects of envy on job performance. While employees in collectivistic cultures may be motivated to increase their job performance so that they can associate with and emulate the target, this is less likely to happen when the envied target is an out-group co-worker (as opposed to an in-group co-worker). Thus, the effect of envy on job performance may be influenced by culture and the group membership of the envied target.

Furthermore, people's perceived similarity towards others may be different across cultures and result in differences in envy and subsequently in job performance. Past research shows that promotion rejectees' perceived similarity to a promotee was positively related to envy towards the promotee, and that envy was positively related to job performance (Schaubroeck & Lam, 2004). Since members of horizontal versus vertical cultures perceive greater similarity to others, it is likely that employees in horizontal cultures may feel more motivated to improve their performance as a result of heightened envy. This difference between horizontal and vertical cultures may be increased for people from individualistic cultures, as they are more competitive than collectivistic cultures and are more likely to express their feelings of envy behaviorally (Gardner et al., 2002).

Fairness Perceptions. Past research suggests that envy is associated with feelings of injustice and perceived unfairness (Cohen-Charash & Mueller, 2007; Heider, 1958; Parrott & Smith, 1993; Smith, 1991). Cultural differences may influence this relationship between envy and fairness perceptions. Recall our earlier arguments that individuals from collectivistic cultures are more likely than those from individualistic cultures to use reappraisal or deep acting as emotional regulation strategies and transform the pain associated with envy into joy. As such, the pain of envy is reduced or no longer present. Thus, employees in collectivistic cultures may be less likely to experience perceived unfairness than those in individualistic cultures.

Since horizontal cultures are more egalitarian than vertical cultures (Triandis & Gelfand, 1998), members in horizontal cultures should be more sensitive about fairness concerns than vertical cultures. When a superior co-worker stands out and deviates from the norm, envy is more likely to be elicited among employees from horizontal cultures than in vertical cultures as it violates the ideals of equality. Hence, in these instances, employees in horizontal cultures may be more likely to experience perceived unfairness than members in vertical cultures.

Research on envy and fairness perceptions has yet to differentiate the effects of envy on different types of fairness. The fairness literature has documented the different types of fairness, such as *distributive fairness* (i.e., the perceived fairness of decision outcomes), *procedural fairness* (i.e., the perceived fairness of organizational procedures used to determine outcomes), and *interactional fairness* (i.e., the perceived fairness of the interpersonal treatment one receives from authorities (see Colquitt, Greenberg, & Zapata-Phelan, 2005, for a review). To advance the research on envy and fairness perceptions, future studies can explore the different foci of fairness perceptions that envy may elicit. For example, since vertical cultures are more likely to be submissive to authority than horizontal cultures are (Triandis & Gelfand, 1998), the effects of envy on interactional fairness may be weaker in vertical cultures than in horizontal cultures.

Interpersonal Level

Interpersonal Citizenship and Counterproductive Work Behaviors. At the interpersonal level, envious employees may respond to envy by altering their levels of interpersonal citizenship behavior (hereafter ICB) and/or interpersonal counterproductive work behavior (hereafter CWB-I) directed at the envied target, and this can be influenced by culture. ICB occurs when co-workers help one another beyond their job requirements in ways that either directly or indirectly increase individual job performance, which ultimately enhances group and organizational functioning (Bateman & Organ, 1983; Settoon & Mossholder, 2002). In contrast,

CWB-I are voluntary behaviors that are aimed at inflicting personal harm on others (Conlon, Meyer, & Nowakowski, 2005; Fox & Spector, 1999; Robinson & Bennett, 1995).

In cultures that are more likely to endorse the benign form of envy, envious employees may be more likely to engage in ICB. Helping the envied co-worker can provide a chance for the envious person to be part of the envied co-worker's successful in-group. Furthermore, such help may enable the envious person to achieve the envied co-worker's accomplishments and, as a result, elevate the envious person's social status (Tai et al., 2012). In contrast, in cultures that are more likely to endorse the malicious form of envy, envious employees may be more likely to engage in CWB-I. This is because cultures that endorse the benign or malicious forms of envy may have different cultural norms of interpersonal harmony. Engagement in either ICB and CWB-I affects interpersonal harmony differently, such that the former increases it while the latter decreases it. Since we proposed earlier that collectivistic cultures are more likely to engage in the benign form of envy, while individualistic cultures are more likely to engage in the malicious form of envy, we can expect that collectivistic cultures are more likely to engage in ICB, while individualistic cultures are more likely to engage in CWB-I.

In addition, employees in certain cultures may regulate or transform their feelings of envy into *firgun* or *mudita*, so that feeling joy for the envied target generally motivates them to be helpful towards the envied target. Therefore, this suggests that in cultures such as collectivistic cultures, where envy is likely to be regulated and transformed into *firgun* or *mudita*, employees are more likely to engage in concomitant increases in ICB and decreases in CWB-I directed at the envied target.

Although we propose that employees in collectivistic cultures are more likely to engage in ICB than are employees in individualistic cultures, envious employees in collectivistic cultures may otherwise respond to the pain of envy by reducing their ICB towards their envied targets. Perhaps those in collectivistic cultures are more likely to do so in a covert way (e.g., withholding help) than do those in individualistic cultures. This is because reducing ICB is more covert than engaging in CWB-I, and it is less likely to be perceived as disrupting interpersonal harmony. Thus, these alternative arguments suggest that in both individualistic and collectivistic cultures, employees may reduce their ICB towards envied targets.

Besides predicting differences in engagement of interpersonal behaviors between individualistic vs. collectivistic cultures, there might be differences in employees' engagement of interpersonal behaviors on the vertical-horizontal dimension as well. For example, there might be differences in engagement of CWB-I between HI and VI cultures. We made the prediction earlier that individuals in HI cultures are less focused on competition and acquisition of status compared to individuals in VI culture (Triandis & Gelfand, 1998), and as a result, that they are less likely to express their feelings of envy behaviorally. Building on this argument, employees in HI cultures may then be less likely to engage in CWB-I compared to employees in VI cultures. Furthermore, with regard to the reduction in ICB in collectivistic cultures, the effect might even be more pronounced for cultures that are also high in the vertical dimension, as there is a focus on status acquisition (Triandis & Gelfand, 1998). Hence, employees in VC cultures are more likely to reduce ICB than employees in HC cultures are.

Leader–Member Exchange. Envy may also influence interpersonal outcomes such as "leader–member exchange" (LMX), which refers to the quality of the exchange relationship between the employee and the leader (Graen & Scandura, 1987; Liden, Sparrow, & Wayne, 1997). Employees with low-quality LMX are likely to envy others in the organization with high-quality LMX relationships (Tai et al., 2012). It is likely that such employees will become demotivated and then engage in deviant behaviors, associated with the malicious form of envy, with the aim to sabotage the exchange relationships of envied targets (Tai et al., 2012). However, at the same time, employees may be likely to take proactive steps, associated with the benign form of envy, to improve the quality of their own LMX relationships so as to reduce the relative disadvantage that they have in terms of their LMX relationship in comparison with the envied co-worker.

Culture can be a factor that influences how envious employees alter their own or the envied targets' LMX relationships. As we saw in the previous arguments, collectivistic cultures that are more likely to endorse the benign form of envy due to norms of interpersonal harmony will improve the quality of their own LMX relations. The reverse will be true for individualistic cultures that are more likely to endorse the malicious form of envy, which will sabotage the LMX of the envied targets.

In addition, we can expect to find that cultural differences in self-construals will influence how envious employees alter their own or the envied targets' LMX relations. In cultures with interdependent self-construals, people value connectedness over uniqueness, and they are motivated to find ways to fit in with relevant others and adjust themselves to the needs and expectations of others in relationships (Kitayama &

Uchida, 2005; Markus & Kitayama, 1991; Triandis, 1995). Furthermore, individuals with interdependent self-construals tend to build their positive self-concept through development and maintenance of close relationships with others (Cross, Bacon, & Morris, 2000). Therefore, in interdependent cultures, envious employees with low-quality LMX may be less likely to engage in the malicious form of envy or to engage in deviant behaviors that undermine the high-quality exchange relationships of envied co-workers.

In contrast, in cultures with independent self-construals, people emphasize separateness and uniqueness and strive for autonomy (Markus & Kitayama, 1991). Individuals with independent self-construals tend to build their positive self-concept by standing out and being better than others on self-defining domains (Blaine & Crocker, 1993; Harter, 1993; Tesser, 1988). Hence, in these cultures, envious employees with low-quality LMX relationships may be more likely to engage in the malicious form of envy and therefore be more likely to undermine the exchange relationships of envied targets.

In a nutshell, employees in independent cultures may be more likely to engage in the malicious form of envy than employees in interdependent cultures are. However, as employees in both cultures are motivated to improve their own LMX relationships, we can expect them to be similar in their engagement in behaviors that are consistent with the benign form of envy.

Group Level

Cooperation and Competition Within Groups. To date, there is little research that examines envy in groups and how it affects group outcomes, with the exception of the study conducted by Duffy and Shaw (2000). The authors found that envy in the group is positively related to "social loafing" and negatively related to group cohesiveness, group potency, and group performance. These findings suggest that envy may be detrimental for group outcomes. Hence, we predict that cultures that have a lower likelihood of elicitation of envy, such as collectivistic and vertical cultures, will engender less negative consequences for group outcomes as a result of envy. In addition, collectivistic cultures may also reduce or transform the experience of envy, which mitigates its negative effects on group outcomes.

Other than group cohesiveness, potency, and performance, we propose that envy experienced in groups is likely to influence cooperation and competition levels in groups. In the following section, we discuss how culture may influence the effects of envy on cooperation versus competition within groups through collective identity.

Collective identity is understood as shared perceptions among group members to the degree in which individuals merge their sense of self with the group (Ashmore, Deaux, & McLaughlin-Volpe, 2004; Pratt, 2003). When people are in social groups, they may define their social selves at a broader level in terms of membership in larger, more impersonal collectives or social categories (Brewer & Gardner, 1996; Breckler, Greenwald & Higgins, 1986; Greenwald & Breckler, 1985). Thus, the collective identity is a social extension of the self, and it may be more salient when people construe their identities within groups (Brewer & Gardner, 1996).

Collective identity may influence the effects of envy on cooperation versus competition within groups because it alters the social comparison processes and outcomes among work group members, especially if the envious target is perceived to be an in-group member. Specifically, collective identity changes the frame of reference from the envied co-worker to the group in which both the envious person and the envied co-worker belong to. It also changes the source of self-evaluation from personal capability to group capability and changes the perceptions of other group members from "they" to "we" (see Brewer & Gardner, 1996; Smith, Coats, & Walling, 1999).

Therefore, when perceived collective identity is high, envied co-workers may no longer be perceived as competitors but instead are perceived as the pride of the group (Kim & Glomb, 2014). Furthermore, when perceived collective identity is high, envious employees are more likely to attribute the success of their work group to their own success (Brewer & Weber, 1994). Based on these observations, we suggest that when perceived collective identity is high, there will be less competition within the group.

We further propose that culture may influence the relationship between envy and cooperation/competition within groups through the influence of collective identities. We contend that culture may affect people's collective identity in groups and subsequently influence envy's effects on cooperation versus competition. To the extent that collectivistic cultures emphasize cooperation and inclusiveness (Chen, Chen, & Meindl, 1998), employees in these cultures may be more likely to possess higher levels of collective identity and as a result be more cooperative in work groups compared to employees in individualistic cultures.

Summary

In summary, we applied our theoretical framework to outline the effect of cultures on envy to organizational settings. Specifically, we propose that the effects of culture on the elicitation, experience, and expression of envy may engender different individual, interpersonal, and group outcomes at the workplace. We summarize our theoretical model and its organizational implications in Figure 11.1.

Conclusion

The empirical study of envy in the social and organizational sciences has been increasing steadily in recent years. In order to broaden the research on envy, future research should consider examining the effects of envy in organizations from a cross-cultural perspective. In particular, future work may explore the elicitation, experience, and expressions of envy across different cultures and how envy may subsequently influence different levels of organizational outcomes. We hope that our chapter provides an appropriate starting point for future inquiry, and we encourage organizational behavior scholars to examine how culture may influence the effect of envy on work outcomes.

References

Adrianson, L., & Ramdhani, N. (2014). Why you and not me? Expressions of envy in Sweden and Indonesia. *International Journal of Research Studies in Psychology*, *3*(3), 43–65.

Anderson, C., Hildreth, J. A. D., & Howland, L. (2015). Is the desire for status a fundamental human motive? A review of the empirical literature. *Psychological Bulletin*, *141*(3), 574–601.

Ashmore, R. D., Deaux, K., & McLaughlin-Volpe, T. (2004). An organizing framework for collective identity: Articulation and significance of multidimensionality. *Psychological Bulletin*, *130*(1), 80–114.

Bateman, T. S., & Organ, D. W. (1983). Job satisfaction and the good soldier: The relationship between affect and employee "citizenship." *Academy of Management Journal*, *26*(4), 587–595.

Bedeian, A. G. (1995). Workplace envy. *Organizational Dynamics*, *23*(4), 49–56.

Belk, R. (2011). Benign envy. *AMS Review*, *1*(3–4), 117–134.

Blaine, B., & Crocker, J. (1993). Self-esteem and self-serving biases in reactions to positive and negative events: An integrative review. In R. F. Baumeister, Ed., *Self-Esteem: The Puzzle of Low Self-Regard* (pp. 55–85). New York: Plenum Press.

Breckler, S. J., Greenwald, A. G., & Wiggins, E. C. (1986). Public, private, and collective self-evaluation: Measurement of individual differences. In *International Researches and Exchanges Board (IREX) Conference on Self and Social Involvement*, Princeton, NJ.

Brewer, M. B., & Gardner, W. (1996). Who is this We? Levels of collective identity and self representations. *Journal of Personality and Social Psychology*, *71*(1), 83–93.

Brewer, M. B., & Weber, J. G. (1994). Self-evaluation effects of interpersonal versus intergroup social comparison. *Journal of Personality and Social Psychology*, *66*(2), 268–275.

Bochner, S. (1994). Cross-cultural differences in the self concept: A test of Hofstede's individualism/collectivism distinction. *Journal of Cross-Cultural Psychology*, *25*(2), 273–283.

Brigham, N. L., Kelso, K. A., Jackson, M. A., & Smith, R. H. (1997). The roles of invidious comparisons and deservingness in sympathy and schadenfreude. *Basic and Applied Social Psychology*, *19*(3), 363–380.

Brown, D. E. (1991). *Human Universals*. New York: McGraw-Hill.

Chen, C. C., Chen, X. P., & Meindl, J. R. (1998). How can cooperation be fostered? The cultural effects of individualism-collectivism. *Academy of Management Review*, *23*, 285–304.

Cohen-Charash, Y., Erez, M., & Scherbaum, C. A. (2008). When Good Things Happen to Others: Envy and *Firgun* Reactions. Symposium presented at the Annual Meeting of the Society for Industrial and Organizational Psychology, San Francisco, CA.

Cohen-Charash, Y., & Mueller, J. S. (2007). Does perceived unfairness exacerbate or mitigate interpersonal counterproductive work behaviors related to envy? *Journal of Applied Psychology*, *92*(3), 666–680.

Colquitt, J. A., Greenberg, J., & Zapata-Phelan, C. P. (2005). What is organizational justice? A historical overview. In J. Greenberg & J. A. Colquitt, Eds., *Handbook of Organizational Justice* (pp. 3–56). Mahwah, NJ: Erlbaum.

Conlon, D. E., Meyer, C. J., & Nowakowski, J. M. (2005). How does organizational justice affect performance, withdrawal, and counterproductive behavior? In J. Greenberg & J. A. Colquitt, Eds., *Handbook of Organizational Justice* (pp. 301–327). Mahwah, NJ: Lawrence Erlbaum Associates, Publishers.

Cross, S. E., Bacon, P. L., & Morris, M. L. (2000). The relational-interdependent self-construal and relationships. *Journal of Personality and Social Psychology*, *78*(4), 791–808.

Crusius, J., & Mussweiler, T. (2012). When people want what others have: The impulsive side of envious desire. *American Psychological Association*, *12*(1), 142–153.

Darley, J. M., & Aronson, E. (1966). Self-evaluation vs. direct anxiety reduction as determinants of the fear-affiliation relationship. *Journal of Experimental Social Psychology*, *1*(Suppl 1), 66–79.

Duffy, M. K., & Shaw, J. D. (2000). The Salieri syndrome: Consequences of envy in groups. *Small Group Research*, *31*(1), 3–23.

Eid, M., & Diener, E. (2001). Norms for experiencing emotions in different cultures: Inter- and intranational differences. *Journal of Personality and Social Psychology*, *81*(5), 869–885.

Ekman, P., & Friesen, W. (1971). Constants across cultures in the face and emotion. *Journal of Personality and Social Psychology, 17*(2), 124–129.

Exline, J. J., Single, P. B., Lobel, M., & Geyer, A. L. (2004). Glowing praise and the envious gaze: Social dilemmas surrounding the public recognition of achievement. *Basic and Applied Social Psychology, 26*(2–3), 119–130.

Feather, N. T. (2012). Tall poppies, deservingness and schadenfreude. *Psychologist, 25*(6), 434–437.

Festinger, L. (1954). A theory of social comparison processes. *Human Relations, 7*(2), 117–140.

Foster, G. M. (1972). The anatomy of envy: A study in symbolic behavior. *Current Anthropology, 13*(2), 165–186.

Fox, S., & Spector, P. E. (1999). A model of work frustration–aggression. *Journal of Organizational Behavior, 20*(6), 915–931.

Gardner, W. L., Gabriel, S., & Hochschild, L. (2002). When you and I are "we," you are not threatening: The role of self-expansion in social comparison. *Journal of Personality and Social Psychology, 82*(2), 239–251.

Gordon, B. F. (1966). Influence and social comparison as motives for affiliation. *Journal of Experimental Social Psychology, 1*(Suppl 1), 55–65.

Gordon, S. L. (1989). Institutional and impulsive orientations in selective appropriating emotions to self. In D. D. Franks & D. McCarthy, Eds., *The Sociology of Emotions: Original Essays and Research Papers* (pp. 115–136). Greenwich, CT: JAI Press.

Graen, G. B., & Scandura, T. (1987). Toward a psychology of dyadic organizing. In B. Staw & L. L. Cumming, Eds., *Research in Organizational Behavior* (vol. 9, pp. 175–208). Greenwich, CT: JAI Press.

Grandey, A. A. (2003). When "the show must go on": Surface acting and deep acting as determinants of emotional exhaustion and peer-rated service delivery. *Academy of Management Journal, 46*(1), 86–96.

Greenwald, A. G., & Breckler, S. J. (1985). To whom is the self presented? In B. Schlenker, Ed., *The Self and Social Life* (pp. 126–145). New York: McGraw-Hill.

Gross, J. J. (1998). The emerging field of emotion regulation: An integrative review. *Review of General Psychology, 2*(3), 271–299.

Gross, J. J. (2001). Emotion regulation in adulthood: Timing is everything. *Current Directions in Psychological Science, 10*(6), 214–219.

Gross, J. J. (2002). Emotion regulation: Affective, cognitive, and social consequences. *Psychophysiology, 39*(3), 281–291.

Gudykunst, W. B., Gao, G., Schmidt, K. L., Nishida, T., Bond, M. H., Leung, K., et al. (1992). The influence of individualism, collectivism, self-monitoring, and predicted-outcome value on communication in ingroup and outgroup relationships. *Journal of Cross-Cultural Psychology, 23*(2), 196–213.

Hakmiller, K. L. (1966). Need for self-evaluation, perceived similarity and comparison choice. *Journal of Experimental Social Psychology, 1*(Suppl 1), 49–54.

Harter, S. (1993). Causes and consequences of low self-esteem in children and adolescents. In R. F. Baumeister, Ed., *Self-Esteem: The Puzzle of Low Self-Regard* (pp. 87–116). New York: Plenum.

Heider, F. (1958). *The Psychology of Interpersonal Relations.* New York: John Wiley.

Hill, S. E., & Buss, D. M. (2006). Envy and positional bias in the evolutionary psychology of management. *Managerial and Decision Economics*, 27(2–3), 131–143.

Hofstede, G. (1980). *Culture's Consequences: International Differences in Work-Related Values.* Beverly Hills, CA: Sage.

Kant, I. (1797). *Die Metaphysik der Sitten.* Königsberg, Germany: Friedrich Nicolovius.

Kashima, Y. & Callan, V. (1994). The Japanese work group. In H. C. Triandis, M. D. Dunnette, & L. M. Hough, Eds., *Handbook of Industrial/Organizational Psychology* (vol. 4, pp. 610–646). Palo Alto, CA: Consulting Psychologists Press.

Kim, E., & Glomb, T. M. (2014). Victimization of high performers: The roles of envy and work group identification. *Journal of Applied Psychology* 99(4), 619-634.

Kitayama, S., & Uchida, Y. (2005). Interdependent agency: An alternative system for action. In R. M. Sorrentino, D. Cohen, J. M. Olson, & M. P. Zanna, Eds., *Culture and Social Behavior: The Ontario Symposium* (vol. 10, pp. 137–164). Mahwah, NJ: Psychology Press.

Leung, K. (1988). Some determinants of conflict avoidance. *Journal of Cross-Cultural Psychology*, 19(1), 125–136.

Liden, R. C., Sparrow, R. T., & Wayne. S. J. (1997). Leader-member exchange theory: The past and potential for the future. In G. R. Ferris, Ed., *Research in Personnel and Human Resources Management* (vol. 15, pp. 47–119). New York: Elsevier Science/ JAI Press.

Lindholm, C. (2008). Culture and envy. In R. H. Smith, Ed., *Envy: Theory and Research* (pp. 227–244). New York: Oxford University Press.

Markus, H. R., & Kitayama, S. (1991). Culture and the self: Implications for cognition, emotion, and motivation. *Psychological Review*, 98(2), 224–253.

Matsumoto, D., Yoo, S. H., Fontaine, J., Anguas-Wong, A. M., Ariola, M., Ataca, B., et al. (2008). Mapping expressive differences around the world: The relationship between emotional display rules and individualism v. collectivism. *Journal of Cross-Cultural Psychology*, 39(1), 55–74.

McClelland, D. C. (1961). *The Achieving Society.* New York: Van Nostrand-Rheinhold.

Menon, T., & Thompson, L. (2010). Envy at work. *Harvard Business Review*, 88(4), 1–6.

Morling, B., Kitayama, S., & Miyamoto, Y. (2003). American and Japanese women use different coping strategies during normal pregnancy. *Personality and Social Psychology Bulletin*, 29(12), 1533–1546.

Murata, A., Moser, J. S., & Kitayama, S. (2013). Culture shapes electrocortical responses during emotion suppression. *Social Cognitive and Affective Neuroscience*, 8(5), 595–601.

Oyserman, D., & Lee, S. W. (2008). Does culture influence what and how we think? Effects of priming individualism and collectivism. *Psychological Bulletin*, 134(2), 311–342.

Parrott, W. G., & Smith, R. H. (1993). Distinguishing the experiences of envy and jealousy. *Journal of Personality and Social Psychology*, 64(6), 906–920.

Plato (2007/360 B.C.). Philebus. (Trans. B. Jowett.) Charleston, SC: BiblioBazaar.

Polman, E., & Ruttan, R. L. (2012). Effects of anger, guilt, and envy on moral hypocrisy. *Personality and Social Psychology Bulletin*, 38(1), 129–139.

Pratt, M. G. (2003). Disentangling collective identity. In J. Polzer, E. Mannix, & M. N. Stamford, Eds., *Identity Issues in Groups: Research in Managing Groups and Teams* (vol. 5, pp. 161–188). Norwalk, CT: Elsevier Science.

Robinson, S. L., & Bennett, R. J. (1995). A typology of deviant workplace behaviors: A multidimensional scaling study. *Academy of Management Journal, 38*(2), 555–572.

Rodriguez Mosquera, P. M., Parrott, W. G., & Hurtado de Mendoza, A. (2010). I fear your envy, I rejoice in your coveting: On the ambivalent experience of being envied by others. *Journal of Personality and Social Psychology, 99*(5), 842–854.

Salovey, P. (1991). *The Psychology of Jealousy and Envy.* New York: Guilford Press.

Salovey, P., & Rothman, A. (1991). Envy and jealousy: Self and society. In P. Salovey, Ed., *The Psychology of Jealousy and Envy* (pp. 271–286). New York: Guilford Press.

Schaubroeck, J., & Lam, S. S. K. (2004). Comparing lots before and after: Promotion rejectees' invidious reactions to promotees. *Organizational Behavior and Human Decision Processes, 94*(1), 33–47.

Schimmel, S. (2008). Envy in Jewish thought and literature. In R. H. Smith, Ed., *Envy: Theory and Research* (pp. 17–38). Oxford, UK: Oxford University Press.

Schoeck, H. (1969). *Envy.* Liberty Press.

Settoon, R. P., & Mossholder, K. W. (2002). Relationship quality and relationship context as antecedents of person-and task-focused interpersonal citizenship behavior. *Journal of Applied Psychology, 87*(2), 255–267.

Singelis, T. M. (1994). The measurement of independent and interdependent self-construals. *Personality and Social Psychology Bulletin, 20*(5), 580–591.

Smith, R. H. (1991). Envy and the sense of injustice. In P. Salovey, Ed., *The Psychology of Jealousy and Envy* (pp. 79–102). New York: Guilford Press.

Smith, E. R., Coats, S., & Walling, D. (1999). Overlapping mental representations of self, in-group, and partner: Further response time evidence and a connectionist model. *Personality and Social Psychology Bulletin, 25*(7), 873–882.

Smith, R. H., & Kim, S. H. (2007). Comprehending envy. *Psychological Bulletin, 133*(1), 46–64.

Smith, R. H., Turner, T. J., Garonzik, R., Leach, C. W., Urch-Druskat, V., & Weston, C. M. (1996). Envy and schadenfreude. *Personality and Social Psychology Bulletin, 22*(2), 158–168.

Stephan, W. G., Stephan, C. W., & De Vargas, M. C. (1996). Emotional expression in Costa Rica and the United States. *Journal of Cross-Cultural Psychology, 27*(2), 147–160.

Stephan, C. W., Stephan, W. G., Saito, I., & Barnett, S. M. (1998). Emotional expression in Japan and the United States: The non-monolithic nature of individualism and collectivism. *Journal of Cross-Cultural Psychology, 29*(6), 728–748.

Tai, K., Narayanan, J., & McAllister, D. J. (2012). Envy as pain: Rethinking the nature of envy and its implications for employees and organizations. *Academy of Management Review, 37*(1), 107–129.

Tajfel, H. (1974). Social identity and intergroup behaviour. *Social Science Information/ Sur les sciences sociales, 13*(2), 65–93.

Taylor, S. E., & Brown, J. D. (1988). Illusion and well-being: A social psychological perspective on mental health. *Psychological Bulletin, 103*(2), 193–210.

Taylor, S. E., Sherman, D. K., Kim, H. S., Jarcho, J., & Takagi, K. (2004). Culture and social support: Who seeks it and why? *Journal of Personality and Social Psychology*, *87*(3), 354–362.

Tesser, A. (1988). Toward a self-evaluation maintenance model of social behavior. In L. Berfcowitz, Ed., *Advances in Experimental Social Psychology* (vol. 21, pp. 181–227). New York: Academic Press.

Triandis, H. C. (1995). *Individualism and Collectivism*. Boulder, CO: Westview.

Triandis, H. C., & Gelfand, M. J. (1998). Converging measurement of horizontal and vertical individualism and collectivism. *Journal of Personality and Social Psychology*, *74*(1), 118–128.

van de Ven, N., Zeelenberg, M., & Pieters, R. (2009). Leveling up and down: The experiences of benign and malicious envy. *Emotion*, *9*(3), 419–429.

van de Ven, N., Zeelenberg, M., & Pieters, R. (2011). Why envy outperforms admiration. *Personality and Social Psychology Bulletin*, *37*(6), 784–795.

van de Ven, N., Zeelenberg, M., & Pieters, R. (2012). Appraisal patterns of envy and related emotions. *Motivation and Emotion*, *36*, 195–204.

Vecchio, R. (2005). Explorations in employee envy: Feeling envious and feeling envied. *Cognition and Emotion*, *19*(1), 69–81.

Wang, C. S., Sivanathan, N., Narayanan, J., Ganegoda, D. B., Bauer, M., Bodenhausen, G. V., et al. (2011). Retribution and emotional regulation: The effects of time delay in angry economic interactions. *Organizational Behavior and Human Decision Processes*, *116*(1), 46–54.

Wheeler, L. (1966). Motivation as a determinant of upward comparison. *Journal of Experimental Social Psychology*, *1*(Suppl 1), 27–31.

Yamagishi, T., Jin, N., & Miller, A. S. (1998). In-group bias and culture of collectivism. *Asian Journal of Social Psychology*, *1*(3), 315–328.

12 | Envy and School Bullying in the Japanese Cultural Context

HIDEFUMI HITOKOTO AND MASATO SAWADA

Introduction

School bullying involves "abuse of power" (Smith & Sharp, 1994) across all societies, and is understood as a "problem of the relationship" among the individuals involved (Pepler, 2006).[1] However, the cultural meanings people attach to the abuse of power or relationship in context—how they carry it out in daily life, the point of engaging in such behavior, and the seemingly subtle meanings conveyed in the actions of bullying—may vary tremendously across cultural contexts. In some cases, understanding the nuances of power abuse and relationships may remedy a problem that is implicitly tied to traditional modes of self, institutionalized values, and the patterns of everyday life that sustain the shared meaning of power and relationship. In this chapter, we argue that cultural context may set the stage for facilitating school bullying, and that focusing on the cultural psychological process of envy may contribute to understanding this longstanding problem in Japanese education.[2] Our review taps into literature on psychology of emotion and cultural psychology, not to localize the problem in Japan (Naito & Gielen, 2005), but to shed light on the problem by framing how it is predicated on the process of envy and entangled with the cultural context so that the abuse of power both in and out of the classroom (i.e., harassment or worker exploitation) can also be integrated under the theory of envy and culture.

The Model

We argue in Figure 12.1 that the abuse of power is often mediated by envy, and that the cultural context surrounding the emotional process may

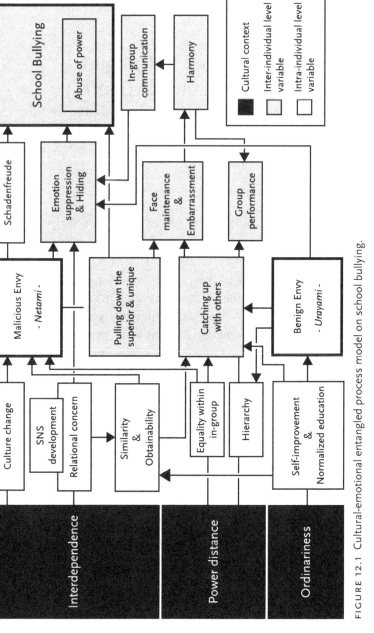

FIGURE 12.1 Cultural-emotional entangled process model on school bullying.

facilitate envy-related bullying. Specifically, malicious envy is considered to mediate the prevalence of school bullying in interdependent cultures. Japanese society has long suffered from school bullying (Toda, Aoyama, & Kanetsuna, 2013), but cultural psychological approaches to the problem have been scarce (Naito & Gielen, 2005). We argue that this problem is in part sustained by traditional cultural practices of interdependence that focus on ordinariness and harmony and power distance, and that, recently, it has been further facilitated by technological development and cultural change.

Cultural Background One: Interdependence and Ordinariness

Japanese cultural understandings of the self and relationships are essentially relational as well as contextual (Markus & Kitayama, 1991). Cultures where individuals mutually understand and share the meanings of the self as such are called *interdependent* cultures.[3] In interdependent cultural settings such as traditional and mainstream Japanese educational institutions and companies, preservation of interpersonal harmony is a requirement for decent social life.

Harmony is achieved by the pursuit of quiescence and of being ordinary: avoiding standing out among others (Hitokoto & Uchida, 2015). The evidence is consistent with this point of view in that Japanese students, when compared to European American students, are quicker to detect a disappearing smile in a target's facial expression (Ishii, Miyamoto, Niedenthal, & Mayama, 2011), encounter more chances to be rejected by their friends (Kashima & Hitokoto, 2009), and show significantly higher scores on diagnostic tests for social phobia symptoms (Dinnel, Kleinkneht, & Tanaka-Matsumi, 2002). These data indicate that interdependence among the Japanese is built on preempting disharmony.

Sensitivity to interpersonal disharmony, particularly to rejection by other in-group members, is considered to be the core element of interdependent self-construal (Dinnel et al., 2002; Okazaki, 1997). When interdependence is the rule, being a full-fledged person requires one to know what the "right way" is, instead of "choosing" one's own way (Markus & Conner, 2014), and to be capable of preserving one's status in one's interpersonal relationships. Because keeping a status requires one to hold up socially acceptable face, or social reputation in the eyes of related others who accept the self, this translates into the motivation to be *normal*. Being normal requires comparison of the self to the general and ordinary others and making the self closer to this shared standard. Japanese social comparison often involves comparison of the self to close friends, and upon noticing the self falling behind, or lacking something, Japanese strive to catch up to the average level (Heine, Kitayama, Lehman, Takata, Ide, Leung, & Matsumoto, 2001; Takata, 1992). This pattern of social comparison varies from that of European Americans', which positions the self in contrast to a higher or a lower comparison target with the motivation to move either closer to (the higher target), or farther away from this person (the lower target) in order to maintain one's self-esteem (Smith, 2000). Japanese social comparison targets can also be ordinary others in general, and the Japanese make efforts to catch up with them out of concern about falling behind, a form of anxiety about the potential disharmony caused by the loss of one's social face.

Deviating from the ordinary can elicit strong anxiety and feelings of discomfort among the Japanese (Sano & Kuroishi, 2009). The ordinariness orientation is developed through egalitarian education that focuses on nurturing the *generalist* instead of the unique *specialist* in the mainstream work context (Toivonen, Norasakkunkit, & Uchida, 2011). Ohashi (2010) measured cross-age differences in the student-rated favorability of being ordinary (*Fu-tsuu* in Japanese). She found that, around the first year of junior high school (i.e., age 12–13), most students recognized themselves as ordinary, favored being ordinary, and thought their friends would favor ordinary individuals. Coincidentally, this is the approximate age at which the reported level of victimization from school bullying is highest compared to that of other age groups (Morita, 2001).

Favoring ordinariness usually functions to preserve one's well-being in this cultural context. Recognition that one is an ordinary person is correlated with interpersonal harmony and the feeling of quiescence. Hitokoto and Uchida (2015) administered a scale of interdependent happiness (IHS), which included items asking about interpersonal harmony, quiescence, and ordinariness among others, to Japanese, Korean, German, and American adults. Results showed that the unique correlation between IHS and subjective well-being was systematically stronger in more collectivistic countries. An ordinary person may experience a higher level of subjective well-being in the cultural context of interdependence by maintaining good harmony in his or her in-group. An interdependent cultural context also often fosters social anxiety because social reputation is something essentially out of one's control: being anxious about how one might appear to others becomes functional. Others' approval is best gained when one behaves according to and is ready to respond to others' expectations, and by being loyal and committed to the standards shared in the group. In Japanese culture, the game is not about being unique, but more about everyone's being capable of doing the same basic things as others, and staying in tune with related others in order to maintain the group's harmony.

Implications for Envy

Two Types of Envy in Interdependent Cultural Contexts

To analyze the relationship between interdependent cultural context and envy, we first need to distinguish between the two types of envy: benign and malicious. While benign envy motivates individuals to improve towards an admired target, malicious envy motivates individuals to decrease the relative superiority of the rival to the self, leading the individual to attempt to pull down the rival. Clearly, malicious envy may cause interpersonal disruption, but this malice is considered to be the proper, core feeling of envy (Smith & Kim, 2007; Miceli & Castelfranchi, 2007). When an interdependent culture requires its members to preserve interpersonal harmony, then, malicious envy is a type of emotion that has to be regulated or prevented (Uchida & Kitayama, 2009).

Interestingly, this cultural focus on the destructive nature of malicious envy can be seen in the "emotion words" of envy communicated among Japanese. Emotion words that are culturally valued or sanctioned may be detailed to describe particular experiences, so that they can be collectively regulated through daily interactions (Mesquita, 2001). In contrast to English, which has only one word for *envy*, two separate Japanese terms are used to denote *benign envy* and *malicious envy* (Hoogland, Thielke, & Smith, Chapter 5; Sterling, van de Ven, & Smith, Chapter 3, this volume) in Japanese: *Urayami* (benign envy) and *Netami* (malicious envy). Explicitly telling others that one is feeling *Netami* is socially unacceptable in Japan, as is expressing malicious envy in English-speaking countries. Among the forms of envy, *Netami* particularly refers to the painful social comparison (Duffy, Scott, Shaw, Tepper, & Aquino, 2012; Yu & Duffy, Chapter 2; Floyd & Sterling, Chapter 7, this volume). However, the fact that the Japanese have developed independent terms for these two types of envy is intriguing. It may point to how Japanese daily social exchanges of envy are culturally focused (Mesquita, 2001), and therefore articulated, so that speakers explicitly hide the darker one for fear of inviting disharmony, much more so than in English-speaking countries.

In Japanese, *Urayami* (benign envy) is the term often used under envy/admiration inducing situations, and the term is used when telling others about the content of social comparison. For example, *Urayamashii,* a variation of *Urayami*, is used when one is admiring another's advantage over oneself. This is publicly stated, and often positively responded to by others with some sympathy or agreement. In contrast, *Netamashii,* a variation of *Netami* (malicious envy), can connote a negative comparison; using this term could lead others to be alarmed that the speaker and his or her target might engage in interpersonal conflict. Interestingly, a seven-year-old (a second-year student of elementary school) can understand the word *Urayami* (benign envy), while not all of the same age group will understand the word *Netami* (malicious envy) (Sawada, 2006), suggesting some collective avoidance of the word denoting malicious envy in Japanese early education.

In an interdependent cultural context, expression of malicious envy is strongly suppressed because of harmony concerns. Beyond suppressing the emotion, the Japanese take preventive steps to protect others from feeling malicious envy when something positive has happened solely to the self. Uchida and Kitayama (2009) argued that Japanese people are strongly concerned about being happy alone in their group, since they do not want close others to maliciously envy them. When researchers collected the meaning of "happiness" from students, some students described the meaning as "something that invite others' malicious envy toward the self." Because Japanese share the meaning of "happiness" as "harmony," they are quick to denote the absence of others' malicious envy (and perhaps other sources of disharmony) as a necessary part of their happiness. Prevention of malicious envy, therefore, seems to be a necessary part of happiness in interdependent cultures.

Such regulation, however, will only remain superficial, or normative, since the emotion is so strong that it burns the individual from inside (Kim & Glomb, 2014). In fact, Japanese do experience malicious envy, which is indirectly expressed via interpersonal violence such as school bullying, or observing (and not stopping) bullying out of schadenfreude (Sawada, 2006; Sawada, Kanetsuna, & Toda, 2014). *Schadenfreude* is a pleasurable emotion experienced over others' misfortune. This other is, quite often the case, a target of one's own envy, so schadenfreude is considered to be a feeling of joy over the misfortune that has befallen someone one envies in some way (Hoogland et al., Chapter 5; Floyd & Sterling, Chapter 7;

Vidaillet, Chapter 8, this volume). Because we believe in this innate intensity of envy, our analysis below is built on the perspective that, when envy shows its violent side in the cultural context of interdependence, more indirect, closed, hidden, and justified types of bullying (Kanetsuna, 2004) will emerge.

When the two types of envy are seen in the Japanese context, they may function differently, depending on the envying agent's relative state of achievement in that agent's in-group. When one is falling behind the standard, he/she is likely to be benignly envious of those who have already achieved the normal standard and become motivated to improve the self (i.e., "I want to be an *ordinary* person, like others"). Here, malicious envy will rarely be felt, because the very point of motivating the self to catch up to the ordinary standard is to preserve group harmony, and malicious envy will be destructive of this end. However, the benign envy might well be mixed with the emotion of *embarrassment* in this situation, because not being able to live up to others' expectations and norms can hint at a potential loss of one's face in the eyes of other members of the group. In other words, when the target of achievement is the normative standard, the state of falling behind will be felt as a genuine lack (i.e., "Everyone normally has it, but *I* don't!"). Benign envy towards those who are clearly superior to oneself is also available among interdependent cultural members, and because the interdependent self is a rooted, related, and *ranked* self (Markus & Conner, 2014), the hierarchical relationship and the powerful individual who is at the center of the group will be especially admired. Also, this benign envy towards an in-group superior tends to be a matter of normative requirement (i.e., "*Admire* your boss!"). However, for reasons we discuss later, when to-be-superior individuals try to rise, they will initially face a great attack of malicious envy from others before being granted a higher status, since the general rule of an interdependent culture is to preserve harmony and not be unique. For example, either benign or malicious envy may explain passive violence in which students observe and neglect school bullying (Sawada, 2013). It seems that envy towards those regarded as normal and the envy towards those regarded as superior can have quite distinct meanings for the Japanese: while the former tends to be benign and mixed with embarrassment, the latter may transform from malicious envy into normative and/or private admiration, depending on the accumulated social reputation of the target person, thus functioning to preserve in-group cohesion at the group level.

The key to understanding the link between envy and school bullying is the role of malicious envy in *maintaining* group harmony when someone in the group breaches or is expected to breach that harmony by standing out (being superior). Because of the salience of "face" and the extent to which group goals are pursued in daily work, a solely individual success that takes place within a group will probably undermine or potentiate conflicts with the group interest, even though the individual success is a positive experience. Because of this, when one becomes superior without paying sufficient attention to preventing disharmony, in-group members will condemn this person, and the individual's success will be regarded as a betrayal of the group.

Narrow Horizons on the Improving Self

The Japanese belief in the significance of self-improvement is so strong that most Japanese success stories involve a plot about how the protagonists constantly improved and upgraded themselves (Heine et al., 2001). Historically retold in such stories are the notion of endless self-improvement, and an almost illusory value ascribed to the *process*, and implicit disregard of the actual *outcome*. Someone's working until they die, for example, can be regarded as a beautiful sacrifice for the group, if not a happy story. Because this improvement is ultimately intended to maximize group harmony, being fundamentally unique or radically different at the expense of harmony is prohibited. As a result, among the majority, endless self-improvement will be tamed and packed into a pursuit of features that are just ordinary: studying hard in cram school to get into a decent (not exactly outstanding) university, working hard until midnight to earn an ordinary salary and a decent (not exactly special) job, and so on. Therefore, especially for the achievements that most people can reach, and thus one's minimally accepted face can be established, commitment to the right effort is believed to be the longest, yet shortest, route to their attainment. In Japanese elementary schools, students are required to set short-term goals to accomplish (i.e., to greet their teachers, pick up trash when they see it, prepare their lunch promptly, and so on), and in daily classroom meetings, every child is required to self-reflect about whether he or she accomplished the goal as a member of a team. They are required to mutually monitor whether someone is falling behind on this campaign in a meeting called a *Hansei-kai* (self-reflection meeting). In Japanese junior high school, students belong to a club activity group and are taught to fulfill the group norms, often provided by their teachers, coaches, or elder students, together with their fellows. Such self-reflective practices are also considered to be a significant part of quality control in major industries such as the automobile industry (Imai, 1986).[4]

As a result of this constant concern about interpersonal harmony, Japanese negative social comparison and envy exclusively involve the focus on the comparison between the self and the surrounding others such as one's friends. Sawada (2005) surveyed 92 children ranging from third-grade elementary school students to third-year junior high school students (ages 8–15 years old) on their experiences of envy. Interviewees were instructed to respond to the question, "Please think back to times when your brothers, sisters, or friends appeared feeling good about something that involved comparison between them and yourself, and you felt bad about the incident" After nominating an incident, students rated the extent to which they felt envy-related emotion words such as "bitterness," "sadness," and "hatred." When correspondence analysis was administered to the emotions, three categories were found: a malicious feeling towards a superior other, a feeling of anguish regarding the inferior self, and a feeling of deficiency focusing on one's lack. Thus, the emotional meaning of envy for Japanese students involved malicious envy, appraisals about the surrounding others and the self, as well as a sense of lack. This is in line with Takata's (1992) argument regarding Japanese social comparison, involving comparison of the self to others, followed by a focus on a lack, to improve. Furthermore, when nominated situations were categorized, the targets of envy ranged from getting a good grade, having better physical education performance scores, receiving praise from teachers, or having better health compared to their friends. All of these comparisons were on the dimensions that are attainable through making an effort in school life. The conception of envy among Japanese students revolves around malicious feelings mixed with negative comparisons with their surrounding others over attainable targets.

Similarity and Obtainability

At first glance, it may appear counterintuitive to argue that malicious envy implies attainability, since past studies show that *low* attainability leads to frustration (Lockwood & Kunda, 1997) and malicious envy (see Sterling, van de Ven, & Smith, Chapter 3, this volume). However, in a context where most of the people/students are provided with a decent life necessities out of the tradition of normalized education such as in Japan, the goal is to live life in a normal way through preserving one's status and keeping one's obligation.

Here, we argue that culture might be a factor in the control/obtainability–malicious envy relationship. Control is an indispensable element of independent cultural practice (Morling, Kitayama, & Miyamoto, 2002). If malicious envy essentially flows from *unexpected despair about one's expected attainment caused by the greater success of a rival* across cultures, and the independent means to avoid this end is control, then low control would be related to malicious envy in independent cultures, because despair will be guaranteed when one lacks control. Therefore, Americans would significantly lose their sense of control during the experience of envy, and this was found to be the case in Smith, Sawada, Hitokoto, Hoogland, Brown, and Cooper (2013). However, in the Japanese educational setting, which is so full of normalized, prepared, and common settings across students, individuals are surrounded by millions of cues persuading them that they are similar to others and can expect to have the same things as others as long as they can preserve a minimum social standing through their efforts. If someone possesses something valuable or special in this context, obtainability, or the expectation that others would also be able to have the valuable thing at some point, may better predict malicious envy than control does, because such similarity-induced obtainability would strongly suggest unexpected despair about the lack of a cooperative and harmonized campaign of efforts with the target person (i.e., "We are supposed to have the same things if we keep trying together, but the fact is that he/she already has it and I don't!"). Thus, in Japan, one may expect to observe a positive correlation between obtainability and malicious envy under circumstances of high similarity.

At first glance, such coexistence of effort and harmony may appear contradictory. Making one's effort in a class, for example, would make the self differ from others, thus ordinariness would be breached as a result. However, Japanese self-improvement is always situated in the in-group context where harmony is the indispensable goal (Heine et al., 2001). Students will be struggling to improve *together* with close others, and the campaign of self-improvement is intended to succeed as a group, and not as an individual (Imai, 1986). These close others are, for example in Japanese formal education, perceived as people sharing the same background, fate, and preferences, and even the same values and ideals, and are thus perceived to be *similar* to the self. They are normatively encouraged to wear the same uniform, use the same utensils, walk to school together, eat the same provided lunch and clean up the classroom at the same time, decide their career path during the same developmental period, and find a job at the same time after undergraduate education. This practice of similarity would give them a strong comparative ground, which would in turn strengthen the perceived obtainability of valuables and goals (e.g. "I should work harder, because I and he/she are supposed to have started at the *same* time and having the *same* things, for he/she is a *similar* student from the *same* school as I am!").

Sawada (2006) surveyed 1,600 elementary school children in terms of how they appraised the hypothetical situation of facing a friend who was better off than themselves. Children rated the extent to which they felt envy-related emotions, along with appraisals of obtainability of the valuable good possessed by this friend, such as a high exam score. He prepared two versions of this better friend: one was described as someone who had obtained a comparable exam score or allowance before (high similarity condition), and the other as someone who had been better off than the self before (low similarity condition). Results showed that children's perceptions of obtainability as well as envy were maximized in the high similarity condition, and the appraisal of obtainability mediated envy. Because this study merely used aggregated scores of benign and malicious envy, it was unclear which type of envy this similarity-induced obtainability predicted. In another study, Sawada (2005) did differentiate between benign and malicious envy and measured both among elementary school children in a hypothetical social comparison situation. He again found that similar others, such as one's classmates, were both benignly and maliciously envied, and he also found that this was differently pronounced by the content of the comparison: students maliciously envied the target person when compared on internal attributes (i.e., test scores or athletic ability), and they benignly envied the target person when compared on external attributes (i.e., having a chance to go on a vacation to a foreign country). It is possible that, for those who believe in self-improvement, or an endless capability to make themselves better, when internal attributes are compared with those of supposed-to-be similar others, the more obtainable they perceive the attribute to be, the more malice they will feel.

Implications for School Bullying

Damping Down the Unique

Despite the importance of ordinariness, some individuals do stand out for their exceptional performance. However, those unique ones are likely to face cultural pressure to conform to the ordinariness imposed by their friends, because being exceptionally unique can *potentiate* a breach of harmony via damaging everyone else's face in the group. Unlike in cultural contexts encouraging uniqueness, diversity, and creativity, where difference is taken as an opportunity (Takemura, 2014), in interdependent contexts, attempts to make the self appear different from others, let alone out-compete others, can be regarded as a sort of insult or betrayal.

Supporting this argument, it has been found that Japanese students are bullied mainly by their classroom friends, rather than by students from other classes (Morita, 2001), and that bullies perceive that their act of violence is a sort of righteous education they should give to the victims, who are perceived by the perpetrators as odd, unique, and therefore breaching classroom order (Kanetsuna, Smith, & Morita, 2006). Also, Sawada (2006) found that malicious envy predicted destructive coping behaviors, such as damaging victims' valuables, a form of relational aggression in the Japanese classroom. When a child student becomes notable, the very class group he or she has been making an effort for will become a hidden threat bearing malicious envy toward that child's further accomplishment (see Adams & Plaut, 2003, for a similar discussion).

The possible cultural background for envy in this context will be that these envious friends are actively disregarding the unique individuals in fear of losing their own face and harmony. This cultural dynamic could lead unique Japanese students to be victimized due to envy as well as the schadenfreude of their friends. This would be especially painful when the unique student conceives of well-being in terms of the harmony of interpersonal relationships. In such a case, he/she will inevitably need to weigh his/her path against relational harmony (Ogihara & Uchida, 2014), or suffer from a double burden of both academic success and preservation of his/her interpersonal harmony. This could explain why harmonious interpersonal relationships are undermined by increased socioeconomic status in interdependent culture (Hitokoto, 2014).

Another motivation of classmates bullying their friends would be the *contempt* or *disgust* (Kanetsuna, 2014) felt towards those who could not catch up to the ordinary level and fell behind the collective campaign of being ordinary. Considering the fact that ordinariness may also disturbed by someone lower than the shared standard, an ordinariness orientation may push the average members to either turn a cold shoulder to those who have failed to be ordinary, or to disregard their social face entirely. Viewed from the perspective of this inferior unique one, ordinary individuals could be captured as a target of envy as well as *resentment* for excluding the self. However, because cultural orientation towards ordinariness is satisfied after achieving the standard that one can at least preserve one's minimum social face as a normal person, there will not be much of an incentive for interdependent cultural members to actively aggress against, if not warmly accept, those lower than the ordinary standard. Such a subtle disregard towards those lower might be another factor that gives "righteousness" to Japanese bullies.

Hidden Violence

Whenever there is news of bullying victims' committing suicide, the teacher who is in charge of the classroom commonly reports that he/she "didn't know that there was bullying going on in the class." Accepting the fact that some of those teachers were actually ignorant of what was going on, among the general Japanese audiences who hear the news, these confessions of the teacher echo like a cliché. Severe Japanese school bullying is very much hidden from the eyes of others outside the bullying.

One culprit in this scenario would be the culturally shaped skills of masking negative emotions among the victims. In Japan, victims show suppressed levels of help-seeking (Kanetsuna et al., 2006), which means that critical interventions often occur late. Fear of disturbing one's social harmony, or concern about stepping on a potentially slippery slope to losing one's social standing, is so strong for the members of interdependent cultures that they hesitate to ask for help from others when face or harmony is at stake (Taylor, Sherman, Kim, Jarcho, Takagi, & Dunagan, 2004). This anxiety is called "relational concern" (Hayashi, 2009; Taylor et al., 2004), and is strongly suspected to be a motivation of victims who are hesitant to speak up publicly about being bullied, which is essentially embarrassing and therefore will lead to the loss of their face. When relational concern is salient, individuals may rather sacrifice themselves in order to preserve the group norm. One result of such habituated behavior is the intentional regulation of negative emotions (Murata, Moser, & Kitayama, 2012). When Japanese students were shown a negative emotional stimulus together with an instruction to suppress the emotion, compared to European American students, they were much more efficient at doing so, even at the neural level of emotion regulation. Such automatic processing should require a lifelong practice of emotional suppression, presumably on behalf of group harmony. Suppression occurs for envy as well, and for this, any social comparison taking place in the Japanese classroom becomes very subtle; therefore, the victims of bullying may not notice that they are the target of others' envy until they are explicitly bullied.

Cultural emotional suppression may also drive up the violence of bullies by increasing the number of bystanders who are also suppressive of their negative emotions about the bullying of their classmates. That is, where observers of the bullying are concerned and trying their best to prevent disharmony in a relationship circle that includes bullies, and are capable of maintaining anonymity within that group which shares an in-group rule to righteously aggress against a certain individual, the number of observers would simply accumulate. What is worse is that those who are willing to stand up to stop bullying may stand out as another anomaly in the bullies' circle. Consistent with this argument, student interventions to stop bullying decrease in Japan, while they increase in England and the Netherlands around the first to the second year of junior high school (Morita, 2001), when the reported victimization reaches the highest level among all age groups. This could also suggest that the Japanese envy-related violence would potentially escalate at around the junior high school level.

A final source of bullying may be rooted in the shared meaning of "bullying" itself. Japanese in-group communication often uses implicit channels such as unwritten norms or extremely subtle perspective-taking. Surely, in every culture, in-group communication almost necessarily involves shared in-group understandings about the topic of conversation, presumably because communicating in a way that leaves an idea unsaid but mutually understandable can make conversing partners feel close to each other. However, in Japan, where harmony is the valued norm, an almost artistic synchronization of perspective-taking is valued and practiced in close relationships (Markus & Kitayama, 1991). In such successful communication, seeming rejection (i.e., saying to your closest friend, "You are an idiot," as a joke) may, in fact imply a very informal, paradoxically accepting message as an in-group member. The reason why the Japanese take such a roundabout way to express attachment towards their close others may be a habituated, overly cautious approach to in-group reputation (Snyzer, Takemura, Delton, Sato, Robertson, Cosmides, & Tooby, 2012), and the resulting automatic concern about losing social face. According to Hayama and Sakurai (2008), bullying may start when a teasee does not catch the benign intensions of the teaser. If the art of good (ideally in-group) communication lies on the fine line where one shares the good intensions of a teaser without exposing oneself to the embarrassment of losing face, then in such a context, mistakes in reading the right intensions of the teaser should be unavoidable, and the teasee may feel especially humiliated.

One linguistic piece of evidence for this interpretation is apparent in the word *Ijime* (bullying). *Ijime* is a conjugation of *Ijiri* (to play, or fumble), a word used to describe in-group joking directed towards someone (i.e., the act of sending the message "you are an idiot" in an in-group context can be described as *Ijiri*). Being the target of *Ijiri* actions (or "*Ijirareru*") may quite often be regarded as one paradoxical proof of being taken good care of by supportive others. Therefore, in Japanese language use, bullying is expressed as a variation of in-group joking. Thus, the reason why Japanese bullying tends to be hidden might be that the ideal form of communication takes place in the most implicit channels. Also, this "articulated" hiding of violence could, if skilled enough, be applied to hide the violence due to malicious envy. For example, it could be used to give the excuse for the bullies damaging the valuables of the victim that they were just playing, or hanging around together.

Anecdotal evidence suggests that when bullying takes place and the victim has been peer-pressured by the bullies not to admit that he/she is being victimized, bullies often report to the teachers that they were just joking/playing with each other: Bullies are clever enough to disguise their abuse with this excuse because they fully understand that the ideal communication exchanged among the *good* friends may sometimes appear abusive to a third person. An interesting hypothesis we can derive from this argument is that Japanese bullies may utilize high *machiavellian intelligence* or related perspective-taking skills in order to abuse their social power under the name of group justice. Then, if a sub-group of bullies in the classroom collaboratively envies someone who possesses a socially desirable attribute, such as academic ability, even a socially valued person such as a brilliant student could also be treated as one who is "unjust."

Cultural Background Two: Power Distance

In high power-distance cultures, members of the culture accept the fact that there are differences in how power is distributed (Hofstede, 2001). In such cultures, people tend to separate themselves into different sets of socially agreed-upon classes in their society. Examples include the caste system in India, and the four classes (warriors to tradesmen in the Edo period) in Japan. Although the four classes are no longer present today, classes based on age, affiliated university/company, and occupational status would be the popular powers recognized by the Japanese today.

When communicating with someone who belongs to a different class than the self, normative behaviors become different, and these repertoires of behavior are strictly coded. It is very common for Japanese junior high school students to learn to use honorifics to address teachers and even to address those who are only one year senior to them. Students from different school years rarely interact with each other, and seniors formally use their power to lead and teach younger students. A breach of those codes can invite severe social punishment, including a superior's righteous anger, deprivation of resources, contempt for a moral violation, or simply isolation.

Surely, not all aspects of cultural power distance are sources of problems; rather, in power-distant cultures, stratified hierarchies may have served certain functions to preserve organizational activities, such as heavy industry in the mid-twentieth century in Japan. However, Japanese individuals with high objective socioeconomic status have more privilege of expressing anger than those of lower status (Park, Kitayama, Markus, Coe, Miyamoto, Karasawa, et al., 2013), lower-status individuals follow cultural rules to either mask or neutralize negative emotional expressions, especially in front of higher-status individuals (Ekman, 1989), and high power-distance cultural members are less critical of an insulter when the insulter has higher status than the self (Bond, Wan, Leung, & Giacalone, 1985); thus, cultural power distance can potentiate power abuse.

Once a higher-status individual starts to abuse his/her power, individuals located at the lower end of the power continuum—such as employees or students—may have less chance to defy the skewed distribution of power. The power structure is maintained in such a way that those of higher status can further extend their power on one hand, and impose upon those of lower status to suppress their negative emotions and be obedient to the other. The fact that a large number of individuals accept power differences may result in people's being overly willing to leave decisions to a leading authority, or may result in subordinates' having no choice but to obey a tyrant. In the latter case, lower-status individuals are often forced to follow behavioral norms that run contrary to their personal feelings. Because these behaviors are essentially norms, sometimes "respectful" behaviors may involve being thoughtlessly agreeable to one's boss, masking the negative feelings one truly has for rude customers, or not registering any accusations when sexually harassed by an elder. These norms may be learned through early education, such as in junior high school, when most of the students participate in-group activities involving power difference, such as club activities, and through the seniority hierarchy in the curriculum.

Implications for Envy

Implications of cultural power distance for envy can be manifold, since power distance may lead to people to sensitive appraisals of status difference and equality, in order to know their own and others' proper place/status. Importantly, when there is a higher-status individual than the self, the norm is to show admiration and respect-related behaviors to the superior. When the superior is considered to be an appropriate occupant of the higher status, respect will be suitable, and as far as this applies, practices of honorifics and seniority can function to enhance organizational performance motivated by respect on the subordinates' side, and communal caring on the superiors' side. Also in this case, superiors will be often admired as a target of benign envy by those of lower status. However, when the higher status is not occupied by someone regarded as appropriate, and subordinates are given a formal chance to climb up the social ladder, then subordinates may suffer from more malicious envy because there are multiple institutionalized means (e.g., freedom to choose the business/training menu in a workplace/club activity, opportunity to communicate with and have their requests granted by the boss) for the superiors to preserve the status quo.

In a worst case, power holders (such as a year-elder student in junior high school), are socially authorized to exercise abusive actions toward subordinates under the auspices of education or teaching, and the lower-status students are deprived of any means to adjust the power equilibrium. The subordinates have no choice but to suppress their aggression following malicious envy. In all probability, accumulation of this emotion may lead to higher hopes among the subordinates to see those of higher status fall. For example, Sawada and Hayama (2012) found that those who are vengeful feel particularly intense schadenfreude towards the fallen superior's plight.

Envy is not only experienced by lower-status holders toward those of higher status. When a superior is envious of someone of lower status for his/her distinguished performance, the felt frustration will strike the higher status even more strongly than a simple defeat. This is because the norm of the subordinate is to be submissive, and because of this, higher-status individuals are rarely exposed to their subordinates' trying to out-compete them. Also, admitting that the self (superior) is falling behind the lower-status person, and admiring his/her abilities, would be a disgrace to one's own face; therefore, benign envy is unlikely to be felt. As a result, higher-status individuals may feel intense humiliation together with envy of the capability that the lower-status individuals possess. Chances of such a "takeover" will increase when educational and working institutions start to encourage individual skills and abilities rather than hierarchically structured group outputs. Taken together, a power-distant cultural context may set a stage to either overly suppress expressions of malicious envy, or to further enhance aggressive intentions in the wake of this emotion.

Another interesting effect of power distance on envy is the members' appraisal of equal-status holders who share the same level in the power hierarchy. Simply sharing the same hierarchical position, such as age, local origin, or occupational rank, is often a sufficient condition for the members of power-distant cultures to assume high similarity between themselves and others. Japanese classroom activities often involve group practices such as sharing an entire curriculum with the same students, eating school lunches with the same students, cleaning up the room with the same students, competing with other classrooms in sports contests and chorus concerts with the same students, and having teachers interact with the same students as a group. Once they are put into the same class, the similarity among individuals is stressed, and hierarchical differences, such as school age, are strictly differentiated in Japanese formal education. One result of these practices is that members' hierarchical ranks remain stable for a long time. If there is a change, those who were originally at the same hierarchical level as the rising individual would feel intensified envy because they have long shared a belief in their similarity and expected to have the same fate as that person. When power distance is societally accepted, it is believed that similar others, in multiple ways, *should* stay the same.

If this hypothetical dynamic holds for children living in the Japanese educational context that stresses equality, then malicious envy can intensify all the more when a should-be-equal friend has succeeded ahead of the self. Sawada (2008) presents anecdotal evidence from Japan suggesting just how serious such envy towards a similar member in a hierarchy is.

At an elementary school festival where children were to put on a staging of *Snow White*, some parents made a claim to the teacher that it was not equal for their own child to play a supporting role in the play. As a result, this class had to rearrange *Snow White* into a play involving 35 Snow Whites, with every student getting to play Snow White. In a school sports contest where the elementary school classes competed with each other, teachers who felt uncomfortable about ranking students from the same grade from first to last required students to first run around the track as usual, and to stop right before the finish line so that everyone could reach the goal at the same time. These actual examples from Japan show how concerned the Japanese are about maintaining equality within a stable hierarchy, and not daring to reveal envy in a should-be-equal classroom.

Implications for School Bullying

Japanese students are bullied by their classroom friends, rather than by elders in other classrooms as often occurs in English school bullying (Kanetsuna, 2004). We believe this is one example of envy towards similar others. When one class contains approximately 35 students who are being taught to focus on similarities such as age or socioeconomic status, these practices are likely to lead to unwanted competition among the should-be-equal students sharing the same level in a hierarchy.

When individual differences arise in such normalized classrooms, the dynamics among students may lead them to preserve their equal status on one hand, and to behave submissively to the power holder—in this case, a bully—on the other hand. This may set the stage for indirect bullying: malicious action towards one's schoolmate by means of name-calling, blackmailing, or spreading rumors, manipulated and commanded by a limited number of true bullies in the class. Consistent with this argument, bullies in Japanese classrooms tend to be those who hold a certain fame among the class members; indirect bullying is the most typical method of bullying in Japan (Kanetsuna, 2004); the number of individuals who always bully someone is extremely limited within a class (Morita, 2001); and the predominance of students who either subject themselves to bullies or stand back increases with school grade, and these observers experience constant fear that they might become the next target (Morita, 2001). Japanese "classroom bullying" may be described as a hidden, passive, bystanders' ostracism of those who are unique. Surely, in any culture, ostracism is sadly one of the very basic forms of collective violence, which can be traced back to the human evolutionary past. However, the interdependent, ordinariness-oriented, and hierarchy-conscious cultural norms and values are compatible with this particular aspect of human violence.

Because of the classroom hierarchy structure, Japanese bullying demonstrates punitive dynamics toward minorities in the class. Onishi, Kurokawa, and Yoshida (2009) used scenarios to examine the types of bullying in Japan among elementary and junior high school children. They found two types of bullying: "anomaly exclusion," defined by bullying to reject and ostracize weak minorities in order to preserve uniformity in one's group; and "punishment," defined as the bullying of victims who are perceived to have made mistakes that have damaged some collective interest. For example, punishment will befall those who have bragged about their high exam scores to other members in the class, or those who do not reply to others' greetings. Importantly, punishment bullying is a type of bullying in which the bullies believe they are doing "justice" by taking punitive control over the faults in the victims.

Sawada (2013) surveyed Japanese elementary and junior high school students to determine the facilitating factor in the "anomaly exclusion" type of bullying. Students read hypothetical scenarios describing the self being asked by other members of the class to bully a member of the class because this person was getting on everyone's nerves by having a big mouth. Using between-participant manipulation, this victim was described as either someone who was bragging about his/her good score (envy condition), telling others about the self's lowered score (hatred condition), or someone simply chatting too much (control condition). Results indicated that in the envy condition, significantly more students responded that they (1) would personally decline to join in the bullying, but (2) would not tell others to stop bullying, compared to other conditions. This indicates that when Japanese students were asked to be passively involved in the "anomaly exclusion" conducted against the envied individual in a class, they were likely to become observers: passive onlookers who account for the largest number of classroom students (in a 35-student classroom environment), and are suspected to be the cause of the increase in school bullying in Japan (Morita, 2001). Taking into consideration the exclusive, punitive orientation in the class, this negative response after envy can be one tool to achieve the cultural goal of the Japanese class: to normalize and maintain ordinariness among the should-be-the-same others.

New Contexts 1: Cyberbullying

Japan's well-known high-technology industry and cell phones with Internet access, used mainly by the young, sadly have been spurring school bullying in unprecedented ways. In Japan, there have been continuous troubles occurring on either bulletin board systems (BBS) on the Web, or more recently, on social networking services such as "LINE." LINE is a chatting application on a smartphone. Junior high school students particularly favor the use of LINE, which provides a group chat function to invite individuals and create an internal chat. If a member texts to the group, all the other group members can see the message.

Useful as it seems, this function is often used as a tool to expel individuals from the group. For example, if one individual is disliked by the rest of the group, others can either create an independent internal chat by themselves, or directly exclude the anomalous one from the existing chat group and send him/her an automated notice of ostracism. When using such technology, people do not need to directly engage in interpersonal conflict to exclude a former member. They can mask, disguise, or hide themselves in anonymity, so they can avoid direct interaction with someone they dislike, or avoid having complicated relationships. This would be especially useful to children with immature interpersonal conflict-resolution skills, who are living in a conflict-preempting culture. Above all, this hidden nature of chatting is nicely compatible with subtle Japanese interaction, which originally should have meant preserving harmony without anyone losing face.

The aforementioned features of text message technology can set a great stage for Japanese students' bullying, known as *cyberbullying*. Cyberbullying is different from traditional bullying in that the perpetrator does not usually see the victim's reaction, at least in the short term; the variety of bystander roles is more complex, and the breadth of the potential audience is increased (Smith, 2015). According to the Ministry of Education, Culture, Sports, Science, and Technology (MEXT, 2014), there were more than 8,787 cyberbullying incidents in 2013 (4.5% of all types of bullying), and this prevalence has not changed for some time. Because of the estimated recent expansion of the technological repertoire in this crime, cyberbullying has now become a serious concern, leading to student problem behaviors including inappropriate postings about their classmates or teachers (Aoyama, Utsumi, & Hasegawa, 2012).

Surely cyberbullying may take place in any culture; however, when the technology is combined with the cultural context of interdependence, some of the incidents may become psychologically more painful. In some cases, LINE-related bullying has escalated to the point where it drives the victim to suicide. Anecdotal evidence suggests that Japanese junior high school students sometimes fear being bullied after receiving a message from their friends. This is facilitated by the fact that LINE provides the function of posting an "already read" notice. When sending a message to another, the sender can see when the recipient has "already read" the message. This was originally provided as a notice to inform the sender to wait for the recipient to reply; however, Japanese students feel anxious that their friends—the senders—would be angry if they do not reply quickly after reading the initial message. Such an obligatory emotional process surrounding Japanese communication, that even receiving a message can impose an obligation to reply, can easily be combined with the anxiety of being rejected by one's friends. We may be able to argue that this produces a modern high-tech version of social anxiety.

Cyberbullying can take place both in and out of school, and it is fairly easy for many individuals to get involved and for perpetrators to remain highly anonymous. Given that Japanese school bullying has been conducted with the use of indirect violence, the features of cyberbullying described above may even facilitate violence caused by a classroom dynamic of ostracism sustained by many *reinforcers* and *bystanders* (e.g., Salmivalli, 1999; Salmivalli, Lagerspetz, Björkqvist, Österman, Kaukiainen, 1996). While some students may be sympathetic to the victim, these subgroups in the classroom "take pleasure in the misery of others," and these students are more likely to reinforce or get involved in the collective accumulation of abusive power resorted to by the perpetrators. These individuals are known to feel joy when observing victims suffer, and thus, their emotional process would resemble taking joy in others' pain: schadenfreude. To investigate this possibility, Sawada, Kanetuna, and Toda (2014) surveyed Japanese junior high school students on the relationship between enviousness towards a hypothetical target and their emotional reactions to cyberbullying conducted against the target. Results showed that envy-prone individuals tend to report increased schadenfreude when they observe the target being bullied on the Internet. The results would point to the possibility that (presumably malicious) envy and its resulting aggression can easily extend to aggression in the cyber space.

New Contexts 2: Culture Change Toward Individualism

Smith, Sawada, Hitokoto, Hoogland, Brown, and Cooper (2013) compared envy experienced by Japanese and North American students. They instructed both Japanese and North American students to recall their experiences of malicious envy and benign envy, and had them retrospectively rate the extent to which they have felt/experienced envy-related emotions and appraisals. They found that benign envy is more frequently felt among the Japanese, while malicious envy is more frequently felt among the Americans. This is in line with the argument that in individualistic cultures, malicious envy is more prevalent than in collectivistic cultures (Tan, Tai, & Wang, Chapter 11, this volume). However, considering school bullying as one form of envy-related aggression, cross-national differences of malicious envy may point to one possible underlying mechanism in the common process of malicious envy across cultures: increased narcissism and resulting relational aggression.

Narcissism increased in the late twentieth century in the United States (Twinge & Foster, 2008), a time when United States became even more individualistic (Greenfield, 2013). If cultural change towards individualism can lead to a heightened sense of hubristic self, and such grandiose sense of the self leads to sensitivity to malicious envy, then culture change towards individualism may accompany malicious envy across national borders. In fact, Onishi, Kawabata, Kurokawa, and Yoshida (2012) found that narcissistic orientations measured by responses to hypothetical scenarios positively correlated with a particular type of relational aggression: punishment bullying among elementary and junior high school students in Japan. Subjective righteousness in bullies is, in this case, merely the bully's arrogant perception based on an egocentric understanding that his or her own perspective must be right. If such egocentric perception accompanies or is even encouraged by the cultural context of individualism, then malicious envy and school bullying may increase when the culture becomes more individualistic.

Japanese culture is changing (Hamamura, 2012), and the change is headed towards increased individualism. Hitokoto and Tanaka-Matsumi (2014) demonstrated that, in more changed regions in Japan, adults exhibited lower levels of well-being, self-worth, and social support compared to adults in unchanged regions.[5] Given the above reasoning, it seems reasonable to expect a link between individualism and school bullying problems in Japan. That is, if school bullying involves malicious envy (Sawada, 2008), and malicious envy is prevalent in individualistic cultural contexts, then even in Japan, a more individualistic context should foster more school bullying.

Based on this hypothesis, we examined whether regional scores of individualism–collectivism in Japan would correlate with reported regional averages of school bullying. We used 47 Japanese prefecture-level collectivism scores calculated by Hitokoto, Murabe, Narita, and Tanaka-Matsumi (2010), and correlated the 47 scores with the reported percentage of junior high school students' reported incidents of either experiencing or observing bullying in their respective schools. Supporting our argument, while even collectivistic regions of Japan showed some reports of school bullying, the prevalence of bullying was pronounced among regions with higher levels of individualism. However, at this point we are not sure if this result is mediated by malicious envy or other closely related emotions such as schadenfreude.

Cultural change in East Asia offers a good opportunity to test whether problems caused by malicious envy might be explained by some societal factors, such as individualism. In a changing context like Japan, the superficial trend would be to be special and to out-compete others for individual success. But because this may only be a superficial trend that is not built upon the long-lasting cultural system that has been articulated throughout history, existing institutionalized systems would not be ready for significant competition (e.g., no grade-skipping, strong seniority systems, and so on). Naturally, the result of the tension between the superficial trend and long-term system would be an increase in collective punishment of the unique, and relentless competition that almost always results in the victory of ordinariness (Naito & Gielen, 2005). If the group-governed punishment of bullying and social comparison leading to meaningless regression to the ordinary is one result of Japanese societal confusion in the era of culture change (Norasakkunkit, Uchida, & Toivonen, 2012), then good regulation of malicious envy will surely be needed in Japanese society today.

Summary

In interdependent cultural contexts, envy will be situated in an environment where many individuals value similarity, feel comfort in ordinariness, and minimize anxiety caused by disharmony. This is when the destructive nature of malicious envy is hidden, but still communicated indirectly to the weak, who are deprived of the means to counter the power imbalance. Such dynamics are predicated on formal education that cultivates a preference for generalists. Recently, aggression caused by envy has extended to cyberspace, where anonymous and collective aggression can easily take place in the hands of children who are living in the age of the grandiose sense of self.

Notes

1. This chapter is partly supported by a Grant-in-Aid for Scientific Research (C) of the Japan Society for the Promotion of Sciences (Grant Number 26380867).

2. Our review is very selective, focusing on the little-explored link between envy, bullying, and culture. School bullying has a universal behavioral definition, and evidence-based coping methods have been extensively studied by educational psychologists (Kanetsuna, Smith, & Morita, 2006; Morita, 2001).

3. As far as our analyses in this chapter are relevant, we will predict that other inter-dependent cultures would also exhibit the same problems of envy.

4. These cultural practices in Japanese formal education are very different from those of Western education (Markus & Conner, 2014), which focuses on nurturing individual creativity, assertiveness, encouraging students to find unity in diverse perspectives, and detecting a child's gifted area of expertise (thus, something stable within the child as an entity) as early as possible through participatory discussion, "show and tell," grade-skipping, and curriculum choice. Japanese formal education does not officially allow the skipping of grades, and even if a child is in need of special education due to an obvious disability, a fair number of parents do not want their child to be treated differently from other students of the same age. For most Japanese parents, formal education is not only about their child's acquisition of academic skills, but also about their child's achieving ordinariness.

5. It is still uncertain whether these undermining effects of cultural change on our mental health are due to a mismatch between the original culture and the new one or simply reveal one downside of the rugged individualism that has already been pointed out in North America (Twenge & Campbell, 2010; Kraus, Piff, Mendoza-Denton, Rheinschmidt, & Keltner, 2012).

References

Adams, G., & Plaut, V. C. (2003). The cultural grounding of personal relationships: Friendship in North American and West African worlds. *Personal Relationships*, *10*, 333–347.

Aoyama, I., Utsumi, S., & Hasegawa, M. (2012). Cyberbullying in Japan: Cases, government reports, adolescent relational aggression, and parental monitoring roles. In Q. Li., D. Cross, & P. K. Smith, Eds., *Bullying in the Global Playground: Research on Cyberbullying from International Perspectives* (pp. 183–201). New York: Wiley-Blackwell.

Bond, M. H., Wan, K. C., Leung, K., & Giacalone, R. A. (1985). How are responses to verbal insult related to cultural collectivism and power distance? *Journal of Cross-Cultural Psychology*, *16*, 111–127.

Dinnel, D. L., Kleinkneht, R. A., & Tanaka-Matsumi, J. (2002). A cross-cultural comparison of social phobia symptoms. *Journal of Psychopathology and Behavioral Assessment*, *24*, 75–84.

Duffy, M. K., Scott, K. L., Shaw, J. D., Tepper, B. J., & Aquino, K. 2012. A social context model of envy and social undermining. *Academy of Management Journal*, *55*, 643–666.

Ekman, P. (1989). The argument and evidence about universals in facial expression of emotion. In H. Wagner & A. Manstead, Eds., *Handbook of Social Psychophysiology* (pp. 143–164). Chichester, UK: John Wiley & Sons, Ltd.

Greenfield, P. M. (2013). The changing psychology of culture from 1800 through 2000. *Psychological Science*, *29*(9), 1722-1731.

Hamamura, T. (2012). Are cultures becoming individualistic? A cross-temporal comparison of individualism-collectivism in the United States and Japan. *Personality and Social Psychology Review*, *16*(1), 3–24.

Hayama, D., & Sakurai, S. (2008). Extreme jokes: The process by which speakers form expectations of communicating benign intentions [in Japanese]. *Japanese Journal of Educational Psychology*, *56*, 523–533.

Hayashi, S. (2009). The effect of relational concern on the decision of help seeking behavior. 2009 Graduation thesis, Kwansei Gakuin University, Department of Integrated Psychological Science.

Heine, S. J., Kitayama, S., Lehman, D. R., Takata, T., Ide, E., Leung, C., et al. (2001). Divergent consequences of success and failure in Japan and North America: An investigation of self-improving motivations and malleable selves. *Journal of Personality and Social Psychology*, *81*(4), 599–615.

Hitokoto, H. (2014). Interdependent happiness: Cultural happiness under the East Asian cultural mandate. *JICA-Research Institute Working Paper*, *79*, 1–29. Tokyo: JICA-Research Institute.

Hitokoto, H., & Tanaka-Matsumi, J. (2014). Living in the tide of change: Explaining Japanese subjective health from the socio-demographic change. *Frontiers in Psychology*, *29*. (published online) doi:10.3389/fpsyg.2014.01221

Hitokoto, H., & Uchida, Y. (2015). Interdependent happiness: Theoretical importance and measurement validity. *Journal of Happiness Studies*, *16*, 211–239.

Hitokoto, H., Murabe, T., Narita, K., & Tanaka-Matsumi, J. (2010, January). Through time and space: Regional variation of individualism–collectivism in Japan. Poster presented at the 11th Annual Meeting of the Society for Personality and Social Psychology, Las Vegas, NV.

Hofstede, G. (2001). *Culture's Consequences: Comparing Values, Behaviors, Institutions, and Organizations Across Nations*. London: Sage.

Imai, M. (1986). *Kaizen: The Key to Japan's Competitive Success*. New York: McGraw-Hill.

Ishii, K., Miyamoto, Y., Niedenthal, P. M., & Mayama, M. (2011). When your smile fades away: Cultural differences in sensitivity to the disappearance of smiles. *Social Psychological and Personality Science*, *2*, 516–522.

Kanetsuna, T., Smith, P. K., & Morita, Y. (2006). Coping with bullying at school: Children's recommended strategies and attitudes to school-based interventions in England and Japan. *Aggressive Behavior*, *32*, 570–580.

Kanetsuna, T. (2004). Pupil Insights into School Bullying: A Cross-National Perspective Between England and Japan. Unpublished Ph.D. thesis, Goldsmiths College, University of London.

Kashima, E., & Hitokoto, H. (2009). Cultural similarities and differences in social identification in Japan and Australia. *Asian Journal of Social Psychology*, *12*, 71–81.

Kim, E., & Glomb, M. T. (2014). Victimization of high performers: The role of envy and work group identification. *Journal of Applied Psychology*, *99*, 617–634.

Kraus, M. W., Piff, P. K., Mendoza-Denton, R., Rheinschmidt, M. L., & Keltner, D. (2012). Social class, solipsism, and contextualism: How the rich are different from the poor. *Psychological Review 119*, 546–72.

Lockwood, P., & Kunda, Z. (1997). Superstars and me: Predicting the impact of role models on the self. *Journal of Personality and Social Psychology*, *73*, 91–103.

Markus, H. R., & Conner, A. (2014). *Clash! Eight Cultural Conflicts That Make Us Who We Are*. New York: Hudson Street Press.

Markus, H. R., & Kitayama, S. (1991). Culture and the self: Implications for cognition, emotion, and motivation. *Psychological Review*, *98*, 224–253.

Miceli, M., & Castelfranchi, C. (2007). The envious mind. *Cognition and Emotion*, *21*, 449–479.

Ministry of Education, Culture, Sports, Science, and Technology. (2014). *Jidou seito no mondai koudou nado seito shidoujou no shomondai ni kansuru chousa ni tsuite.* [*Survey on children's problem behaviors and issues on student guidance*] [in Japanese].

Morita, Y. (2001). *Ijime no kokusai hikaku kennkyuu* [*International comparison study of school bullying*]. Tokyo: Kaneko Shobo.

Morling, B., Kitayama, S., & Miyamoto, Y. (2002). Cultural practices emphasize influence in the United States and adjustment in Japan. *Personality and Social Psychology Bulletin*, *28*, 311–323.

Naito, T., & Gielen, U. P. (2005). Bullying and *ijime* in Japanese schools: A sociocultural perspective. In F. L. Denmark, H. H. Krauss, R. W. Wesner, E. Midlarsky, & U. P. Gielen, Eds., *Violence in Schools: Cross-National and Cross-Cultural Perspectives* (pp. 169–190). New York: Springer Science + Business Media.

Norasakkunkit, V., Uchida, Y., & Toivonen, T. (2012). Caught between culture, society, and globalization: Youth marginalization in post-industrial Japan. *Social and Personality Psychology Compass*, *6*, 361–378.

Ogihara, Y., & Uchida, Y. (2014). Does individualism bring happiness? Negative effects of individualism on interpersonal relationships and happiness. *Frontiers in Psychology*, *5*. (published online) doi:10.3389/fpsyg.2014.00135

Ohashi, M. (2010). Asian American and white American differences on affective distress symptoms: Do symptom reports differ across reporting methods? *Tokyo Future University Bulletin*, *3*, 29–36.

Okazaki, S. (1997). Sources of ethnic differences between Asian American and white American college students on measures of depression and social anxiety. *Journal of Abnormal Psychology*, *106*, 52–60.

Onishi, A., Kawabata, Y., Kurokawa, M., & Yoshida, T. (2012). A mediating model of relational aggression, narcissistic orientations, guilt feelings, and perceived classroom norms. *School Psychology International*, *33*, 367–390.

Onishi, A., Kurokawa, M., & Yoshida, T. (2009). Influences of students' teacher recognition on abuse [in Japanese]. *Japanese Journal of Educational Psychology*, *57*, 324–335.

Park, J., Kitayama, S., Markus, H. R., Coe, C. L., Miyamoto, Y., Karasawa, M., et al. (2013). Social status and anger expression: The cultural moderation hypothesis. *Emotion*, *13*(6), 1122–1131.

Pepler, D. (2006). Bullying interventions: A binocular perspective. *Journal of the Canadian Academy of Child and Adolescent Psychiatry, 15*, 16–20.

Salmivalli, C. (1999). Participant role approach to school bullying: Implications for interventions. *Journal of Adolescence, 22*, 453–459.

Salmivalli, C., Lagerspetz, K., Björkqvist, K., Österman, K., & Kaukiainen, A. (1996). Bullying as a group process: Participant roles and their relations to social status within the group. *Aggressive Behavior, 22*, 1–15.

Sano, Y., & Kuroishi, N. (2009). The effect of being in the "middle" in Japan: From the perspective of self-improving motivation. *Japanese Journal of Interpersonal and Social Psychology, 9*, 63–72.

Sawada, M. (2006). *Kodomo no netami kanjo to sono taisyo* [Envy and its coping in childhood]. Tokyo: Shinyo Sya.

Sawada, M. (2008). From envy to admiration: Education of positive competitiveness [in Japanese]. *Child Study, 62*, 754–759.

Sawada, M. (2013). Ijime higaisya ni taisuru netami to urami ga sankayakuwari ni oyobosu eikyou [Participant role affected by envy and resentment towards bully victims]. Poster presented at the 55th Annual Meeting of the Japanese Association for Educational Psychology (August, 17th–19th), Tokyo, Japan.

Sawada, M., & Hayama, D. (2012). Dispositional vengeance and anger on schadenfreude. *Psychological Reports, 111*, 322–334.

Sawada, M., Kanetsuna, T., & Toda, Y. (2014). How envy of the victim of bullying is associated with the schadenfreude of witnesses. Paper presented at 14th Biennial Conference of the European Association for Research on Adolescence (September, 3rd–6th), Izmir, Turkey.

Smith, P. K. (2015). The nature of cyberbullying and what we can do about it. *Journal of Research in Special Educational Needs, 15*, 176–184.

Smith, R. H., & Kim, S. H. (2007). Comprehending envy. *Psychological Bulletin, 133*, 46–64.

Smith, R. H., Sawada, M., Hitokoto, H., Hoogland, C., Brown, E., & Cooper, C. (2013). Cross-cultural support for the emotion construct of *glückschmertz*, displeasure over another's good fortune. Poster presented at the 14th Annual Meeting of the Society for Personality and Social Psychology (January, 17th–19th), New Orleans, LA.

Smith, P. K., & Sharp. S. (1994). *School Bullying: Insights and Perspectives*. London: Routledge.

Smith, R. H. (2000). Assimilative and constructive emotional reactions to upward and downward social comparison. In J. Suls & L. Wheeler, Eds., *Handbook of Social Comparison: Theory and Research* (pp. 173–200). New York: Kluwer Academic/Plenum Publishers.

Snyzer, D., Takemura, K., Delton, A. W., Sato, K., Robertson, T., Cosmides, L., et al. (2012). Cross-cultural differences and similarities in proneness to shame: An adaptationist and ecological approach. *Evolutionary Psychology, 10*, 352–370.

Takata, T. (1992). *Self in Social Comparison* [in Japanese]. Tokyo: Saiensu Sha.

Takemura, K. (2014). Being different leads to being connected: On the adaptive function of uniqueness in "open" societies. *Journal of Cross-Cultural Psychology, 45*(10), 1579–1593.

Taylor, S. E., Sherman, D. K., Kim, H. S., Jarcho, J., Takagi, K., & Dunagan, M. S. (2004). Culture and social support: Who seeks it and why? *Journal of Personality and Social Psychology*, *87*, 354–362.

Toda, Y., Aoyama, I., & Kanetsuna, T. (2013). Cyberbullying and its prevention: International perspectives [in Japanese]. *Studies on Education and Society*, *23*, 29–39.

Toivonen, T., Norasakkunkit, V., & Uchida, Y. (2011). Unable to conform, unwilling to rebel? Youth, culture, and motivation in globalizing Japan. *Frontiers in Psychology*, *2*, 1–9.

Twenge, J. M., & Campbell, W. K. (2010). *The Narcissism Epidemic: Living in the Age of Entitlement*. New York: Atria Books.

13 | "Storms of Slander"

RELATIONAL DIMENSIONS OF "ENVY" IN JAVA, INDONESIA

THOMAS STODULKA

Introduction

This chapter considers a social anthropological perspective on "envy."[1] Anthropologists have predominantly approached envy and related phenomena as cultural performances that target the avoidance of inducing envy in fellow others (Foster, 1972; Lindholm, 2008; Taggart, 2011, 2012). This chapter takes an actor-centered perspective and emphasizes the relational aspects of envy in analyzing encounters between "enviers" and the "envied" with regard to social and economic power asymmetries. It highlights envy as a motivational force that originates from human "inequity aversion" and aims at the preservation of the social and cosmological order and equanimity of neighborhoods, communities, and organizations in Java, Indonesia.

Anthropology has so far prioritized symbolic and structural analyses of envy-related cultural phenomena like the evil eye, witchcraft, or black magic (Ansell, 2009; Evans-Pritchard, 1937; Lindholm, 2008; Siegel, 2006) and marginalized the more mundane psychological, experiential, and relational dimensions of envy-related behavior and speech (Burbank, 2014; Castellanos, 2015). This chapter considers envy as explanatory model for publicly denied, yet covertly endorsed, actions directed at those who are considered more successful but are believed to neglect their status-related social and economic obligations to the wider community. I will allow myself considering psychological envy theory as gateway into the anthropological analysis of the motivations behind public articulations of "moral lessons" (*pelajaran moral*) in the context of power asymmetries.

By integrating a more robust psychology, I will elaborate that rhetorically camouflaged envy is far from exceptional within a contemporary Javanese social fabric that encompasses inflated material desires and conspicuous consumption promoted by a nationalist discourse of modernity (Herriman, 2014).

The omnipresence of envy might sound surprising, considering that the everyday social life in Java explicitly targets its cultural management through feeling and display rules that proscribe envious behavior and speech. Although the envy-related emotion words *iri* ("envy"), *dengki* ("hate-envy"), or *sirik* ("envious"), like other negative emotions, are paraphrased and euphemized in both Indonesian and Javanese everyday language when a person refers to her or his feelings (e.g., by praising third persons' socioeconomic success in a conversation, but not commenting on their moral qualities as cultural beings, which is publicly considered more important),[2] I intend to demonstrate that envy-related acts are tacitly encouraged if they target persons who are blamed to jeopardize neighborhoods' or organizations' equanimity (*tentram*), and social and cosmological harmony (*rukun*). Blame is conveyed by questioning a person's humanity (*dadi wong*), morality (*wong jawa*), and cultural refinement (*halus*) (see also Gressel, Chapter 17, this volume).

I will briefly review the concepts of "benign" and "malicious" envy (see Sterling et al., Chapter 3, this volume) and discuss whether envy might be best defined as human experience that is related to the essential human capacity of inequity aversion. I will then relate these theoretical considerations to an ethnographic case study and contend that envy is highly relational. The anthropological perspective oscillates between the moral judgements of those involved within envy-episodes and reveals that the dichotomy of benign and malicious envy is analytically important, but the labeling of envy-prone acts and words by those we study always depends on our interlocutors' position within envy-episodes (see also Hoogland et al., Chapter 5; Yu & Duffy, Chapter 2, this volume). Furthermore, envy's widespread moral stigmatization renders its ethnographic study particularly challenging.

Envy: Benign and/or Malicious?

Research in sociology, psychology, economics, and philosophy has revealed a remarkable body of work that clearly contributes to our understanding of envy (see Cohen-Charash and Larson, Chapter 1, this volume). Research converges on the idea of envy as a universal emotion (Castellanos, 2015; Foster, 1972; Hill & Buss, 2008; Lindholm, 2008; Schoeck, 1969). Even studies on non-human primates and non-primate species report experimentally induced behavior that can be interpreted as envious (de Waal, 2009). At the same time, envy is defined as a relational phenomenon that is at stake in processes of mostly upward social comparison. The occurrence and appraisal of social comparison and related communicative acts are intertwined with cultural beliefs about social hierarchies, ethics, morality, fairness, and justice.

Moreover, envy is considered an emotion that has positive as well as negative effects for individuals, their social relationships, social organizations, or the larger society. On one hand, envy—or more precisely, the norms and rules targeting its regulation—is thought to be fundamental to social orders and structures and a strong motivational incentive to increase one's performance (Foster, 1972; Simmel, 1908; Schoeck, 1969; Smith & Kim, 2007). At the same time, envy is ambiguous, since it can withhold effort and performance, subdue innovation and creativity, or lead to outright hostility and conflict (Smith & Kim, 2007). In many societies, envy and related phenomena are considered reprehensible, egoistic, unethical, or shameful (Foster, 1972) and are regulated by strict feeling and display rules.[3]

Despite a rich research tradition on the various aspects of envy, surprisingly little effort has been put into comparative empirical analysis of the direct effects of cultural and social-structural conditions and changes on the experiential qualities of envy (Neckel, 1999; von Scheve et al., 2013). This is remarkable, because subtle differences in the experience of envy are supposed to have profound behavioral consequences. Socially as well as individually, the most striking difference can be found in the distinction between benign and malicious envy (Smith & Kim, 2007; van de Ven et al., 2009). Envy is usually defined as arising "when a person lacks another's superior quality, achievement, or possession and either desires it or wishes that the other lacked it" (Parrott & Smith, 1993: 908). Most definitions also encompass unpleasant feelings of inferiority, hostility, and resentment towards the party enjoying a desired possession. Clore and associates subsume envy (together with jealousy and resentment) under the class of emotions defined as "ill-will" towards the "fortunes of others" (1988:99). Smith and Kim (2007) have defined this as "envy-proper," and D'Arms and Kerr (2008) argue that there is no such thing as benign envy, which is more aptly described as either "desire" or "longing."

There is considerable debate over the issue of whether envy necessarily entails hostile feelings and motivations, or whether feelings of frustration, longing, and inferiority are sufficient components (Foster, 1972; Rawls, 1971; Parrott, 1991; van de Ven et al., 2009). It has been argued that the former is too close to resentment and the latter too close to admiration, whereas both forms are clearly dubbed "envy" throughout the literature. Interestingly, some languages only have one word, probably encompassing both kinds of experiences (e.g., English [*envy*], Spanish [*envidia*], Italian [*invidia*]; Pidgin Aboriginal [*jealous*]), whereas others have two (e.g., Dutch [*benijden, afgunst*], German [*Neid, Missgunst*]) dedicated words. Van de Ven and colleagues (2009) argue that people have two basic behavioral propensities in dealing with experiences of envy: because envy results from unfavorable upward social comparisons, one option is to level down the object of comparison (malicious) or level up one's own position (benign). In their study, they show that, even in cultures with languages that only have one dedicated word for envy, both kinds of envious experience are well known and clearly related to different action tendencies: benign envy leads to the motivation to improve one's own standing, whereas malicious envy leads to the motivation to destroy an envied person's possessions.

Whether both concepts can be neatly separated in the Javanese-Indonesian context, where there are *four* different words[4] related to envy-like feelings—*dengki* ("hate-envy"), *iri* or *iri hati* ("envy"), *sirik* ("envious"), and *cemburu* ("jealous"[5]; "jealous love")—shall be scrutinized in the following discussion. By means of a methodology that prioritizes both participant and systematic observation, in-depth and repetitive interviewing and conversation, that works with samples (most anthropologists prefer the term "communities") within their actual social and local worlds, and that is less focused on testing hypotheses, but open-ended regarding its results, anthropology contributes to interdisciplinary research by rooting emotions within their lived social, political and cultural matrices.

Envy and Inequity Aversion as Essential Human Capacities

Whether envy is a universal emotion can only be shown by means of thorough empirical in-depth analyses of social comparison that complement exclusively lexicographic and questionnaire-based studies (Fessler, 2004; Heider, 1991) across cultures and across different social groups within cultures. Alan Fiske (1992), who has combined results from his fieldwork in West Africa with an analysis of the cross-cultural record, concluded that social comparison is a panhuman potential, one of four cognitive models employed in all societies to structure social relationships. Relating to Fiske, Victoria Burbank (2014) proposes an analytical framework that does not narrow our focus on envy in terms of its exclusively Western understanding. In order to avoid the "thorny issue of human universals" (Burbank, 2014, p. 5), the anthropologist asks whether a more fundamental inequity aversion (Fehr & Schmitt, 1999) might be an essential human potential, or "inherited disposition" to use Bloch and Sperber's (2002) term, within humanity's evolutionary frameworks.

In an extension to Burbank and Fiske, I propose a relational and episodic framework to the study of envy. A relational ethnographic approach promises to add social experiences to cultural typologies that ascribe envy to particular forms of social structure (Foster, 1972; Lindholm, 2008; Stein, 1974). Not only are human emotions more complex than can be accounted for simply by being tied to social structures, but also the lives of those who continuously create, challenge, resist, and subvert these social structures are more dynamic than the cross-cultural study of emotions has suggested (Henrich et al., 2010). Moreover, the very few recent contributions from anthropology have promoted the misconception that envy-like phenomena in so-called "non-Western societies" are predominantly related to "the evil eye" or superstition (Castellanos, 2015; Taggart, 2011, 2012), witchcraft, black magic, and sorcery (Siegel, 2006). For example, Harris and Salovey (2008) write that anthropologist Charles Lindholm

> raises some intriguing predictions regarding cultural differences. He notes ... that evil eye is particularly likely to exist in midlevel, "part societies" (i.e., those whose structure is between simple societies such as hunter and gatherers and complex societies). In building on this, Lindholm proposes that fear of being envied and "envy" are likely to recede in complex societies, such as those of the United States, which have extensive government and judicial systems, growing economies, and impersonal distribution of resources (e.g., in contrast to the personal sharing that takes place in hunter-gatherer societies) (2008, p. 351).

I would suggest that this argument is difficult. First, there is no ethnographic evidence for such claims, because there are not enough studies to support the hypothesis. *If* empirical studies are conducted, they are typically based on laboratory experiments with limited and homogenous samples (i.e., "WEIRD"[6] subjects). Secondly, Lindholm's typology can serve as a compelling vantage point for further anthropological studies, but it implies a Xerox model of intergenerational and peer emotion socialization. The lifeworlds of people, even those who live within comparatively closed communities, are likely to be constantly changing regarding locally and globally circulating desires, imaginations, and needs. Third, there are too many exceptions. For example, I would argue that the works of Victoria Burbank (2014) or Sighard Neckel (1999) are cultural misinterpretations of so-called "egalitarian" and "complex" societies, where envy is more quotidian than extraordinary.

Envy in Javanese Neighborhoods and Workplaces

The Public Nonexistence of Envy

The following case study is located in the Indonesian city of Yogyakarta (Java). The proud "authentic Yogyakartans" (*Jogja asli*) and their political and cultural elites promote the city and its surroundings, which are home to around 3.5 million people, as the archipelago's capital of higher education, cultural heritage, tourism, and the center of fine arts. The city's residents stress that "Jogja," as they call it, is the cradle of "Javanese-ness" (*kejawèn*) and Javanese culture (*budaya Jawa*), which promotes refined, respectful, and harmonious social interactions. Despite the dynamism of everyday life in Javanese neighborhoods and workplaces, where people from different social strata, ethnicities, and educational backgrounds interact in culturally resourceful and blended ways, people allude to a way of life that is endorsed as the "Javanese way" (*cara Jawa*) and is best encapsulated in what is locally understood as *budi pekerti*.[7] This idealized folk model links moral norms of social conduct with a good and virtuous life, and socially embodies metaphysical dichotomies (*halus*, "refined," and *kasar*, "rough") and the balancing of the inner and outer self (*lahir dan batin*) in order to achieve and maintain the cultural aspiration of social harmony (*rukun*) and intersubjective equanimity (*tentram*) (Beatty, 1999; Geertz, 1960; Stodulka, 2016). The *budi pekerti* is a dynamic guidance of proper conduct and consists of the following principles:

1. Honesty (*kejujuran*), sincerity (*ketulusan*), obedience, and compliance (*kepatuhan,* or *manut*) with social and cultural norms.

2. A good name (*nama baik*). Protect the reputation of a good name so as not to experience or induce feelings of *malu* ("shame"/"embarrassment") in oneself and others, which can equate to the loss of one's "respectability" (*hormat*).

3. Social harmony (*rukun*). Avoid conflicts in the family, and among neighbors, the village, and the larger society. It is said that destruction and chaos emerge when people ignore *rukun* and *tentram*.

4. Patience (*sabar*) and wholehearted (*ikhlas*) acceptance (*nrimo*) of life's adversities.

5. No envy (*iri*) of other people's achievements. One must work hard and be rewarded only with God's blessings.

6. No profit (*tanpa pamrih*) or "egoism." The focus on one's own success and profit (*pamrih*) is misleading in a person's path to becoming "a good Javanese." Instead, cooperation (*gotong royong*) on various social scales and collective enjoyment of achievements are valued.

In order to deal with the complexities of community and work life, people are expected to know their position within society and behave accordingly. Acting as if one doesn't know one's place within Javanese hierarchical social order is perceived as "ignorant" (*cuek*), "wild" (*liar*), "not-yet-Javanese" (*durung Jawa*), and even "not-yet-human" (*durung wong*). Being aware of one's social position in social encounters, one is to behave deferentially and is never "loud" (*keras*) or "self-confident" (*tidak tahu diri*) to those of higher status; and is generous but never "arrogant" (*sombong*) or too "proud" (*bangga*), to those of lower status.

Although envy is silenced in public social life, the intense fear of one's own and others' envy is more out in the open. For example, it is powerfully depicted in two popular songs from the 1980s. Koes Plus, Indonesia's "Beatles," have dedicated a whole song to envy-like feelings, titled "*Jangan iri hati*" (1974)—"Don't 'Envy'!" The song consists of only two lines that repetitively warn the listeners, "over and again, I remind you, do not follow the feelings (*rasa*) of hate-'envy' (*dengki*) and 'envy' (*iri*) / Cultivate yourself for your future / If you don't understand, you will keep being envious (*iri hati*), your time will be up, and you will still be like that." Indonesia's "king of *dangdut*,"[8] controversial polygamist Rhoma Irama, sermonized in his song *Badai fitnah*—"Storm of Slander":

It is difficult to reach prosperity in this life, and to retain it is even more difficult, because there is many who hate-envy (*dengki*) and envy (*iri*), for those who hate-envy, they will never stop / Many ways are used to make one fall, to reach this target everything else is sacrificed, to make those who are hated (*dibenci*) not prosper any longer, whatever happens, he does not care.[9]

Both songs were composed and performed during the heyday of the so-called New Order (1965–1998), a dictatorship that was established under then-President Suharto, whose family and cronies controlled and manipulated Indonesia's mass media in their aspiration to create obedient "modern citizens." By opening Indonesia to Western investment, the New Order promoted a capitalist market economy with an emerging middle class that defined itself through conspicuous patterns of consumption. This mock modernity was built on the exploitation of the *masyarakat* ("people") who were told to work hard in the paddy fields in order to contribute to the prosperity and modernity of the nation (Friend, 2003; Vickers, 2005). The hijacking of the *budi pekerti* (the principles of being "a good Javanese") for the sake of national harmony, prosperity, and progress, arguably planted the seeds for a 'modernized cultural climate' in which the conspicuous consumption of material goods continue to challenge the social balance of neighborhood communities (Antlöv & Hellman, 2005; Guinness, 2009; Newberry, 2006), and expand envy in Java's emotional landscape.

"Backdoor Java": Encountering Gossip, Slander, and Witch-hunts

I came across Rhoma Irama's above-mentioned song "Storm of Slander" when it was played at full volume from a neighbor's karaoke machine while I was typing up field notes during my last fieldwork between July 2014, and June 2015. My family and I had rented a house at the outskirts of Yogyakarta from an elderly Javanese couple. Retired 70-year-old Pak Romy[10] had worked for an international organization in Europe most of his life. Together with his wife, he continued living abroad, but he returned to his Yogyakarta home, a big house with a lush garden that was located behind the smaller house we had rented from them, twice a year. It was difficult to meet them during their visits. Their housekeeper and his wife, who lived in the house when the elderly couple returned to their European home, explained that Pak Romy was busy receiving extended family members, neighbors, and friends. When I finally met our landlord, he apologized for his elusiveness. He emphasized that he was managing his social and economic responsibility towards his extended family and neighbors. He supported a local orphanage with donations, distant nieces and nephews with scholarships, and paid a significant amount of money to the head of our neighborhood (*Pak RT*) in order to provide for disadvantaged *kampung*[11] residents and host adequate ceremonies during national holidays. "The money from your rent, for example, is directly distributed to our neighborhood. We keep nothing for ourselves," he added. He then advised me to always be aware of our neighbors' opinion about my family. "You know, these two older ladies, who live opposite your house, they gossip about neighbors with the vegetable vendors that pass through here every morning. You should not pay too much attention, but keep your eyes and ears open. Although some of the neighbors are really naughty, try to be nice to them. This is not Germany," he emphasized and smiled.

Although I had previously conducted four years of fieldwork in Yogyakarta, the *kampung* was a new experience. Having been involved with so-called street children during previous research, I had found that appropriate social conduct was equally important, but its parameters were different. In a *kampung*, the door of one's house is to be kept open from dawn until dusk; when people approach one's house, one would offer tea and snacks, have a chat (*ngobrol*), and show that one cares for the neighborhood; when one hosts a party or a dinner with friends, one invites the neighbors; if one cooks a meal, one would talk to the neighbors, who might just sit half a meter next to the stove on their side of the wall, and announce that one cooks; when the meal is served, one would shout "*Makan, makan*" (Eat, eat), and the neighbors would reply "*Monggo makan*" (Please, eat) in a mix of Javanese and Indonesian; in case one goes on vacation, one is expected to bring souvenirs (*oleh-oleh*) from distant places. These sociocultural practices make the anthropologist think of Foster's (1972) typology of neighborhood appeasement in order to prevent others' envy towards oneself and one's family.

With this brief description of *kampung* life as a backdrop, let me illustrate a case study that demonstrates the relational aspects of envy in encounters between neighbors of disparate social and economic status.

I had met Jerome (51 years old), an expatriate entrepreneur in the lobby of the Yogyakarta airport on a clear morning at the onset of the rainy season in November 2014. We both waited for the early morning flight to Singapore, the only international flight leaving the small airport, which accounts for less than a tenth of Singapore's passenger and aircraft movement ratio. This proportion also reflects Yogyakarta's minor role in international economic transactions and business corporations compared to its cosmopolitan international hub, located only two hours away.

Since we were the only two foreigners (*bule*)¹² in the waiting hall, Jerome seemed to have felt an urge to get some of his recent experiences in a Javanese *kampung*, where he had lived together with his Indonesian wife for three years, off his chest. After I had introduced myself as an anthropologist who had lived and worked in Yogyakarta for altogether more than five years since 2001, he was curious whether I could explain to him what was at stake behind his neighbors' "stupid," he even repeated the word in Indonesian, "*bodoh*," behavior. I was trapped in a situation of assumed similarity, which was not unfamiliar to me. I had heard similar stories told by foreigners, so-called upper- and middle-class Javanese, and other Indonesian entrepreneurs a few dozen times over the last decade, because they were convinced that our shared social identities as non-Javanese or non-villagers produced similar experiences of encountering others' envy.

Jerome lived in an urban, yet village-like neighborhood at the city's outskirts. Together with another foreigner, he had set up a company that had a turnover of around 300,000 US dollars per year. In his own words, Jerome's annual share of $150,000 equals sixty times the average salary of an elementary school teacher. He had a nice villa built at the end of a road, from which he could overlook the paddy fields of his neighbors, where some of them worked as farmers. Others had rented their parcels to hired laborers from the countryside, because they worked as teachers, policemen, administration officers, shop owners, or taxi drivers. Jerome and his Jakarta-born wife, who was an accountant, had decided to build a wall around their villa in order to encapsulate themselves from nosy neighbors and to avoid provoking envy. To further avoid the envy of his neighbors and the head of his neighborhood unit (*Pak RT*), the businessman had learned from his wife "to share with the local community the Javanese way," as he had put it. He contributed an amount equal to a school teacher's yearly salary to the neighborhood festivities of the national independence day on August 17, which he gave to the *Pak RT*. Furthermore, he paid for the asphalt coating of the main road through the neighborhood, including all expenses at the festivities (*slametan*) accompanying the inauguration of the road. He arranged for four high school scholarships, and bought shoes for the children of his direct neighbors. I kept nodding and smiling, while anticipating his verbal vengeance. I did not have to wait for too long: "Do you know what they did to me after all these investments, Thomas?" Before I could reply, Jerome started a monologue on the "backwardness" and "ungratefulness" of his Javanese neighbors.

When Jerome and his wife returned to their villa late one evening in the peak of the dry season, their security guard, Budi, awaited them at the entrance gate. He was worried that something uncanny might happen to the couple. The young man was very agitated and afraid that the neighbors had hired a *dukun santet* (black magic specialist) who had sent luminescent "energy bullets" to sabotage and put a spell on his business. After Jerome found out that his garden was flooded with the smelly sewage water of the whole neighborhood, he wanted to see the head of the *kampung* and ask for clarification. Budi, the oldest son of one of his neighbors, held him back and told him that it was better to go to bed first and calm down. If Jerome visited the head of the neighborhood (*Pak RT*) in a state of *emosi* ("anger," "enragement"), things would only get worse.

Budi accompanied Jerome to the *Pak RT* the next morning in order to *jaga emosi* ("monitor enragement") and help inquire into the cause and solution of the incident. The *Pak RT* assured Jerome that the leakage of the waste pipes was an accident due to heavy rain in the surroundings of the nearby volcano, Mt. Merapi. In the manner of good Javanese tradition of the *gotong royong* (mutual help and communal work), neighbors would help in taking care of the damage. After nothing had happened during the following three days, during which Jerome's house "smelled worse than a purification plant," the expatriate ordered a professional crew of cleaners from another part of the city to take care of the damage. A few days later, the garden was filled with sewage water again. Even worse, someone broke into his house and stole his motorbike. The entrance gate was demolished, and his wife's flowerbed was trashed. Budi, the security guard, had disappeared. His parents assured Jerome that this was a coincidence, because the young man needed to take care of his ill grandmother in a small village in central Java. The gardener and the housekeeper, both neighbors, never showed up for work again after these incidents.

Jerome looked at me with big eyes, waiting for a reaction. I sighed. The tall entrepreneur smiled: "You know what I did?—This time, I invited the whole neighborhood personally. I promised them a communal meal and prayers and new shoes for every school kid whose parents helped clean up the mess." He raised his eyebrows and started nodding his head, "You know how many of them came?—All of them!" After they jointly cleaned up his garden and enjoyed the catered food, the *Pak RT* made an announcement. In order to protect the neighborhood from further sewage disasters, Jerome was invited to initiate a project that would result in the most modern canalization system of the whole city. All residents promised their help, if the businessman agreed to pay for their work and the materials. The request was concluded with a communal prayer, so *Allah* would protect the project from hostile acts of sabotage, evil spirits, and natural disasters. Jerome finished his coffee with a big gulp, crumpled the empty plastic cup, threw it over his shoulder aiming for a dustbin (which he missed), shrugged his shoulders and laughed: "You know what I did?— I moved out of that bloody *kampung* into a more civilized area, where people don't envy or hate me. I love it! You should come and visit me."

After I returned from Singapore to Yogyakarta a few days later, I visited Jerome's new neighborhood. It was located in the city's center next to an international neighborhood, which was crowded with restaurants, bars, and hotels. The Australian businessman had given up his dream to live at the outskirts, overlooking paddy fields and enjoying his view of distant Mt. Merapi on a cloudless day. He had moved into a housing complex that was built for Dutch-speaking Javanese bureaucrats before Indonesia's declaration of independence in 1945. The very quiet and somewhat loosely guarded complex comprised of 15 houses that looked almost identical from the outside. Two houses accommodated small non-governmental organizations (NGOs), but the other 13 were rented out to expatriate businessmen. Jerome's entrance door was hidden behind an immense black SUV and an antique Japanese motorbike. A fancy automatic sprinkler watered his well-kept lawn and flowerbeds.

Compared to other disciplines (see Hoogland et al., Chapter 5, this volume), ethnography can unfold over days, weeks, months, even years and extend its focus from envy episodes to case studies of repetitive envy-related social interactions of the same persons. When I returned to Jerome's former neighborhood four months later to attend a public performance of contemporary puppet theatre, the events related to Jerome's moving were not a hot topic any longer. While enjoying the puppet performances on the neighborhood's volleyball field, and having tea and snacks, I could talk to different *kampung* residents and acquire a more diverse picture of what Jerome had exposed as envy. One man, a teacher, who was in his fifties, explained to me that the expatriate businessman was "a snob" (*sombong*), who thought that he could compensate for his rude (*kasar*) behavior with his money. Another man, who owned a small laundry, added that Mister Jerome did not care (*tidak peduli*) about anything but his money. Even worse, he only shared with his other *bule* friends, who came once a week with their big cars and had drinking parties (*pesta mabuk*), without ever inviting "one of us," referring to the circle of five men. Another man, who was in his late thirties, expressed his suspicion that something "was wrong" (*tidak beres*) with this odd neighbor, because his gate was always closed. When I asked the teacher again whether he thought that Mister Jerome deserved what he got, he answered that he didn't really know what I was referring to, but in case something had happened to him or his house, it might have been a lesson to teach him morals (*pelajaran moral*). During our four-hour conversation, none of the men talked about their own feelings towards Jerome, let alone *dengki* (hate-envy) or *iri* (envy), but they constantly gossiped about him and pointed out his poor moral conduct. In their opinion, he not only behaved morally wrongly, but he also did not share enough with his surrounding neighbors either. No one felt respected (*dihormati*) by his egoistic (*egois*) behavior except the *Pak RT*, who got a big amount of money every year just before the independence celebrations. When I asked whether there were people in the *kampung* who thought that it was unfair that Jerome was so rich, Pak Rudy, who owned the laundry, answered that it was unfair (*enggak adil*) that "the *Pak RT* got all the money and we got nothing." Pak Herman, the teacher added, "Mister Jerome should have invited us once in a while." Finally, I asked directly whether one of the men thought that someone in the neighborhood had "envied" (*iri*) or was "envious" (*sirik*) of Jerome. The answer was unanimous, "No!". After a few moments of silence, though, Pak Slamet, a young taxi driver added that there was no envy in his *kampung*, but that Mister Jerome actually deserved (*pantas*) his garden to be flooded and motorbike stolen.

During our conversations, my interlocutors never voiced feelings and emotions in relation to themselves. Although the cultural practices of intense rhetoric and bodily emotion-control have changed among younger generations, and particularly in the virtual space of the social media where emotion terms circulate unmasked (Slama, 2010; Thajib, 2014), talking about oneself or one's feelings in direct social encounters was considered inappropriate and non-Javanese. This applies to positive, but even more so to negative emotions like envy, hate, or anger. The motivation for (malevolent) actions was rhetorically externalized and related to the disrespectful behavior of Jerome.

This episode relates to James Siegel's (2006) study on witch-hunts in East Java[13] that resulted in mob executions of 120 assumed "witches" in different villages throughout the area between December 1998 and February 1999. The father of Udi, a young man who had recently returned to his village after having worked in the megacity of Jakarta for ten years, was accused to be a *dukun santet* (black magic specialist) who bewitched village residents. Before Udi had returned from Jakarta, his father was a well-respected healer and religious teacher. After Udi and his father had set up a business in the village from the money that the son had earned in Jakarta, bought a truck and a motorbike, and refurbished their house to look more modern than the neighbors', things started to happen. People in the village started getting ill with symptoms that doctors at the nearest health center were not able to explain. Udi's father became the target of aggression. Instead of initiating dialogue with Udi's father and family, infuriated neighbors showed up at their house with machetes, chased Udi's father through the village, and cut him into pieces. When the anthropologist asked Udi why he thought his father was killed, he answered, "There is someone here who envies (*iri*) us. So far the *santet* issue goes, there is no truth in it. Just envy. He wants to smash this family" (Siegel, 2006, p. 126). The young entrepreneur was convinced that there was an instigator (*provokator*) behind the killing who was envious of his family. Later, Udi found out that the cause for envy was their sudden wealth and the fact that it was publicly displayed. Since, so says public opinion, no one can become rich without working (in the paddy fields), their prosperity must have been related to black magic.

In the workplace, the ascription of improper conduct like cheating and taking advantage of one's position arises from feelings related to the same aversion to inequity. These feelings can transform into severe ill-will and malicious acts by means of slander and also witchcraft. Compared to cultural contexts discussed in other chapters in this volume, a distinction between workplace, organization, community, and neighborhood is difficult in Javanese contexts. Java and Indonesia comprise modern and globally operating enterprises sometimes similar to those of Singapore. Furthermore, Indonesia is a global exporter of oil, palm oil, ores, and rubber, and hosts an abundance of factories that manufacture textiles, shoes, motor vehicle parts, and electrical machineries. But Java's economy also encompasses household ventures, neighborhood corporations, and family businesses that are often described as economies of the informal sector. Since working and socializing are not per se oppositional qualities of life, Javanese business organizations work along parameters similar to those at stake in the *kampung*. To avoid confusion, I do not insinuate that Javanese enterprises are economically inefficient. But once a colleague's moral respectability is questioned, sanctions can operate in "Javanese ways" that might seem anachronistic if the cultural context is left aside. In the case of corruption, for example, only the corruptors who do not share "slices of their cake" with their colleagues, associates, or business partners are publicly denigrated and stigmatized as immoral. Retaliation includes gossip, slander, and increasingly overt threats until the moral transgressors give in and share. Since contemporary "witches" (*dukun santet*) have become aware of the feelings related to this moralized inequity aversion within organizations and workplaces, they have started offering paid services to ruin competitors' businesses through online magic.[14] In lifeworlds where spirits are omnipresent and the social proximity to the assumed powerful and the elites is a vivid source of social esteem, moral status, and upward social mobility, malicious gossip, backstabbing, and witchcraft are commanding coercive threats.

Is Envy on the Rise?

That envy is rhetorically nonexistent does not mean that it cannot be a part of Javanese experience. The *budi pekerti* promotes partial sharing of wealth and achievements and provides a cultural rhetoric that explicitly targets the avoidance of envy recognition. Foster has defined such rules as the "cultural control of the fear of envy" (1972, p. 175). The five men I talked to during the puppet theatre performance demonstrated their "patience" (*sabar*), "sincerity" (*ikhlas*), and "acceptance" (*nrimo*) of Jerome's behavior in order to preserve the neighborhood's social harmony (*rukun*). But "Javanese ways" with their public denial of conflict and the silencing of negative emotions provide a space for gossip and slander. If persons, and particularly those who expose themselves publicly due to their social, political or economic achievements and material wealth, do not conform to the idealized expectations of surrounding workplaces or neighborhoods and share their achievements by symbolic or factual sharing and paying respect to those less fortunate (*yang kurang beruntung*) by means of visits or invitations, their inadequate behavior can be commented on vigorously. I have described above and in relation to the *budi pekerti* that it is inappropriate to express negative emotions directly. This would only indicate one's own immorality and impurity of thoughts and put the reputation of one's own name at a risk. Hence, the motivation and cause for gossiping and hostility are externalized and linked to the behavior of those who are exposed to the malicious acts. Successful persons (*orang sukses*) who arouse negative feelings in others by violating the social and cultural rules of adequate sharing are blamed for jeopardizing social harmony (*rukun*) and labeled as "arrogant" (*sombong*) or "ignorant" (*cuek*). The obsession with gossip among those who consider themselves deprived can foster an emotional climate that creates hostility towards those who are ascribed "egoism" (*egois*) in relation to their prosperity. Gossip can transform into aggression once the gossiped-about person refuses to improve her or his improper conduct. Since envy is masked as moral concern that is never expressed directly, but communicated through subtle looks, gestures, and comments either while passing or behind one's back, it is difficult for the gossip-target to anticipate others' boiling malevolence. But turning a blind eye to even the subtlest hints of envy, masked as moral concerns or the questioning of one's integrity by a neighbor or a colleague, can be interpreted as evidence (*bukti*) of the envied person's ignorance, arrogance and egoism. In a climate of insinuations of immorality in those who are considered prosperous but ignorant, retaliation, hostility, and malignant acts become legitimized punishments, ranging from social ostracism to witchcraft and physical violence.

With proliferating practices of those that have achieved material wealth by means of their involvement in local, national, or international market economies to candidly display their accumulated material wealth, the urban *kampung*'s narrow alleys and lacking spaces of privacy are inclined to nourish a climate of insinuation, camouflaged envy and moral blaming of those considered prosperous. The rapid expansion of 'modern' mind-sets by means of a ubiquitous use of social media (Indonesia is the world's third largest Facebook country[15]) that targets the virtual public display of achievements and upward social mobilities, a continuing elitist nepotism, and a commercial credit system that enables the "less fortunate" or "poorer" strata (*wong cilik*) of Javanese society to lease or buy new commodities (but traps many into vicious circles of debt and dependence), fuels the desire to compete on grounds of consumptive display. The proliferation of the idioms "*jangan sirik!*" (Don't be envious!), or "*sirik tanda tak mampu!*" (You envy, because you cannot achieve what the other has!), voiced among the younger generations of urban neighborhoods, suggests a considerable salience of envy. The phrases are expressed in social situations, where another person is gossiped about too harshly in relation to her or his economic, educational, or social achievements. Both idioms are expressed as compassionate mockery, countered with a joke by the person that appears all too envious. Although these situations are colored positively in order not to offend the envier overtly, once identified as potentially envious even within a joke, envy ascriptions can hardly be revoked. The rhetorical and social management of negative emotions is a mastery that needs to be parceled up carefully as collective (and not individual) concern for the envied persons' morality. Although public envy articulations are on the rise in the virtual spaces of the social media and in the joking and mocking of urban slang, appearing all too emotional (*lebai*) is detrimental to one's own good name (*nama baik*), respectability (*hormat*), and equanimity (*tentram*).

Conclusion

One important lesson that anthropology teaches since its formative years is to remain cautious about the differences between what people say (to one another), what people do (to one another), what they say they do (to one another), and how all this changes depending on whom they converse or interact with (Bruner, 1986; Stodulka, 2015a, 2015b). This reminder is important when one is studying socially or culturally undesirable or negative experience and behavior, as is often the case with envy-related phenomena. As researchers, we need to consider that envy occupies different moral spaces in different social contexts and different cultural psyches. Thus, a too-narrow definition of envy can be considered one reason why its anthropological study has progressed slowly compared to other disciplines. Envy is not a concrete and isolated feeling state that can be ascribed easily or tested cross-culturally. The chapters in this volume show that there is no single definition of envy in psychology and related disciplines. This can be read as an invitation to anthropologists to contribute to the study of envy. Exaggerated anthropological skepticism towards psychology seems counterproductive, since contemporary emotion research, regardless of its scholarly origin, agrees that emotions are bio-cultural processes that emerge when persons negotiate, engage, or interact with someone or something, be that real or imaginary, be it related to the past, present, or anticipated future (Engelen et al., 2009; Izard, 2010, 2011; Mesquita & Boiger, 2014; Mulligan & Scherer, 2012; Russell, 2014). Emotions are considered relational phenomena that never exist without the other (Beatty 2013; Barbalet, 2011; Burkitt, 2014; Röttger-Rössler & Stodulka, 2014). Furthermore, envy is relational, since it arises between at least two parties, the envied and the enviers, within a social context of comparison and competition, be that imagined or socially manifest within direct encounters and interactions. But envy comprises another relational dimension: in cultures[16] where envy is considered inappropriate and immoral, the respective words for envy are predominantly circumscribed or expressed in a mocking or joking tone. Only the envied and distant bystanders are entitled to identify others' acts as envy-driven. In contrast, the envier adorns her or his motivation with socially appropriate words that refer to a standardized cultural rhetoric of public moral concern.

Since researchers are part of the social and cultural contexts in which they study envy (this is true for laboratory experiments, questionnaire-based studies, and ethnographies), envy's relationality also applies to our empirical assessments and research methodologies. What psychologists define as the social acceptability or social desirability of their participants' responses, or what has been scrutinized as the epistemic discrepancy between ideal and actual affect (Tsai, 2007), is discussed as situated knowledge (Davies 2010; Dilger et al., 2015; Stodulka, 2015a) in anthropological terms. This becomes especially evident when studying silenced and rhetorically circumnavigated negative emotions. I argue that it is precisely this multiple relationality and sociocultural entanglement of envy in the lives of those we study that invites anthropologists to engage in disciplinary and interdisciplinary research on a social, cultural, economic, and psychological phenomenon that our discipline has ignored for decades.

The disparate interpretations of those who are related within potential envy episodes have illustrated the epistemic challenges to conducting research on negative and muted emotions. Again, I argue that it is this disparity, where the envied accuse others of envy and the potential enviers deny such an emotion but hint at the targets' moral transgressions instead, is a vantage point from which to engage in an open-ended and relational epistemology to study envy and related phenomena. The anthropological study of envy might become more tangible if psychological concepts of envy are not rejected per se, but considered as theoretical gateways that open up new perspectives once altered according to particular ethnographic contexts. In regard to the above-described sewage incident, the witch-hunt, or the online witchcraft services, the envy-proper (Smith & Kim, 2007) provides a powerful analytical framework to explain the motivations and emotions underlying these acts. The case study suggests that envy in Java can be conceived as (1) ill-will that (2) manifests in malicious acts, (3) which are legitimized based on local ideas of sociality, (4) and directed at persons who do not compensate according to moralized cultural standards of symbolic or actual sharing.

I have opened this chapter with a self-critical assessment of anthropological perspectives on envy, and I would like to conclude with a constructive critique of the psychological literature. The supposition that benign envy is a strong motivational incentive to increase one's individual performance does not manifest in the context of the Javanese case study. The distinction between benign and malicious envy is not of a motivational quality. It is a matter of perspective. What most of the psychological literature considers benign envy might be defined as "admiration" in the

Javanese context. The case study suggests that envy motivates those who evaluate their social position and economic potential as inferior in order to design collective actions until the socially and economically superior give in and compensate accordingly, but there is no evidence that it "devours the self ... and gnaws away at itself, eroding self-worth and self-esteem. (Harris & Salovey, 2008, p. 336)

In line with the editors and authors of this volume, I am convinced that interdisciplinary research is a promising avenue to understanding the interplay between human experience, emotion, society, and culture. Isolated laboratory approaches or particularist ethnographies that resist cross-cultural juxtaposition and comparison might increase our knowledge about solitary matters, but they are of limited value in understanding the human condition. Regarding envy's relational and volatile dimensions, it seems reasonable that social scientists of different disciplines keep each other in check for the sake of advanced knowledge regarding the transcultural dimensions of social comparison, inequity aversion, and related emotions.

Acknowledgments

I am very grateful to Christian von Scheve, Victoria Sakti, Samia Dinkelaker, Ferdi Thajib, and the editors of this book. They have sharpened my awareness of past and current debates on the issues I address in this article, and have substantially contributed to helping me focus my argument. Fieldwork (2014–2015) underlying this article has been generously supported by the VolkswagenFoundation.

Notes

1. Although I advocate the transcultural study of affects and emotions, I consider scientific concepts that have ontogenetically emerged from English-speaking social environments—like, for example, "love," "shame," "anger," "sadness," "fear" or "envy"—as constructed theoretical templates that facilitate the study of complex and multidimensional human experiences. This does not mean that I reject the concept of concise emotions as "Western biases." On the contrary, I believe in a psychic unity (Burbank 2014) of humanity and the necessity to use common scientific concepts of emotions, because they translate observed phenomena and otherwise collected data into a language that enables us to continuously feed on each other's interdisciplinary insights.

2. The "egalitarian" lingua franca *Bahasa Indonesia* (Indonesian) has continuously replaced the complex *Basa Jawa* (Javanese) since its introduction into the national

curricula of schools in the 1950s, not only in many urban, middle-class households, but also in the *kampung*. And yet, with over 100 million potential speakers, *Basa Jawa* still is a central pillar of being Javanese. *Basa Jawa* is categorized into the three speech levels: *krama* (which is further distinguished into the ceremonial speeches of *andhap* and *inggil*), *krama madya*, and *ngoko* (Berman, 1998). The level that is applied in conversations depends on the interactants' relational social position.

3. For exceptions, see Burbank (2014) and Castellanos (2015), who have illustrated that envy is a central part of everyday life and ethnic identity formation in Australian Aboriginal communities and in Aguabuena communities of Colombia.

4. More than 700 languages are spoken in Indonesia. These four emotion words are from the dominant Javanese-Indonesian language. There might even exist different words for envy in different slangs of Javanese.

5. The four words are used interchangeably. As in other cultural contexts, the emotion word *cemburu*, which directly translates as "jealousy," is used in a way that emotion researchers would define as "envy." Since there is considerable debate about the similarities and differences of envy and jealousy as analytical concepts, see, for example, Burbank, 2014; Foster, 1972; Harris & Salovey, 2008; Parrott, 1991; or Schimmel, 2008, for concise discussions.

6. WEIRD is an acronym for "Western," "Educated," "Industrialized," "Rich," "Democratic" and refers to psychology's research practice of predominantly studying its own students. See Henrich et al. (2010) and comments for a critical discussion.

7. *Budi pekerti*'s literary translation from *Basa Jawa* (Javanese): deeds that originate in pure and good thoughts.

8. *Dangdut* is a popular Indonesian music genre that is influenced by Malay, Arabic, and Hindi music. Due to its popularity among the "little people," it is also described as "music for the masses."

9. Translations by the author; retranslated by anthropologist Victoria K. Sakti.

10. The names of persons and places are pseudonyms and have been anonymized for reasons of confidentiality.

11. *Kampung* is a sociospatial community, which is organized along strict social and cultural rules and norms of conduct. Java's cities are both geographically and socially structured as mega-clusters of thousands of *kampung*, now increasingly interrupted by commercial units and other more encapsulated housing styles.

12. *Bule* can be translated as "Whitey." The fairly negative word mostly refers to (Caucasian) "Westerners."

13. See also Beatty (2009) for further reading.

14. See https://dukunsantet.wordpress.com for a very offensive advertisement.

15. See the article in Indonesia's largest English-speaking newspaper, www.thejakartapost.com/news/2013/06/18/facebook-has-64m-active-indonesian-users.html, or the statistics in the blog network, http://www. adweek.com/socialtimes/indonesia-facebook-english/242044.

16. I use the term "culture" here with the full confidence of a post-modernist. Contrary to many transcultural psychiatries (Han & Northoff, 2008; Han et al., 2012), cultural neurosciences (Chiao, 2010) and cross-cultural psychologies (Kitayama & Uskul, 2011), I do not refer to "culture" as a camouflage term for "race" (Heinz et al., 2014), nation-state, or locality. "Culture" is what emerges when persons of similar and

dissimilar "differences" (Moore, 1994) (start to) understand, empathize, and act upon each other's thoughts and feelings.

References

Ansell, A. (2009). "But the winds will turn against you": An analysis of wealth forms and the discursive space of development in northeast Brazil. *American Ethnologist, 36*(1), 96–109.

Antlöv, H., & Hellman, J. (2005). Introduction: Images of Java in academic discourses. In H. Antlöv & J. Hellman, Eds., *The Java That Never Was: Academic Theories and Political Practices* (pp. 1–20). Münster, Germany: LIT Verlag.

Barbalet, J. (2011). Emotions beyond regulation: Background emotions in science and trust. *Emotion Review, 3*(1), 36–43.

Beatty, A. (1999). *Varieties of Javanese Religion. An Anthropological Account.* Cambridge, UK: Cambridge University Press.

Beatty, A. (2013). Current emotion research in anthropology: Reporting the field. *Emotion Review, 5,* 414–422.

Bloch, M., & Sperber, D. (2002). Kinship and evolved psychological dispositions: The mother's brother controversy reconsidered. *Current Anthropology, 43*(5), 723–748.

Bruner, E. M. (1986). Experience and its expressions. In V. Turner & E. M. Bruner, Eds., *The Anthropology of Experience* (pp. 3–31). University of Illinois Press.

Burbank, V. (2014). Envy and egalitarianism in Aboriginal Australia: An integrative approach. *The Australian Journal of Anthropology, 25*(1), 1–21.

Burkitt, I. (2014). *Emotions and Social Relations.* London: Sage.

Castellanos, D. (2015). The ordinary envy of Aguabuena people: Revisiting universalistic ideas from local entanglements. *Anthropology and Humanism, 40*(1), 20–34.

Chiao, J. Y. (2010). At the frontier of cultural neuroscience: Introduction. *Social Cognitive and Affective Neuroscience, 5,* 109–110.

Collins, A., Ortony, A., & Clore, G. L. (1988). *The Cognitive Structure of Emotions.* Cambridge University Press.

D'Arms, J., & Kerr, A. D. (2008). Envy in the philosophical tradition. In R. H. Smith, Ed., *Envy: Theory and Research* (pp. 39–59). New York: Oxford University Press.

Davies, J. (2010). Disorientation, dissonance, and altered perception. In J. Davies & D. Spencer, Eds., *Emotions in the Field: The Anthropology and Psychology of Fieldwork Experience* (pp. 79–97). Palo Alto, CA: Stanford University Press.

De Waal, F. (2009). The origins of fairness. *New Scientist, 204*(2734), 34–35.

Dilger, H., Huschke, S., & Mattes, D. (2015). Ethics, epistemology, and engagement: Encountering values in medical anthropology. *Medical Anthropology, 34*(1), 1–10.

Engelen, E.-M., Markowitsch, H. J., von Scheve, C., Röttger-Rössler, B., Stephan, A., Holodynski, M., et al. (2009). Emotions as bio-cultural processes. Disciplinary approaches and interdisciplinary outlook. In B. Röttger-Rössler & H. J. Markowitsch, Eds., *Emotions as Bio-cultural Processes* (pp. 23–53). New York: Springer.

Evans-Pritchard, E. E. (1937). *Witchcraft, Oracles and Magic Among the Azande.* Oxford University Press.

Fehr, E., & Schmitt, K. (1999). A theory of fairness, competition, and cooperation. *The Quarterly Journal of Economics*, *114*, 817–868.

Fessler, D. M. T. (2004). Shame in two cultures: Implications for evolutionary approaches. *Journal of Cognition and Culture*, *4(2)*, 207–262.

Fiske, A. (1992). The four elementary forms of sociality: Framework for a unified theory of social relations. *Psychological Review*, *99*(4), 689–723.

Foster, G. M. (1972). The anatomy of envy: A study in symbolic behavior. *Current Anthropology*, *13*(2), 165–186.

Friend, T. (2003). *Indonesian Destinies*. Cambridge, MA: Harvard University Press.

Geertz, C. (1960). *The Religion of Java*. Chicago, IL: The University of Chicago Press.

Geertz, H. (1961). *The Javanese Family: A Study of Kinship and Socialization*. New York: Free Press of Glencoe.

Guinness, P. (2009). *Kampung, Islam and State in Urban Java*. Singapore: NUS Press.

Han, S., & Northoff, G. (2008). Culture-sensitive neural substrates of human cognition: A transcultural neuroimaging approach. *Nature Reviews Neuroscience*, *9*, 646–654.

Han, S., Northoff, G., Vogeley, K., Wexler, B. E., Kitayama, S., & Varnum, M. E. W. (2012). A cultural neuroscience approach to the biosocial nature of the human brain. *Annual Review of Psychology*, *64*, 335–359.

Harris, C. R., & Salovey, P. (2008). Reflections on envy. In R. H. Smith, Ed., *Envy: Theory and Research* (pp. 335–356). New York: Oxford University Press.

Heider, K. (1991). *Landscapes of Emotion: Mapping Three Cultures of Emotion in Indonesia*. Cambridge, UK: Cambridge University Press.

Heinz, A., Müller, D. J., Krach, S., Cabanis, M., & Kluge, U. P. (2014). The uncanny return of the race concept. *Frontiers in Human Neuroscience*: Research Topic: Critical Neuroscience—the context and implications of human brain research. Available at http://dx.doi.org/10.3389/fnhum.2014.00836.

Henrich, J., Heine, S. J., & Norenzayan, A. (2010). The weirdest people in the world? *Behavioral and Brain Sciences*, *33*(2/3), 1–75.

Herriman, N. (2014). The morbid nexus: Reciprocity and sorcery in rural East Java. *The Australian Journal of Anthropology*, *26*(2), 255–275.

Hill, S. E., & Buss, D. M. (2008). The mere presence of opposite-sex others on judgments of sexual and romantic desirability: Opposite effects for men and women. *Personality and Social Psychology Bulletin*, *34*(5), 635–647.

Izard, C. E. (2010). The many meanings/aspects of emotion: Definitions, functions, activation, and regulation. *Emotion Review*, *2*, 363–370.

Izard, C. E. (2011). Forms and functions of emotions: Matters of emotion–cognition interactions, *Emotion Review*, *3*, 371–378.

Kitayama, S., & Uskul, A. K. (2011). Culture, mind, and the brain: Current evidence and future directions. *Annual Review of Psychology*, *62*, 419–449.

Lindholm, C. (2008). Culture and envy. In R. H. Smith (Ed.) *Envy: Theory and Research* (pp. 227–246). New York: Oxford University Press.

Mesquita, B., & Boiger, M. (2014). Emotions in context: A sociodynamic model of emotions. *Emotion Review*, *6*, 298–302.

Moore, H. L. (1994). *A Passion for Difference: Essays in Anthropology and Gender*. Cambridge, UK: Polity Press.

Mulligan, K., & Scherer, K. R. (2012). Toward a working definition of emotion. *Emotion Review, 4*, 345–357.

Neckel, S. (1999). Blanker Neid, blinde Wut? Sozialstruktur und kollektive Gefühle [Bare envy, blind rage? Social structure and collective feelings]. *Leviathan, 27*(2), 145–165.

Newberry, J. (2006). *Back Door Java: State Formation and the Domestic in Working Class Java*. Peterborough, ON: Broadview Press.

Parrott, G. W. (1991). The emotional experiences of envy and jealousy. In P. Salovey, Ed., *The Psychology of Jealousy and Envy* (pp. 3–30). New York: Guilford Press.

Parrott, G. W., & Smith, R. H. (1993). Distinguishing the experiences of envy and jealousy. *Journal of Personality and Social Psychology, 64*(6), 906–920.

Rawls, J. (1971). *A Theory of Justice*. Cambridge, MA: Belknap Press of Harvard University Press.

Röttger-Rössler, B., & Stodulka, T. (2014). Introduction: The emotional make-up of stigma and marginality. In T. Stodulka & B. Röttger-Rössler, Eds., *Feelings at the Margins—Dealing with Violence, Stigma and Isolation in Indonesia* (pp. 11–29). Frankfurt, NY: Campus.

Russell, J. A. (2014). Four perspectives on the psychology of emotion: An introduction. *Emotion Review, 6*, 291.

Schimmel, S. (2008). Envy in Jewish thought and literature. In R. H. Smith, Ed., *Envy: Theory and Research* (pp. 17–38). New York: Oxford University Press.

Schoeck, H. (1969). *Envy: A Theory of Social Behavior*. (Trans. M. Glenn & B. Ross.) Berlin: De Gruyter.

Siegel, J. (2006). *Naming the Witch*. Palo Alto, CA: Stanford University Press.

Simmel, G. (1908). *Soziologie: Untersuchungen über die Formen der Vergesellschaftung* [Sociology: Studies on the Forms of Public Ownership]. Leipzig, Germany: Duncker & Humblot.

Slama, M. (2010). The agency of the heart: Internet chatting as youth culture in Indonesia. *Social Anthropology, 18*(3), 316–330.

Smith, R. H. (1991). Envy and the sense of injustice. In P. Salovey, Ed., *Psychological Perspectives on Jealousy and Envy* (pp. 79–99). New York: Guilford.

Smith, R. H., & Kim, S. H. (2007). Comprehending envy. *Psychological Bulletin, 133*, 46–84.

Smith, R. H., Ed. (2008). *Envy: Theory and Research*. New York: Oxford University Press.

Stein, H. F. (1974). Envy and the evil eye among Slovak-Americans: An essay in the psychological ontogeny of belief and ritual. *Ethos, 2*(1), 15–46.

Stodulka, T. (2016). *Coming of Age on the Streets of Java: Coping with Stigma, Marginality and Illness*. Bielefeld: transcript.

Stodulka, T. (2014). "Playing it right": Empathy and emotional economies on the streets of Java. In T. Stodulka & B. Röttger-Rössler, Eds., *Feelings at the Margins—Dealing with Violence, Stigma and Isolation in Indonesia* (pp. 103–127). Frankfurt, NY: Campus.

Stodulka, T. (2015a). Emotion work, ethnography and survival strategies on the streets of Yogyakarta. *Medical Anthropology, 34*(1), 84–97.

Stodulka, T. (2015b). Spheres of passion: Fieldwork, ethnography and the researcher's emotions. *Curare—Journal for Medical Anthropology 38*(1+2), 103–116.

Taggart, J. M. (2011). Interpreting the Nahuat dialogue on the envious dead with Jerome Bruner's theory of narrative. *Ethos*, *40*(4), 411–430.

Taggart, J. M. (2012). Narratives of emotional experience and long-term fieldwork among the Nahuat of Mexico. *Anthropology and Humanism*, *36*(1), 47–54.

Thajib, F. (2014). Navigating inner conflict: Online circulation of Indonesian Muslim queer emotions. In T. Stodulka & B. Röttger-Rössler, Eds., *Feelings at the Margins— Dealing with Violence, Stigma and Isolation in Indonesia* (pp. 159–179). Frankfurt, NY: Campus.

Tsai, J. L. (2007). Ideal affect: Cultural causes and behavioral consequences. *Perspectives on Psychological Science*, *2*(3), 242–259.

van de Ven, N., Zeelenberg, M., & Pieters, R. (2009). Leveling up and down: The experiences of benign and malicious envy. *Emotion*, *9*(3), 419–429.

Vickers, A. (2005). *A History of Modern Indonesia*. Cambridge, UK: Cambridge University Press.

Von Scheve, C., Stodulka, T., & Schmidt, J. (2013). Von der "Neidkultur" zu Kulturen des Neides [From "envy cultures" to the cultures of envy]. *Aus Politik und Zeitgeschichte*, *63*(32-33), 41–46.

14 | The Behavioral Economics of Envy
WHAT CAN WE LEARN FROM IT?

JÉRÉMY CELSE

Introduction

The Standard Economic Agent Is Free of Envy

Theodore Roosevelt perceived envy as an obstacle to the good working of modern societies by claiming that: "Probably the greatest harm done by vast wealth is the harm that we of moderate means do ourselves when we let the vices of envy and hatred enter deep into our own natures."[1] Surprisingly, the emotion is completely omitted in Standard Economic Theory (SET afterwards), the traditional approach to economics. SET describes the framework traditional economists refer to when conceptualizing the world and analyzing human behavior. Because its assumptions can be seen as too simplistic and unrealistic, SET is often criticized as failing to fully explain and predict the diversity and complexity of human decisions such as why people trust perfect strangers (Berg, Dickhault, & McCabe, 1995) or why people reject unequal bargaining proposals and prefer to quit a negotiation with nothing (Güth, Schmittberger, & Schwarze, 1982). Economists typically consider that the standard economic agent does not compare his or her situation to others' situations and hence does not suffer from envy. Indeed, SET relies on two main assumptions: self-interest and rationality. The former assumption suggests that the utility of an agent depends exclusively on his or her own material resources and situation (e.g., consumption under income and leisure constraints), regardless of the situation of other agents.[2] The latter assumption implies that rational agents always opt for the choice or strategy that maximizes their utility; namely, those that increase their own material resources. Nevertheless, SET fails to capture the diversity and complexity of human motivations, as demonstrated by the many mismatches found between the predictions of SET and observations from real life, or results from both laboratory and field experiments (Khaneman, Knetsch, & Thaler, 1986; Güth, Schmittberger, & Schwarze, 1982).

To illustrate this limited characterization of human motivations, imagine you received two job propositions for two similar firms, named Firm A and Firm B. Both propositions are similar in all points except in the wage offered: Firm A proposes to pay you a higher wage than Firm B does. In such a setting, it is very likely that you would favor Firm A's proposition. Based on the assumptions that standard agents are rational and self-interested, SET also conjectures that people will prefer Firm A's wage since the wage offered is the highest. Now, imagine that, before accepting the offer, you realize that the wage offered by Firm A is the lowest within the distribution of wages in Firm A, whereas the wage proposed by Firm B is the highest within the distribution of wages in Firm B. Would you still favor Firm A's proposition? Despite that new information, SET would still make the same prediction, since the wage offered is, in absolute terms, the highest. Assuming that people have relative concerns and may experience emotions as envy, Behavioral Economics would be more nuanced (see below).

Solnick and Hemenway (1998) investigated this dilemma by asking respondents to indicate in which state they would prefer to live in. The two presented states were strictly identical (and so are prices and purchasing power in the two states), except in one dimension. In one state (the absolute state), the respondent earned a yearly income of $100,000, whereas other people in that state earned a yearly income of $200,000. In the second state (the positional state), the respondent earned a lower yearly income ($50,000) but twice the yearly income others earned in this second state ($25,000). In the first state, the respondent has a large amount (in objective terms) but is poorly endowed compared to others. In the second state, the respondent has now a smaller amount (in objective terms) but is better endowed than others. Based on the assumption that standard economic agents are self-interested and rational, SET predicts that respondents would prefer the first state since it offers the highest yearly income (or highest amount of a good, e.g., whether it be money, intelligence, or some other valued thing, etc.). Nevertheless, Solnick and Hemenway (1998) found that more than half of the respondents picked the Positional state, indicating that they preferred to incur a cost (i.e., having a smaller absolute amount of good) rather than being relatively disadvantaged (see also Frank, 1997; Solnick & Hemenway, 2005, 2007; Carlsson, Johansson-Stenman, & Martinsson, 2007; Grolleau & Said, 2009; Wouters et al., 2015). In the same line, observations derived from laboratory experiments suggest that people are often willing to sacrifice own monetary resources to prevent others from receiving higher benefits than they (Beckmann, Formby, Smith, & Zheng, 2002; Celse, 2010, 2016; Charness & Grosskopf, 2001; Güth, 1995; Zizzo & Oswald, 2001; Zizzo, 2003, 2004).[3]

Why are agents willing to spend or sacrifice resources in order to prevent others from being above them? Envy is one good explanation (see Cohen-Charash & Larson, Chapter 1, this volume). Envy arises from relative inferiority; i.e., when one lacks and desires others' superior possessions or situations (Parrott & Smith, 1993). Because agents are capable of envy, they dislike being below others, and as a consequence they are willing to spend resources to avoid a situation of relative inferiority. But, as just noted, emotions such as envy are completely ruled out in SET. Behavioral Economics (BE) aims at filling this gap. BE is a new branch of economics aiming at enhancing the empirical base and explanatory power of economics "by providing it with more realistic psychological foundations" (Camerer & Loewenstein, 2004, p. 3). To seek a richer description of the behavior of economic agents, BE relaxes the traditional assumptions of rationality and self-interest. The notion of bounded rationality (namely, that agents do not always behave to maximize their utility) substitutes for the notion of rationality, and the notion of social preferences (see below) replaces self-interest.[4] Through analytical models and experiments (either laboratory or field experiments), BE helps by improving our understanding of individuals' decision-making. The aim pursued in this chapter is to tackle envy from a BE perspective. Throughout this chapter, we will address the following questions: (1) How do economists conceptualize envy within their models? (2) What important changes highlighted by recent findings in BE may be addressed to refine these models? (3) What are the main lessons one can draw from the BE of envy? We will answer these questions by referring to recent findings from BE. This chapter consists of three parts, addressing each question consecutively.

Part One: A Behavioral Model of Envy

To explain the mismatch between predictions made by SET and empirical observations, behavioral economists have developed new theories that allow the introduction of additional motivations other than self-interest, into agents' decision-making, such as considering:

1. Agents' concerns for the payoffs allocated to other relevant reference agents in addition to the concern for one's own payoff (social preference models);
2. Agents' reactions to others' expected or observed behavior (reciprocity models);
3. Agents' concerns over others' expectations (guilt-aversion models); or
4. Agents' reactions toward the preferences (and type) of other agents (type-based models).

For envy to arise, an agent must compare his or her situation to another and suffer from the unflattering diagnosis he or she derives from this comparison (Cohen-Charash & Larson, Chapter 1, this volume). Hence, a condition required to generate envy is to engage in social comparison; i.e., to take into account others' situation. Thus, envy entails what behavioral economists label a social "preference." Preferences form the foundation of all choice theory in economics. The term "preference" refers to how agents, when they are presented different alternatives (such as allocations of material resources), value and order these alternatives. In other words, if agents are facing two potential allocations of material resources, they should be able to indicate their preferences; i.e., whether they prefer one allocation to another or if they are indifferent between them. Social preferences are a particular class of preferences; meaning that agents do value their material resources allocated to them as well as the material resources allocated to other relevant reference agents (either positively if altruism, or negatively if envy). We provide below an example of a social preference model. These models relax the assumption of self-interest while retaining the assumption of rationality. In a formal way, let $\{1, 2, \ldots, N\}$ denote a set of agents and $x = (x_1, x_2, \ldots, x_N)$ an allocation of material resources (e.g., income) out of some set X of feasible allocations. Social preferences are then defined by:

$$U_i(x_i, x_j); \quad \text{with } i \neq j \tag{1}$$

In equation (1), U_i represents the utility of agent i, i.e., agent i's satisfaction. Based on SET, the utility of agent i only depends on x_i (i.e., $U(x_i)$) whereas, based on a social preference model as described in equation (1), the utility of agent i, for any given x_i, is affected by variations of x_j ($j \neq i$), x_j representing the material resources owned by agent j. In other words, an agent is said to exhibit social preferences if and only if, in addition to his or her own material resources, the agent cares also about the material resources allocated to relevant reference agents. Based on equation (1), if agent i is altruistic, then his or her utility (U_i) is directly related to x_j: the utility of agent i increases with x_j. Conversely if agent i is envious, his or her utility is inversely related to x_j: the utility of agent i decreases (resp. increases) as x_j increases (resp. decreases).

Social preferences, such as envy, can be conceptualized in a variety of ways (Fehr & Schmidt, 2006; Sobel, 2005). Such diversity leads to multiple models of social preferences. It is worth pointing out that there is no a unique behavioral model used to characterize envy, but rather various models, each using a different approach to describe the emotion. One very simple approach to conceptualize envy is to consider that agents value differently their own material resources and others' material resources, as summarized in equation (2) (Bolton, 1991; Mui, 1995; Kirchsteiger, 1994). "*Pure*" envy models use this approach and are summarized by this example:

$$U_i(x_i, x_j) = u(x_i) + sv(x_j) \tag{2}$$

Equation (2) belongs to the family of "*pure*" envy models (Zizzo, 2009, p. 192). Equation (2) pictures the trade-off that agent i makes between social preferences and self-interest. The self-interest dimension is captured by the first term of the equation, $u(x_i)$, which represents the utility agent i derives from his or her own material resources (x_i). Social preferences are symbolized by $v(x_j)$, which represents the utility agent i derives from the material resources allocated to another agent j (x_j). The coefficient s characterizes the weight agent i attributes to social preferences. A purely self-interested agent will be characterized by $S = 0$, an altruistic agent by $s > 0$, and an envious agent by $s < 0$. With $s < 0$, the model states that agent i's values positively his or her own material resources and negatively the material resources allocated to agent j. A "*pure*" envy model only considers envy; i.e., imposes $s < 0$.

In a more sophisticated class of social preference models, preferences are expressed in terms of the distribution of material resources to all referent agents. Such models presuppose that an agent compares his or her material resources to another and that the agent's utility increases when the allocation of material resources gets close to a certain level (and vice versa). Several models of this type have been developed: Fehr and Schmidt (1999), Bolton and Ockenfels (2000), and Charness and Rabin (2002). Each model has advantages and disadvantages and can propose a definition of envy. Rather than presenting all models and how they define envy, in this chapter, we will focus on the first model. In comparison to the other two models, the Fehr and Schmidt model is mathematically more accessible (i.e., analytically simpler), intuitive (since based on empirical observations), and more flexible (i.e., it can fit to different contexts and can serve as a base to introduce additional motivations). In addition, its predictive power has been corroborated empirically in various contexts (Blanco, Engelmann, & Normann, 2011; Leibbrandt & Lopez-Perez, 2011, 2012). Finally, relative to "*pure*" envy models, this model is better able to include additional motivations along with envy.

The Inequity Aversion Model (or Envy and Compassion Model)

The Inequity Aversion model (IA model afterwards) proposed by Fehr and Schmidt (1999) originates from Bolton (1991). Whereas the latter approach supposes that an agent's utility is either monotonously increasing or decreasing depending on the utility of others (see previously), the former approach assumes that agents compare their allocation of material resources to an equitable allocation and that the diagnostic resulting from this comparison generates direct consequences for their utility function.

The IA model considers that agents are inequity-averse. Being inequity-averse means that the agent dislikes allocations of material resources that are perceived as inequitable. In the IA model, agents are motivated to achieve equitable outcomes, and they can feel envy when the relevant others' material resources exceed an equitable allocation of material resources. Conversely, an agent can feel compassion when his or her own material resources exceed an equitable allocation of material resources. As noted earlier, there are multiple ways to conceptualize envy, and each behavioral model can propose its version of envy. In the IA model, envy can be conceptualized as a utility loss (e.g., dissatisfaction) that arises when agents are exposed to a disadvantageous distribution of material resources.[5] From now on, we will define envy as above; i.e., as an aversion to inferiority.

To detail the IA model, we have to consider a set of N agents indexed by $i \in \{1, 2, \ldots, N\}$. Let $x = (x_1, x_2, \ldots, x_N)$ denote the vector of monetary resources. The utility function of player i, $i \in \{1, 2, \ldots, N\}$ is represented by:

$$U_i(x_1, x_2, \ldots, x_N) = x_i - \frac{1}{N-1} \alpha_i \sum_{j \neq i} \max\{x_j - x_i, 0\}$$
$$- \frac{1}{N-1} \beta_i \sum_{j \neq i} \max\{x_i - x_j, 0\} \tag{3}$$

The model states the following assumptions regarding α_i and β_i:

$$0 \leq \beta_i \leq 1 \tag{4}$$

$$\alpha_i \geq \beta_i \tag{5}$$

The first term of equation (3) captures the self-interest dimension and measures the utility agent i derives from his own material payoff. This utility increases and decreases with agent i's own material resources. The second term of the equation determines the "disutility" resulting from being below others. This term catches the aversion from disadvantageous inequity; namely agent i's envy. Finally, the last term of the equation captures the aversion from advantageous inequity (i.e., agent i's compassion); namely, the disutility resulting from being above others.

In the model, each agent i is defined by a pair of parameters (α_i, β_i). The first parameter measures agent i's envy at being worse off than relevant referent others. The second parameter captures agent i's compassion at being better off than relevant referent others. The model presupposes some conditions to these parameters. Condition (4) excludes the existence of agents' deriving a utility from being above others; namely, agents that enjoy having more than others.[6] Condition (5) expresses the idea that agents suffer more from disadvantageous inequalities than from advantageous ones. Saying it differently, the disutility agent i derives from inequality is larger if another person is better off than agent i than if another person is worse off. This condition underlines the importance of envy over compassion.

Main Characteristics of the IA Model

Despite its analytical simplicity, the IA model has multiple advantages. Firstly, and in contrast to SET, it presupposes agents' preferences to be heterogeneous by defining for each agent a pair of parameters (α_i, β_i). Agents' decisions depend on their personal characteristics based on the pair (α_i, β_i). This perspective refines our understanding of why some agents are willing to sacrifice resources to prevent others from having more than they, whereas others are not.

Another key component of the model is that each agent compares his or her situation to each other agent within his or her reference group. As a consequence, agent i's behavior will depend on the income difference toward a particular agent $j, (j \neq i)$, rather than toward a more global aggregate as the average position of agent i within his or her reference group (as presupposed by Bolton and Ockenfels) or rather than the income differences between the agent and the least-well-off agent within his or her reference group (as presupposed by Charness and Rabin).

Finally, the IA model is flexible, since the specificity of the model can predict both positive and negative decisions. On one hand, agents can engage in antisocial behavior (e.g., sabotaging, destroying, etc.) toward relevant referent others if they are envious; namely, if their own material resources are below the equitable level. On the other hand, agents can engage in prosocial behavior (e.g., giving, cooperating, etc.) toward relevant others if they feel compassionate.

Main Limitations

In the IA model, envy can be defined as a disutility in presence of disadvantageous inequality. This definition proposes a stylized version of envy that differs from the emotion itself in many aspects (Wobker & Kenning, 2013). Since behavioral economists typically focus on agents' decisions and on their consequences in terms of utility, they develop behavioral models satisfying a limited number of conditions. Firstly, models aim at explaining and predicting agents' behavior as much as possible, knowing that the emphasis is on predicting rather than on explaining. Secondly, models must remain as simple as possible from an analytical perspective so as to be easily understandable and interpretable. Refinement is considered only if it leads to a significant increase in the model's explanative and predictive power. To fulfil such a goal, behavioral models are characterized by this stylized approach; they capsulate the object of investigation to its simplest form.

The IA model suffers from this stylized approach, and it creates a number of potential problems. The first problem is that the way envy is conceptualized in the IA model creates some ambiguity about the definition of envy itself: Does the IA model refers to envy as an emotion, as a mood, or as a personality trait? Such distinctions are ignored in the economic vision of envy. A second problem is that by using such a reductionist approach, the IA model does not ensure a clear distinction between other emotions, such as resentment, indignation, jealousy, or *schadenfreude*. In the IA model, all these emotions would be conceptualized through $\alpha_i > 0$, i.e., by a dis-utility at being below others. The IA model assumes that these similar emotions lead to the same disutility and behavior.[7]

A second limitation of the IA model relates to the definition of the relevant reference agents. Most social preferences models assume that agents compare their situation with a set of reference agents. The IA model assumes that an agent compares his or her situation to the situation of all other $(n-1)$ relevant reference agents in his or her environment (e.g., game, experiment, firm). The question is, who are these relevant reference agents? The IA model postulates that an agent i is defined as a relevant reference for agent j $(i \neq j)$ if agent i's decisions affect agent j's situation. Thus, the definition of "relevant reference agents" depends on the situation: in the context of a firm, the relevant reference agents may be the colleagues or co-workers in the firm with whom a person interacts most frequently, in a family context it can be a person's relatives, in a social context one's neighbors, and trading partners in a professional context. Finally, in a laboratory experiment context, all participants in an experimental session are relevant reference agents to each other. To summarize, an agent's reference group is the whole group, independent of x_i, rather than any particular subset of the whole.[8] Such an assumption would imply that, for illustration, an employee would suffer from a more intense envy towards his or her boss who lies far above him or her in the wage distribution rather than towards an immediate colleague who lies just above him or her in the wage distribution.

Another limitation relates to the source of envy. The IA model proposes a conditional form of envy: an agent is envious if and only if, in addition to his or her material resources, the agent's utility decreases as the allocation of material resources becomes less equitable. Envy is conditional since it is assumed to disappear as soon as agent i's material resources become inequitable (then the agent feels compassion toward others). The definition of equity is at the core of the model: agents are considered as inequity-averse if they dislike material resources that are perceived as inequitable.

What constitutes an equitable allocation? How does the model define fairness? Equity and fairness judgements are grounded on a neutral reference point or allocation that serves as a basis to evaluate a given situation.

To define this reference point, Fehr and Schmidt refer to the literature showing the importance of relative income comparisons for individual well-being and behavior (e.g., Clark & Oswald, 1996; Neumark & Postlewaite, 1998). This literature mainly conveys how individuals are strongly averse to inferiority (Loewenstein et al., 1989). As the IA model was initially designed for laboratory experimentation, authors used a simple definition of an equitable allocation: they consider that agents compare their allocation to others and that an equitable allocation is defined as an egalitarian allocation; namely, a situation in which allocations are identical. In the IA model, equity is defined as equality of monetary payoffs—more precisely, equality is assessed in terms of the absolute differences between the agent's material resources and the material resources of all relevant reference.[9] Namely, agent i suffers a utility loss from existing differences between his or her material resources (x_i) and agent j's material resources (x_j). Any increase of ($x_j - x_i$) adds to his or her envy.

A final problem relates to the assumption of linear preferences. The IA model predicts "corner" solutions; that is, extreme solutions. This analytical simplicity ignores the likelihood that many decisions lie between extremes. For example, consider the Dictator Game, in which one player (the dictator), is required to choose whether to send to an anonymous participant (the receiver) a part of the amount of money he or she received from the experimenter (Kahneman et al., 1986; Hoffman et al., 1994). In such a setting, the IA model predicts that, depending on the pair (α_i, β_i), participants would either send nothing to the receiver ($\beta_i > 0.5$) or would share equally with the receiver if ($\beta_i > 0.5$) (Fehr & Schmidt, 2006).

Part Two: Pointing in New Directions

We presented and discussed a behavioral model of envy in which envy can be conceptualized as a utility loss resulting from disadvantageous inequalities. This definition may be considered coarse, since it lacks the ability to capture the complex and protean nature of envy as shown in many chapters in this volume. We now point out two major directions that should deserve further attention and may serve as a basis to further transform the model: fairness perceptions and the concept of the reference group. We now examine how can recent findings from BE may help in transforming the model so as to capture envy with more accuracy and to disentangle the latter from other emotions.

Disentangling Envy from Other Emotions: The Role of Perceived Fairness

A recurrent problem in economics is that the definition of envy confuses the emotion with other, related, emotions (Zizzo, 2009). In the IA model, agents care about inequalities, and envy is thought to arise when agents are exposed to unfavorable inequalities. This is an advance over the traditional view embraced by economics (SET) in which envy, like other emotions, is absent. Nevertheless, in the IA model, there is a rudimentary characterization of envy. Distinctive components of envy (especially in contrast to other related emotions) are ignored, however, as are the distinctive inequalities (e.g., aspects of the envied other) leading to envy. As behavioral models focus on predicting at the expense of explaining, confusing envy with resentment or indignation is not a preoccupation for behavioral modelers. Nevertheless, as shown in other chapters (see Hoogland, Thielke, & Smith, Chapter 5; Annoni et al., Chapter 20, this volume), these emotions may lead to very different behaviors. Without considering all the distinctive aspects of envy and other emotions, models may try to incorporate factors in order to make such an insightful distinction between envy and related emotions (like resentment) and even between different behavioral manifestations of envy. At present, no changes in equations have been proposed to disentangle envy from other related emotions.

Next, we present recent empirical evidence suggesting the complexity of envy and thus showing that envy cannot be summarized as an emotional reaction to inferiority aversion. A promising avenue for future research would be to incorporate changes in the model so as to take into account these factors.

There are notions that are central in envy, such as agents' perception of control and fairness (see Hoogland, Thielke, & Smith, Chapter 5, this volume; Lockwood & Kunda, 1997; Testa & Major, 1990). Such notions are completely omitted in the IA model. The fairness of how valued resources are distributed is an important factor in how people react to their outcomes. As a long tradition of research shows (see Hoogland, Thielke, & Smith, Chapter 5; Mishra, Whiting, & Folger, Chapter 16, this volume; Konow, 1996, 2000, 2003), agents react differently, depending on whether they perceive inequalities to be deserved or not. One determinant of perceived fairness relates to effort (Burrows & Loomes, 1994; Dickinson & Tiefenthaler, 2002; Hoffman & Spitzer, 1985; Konow, 2003; Leventhal & Michaels, 1971; Ruffle, 1998; Schokkaert & Capeau, 1991). Despite an income distribution's being unequal or the agent's being relatively worse off, an agent is assumed to consider a situation or an income distribution as fair if the latter corresponds to degree of the agent's effort. This relates to equity theory, a social psychological theory of fairness suggesting that the equitable ratio of outcomes is proportional to the ratio of inputs. Adams (1965) proposed a reformulation and suggested that "when [an individual] finds that his outcomes and inputs are not in balance in relation to those of others, feelings of inequity result" (p. 280).

To summarize, agents should accept inequalities (and thus be less likely to feel envy) if inequalities are deserved, i.e., if inequalities are effort-dependent. In contrast, the IA model does not ensure such a distinction, since equity is defined by payoff differences alone. For illustration, consider two situations: one in which agents are paid according to their effort-related performance, whereas in the other situation, agents are paid according to randomness (such as a gamble draw). Based on equity theory, inequalities in the first situation would be considered fair (since they are effort-dependent), and agents should not suffer from envy but rather from resentment or indignation. In the IA model, equity is defined and measured in terms of the absolute income differences between the agent and all relevant reference agents. Thus in both situations agents should suffer from the same envy, i.e., disutility from being below others. The IA model considers envy to increase (resp. decrease) with the distance between agents' income. While envy, in the IA model, is associated with a willingness to restore equality (envy disappears when the agent possesses at least the same situation as referent relevant others), as many chapters in this book show, the relationship between envy and equality is complex. Envy does not necessarily involve equality per se: an envious person is likely to prefer a situation in which neither he nor his rival enjoy the desired attribute (i.e., object of envious feelings) to a situation in which both the envier and the rival possess it (D'Arms & Kerr, 2009). Some empirical evidence supports this suggestion (Celse, 2012; Bolle & Kemp, 2013).

There are, to our knowledge, few attempts to introduce fairness perceptions into a theoretical model (Konow, 2000, 2010; Gill & Stone, 2010) and more particularly into a behavioral model of envy despite the existence of empirical literature supporting the idea that agents do incorporate fairness considerations in their decisions. Through a money-burning experiment, Zizzo (2004) showed that agents express more negative social preferences (such as envy, although the emotional reaction is likely to also contain resentment) when (perceived) inequalities are undeserved. He found that participants burned significantly more participants who were initially given an advantage over the others by the experimenter than other participants. Recent findings also suggest the complexity of possible reactions to disadvantages. Celse (2010), in a variant of a money-burning experiment, found reduction decisions from worse-off participants to be more intense when inequalities originated from differences in performance than when inequalities were generated by a random process (Rustichini & Vostroknutov, 2014). Thus, it would appear that understanding emotional reactions to inequality ultimately entails taking into account perceptions of fairness, which in turn has complex associations with envy (e.g., see Smith & Kim, 2007).

A first step to sketching with more accuracy envy and its manifestations, as well as disentangling the latter from other emotions, would consist of introducing a moral dimension in theoretical models. Gil and Stone (2009) propose to model agents' perception of fairness in a tournament setting, assuming that agents care about their own monetary resources as well as the comparison of that monetary resource with an endogenous reference point representing the monetary resource the agent perceives to deserve. In their model, the harder an agent works relative to her rival, the more the agent feels she deserves. They found that deservingness concerns explain why agents engage in different levels of efforts. More particularly with asymmetrical agents, they showed that the strength of deservingness preferences, i.e., the difference between their current monetary resource and the monetary resource they perceive to deserve, explains the differences in effort between the advantaged and disadvantaged agents. They also show that deservingness concerns explain why agents compete for status in tournaments, which may help managers choose between different reward schemes (e.g., flat payment or rank-dependent payment). For instance, Gill and Stone (2009) found that, in the absence of fairness considerations, managers are indifferent between wage schemes, but when desert concerns are weak, managers should opt for a rank-dependent payment (i.e., a tournament). Their results show how important are deservingness concerns and suggest that additional changes in the equation may be addressed to refine the economic definition of envy.

The Concept of a Reference Group in Envy

All models of social preferences assume that agents are influenced by social comparisons with a set of relevant agents. The IA model, based on linear preferences, states that the reference group of individual i is the whole group, independent of (x_i), rather than any subset of the group; that is, it is independent of the individual's category. The IA model postulates a linear relationship between income inequalities and envy: the higher the income differences $(x_j - x_i)$, the more envious agent i will feel toward agent j, and the greater the likelihood that agent i will concede to his or her envious feelings by taking action (e.g., engage in destructive behavior, choosing envious allocations, etc.). Thus a standard economic agent should experience a more intense envy toward Bill Gates rather than toward his or her colleague or close neighbor. Although there is little work on who are the relevant reference agents, results from experiments tend to show a more complex pattern.

Celse (2016) did not observe such a linear relationship between income inequalities and envy. In a variant of a money-burning experiment, and by allocating various combinations of endowments, Celse (2016) could investigate the impact of income inequalities, measured in both absolute $(x_j - x_i)$ and relative terms x_j/x_i, on individuals' decisions to reduce others' income. In the experiment, participants were asked to report their satisfaction twice: after being informed of their endowment and after being informed of another participant's endowment. Celse (2016) showed that participants exposed to better endowed opponents expressed envy: their satisfaction shrank when learning others' higher endowment. He found a positive relationship between reported envy and absolute inequalities between endowments: participants reported more intense envy as absolute inequalities between endowments increased. However, there was a negative relationship between decisions to reduce others' endowments and relative inequalities between endowments: the higher the relative inequality between endowments, the lower the probability for a participant to reduce the endowment of the participant he was paired with. Counter to the IA model's prediction, the greatest number of reduction decisions was found in presence of slight relative inequalities. Other laboratory experiments also showed similar results: people were more likely to reduce their income in the presence of slight income differences rather than high differences (Abbink, Masclet, & Mirza, 2010; Hoff, Kshetramade, & Fehr, 2008). Thus, whereas the IA model states envy and associated negative behaviors are positively correlated to income differences, it appears that individuals are responsive to factors beyond simply the degree of income inequality: envy and related behaviors are more intense in small income gaps than in large ones. As would be expected based on work on social comparisons in general (see Suls & Wheeler, 2000), similarity in important social dimensions (Grossman & Komai, 2013; Clark, Masclet, & Villeval, 2006) and closeness (Jimenez & Cobo-Reyes, 2012) is likely to affect envy and envy-related behaviors. Hence the relationship between degree of income inequality and envy does not seem to be straightforward but is more complex than assumed by the IA model, suggesting another areas in which future models might be adjusted (see Grossman & Komai, 2013).

Part Three: Main Lessons from the Behavioral Economics of Envy

As the chapters in this volume show, the workplace gathers all the required ingredients for envy to arise naturally: by assigning limited organizational resources, firms generate inequalities among co-workers that often result in envy (Bedeian, 1995; Vecchio, 2000; Vidaillet, 2007, 2008) and that can negatively affect organizational climate and job performance. As we will show, envy may also constitute a powerful motivation to enhance employees' performance. Because of its motivational potential, BE has focused on envy and artificially induced the emotion in a variety of experimental contexts.

What are the main lessons to learn from the BE of envy that may have relevant managerial implications? Based on what I presented in previous sections, I now detail the findings whose insights may provide a better understanding of envy in the workplace.

Envy Is a Powerful Motivation

The IA model considers individual income to play a key role in agents' decisions but points out the necessity to introduce other factors in order to better explain individuals' decisions. In addition to individual income, the IA model outlines the importance of income comparisons in agents' decision-making process. This intuition is supported by a large amount of evidence suggesting the importance of others' income and more particularly of relative income (i.e., the rank of one's income in the income distribution) over individual income in shaping individual well-being and behavior (see Senik, 2005; Clark, Frijters, & Shields, 2008; Brown, Gardner, Oswald, & Qian, 2008). These cited studies show that, controlling for an agent's own income, higher earnings of other referent agents are associated with lower levels of subjective well-being. Thus, assuming that income will be the major determinant of individual satisfaction and behavior would be misleading. Managers should be sensitive to employees' concerns over relative income in their organization: employees care about their wage and also about where their remuneration lies within the wage hierarchy in their office or factory (see also Clark & Oswald, 1996; Groot & Van den Brink, 1999). Thus, as suggested by Frank (1985), firms might trade off status (or relative income) and wages, since people are envious, they should opt for lower-wage jobs in one company, in order not to be below others in an alternative company.

Social comparison is an inevitable process that may have dramatic consequences in the workplace if ignored by managers. For example, recent results show that unhappy individuals chose more often to reduce others' income at their own expense in order to be above others (Charness & Grosskopf, 2001). If one's rank in the wage distribution modulates individual well-being and job satisfaction and may generate envy, it is likely that envy, as Frank (1985) highlighted, may serve as a motivation to engage in action so as to improve one's position within the wage hierarchy. Particularly when one's income is below that of others, envy represents a natural and good candidate for organizing and coordinating behavioral processes (de Vries, 1992).

Clearly, the IA model supports the basic power of social comparisons to affect a person's sense of well-being by suggesting that envy (i.e., the disutility resulting from being below others) as a powerful motivation to explain and to make sense of agents' decisions and observed behaviors. For example, the IA model considers envy to exert a larger influence on agents' decisions and behaviors than compassion (i.e., the disutility resulting from being above others). This assumption finds support from many studies showing the aversion people had for receiving inferior material resources than referent agents, but less aversion when reference agents receive less (Loewenstein, Thompson, & Bazerman, 1989; Fliessbach et al., 2007; Bault, Coricelli, & Rustichini, 2008). Overall, BE regards envy as a powerful motivation since the emotion is known to have affective (Bault et al., 2008; Lehmann, 2001; Miles & Rossi, 2007; Smith & Kim, 2007) and cognitive (Fliessbach et al., 2007) implications.

Envy as a Managerial Strategy

Although some findings in BE highlight the negative effects of envy on well-being, other findings suggest that fostering it can also serve as a managerial strategy to spur employees to work harder and better. The literature on relative-feedback provision (informing an agent about his or her absolute level of performance and about others' performance levels) provides a good illustration of the larger motivational influence of envy to foster individual performance. Feedback provision may generate envy by revealing one's relative inferiority (i.e., negative feedback), but it may then increase one's performance. In a field experiment in a Japanese bank, Gino and Staats (2012) showed that, when employees learned that their own performance was among the lowest of their reference group, they often increased their performance. Conversely, when they learned that their performance was among the highest of their reference group, they often failed to improve their performance (see also Charness, Masclet, & Villeval, 2013; Azmat & Iriberri, 2010, 2016).

Results from the Gift-Exchange game, which reproduces a simplified version of the interaction between a manager and its employee, provide a good illustration of how envy can be used as a managerial lever to motivate employees' behaviors. The Gift-Exchange game (Fehr, Kirchsteiger, & Riedl, 1993) is a two-stage game in which two paired participants are interacting: a manager and an employee. In the first stage, the manager proposes a wage to the employee. In the second stage, the employee is informed about the wage proposed and can either reject (then both participants receive null payoffs) or accept the wage. In that latter case, the employee has to choose an effort level that is costly for the employee and generates benefits to the manager. In their seminal paper, Fehr, Kirchsteiger, and Riedl (1993) found a positive relationship between the wage proposed by the manager and the effort provided by the employee: employees reacted to low wages with low effort levels, and vice versa. Clark, Masclet, and Villeval (2010) used a variant of the Gift-Exchange game in which, at the beginning of the second stage, the employee is told about the wage proposed by his or her manager as well as the wage proposed by four other managers to their respective employees. As suggested by the IA model, they found that the effort level provided by employees depended both on individual income (i.e., employees exerted more effort as their own wage increased and vice versa) and on relative income (i.e., the position of their own wage in the wage distribution). Their most interesting result was that rank within the wage distribution seemed to matter more than absolute income: employees worked harder as their position within the wage distribution increased, independently of the wage received (Gneezy & Rustichini, 2000).

Other studies show that envy can induce employees to work less. In a study conducted by Gächter and Thöni (2010), employees could learn the wages proposed by the manager as well as the wage their manager proposed to another, similar, employee. They showed that 28% of participants were envious (as defined by the IA model); namely, when they realized that their co-worker earned a higher wage than they had, they significantly reduced their own level of effort, irrespective of the wage received. Similar results were obtained by Cohn, Fehr, Herrmann, and Schneider (2011), who examined the impact of wage cuts on the performance of paired workers. They discovered that cutting the wage of one worker out of the two causes the highest drop in performance (34%).

To summarize, whereas envy may constitute a powerful motivator, it can be a double-edged sword. On one hand, generating envy in the workplace can foster productivity by pushing employees in a positive spiral of continual improvement (Kragl & Schmidt, 2009; Grund & Sliwka, 2005; Gino & Staats, 2012). On the other hand, it can push employees to engage in counterproductive efforts and even pit employees against one another (Cohn et al., 2011; Gachter & Thoni, 2010; Mui, 1995; see Sterling, van de Ven, & Smith, Chapter 3, this volume). Most typically, studies in BE have shown that an increase in wage inequalities reduces the likelihood of envious, destructive behaviors.

Clearly, further studies are required to investigate the impact of other factors on envy and its expressions. Achieving the optimal balance of providing performance-enhancing feedback and at the same time minimizing the negative effects of envy on well-being raises complex issues, and, indeed, much work needs to be done in this area. Direct comparisons between existing studies are difficult, for instance, since they often use different environments and different methods. It is likely that culture (see Tan, Tai, and Wang, Chapter 11, this volume), is another important factor in determining how envy operates in both positive and negative ways. Managers should also pay close attention to the factors modulating the expressions of envy, such as perceived fairness (Smith et al., 1994), perceived control (Testa & Major, 1990), and the relevance of the desired attribute (Lockwood & Kunda, 1997).

The Nature of Envy

We showed studies suggesting that envy motivates agents' behavior in a variety of directions, either by inciting them to make constructive efforts or by pushing them to engage in counterproductive activities. A last question remains—how envy is perceived in BE: Is envy viewed as a positive emotion leading to constructive efforts or as a negative emotion driving to destruction? A traditional view in economics shared about envy is that the emotion is intrinsically bad, and, as a consequence, socially condemned and individually restrained. In BE, the majority of studies focuses on the association between envy and antisocial behavior (Beckman et al., 2002; Gächter & Thöni, 2010; Cohn et al., 2011; Celse, 2016; Zizzo & Oswald, 2001). A substantial number of studies showing that an important fraction of people (up to 60%) are willing to pay in order to reduce others' income (e.g., Zizzo, 2009). However, through an economic prism, the emotion of envy is not pictured as a resolutely negative or positive emotion. Whereas psychologists often point out the importance of disentangling two notions of envy (e.g., see Cohen-Charash & Larson, Chapter 1; Sterling, van de Ven, & Smith, Chapter 3; Hoogland, Thielke, & Smith, Chapter 5, this volume), such a distinction is pointless in BE: envy can be pictured as positive or negative, depending on the consequences the emotion generates for the utility function. Envy is conceptualized as a preference, a component of an agent's utility function.

Thus, the perception of envy as a destructive or as an emulative force depends on the context; i.e., on the conditions in which agents interact with others and on agents' perceptions of this context (see Zizzo, 2009). Almost all models picture envy as a utility loss; i.e., they consider that envy damages an agent's utility function. It is acknowledged that envy is associated with several important decisions such as whether to reject gain improvements: envious people prefer to receive lower allocations rather than obtaining higher allocations, if such higher allocations benefit others more (Solnick & Hemenway, 1998; Beckman et al., 2002). Envy explains why agents refuse low proposals in bargaining interactions (Güth, 1995; Kirchsteiger, 1994). Envy is known to be associated with lying behaviors: envy pushes individuals to lie in order to hurt others (Gino & Pierce, 2009, 2010). Envy prevents agents from coordinating efficiently (Jimenez & Cobo-Reyes, 2007) and affects risk attitude (Sonnemans & Linde, 2011; Gamba & Manzoni, 2014; Zizzo & Kebede, 2011).

The main conclusion from the behavioral economics of envy is that envy is a strong motivational force that can be directed to promote a variety of behaviors: exert more effort (Clark et al., 2010), engage in prosocial behavior (Tai, Naranayan, & McAllister, 2012), or refrain from antisocial behavior (Celse, Chang, Max, & Quinton, forthcoming). For illustration, Celse, Chang, Max, and Quinton (2016) showed how envy can serve as a motivational mechanism to promote moral behavior; namely, to prevent individuals from lying (see Lee & Gino, Chapter 15, this volume). They gave participants an opportunity to lie and to gain higher benefits from that lie without being identified. They found that most participants took that opportunity to lie and gained higher earnings. Interestingly, they found that participants did not lie in presence of envy (as defined by the IA model): when lies generate higher benefits for others rather than for the liar, he refrains from lying. This result indicates that envy can be regarded as a micro-motivation to reduce the tendency to lie. Without implementing mechanisms to fight immoral behaviors (monitoring, sanctions, etc.), envy was powerful enough to curb participants' tendency to lie.

To summarize, three main lessons can be derived from the BE of envy. First, focusing on individual income to motivate employees may be misleading. Second, envy may be used as a managerial strategy since it is a powerful motivation. Finally, its motivational power can work in different directions: envy can serve to promote prosocial behavior (like being honest) or to promote anti-social behavior (like refusing gain improvements if these improvements give higher benefits to others). Managers could use envy to motivate their employees toward an objective, but they should be attentive to the context in which envy occurs so as to control for its behavioral implications and expressions.

Conclusion

Through this chapter, we presented a behavioral model in which decision-makers compare their situation to others, and derive utility (namely satisfaction) from their allocation of resources and disutility from any existing differences between their allocation of resources and others'. In this model, envy can be conceptualized as a dissatisfaction that arises when the agent faces unflattering comparisons. The greater the difference between his or her allocation and the allocation given to another agent, the more the agent suffers from envy. We highlighted the main features of this model and suggested its main limitations as well. We presented studies suggesting answers to these limits and discussed some elements that could be introduced to improve the economic definition of envy. Finally, we listed the main lessons from the BE of envy that can refine our understanding of envy in the workplace.

From an economic viewpoint, envy is acknowledged to be an important feature in human motivation. Despite its motivational power, the economic definition of envy may be considered sloppy and imprecise. As a consequence, the economic definition of envy and the emotion itself are different constructs. However, it is worth pointing out that, in economics, the emphasis is neither on the definition nor on the description of an element, but on the prediction of behavior. In economics, behavioral models seek to explain and consequently predict agents' behaviors as much possible. Economists consider a refinement in a theory if it leads to a significant increase in its predictive power. It is acknowledged that behavioral models incorporating envy (such as the one we described) have an important predictive power in explaining agents' behavior and more precisely agents' decisions to punish others (Leibbrandt & Lopez-Perez, 2011, 2012). As we highlighted throughout this chapter, research on envy is a promising avenue, and there is still room for further investigation on the topic.

Notes

1. Presidential speech at Kennedy Plaza, Providence, Rhode Island (August 1902), *Presidential Addresses and State Papers* (1910), p. 103.

2. Economists refer to the term *utility* to represent the satisfaction agents derive from their situation and actions. For a convenient reading, one can replace the term *utility* with *satisfaction*.

3. Celse (2016) reviews the existing literature on money-burning experiments.

4. See Simon (1991) for a definition of bounded rationality, and Sobel (2005) for social preferences.

5. Although in its original version, the IA model considered envy indirectly, the model has been widely adopted by economists to represent envy (Camerer, 2003). Victim of his success, the model is also known as the "envy and compassion model."

6. Such individuals would be characterized by $\beta_i < 0$.

7. The same problem occurs in a "pure" envy model: these emotions would be captured by $s < 0$. This problem is recurrent in behavioral economics (Zizzo, 2009). Behavioral economists typically consider that both an envious agent and, for instance, a spiteful one are characterized by the same utility function that values negatively the material resources allocated to other relevant agents (Kirchsteiger, 1994; Mui, 1995).

8. This viewpoint contrasts with Social Comparison Theory (Festinger, 1954; Suls & Wheeler, 2000), which assumes individuals define reference groups and compare themselves with individuals who belong to these reference groups. Only social comparisons involving referent agents are prone to generating envy.

9. Some models define "equality" in terms of the existing differences between the agent's payoff and the worst-off agent belonging to his reference group (Charness & Rabin, 2002); or equality can also be defined in terms of the agent's relative share of the overall surplus (Bolton & Ockenfels, 2000). See Sobel (2005) for a comprehensive overview.

References

Abbink, K. Masclet, D., & Mirza, D. (2010). Inequality and inter-group conflicts: An experimental evidence. CIRANO Working Papers 2011s-10, CIRANO.

Adams, J. S. (1965). Inequity in social exchange. In L. Berkowitz, Ed., *Advances in Experimental Social Psychology* (Vol. II, pp. 267–299). Academic Press.

Azmat, G., & Iriberri, N. (2010). The importance of relative performance feedback information: Evidence from a natural experiment using high school students. *Journal of Public Economics*, 94(7–8), 435–452.

Azmat, G., & Iriberri, N. (2016). The provision of relative feedback: An analysis of performance and satisfaction. *Journal of Economics & Management Strategy*, *25*(1), 77–110.

Bault, N., Coricelli, G., & Rustichini, A. (2008). Interdependent utilities: How social ranking affects choice behavior. *PLoS One*, *3*(10) e3477, Epub Oct. 22, 2008.

Beckman, S. R., Formby, J. P., Smith, W. J., & Zheng, B. (2002). Envy, malice and Pareto efficiency: An experimental investigation. *Social Choice and Welfare*, *19*, 349–367.

Bedeian, A. G. (1995). Workplace envy. *Organizational Dynamics*, *23*(4), 49–56.

Blanco, M., Engelmann, D., & Normann, H. (2011). A within-subject analysis of other-regarding preferences. *Games and Economic Behavior*, *72*, 321–338.

Bolle, F., & Kemp, S. (2013). Are egalitarian preferences based on envy? *Journal of Behavioral and Experimental Economics*, *45*, 57–63.

Bolton, G. (1991). A comparative model of bargaining: Theory and evidence. *American Economic Review*, *81*, 1096–1136.

Bolton, G., & Ockenfels, A. (2000). ERC: A theory of equity, reciprocity and competition. *American Economic Review*, *90*, 166–193.

Brown, G. D. A., Gardner, J., Oswald, A., & Qian, J. (2008). Does wage rank affect employees' well-being? *Industrial Relations*, *47*(3), 355–389.

Burrows, P., & Loomes, G. (1994). The impact of fairness on bargaining behavior. *Empirical Economics*, *19*, 201–221.

Camerer, C. F. (2003). *Behavioral Game Theory: Experiments in Strategic Interaction*, Princeton, NJ: University Press.

Camerer, C. F., & Lowenstein, G. (2004). Behavioral economics: Past, present, future. In C. Camerer, G. Lowenstein, and M. Rabin, Eds., *Advances in Behavioral Economics* (pp. 3–53). New York: Russell Sage.

Carlsson, F., Johansson-Stenman, O., & Martinsson, P. (2007). Do you enjoy having more than others? Survey evidence of positional goods. *Economica*, *74*, 586–598.

Celse, J. (2010). Envy in *Othello*: Can effort explain such a tragic issue? *LAMETA Working Papers*, DT2010-23.

Celse, J. (2012). Is the positional bias an artefact? Distinguishing positional concerns from egalitarian concerns. *The Journal of Socio-Economics*, *41*, 277–283.

Celse, J. (2016). Will Joe the Plumber envy Bill Gates? The impact of absolute and relative differences on both individual satisfaction and behavior. *Revue d'Economie Politique*, *126* (2), 65–92.

Celse, J., Chang, K., Max, S., & Quinton, S. (2016). The reduction of employee lying behavior: Inspiration from a study of envy in part-time employees. *Journal of Strategy and Management*, *9* (2), 118–137.

Charness, G., & Grosskopf, B. (2001). Relative payoffs and happiness: An experimental study. *The Journal of Economic Behavior and Organization*, *45*, 301–328.

Charness, G., & Rabin, M. (2002). Understanding social preferences with simple tests. *Quarterly Journal of Economics*, *117*, 817–869.

Charness, G., Masclet, D., & Villeval, M. C. (2013). The dark side of competition for status. *Management Science*, *60*(1), 38–55.

Clark, A., & Oswald, A. (1996). Satisfaction and comparison income. *Journal of Public Economics*, *61*, 359–381.

Clark, A., & Oswald, A. (1996). Satisfaction and comparison income. *Journal of Public Economics*, *61*, 359–381.

Clark, A., Frijters, P., & Shields, M. (2008). Relative income, happiness and utility: An explanation for the Easterlin paradox. *Journal of Economic Literature*, *46*(1), 95–144.

Clark, A., Masclet, D., & Villeval, M. C. (2010). Effort and comparison income: Experimental and survey evidence. *Industrial and Labor Relations Review*, *63*(3), 407–426.

Cohn, A., Fehr, E., Herrmann, B., & Schneider, F. (2011). Social comparison in the workplace: Evidence from a field experiment. IZA Discussion Papers 5550, Institute for the Study of Labor (IZA).

D'Arms, J., & Duncan Kerr, A. (2009). Envy in the philosophical tradition. In R. H. Smith, Ed., *Envy: Theory and Research* (pp. 39–59). Series in Affective Sciences. New York: Oxford University Press.

De Vries, M. F. R. (1992). The motivating role of envy: A forgotten factor in management. *Administration & Society*, *24*(1), 41–60.

Dickinson, D. L., & Tiefenthaler, J. (2002). What is fair? Experimental evidence. *Southern Economic Journal*, *69*(2), 414–428.

Fehr, E., & Schmidt, K. (1999). A theory of fairness, competition and cooperation. *Quarterly Journal of Economics*, *114*, 817–868.

Fehr, E., & Schmidt, K. M. (2006). The economics of fairness, reciprocity and altruism—experimental evidence and new theories. In S. Kolm & J. Mercier Ythier, Eds., *Handbook on the Economics of Giving, Reciprocity and Altruism* (pp. 616–684). New York: Elsevier.

Fehr, E., Kirchsteiger, G., & Riedl, A. (1993). Does fairness prevent market clearing? An experimental investigation. *Quarterly Journal of Economics*, *89*, 437–459.

Festinger, L. (1954). A theory of social comparison processes. *Human Relations*, *7*, 117–140.

Fliessbach, K., Weber, B., Trautner, P., Dohmen, T., Sunde, U., Elger, C. E., & Falk, A. (2007). Social comparison affects reward-related brain activity in the human ventral striatum. *Science*, *318*(5854), pp. 1305–1308.

Frank, R. (1985). *Choosing the Right Pond*. Oxford, UK: Oxford University Press.

Frank, R. H. (1997). The frame of reference as a public good. *The Economic Journal*, *107*(Nov), 1832–1847.

Gächter, S., & Thöni, C. (2010). Social comparison and performance: Experimental evidence on the fair wage-effort hypothesis. *Journal of Economic Behavior & Organization*, *76*(3), 531–543.

Gamba, A., & Manzoni, E. (2014). Social comparison and risk taking behavior. *Jena Economic Research Papers*, *1*, 1–28.

Gill, D., & Stone, R. (2010). Fairness and desert in tournaments. *Games and Economic Behavior*, *69*, 346–364.

Gino, F., & Pierce, L. (2009). Dishonesty in the name of equity. *Psychological Science*, *20*(9), 1153–1160.

Gino, F., & Pierce, L. (2010). Lying to level the playing field: Why people may dishonestly help or hurt others to create equity. Special issue on regulating ethical failures: Insights from psychology. *Journal of Business Ethics*, *95*(1), 89–103.

Gino, F., & Staats, B. (2012). Specialization and variety in repetitive tasks: Evidence from a Japanese bank. *Management Science*, *58*(6), 1141–1159.

Gneezy, U., & Rustichini, A. (2000). Pay enough or don't pay at all. *Quarterly Journal of Economics*, *115*(3), 791–810.

Grolleau, G., & Said, S. (2009). Do you prefer having more or more than others? Survey evidence on positional concerns in France. *Journal of Economic Issues*, *42*(4), 701–717.

Groot, W., & Van den Brink, H. (1999). Overpayment and earnings satisfaction: An application of an ordered response tobit model. *Applied Economics Letters*, *6*, 235–238.

Grossman, P. J., & Komai, M. (2013). Within and across class envy: Anti-social behavior in hierarchical groups, Monash Economics Working Papers 02-13, Monash University, Department of Economics.

Grund, C., & Sliwka, D. (2005). Envy and compassion in tournaments. *Journal of Economics and Management Strategy*, *14*(1), 187–207.

Güth, W. (1995). On bargaining—a personal review. *Journal of Economic Behavior & Organization*, *27*, 329–344.

Hoff. D., Kshetramade, M., & Fehr, E. (2008). Spite and development. *American Economic Review*, *98*(2), 494–499.

Hoffman, E., & Spitzer, M. L. (1985). Entitlements, rights, and fairness: An experimental examination of subjects' concepts of distributive justice. *Journal of Legal Studies*, *14*, 259–297.

Jimenez, N., & Cobo-Reyes, R. (2012). The dark side of friendship: Envy. *Experimental Economics*, *15*(4), 1–24.

Kahneman, D., Knetsch, J., & Thaler, R. (1986). Fairness and the assumptions of economics. *Journal of Business*, *59*(4), 285–300.

Kirchsteiger, G. (1994). The role of envy in ultimatum games. *Journal of Economic Behavior & Organization*, *25*, 373–389.

Konow, J. (1996). A positive theory of economic fairness. *Journal of Economic Behavior and Organization*, *31*, 13–35.

Konow, J. (2000). Fair shares: Accountability and cognitive dissonance in allocation decisions. *American Economic Review*, *90*, 1072–1091.

Konow, J. (2003). Which is the fairest one of all? A positive analysis of justice theories. *Journal of Economic Literature*, *41*, 1188–1239.

Konow, J. (2010). Mixed feelings: Theories of and evidence on giving. *Journal of Public Economics*, *94*(3-4), 279–297.

Kragl, J., & Schmidt, J. (2009). The impact of envy on relational employment contracts. *Journal of Economic Behavior & Organization*, *72*, 766–779.

Lehmann, D. R. (2001). The impact of altruism and envy on competitive behavior and satisfaction. *International Journal of Research in Marketing*, *18*, 5–17.

Leibbrandt, A., & Lopez-Perez, R. (2011). The dark side of altruistic third party punishment. *Journal of Conflict Resolution*, *55*, 761–784.

Leibbrandt, A., & Lopez-Perez, R. (2012). An exploration of third and second party punishment in ten simple games. *Journal of Economic Behavior and Organization*, *84*(3), 753–866.

Leventhal, G. S., & Michaels, J. W. (1971). Locus of cause and equity motivation as determinants of reward allocation. *Journal of Personality and Social Psychology*, *17*(3), 229–235.

Lockwood, P., & Kunda, Z. (1997). Superstars and me: Predicting the impact of role models on the self. *Journal of Personality and Social Psychology*, *73*, 91–103.

Loewenstein, G. F., Thompson, F. L., & Bazerman, M. H. (1989). Social utility and decision making in interpersonal contexts. *Journal of Personality and Social Psychology*, *57*(1989), 426–441.

Miles, D., & Rossi, M. (2007). Learning about one's relative position and subjective well-being. *Applied Economics*, *39*(13), 1711–1718.

Mui, V. L. (1995). The economics of envy. *Journal of Economic Behavior & Organization*, *26*, 311–336.

Neumark, D., & Postlewaite, A. (1998). Relative income concerns and the rise in married women's employment. *Journal of Public Economics*, *70*, 157–193.

Parrott, W. G., & Smith, R. H. (1993). Distinguishing the experiences of envy and jealousy. *Journal of Personality and Social Psychology*, *64*, 906–920.

Ruffle, B. (1998). More is better, but fair is fair: Tipping in dictator and ultimatum games. *Games and Economic Behavior*, *23*, 247–265.

Rustichini, A., & Vostroknutov, A. (2014). Merit and justice: An experimental analysis of attitude to inequality, PLOS One, December.

Schokkaert, E., & Capeau, B. (1991). Interindividual differences in opinions about distributive justice. *Kyklos*, *44*(3), 25–45.

Senik, C. (2005). Income distribution and well-being: What can we learn from subjective data?. *Journal of Economic Surveys*, *19*(1), 43–63.

Simon, H. A. (1991). Bounded rationality and organizational learning. *Organization Science*, *2*(1), 125–134.

Smith, R. H., & Kim, S. H. (2007). Comprehending envy. *Psychological Bulletin*, *133*(1), 46–64.

Smith, R. H., Parrott, W. G., Ozer, D., & Moniz, A. (1994). Subjective injustice and inferiority as predictors of hostile and depressive feelings in envy. *Personality and Social Psychology Bulletin*, *20*(6), 705–711.

Sobel, J. (2005). Interdependent preferences and reciprocity. *Journal of Economic Literature*, *43*, 392–436.

Solnick, S. J., & Hemenway, D. (1998). Is more always better? A survey on positional concerns. *Journal of Economic Behavior & Organization*, *37*, 373–383.

Solnick, S. J., & Hemenway, D. (2005). Are positional concerns stronger in some domains than in others? *American Economic Review*, *95*(2), 147–151.

Solnick, S. J., & Hemenway, D. (2007). Positional goods in the United States and China. *Journal of Socio-Economics*, *36*(4), 537–545.

Sonnemans, J., & Linde, J. (2011). Social comparisons and risky choices. *Journal of Risk and Uncertainty*, *44*, 45–72.

Suls, J. M., & Wheeler, L., Eds. (2000). *Handbook of Social Comparison: Theory and Research*. New York: Plenum Press.

Tai, K., Naranayan, J., & McAllister, D. J. (2012). Envy as pain: Rethinking the nature of envy and its implications for employee and organizations. *Academy of Management Review*, *37*(1), 107–129.

Testa, M., & Major, B. (1990). The impact of social comparison after failure: The moderating effects of perceived control. *Basic and Applied Social Psychology*, *11*, 205–218.

Vecchio, R. P. (2000). *Organizational Behavior: Core Concepts*. 4th edn. Fort Worth, TX: Dryden Press.

Vidaillet, B. (2007). Lacanian theory's contribution to the study of workplace envy. *Human Relations*, *60*(11), 1669–1700.

Vidaillet, B. (2008). *Workplace Envy*. London: Palgrave McMillan.

Wobker, I., & Kenning, P. (2013). Drivers and outcome of destructive envy behavior in an economic game setting. *Schmalenbach Business Review*, *65*, 173–194.

Wouters, S., van Excel, N. J. A., van de Donk, M., Rhode, K. I. M., & Brouwer, W. B. F. (2015). Do people desire to be healthier than other people? A short note on positional concerns for health. *European Journal of Health Economics*, *16* (1), 47–54.

Zizzo, D. J. (2003). Money burning and rank egalitarianism with random dictators. *Economics Letters*, *81*(2), 263–266.

Zizzo, D. J. (2004). Inequality and procedural fairness in a money burning and stealing experiment. In F. Cowell, Ed., *Inequality, Welfare and Income Distribution: Experimental Approaches*, Vol. 11 of *Research on Economic Inequality* (pp. 215–247). New York: Elsevier.

Zizzo, D. J. (2009). The cognitive and behavioral economics of envy. In R. H. Smith, Ed., *Envy: Theory and Research* (pp. 190–210). Series in Affective Sciences. New York: Oxford University Press.

Zizzo, D. J., & Kebede, B. (2011). Envy and agricultural innovation: An experimental case study from Ethiopia. *CSAE Working Paper Series 2011-06*, Centre for the Study of African Economies, University of Oxford.

Zizzo, D. J., & Oswald, A. (2001). Are people willing to reduce others' incomes? *Annales d'Economie et de Statistiques*, *63*–64, 39–62.

15 | Envy and Interpersonal Corruption

SOCIAL COMPARISON PROCESSES AND UNETHICAL BEHAVIOR IN ORGANIZATIONS

JULIA J. LEE AND FRANCESCA GINO

Introduction

In an influential 1986 article, Treviño proposed an interactionist model that combined individual and situational variables to predict unethical behavior in the workplace (Treviño, 1986). As Treviño noted, despite receiving widespread attention, the issue of ethical decision-making in organizations had been the subject of little empirical investigation.

Since then, the situation has improved. In fact, as reported in a recent meta-analysis of the sources of unethical behavior in organizations, "behavioral ethics has become a legitimate and necessary field of social scientific inquiry" (Kish-Gephart, Harrison, & Treviño, 2010). Over the last three decades, not only have many scholars investigated both theoretically and empirically the conditions under which employees are likely to cross ethical boundaries (Ford & Richardson, 1994; O'Fallon & Butterfield, 2005; Tenbrunsel & Crowe, 2008; Tenbrunsel, Diekmann, Wade-Benzoni, & Bazerman, 2010), but dramatic instances of unethical behavior in organizations have increasingly populated the news, thus highlighting the practical importance of the study of behavioral ethics.

A review of the literature on unethical behavior indicates that researchers generally maintain that two main sets of factors influence employees' decisions to act unethically: (1) situational forces (related to the context the person is operating in), and (2) dispositional forces (related to the person's personality). Research on unethical behavior has mainly examined antecedents consistent with these theoretical bases. Examples of such antecedents include demographic variables (O'Fallon & Butterfield,

2005), an individual's concern for self-presentation (Covey, Saladin, & Killen, 1989), his or her stage of moral development (Treviño & Youngblood, 1990), ethics training (Delaney & Sockell, 1992), ethical climate and culture (Treviño, 1986; Victor & Cullen, 1988), codes of conduct (Brief, Dukerich, Brown, & Brett, 1996; Helin & Sandström, 2007; McCabe, Treviño, & Butterfield, 1996), reward systems and incentives (Flannery & May, 2000; Hegarty & Sims, 1979; Tenbrunsel, 1998; Treviño & Youngblood, 1990), the nature of the goals driving one's actions (Schweitzer, Ordóñez, & Douma, 2004), and environmental wealth (Gino & Pierce, 2009b). The common denominator across these studies is the notion that unethical behavior stems from an individual's desire to advance his or her self-interest because of dispositional or situational forces, even when self-interest conflicts with organizational goals.

Several researchers recently have noted that engaging in unethical behaviors might be the results of social comparison processes; that is, people who engage in unethical behavior may be motivated, not only by pure self-interest, but also by producing costs to others (e.g., co-workers) in their organizations (e.g., those who seem superior or advantaged). For example, recent research identified interpersonal motivation to *hurt* others (i.e., involving a potential harm to others, such as taking more credit for the work than one deserves) as a factor when individuals engage in unethical behavior, and that this motivation may be linked to social comparisons (Gino & Pierce, 2009a, 2010a). In particular, a series of studies involving wealth-based inequity demonstrated that emotional reactions such as envy (linked to a social comparison by definition) and guilt (which is often linked to a social comparison, such as when someone is over-benefitted compared to others) can lead to unethical helping or hurting behavior. Gino and Pierce (Gino & Pierce, 2009a, 2010a) showed that individuals engage in dishonest behavior to relieve the emotional distress of envy from wealth-based inequity. When participants were made worse off than the referent other, they increased their hurtful behavior. Furthermore, this effect was persistent even at the expense of their self-interest, which involves forgoing either material rewards or financial benefits to oneself, as it could relieve emotional distress from feeling envy (Gino & Pierce, 2009a). In the context of vehicle emissions testing, for example, Gino and Pierce (Gino & Pierce, 2010b) found that the emission inspectors were less lenient toward wealthy customers who had been identified as having luxury vehicles. A laboratory study confirmed the psychological mechanisms explaining this wealth-based discriminatory behavior, by demonstrating that individuals were more likely to feel envious of peers who drive luxury cars, compared to those who drive standard cars, and thus were less likely to help the wealthy peers. Thus, this recent stream of work highlights a different motivation for unethical behavior in organizations, one that focuses on either the relationship between two employees, or on the relationship between an employee and the organization.

Our purpose in this chapter is to explore the role of upward social comparisons and the emotional reactions they trigger in the context of unethical behavior. Under what conditions do the potential benefits and costs of an action to others (motivated at least in part by social comparisons and the invidious emotions that these social comparisons can produce) cause an employee to cross ethical boundaries? An understanding of the motives underlying unethical behavior is essential in order for research on unethical behavior in organizations to progress. In exploring this issue, we seek to further the understanding of envy, social comparison processes, and unethical behavior in organizations in three main ways.

First, we review the relevant literature on envy, social comparison processes, and unethical behavior in organizations, highlighting the conceptual links and potential overlaps among them. We then present a model of unethical behavior in organizations that provides an overview of how motives that are interpersonal, and their interactions with characteristics of an organization's structure, influence unethical actions and the consequences associated with them in organizational contexts. Thus, in this model we conceptualize motivational bases of unethical behavior in organizations and its potential consequences. This approach seeks to improve our understanding of the intentionality of unethical behaviors by examining how interpersonal motives linked to social comparison processes interplay with the characteristics of an organization's structure.

Second, based on Festinger's (1954) social comparison theory and its extensions, we outline specific antecedents of unethical behaviors that hurt others, driven by upward social comparison processes and the emotional reactions they trigger, such as envy. Following the main tenets of social comparison research (Garcia, Tor, & Gonzalez, 2006; Goethals & Darley, 1977), we propose that individuals will be motivated to engage in unethical behavior that hurts others in organizations (what we refer to as *interpersonal unethical behavior*) when (1) they make an upward comparison to co-workers on a relevant dimension, (2) they believe the comparison is commensurable, (3) they feel (or are) close and similar to the comparison target. We then detail the effects of interpersonal unethical behaviors, in turn, upon organization/work group effectiveness and an individual's reputation as a reliable and trustworthy organizational member, especially when this unethical behavior is linked to invidious motives (Guimond, 2006; Suls & Wheeler, 2000; Suls & Miller, 1977). Thus, we seek, not only to explore the role of interpersonal motives related to social comparison processes underlying interpersonal unethical behaviors, but also to examine the outcomes of such behaviors in this context.

Third, and finally, we offer recommendations for implementing changes in organizations designed to limit, if not eliminate, the detrimental impact of interpersonal unethical behaviors. We also discuss implications for future theory development and practical implications.

Defining Interpersonal Unethical Behavior in Organizations

Researchers in behavioral ethics have focused on motives that emphasize a self-serving or self-oriented motivation for unethical behavior. For example, Gneezy (2005) noted that people tell lies whenever it is beneficial for them, regardless of the lies' effect on the other party. This statement is consistent with prior work conceptualizing the decision to behave unethically as a pure product of economic incentives, in which individuals mainly weigh the financial benefits of unethical behavior against the costs—such as the financial penalty that could arise from getting caught (Allingham & Sandmo, 1972). Similarly, Tenbrunsel (1998) showed that monetary incentives increase individuals' willingness to misrepresent information to another party in a social exchange, consistent with Lewicki's (1983) argument that individuals lie to the extent that lying benefits them. Individuals driven by egoistic motives have been shown to ignore others' interests and to be reluctant to sacrifice their personal outcomes to benefit a counterpart (Van Lange, 1999).

Yet employees often act dishonestly in order to hurt co-workers, even when they receive no personal financial benefits from doing so (see Celse, Chapter 14, this volume, for envy-driven behaviors that are not consistent with standard economic assumptions of self-interest). For instance, an employee may try to sabotage a co-worker in order to appear to be the best-performing member in the eyes of their supervisor. Thus, the motivation to act unethically in such cases is not driven purely by financial self-interest, even though it is possible that crossing ethical boundaries to help or hurt others may benefit the self psychologically and materially (e.g., In a zero-sum situation where a cost to one's comparison target is a benefit to oneself). Rather, we characterize this motivation as *interpersonal* to the extent that it involves one's social comparison to *others*. This interpersonal motivation may drive a decision to behave unethically, due to one's attempt to reduce an aversive state of experiencing envy. We refer to unethical behavior motivated by potential costs to others as "*interpersonal* unethical behavior." This focus on others often occurs when employees engage in social comparisons with their co-workers (Gino & Pierce, 2010b).

Given our focus on interpersonal unethical behavior in organizational settings, it is important to make a clear distinction between interpersonal unethical behavior and two closely related constructs (Duffy, Ganster, & Pagon, 2002; Kish-Gephart et al., 2010): workplace deviance and social undermining.

First, the definition of interpersonal unethical behavior is different from the construct of workplace deviance or counterproductive work behavior (Sackett, Berry, & Wiemann, 2006), even if this distinction may seem subtle. "Workplace deviance" and "counterproductive work behavior" refer to behaviors that violate *organizational* norms (Bennett & Robinson, 2003), while "interpersonal unethical behavior" refers to behaviors that violate widely accepted *societal* norms, pertaining to the set of behaviors that is considered socially unacceptable (e.g., taking credit for your co-worker's work). There are certainly areas of overlap in these types of behaviors. For instance, lying to customers and misreporting work expenses are generally considered behaviors that violate both widely accepted societal norms and organizational norms. However, other (often less serious) forms of workplace deviance (e.g., gossiping, taking exceptionally long lunch breaks, working slowly) violate organizational norms but may not be considered inappropriate within the set of widely accepted societal norms (Dalal, 2005; Robinson & Bennett, 1995). As these examples suggest, some overlap exists between the set of counterproductive or deviant work behaviors and the set of unethical behaviors, but several forms of counterproductive or deviant work behavior cannot be categorized as interpersonally unethical. In this chapter, we refer only to forms of counterproductive or deviant work behaviors that can be clearly labeled "unethical."

Second, the definition of social undermining can also be differentiated from interpersonal unethical behavior. "Social undermining" refers to behaviors that are intended to hinder the ability to establish and maintain positive interpersonal relationships, work-related success, and one's favorable reputation in the workplace (Duffy, Ganster, & Pagon, 2002). Although both social undermining and interpersonal unethical behavior are *interpersonal* by nature, we focus specifically on the set of behaviors that are not only hurting and undermining other employees, but also clearly violate the societal norms. For example, an employee's action of actively hiding a key piece of information to sabotage others can be both social undermining and interpersonal unethical behavior. However, making a joke about a co-worker (to the extent that it does not cross ethical boundaries) and making him or her feel bad would be an example of social undermining rather than interpersonal unethical behavior.

Upward Social Comparisons, Envy, and Interpersonal Unethical Behavior

Social comparison refers to the "process of thinking about information about one or more other people in relation to the self" (Wood, 1996). As a basic aspect of human experience, social comparisons have been studied by psychologists in many areas of human functioning (Crosby, 1976). In fact, social comparisons are widely considered an "almost inevitable element of social interaction" (Brickman & Bulman, 1977), helping individuals reduce uncertainty and create meaning (Suls & Wheeler, 2000), and affecting so much of everyday experience from self-evaluations (e.g., Lockwood & Kunda, 1997; Tesser, 1991) to emotions such as anger, resentment, and envy (Smith, Pettigrew, Pippin, & Bialosiewicz, 2012; Smith, 2000; Smith & Kim, 2007).

Social psychologists have studied social comparison processes for more than 50 years, but despite early calls to explore social comparison processes in the workplace (Goodman, 1977), the topic has only recently received the attention of organizational scholars outside of the organizational justice and fairness literature (Ambrose, Harland, & Kulik, 1991; Greenberg, Ashton-James, & Ashkanasy, 2007). Notably, organizational contexts are both uncertain and competitive (Kay, Wheeler, Bargh, & Ross, 2004). Employees often compare themselves to co-workers or peers on various dimensions, including ability, salary, and level of allocated resources (Brown, Ferris, Heller, & Keeping, 2007).

People may compare downward to an individual who is perceived to be worse off on some characteristic or dimension (e.g., resources allocated, salary, ability, reputation, or relationship with supervisor), or upward to an individual who is perceived to be better off on some characteristic or dimension. We here focus on upward comparisons, in particular, that may lead employees to feel envious of co-workers' fortunes and abilities. For instance, an employee's upward social comparisons can lead to competitive behavior and arousal (Festinger, 1942, 1954; Hoffman, Festinger, &

Lawrence, 1954), or even envy (Gino & Pierce, 2009a; and see Cohen-Charash & Larson, Chapter 1, and other chapters in this volume for in-depth conceptualizations of envy), which in turn could result in the desire to sabotage the comparison target.

Traditionally, models used to explain unethical behavior have focused on rational effortful processing related to a person's cognition. For example, Rest (1986) proposed a four-step model of ethical decision-making that includes moral awareness, judgment, motivation, and ultimately behavior. However, recent theorizing in behavioral ethics and moral psychology suggests that many reactions to ethical dilemmas are automatic and affective (Haidt, 2001; Sonenshein, 2007). Building on this research, we conceptualize unethical behavior, not only as a product of rational calculation of cost and benefit (e.g., employees steal from the company when there is no risk of getting caught), but also as a response to emotional reactions such as envy. Here we suggest that interpersonal unethical behavior can result from the emotional reactions employees experience after comparing themselves to co-workers, particularly if the comparison produces envy.

The experience of envy can motivate interpersonal unethical behavior aimed at hurting close others (e.g., co-workers). Envy has been shown to lead employees to directly sabotage co-workers' efforts, to behave competitively with them in collaborative settings, or simply to lobby the managers who assign them compensation (Cropanzano, Goldman, & Folger, 2003; Pruitt & Kimmel, 1977). Similarly, feelings of envy toward peers lead to target-derogation (Salovey & Rodin, 1984) and social undermining (i.e., behavior intended to hinder the ability of others) through moral disengagement, and this effect is more pronounced when there is a high sense of social identification (Duffy, Scott, Shaw, Tepper, & Aquino, 2012). This envy also decreases the likability of the promoted co-worker, which suggests a possibility that the envious ones may engage in an unethical behavior to hurt the target of their envy. These results suggest that envy can be a powerful motivator that could help rationalize one's unethical actions toward others.

Figure 15.1 illustrates these interpersonal forces behind unethical behavior in organizations. According to this model, one set of forces reflects the interpersonal motive behind unethical behavior: interpersonal unethical behaviors result from an individual's desire to hurt comparison targets as a result of social comparisons and the emotions associated with them (i.e., envy). The second set of forces leading to interpersonal unethical behavior encompasses characteristics of an organization's structure

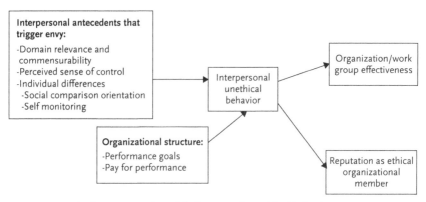

FIGURE 15.1 An interpersonal model of envy and unethical behavior.

related to performance goals and pay for performance. The model indicates that interpersonal motives interact with these organizational features in predicting interpersonal unethical behavior. That is, interpersonal motives moderate the relationship between organizational characteristics and interpersonal unethical behaviors, such that the relationship between organizational characteristics and interpersonal unethical behaviors is weaker in the presence of interpersonal motives. Building on previous work, we also propose that interpersonal unethical behaviors negatively impact organization and work group performance, as well as an organization's reputation.

Antecedents of Interpersonal Unethical Behavior from Social Comparison

Scholars doing work on social comparison processes have identified several factors that influence the behaviors and emotions resulting from social comparisons. As antecedents of interpersonal unethical behavior, consistent with prior theorizing, we propose that social comparisons (upward comparisons, for the present analysis) are more likely to lead to invidious emotional and often unethical behavioral consequences in the presence of a number of conditions.

Domain Relevance and Commensurability. There are two areas in which employees may identify their comparison target. First, the performance dimension has to be personally relevant and important to the self. According to the Self-Evaluation Maintenance Model (Tesser, 2000), comparison can increase competitive, contrastive reactions only when the dimension is relevant to the self. The higher the relevance of the performance dimension involved for the person making the comparison, the more likely this comparison process is to occur. And the more likely it is for the comparison to occur, the more likely the person making the comparison is to experience strong emotions of envy. Thus, outperforming a close other on a dimension high in self-relevance bolsters self-evaluation (Beach & Tesser, 2000; Tesser, 1988).[1] Examples of such negative comparisons are quite common, as in the case of an employee who feels threatened because he perceives another co-worker within the same team to be smarter, more able, or harder-working, or because the co-worker earns more money for the same type of job.

Second, the comparison target is commensurable, in that he or she shares related attributes. According to the "related attributes" hypothesis (Goethals & Darley, 1977), individuals have a tendency to choose a comparison target who is "close to one's own performance or opinion, given his standing on characteristics related to and predictive of performance or opinion." This comparison target is a person with similar characteristics who motivates one to perform just as well as, if not better than, this commensurate other. Thus, the emotions of envy resulting from social comparisons and interpersonal unethical behaviors are more likely to occur when a comparison target is commensurate. In an organizational setting, for example, this commensurability (e.g., self-similarity) to the promoted co-worker increased envy among those who were rejected for promotion (Schaubroeck & Lam, 2004).

Thus, individuals who engage in upward social comparisons on a relevant performance dimension (i.e., the domain of comparison is important to the self) and with a commensurate and similar comparison target on comparison-related attributes may be more likely to experience envy, and such processes can lead to more unethical behavior in an attempt to outperform a target.

Low Sense of Perceived Control. Any relevant upward social comparison is likely to produce invidious emotions; however, another factor may be important in determining whether the emotions are likely to be malicious (and thus be linked with unethical behavior) or relatively benign (and not so likely to be linked with unethical behavior)—and this comes down to whether closing the gap between the self and the advantaged target is perceived to be within one's control. Lockwood and Kunda (1997) build on the idea that the target of upward comparison is most likely to influence self-concepts when they are considered relevant. As an additional moderator, they showed that the consequences of having relevant "superstars" depend on the perceived attainability of their success. They posited that when the superstar's success seems attainable and within one's control, it will inspire and motivate individuals to set higher goals for themselves. On the other hand, when the superstar's success seems unattainable, it will make one's inferiority and failures more salient, thereby discouraging and demoralizing the self. This work maps substantially onto the distinction between benign and malicious envy. That is, experiencing benign envy leads to self-improvement, whereas experiencing malicious envy leads to a "pulling-down" motivation aimed at damaging the position of the target of upward comparison (van de Ven, Zeelenberg, & Pieters, 2009). They further examined how the emotional responses to the upward comparison target are influenced by the perceived attainability (van de Ven, Zeelenberg, & Pieters, 2011). Only when individuals thought self-improvement was attainable would an upward social comparison trigger benign (vs. malicious) envy and subsequently, better performance.

Thus, one's perceived control over the attainability of the outcomes may play a significant role in the type of envy, and its behavioral consequences in the moral dimension. When the outcome is perceived as unattainable, it can increase the likelihood of experiencing strong emotions of malicious envy and motivate individuals to reduce the threat to their self-evaluation of competence (Beach & Tesser, 2000). Imagine an employee who has a comparison target who brings in many high-level clients at a law firm. If the success of this employee is viewed as attainable (e.g., they became successful by putting in the most billable hours), then the feelings of envy may not necessarily lead to interpersonal unethical behavior, because there is a way to achieve a similar goal by exerting more effort without undermining the comparison target. However, if the target's success is viewed as unattainable (e.g., successful because he or she had good family connections), this is more likely to motivate individuals to harm the comparison target, even if it involves crossing the ethical boundaries.

Individual Differences. Whereas the first set of factors addresses individuals' desire to engage in interpersonal unethical behavior due to influences related to the increased likelihood that they will engage in upward social comparisons with others in the workplace and experience envy (i.e., due to the high self-relevance—domain importance, commensurability, and closeness—and low attainability), the second set of factors related to interpersonal motivation is the value individuals place on self-evaluation and self-enhancement. That is, individuals are more likely to engage in unethical behavior that hurts others as a result of social comparisons as the value they place on seeing themselves in a positive light increases. We suggest here that two dispositional factors are likely to influence such value: social comparison orientation and self-monitoring.

Several scholars have suggested that some individuals are more predisposed than others to engage in social comparisons (Gilbert, Giesler, & Morris, 1995; Hemphill & Lehman, 1991; Steil & Hay, 1997). Gibbons and Buunk (1999) describe social comparison orientation (SCO) as the tendency to be strongly oriented to social comparison, to be particularly sensitive to one's own standing relative to others, and to be interested in learning about others' thoughts and behavior in similar situations. According to Gibbons and Buunk (1999), individuals high in SCO are characterized by a heightened uncertainty about themselves and a relatively strong dependency upon other people for their self-evaluation. Thus, relative to those low in SCO, individuals high in SCO are more likely to be sensitive to comparisons with others (Michinov & Michinov, 2001), which may amplify one's experience of envy, thus increasing the likelihood of engaging in interpersonal unethical behavior.

Self-monitors are individuals who are sensitive to the social appropriateness of their self-presentations. These "social chameleons" change their attitudes, perspectives, and behaviors to suit the social setting they are in at any given moment (Snyder, 1974). More specifically, compared to low self-monitors, high self-monitors are (a) more concerned about behaving in a socially appropriate manner, (b) more sensitive to the expression and self-presentation of others in social situations, and (c) more skillful in using these and other situational cues as guidelines for monitoring and managing their own self-presentation and expressive behavior (Snyder, 1974). Ickes and Barnes (1977) have argued that high self-monitors, relative to low self-monitors, are more likely to seek out and use relevant social comparison information in a self-presentation situation and to express and communicate an arbitrarily chosen emotional state more accurately. These scholars propose that high self-monitors make better organizational members than low self-monitors because they are more likely to be sensitive to others' need for help and to be able to adjust their behavior. However, being sensitive to others' needs may in turn translate to a higher likelihood to feel envy toward others, and therefore to take actions that can hurt others, even when such actions are unethical. Thus, we suggest that high self-monitors may be more likely to engage in interpersonal unethical behavior because they tend to be more sensitive to social cues and interpersonal contexts that may fuel their upward social comparisons.

Organizational Characteristics, Envy, and Interpersonal Unethical Behavior

The final set of factors that we suggest directly affect employees' likelihood to engage in interpersonal unethical behavior is related to the characteristics of an organization. We considered two main features—an organization's performance goals and its pay for performance—that may be particularly relevant, because these features can make the performance domain particularly important and salient, creating a situational cue that gives rise to upward social comparisons.

Researchers have described performance goals as important tools that organizations and their managers can effectively use to motivate employees' performance. Several studies have demonstrated that specific, challenging goals are more likely to motivate performance than "Do your best" exhortations or vague goals lacking specific targets (see Locke & Latham, 1990, 2002, 2006). These benefits in motivation and performance are driven by the fact that specific goals provide a clear and unambiguous means of evaluating employee performance, while at the same time focusing employees' attention. Yet recent research has documented a link between specific, challenging goals and unethical behavior. Specifically, Schweitzer, Ordonez, and Douma (2004) found that people with unmet goals are more likely to engage in unethical behavior than are people attempting to do their best, in both the presence and the absence of economic incentives. Furthermore, they found that the relationship between goal setting and unethical behavior was particularly strong when people fell just short of reaching their goals.

Thus, we suggest that specific, challenging goals may lead to increasing the employees' attention to the goal, and as a result, the employees may be more likely to evaluate themselves and others in terms of how close they are to meeting the goal. This would increase the salience of other employees who are closer to the goal than they are, and the upward social comparisons and resulting envy could lead to interpersonal unethical behavior. In fact, we expect employees to be more likely to sabotage others they envy (e.g., comparison targets who are closer to the goal than they are) when they are close to reaching their specific performance targets, by engaging in an unethical behavior. However, caution must be taken when theorizing about the relationship between performance goals, upward social comparisons, and interpersonal unethical behavior. Depending on the type of envy that the comparison target's performance levels trigger, it may not necessarily lead to unethical behavior. That is, if the performance goals are perceived to be within the envier's control, then these feelings may qualify as benign envy, which often leads to a strong motivation to exert effort to achieve goals. On the other hand, when the performance goal seems unattainable, individuals may experience malicious envy, and thus be more likely to actively harm or sabotage their comparison target by engaging in unethical behaviors (see Sterling, van de Ven, & Smith, Chapter 3, this volume, for the typology of benign vs. malicious envy). Thus, we suggest that specific, challenging goals can lead to interpersonal unethical behavior, especially when such goals are viewed as unattainable and thus trigger malicious envy.

Another potentially important factor related to an organization's structure that may influence interpersonal unethical behavior is individual-pay performance. Similar to the effects of specific and challenging goals, individual-pay performance may lead employees to focus too much on their own targets and to engage in competitive behavior, compared to performance goals that are shared by work teams. Consider a workplace where an employee's monetary incentives are closely aligned with his or her observable performance, but other factors such as the employee's ability to work in teams and willingness to learn are not taken into account. Under this individual pay-for-performance system, pay will inevitably vary across employees, which will lead to more social comparisons among peers (Larkin, Pierce, & Gino, 2012). As discussed earlier, competition and the emotions it brings about (e.g., envy) are likely to highlight the importance of reaching performance levels associated with given levels of pay.

Consequences of Envy and Interpersonal Unethical Behavior

Shu, Gino, and Bazerman (2011) noted that, since its introduction, most research on unethical behavior has examined it as a dependent variable. Although confirming empirical work is lacking, in theory, unethical behaviors are thought to be destructive to organizational health, functioning, and performance (Gino & Pierce, 2010b). Consistent with this perspective, we suggest that interpersonal unethical behaviors are negatively related to organizational and work group effectiveness. However, as Cialdini (1996) argued as one of the "Triple Tumors of Dishonesty," unethical behaviors can lead to a bad reputation in the long term. Drawing upon research on trust and reputation, we propose that unethical actions also have important destructive effects on an employee's reputation as a reliable and trustworthy organizational member. In this next section, then, we discuss the relationship between interpersonal unethical behaviors and both organization/work group effectiveness and employee reputation.

Envy, Interpersonal Unethical Behavior, and Organization/Work Group Effectiveness

There are two ways in which organizational functioning and work group effectiveness can be harmed by upward social comparisons and interpersonal unethical behavior.

First, the envy that is triggered by upward social comparisons at work can be detrimental to employee behavior by itself, even when it does not necessarily lead to unethical behavior. Envious individuals who do not have a sense of control may be more likely to seek alternative employment to cope with their aversive emotions, which could lead to higher turnover (Vecchio, 2000). For example, employees who engage in upward social comparison are more likely to leave their job (Card, Mas, Moretti, & Saez, 2012), to exert less effort into the task at hand (Greenberg, 1987), and to be absent more often (Schwarzwald, Koslowsky, & Shalit, 1992) than those who did not. Although past studies did not directly test the mediating hypothesis on what type of envy employees felt, and how this led to negative employee behaviors, they suggest that upward social comparison may be costly to organizational functioning. More specifically, envy has been shown to decrease team cohesiveness and team efficacy, thus leading to lower group performance and group satisfaction and higher absenteeism (Duffy & Shaw, 2000).

Second, unethical behavior plays an important yet destructive role in organization and work-group functioning. Unethical behavior (independent of the motives behind it) could reduce organizational performance by increasing the need to allocate scarce resources to maintenance functions within firms, thereby reducing the availability of such important resources for more productive purposes that may be vital to an organization's functioning and performance. In addition, unethical behavior can erode trust among employees (Cialdini, 1996), thus increasing the likelihood of potential friction and conflict within organizations and resulting in reduced effectiveness. Finally, by reducing the attractiveness of the organization as an ethical place to work, organizations where unethical behavior is prevalent may be less able to attract and retain the best employees, thereby worsening their performance. Similarly, Cialdini (1996) posited that unethical business practices might lead to a higher rate of employee turnover.

Taken together, growing evidence points to that engaging in upward social comparison (and potential malicious envy that arises from it) and interpersonal unethical behavior would be detrimental to organizational functioning and work-group effectiveness.

Envy, Interpersonal Unethical Behavior, and Reputation

Engaging in upward social comparison and interpersonal unethical behaviors can have detrimental effects on one's own reputation as a trustworthy and reliable organizational member.

First, the reputational costs associated with upward social comparisons are well-established for individuals who are the targets of upward social comparison. Exline and Geyer (2004) argued that individuals who outperform others may experience discomfort and unease as they are concerned about how their achievements are perceived, or envied by others. In fact, targets of upward social comparison (via promotion) became envied by co-workers, and even disliked by those who were rejected for promotion (Schaubroeck & Lam, 2004). Such concerns over being envied are costly for organizations, as the targets deliberately reduce their performance or effort levels to avoid future upward social comparison, or under-report their own performance (Henagan & Bedeian, 2009). On the other hand, much less attention has been paid to the reputation of those who experience envy. Given that envy often occurs along with feelings of hostility and ill will toward the target of upward social comparison (Smith, Parrott, Ozer, & Moniz, 1994), we posit that envious employees may be viewed by others as threatening, and thus have negative reputations when being considered for team selection or promotion.

Second, employees who engage in unethical behaviors are more likely to be viewed as problematic organizational members by others. Research has examined the questions of how observers judge the behavior of wrongdoers. Prior empirical studies have demonstrated that such judgements are influenced by characteristics of the crime, such as the seriousness of the offense (Carlsmith, Darley, & Robinson, 2002; Feather, 1996; Walster,

1966) and the severity of the consequences (Shaver, 1970), the difficulty of detecting the crime (Carlsmith et al., 2002), and the characteristics of the criminal, such as the wrongdoer's history of transgressions (Carroll & Payne, 1977; Ebbesen & Konecni, 1975), or the wrongdoer's reasons for committing the transgression (Savitsky & Babl, 1976). Thus, employees who engage in interpersonal unethical behaviors, even when such behaviors may benefit co-workers, are likely to be viewed as unreliable and untrustworthy.

Implications and Directions for Future Research

In this chapter, we have contended that upward social comparison processes and the emotional reactions (i.e., envy) associated with them are an important motivational force underlying interpersonal unethical behaviors. We have offered a framework for understanding (1) how factors that give rise to one's upward social comparison may drive individuals' unethical behavior through envy, (2) the effects of interpersonal unethical behaviors on organizational functioning and work-group effectiveness, and (3) reputational effects that result from interpersonal unethical behaviors.

Understanding the underlying motivation for unethical behavior in organizations is important in advancing research on this topic, for several reasons. First, Kish-Gephart et al.'s (2010) meta-analysis highlights the generally weak and inconsistent predictive power of dispositional antecedents in accounting for unethical behavior in organizations. Likewise, job attitudes explain only small amounts of variance in unethical behavior in organizations (Tenbrunsel & Crowe, 2008). A possible explanation for these disappointing results is the overlap between interpersonal motives resulting from feelings of envy from upward social comparisons, and unethical behavior in the workplace. By separating purely financial motives that benefit the self from interpersonal motives that may or may not lead to financial benefits, researchers may be better able to predict different types of unethical behavior in the workplace. Second, because such motivation is likely to modulate the relationship between interpersonal unethical behaviors and organization/work-group effectiveness and organizational reputation, gaining a better understanding of these effects is relevant for management scholars and practitioners alike.

This chapter enhances our understanding of social comparison processes as well. It provides a framework for examining a widely studied and important topic: the role of interpersonal concerns related to social comparisons and envy resulting from them in the context of unethical behavior in organizations. Furthermore, we suggest that, like behavioral ethics scholars, researchers interested in emotions and social comparison processes need to examine their key constructs to ensure that they are theoretically and empirically sound. Last, work on social comparison processes has been aimed mainly at studying the effects of such processes on individuals. In contrast, we suggest that social comparison processes and the emotions associated with them ultimately have organizational implications as well. Thus, in future research on social comparison processes, researchers should consider the consequences such processes pose for organizational functioning and performance.

In the discussion of our model, we have raised some theoretical questions that must be dealt with in the future. First, what is the nature of the relationship between interpersonal motives for interpersonal unethical behavior and the features of an organization's structure? Further exploration of the interplay of social comparisons and an organization's structure would enhance our knowledge of interpersonal unethical behavior, as well as the benign vs. malicious envy resulting from comparisons employees engage in at work.

Second, what is the role of observer attributions regarding acts of interpersonal unethical behavior? Gino, Moore, and Bazerman (2008) note that judging a given behavior as unethical, and determining the motives behind it, are often subjective processes. More theoretical work is needed to explain how attributions regarding interpersonal unethical behaviors are formed, especially in cases in which the actions produce costs to other organizational members. The nature of the behavior itself (e.g., sabotaging), in addition to organizational factors and individual factors that trigger envy may affect such attributions. For example, a person's status as a peer or supervisor may influence how that person interprets others' motives (Fragale, Rosen, Xu, & Merideth, 2009). Similarly, situational factors such as the ethical, competitive, or corporate climate (Cohn, Fehr, & Maréchal, 2014) may bias one's attributions. Because attributions of the potential benefits and costs that interpersonal unethical behaviors encompass are likely to affect the nature of the reputational effects on the wrongdoer, an improved understanding of these issues is necessary.

Finally, if the arguments we have made here are true, there seem to be important implications for practicing managers. First, the chapter illustrates why managers must be careful in assessing the unethical behaviors of their subordinates and why they should carefully consider the types of envy and resulting behavioral tendencies. Likewise, if the unethical behaviors motivated by upward social comparisons and the emotions associated with them are less likely to facilitate an organization's functioning, health, and performance, organizations and their managers should be cautious in how they respond to such behaviors. Finally, as noted by Gino and Pierce (2009a), unethical behaviors are particularly worrisome for organizations when they consist of an employee's hurting the performance of a co-worker. Therefore, managers should think carefully about their organizational policies, since, like other features of an organization's structure, policies may have a direct impact on employees' envy and interpersonal unethical behavior.

Note

1. It is important to note that these comparison processes appear to be automatic and require minimal awareness and attention (Pilkington, Tesser, & Stephens, 1991; Pleban & Tesser, 1981; Tesser & Collins, 1988; Tesser & Paulhus, 1983; Tesser, Millar, & Moore, 1988).

References

Allingham, M. G., & Sandmo, A. (1972). Income tax evasion: A theoretical analysis. *Journal of Public Economics*, *1*(3–4), 323–338. Available at http://doi.org/10.1016/0047-2727(72)90010-2.

Ambrose, M. L., Harland, L. K., & Kulik, C. T. (1991). Influence of social comparisons on perceptions of organizational fairness. *Journal of Applied Psychology*, *76*(2), 239–246. Available at http://doi.org/10.1037/0021-9010.76.2.239.

Beach, S. R. H., & Tesser, A. (2000). Self-evaluation maintenance and evolution. In J. Suls & L. Wheeler, *Handbook of Social Comparison* (pp. 123–140). Boston, MA: Springer US. Available at http://doi.org/10.1007/978-1-4615-4237-7_7.

Bennett, R. J., & Robinson, S. L. (2003). *The Past, Present, and Future of Workplace Deviance Research*. Mahwah, NJ: Lawrence Erlbaum Associates Publishers.

Brickman, P., & Bulman, R. J. (1977). Pleasure and pain in social comparison. In *Social Comparison Processes: Theoretical and Empirical Perspectives* (Vol. 149, p. 186). Washington, DC: Hemisphere.

Brief, A. P., Dukerich, J. M., Brown, P. R., & Brett, J. F. (1996). What's wrong with the Treadway Commission report? Experimental analyses of the effects of personal values and codes of conduct on fraudulent financial reporting. *Journal of Business Ethics*, *15*(2), 183–198. Available at http://doi.org/10.1007/BF00705586.

Brown, D. J., Ferris, D. L., Heller, D., & Keeping, L. M. (2007). Antecedents and consequences of the frequency of upward and downward social comparisons at work.

Organizational Behavior and Human Decision Processes, 102(1), 59–75. Available at http://doi.org/10.1016/j.obhdp.2006.10.003.

Card, D., Mas, A., Moretti, E., & Saez, E. (2012). Inequality at work: The effect of peer salaries on job satisfaction. *American Economic Review, 102*(6), 2981–3003. Available at http://doi.org/10.1257/aer.102.6.2981.

Carlsmith, K. M., Darley, J. M., & Robinson, P. H. (2002). Why do we punish? Deterrence and just deserts as motives for punishment. *Journal of Personality and Social Psychology, 83*(2), 284–299. Available at http://doi.org/10.1037/0022-3514.83.2.284.

Carroll, J. S., & Payne, J. S. (1977). Judgments about crime and the criminal. In B. D. Sales, *The Criminal Justice System* (pp. 191–239). Springer, US.

Cialdini, R. B. (1996). Social influence and the triple tumor structure of organizational dishonesty. In D. M. Messick & A. E. Tenbrunsel, *Code of Conduct: Behavioral Research into Business Ethics* (pp. 44–58). Russell Sage Foundation.

Cohn, A., Fehr, E., & Maréchal, M. A. (2014). Business culture and dishonesty in the banking industry. *Nature, 516*(7529), 86–89. Available at http://doi.org/10.1038/nature13977.

Covey, M. K., Saladin, S., & Killen, P. J. (1989). Self-monitoring, surveillance, and incentive effects on cheating. *The Journal of Social Psychology, 129*(5), 673–679. Available at http://doi.org/10.1080/00224545.1989.9713784.

Cropanzano, R., Goldman, B., & Folger, R. (2003). Deontic justice: The role of moral principles in workplace fairness. *Journal of Organizational Behavior, 24*(8), 1019–1024. Available at http://doi.org/10.1002/job.228.

Crosby, F. (1976). A model of egoistical relative deprivation. *Psychological Review, 83*(2), 85–113. Available at http://doi.org/10.1037/0033-295X.83.2.85.

Dalal, R. S. (2005). A meta-analysis of the relationship between organizational citizenship behavior and counterproductive work behavior. *Journal of Applied Psychology, 90*(6), 1241–1255. Available at http://doi.org/10.1037/0021-9010.90.6.1241.

Delaney, J. T., & Sockell, D. (1992). Do company ethics training programs make a difference? An empirical analysis. *Journal of Business Ethics, 11*(9), 719–727. Available at http://doi.org/10.1007/BF01686353.

Duffy, M. K., & Shaw, J. D. (2000). The Salieri syndrome: Consequences of envy in groups. *Small Group Research, 31*(1), 3–23. Available at http://doi.org/10.1177/104649640003100101.

Duffy, M. K., Scott, K. L., Shaw, J. D., Tepper, B. J., & Aquino, K. (2012). A social context model of envy and social undermining. *Academy of Management Journal, 55*(3), 643–666. Available at http://doi.org/10.5465/amj.2009.0804.

Ebbesen, E. B., & Konecni, V. J. (1975). Decision making and information integration in the courts: The setting of bail. *Journal of Personality and Social Psychology, 32*(5), 805–821. Available at http://doi.org/10.1037/0022-3514.32.5.805.

Exline, J. J., & Geyer, A. L. (2004). Perceptions of humility: A preliminary study. *Self and Identity, 3*(2), 95–114. Available at http://doi.org/10.1080/13576500342000077.

Feather, N. T. (1996). Reactions to penalties for an offense in relation to authoritarianism, values, perceived responsibility, perceived seriousness, and deservingness. *Journal of Personality and Social Psychology, 71*(3), 571–587. Available at http://doi.org/10.1037/0022-3514.71.3.571.

Festinger, L. (1942). Wish, expectation, and group standards as factors influencing level of aspiration. *The Journal of Abnormal and Social Psychology*, *37*(2), 184–200. Available at http://doi.org/10.1037/h0060328.

Festinger, L. (1954). A theory of social comparison processes. *Human Relations*, *7*, 117–140.

Flannery, B. L., & May, D. R. (2000). Environmental ethical decision making in the U.S. metal-finishing industry. *Academy of Management Journal*, *43*(4), 642–662. Available at http://doi.org/10.2307/1556359.

Ford, R. C., & Richardson, W. D. (1994). Ethical decision making: A review of the empirical literature. *Journal of Business Ethics*, *13*(3), 205–221. Available at http://doi.org/10.1007/BF02074820.

Fragale, A. R., Rosen, B., Xu, C., & Merideth, I. (2009). The higher they are, the harder they fall: The effects of wrongdoer status on observer punishment recommendations and intentionality attributions. *Organizational Behavior and Human Decision Processes*, *108*(1), 53–65. Available at http://doi.org/10.1016/j.obhdp.2008.05.002.

Garcia, S. M., Tor, A., & Gonzalez, R. (2006). Ranks and rivals: A theory of competition. *Personality and Social Psychology Bulletin*, *32*(7), 970–982. Available at http://doi.org/10.1177/0146167206287640.

Gibbons, F. X., & Buunk, B. P. (1999). Individual differences in social comparison: Development of a scale of social comparison orientation. *Journal of Personality and Social Psychology*, *76*(1), 129–142. Available at http://doi.org/10.1037/0022-3514.76.1.129.

Gilbert, D. T., Giesler, R. B., & Morris, K. A. (1995). When comparisons arise. *Journal of Personality and Social Psychology*, *69*(2), 227–236. Available at http://doi.org/10.1037/0022-3514.69.2.227.

Gino, F., & Pierce, L. (2009a). Dishonesty in the name of equity. *Psychological Science*, *20*(9), 1153–1160. Available at http://doi.org/10.1111/j.1467-9280.2009.02421.x.

Gino, F., & Pierce, L. (2009b). The abundance effect: Unethical behavior in the presence of wealth. *Organizational Behavior and Human Decision Processes*, *109*(2), 142–155. Available at http://doi.org/10.1016/j.obhdp.2009.03.003.

Gino, F., & Pierce, L. (2010a). Lying to level the playing field: Why people may dishonestly help or hurt others to create equity. *Journal of Business Ethics*, *95*(S1), 89–103. Available at http://doi.org/10.1007/s10551-011-0792-2.

Gino, F., & Pierce, L. (2010b). Robin Hood under the hood: Wealth-based discrimination in illicit customer help. *Organization Science*, *21*(6), 1176–1194. Available at http://doi.org/10.1287/orsc.1090.0498.

Gino, F., Moore, D. A., & Bazerman, M. H. (2008). See no evil: When we overlook other people's unethical behavior. In R. M. Kramer, A. E. Tenbrunsel, & M. H. Bazerman, *Social Decision Making* (p. 29).

Gneezy, U. (2005). Deception: The role of consequences. *American Economic Review*, *95*(1), 384–394. Available at http://doi.org/10.1257/0002828053828662.

Goethals, G. R., & Darley, J. M. (1977). Social comparison theory: An attributional approach. *Social Comparison Processes Theoretical and Empirical Perspectives*, 259–278.

Goodman, P. S. (1977). Social comparison processes in organizations. In G. Salancik & B. Staw, *New Directions in Organizational Behavior.* Available at http://doi.org/10.2172/7318201.

Graham, C., Litan, R. E., & Sukhtankar, S. (2002). *The Bigger They Are, the Harder They Fall: An Estimate of the Costs of the Crisis in Corporate Governance.* Washington, DC: The Brookings Institution.

Greenberg, J. (1987). Reactions to procedural injustice in payment distributions: Do the means justify the ends? *Journal of Applied Psychology, 72*(1), 55–61. Available at http://doi.org/10.1037/0021-9010.72.1.55.

Greenberg, J., Ashton-James, C. E., & Ashkanasy, N. M. (2007). Social comparison processes in organizations. *Organizational Behavior and Human Decision Processes, 102*(1), 22–41. Available at http://doi.org/10.1016/j.obhdp.2006.09.006.

Guimond, S. (2006). *Social Comparison and Social Psychology.* Cambridge University Press.

Haidt, J. (2001). The emotional dog and its rational tail: A social intuitionist approach to moral judgment. *Psychological Review, 108*(4), 814–834. Available at http://doi.org/10.1037/0033-295X.108.4.814.

Hegarty, W. H., & Sims, H. P. (1979). Organizational philosophy, policies, and objectives related to unethical decision behavior: A laboratory experiment. *Journal of Applied Psychology, 64*(3), 331–338. Available at http://doi.org/10.1037//0021-9010.64.3.331.

Helin, S., & Sandström, J. (2007). An inquiry into the study of corporate codes of ethics. *Journal of Business Ethics, 75*(3), 253–271. Available at http://doi.org/10.1007/s10551-006-9251-x.

Hemphill, K. J., & Lehman, D. R. (1991). Social comparisons and their affective consequences: The importance of comparison dimension and individual difference variables. *Journal of Social and Clinical Psychology, 10*(4), 372–394. Available at http://doi.org/10.1521/jscp.1991.10.4.372.

Henagan, S. C., & Bedeian, A. G. (2009). The perils of success in the workplace: Comparison target responses to coworkers' upward comparison threat. *Journal of Applied Social Psychology, 39*(10), 2438–2468. Available at http://doi.org/10.1111/j.1559-1816.2009.00533.x.

Hoffman, P. J., Festinger, L., & Lawrence, D. H. (1954). Tendencies toward group comparability in competitive bargaining. *Human Relations, 7*(2), 141–159. Available at http://doi.org/10.1177/001872675400700203.

Ickes, W., & Barnes, R. D. (1977). The role of sex and self-monitoring in unstructured dyadic interactions. *Journal of Personality and Social Psychology, 35*(5), 315–330. Available at http://doi.org/10.1037/0022-3514.35.5.315.

Jensen, M. C. (2001). Value maximization, stakeholder theory, and the corporate objective function. *Journal of Applied Corporate Finance, 14*(3), 8–21. Available at http://doi.org/10.1111/j.1745-6622.2001.tb00434.x.

Jones, T. M. (1995). Instrumental stakeholder theory: A synthesis of ethics and economics. *Academy of Management Review, 20*(2), 404–437. Available at http://doi.org/10.5465/amr.1995.9507312924.

Kay, A. C., Wheeler, S. C., Bargh, J. A., & Ross, L. (2004). Material priming: The influence of mundane physical objects on situational construal and competitive behavioral choice. *Organizational Behavior and Human Decision Processes*, *95*(1), 83–96. Available at http://doi.org/10.1016/j.obhdp.2004.06.003.

Kish-Gephart, J. J., Harrison, D. A., & Treviño, L. K. (2010). Bad apples, bad cases, and bad barrels: Meta-analytic evidence about sources of unethical decisions at work. *Journal of Applied Psychology*, *95*(1), 1–31. Available at http://doi.org/10.1037/a0017103.

Larkin, I., Pierce, L., & Gino, F. (2012). The psychological costs of pay-for-performance: Implications for the strategic compensation of employees. *Strategic Management Journal*, *33*, 1194–1214, Available at http://doi.org/10.1002/smj.1974.

Lev, B., Petrovits, C., & Radhakrishnan, S. (2009). Is doing good good for you? How corporate charitable contributions enhance revenue growth. *Strategic Management Journal*, *31*(2), 182–200. Available at http://doi.org/10.1002/smj.810.

Lewicki, P. (1983). Self-image bias in person perception. *Journal of Personality and Social Psychology*, *45*(2), 384–393. Available at http://doi.org/10.1037/0022-3514.45.2.384.

Locke, E. A., & Latham, G. P. (1990). *A Theory of Goal Setting and Task Performance*. Englewood Cliffs, NJ: Prentice-Hall.

Locke, E. A., & Latham, G. P. (2002). Building a practically useful theory of goal setting and task motivation: A 35-year odyssey. *American Psychologist*, *57*(9), 705–717. Available at http://doi.org/10.1037/0003-066X.57.9.705.

Locke, E. A., & Latham, G. P. (2006). New directions in goal-setting theory. *Current Directions in Psychological Science*, *15*(5), 265–268. Available at http://doi.org/10.1111/j.1467-8721.2006.00449.x.

Lockwood, P., & Kunda, Z. (1997). Superstars and me: Predicting the impact of role models on the self. *Journal of Personality and Social Psychology*, *73*(1), 91–103. Available at http://doi.org/10.1037/0022-3514.73.1.91.

McCabe, D. L., Treviño, L. K., & Butterfield, K. D. (1996). The influence of collegiate and corporate codes of conduct on ethics-related behavior in the workplace. *Business Ethics Quarterly*, *6*(4), 461. Available at http://doi.org/10.2307/3857499.

Michinov, E., & Michinov, N. (2001). The similarity hypothesis: A test of the moderating role of social comparison orientation. *European Journal of Social Psychology*, *31*(5), 549–555. Available at http://doi.org/10.1002/ejsp.78.

O'Fallon, M. J., & Butterfield, K. D. (2005). A review of the empirical ethical decision-making literature: 1996–2003. *Journal of Business Ethics*, *59*(4), 375–413. Available at http://doi.org/10.1007/s10551-005-2929-7.

Pilkington, C. J., Tesser, A., & Stephens, D. (1991). Complementarity in romantic relationships: A self-evaluation maintenance perspective. *Journal of Social and Personal Relationships*, *8*(4), 481–504. Available at http://doi.org/10.1177/026540759184003.

Pleban, R., & Tesser, A. (1981). The effects of relevance and quality of another's performance on interpersonal closeness. *Social Psychology Quarterly*, *44*(3), 278. Available at http://doi.org/10.2307/3033841.

Pruitt, D. G., & Kimmel, M. J. (1977). Twenty years of experimental gaming: Critique, synthesis, and suggestions for the future. *Annual Review of Psychology*, *28*(1), 363–392. Available at http://doi.org/10.1146/annurev.ps.28.020177.002051.

Robinson, S. L., & Bennett, R. J. (1995). A typology of deviant workplace behaviors: A multidimensional scaling study. *Academy of Management Journal*, *38*(2), 555–572. Available at http://doi.org/10.2307/256693.

Sackett, P. R., Berry, C. M., & Wiemann, S. A. (2006). Citizenship and counterproductive behavior: Clarifying relations between the two domains. *Human Performance*, *19*(4), 441–464. Available at http://doi.org/10.1207/s15327043hup1904_7.

Salovey, P., & Rodin, J. (1984). Some antecedents and consequences of social-comparison jealousy. *Journal of Personality and Social Psychology*, *47*(4), 780–792. Available at http://doi.org/10.1037/0022-3514.47.4.780.

Savitsky, J. C., & Babl, J. (1976). Cheating, intention, and punishment from an equity theory perspective. *Journal of Research in Personality*, *10*(1), 128–136. Available at http://doi.org/10.1016/0092-6566(76)90091-X.

Schaubroeck, J., & Lam, S. S. K. (2004). Comparing lots before and after: Promotion rejectees' invidious reactions to promotees. *Organizational Behavior and Human Decision Processes*, *94*(1), 33–47. Available at http://doi.org/10.1016/j.obhdp.2004.01.001.

Schwarzwald, J., Koslowsky, M., & Shalit, B. (1992). A field study of employees' attitudes and behaviors after promotion decisions. *Journal of Applied Psychology*, *77*(4), 511–514. Available at http://doi.org/10.1037/0021-9010.77.4.511.

Schweitzer, M. E., Ordóñez, L., & Douma, B. (2004). Goal setting as a motivator of unethical behavior. *Academy of Management Journal*, *47*(3), 422–432. Available at http://doi.org/10.2307/20159591.

Shaver, K. G. (1970). Defensive attribution: Effects of severity and relevance on the responsibility assigned for an accident. *Journal of Personality and Social Psychology*, *14*(2), 101–113. Available at http://doi.org/10.1037/h0028777.

Shu, L. L., Gino, F., & Bazerman, M. H. (2011). Dishonest deed, clear conscience: When cheating leads to moral disengagement and motivated forgetting. *Personality and Social Psychology Bulletin*, *37*(3), 330–349. Available at http://doi.org/10.1177/0146167211398138.

Smith, H. J., Pettigrew, T. F., Pippin, G. M., & Bialosiewicz, S. (2012). Relative deprivation: A theoretical and meta-analytic review. *Personality and Social Psychology Review*, *16*(3), 203–232. Available at http://doi.org/10.1177/1088868311430825.

Smith, R. H. (2000). Assimilative and contrastive emotional reactions to upward and downward social comparisons. In J. E. Suls & L. E. Wheeler, *Handbook of Social Comparison* (pp. 173–200). Boston, MA: Springer US. Available at http://doi.org/10.1007/978-1-4615-4237-7_10.

Smith, R. H., & Kim, S. H. (2007). Comprehending envy. *Psychological Bulletin*, *133*(1), 46–64. Available at http://doi.org/10.1037/0033-2909.133.1.46.

Smith, R. H., Parrott, W. G., Ozer, D., & Moniz, A. (1994). Subjective injustice and inferiority as predictors of hostile and depressive feelings in envy. *Personality and Social Psychology Bulletin*, *20*(6), 705–711. Available at http://doi.org/10.1177/0146167294206008.

Snyder, M. (1974). Self-monitoring of expressive behavior. *Journal of Personality and Social Psychology*, *30*(4), 526–537. Available at http://doi.org/10.1037/h0037039.

Sonenshein, S. (2007). The role of construction, intuition, and justification in responding to ethical issues at work: The sensemaking-intuition model. *Academy of Management Review*, *32*(4), 1022–1040. Available at http://doi.org/10.5465/AMR.2007.26585677.

Steil, J. M., & Hay, J. L. (1997). Social comparison in the workplace: A study of 60 dual-career couples. *Personality and Social Psychology Bulletin*, *23*(4), 427–438. Available at http://doi.org/10.1177/0146167297234008.

Suls, J. E., & Wheeler, L. E. (2000). *Handbook of Social Comparison: Theory and Research*. Dordrecht, The Netherlands: Kluwer Academic Publishers.

Suls, J. M. E., & Miller, R. L. E. (1977). *Social Comparison Processes: Theoretical and Empirical Perspectives*. Oxford, England: Hemisphere.

Tenbrunsel, A. E. (1998). Misrepresentation and expectations of misrepresentation in an ethical dilemma: The role of incentives and temptation. *Academy of Management Journal*, *41*(3), 330–339. Available at http://doi.org/10.2307/256911.

Tenbrunsel, A. E., & Crowe, K. S. (2008). Ethical decision making: Where we've been and where we're going. *The Academy of Management Annals*, *2*(1), 545–607. Available at http://doi.org/10.1080/19416520802211677.

Tenbrunsel, A. E., Diekmann, K. A., Wade-Benzoni, K. A., & Bazerman, M. H. (2010). The ethical mirage: A temporal explanation as to why we are not as ethical as we think we are. *Research in Organizational Behavior*, *30*, 153–173. Available at http://doi.org/10.1016/j.riob.2010.08.004.

Tesser, A. (2000). On the confluence of self-esteem maintenance mechanisms. *Personality and Social Psychology Review*, *4*(4), 290–299. Available at http://doi.org/10.1207/S15327957PSPR0404_1.

Tesser, A., & Collins, J. E. (1988). Emotion in social reflection and comparison situations: Intuitive, systematic, and exploratory approaches. *Journal of Personality and Social Psychology*, *55*(5), 695–709. Available at http://doi.org/10.1037/0022-3514.55.5.695.

Tesser, A., & Paulhus, D. (1983). The definition of self: Private and public self-evaluation management strategies. *Journal of Personality and Social Psychology*, *44*(4), 672–682. Available at http://doi.org/10.1037/0022-3514.44.4.672.

Tesser, A., Millar, M., & Moore, J. (1988). Some affective consequences of social comparison and reflection processes: The pain and pleasure of being close. *Journal of Personality and Social Psychology*, *54*(1), 49–61. Available at http://doi.org/10.1037/0022-3514.54.1.49.

Treviño, L. K. (1986). Ethical decision making in organizations: A person-situation interactionist model. *Academy of Management Review*, *11*(3), 601–617. Available at http://doi.org/10.5465/AMR.1986.4306235.

Treviño, L. K., & Youngblood, S. A. (1990). Bad apples in bad barrels: A causal analysis of ethical decision-making behavior. *Journal of Applied Psychology*, *75*(4), 378–385. Available at http://doi.org/10.1037/0021-9010.75.4.378.

van de Ven, N., Zeelenberg, M., & Pieters, R. (2009). Leveling up and down: The experiences of benign and malicious envy. *Emotion*, *9*(3), 419–429. Available at http://doi.org/10.1037/a0015669.

van de Ven, N., Zeelenberg, M., & Pieters, R. (2011). Why envy outperforms admiration. *Personality and Social Psychology Bulletin*, *37*(6), 784–795. Available at http://doi.org/10.1177/0146167211400421.

Van Lange, P. A. M. (1999). The pursuit of joint outcomes and equality in outcomes: An integrative model of social value orientation. *Journal of Personality and Social Psychology*, *77*(2), 337–349. Available at http://doi.org/10.1037/0022-3514.77.2.337.

Vecchio, R. P. (2000). Negative emotion in the workplace: Employee jealousy and envy. *International Journal of Stress Management*, 7(3), 161–179. Available at http://doi.org/10.1023/A:1009592430712.

Victor, B., & Cullen, J. B. (1988). The organizational bases of ethical work climates. *Administrative Science Quarterly*, 33(1), 101. Available at http://doi.org/10.2307/2392857.

Walster, E. (1966). Assignment of responsibility for an accident. *Journal of Personality and Social Psychology*, 3(1), 73–79. Available at http://doi.org/10.1037/h0022733.

Wood, J. V. (1996). What is social comparison and how should we study it? *Personality and Social Psychology Bulletin*, 22(5), 520–537. Available at http://doi.org/10.1177/0146167296225009.

16 | Envy and Injustice

INTEGRATION AND RUMINATIONS

PARESH MISHRA, STEVEN WHITING, AND ROBERT FOLGER

Salieri (Addressing a crucifix): From now on we are enemies, You and I. Because You choose for Your instrument a boastful, lustful, smutty, infantile boy [referring to Mozart] and give me for reward only the ability to recognize the incarnation. Because You are unjust, unfair, unkind, I will block You, I swear it. I will hinder and harm Your creature on earth as far as I am able. I will ruin Your incarnation.

—*From the movie* Amadeus *(Shaffer, 1984)*

Introduction

In the above quote, the composer Antonio Salieri cries out to God that Mozart's possession of superior musical talent is "unjust, unfair, (and) unkind." In this work of fiction, Salieri is portrayed as a tormented, envious colleague of Mozart, obsessed with Mozart's superior talent and driven to get back at God by destroying His "incarnation." Although a work of fiction, Salieri's statement demonstrates aptly how feelings of envy and injustice can often co-occur in life, a phenomenon that has been noted and observed by many scholars (for example, by Ben-Ze'ev, 1992; Cohen-Charash & Mueller, 2007; Schaubroeck & Lam, 2004; Smith, 1991).

Even though envy and injustice might frequently co-occur in life, they have not as frequently co-occurred in the academic literature. Systematic work on the emotion of envy and work on the experience of injustice (particularly in organizational settings) have developed along largely separate lines, in different disciplines with little overlap or cross-fertilization. Although this separation is certainly understandable, we believe the integration of these two literatures would offer tremendous potential for improved understanding. In particular, we are interested in how theoretical models of organizational justice can inform and advance an understanding of envy.

Envy and justice have concerned civilization for millennia. The topic of envy has been treated in the scriptures of major world religions, in the works of philosophers from Aristotle to Adam Smith, and has of course been a prominent theme in literature as well. Similarly, the topic of justice has a long history. Major religions comment on what is just and unjust, and philosophers in ancient and modern times alike have deliberated scrupulously on the topic of justice. Many philosophers have written on both envy and justice, often viewing the concepts as interrelated (e.g., Plato, Aristotle, Aquinas, Hume, Kant, Nietzsche, Freud, Francis Bacon, Adam Smith, John Rawls, etc.). For example, Aristotle, Freud, and Nietzsche described envy as the psychological foundation behind people's concern for justice (D'Arms, 2013; Schoeck, 1969), while Rawls viewed envy as an outcome of high inequalities in society (D'Arms, 2013).

Compared to this ancient tradition, the systematic and scientific investigation of justice and envy is rather recent. According to Colquitt, Greenberg, and Zapata-Phelan (2005), the first wave of research on organizational justice began in sociology with Stouffer's groundbreaking work on relative deprivation (Stouffer, Suchman, DeVinney, Starr, & Williams, 1949). This led to Homan's (1961) work on distributive justice, Blau's (1964) ideas on fairness in exchanges, and Adams' (1965) publications on equity theory. These models have led to a rather substantial amount of research on organizational justice in the fields of industrial/organizational psychology and organizational behavior (Colquitt et al., 2005). Similarly, the systematic investigation of envy can be traced to sociology (Schoeck, 1969) and anthropology (Foster, 1972), leading to a considerable development of this topic in the field of social psychology (e.g., Smith, 1991; Smith, Parrott, Ozer, & Moniz, 1994). Given the different objectives and traditions of these two disciplines (social psychology and industrial/organizational psychology), the topics of envy and organizational justice have been largely separated from each other.

In contrast to religious and philosophical treatments of justice, which are largely prescriptive in nature, organizational justice research has been mostly descriptive, attempting to determine how and why people view certain events as just or unjust (Cropanzano, Bowen, & Gilliland, 2007). This work has focused on the appropriateness and fairness of outcome distributions (Adams, 1965; Blau, 1964; Homans, 1961), often termed "distributive justice," the fairness of workplace procedures (Leventhal, 1980) frequently termed "procedural justice," and the fairness of workplace interactions (Bies & Moag, 1986) termed "interactional justice." Empirical work has largely sought to establish that these various perceptions of justice are distinct from one another, and to investigate the antecedents and consequences of such fairness judgments. In short, organizational justice has focused on the judgments and perceptions of individuals regarding what they view as fair and unfair in work settings. Of course, there has often been an emotional component to justice research, but emotions have most frequently been viewed as outcomes of justice perceptions. For example, Adams (1965) argued that receiving underpayment would result in anger, and overpayment in guilt. This view of emotions as outcomes of distributive, procedural, and interactional justice is arguably the most common perspective (e.g., Weiss, Suckow, & Cropanzano, 1999). Not surprisingly, this view has come under criticism, with some arguing that justice has not adequately considered the role of emotions (e.g., Barclay, Skarlicki, & Pugh, 2005; Bies & Tripp, 2002; Weiss et al., 1999). Nevertheless, it is fair to say that emotions have been viewed largely as outcomes of justice perceptions, and that emotions have not taken center stage in theoretical models of organizational justice (Dr. Cremer & van den Bos, 2007; Cropanzano, Stein, & Nadisic, 2011).

In comparison, envy has been studied from two distinct perspectives: trait and state. From the trait perspective or the dispositional view of envy (Krizan & Johar, 2012; Smith, Parrott, Diener, Hoyle, & Kim, 1999), certain people are chronically predisposed to feeling envy. On the other hand, the state perspective of envy or episodic envy (Cohen-Charash, 2009) focuses on the discrete experience of envy. Our focus in this chapter is on the concept of state envy. There are many definitions of state envy, but perhaps the most widely cited is that by Parrott and Smith (1993) which defines envy as an unpleasant, often painful emotion characterized by feelings of inferiority and hostility that is produced by comparing oneself with another person or group of persons who enjoy a desired possession, social position, attribute, or quality of being.

According to this definition, envy has three main components: upward social comparison, unpleasant emotion, and hostility. The first component of upward social comparison provides a description of the condition in which envy is experienced. We experience envy when we compare ourselves with someone who is similar to us but is better endowed or advantaged than us on a parameter that is relevant and important to our self-worth. Thus, envy is only experienced during upward social comparison. We don't envy someone who is worse off than us.

The second element of Parrott and Smith's (1993) definition of envy is that envy is an unpleasant or painful emotion. The pain is seen to come from feelings of inferiority in relation to the envied. In other words, the better attributes, possessions, and achievements of the envied are magnified in the envier's mind as a "lack" that is unpleasant or painful to the envier.

Lastly, Parrott and Smith's (1993) definition also emphasizes that envy is characterized by feelings of hostility towards the envied. The envier feels hostility towards the envied because the latter is the reason behind the envier's feeling of inferiority.

It would be fair to say that there is a general consensus in the literature regarding the first two components of Parrott and Smith's (1993) definition of envy, but that the final component of hostility has been the source of some controversy. This controversy has led to the concept of two different varieties of envy: malicious envy (envy including hostility) and benign envy (envy lacking hostility). Researchers subscribing to the malicious view of envy call malicious envy "envy proper" (e.g., Miceli & Castelfranchi, 2007; Schoeck, 1969; Smith & Kim, 2007), whereas those promoting the idea of benign envy insist that envy need not always be malicious and can even help in the positive growth of individuals (e.g., van de Ven, Zeelenberg, & Pieters, 2009).

Having said this, and given our general purpose of investigating how organizational justice research and envy research can inform each other, we are ready to break with tradition. In particular, we steer away from a basic-emotions-as-categories approach when it comes to envy (cf. Ekman, 1992; Izard, 2007) and instead pursue the implications of the appraisal theories (e.g., Ellsworth & Scherer, 2003). The important implication of appraisal theories is that "the boundary between qualitatively different emotions is continuous" (Wondra & Ellsworth, 2015, p. 417). Although not focused specifically on envy as a discrete and distinctively identifiable emotion, the following passage illustrates our approach:

> There are no separate emotion systems. Because our appraisals of situations occur along a continuum [e.g., pleasant—unpleasant] and what we feel is based on our appraisals, so too our emotional experiences occur along a continuum. When we say that we feel angry we are really describing a variety of emotional experiences that shade into each other with no clear boundaries. There can be many different kinds of anger that vary somewhat in the

pattern of appraisal, but that are similar enough for us to use the same word to describe them. Even the boundary between experiences that we call anger and experiences that we call fear or any other emotion is fuzzy. (Wondra & Ellsworth, 2015, pp. 417–418)

William James used the analogy of the color spectrum or the weather, referring to "shadings of emotional feeling . . . [that] merge endlessly into each other" with "subdivisions . . . to a great extent either fictitious or un-important" (James, 1850/1950, p. 448), as quoted in a related commentary (Ellsworth, 2014, p. 22). We certainly don't think of envy as a fictitious or unimportant way of referring to a common phenomenological experience. Nevertheless, we take from these commentaries a way of thinking about envy that opens it up to diverging possible interpretations rather than a canonical description. We do so in part as a literary device: It allows us to be more playful and creative as we seek possible connections between organizational justice and envy. By thinking of envy in a broad way, along a continuum of related affective/cognitive mixes, we hope to find more points of contact with organizational justice.

Our journey starts where some progress has already been made; namely, by exploring some implications of distributive-justice concepts in their relationship to envy. These concepts trace back to the seminal work by Adams (1965) on inequity. Justice research has been a very active area of inquiry ever since then, however, so we continue by borrowing from subsequent advances as well. Among them are notions of counterfactuals rather than social comparisons, and extensions from distributive justice into procedural justice.

The Case of Envy and Distributive Justice

As a starting point for considering how models of organizational justice can inform envy, we begin with the case of distributive justice and envy, particularly the experience of distributive *injustice*. An important common element to most views of envy and distributive injustice is the concept of upward social comparisons (Colquitt et al., 2005; Greenberg, Ashton-James, & Ashkanasy, 2007; Parrott & Smith, 1993). Social comparison forms the foundation of distributive-justice theories such as the relative deprivation theory and equity theory. According to the relative deprivation theory, people feel resentment and dissatisfaction when they believe that they have been deprived of a desired and deserved outcome compared with some referent (Crosby, 1976). Similarly, according to Adams (1965), people experience inequity when they perceive that their– input–outcome ratios are lower than the input–outcome ratios of others. As such, distributive injustice experiences involve upward social comparisons.[1]

Of course, envy has the notion of upward social comparisons built into its most common definition (Parrott & Smith, 1993); thus, by definition, one cannot experience envy without an upward social comparison. In this regard, the experience of envy and distributive injustice would seem rather similar. However, we believe new insights can be developed by considering what is being compared in envious situations compared to distributively unjust situations. As we argue here, and as has been argued elsewhere by the first author (Mishra, 2012a, 2012b), people experience distributive injustice when they make upward social comparisons of input–outcome ratios (as per equity theory), but they can experience envy when they make upward social comparisons of outcomes or inputs *separately*. That is to say, from the perspective of equity theory, to experience distributive injustice, one needs information about *both* the inputs and the outcomes of a social other, but it could be the case that to be envious requires only information about one of these two factors.

As outlined by Adams (1965) and as follows in the distributive justice literature, the social comparison of inputs and outcomes happens together in the form of input–outcome ratios. It is certainly reasonable to take both inputs and outcomes into account while evaluating fairness. However, since envious comparisons evaluate one's self-worth (Tesser, 1986, 1991), they need not take the form of input–outcome ratios. Although many of the factors on which people make envious comparisons (e.g., abilities, personality characteristics, social positions, possessions, achievements, rewards) could be classified as work inputs and outcomes in a classic distributive-justice fashion, we argue that the experience of envy does not require comparisons of these factors in input–outcome ratios. In contrast to judgments of distributive injustice, individuals can feel envious with knowledge of *only* inputs (e.g., I feel envious of my colleague who is smarter than me), or *only* outcomes (e.g., I feel envious of my colleague who got a promotion). Mishra (2012a) termed these envious comparisons *input-envy* and *outcome-envy,* respectively.

As an example, when people compare an input variable such as intelligence, they are trying to answer questions such as, "Am I as smart as my co-worker?" If intellectual ability is a valued attribute, then not being as smart as one's co-worker is perceived as a lacuna and is painful. Jobs represent a major part of personal identities (Chreim, Williams, & Hinings,

2007), so it matters to people how well or poorly they perform in work settings. A strategy individuals might use to evaluate their performance at work is to compare their own inputs with those of their colleagues (Festinger, 1954). A researcher, for example, may regularly compare his writing skills, research productivity, and time investments in research with those of his peers to draw inferences about his own overall strength as a researcher. If the researcher feels that his work inputs are significantly lower than his colleague's, he may begrudge his colleague's superior skills or work-ethic, because they make the researcher feel inferior. Mishra (2012a) describes this as "input-envy." Input-envy is the feeling of pain experienced during upward social comparison of work inputs. This is an interesting notion, since employing input-envy can lead to predictions that are the reverse of what we would expect from equity theory. From the perspective of equity theory, when people perceive their peers' inputs to be higher than their own, this should lead to more equity, since higher comparison inputs of a peer mathematically make the input–outcome ratio more favorable for the comparing person. However, from the perspective of input-envy, higher inputs of a colleague can cause the comparing person to be emotionally distressed and resentful, because they make the person feel inferior to the comparison other. Notably, such envious emotions could result from comparing inputs that are controllable (e.g., effort), as well as those that are not controllable (e.g., intelligence).

Similarly, Mishra (2012a) argued that standalone comparisons of outcomes can generate envious emotions. When people compare outcomes without taking into account, or perhaps even without possessing knowledge of, the inputs of a social other, such a comparison could nevertheless result in envy. This happens because outcomes, when seen in isolation, hide from us the struggles, failures, and sacrifices that people undertake to achieve them. Without conscious consideration of any of the unpleasant inputs/efforts that go into the process of acquiring valued outcomes, the outcomes can become unrealistically attractive, and not possessing them can become symbolic of something lacking within the self. This form of inferiority that arises from the standalone comparison of outcomes is called "outcome-envy" (Mishra, 2012a). An example of outcome-envy would be an employee resenting a peer for winning a prestigious award. Notably, such an envious comparison could be made without possessing any knowledge of the inputs (e.g., hard work, intelligence) required to achieve the award.

Initial empirical investigations of these ideas support the notion that envious comparisons and emotions can be generated with knowledge of inputs alone (input-envy) and outcomes alone (outcome-envy), but that such isolated knowledge does not produce distributive-injustice perceptions (Mishra, 2012a). Mishra had raters review scenarios that variously contained information about inputs only, outcomes only, or information about both inputs and outcomes. When information about both inputs and outcomes was provided, raters judged these scenarios to be indicative of unfairness or injustice, but not of envy. Conversely, when the scenarios contained information about only inputs or only outcomes (but not inputs and outcomes together), raters reported that these scenarios were indicative of envy, but not unfairness.

Of course, such reports are limited in that they come from third-party observers and not from individuals experiencing feelings of injustice or envy themselves. However, obtaining self-reports of an emotion like envy is a tricky proposition, since envy is a socially undesirable emotion (Foster, 1972; Parrott & Smith, 1993; Schoeck, 1969; Smith & Kim, 2007). In contrast, feelings of injustice are often described as unpleasant, but these feelings are not likely to be socially undesirable, since they involve unfairness and violations of fundamental moral principles (Folger, 1998; Folger & Cropanzano, 2001). However, the original problem remains that those who are envious are not particularly likely to tell us so. Therefore, determining whether information about inputs only, outcomes only, or inputs and outcomes in combination produces various envious emotions and injustice perceptions requires looking beyond self-reports of emotions to actual behavior in response to these conditions.

As has been observed by those subscribing to the malicious view of envy, envy involves hostility toward the envied person. Both anecdotal and empirical evidence supports the notion that those experiencing envy may attempt to harm the envied individual (Cohen-Charash & Mueller, 2007; Foster, 1972; Moran & Schweitzer, 2008; Schoeck, 1969), or may experience schadenfreude toward the envied (van de Ven et al., 2015; van Dijk, Ouwerkerk, Goslinga, Nieweg, & Gallucci, 2006). Although feelings of injustice have also been associated with hostile behavior (Bowling & Beehr, 2006; Fox, Spector, & Miles, 2001; Mitchell & Ambrose, 2007) and schadenfreude (Feather & Nairn, 2005; Feather & Sherman, 2002), we argue that a fundamental difference between hostility in envious and unjust situations will be in the *target* of hostility. That is to say, the envious should direct their behaviors primarily toward the envied individual, whereas those experiencing injustice are more likely to primarily target the system that generated an unfair result (i.e., the organization) or the supervisor or authority figure responsible for the distribution of outcomes (except perhaps in cases where the individual acted unfairly to gain an advantage, which we would argue is rarer).

Using this logic, Mishra (2012a) investigated whether information about inputs only, outcomes only, or combinations of inputs and outcomes would generate differences in helping-behavior directed toward a target social other. Put simply, Mishra hypothesized that those experiencing envy would be less likely to help the target, while those experiencing feelings of injustice would be more likely to help the target (since their hostility would be directed toward the system or the authority figure, not the social other). Across two experimental studies, Mishra (2012a, 2012b) found that information about inputs alone or outcomes alone produced less helping than did information about inputs and outcomes in combination.

In the first study, Mishra (2012a) used a computer simulation in which participants were led to believe that they were participating in the study along with another student who could send them chat or text messages during the course of the session. These messages were used variously to manipulate information about inputs only, outcomes only, or inputs and outcomes in combination. For example, all participants completed a supposed test of managerial aptitude and were told that they had achieved an average score. In the input-only condition, after completing this portion of the study, participants received a text message from their partner indicating that the partner had obtained a much higher score, indicating far-above-average managerial aptitude. In the outcome-only condition, participants were led to believe that their partner would be receiving more extra credit points than they would after both finished a difficult anagram task (no information about the partner's managerial aptitude score was included). Finally, an unjust situation involving information about both inputs and outcomes was manipulated by providing participants information that they had equivalent average managerial aptitude to their partner (inputs), but that their partner would receive more extra credit for the session in question (outcome) because their partner was randomly assigned to complete a much easier anagram task than the participant, resulting in a higher score.

At the end of the study, all participants had an opportunity to help their partner. Participants were led to believe that they would be eligible for a $25 raffle based on the amount of points they obtained in a separate card game that was based entirely on luck. Participants needed 25 points to be entered in the raffle, and they always "earned" 32 points. At the end of the study, they were told that their partner had only 20 points and were asked if they were willing to transfer five of their seven spare points to the partner so that the partner could be entered in the raffle. Even though the outcome was unfair in the injustice condition (i.e., the partner was going to get more extra credit than the participant because the partner had been randomly given an easier anagram task), participants were highly likely to help the partner. with 89% of participants providing extra raffle points. However, when information about inputs only was provided, and the only thing the participants knew was that their partner was superior in terms of managerial aptitude, participants were much less likely to help that target, giving away their spare points only 64% of the time. In the outcome-only condition (no information about partner's managerial ability), participants helped their partner 78% of the time.

In a second study, Mishra (2012b) investigated a similar set of questions, using confederates as peer rather than an electronically manipulated peer. Participants in this study were told that they would be helping to validate a new intelligence test by investigating whether practicing for the test would influence test performance. Individual participants and a gender-matched confederate were told that a coin flip would determine who would get a chance to practice the test before taking the test. The test in question was actually a puzzle task that involved the completion of geometrical shapes to recreate a given silhouette.

When the coin flip determined that the participant would be given an opportunity to practice, the participant was given that chance, while the confederate engaged in an alternative meaningless task. Then, the actual test was administered. Even though the participant had a practice session, the confederate (who knew the solutions to the puzzles in advance) performed much better than the participant did on the task. This should generate envy, since the "superior intelligence" of the confederate made it easy for them to solve the puzzles without practice.

When the coin flip determined that the confederate would get a chance to practice, the participant was given the irrelevant task, and subsequently the actual test took place. Once again, the confederate far outperformed the participant. However, in this condition, that superior performance was attributable to the unfair chance that the confederate received to practice the task. As such, this condition should generate a sense of injustice rather than envy of the target.

At the conclusion of the puzzle test, the participant and confederate were then assigned to a new and seemingly unrelated experimental task on computers. In the course of completing that task, an opportunity for the participant to help the confederate was provided. At an appointed time, the confederate began to cough rather violently, and got up from the chair to retrieve his/her water bottle. Upon doing so, s/he "accidentally" knocked over a tray of puzzle pieces, but did not stop to pick the pieces up, continuing instead to retrieve his/her water to alleviate coughing. As the confederate slowly took a drink, it was then observed whether or not the participant would assist the confederate by picking up the puzzle pieces.

In the condition manipulating injustice, where the confederate had unfairly received a practice opportunity not afforded the participant, the participant helped the confederate 63% of the time. By contrast, in the envy condition, where the confederate demonstrated superior intelligence (outperforming the participant on the puzzle task despite the participant's having had a practice opportunity not afforded the confederate), the participant helped only 37% of the time.

Together, these results from Mishra (2012a, 2012b) seem to suggest that information related only to inputs or outcomes can by itself generate envious comparisons, but that information related to both inputs and outcomes is required to generate perceptions of unfairness. Interestingly, the results also suggest that feelings of envy seem to be particularly likely on the input side of the equation. Although we argued that knowledge of inputs or outcomes alone could generate envy, Mishra's results seem to indicate that perceived differences in inputs are particularly likely to lead to envy.

Naturally, these initial results generate at least as many questions as they answer (including potential differences between varieties of inputs— controllable factors such as effort vs. non-controllable factors such as intelligence; or the complexity of classifying some factors as either inputs or outcomes). However, we believe that these results highlight the potential benefits of considering how models of organizational justice and envy can inform each other and lead to new insights. Starting from the base of distributive justice and considering the comparison of input and outcome ratios, Mishra (2012a, 2012b) was able to generate new ideas and evidence concerning how envious comparisons might arise, how these may differ from perceptions of unfairness, and (importantly) the behavioral consequences of these variations in terms of helping, and the target of hostility for envy as opposed to injustice. We propose here that other models from the justice literature have a similar potential to inform the study of envy.

Envy, Counterfactuals, and Procedural Justice

Having addressed the case of envy and distributive justice, we turn now to consider other ways in which justice and fairness research might inform work on envy. Specifically, we address two areas where circumstances of fairness perceptions might fruitfully inform envy-like emotions. First, we'll consider the potential for using counterfactual thinking (rather than relying solely on the logic of social comparisons) to understand fairness and envious emotions. Second, we'll consider how the concept of procedural justice informs envy.

"Counterfactual thinking" refers to the manner in which people are influenced by alternatively imaginable versions of actual circumstances (Kahneman & Tversky, 1982). Counterfactual thinking presents a compelling model for analyzing perceptions of injustice and feelings of envy. Of course, we are not the first to recognize the potential importance of counterfactual thinking to envious experiences (Ben-Ze'ev, 1992; Elster, 1991), and recent research by van de Ven and Zeelenberg (2015) explores the notion that counterfactuals are linked to the intensity of envy that people experience. We will address some of the van de Ven and Zeelenberg (2015) findings subsequently, but first we'll build the general case for considering counterfactual thinking as a perspective on justice perceptions and envious emotions.

In addressing counterfactuals in relation to fairness perceptions and envy, we draw on the closely related frameworks of referent cognitions theory, or RCT (Folger, 1987), and fairness theory (Folger & Cropanzano, 2001). Rather than make fine-grained distinctions between these, we use the simplification of combining them as the RC/FT acronym. Three varieties of counterfactuals—Would, Could, and Should—are central to RC/FT. The first refers to an outcome-related comparison. As pertains to both envy and a sense of unfairness, the relevant counterfactual is one that casts a person's actual condition in an unfavorable light by comparison. In some sense, the qualitative dimensions of any actual experience bear the stamp of implicit counterfactuals: A temperature is warm relative to those that are colder or hotter than it, for example. The construct of a *comparison level* or CL is a conceptual predecessor. Its description could just as well fit the idea of Would counterfactuals because it refers to the determinants of feelings of relative satisfaction, as follows:

> The location of CL on the person's scale of outcomes will be influenced by all of the outcomes known to the member, either by direct experience or symbolically. It may be taken to be some modal or average value of all known outcomes, each outcome weighted by its "salience," or strength of instigation, which depends, for example, upon the recency of experiencing

the outcome and the occurrence of stimuli which serve as reminders of the outcome. (Thibaut & Kelley, 1959, p. 21)

The significance of CL in regard to Would counterfactuals is that the former articulated clearly just how many different kinds of environmental features can affect the feelings associated with actual states or conditions. Another passage, well worth quoting at length, brings this out.

In defining the CL the primary intention is to locate a psychologically mean-ingful mid-point for the scale of outcomes—a neutral point on a scale of satisfaction-dissatisfaction. . ... We have chosen to define the CL as being some modal or average value of all the outcomes known to the person (by virtue of personal or vicarious experience), each outcome weighted by its salience (or the degree to which it is instigated for the person at the moment). A person's CL depends not only upon outcomes he has experienced or *seen others experi-encing* [emphasis added] but also upon which of these are actively stimulating to him—are obtruded on him, are vivid and perhaps implicitly rehearsed as he makes an evaluation of his circumstances. This salience depends in part upon momentary cues which serve as reminders of ... alternatives. To the degree this is true, CL is subject to situation-to-situation and moment-to-moment variations. Perhaps more important, because of their relative stability, are the outcomes the salience of which is independent of the immediate situation— outcomes for which the person provides dependable self-instigations or, so to speak, self-reminders. (Thibaut & Kelley, 1959, pp. 81–82)

Clearly this describes a very rich set of stimuli that can influence how people feel about their actual situations! Would-counterfactuals reflect the same richness in the following way. The RC/FT framework focuses on feel-ings of dissatisfaction as a necessary component of unfairness perceptions. To be dissatisfied is to have a sense of something other than the actual state that would be better than it, making the actual seem inferior by virtue of the comparison to something more favorable (whether explicitly or only as the object of implicit awareness). A succinct reference to CL as especially influenced by "favorable unattained outcomes" also captures the relation-ship between Would counterfactuals and the potential for an experienced sense of (disadvantageous) unfairness. The difference is that, whereas the CL is a neutral baseline or dividing point that separates the qualities of favorable and unfavorable, Would counterfactuals associated with unfair-ness involve a specific actual (current) state and alternatively imaginable states that make it seem relatively unsatisfactory by comparison.

Before discussing the Could and Should counterfactuals, we must note how our use of the notion of counterfactuals differs from one that is more common. Ours is in fact very broad. We can illustrate by first referring to a very classic reference to counterfactuals in the context of envy; namely, the description of "counterfactual emotions ... [including] frustration, regret, and some cases of indignation, grief, and envy" (Kahneman & Tversky, 1982, p. 206). That description was given in conjunction with an analysis of emotions that "arise when reality is compared with a favored alternative" (Kahneman & Tversky, 1982, p. 202). So far, the conceptualization is consistent with our broad sense of (negative) counterfactuals as mental contrasts involving upward comparisons toward some condition better than one's current state. The narrower—and more commonly used—concept of counterfactuals, however, comes from a phrase we omitted from the quotation we just cited. In full, it referred to "a favored alternative, which one had *failed to reach* but could *easily imagine* reaching" (Kahneman & Tversky, 1982, p. 202, emphasis added).

The narrower versus broader conceptualization of upward counterfactual comparisons is important because, in the narrower case, the actual condition is an end state resulting from one's unsuccessful efforts to achieve some other condition instead. The ease of imagining the unattained counterfactual state, therefore, seems as if it would be primarily affected by speculating about how it might have been possible to be successful. Put another way, one possible implication is a type of self-criticism, even if only about something as temporary and mutable (perhaps with compensating results soon to come!) as a momentary lapse.

Envy, however, is not ordinarily thought of as an emotion associated with self-blame. For example, Salieri presumably placed more blame on God than he did on himself—it wasn't his fault that his talents paled in comparison to Mozart's, because he was in fact the more devout follower of God. Here, then, is how the Would counterfactual operates similarly in the cases of envy and of perceived unfairness: In neither case is the upward counterfactual a negative reflection on the efforts of the person making that comparison, whether it is associated with envy, perceived unfairness, or both.[2]

The RC/FT conceptualization of the Could and Should counterfactuals brings further considerations to bear on counterfactual thinking in general as well as on envy and perceived unfairness in particular. From the RC/FT perspective, these two counterfactuals are important, specifically as they relate to ways that someone else might be held accountable for the state of a person who feels disadvantaged (i.e., experiences negative feelings because of an unfavorable Would counterfactual comparison). If some other agent might have been responsible for the negative outcome, the possibility of various Could counterfactuals refers to presumptions about ways such an agent might have been able to behave in a manner other than the one actually manifested. No doubt Salieri had such thoughts without difficulty—after all, an omnipotent being could make an infinite number and variety of Mozarts and Salieris, including ones in which the latter was more gifted than the former!

Note that, although the versions of envy-related emotions we are focusing on involve the absence of self-blame, that shared feature with perceived unfairness nonetheless still allows for a differentiation of the two types of experience. The absence of self-blame is a necessary condition for both states, but it is not sufficient for either. In fact, it is the potential for other-blame that allows for some shadings of difference. Other-blame in the RC/FT framework is a necessary condition for someone to be held accountable for perceived unfairness, whereas it is perhaps not so closely tied to envy. In fact, we propose that envy-like emotions can vary in the extent to which other-blame is present. Moreover, we have articulated things this way in order to allow for instances in which envy and resentment (of perceived unfairness) might be experienced simultaneously or cyclically—or not.

An other-blame Could counterfactual reflects the common intuition that people are not blamed for failing to do things that are impossible, or for doing things impossible not to have done. An other-blame Could counterfactual is a necessary condition in order to hold someone accountable for conditions deemed unfavorable. Reference to blame, however, is not the same as mere causation. People in one sense are not considered causally responsible for failing to bring about some condition that was impossible to attain, whereas that aspect of causal reasonability holds when they have exercised their discretion to pursue one course of action rather than others also open to them because of their capabilities. Choosing one option rather than another equally viable one suffices to establish that someone could have acted differently, but words with socially undesirable connotations (e.g., "blame") need not come with the territory.

For example, Rob and Steve compete in a chess tournament. Steve beats Rob, who has previously been successful in other tournaments and knows how it feels to win—hence he has the basis for dissatisfaction that can come from upward Would counterfactuals (e.g., "Oh how much better it would feel if I were the one carrying home that trophy, which is so much more impressive than the trophies I've won in other tournaments"). Notice that, without further elaboration, the possibility of such Would counterfactuals in and of themselves does not dictate either envy or perceived unfairness. If an elaborated narrative involved stipulating that Rob had no sense of self-blame (e.g., "I played as well as I'm capable of playing and don't regret a single move I made"), that still need not entail either of those emotions. Steve is "to blame" for Rob's defeat in the sense of mere causal responsibility, but it makes more intuitive sense to make that the basis for praising Steve rather than blaming him.

There are many ways to lose a game of chess. Likewise, there are many ways that Steve could have played differently, and thus he could have (deliberately or unintentionally) caused Rob to win. This shows that Steve's possession of discretionary control—the basis for Could counterfactuals attributed to him by Rob—is also insufficient for Rob to feel unfairly treated by Steve, despite the dissatisfying Would counterfactual of losing rather than winning.

Suppose, however, that Steve had an earpiece that allowed him to be coached secretly while playing. Suppose also that Rob later hears Steve bragging about this method of cheating, but can't prove it. That provides the Should counterfactual as the third ingredient of unfairness identified by the RC/FT analysis: Knowing about a player who cheats makes it easy to bring to mind the Should-not-cheat counterfactual, which Steve Could have abided by, and which perhaps Would have allowed Rob to win. Workplace analogs occur when, for example, an employee believes that a co-worker is better off (e.g., got the promotion the employee wanted) only because of favoritism by the boss, which the boss should not have allowed to influence the decision.

Knowledge of all three of the requisite counterfactuals might make Rob envious (or more envious) and might also make him feel unfairly treated, which goes to our point that the two types of emotions can overlap. One difference between them, however, involves the potential reactions of third parties. Suppose Paresh had watched the game. Afterward he might have no feelings of envy vis-à-vis Steve—even if at that point the "win" (and trophy) might be something that Paresh does not have and never has had. That would be true if Paresh had no desire to do well playing chess; perhaps he also would not even desire the celebrity status that can go with winning competitive contests. On the other hand, Paresh might well have feelings akin to moral outrage about Steve's unfair way of achieving his "win" (just as might occur when people boycott a company not because of any effects on them personally, but because of some basis for outrage about the way that company treats its employees).

The Would/Could/Should counterfactuals represent three parameters relevant to both (un)fairness perceptions and envy. Individually and in various combinations, they can not only differentiate envy from unfairness but also account for instances of their overlap. Moreover, they can represent discrete values of variables ("If only I'd won that trophy") as well as influences from along a continuum (e.g., different alternatively imaginable states, weighted to various degrees affecting the location of some satisfaction/dissatisfaction divide such as a CL). Rather than mapping out numerous permutations and combinations of these counterfactual variables, we provide a sampling of illustrations (see also Folger, 1987; Mark & Folger, 1984):

1. Tami and Pam are professional golfers, both lying 140 yards away from the flagstick. Tami hits first, using a pitching wedge, and the ball lands short of the green. Pam uses a 9-iron and puts the ball in the hole. Tami is immediately reminded of how good it feels to hit such a shot (upward Would) and experiences a degree of envy or an envy-like emotion. She had also been wavering between hitting a 9 or a wedge (upward Could) and thinks perhaps she did not make an accurate enough assessment of the wind (ease or difficulty of various degrees of Coulds), which becomes another factor influencing the nature of experiences with envy-like qualities. Maybe she won't feel so envious, for example, if she internalizes self-blame about her club-selection as a dumb mistake on her part. Similarly, the nature of an employee's envy-like emotional reaction can vary as a function of (a) the salience and extent of a co-worker's superior state on some occasion, and (b) whether or not it seems as if the employee could have done just as well "if only. . ." (e.g., he or she had tried harder).

2. Brigitte and Louise face similar circumstances when playing in a tournament. Louise is the second to play, and holes her shot. Brigitte had hit one only inches away—an instance of a close upward-Would counterfactual, also easily brought to mind because of a very mutable Could counterfactual. Perhaps these circumstances make Brigitte especially envious; perhaps not (she is used to lucky and unlucky bounces on the green by herself as well as other players, so this instance is not so exceptional or abnormal as to make holing the shot the "normal" counterfactual that comes immediately to mind). Similarly, the basis for Could attributions in the workplace can seem clear-cut (e.g., regarding how much control over the situation the envying and the envied persons might have been able to exercise) or

ambiguous to various degrees (e.g., unclear how much "luck" might have played a role, and what the source of good—or bad—luck might have been).

3. Paul and Sam's experience is similar to those above; Sam holes the shot, whereas Paul (who hit first) is a few yards away. Paul is convinced Sam's caddy cheated (i.e., the caddy used a device, outlawed by the rules of golf, to measure wind and distance) but cannot prove it (doesn't know where the caddy hides it). Paul is not only envious but also has a sense of injustice. On the other hand, he does not hold it against Sam, who he is convinced did not know of his caddy's unethical tactics. Workplace examples include those in which an employee is envious of an advantaged co-worker but suspects the blame lies with someone higher in the chain of command (e.g., a perceived "glass ceiling" discrepancy that can't be verified as having been caused by deliberate bias).

4. George and Ramone's circumstances are like those of Brigitte and Louise. It is the last hole, and George—who hit first—loses the tournament by a single stroke. This illustrates a way the emotion he feels, whatever it is, might be more intense than Brigitte's (Could and Would are unchanged as far as mutable closeness, but there is a greater valence discrepancy between George's actual outcome and the bounteous alternative reality he can easily imagine experiencing). Similarly, there can be workplace circumstances like those we alluded to in conjunction with the Brigitte/Louise vignette, but where the stakes are enormous (e.g., being among those laid off rather than being one of the "survivors").

5. Nathan and Phillip's case is just like George and Ramone's, except it is only the first day of the tournament. Nathan thinks Phillip's ball went in the hole because the greens are soft and keeping balls hit on them from rolling off. He realizes that because his ball was only inches short, taking into account (more accurately) the condition of the greens is an easy adjustment to make. In this case, the closeness and mutability of the Could counterfactual works to inspire Nathan to be willing to do what golfers call "grinding it out" (ignoring mistakes and just keep playing ever harder) because he thinks his chances of winning the tournament are still quite good. Similar circumstances in the workplace might exist when the next performance appraisal is still a long way off, and there's plenty of time to learn how to make the simple adjustments needed so as not to be compared unfavorably to a co-worker.

And so on, but with some variations that might be unique to a head-to-head competition between two rivals (or to the nexus of workplace relations). The point is that it might be necessary to take into account many other possible Would/Could/Should variations in other types of situations.

Our golfing illustrations have involved primarily variations in Would and Could counterfactuals (other than the case of Sam's rule-breaking caddy). When Should counterfactuals are also taken into account, other interesting possibilities can be illustrated. In particular, this brings potential fairness considerations into the mix when something *Should* not have occurred and *Could* have been prevented, tying into the framework of *procedural justice*.

The psychology of procedural justice was first mapped out by Thibaut and Walker (1975), especially regarding the context of dispute resolutions arbitrated by a third-party decision maker (e.g., a judge who can decide the merits of a plaintiff's case in civil proceedings). Right away, this brings out what we just said about variations on the theme of head-to-head competition. On one hand, a plaintiff-versus-defendant dispute is not totally unlike the case of competing golfers (e.g., both dyadic and zero-sum). On the other hand, they differ in such matters as resolution on the basis of the facts of the case relative to legal precedents rather than the relative skills of the two disputants. Moreover, the third party who acts as decision-maker can play a role that itself has numerous parameters—again creating the possibility for permutations and combinations that allow for a range of envy-like emotional experiences, along with or independent of feeling about the fairness or unfairness of the situation.

Subsequent to the seminal contributions of Thibaut and Walker, the literature on procedural justice spread to the context of work organizations (Folger, 1977; Folger & Greenberg, 1985), and it has by this point become quite voluminous. Based on that, we can point to several specific types of situations to illustrate procedural justice variations (with or without accompanying envious feelings) in relation to Should counterfactuals.

To begin with, there are many elements of decision-making that can vary in terms of their possible effects on procedural justice perceptions. A list by Leventhal (1980), for example, includes consistency, bias suppression, accuracy, and correctability. Each can represent a salient normative standard for what is perceived to be the proper way of conducting a decision-making process. If one such standard seems applicable in a given context, it is thus the relevant Should. The enactment of the actual process may or may not fully adhere to this standard. To the extent that it falls short, there is a negative (aversive) gap between reality and the Should counterfactual.

Moreover, people can apply their own idiosyncratic standards for the perceived justice of procedures. Suppose, for example, Fred receives a score of "Below expectations" on his quarterly performance appraisal at work. His friend Matt, who works the same job but a different shift with a different supervisor, receives a score of "Exceeds expectations." Fred learns not only about Matt's rating (there's a possible Would discrepancy) but also that it was based on scores from customer satisfaction surveys, whereas Fred's was based on subjective supervisor ratings. Fred believes that using customer feedback is a procedurally fairer way of determining evaluations (and that he would perform well on such a measure). This idiosyncratic procedural standard for decision-making correctness (whereby Fred assumes customer feedback occupies a more privileged position on an implicit scale that has accuracy as a fairness criterion) creates a salient Should. Fred concludes that his lower evaluation was the product of a flawed, procedurally unjust evaluation system.

We would describe that situation as follows. To begin with, Fred might be envious because of his "Below Expectations" relative to Matt's "Exceeds." What makes it even worse, and hence the basis for amplified envy, is that Fred thinks the evaluation procedures are flawed. To put it another way, his envy might have been attenuated if he didn't have such a quarrel with the appraisal system. The reason is that counterfactuals to reality tend to run from an inappropriate state in a direction toward one imagined as being more appropriate. Fred thinks of supervisor evaluations as an unfair appraisal method and can easily imagine, not only an alternative procedure that seems more appropriately situated on the accuracy continuum (customer feedback), but also that Would have given him—in the simulated world of his imagination—a higher evaluation. But, although envious of Matt, Fred seems unlikely to bear him a grudge. He experiences both a form of envy and a sense of injustice, but associated with two different elements of evaluation; anger about feeling unfairly mistreated, in other words, would be directed toward his supervisor.

Bringing in the element of procedural justice has at least two implications regarding envy-like psychological states. First, as an additional counterfactual, it brings into play another basis for making envious comparisons possible or for amplifying the intensity associated with those already instigated. If it is easy to imagine a better, fairer process, the search for evidence about what Would have happened otherwise takes on a sense of urgency ("I've got to find out Matt's evaluation, so I'll know whether my evaluation would have been better with his boss"); if such evidence is discovered, it seems to take on a greater truth value as an indicator of "what might have been," and hence it feeds into envy more readily and perhaps with greater intensity.

A study by van de Ven and Zeelenberg (2015) produced evidence for an amplification of the emotional intensity associated with an envious state. Control-condition participants read a vignette and were asked to imagine how they might feel about not being promoted from junior to senior sales representative, given that a comparable colleague was promoted. They also read that "there does not seem to be a strong reason to favor one over the other." When van de Ven and Zeelenberg obtained ratings on a measure of envy that ranged from not at all (0) to very much (10), the average was 6.6 in this condition.

Two other conditions added another sentence after the one that said there was not a strong reason to prefer one candidate over the other (themselves vs. the colleague). These sentences introduced variations in the decision-making procedure that coincided with the authors' predictions based on the logic of counterfactuals. In a condition involving a "close" counter-factual (the easier to imagine as an alternative procedure that would have reversed the promotion results), the added sentence indicated that *typically* in such toss-up cases, the promotion would go to the employee who had worked longer at the company—the participant! That statement produced an average rating of 7.3 on the measure of envy, indicating an amplifica-tion effect significantly higher than was present in the control condition. A "far" counterfactual condition added the same sentence about longevity as the typical tie-breaker, but indicated that the colleague was the one with the longer tenure. The score there dropped to 5.8, which was significantly below the control level. Moreover, an analysis of mediation showed that these differences across conditions varied as a function of answers to an "it could have been me" question (van de Ven & Zeelenberg, 2015, p. 960). In other words, differences in counterfactual "closeness" (how easy it made it to think about the missed-out-on promotion)—based on procedural differences—led to differences obtained for envy.

The element of procedural justice also has a second implication regard-ing envy-like psychological states. As we see it, procedural justice can be part of a chicken-and-egg combination that allows for causal relations in either of two directions as well as in reciprocal loops. One causal direction occurs when perceived procedural injustice sets in motion a search for invidious comparisons, and envy results when they are found. Valid pro-cedures are less likely to make counterfactual alternatives come to mind than questionable procedures are. The latter instead can have a tendency to cause "If only . . ." or "I wonder what if . . ." thoughts. We suspect that the more someone looks for evidence that something unfair might have resulted from procedural improprieties, such as another person's getting (undeservedly) a better outcome, the higher the odds of "finding" that type of basis for envy.

A causal sequence might run in the other direction when people find themselves being envious of others because of something the latter have received as the outcome of some process. In this case, there might be a temptation to rationalize that someone else's better state was not because of one's own deficiencies (self-threatening cognitions) but instead could be attributed to an unfair procedure (ego-defensive conclusions). Because both kinds of causal directions are possible, therefore, one might in turn trigger the other and thus foster a pattern of reciprocal-causation thoughts (e.g., "I got less than they did. I think that means the decision-making process might have been unfair. If so, then I not only got less than them but also perhaps less than I might have gotten. That's even more reason to feel envious").

Conclusion

In this chapter, we have attempted to explore how models of organizational justice and envy can inform each other and advance our understanding of both phenomena. In some instances, we have addressed empirical results that inform these questions, and in others we have speculated on fruitful ways to think about both areas of study. Naturally, this effort has not been exhaustive, and multiple other approaches to combining these areas and drawing insights one from the other could be imaginable. It is our hope that this effort to integrate these two research traditions will lead to new insights and research that will advance the understanding of both.

Notes

1. Strictly speaking, Adams (1965) also allowed for feelings of inequity based on non-social comparisons such as self at a previous time. Similarly, the theory of *deonance* (Folger, 2001; Folger & Glerum, 2015) identifies reasons why a sense of injustice might be experienced even in the absence of social comparisons—such as with violations of principle, or based on harmful intent without actual harm (Umphress, Simmons, Folger, Ren, & Bobocel, 2013). We restrict our discussion of inequity to cases involving social comparison here, however, because of their particular relevance to envy.

2. Of course, perceptions can take twists and turns that don't always fit an abstract conceptual scheme (such as this one). An example is that envy also can often be linked with shame. The envying person may not feel "at fault" (in an attributionally straightforward, rational way) and yet still feel *ashamed* in the sense of perceived inferiority relative to the other person's superiority. In cases such as being born with an affliction and envying those who don't have it, for instance, someone might feel ashamed about the affliction but not harbor self-blame about it.

References

Adams, J. S. (1965). Inequity in social exchange. In L. Berkowitz, Ed., *Advances in Experimental Social Psychology* (vol. 2, pp. 267–299). New York: Academic Press.

Barclay, L. J., Skarlicki, D. P., & Pugh, S. D. (2005). Exploring the role of emotions in injustice perceptions and retaliation. *Journal of Applied Psychology, 90*, 629–643.

Ben-Ze'ev, A. (1992). Envy and inequality. *The Journal of Philosophy, 89*, 551–581.

Bies, R. J., & Moag, J. F. (1986). Interactional justice: Communication criteria of fairness. In R. J. Lewicki, B. H. Sheppard, & M. H. Bazerman, Eds., *Research on Negotiations in Organizations* (vol. 1, pp. 43–55). Greenwich, CT: JAI Press.

Bies, R. J., & Tripp, T. M. (2002). "Hot flashes, open wounds": Injustice and the tyranny of its emotions. In D. D. Steiner, D. P. Skarlicki, & S. W. Gilliland, Eds., *Emerging Perspectives on Managing Organizational Justice* (pp. 203–221). Greenwich, CT: Information Age Publishing.

Blau, P. M. (1964). *Exchange and Power in Social Life*. New York: Wiley.

Bowling, N. A., & Beehr, T. A. (2006). Workplace harassment from the victim's perspective: A theoretical model and meta-analysis. *Journal of Applied Psychology, 91*, 998–1012.

Chreim, S., Williams, B. E., & Hinings, C. R. (2007). Interlevel influences on the reconstruction of professional role identity. *Academy of Management Journal, 50*, 1515–1539.

Cohen-Charash, Y. (2009). Episodic envy. *Journal of Applied Social Psychology, 39*, 2128–2173.

Cohen-Charash, Y., & Mueller, J. S. (2007). Does perceived unfairness exacerbate or mitigate interpersonal counterproductive work behaviors related to envy? *Journal of Applied Psychology, 92*, 666–680.

Colquitt, J. A., Greenberg, J., & Zapata-Phelan, C. P. (2005). What is organizational justice: A historical overview. In J. Greenberg & J. A. Colquitt, Eds., *Handbook of Organizational Justice* (pp. 3–56). Mahwah, NJ: Lawrence Erlbaum Associates.

De Cremer, D., & van den Bos, K. (2007). Justice and feelings: Toward a new era in justice research. *Social Justice Research, 20*, 1–9.

Cropanzano, R., Bowen, D. E., & Gilliland, S. W. (2007). The management of organizational justice. *Academy of Management Perspectives, 21*, 34–48.

Cropanzano, R., Stein, J. H., & Nadisic, T. (2011). *Social Justice and the Experience of Emotion*. New York: Routledge.

Crosby, F. (1976). A model of egoistical relative deprivation. *Psychological Review, 83,* 85–113.

D'Arms, J. (2013). Envy. In E. N. Zalta, Ed., *The Stanford Encyclopedia of Philosophy* (Winter 2013 ed.). Retrieved from http://plato.stanford.edu/archives/win2013/entries/envy/.

Ekman, P. (1992). Are there basic emotions? *Psychological Review, 99,* 550–553.

Ellsworth, P. C. (2014). Basic emotions and the rocks of New Hampshire. *Emotion Review, 6,* 21–26.

Ellsworth, P. C., & Scherer, K. R. (2003). Appraisal processes in emotion. In R. J. Davidson, H. Goldsmith, & K. R. Scherer, Eds., *Handbook of Affective Sciences* (pp. 572–595). New York: Oxford University Press.

Elster, J. (1991). *Envy in Social Life.* Cambridge, MA: MIT Press.

Feather, N. T., & Nairn, K. (2005). Resentment, envy, schadenfreude, and sympathy: Effects of own and other's deserved or undeserved status. *Australian Journal of Psychology, 57,* 87–102.

Feather, N. T., & Sherman, R. (2002). Envy, resentment, schadenfreude, and sympathy: Reactions to deserved and undeserved achievement and subsequent failure. *Personality and Social Psychology Bulletin, 28,* 953–961.

Festinger, L. (1954). A theory of social comparison processes. *Human Relations, 7,* 117–140.

Folger, R. (1977). Distributive and procedural justice: Combined impact of "voice" and improvement on experienced inequity. *Journal of Personality and Social Psychology, 35,* 108–119.

Folger, R. (1987). Reformulating the preconditions of resentment: A referent cognitions model. In J. C. Masters & W. P. Smith, Eds., *Social Comparison, Justice, and Relative Deprivation: Theoretical, Empirical, and Policy Perspectives* (pp. 183–215). Hillsdale, NJ: Lawrence Erlbaum Associates.

Folger, R. (1998). Fairness as moral virtue. In M. Schminke, Ed., *Managerial Ethics: Moral Management of People and Processes* (pp. 13–34). Mahwah, NJ: Erlbaum.

Folger, R. (2001). Fairness as deonance. In S. W. Gilliland, D. D. Steiner, & D. P. Skarlicki, Eds., *Research in Social Issues in Management* (pp. 3–31). Greenwich, CT: Information Age Publishers.

Folger, R., & Cropanzano, R. (2001). Fairness theory: Justice as accountability. In J. Greenberg & R. Cropanzano, Eds., *Advances in Organizational Justice* (pp. 1–55). Stanford, CA: Stanford University Press.

Folger, R., & Glerum, D. R. (2015). Justice and deonance: "You ought to be fair." In R. Cropanzano & M. Ambrose, Eds., *The Oxford Handbook of Justice in the Workplace* (pp. 331–350). New York: Oxford University Press.

Folger, R., & Greenberg, J. (1985). Procedural justice: An interpretive analysis of personnel systems. In K. Rowland & G. Ferris, Eds., *Research in Personnel and Human Resources Management* (vol. 3, pp. 141–183). Greenwich, CT: JAI Press.

Foster, G. M. (1972). The anatomy of envy: A study in symbolic behavior. *Current Anthropology, 13,* 165–186.

Fox, S., Spector, P. E., & Miles, D. (2001). Counterproductive work behavior (CWB) in response to job stressors and organizational justice: Some mediator and moderator tests for autonomy and emotions. *Journal of Vocational Behavior*, *59*, 291–309.

Greenberg, J., Ashton-James, C. E., & Ashkanasy, N. M. (2007). Social comparison processes in organizations. *Organizational Behavior and Human Decision Processes*, *102*, 22–41.

Homans, G. C. (1961). *Social Behavior: Its Elementary Forms*. London: Routledge & Kegan Paul.

Izard, C. E. (2007). Basic emotions, natural kinds, emotion schemas, and a new paradigm. *Perspectives on Psychological Science*, *2*, 260–280.

James, W. (1850/1950). *The Principles of Psychology*. New York: Dover.

Kahneman, D., & Tversky, A. (1982). The simulation heuristic. In D. Kahneman, P. Slovic, & A. Tversky, Eds., *Judgement Under Uncertainty: Heuristics and Biases* (pp. 201–208). New York: Cambridge University Press.

Krizan, Z., & Johar, O. (2012). Envy divides the two faces of narcissism. *Journal of Personality*, *80*, 1415–1451.

Leventhal, G. S. (1980). What should be done with equity theory? New approaches to the study of fairness in social relationships. In K. Gergen, M. Greenberg, & R. Willis, Eds., *Social Exchange: Advances in Theory and Research* (pp. 27–55). New York: Plenum.

Mark, M. M., & Folger, R. (1984). Responses to relative deprivation: A conceptual framework. *Review of Personality and Social Psychology*, *5*, 192–218.

Miceli, M., & Castelfranchi, C. (2007). The envious mind. *Cognition and Emotion*, *21*, 449–479.

Mishra, P. (2012a). *Wicked Justice: Differentiating Between Unfairness and Envy.* (Ph.D. dissertation.) Bloomington, IN: Indiana University.

Mishra, P. (2012b). Wicked justice: Differentiating between unfairness and envy. *Academy of Management Proceedings*, *1*, 1-6. doi: 10.5465/AMBPP.2012.306

Mitchell, M. S., & Ambrose, M. L. (2007). Abusive supervision and workplace deviance and the moderating effects of negative reciprocity beliefs. *Journal of Applied Psychology*, *92*, 1159–1168.

Moran, S., & Schweitzer, M. E. (2008). When better is worse: Envy and the use of deception. *Negotiation and Conflict Management Research*, *1*, 3–29.

Parrott, W. G., & Smith, R. H. (1993). Distinguishing the experiences of envy and jealousy. *Journal of Personality and Social Psychology*, *64*, 906–920.

Schaubroeck, J. M., & Lam, S. S. K. (2004). Comparing lots before and after: Promotion rejectees' invidious reactions to promotees. *Organizational Behavior and Human Decision Processes*, *94*, 33–47.

Schoeck, H. (1969). *Envy: A Theory of Social Behavior.* (Trans. M. Glenny & B. Ross.) London: Secker & Warburg.

Shaffer, P. (1984). IMDB: *Amadeus*. Retrieved from http://www.imdb.com/title/tt0086879/quotes

Smith, R. H. (1991). Envy and the sense of injustice. In P. Salovey, Ed., *The Psychology of Jealousy and Envy* (pp. 79–99). New York: The Guilford Press.

Smith, R. H., & Kim, S. H. (2007). Comprehending envy. *Psychological Bulletin*, *133*, 46–64.

Smith, R. H., Parrott, W. G., Diener, E. F., Hoyle, R. H., & Kim, S. H. (1999). Dispositional envy. *Personality and Social Psychology Bulletin, 25*, 1007–1020.

Smith, R. H., Parrott, W. G., Ozer, D., & Moniz, A. (1994). Subjective injustice and inferiority as predictors of hostile and depressive feelings in envy. *Personality and Social Psychology Bulletin, 20*, 705–711.

Stouffer, S. A., Suchman, E. A., DeVinney, L. C., Starr, S. A., & Williams Jr., R. M. (1949). *The American Soldier: Adjustment to Army Life* (Vol. I). Princeton, NJ: Princeton University Press.

Tesser, A. (1986). Some effects of self-evaluation maintenance on cognition and action. In R. M. Sorrentino & E. T. Higgins, Eds., *The Handbook of Motivation and Cognition: Foundations of Social Behavior* (pp. 435–464). New York: Guilford Press.

Tesser, A. (1991). Emotion in social comparison and reflection processes. In J. M. Suls & T. A. Wills, Eds., *Social Comparison: Contemporary Theory and Research* (pp. 115–145). Hillsdale, NJ: Erlbaum.

Thibaut, J. W., & Kelley, H. H. (1959). *The Social Psychology of Groups*. New York: John Wiley & Sons.

Thibaut, J. W., & Walker, L. (1975). *Procedural Justice: A Psychological Analysis*. New York: Erlbaum/Halstead.

Umphress, E. E., Simmons, A. L., Folger, R., Ren, R., & Bobocel, R. (2013). Observer reactions to interpersonal injustice: The roles of perpetrator intent and victim perception. *Journal of Organizational Behavior, 34*, 327–349.

van de Ven, N., & Zeelenberg, M. (2015). On the counterfactual nature of envy: "It could have been me." *Cognition and Emotion, 29*, 954–971.

van de Ven, N., Hoogland, C. E., Smith, R. H., van Dijk, W. W., Breugelmans, S. M., & Zeelenberg, M. (2015). When envy leads to schadenfreude. *Cognition and Emotion, 29*, 1007–1025.

van de Ven, N., Zeelenberg, M., & Pieters, R. (2009). Leveling up and down: The experiences of benign and malicious envy. *Emotion, 9*, 419–429.

van Dijk, W. W., Ouwerkerk, J. W., Goslinga, S., Nieweg, M., & Gallucci, M. (2006). When people fall from grace: Reconsidering the role of envy in schadenfreude. *Emotion, 6*, 156–160.

Weiss, H. M., Suckow, K., & Cropanzano, R. (1999). Effects of justice conditions on discrete emotions. *Journal of Applied Psychology, 84*, 786–794.

Wondra, J. D., & Ellsworth, P. C. (2015). An appraisal theory of empathy and other vicarious emotional experiences. *Psychological Review, 122*, 411–428.

17 | Disposable Diapers, Envy and the Kibbutz

WHAT HAPPENS TO AN EMOTION BASED ON DIFFERENCE IN A SOCIETY BASED ON EQUALITY?

JOSH GRESSEL

Introduction

Her tone was clipped, her speech rapid-fire as she described anecdotes from nearly 30 years earlier. I quickly gave up any attempt to translate and type as she talked, trusting the recorder to take over while I sat back and listened.

Yocheved is in her late fifties and now 15 years removed from more than two decades as a kibbutz member. I opened our interview with a safe, generic question: "Did you ever witness incidents of envy between members on your kibbutz?" She practically spluttered in her hurry to respond, giving example after example. I found most compelling the story of the disposable diapers:

> When our children were small, we were helped financially by my parents in the city. And our standard of living was higher because of that. For example, we had disposable diapers when no one had anything like that. My father would always buy them for us.... And because of this I was treated with coldness and hostility in the baby house. I got the oldest baby buggy, and they told me I'm not a good enough mother.

Nathan is a 55-year-old kibbutz member. Born and raised on a struggling kibbutz in one part of the country, he moved to the United States for seven years before returning to live with his wife on her wealthy kibbutz in a different part of the country, where he has now lived for over 20 years:

> So long as there's a single standard in things, everyone has the same amount more or less, things are calm. But as soon as someone breaks that standard, it starts to bother people. When a former factory manager retired a few years ago, he said, "I gave my time to the kibbutz." He managed the factory for 10 years and did a good job. And he decided he wanted a car, but not just any car: a 4 x 4. You think that didn't cause an uproar? It caused a big uproar! People were envious that he had a 4 x 4. He demanded it and they gave in to him. He went to work off the kibbutz and he made a lot of money and threatened to keep the money if they didn't give him a 4 x 4.[1]

It is a truism that there is always more than one side to any story. It is especially evident on a kibbutz, where one often is privy to many different versions of what happens between people. But if we simply take these two accounts at face value, we are gifted with two examples of envy from opposite ends of the material continuum. How would we account for such incidents? Are they unique to the kibbutz? Or can the kibbutz, because of its social propinquity[2] on multiple levels, give us a clearer view of envy than we can see elsewhere?

The Kibbutz: An Overview

The kibbutz is a socialist collective community first established in pre-state Palestine in 1910 (Near, 1992). Today numbering 270 separate kibbutzim (plural of "kibbutz") with approximately 140,000 people, they are a long-running experiment in social engineering. The main values on which the kibbutz were based included equality among members, direct democracy in local governance, self-labor, common ownership, and reciprocal responsibility (Near, 1992; Russell, Hanneman, & Getz, 2013).

Though their total population has never exceeded 7.6% of the Jewish population of Israel, for decades, kibbutz members were over-represented in the elite echelons of Israeli society (Palgi & Getz, 2014). This skewing is still true today economically, if no longer socially. In 2009, while kibbutz members were only 2% of the Israeli Jewish population, their contribution to the national economy amounted to 40% in agriculture, 7% in industrial output, 9% in industrial export, and 10% in tourism (The Economic Unit of the Kibbutz Movement, 2009, as cited in Palgi & Reinharz, 2011).

Micro Changes on the Kibbutz: Is a Bicycle a Horse or Is It a Dog?
The kibbutz has always been an evolving experiment, and throughout its history even the smallest change was hotly debated as to whether it threatened core kibbutz values. Many of these debates, so intense at the time, can today seem quaint or even comical. One kibbutz historian related to me (Y. Riemer, personal communication, April 12, 2015) how the introduction of the first bicycle into a kibbutz in the 19fifties was accompanied with a discussion about whether individual members' having bicycles would disrupt the social fabric, because perhaps a member could bicycle to a nearby town whenever he so chose. The discussion crystalized into the following question: Is the bicycle a horse or is it a dog? If it's a horse, it's a dangerous incursion into the socialist lifestyle, as it would allow independent transport. If it's a dog, it is something more for the personal and local pleasure of the owner, with no significant change in day-to-day lifestyle. In the end, this particular kibbutz decided that a bicycle is a dog.

Similarly intense discussions greeted the first electric teakettle, the first radio, the first television, the first car, etc. One third-generation kibbutz member I spoke with reported that when his grandparents received a Zenith radio from relatives off the kibbutz, they gave it to the kibbutz. Subsequently, the kibbutz decided to allow the four families who were classical music lovers to share it in three-month rotations.

Macro Changes: When Does a Kibbutz Stop Being a Kibbutz? With the benefit of over one hundred years of history, several major shifts in the kibbutz can be discerned. Its leadership role in Israeli society lessened over time, from its heroic first decades in building the country to a smaller role after the state's founding in 1948, and then to an almost defensive posture after 1977 when the Likud, a political party not as sympathetic—and sometimes openly antagonistic—to its socialist ideals, came to power and remained there (Near 1992; Pauker, 2011). Communal child-rearing, with children sleeping together in dormitories from as young as six weeks old, was gradually replaced with the practice of all children sleeping at home by the 1990s. The social network changed from an emphasis on connection between members to an emphasis on the nuclear family unit. Budgets were gradually privatized so that members were given larger budgets, but they were then required to pay for things the kibbutz once provided free of charge, such as electricity, food, laundry, clothing, and health care. Nonmembers were allowed to build housing on the kibbutz, in order to revitalize the aging kibbutz population and reverse the population drop (Charney & Palgi, 2011; Greenberg 2011).

Kibbutz scholars agree that no change has been as dramatic and, some would say, antithetical to kibbutz ideology, as the introduction of differential salaries. One of the main features of the kibbutz throughout its history was that the mechanic fixing tractors, the daycare worker, and the factory manager all received the same budget and the same goods. Today, in two-thirds of the kibbutzim, this is no longer true (Palgi & Getz, 2014). In the kibbutzim that have gone to differential salaries, every kibbutz function has been priced according to a formula, and some kibbutz members can now make more than others, either by working longer hours and/or by working in a position the kibbutz values more highly than another.

So significant is this change that a joint government/kibbutz committee was convened to explore when a kibbutz can no longer be considered a kibbutz (Ben-Rafael & Topel, 2011). This is not simply an ideological or philosophical question, since the kibbutz receives special tax breaks from the government because it is a kibbutz. The conclusion this joint committee reached was that a kibbutz remains a kibbutz as long as there remains an emphasis on *arvut hadadit*: reciprocal responsibility. With all the different variations individual kibbutzim have implemented as they have gone to differential salaries, nearly all have kept this concept of *arvut hadadit*. The few kibbutzim that did not disbanded as kibbutzim. This *arvut hadadit* takes different forms, but in terms of economics, there are balance taxes in place to protect the more vulnerable on the kibbutz, such as those who were nearly at retirement age at the time the change took place. For this reason, even the new kibbutz, called the "renewing kibbutz" (*kibbutz mitchadesh*, Ben-Rafael & Topel, 2011) remains a more socialist society than the rest of Israel, with a higher level of reciprocal responsibility.

Interestingly, the remaining one-third of kibbutzim that have stayed with the original system, called the "collective kibbutz" (*kibbutz shitufi*) are typically the kibbutzim that are wealthy enough to be able to afford to keep it in place (Ben-Rafael & Topel, 2011; Palgi & Getz, 2014). Sociology professors Russell, Hanneman, and Getz (2013, p. 111) write that many kibbutz members "comment on the irony in seeing the kibbutz turn into a system of socialism for the rich and capitalism for the poor. Some wryly joke that kibbutz members still like socialism, but now they are forced to ask themselves how much socialism can they afford."

For someone who has never lived on or even visited a kibbutz, particularly someone born and raised in a capitalist society, it can seem puzzling why anyone would voluntarily submit to the sacrifices, frustrations, and, in the earlier years, deprivation, of the kibbutz lifestyle. Having lived as a kibbutz member for seven years, I can tell you what I miss about it. I miss the total commitment to a community in all its aspects; the sense of security that comes when the basics are handled; the knowledge that the larger community is there to support you should you need it at an existential level, and the beauty of seeing the ways in which the kibbutz *does* succeed more than capitalist societies, such as in its treatment of the old, the young, and the infirm. I mention all this because this chapter will be highlighting some of the petty and mean ways in which the kibbutz doesn't work, with less focus on how it does. Because of my emotional attachment to this lifestyle and the people who still live there, I ask the reader to remember there is much more to a kibbutz than what will be presented here.

Envy and the kibbutz: why should we care? Before plunging further into this topic, it makes sense to pause and ask some basic questions: Why should we care about envy? Why should we want to see how it does or doesn't show up on a kibbutz?

All emotions, such as anger, or love, or anxiety, can serve as individual doorways into our internal worlds. Each strong emotion creates a sort of disruptive static to the otherwise routine surface of our existence, opening us up to internal depths we often ignore. If we are comfortable with the emotion, we can be swept along effortlessly and ride its waves: the ecstasy of a concert, the joy of a wedding, the overwhelming love when holding our newborn child. In these moments, we feel ourselves part of a much larger and more meaningful fabric of life. Such experiences can serve as spiritual tether points for us, giving direction to our day-to-day existence when we often may wonder if there is an overarching purpose to our struggle.

Envy, as I suggest elsewhere (Gressel, 2014), can be an equally powerful emotion giving us direction, even though it seems to have little to recommend it. For me to say "I envy you" is to say "I feel less than you, not as good as you, inadequate, smaller." What possible benefit can there be to exploring such a negative feeling?

The answer, I propose, is this: *Envy is not a sign there is something wrong with you. Envy is a sign there is something right with you that you aren't claiming.* The diamond-in-the-rough experience of our envy can only be seen in its multifaceted beauty when we are able to discern what our envy is about on an internal level. Envy is a remarkably accurate pointer toward where we need and want to grow, if only we are able to stop focusing on the other long enough to discern the internal roadmap of our yearnings.[3]

Think about it for a minute: envy has been with us through all of recorded history. Every language, to my knowledge, has a word for it. If it is indeed a universal human emotion, why would it exist unless there is some higher purpose for it? I propose this higher purpose is the same as that for all of our emotions: to help us grow and develop into ever greater wholeness.

We like to think we are individual beings charting our individual courses through our individual lives. We maintain a sense of separation, whether it is the fence that divides our yard from our neighbor's, the invisible line of demarcation between seats on an airplane, or even the skin that covers our bodies. I am me and not you; you are you and not me.

Envy burrows beneath these more superficial distinctions, stops us in our tracks and says: "Hey! You're connected more than you like to pretend. You care about your neighbor more than you like to believe. You want what she has, you wish you could do what he does, you admire the way they pull that off." Or it can sound like this: "What does her being able to do/have that say about me?" Whatever the specifics of the way it pokes us, envy can, if viewed with compassion and curiosity, alert us to a way in which we need to grow and develop. Despite our illusion of separation, we are social beings connected in visible and invisible ways, and we need these points of conscious and sometimes painful contact to help us grow into larger versions of ourselves. This is the reason social propinquity is so important: we need others who are like us to help us become more like ourselves, the selves we were born to become. If you have a talent for the violin, you are not going to envy the expert tennis player, but you probably will envy the first chair in your orchestra if you've been relegated to second chair. This is your soul's signal to you that you want to continue to grow and develop as a violin player.

Now take this archetypal social propinquity dynamic for creating envy and intensify it along the multiple aspects of a kibbutz: you live in a small, usually geographically isolated community that espouses socialist values of connection and reciprocal responsibility. You know almost everyone by sight if not by name. You see each other daily in the dining room, the local grocery, or at work. You are dependent on each other, not only for your collective financial well-being, but also to get permission from each other for things your average city dweller would never think to ask permission for: going overseas to be at your brother's wedding, wanting funds to pay for an elective (but critically important to you) medical test, or going off the kibbutz to study a profession the kibbutz may or may not deem necessary. The person who decides may be your actual physical neighbor, or he may be the person you angered last year when you complained about his dog digging up your flowerbed, or she may even be the woman who gave you that crappy baby buggy so many years ago that you still haven't fully forgiven her for. Or it may be someone to whom you granted permission for something he requested five years ago when you chaired a different committee, even though you thought at the time he didn't deserve it, and you think he'd better remember he owes you. Your children may be in the same class in the small elementary school on the kibbutz, and they may or may not get along.

Multiply these energetically charged points of contact by years or decades of frequently unresolved grievances, some of which can be generational. Throw in some extra seasoning of wondering if you really want to be on the kibbutz each time you have to ask permission for something adults off the kibbutz decide for themselves. Or perhaps you're doubting you're capable of living off the kibbutz at this stage of your life because you invested your formative years in doing things that have little marketable value off the kibbutz, or because of a general sense of impotence that comes from having your life so structured by a larger system for so many years. Add an overlay of dwindling kibbutz ideology—how the history books and the rest of Israeli society tells you you're supposed to feel in this intentional and voluntary community and comparing that to the reality of your day-to-day existence in living with these people you sometimes are angry at and often feel hurt by. Does this sound like a recipe for envy? If so, what would it look like, feel like, and how might it be the same or different than the envy your brother or sister feels in the city?

Methodology

A review of the English and Hebrew psychology and sociology databases produced zero matches for "envy and the kibbutz," and my review of extant literature on the kibbutz revealed nothing specific to the topic of envy. I am aware of one book on emotions, including envy, which has a small section on envy on the kibbutz (Ben-Ze'ev, 2000, pp. 316–321) and this same author mentions it parenthetically in one other article (Ben-Ze'ev, 1992, p. 579). Therefore, this chapter is based on semi-structured interviews about envy with current and former kibbutz members, each of which lasted from 30 to 60 minutes. The goal was diversity of opinion; I spoke to men and women from six different kibbutzim, ranging in age from 34 to 85, in 17 interviews. I interviewed those who were born, raised in, and had never left the kibbutz; those who started on the kibbutz and moved to the city; some who started on the kibbutz, moved to the city, and then moved back to the kibbutz; and some who started in the city, moved to a kibbutz, and then moved back to the city.

The sampling is skewed in favor of kibbutz members living on collective kibbutzim (15 of 17 respondents, though only one-third of kibbutzim are today still collective) vs. a renewed kibbutz (just two of 17, while two-thirds of all kibbutzim today are renewed kibbutzim).

My reasoning for this is as follows: I am attempting to investigate envy in conditions of greater social equality. I am not attempting to give an accurate snapshot of the kibbutz of today. Therefore, I wanted to hear from people who still live or formerly lived in conditions of greater social equality to learn what happens to an emotion based on difference in a society based on equality. My assumption is that kibbutz members living on the earlier model of the kibbutz would be better able to provide this information.

All but one of the interviews were conducted in Hebrew, and all quotes that appear are my translations. I have changed all names and other identifying information to protect respondents' confidentiality.

Findings

Based on my interviews, the following themes emerged:

1. Every respondent agreed that envy exists on the kibbutz
2. The majority of respondents felt that envy is, if anything, stronger on the kibbutz than elsewhere.
3. Various factors unique to the kibbutz were suggested for why envy might be stronger on the kibbutz than elsewhere:
   a. The basic playing field is leveled between kibbutz members so small differences are more visible
   b. The kibbutz espouses an ideology of equality, which sets up an expectation that when it's not met is a cause for envy
   c. The ideology of equality can make standing out from the norm an opportunity for envious criticism
   d. The ideology of equality and calls for fairness and justice stemming from this ideology can often be a camouflage for envy
   e. There is tremendous interdependence between members on the kibbutz on multiple levels, and the friction this causes can both be a source of envy as well as a means of exacting punishment because of it

4. Of those who did not believe envy to be stronger on the kibbutz, but perhaps weaker:
   a. The primary reason given was that envy is a universal human emotion and therefore envy will be found on the kibbutz just like it is found elsewhere
   b. A secondary reason given was that because of the reduced economic disparity on the kibbutz there was less reason for envy.

Analysis

Let us now clump these separate points into major themes, and hear in respondents' words how they show up in everyday kibbutz life. I will also include some outside resources to place their views in a broader context.

1. Envy exists on the kibbutz: Some of the research literature and opinion pieces that decry envy in modern society blame capitalism for creating a system of haves and have-nots. Starting with Marx and Engels (1932/1988), who wrote that communism would create "the positive transcendence of private property, or human self-estrangement, and therefore the real appropriation of the human essence by and for man ... the complete return of man to himself as a social being," there exists a theory that an increase in economic equality would result in a decrease in envy in a more cohesive and healthy society. Even with the failure of communism to create a more just society, such views continue to be heard from the more liberal side of the political spectrum. As one contemporary writer (Wright, 1999) put it: "income inequality may be objectionable in part because it fractures community, generates envy and resentment and makes social solidarity more precarious." Foster (1972) writes about a system he calls "encapsulation," where:

> There are ... institutional forms more rigid than ceremonial systems that compel, or very nearly compel, an individual to adopt or conform to envy-reducing rules. I speak here of mechanisms that break complex societies into smaller, more homogeneous units.... In theory, if not always in practice, a major strength of an egalitarian society derives from the fact that since differences in access to good things are slight, envy is reduced to a level where it is not a seriously disruptive force in the society (p. 185).

According to these writers, a kibbutz, which is both a smaller and more homogenous society with few disparities in income, should have reduced envy as a result.

Opposing these views are those who remind us that we envy those who are most like ourselves and that therefore the smaller and more homogenous the society, the greater the envy. Schoeck (1966/1969) gives many examples of the debilitating effects of envy in smaller societies that were isolated by geography. Cooper (1982, p. 36) writes that "the tendency to compare is most marked among people at very similar levels of income, status, education and the like" and that "the removal of one occasion for envy merely makes people turn to some other dimension of comparison which then becomes a new occasion for envy."

By Schoeck's and Cooper's parameters, the kibbutz should become a hothouse of envy because there is a greater degree of economic equality than in most Western societies and because most kibbutzim are geographically isolated, since they were strategically placed on the borders or in outlying areas of Israel as part of the country's development (Near, 1992).

So who's right?

Not one respondent claimed that the kibbutz had eliminated envy, and the majority reported that in their view envy is even stronger on the kibbutz. When I asked Avi, who was born and lived until age 40 on a kibbutz, what he thought about the claim that eliminating economic disparity would eliminate envy, he responded as follows:

It [the notion that increased economic equality would decrease envy] is a simplistic conception of envy. It's simplistic for a few reasons. One reason is that you never will eliminate envy.... On the kibbutz, equality exists at the macro level, but there are small things that are different, and those small things take on meaning.... The second thing is that there is no equality in individual differences, which are the most important. So [for example] she's prettier, so what, so the ugly woman deserves more? It's a problem: she's smarter, achieves more, is more successful, what are you going to do? Give everyone the same salary? There's no equality on the individual level.

Martin Buber said that the problem [on the kibbutz] will be between people, and not on the economic front. And he's right. The problem on the kibbutz is that you don't have personal space. Less autonomy. That's why what's happening now in the new developments on the kibbutz [referring to the renewed kibbutz], are in general in my opinion in the right direction. That is that they will reduce the force of the feelings that everyone is mixed up with everyone, that everyone resembles each other, that everyone deserves like each other, but that in the area most important—in individual differences—people are all different.

2. Envy is Stronger on the Kibbutz than Elsewhere: Clearly, with all 17 of my respondents saying that envy exists on the kibbutz, it is safe to say that creating a structure of greater economic and social equality does not eliminate envy from human interactions. But could it reduce it? Not according to the majority of my respondents, who report that, if anything, envy is stronger on the kibbutz than off it. Why would this be so?

Naomi is in her mid-fifties. She was born and raised on the kibbutz, and then lived in the city for approximately 18 years until returning to the kibbutz in her mid-forties. She describes a few different reasons that contribute to envy's being stronger on the kibbutz than off it:

> I think what makes feelings harder on the kibbutz is the expectation that people will treat us better. . . . I think that on the kibbutz there's an expectation that people will understand us, will make allowances for us, like an expanded family. We expect that they'll cooperate with us; we have different expectations. Outside we know the world is cruel. Here on the kibbutz we have a different expectation. When it isn't met, then the shock, the anger, the disappointment—I don't know what—the sadness, the hurt is simply larger. You feel it more. . . .
>
> [But] on the kibbutz envy is not only for those who stand out. It's also for those who don't stand out. They're angry at them. "Why are they sitting at home and not working?" But I don't know if it's envy or just anger. A lot of time people feel taken advantage of. "He sits at home and doesn't work." But I'm not sure this is envy.

In her last comment, Naomi is putting her finger on the difficulty of differentiating between envy and resentment, a struggle that is noted throughout the envy literature (see, for example, Feather, 2015; Feather & Nairn, 2005; Miceli & Castelfranchi, 2007; Smith & Kim, 2007). Resentment is generally considered a less morally suspect emotion and therefore a more comfortable one to express openly. When I resent you, I tell myself it is because of something unfair in our respective situations, and this unfairness usually means you have something more than I, and I resent that.

One piece of research (Smith, Parrott, Ozer, & Moniz, 1994) might be applied to Naomi's examples of the kibbutz members who work less hard. The authors of this study focus on the nature of the hostility involved in envy vs. the hostility in resentment or injustice. They parse it as follows: The more objective the sense of injustice, the more vocal and explicit the hostility. The more subjective the sense of injustice, the less it would be expressed, presumably because of fears of social sanctions, such as being criticized for being envious.

Based on these findings, it would seem that Naomi's last example was resentment, because the hostility she reported was openly expressed. The confounding variable here is that there is a tremendous amount of social hostility openly expressed on every kibbutz I have ever visited and certainly on the one where I lived. I am repeatedly shocked when visiting kibbutzim by how readily people will speak negatively about others to just about anyone. Perhaps this is because people who are openly critical of each other feel justification, and therefore lowered social sanctions, for doing so. Certainly having equality as a guiding ideal would lend legitimacy to difficult feelings of comparison and create a greater willingness to vocalize them. If I were to give testimony as to what Naomi's example is, I would say "Both." It is resentment of people who don't seem to contribute as much to the kibbutz. It is envy of those same people for their ability to live the kibbutz life in a way that doesn't seem to involve so much strain.

Let's come back to Nathan, who spoke of the 4 x 4 at the opening of this chapter. Nathan gives more reasons why envy may be stronger on the kibbutz than off it, and his statements nicely demonstrate the similarity of dynamics between two entirely different kibbutzim—Naomi's kibbutz is small, poor, geographically isolated, and struggling demographically. Nathan's kibbutz is large, wealthy, centrally located, and so successful there's a waiting list to become a member.

On the kibbutz, because there's the pretension of equality, people are very sensitive to feelings of inequality. Besides that, it's a private decision. Someone who decides to be envious, it's personal. If a person decides to be envious, and to deal with what he has compared to others, on the kibbutz he'll be really miserable. Because there's a background ideology that justifies the envy and feelings of discrimination and injustice. In the city every person is responsible for his life, and what he achieves he achieves, and that's it. . . .

There's bitterness, for example, there's a lot of fomenting, the managers of the [kibbutz] factory, who work long hours and long days, and they see members who work less hard and much shorter days and are more free to be with their families and their children, so they're envious and they want some monetary compensation or car or some kind of benefit that will compensate them for their big investment that they're investing in the kibbutz. Otherwise they say they're financing the kibbutz and a lot of members are parasites. I think here's envy—it will be camouflaged as a demand for compensation. But it's envy. So members on the one hand want interesting and challenging work, important and a managing position, but on the other hand they're envious of those who have less responsibility and more time at home. There's that element. . . .

You would think when you get to this kibbutz that you've arrived in the Garden of Eden. But if you're not connected to your heart, it doesn't matter how much money you have, if there's no connection to the heart there's no Garden of Eden. . . . So long as the community was intimate—200 members, 300 members—But [this kibbutz] is already close to 900 members and 2,000 people. On one side the intimacy got lost, so a lot of time people aren't clear what we're doing with this equality. It's not the dream of long ago. So people are here for material reasons primarily. So a lot of the effort goes to the material. So there's a lot of envy that's connected to the material.

Nathan is broadening the question of envy on the kibbutz to a more existential one: What are we searching for as humans? Many people, in searching for a life of meaning, might be drawn to live in an alternative community like a kibbutz, hoping that in making such a choice their day-to-day existence will be infused with a greater sense of purpose. Utopian communities have been attempted in all kinds of shapes and sizes, in part to fulfill this yearning, and the kibbutz may be one of the more long lasting, if not the most successful. But what Nathan is reminding us of here is that an external structure of equality cannot eliminate a need to do an internal piece of work around our tendency to envy.

3a. Interdependence on the Kibbutz: As noted above, reciprocal responsibility is one of the main things that makes a kibbutz a kibbutz and different from other societies. The kibbutz takes it as an explicit part of its mandate that its members are responsible for each other and that those less productive because of age or infirmity have a right to live in the same society at the same level. The kibbutz has long aspired to the socialist ideal of each member giving according to her abilities and receiving according to her need. Even with more recent moves to differential salaries, for a kibbutz to stay a kibbutz, this element of reciprocal responsibility must remain in place, though there are now larger gaps in equity between members on the renewing kibbutzim.

This reciprocal responsibility and the communal living arrangements that support it should, according to the cross-cultural literature on envy, reduce the likelihood of envy occurring on the kibbutz. For example, Tan, Tai, and Wang (Chapter 11, this volume) write that

> individualistic cultures, which tend to be competitively oriented, should elicit more envy than collectivistic cultures, which tend to be more cooperatively oriented. Furthermore, in collectivistic cultures, envy is less likely to emerge when the envious target is perceived to be an in-group [e.g. kibbutz] member.

The interviews I conducted did not support these conclusions, however. What I found instead is that along with reciprocal responsibility comes a high degree of interdependence. I attempted to give examples for this above when writing about the multiple aspects of social propinquity. Many respondents I spoke with gave some painful example of how this interdependence could play out, when they or someone they cared about was forced to ask the kibbutz for permission, funding, or both for something an adult living in a city could decide for themselves. "The kibbutz," of course, is an institutional body composed of people, just like in English we might speak of "the system." The difference is that the people who make up the kibbutz are known in intimate ways by those who turn to them for help; and therefore, these interactions can be more charged and more prone to feelings of hurt, injustice, and envy.

Shlomit is in her fifties and has lived her entire life on the same kibbutz, though she acknowledges that for many years she envied those who left the kibbutz (her kibbutz-born husband refused to consider leaving). In talking about this interdependence and how it plays out for members who ask the kibbutz for different things, she said:

> There's a lot more dependency on the kibbutz than there is in the city. If you want to go off to study.... and if someone wants to do something sometimes he has to go to committee and be voted on and it requires a lot more of the agreement of other members. And I believe that dependency creates envy. Sometimes it creates an experience of justice, or of injustice. But let's say a person didn't get what he requested. It creates an experience of frustration and injustice and sometimes envy: "Why didn't I get it and someone else did?" Things are much more connected to each other as compared to the city. I think independence produces a lot less envy. I think if there's an experience of enough space, of enough resources, enough place for everyone it reduces the envy. You don't have to live comparing yourself to another.

In her interview Shlomit paints a picture of subtle colors and shadings on the kibbutz. There are issues that are intermingled, and at another point she also stated, "I don't only want to speak about the difficulty. I think there are also good things that occur on the kibbutz" and mentioned how even with all of its struggles, the kibbutz still is a more just society than the rest of Israel or the West. But included within these subtle shades is the green of envy, which she thinks might show up more strongly in the kibbutz picture than in a similar scene in the city, because there is a less overt competition for resources in the city.

Yocheved, who opened this chapter with the example of the disposable diapers, paints a picture of kibbutz interdependence in very stark colors:

> When I was pregnant [with my youngest daughter] I wanted to get an amniocentesis.[4] It cost 600 shekels [$150]. Listen to that amount. I had to go through a lot because I wasn't the standard age for them to authorize it. I had to go through committee after committee: the first medical committee, the second medical committee so they would authorize me those crappy 600 shekels. And my father saw me go through it, and saw me getting angry. Because I was working, and they'll tell me whether or not I can have an amniocentesis, and afterwards I have a deformed child? How much I cried over this and my father would say "Take the 600 shekels and do the test." And I said "No, I'm an adult, I work, why should I take money from you?" Today I think to myself, "what did I waste time on?" In the end the kibbutz agreed, but they nitpicked me with tweezers until they agreed. That's why I remember it so well. That's why now when I look back on it I remember why I got so mad and why it bothered me so much, that they don't understand me, but it also bothered me that I have to explain myself to other people. Something you and your spouse [in the city] could decide amongst yourselves in your kitchen.

I wasn't clear how something like what Yocheved just described could be envy-related. In explaining, she said that:

> I can tell you definitively that today for sure there's less envy in the city than I felt on the kibbutz. I live now in a community that has people who are very wealthy and there are also people like us, who do all right. And not for one minute do I compare, there's just not that dependency. I go to have coffee with people who own 15 houses, and I really don't care. I simply don't care. I'm not dependent on anyone.
>
> All the things that on the kibbutz seemed like the end of the world, why does someone go overseas[5] and I don't, today don't seem to me important

at all. It could be because I matured. But it could be because everyone lives in their own corner, at their own expense, and their needs are different each from the other. And you don't make those calculations all the time. On the kibbutz you're all the time comparing. Now I don't compare my neighbor's house or their garden or their car. I really don't, in all honesty. On the kibbutz you always compare.... You see these people [on the kibbutz], and who they are and what they are, you see what their abilities are, and what their ability is to get things they want.... My husband works from morning to night and they're loafing. And on top of this they tell me what to do—if I can get an amniocentesis or not. This connection, this dependency, this communal decision making, is the basis for comparing. Who are they to tell me what to do, what to buy, what is my order of priorities?

Let's finish this segment on interdependence and its impact on envy with a story from Ofra, a 70-year-old woman who has lived for the past 50 years on a kibbutz after marrying a "kibbutz son." A "kibbutz son/daughter" is someone born on a kibbutz, and when the kibbutz son or daughter stays on the kibbutz where they were born, it confers a particular lifelong status and identity.

My husband is an anthropologist. I was already a student when we were set to get married and I studied in Jerusalem. He wanted to study anthropology. The kibbutz told him, "No, no, no. If you want to study something, study to become a teacher." He said he didn't want to be a teacher. But in the end he went and studied to become a teacher and worked as a teacher in the kibbutz for three or four years and then he said he wanted to study anthropology. They told him "there's no point to study anthropology but okay, study anthropology and Bible" so that he could be a Bible teacher. In the end he studied just anthropology for his BA.

But you can't work with just a BA, you need at least an MA. In asking for permission to get his master's at the kibbutz general assembly, one of his classmates got up and said, "And how do I know, and how can you promise us, that after we pay for your studies in anthropology you'll come back afterwards and work on the kibbutz and you won't go someplace else to make money?" So someone else told this classmate "in anthropology you don't make money." The kibbutz didn't agree for him to get his MA in anthropology. They said "We don't need anthropologists."

We were ready to leave the kibbutz but then the person who was responsible for the committee on additional training said "We'll go to the university and speak with the anthropology department." And they went to the anthropology department in Tel Aviv and said, "Listen, the kibbutz didn't agree for him to study this year." It was supposed to be four days a week. The university agreed to save his spot if he would study one day a week. That was the compromise. Five days a week he worked as a gardener and one day a week he studied anthropology. And only the next year he went and studied four days a week anthropology. So I think that in this whole process of decision making there was envy mixed in. A lot of different things were said that show there was envy.... By the way, the same classmate who wanted him to make a commitment to return to the kibbutz left the kibbutz himself later.

To anyone attuned to kibbutz dynamics, there is an enormous amount of information in this last anecdote, which is why I like to use concrete examples to illustrate abstract principles such as "interdependence." Certainly, on the surface, we all can recognize the difficulty of needing to ask permission from others to follow your passion, as well as having to contend with comments from people who have known you your whole life who are trying to get you to conform to social norms—in this case, his classmate.

Just to suggest a few other elements that might not be as obvious: this almost certainly was a struggle for Ofra's husband within himself. He was born and nurtured in this kibbutz system, and being "*beseder*" with the kibbutz is enormously important to any kibbutz child, which probably explains why he agreed to be a teacher initially. *Beseder* in Hebrew literally means "in order," and it is an all-purpose word wielded on the kibbutz to mean whatever the speaker wants it to mean to induce social conformity. Questions of social value are determined based upon whether or not and how much they are *beseder*. This produces a community of people who genuinely try to do the right thing for the collective good while struggling to find a *beseder* way to express their individual aspirations as well. The best English equivalent would be "appropriate," a word that means essentially whatever the speaker determines is appropriate for the situation.[6]

Yet a further layer here is the justification of the kibbutz. Anyone living in the city and needing to finance her own studies would need to make a careful calculation as to whether a degree in anthropology made financial sense. Why shouldn't the people in charge of the kibbutz's study funds make a decision based on similar parameters? Wouldn't they be irresponsible if they didn't? This particular person in charge of kibbutz studies, perhaps because of the threat of losing a kibbutz son and his wife—which would undoubtedly have alienated her from the kibbutz son's parents, siblings, and friends—took the added step of going with him to the university to work out a compromise. This appears to have salvaged the situation. Yet it is also infantilizing to have to bring your "kibbutz mommy" to the university where you want to study your MA.

Finally, these committee discussions are public and are discussed further the next day on the kibbutz sidewalks and in the kibbutz dining room, with members aligning themselves along various lines of social or ideological affinity.

I mention just a few of these dynamics more explicitly in order to help the reader appreciate some of the intensity of experience that is possible on the kibbutz that would never occur, or would occur in a more attenuated form, in the city. The kibbutz, in making reciprocal responsibility an explicit value, both corrects some of the egregious excesses of our more capitalistic societies and creates some issues of its own in the process. According to respondents, an increase in envy between kibbutz members may be one such issue.

3b. Envy Camouflaged as Ideology: According to respondents, envy on the kibbutz is frequently camouflaged by ideological outrage. One brief example comes from Mira, a woman in her early seventies who lived most of her life on a kibbutz before leaving at a late age to live in the city. Her story also contains that common kibbutz refrain of who works harder and who doesn't:

> I remember a classic example of envy on the kibbutz. There weren't yet TVs on the kibbutz, and a new family arrived at the kibbutz and brought with them a television. They were given two options: either to put it in the community center for all the members to watch or to put it under the bed and not to watch it at home. People who said it may have thought it was social justice, but for us common folk, who don't think all day about social justice—and let's acknowledge that on the kibbutz there were a lot of other social distortions a lot more significant—we see in it envy. If someone really thought about social justice they would have thought of other things: equality in work for example. There was no equality in work. Some worked hard and some didn't.

Another example comes from Nitzan, who first talks about why she thinks envy is stronger on the kibbutz before explaining how ideology may be used to cover it. Nitzan is in her mid-sixties and has lived for the past 40 years on the kibbutz. I asked her if she thought the kibbutz had succeeded in reducing envy because of the increase in equality:

> I think the opposite. In the city you don't compare yourself to anyone else. Whatever you have is whatever you have. At least at the individual level,

not the political level. On the kibbutz, because of the declaration that we're all equal and we all know we're not, it accentuates the comparison. And because of the comparison there's envy. . . .

There's more envy on the kibbutz because of the gap between what's declared and the reality. There are these classic kibbutz stories: how this one brought a teakettle, and how that one brought nice clothes in his suitcase, these are the kibbutz classic myths ... how all the members went nuts—why should this person have that? Or someone who got a shirt from the U.S. or overseas and kept it. It could be that [these discussions] were under cover of ideology but there's a good chance it was envy, which would reduce the value of the ideology.

Certainly, the vast majority of kibbutz members complaining about inequality, whether it was of someone having a bicycle in the 1950s or a private car today, would claim and perhaps believe that their complaint is based on issues of justice, equality, reciprocal responsibility, or some other value that is an explicit part of the kibbutz charter. How could we tell what's talking—ideology or envy?

Ben-Ze'ev (1992) suggests that one way to discern whether it's genuine outrage over inequality or simply envy speaking is to see whether or not the person complaining attempts to right a systemic wrong or simply carps about individual deviations from the norm. In other words, in Mira's example of the TV set or Nitzan's example of the shirt in the suitcase, someone genuinely concerned about upholding kibbutz values would suggest a community-wide process to establish parameters for how to deal with individual material goods brought in by new members from off the kibbutz: a guiding set of principles to govern how to handle the inevitable challenges of upholding kibbutz ideology. That is, the person genuinely concerned about inequality would attempt to do something about it at a broader level. Someone who is simply envious will speak negatively about the person or the item the person has, and do nothing further. Based on this criterion and the information we have in these two anecdotes, they may indeed be examples of envy dressed up as ideology.

An interesting twist on the role of ideology and envy comes from Arnon, a 34-year-old kibbutz son who now lives in the city teaching special-needs children:

I think that in the city envy is a kind of feeling that comes from not being able to do something, or being unlucky compared to someone else. You were born in place where you don't have and someone else does. Or you're born in a place where you're not able to actualize yourself and someone else is able to do so.

On the kibbutz, you envy someone who blows off the system, the ideals. As opposed to someone who tries to uphold the ideals and strives for equality, who's not able to hold himself apart from the standards of the community, and it's hard for him to see someone else who's able to do so. On the kibbutz it's more a question of ideals and ethics and belief in the path and frustration in how these are or are not being upheld. In the city it's more about frustration that comes from not being lucky or able. On the kibbutz you have the chance to be more than everyone else. It's easy. Everyone gets the same amount and to have more you only need to work on a Friday afternoon at some other place in the city and already you have more. Or you take your inheritance and spend it. Already you would have more. You don't have to invest that much so that you would have more.

On the one hand I envy them, on the other hand I say I couldn't do it—there's nothing for me to envy. It would be hard for me to live with myself doing something like that. But they are able to do it. It's like envying a tycoon who's capable of living off a whole city where he employs the whole town at a minimum wage for his cash cow factory. I can't see myself doing it, but the fact that he's able to do so causes me envy because of what he has.

What I appreciate about Arnon's quote is that from the outside, simply hearing him speak about people who "blow off the system" and work off the kibbutz for extra money, one could conclude that this is another example of a person using ideology as a cover for his envy. But because Arnon explicitly acknowledges his envy ("On the one hand I envy them, on the other hand I say I couldn't do it") it's easier to accept his moral outrage as just that: a rejection of the lack of "walking the talk" of the kibbutz ideology, even while admitting "I can't see myself doing it, but the fact that he's able to do so causes me envy because of what he has."

3c. Standing out from the norm as a cause of envy: When I lived on the kibbutz there was a saying that would be used, with some bitterness, about the "need to cut the grass to a uniform height." This meant that standing out from the norm would result in getting mowed down in one way or another. There is a similar expression in Australia and New Zealand, called the "tall poppy syndrome" (Feather, 1999; Mouly & Sankaran, 2002). A "tall poppy" is anyone who stands out because of rank, success, good looks, or any other characteristic that might incite envy in other people. To "tall poppy" someone is to cut this person down to size, and "tall poppy syndrome" refers to the tall-poppying of tall poppies. It is interesting how both metaphors describe the cutting down of something natural and beautiful to a uniform height so that a human-made sense of order and aesthetic is imposed.

Schoeck (1966/1969) reports a multitude of frightening examples of the destructive force of envy within small communities in many different cultures. It is his thesis that the reason these isolated communities inevitably were backward technologically (and possibly culturally, depending upon one's perspective) was because innovation was squelched by the villagers' ubiquitous fear of the envy of their neighbors.

According to authors Hitokotu and Sawada (Chapter 12, this volume), Japan also strongly emphasizes the social desirability of being normal (*fu-tsuu*). The Japanese *fu-tsuu* may correspond to the Hebrew *beseder* defined earlier. But these authors suggest that standing out from the norm creates internal tension in Japan and being "normal" is not just a social ideal but ego-syntonic at the individual level as well. Based on my interviews, it does not appear that this normalizing/*beseder* ethos has taken root quite so deeply on the kibbutz as it has in Japan, which has thousands of years of cultural history compared to the 100+ years of the kibbutz.

Naomi was quoted earlier when discussing why envy might be stronger on the kibbutz than off it. In explaining this further, she also said:

> When I think about the kibbutz, what increases the envy paradoxically is the aspiration that all of us will be alike, that we'll all be equal, that we'll all be the same. The attempt to bring equality and to make us alike, actually that attempt to do so, it increases the envy even more. "Why are you not like all of us?" "Why all of a sudden do you give yourself permission to stand out?" In the city it's legitimate to be different, to stand out, to excel or not to excel.

One person who apparently was able to buck this dynamic is Yitzhak, a man in his late seventies who has lived since the age of 20 on a kibbutz. Because of his talents in business and economics, he has long been sought after by various organizations and companies outside the kibbutz and has therefore lived a different kind of kibbutz life than the norm, involving frequent travel overseas, a car to get to his various jobs in the city, and other perks of a corporate lifestyle. He speaks first about how the kibbutz creates a set of equal opportunities, and then what happens when people see themselves in unequal places despite these equal opportunities:

> What the kibbutz can definitely give people, especially kibbutz kids, and every kibbutz member from the standpoint of what the kibbutz provides him, is the platform to achieve in maximal ways his potential. Up to this point it's potential.... At the end of things, the gap between the definition of a kibbutz wanting to create equality between people and the reality doesn't allow for a reduction of envy. The gap between definitions and reality, is that if people would have illusions that things should be different, it then increases the feelings of frustration and envy and begrudging (*tzarut ayin*[7]). People have their house, the education from their parents, the community supporting the family, and on top of that the kibbutz can give them the same opportunities, an equal starting point, but in life the manifestation is very different and the collective doesn't give them an excuse and then it creates these feelings. The fact is some have a lower than average IQ and some way above. So in the end wherever you put a person after a period of time you're going to see differences. Most people are aware of these differences and amongst other things you're going to have feelings of frustration and envy. There's nothing to do about it....

When I asked Yitzhak if he ever felt the object of envy from others on the kibbutz because of his achievements off the kibbutz, he answered:

> I'll put it to you like this: Of course envy is a characteristic of humanity and it exists in every society, including the kibbutz. I'm a person who's very satisfied with my functioning my whole life and deal with my things and I don't devote time to what people think, or if they envy me or don't envy, or if they're angry or not angry. I'm a satisfied person, and free of complexes. I deal with my own stuff, period. I don't get stuck in conversations of local gossip; it's a waste of time.... On what do they waste their time, these people on the margins? They're frustrated and it causes them to be stingy, envious, and that's how they explain their problems. But that's their issue. That's not where I invest my time. That's their problem.

In a follow-up email exchange, I asked Yitzhak if it would be right to assume that his ability to succeed so brilliantly in the larger world while living in a small and sometimes envious community was connected to this capacity to ignore the envy of others. Researchers have found that people high in "sociotropy" (excessive concern with pleasing others) experience distress when they outperform others (Exline & Zell, 2012). Yitzhak responded as follows:

> I would both validate and complete that assumption. A person's attention is limited and it's simply a waste of time, which is a very rare commodity, to give it to the random disturbances [of people's envy] which don't advance anything.

4. Envy is not Stronger on the Kibbutz but Perhaps Weaker: Not everyone I spoke with thought that envy was stronger on the kibbutz. A minority explicitly said it's weaker, and even those who thought it was stronger sometimes presented a more nuanced view than has been apparent thus far. Some people said one thing at the beginning of an interview and another at the end, and many of them hedged what they said with qualifiers such as "I'm not sure."

Let's start with one person who was very clear in his view that envy is weaker on the kibbutz than off it. David is in his mid-seventies and has been on the kibbutz nearly all of his life, arriving at the age of eight.

> I think in principle there's less envy on the kibbutz than off the kibbutz. And the reason is that the criterion that people use to measure themselves is much less toward others and much more relative toward themselves. And therefore there's not a very strong basis for envy. You have envy when you compare yourself to others. And it seems to me that kibbutz life, certainly in its ideal expression, has less envy.
>
> For example, during the period when I studied as a child on the kibbutz there weren't grades. But the judgement of the teacher on your work, of the assignment you turned in, was relative to your abilities. So a gifted child who would turn in mediocre work would get a comment in a red marker, "I think you can do better." And a weak student who would turn in something that was barely acceptable, but it was according to his abilities, the teacher would write, "I see you put a lot of work into this." In a society where the criterion for judgement is not others, but you yourself, your abilities, your needs, then there's less room for envy.... The closer you are to embodying the ideal of every person giving according to their ability, and receiving according to their need, the basis for envy of others shrinks....

There's greater economic and social equality [on the kibbutz]. Social equality, for example in the sense that it doesn't matter if you're a professor in the university or a mechanic in the garage you're the same status on the kibbutz. That's very different from the non-kibbutz society.... That's what's different: the equality of the person as he is.

Here we are given an example of a person for whom the kibbutz appears to have lived up to its aspirations as a more just society, with each member looking more inward than outward for a sense of value. Another example comes from Efrat, an 85-year-old woman who has lived on a kibbutz since age 14, after escaping from Europe toward the end of World War II. She spent many years as an educator in the local kibbutz elementary school, and some of her comments seem to echo David's:

You often don't know what causes tension between people because you're not their therapist, you only see it from the side. It can be that there are a lot of causes that create tension between people. Envy is one of the causes. I think that on the one hand, on the kibbutz or in education, we tried to minimize the envy between the children. We tried to tell each child that there's something they're good in. "You're good in this and he's good in that." We didn't encourage the envy in education. That's on one side. On the other hand, in Hebrew there's the saying "*kinat sofrim.*"[8] Something to encourage to achieve more, to do more. The envy challenges people to do more, to do things....

Not all children are the same. So you have to encourage them. You say, "Yes he's good in mathematics but you're very good in soccer." You need to do this in order to encourage them. Also the thing of equality, which is not absolute and can't be absolute, you need to explain it. And that's the way to explain the non-absolute equality. I remember one child I let do something and another child was upset and said "You told us we're all equal." But I answered "We're all equal in that we're all worthy. Every person is worthy. But you can't all be the same."

Maybe [there is less envy on the kibbutz], because there were at least equal opportunities for everyone. Maybe it shrunk the envy but it can't shrink it completely.... The opportunities were equal and I think that did increase the equality and that can minimize the envy.

I think what David and Efrat are gifting us with is a portrait of the kibbutz making a positive difference in how people treat each other. Clearly it hasn't eliminated envy, and the majority of the people I spoke with felt that, if anything, it increased it. But that is not the same as saying the kibbutz has had no positive impact on how people experience themselves day-to-day.

I believe David and Efrat are more right than many of the other respondents explicitly acknowledged, in that there is a certain baseline equality the average kibbutz member takes for granted that is different from the experience of a person living in the city. For example, at least before moving to differential salaries, those who worked on the kibbutz and in manual labor enjoyed a certain status of embodying the historic kibbutz ideal of returning to the land and self labor. No one need be embarrassed coming into the communal dining room in the kibbutz blue worker's uniform covered from head to toe in dirt from a day's work on a combine in the fields. If anything, such an appearance would be a status symbol, and the college professor in his clean city clothes at the same table would be the second-class citizen.

Furthermore, there is a certain baseline treatment of each other as equals that comes from having the playing field leveled out, a democratization of experience that causes most kibbutz-bred people to be less impressed by outside symbols of status, such as fame or money. This leveled playing field may even explain, to some extent, the degree to which kibbutz members feel free to criticize each other. No one is seen as better by standard criteria, no one is afforded automatic respect by positions of status or money, so people may feel more free to voice negative opinions.

Conclusion

The kibbutz offers a unique opportunity to look at envy. In its social and economic structure, there are two main differences from most of Western society, and each difference seems as though it would pull envy in a different direction. First, there is an increase in opportunities for comparison because of the greatly increased level of social propinquity. This would seem to increase the potential for envy. Second, the explicit mandate of the kibbutz is to equalize the social and economic standing of its members. Relative to most of Western society, even the kibbutz' greatest detractors would agree it has somewhat succeeded in these goals. This should cause a decrease in the amount of envy between its members.

But we have seen that, as Ben-Ze'ev notes (1992, p. 579), "Whatever social and moral advantages reduced inequality [on a kibbutz] has, reduced envy is not one of them." All 17 kibbutz members interviewed agree that envy exists on the kibbutz, and the majority feel that, if anything, it is even stronger. Why should this be so?

At the everyday level, I think it is safe to agree with what both Avi and Yitchak said in this chapter: the real issue with envy is the individual differences between people. That is, while you can more or less succeed at providing equality of opportunity and equality of distribution of material, you cannot equalize ambition, intelligence, or personality. These are innate to each person, and no amount of social engineering, whether in the Soviet Union, Cuba, or the kibbutz, is going to change that. It doesn't mean the different social structure is meaningless or has no effect on the day-to-day lives of the kibbutz members, and it doesn't mean that the kibbutz hasn't succeeded in better addressing some of the injustice of capitalist societies. But it does mean that an external structure cannot override innate internal differences. It appears that when these internal differences manifest in different external lives, the closer proximity of kibbutz members to each other increases the opportunity for envy. "Why is he able to work off the kibbutz?" "Why is she able to travel overseas for her job?" "Why are they getting to study?" The kibbutz also provides a ready ideology in which this envy can cloak itself, as it can be couched as an issue of injustice relative to the kibbutz ideals. But many kibbutz members interviewed felt that these ideological statements had their source, at least in part, in envy.

At a deeper level, I think what is most remarkable is how unremarkable these findings are: Envy remains an issue on the kibbutz just like it is in the rest of Western society. It gets reshaped into new contours and perhaps intensified by the different social and economic structure of the kibbutz, just as each organization and workplace will have its own particular variations on envy, as many of the chapters in this book explain. But envy on the kibbutz still remains essentially true to itself, in all its shape-shifting variability. The kibbutz simply creates new forms and situations in which it can appear.

I find something very meaningful and satisfying in this. If envy has been with us throughout all of recorded history, there must be some higher purpose to it, and this higher purpose cannot be obviated through external human social engineering. I come back to the thesis I mentioned earlier (Gressel, 2014): *Envy is not a sign that there is something wrong with you. It is a sign there is something right with you that you aren't claiming.* To me, the fact that envy continues to exist in a situation of greater social and economic equality on the kibbutz simply means that we as human beings have enormous potential for internal growth. Our potential for growth will not be eliminated, no matter where we find ourselves, and the fact that we still envy our neighbor even when our social and economic standings are more equal simply reinforces my contention that the envy of your neighbor is not about the "thing," but about what the thing means to you on an internal level.

If we don't recognize the internal dimensions to the external things we envy, we will get myopically focused on objects that from an outside perspective can seem comical, whether it's disposable diapers or a new four-wheel-drive car in a country with no snow. We have both the ability to become conscious of the internal dimensions we envy, as well as the responsibility to do so. Rather than focus on why someone else shouldn't have what they have, we should focus instead on what we need to do to develop the internal parts of ourselves that are shouting "ouch" when we envy our neighbor or another kibbutz member. Without exercising that potential to learn the internal lessons from our external envy, we lose an opportunity to grow into a larger and truer version of who we were born to become.

Notes

1. A 4 x 4 refers to a four-wheel-drive vehicle. There is symbolic beauty in this example, as Israel gets almost no snow, so there is never an actual need for such a vehicle there.

2. "Propinquity" means closeness, and "social propinquity" is a term used in the social sciences to explain the effect that physical or psychological proximity has on people: usually causing a sense of attraction or relationship. Riding next to someone on an airplane, sharing an elevator or taxi, discovering you share a similar profession or hobby, or attending the same class, are all instances of social propinquity. It has been correlated with a wide variety of social phenomena, such as marrying someone from nearby (Davie & Reeves, 1939), friendship formation (Nahemow & Lawton, 1975), and the formation of community by neighborhood (Hipp & Perrin, 2009). Social propinquity is considered one of the major ingredients in envy formation: we must feel a sense of kinship or identification with a person before we will feel envy. Already in the eighth century BCE, Hesiod wrote: "Potter bears a grudge against potter, and craftsman against craftsman, and beggar is envious of beggar, the bard of bard."

3. I am using different language to expand upon what is elsewhere described as "benign envy." Benign envy is envy that inspires us to constructive emulation rather than the more negative emotional reaction we typically associate with envy (for more information on the distinction between the two types of envy, see, for example, Crusius & Lange, Chapter 4; Hoogland, Thielke, & Smith, Chapter 5; Sterling, van de Ven, & Smith, Chapter 3, this volume). I do not disagree with the current division of envy into benign and malicious subcategories. Yet I believe we should aspire to see *all* of our envy as potentially constructive. My thesis, therefore, is prescriptive rather than descriptive.

4. An amniocentesis is a medical test for pregnant women of older age where a small amount of amniotic fluid is extracted and used to test for the likelihood of genetic abnormalities.

5. The reader may wonder at the frequency with which overseas travel is mentioned as a source of envy by respondents. Israel is a small country, about the size of New Jersey. Because for most of its history it was impossible to travel to neighboring countries, the only way for an Israeli to get away would be to fly elsewhere. For decades this was a luxury only the wealthy could afford.

6. My wife, born and raised on a kibbutz, read an early draft of this chapter. When she got to this part, she said, "You write that the best English word for *beseder* is 'appropriate.' I always thought *beseder* meant 'good.'"

7. Hebrew contains a wonderful expression, *tzarut ayin*, for which we don't have an exact equivalent in English. It literally translates as "narrowing of the eye" and it means not only to envy but also to want the other person not to have what they have. It is stronger than envy and weaker than *schadenfreude* (taking joy in another person's pain) on the envy continuum. I have translated it as "begrudging."

8. *Kinat sofrim* translates loosely as "envy of scholars." In the Jewish religious world, this might mean that an exceptional Talmud scholar would inspire students and colleagues to achieve a comparable level of erudition. The closest English equivalent would be "emulation."

References

Ben-Rafael, E., & Topel, M. (2011). Redefining the kibbutz. In M. Palgi & S. Reinharz, Eds., *One Hundred Years of Kibbutz Life: A Century of Crises and Reinvention* (pp. 249–258). New Brunswick, NJ: Transaction Publishers.

Ben-Ze'ev, A. (1992). Envy and inequality. *The Journal of Philosophy*, *89*(11), 551–581.

Ben-Ze'ev, A. (2000). *The Subtlety of Emotions*. Cambridge, MA: The MIT Press.

Charney, I., & Palgi, M. (2011). Reinventing the kibbutz: The "community expansion" project. In M. Palgi & S. Reinharz, Eds., *One Hundred Years of Kibbutz Life: A Century of Crises and Reinvention* (pp. 259–270). New Brunswick, NJ: Transaction Publishers.

Cooper, D. (1982). Equality and envy. *Journal of Philosophy of Education*, *16*(1), 35–47.

Davie, M., & Reeves, R. (1939). Propinquity of residence before marriage. *American Journal of Sociology*, *44*(4), 510–517.

Foster, G. (1972). The anatomy of envy: A study in symbolic behavior. *Current Anthropology*, *13*(2), 165–202.

Exline, J., & Zell, A. (2012). Who doesn't want to be envied? Personality correlates of emotional responses to outperformance scenarios. *Basic and Applied Social Psychology*, *34*(3), 236–253.

Feather, N. (1999). Judgements of deservingness: Studies in the psychology of justice and achievement. *Personality and Social Psychology Review*, *3*(2), 86–107.

Feather, N. (2015). Analyzing relative deprivation in relation to deservingness, entitlement and resentment. *Social Justice Research* 28:7–26.

Feather, N., & Nairn, K. (2005). Resentment, envy, schadenfreude, and sympathy: Effects of own and other's deserved or undeserved status. *Australian Journal of Psychology*, *57*(2), 87–102.

Greenberg, Z. (2011). Kibbutz neighborhoods and new communities: The development of a sense of belonging among the residents of new community neighborhoods on kibbutzim. In M. Palgi & S. Reinharz, Eds., *One Hundred Years of Kibbutz life: A Century of Crises and Reinvention* (pp. 271–288). New Brunswick, NJ: Transaction Publishers.

Gressel, J. (2014). *Embracing envy: Finding the Spiritual Treasure in Our Most Shameful Emotion*. Lanham, MD: University of America Press.

Hipp, J., & Perrin, A. (2009). The simultaneous effect of social distance and physical distance on the formation of neighborhood ties. *City and Community, 8*(1), 5–25.

Marx, C., & Engels, F. (1988). *Economic and Philosophical Manuscripts of 1844.* (Trans. M. Milligan.) Amherst, NY: Prometheus Books. (Original work published 1932.)

Miceli, M., & Castelfranchi, C. (2007). The envious mind. *Cognition and Emotion, 21*(3), 449–479.

Mouly, V., & Sankaran, J. (2002). The enactment of envy within organizations. *The Journal of Applied Behavioral Science, 38*(1), 36–56.

Near, H. (1992). *The Kibbutz Movement: A History, Volume I*. Oxford, UK: Oxford University Press.

Nahemow, L., & Lawton, M. (1975). Similarity and propinquity in friendship formation. *Journal of Personality and Social Psychology, 32*(2), 205–213.

Palgi, M., & Getz, S. (2014). Varieties in developing sustainability: The case of the Israeli kibbutz. *International Review of Sociology, 24*(1), 38–47.

Palgi, M., & Reinharz, S. (2011). The kibbutz at one hundred: A century of crises and reinvention. In M. Palgi & S. Reinharz, Eds., *One Hundred Years of Kibbutz Life: A Century of Crises and Reinvention* (pp. 1–14). New Brunswick, NJ: Transaction Publishers.

Pauker, A. (2011). The early roots of a later crisis—the kibbutz crisis of the 1980s and its roots at the time of the establishment of the state of Israel. In M. Palgi & S. Reinharz, Eds., *One Hundred Years of Kibbutz Life: A Century of Crises and Reinvention* (pp. 19–32). New Brunswick, NJ: Transaction Publishers.

Russell, R., Hanneman, R., & Getz, S. (2013). *The Renewal of the Kibbutz*. New Brunswick, NJ: Rutgers University Press.

Schoeck, H. (1969). *Envy: A Theory of Social Behavior* (Trans. M. Secker & Warburg Limited) Indianapolis, IN: Liberty Fund. (Original work published in 1966.)

Smith, R., & Kim, S. (2007). Comprehending envy. *Psychological Bulletin, 133*(1), 46–64.

Smith, R., Parrott, W., Ozer, D., & Moniz, A. (1994). Subjective injustice and inferiority as predictors of hostile and depressive feelings in envy. *Personality and Social Psychology Bulletin, 20*(6), 705–711.

Wright, E. (1999). Real utopian proposals for reducing income and wealth inequality. Retrieved April 3, 2015, from http://webcache.googleusercontent.com/search?q=ca che:yXk5b1zAvSYJ:https://www.ssc.wisc.edu/~wright/Inc-equal.pdf+&cd=3&hl=e n&ct=clnk&gl=us

18 | Envy and Inequality in Romantic Relationships

AARON BEN-ZE'EV

The flower which is single need not envy the thorns that are numerous.

—*Rabindranath Tagore*

Introduction: The Nature of Envy

The Major Concern: Undeserved Inferiority

Envy is a very common emotion, yet its basic characteristics are disputable. Two major issues are prominent in envy: inferiority and undeservingness. There have been disputes regarding whether envy is concerned with the other's superior position or with the subject's inferior position, and whether envy is concerned with the deserved or undeserved position of either the other or the subject. Thus, following Aristotle, Adam Smith believes that the other's deserved superiority underlies envy, and argues that "Envy is that passion which views with malignant dislike the superiority of those who are really entitled to all the superiority they possess" (1759, p. 244). In contrast, Descartes emphasizes the unwarranted position of others: in envy, "we judge the others unworthy of their good" (1649, art. 62).

This chapter discusses the nature of envy in the small social group (or organization) of romantic relationships. I first analyze the nature of envy and argue that the major concern in envy is neither *our deserved inferiority* nor *the other's (undeserved or deserved) good fortune*. Envy is rather mainly concerned with *our undeserved inferiority*; hence, two main sub-concerns can be detected in envy: the inferiority concern (expressing the more general comparative concern in emotions), and the undeserved concern (expressing the more general equity concern in emotions) (Ben-Ze'ev, 2000, Chapter 10). In the following sections, I will further support this claim.

Our relative inferiority (or deprivation), rather than all types of inferiority, is what bothers us most in envy. A rich person can be envious of another person's having a bit more, and a beautiful movie star can be envious of another star's beauty. Accordingly, enviers want to be *better* more than they want to be *better off*. The notion of relative deprivation implies a distinction between the objective and subjective well-being of the agent, and the claim that the two are not isomorphically related; sometimes the better-off from an "objective" viewpoint feels subjectively worse off. It is often true that those who are the most deprived in an objective sense are not the ones most likely to experience deprivation (Crosby, 1976; Stouffer et al., 1949a, 1949b). The centrality of the notion of relative deprivation in envy is another indication of the significance of the presence of both the inferiority and the equity concerns in envy (Smith et al., 1994). Equity considerations are also salient in the workplace (see, e.g., Pepper, Gosling, & Gore, 2015, for the role such considerations play among senior executives).

The Inferiority Concern

Closeness is a crucial element in determining emotional relevance. Greater closeness typically implies greater significance and greater emotional intensity. Closeness sets the conditions for meaningful relationships and comparisons. Closeness may be broken down into two factors: (a) similarity in background—for example, biological background, place of birth, education, significant experiences, and opportunities; and (b) proximity in current situation—for example, proximity in time, space, age, status, salary, or possession of a certain object (Ben-Ze'ev, 2000, pp. 132–134).

Claiming that our undeserved inferiority is at the heart of envy stresses the importance of the comparative concern in general, and of closeness in particular, in envy. Greek poet Hesiod wrote that "the potter is angry with the potter and the craftsman with the craftsman, and the beggar is jealous of the beggar" (Evelyn-White, 1914, II, 24). Aristotle argued that we envy those who are near us in time, place, age, or reputation (Aristotle, *Rhetoric:* II, 10). In envy, our attention is focused on those perceived to be immediately above us, since these people occupy the first rungs we will have to climb on fortune's ladder. These are the people we are most likely to be compared with or whose accomplishments are most likely to demean us. Jon Elster (1991) describes this as "neighborhood envy." When there is a great difference, we cannot conceive of ourselves as being similar to the fortunate person, so we find it easier to accept the given situation; consequently, we attach little emotional significance to the good fortune of those whose situation seems very different from ours.

Like other emotions, envy is partial and addresses people of emotional significance for us. We neither compare ourselves with everyone, nor do we compare everything. We do not envy those who succeed in areas insignificant to us; or we may envy only one aspect of another person, continuing to consider ourselves superior in general. We may envy someone for being rich, but if we know this person to be dishonest, we consider ourselves superior.

Although envy typically exists between people who are close to each other, in very close relationships envy may not exist, or at least not in its malicious form aimed at harming the superior person. The social comparison underlying envy requires not only closeness, which enables placing the two parties in the same comparative framework, but also a certain distance, enabling us to see them as distinct. As social comparison is chiefly limited to those who are similar and close to us, envy should be more typical of smaller subject–object gaps where the issue of deservingness is indeed more prominent.

The Undeservingness (Inequity) Concern

According to the equity theory, people feel most comfortable when they are getting exactly what they deserve from their relationships—no more and certainly no less. They are most content when they consider that they are getting roughly what they deserve from life (and love). If people feel over-benefited (receiving more than they deserve), they may experience pity, guilt, and shame; if under-benefited (receiving less than they deserve), they may experience anger, sadness, and resentment (Hatfield, Rapson, & Aumer-Ryan, 2008; Hatfield et al., 1985; Hatfield, Walster, & Berscheid, 1978). The combination of the comparative and equity concerns is significant in the workplace as well (see, e.g., Duffy et al., 2012; Folger & Cropanzano, 2001; Taris et al., 2001).

The perceived deservingness of our situation or that of others is of great importance in determining the nature and intensity of emotions. No one wants to be unjustly treated, or to receive what is contrary to one's wish. The characterization of deservingness is complex due to its similarity to, yet difference from, *moral entitlement*. Entitlement requires *eligibility* and satisfying some *general* rules, whereas deservingness requires satisfying certain conditions of *personal worthiness,* which are not written down in any legal or official regulation. Claims based on *moral right* refer to some mode of *treatment* by other persons, whereas claims of *desert* also refer to the *fairness* of the situation. When we perceive our situation to be undeserved, we do not necessarily accuse someone else of criminal or immoral behavior; we assume, however, that for us to be in such a situation is in some sense unfair.

Claims of desert, such as "I deserve to win the lottery," are based on our sense of the value of our attributes and actions; claims based on moral right, such as "She is entitled to receive a raise in her salary," often refer to obligations constitutive of the relationships with other agents. Claims of desert are not necessarily grounded in anyone's obligations, but rather in the value persons perceive themselves to deserve. Claims of desert are based on *perceived* undeserved or deserved situations that are not necessarily undeserved or deserved in a more objective sense. Perceived undeserved situations may be due to impersonal, arbitrary circumstances. Being unlucky may not involve any criminal or immoral deeds or attitudes of a particular agent, but the unlucky person may still be right to regard bad luck as undeserved. It is not immoral for a rich person to win a big prize in the lottery or to marry another rich person; nevertheless, many poor people may consider it to be unfair. Similarly, being born with a handicap may be considered unfair in the sense that no-one deserves such a misfortune, but it does not entail a criminal or immoral deed.

The feeling of undeserved inferiority in envy may stem from: (a) Perceived or actual immoral *behavior* by the superior agent (or by those made the agent superior); and (b) Unfavorable *background circumstances* of the inferior agent. In both cases, the agent feels undeserved inferiority, but whereas in the first case the agent considers the other person to be undeserving of her superiority, in the second case the other person may be considered to deserve her superiority.

Take, for example, a situation in which two people are competing for an academic prize. In the first case, the winner receives the prize, not because he has better publications, but because two of the judges are his friends. In the second case, the winner's publications are indeed better, and the envious agent is fully aware of this superiority and believes that the winner deserves the prize. However, the agent may attribute her failure to have achieved similar publications to her unfavorable background circumstances, such as an inferior education or time spent on family responsibilities, raising children, or taking care of an elderly parent. In this situation, though the other deserves the prize, the agent still envies the other and considers her own situation to involve undeserved inferiority.

Benign and Malicious Envy

Various classifications of the different types of envy have been suggested (Cohen-Charash & Larson, Chapter 1, this volume). The most relevant classification for my discussion is that which distinguishes between benign and malicious envy (Lange & Crusius, 2015; Sterling, van de Ven, Smith, Chapter 3, this volume). In both types of envy, there is the desire to eradicate one's inferiority, especially since this inferiority is perceived to be undeserved. As indicated above, the other's superiority may be considered deserved; nevertheless, the agent might still regard his own overall situation as undeserved. The main difference between the two types is in their motivational component regarding how to eliminate this sense of inferiority. Malicious envy is associated with the motivation to harm the position of a superior other, and benign envy is associated with the motivation to improve oneself by moving upward (van de Ven, Zeelenberg, & Pieters, 2009). This motivational difference is expressed in other aspects; for example, the cognitive component may differ as well. Thus, while within malicious envy the cognitive system is geared more strongly toward the other person than toward the superior fortune of the other, within benign envy, the cognitive system is geared toward the agent's opportunities to raise his or her own position (Crusius & Lange, 2014).

Malicious envy includes a profoundly hostile attitude; it is nicely illustrated in the proverb, "The envious man thinks that he will be able to walk better if his neighbor breaks a leg." Benign envy involves a positive attitude toward the other, but a negative attitude toward one's own situation; hence, a non-acceptance of the situation. A romantic relationship in which malicious envy is present is likely to be very low in its quality and survival chances. The presence of benign envy expresses a better quality of romantic relationship, but here, too, the agent's attitude toward her own situation is negative. Only when the person who is in the inferior position (in a particular aspect) admires his partner's superior position can we describe their romantic relationship as good.

Malicious envy is typically associated with a situation in which the agent perceives the other's superiority as undeserved and sometimes even immoral. Benign envy is usually related to a situation in which the other's superiority is perceived as deserved, though the agent's own situation is still regarded as undeserved.

Malicious envy is related to the emotion of resentment, while benign envy is related to the emotion of admiration. *Resentment*, which is a kind of moral protest against perceived injustice, is often associated with both anger and (malicious) envy. Resentment can either stand on its own or be part of the emotional experience of envy (and other emotions, such as frustration). Thus, one can say that someone resents the immoral behavior of a certain politician. In this case, resentment is less personal than both envy and anger; hence, the feeling dimension of resentment is less intense. When resentment is part of the experience of envy, the issue of undeserved inferiority becomes central as well, and the whole experience becomes more personal and intense.

In the same vein, admiration can stand on its own or be part of the emotional experience of envy (and of other emotions, such as love). In both envy and admiration, the emotional object is superior to us, but in one case we evaluate this fact in a negative manner, and in the other, in a positive one. The difference in the evaluation mainly stems from the relevance to one's self-esteem; in envy, the relevance is significant (Salovey & Rodin, 1991); hence, we do not envy "trees for their height, or lions for their strength" (Spinoza, 1677, IIIp55c2s). In admiration, we perceive the other's good fortune as enhancing our self-esteem, a kind of basking in reflected glory, in which we feel that we share in the glory of a successful person with whom we are somehow associated (Cialdini et al., 1976). In envy, the subject–object relationship is characterized by high relevancy, great background similarity, and significant current proximity. In admiration, one of these factors is low. In typical admiration, relevancy to our self-esteem is low; therefore, we can enjoy the other person's success. A low degree of relevancy often stems from a low degree of proximity in current situation, although similarity in background may be high (Ben-Ze'ev, 2000).

To illustrate the difference between admiration and benign envy, I offer the following two examples. I admire Immanuel Kant for his profound philosophy, but I do not envy him. The gap between us is too great to be abolished, and in any case, I do not want to be in Kant's situation— for instance, I do not want to live my whole life in a small town, hardly ever leaving it. The second example involves a lecture I once gave about envy and pity in close relationships. In this lecture, I cited a Hebrew proverb stating that a man is never envious of his son or his pupil. (Some of us doubt if this is even remotely true concerning our pupils.) During the discussion period, Bernard Williams challenged the claim concerning the son, adding that he envies his son for bringing home a different girlfriend each weekend. I replied that his envy is benign, not malicious, as he does not want to harm his son's situation, but merely to promote his own. Nevertheless, Williams seems to have experienced envy, rather than admiration, and this envy may have indicated that he was sorry that he was not young anymore and is not able to date many women, as his son does.

The above differences in the motivational aspect may explain findings elucidating why benign envy, but not admiration and other emotions, is associated with upward social comparisons and stimulates better performance due to an upward comparison; this occurs only when people think that self-improvement is attainable. When self-improvement is difficult, an upward social comparison typically leads more to admiration than to motivation to do better. Thus admiration feels good, but it does not lead to a motivation to improve oneself (van de Ven, Zeelenberg & Pieters, 2011).

The dichotomy between feeling better and performing better does not exist in profound romantic love that involves admiration rather than benign envy. Unlike the case of admiring a stranger, which lacks the motivation to do better, in profound love, as I claim below, the central motivation is to enhance the joint togetherness of the couple, as well as the individual flourishing of each partner. In such love, there is a good combination of feeling good and the motivation to improve. This combination is absent in both benign envy and admiration from a distance.

Undeserved Inequality

Envy and Inequality

The centrality of inferiority and deservingness in generating envy emphasizes the role of inequality and inequity in envy. Inequality is often perceived to be negative. Thus, we speak negatively about the growing inequality between the rich and poor. In fact, a dictionary definition of *inequality* is "an unfair situation in which some people have more rights or better opportunities than other people" (*Merriam-Webster Dictionary*). Inequality is often expressed in socioeconomic terms as the gap between those who have and those who do not. Various egalitarian societies have tried to eliminate such gaps by allocating similar resources for fulfilling their members' basic needs, such as food, health, education, and living accommodations. The kibbutz movement in Israel is a prime example. Such equality, however, has not reduced, and in my view has even increased, the level of envy in the kibbutzim (Ben-Ze'ev, 1992; see also Gressel,

Chapter 17, this volume; Amos Oz, 2013, "Deir Ajloun"). Whatever the social and moral advantages of reducing inequality may be, a decrease in envy is not part of them. When social and economic gaps are large, the likelihood of resentment, rage, hate, frustration, and other types of negative emotional reactions is greater, since the moral violation is perceived to be greater.

One reason for the failure to eliminate or even to reduce envy in egalitarian societies is their inability to reduce the inequality associated with natural differences and impersonal causes. Since such inequality does not entail the immoral behavior or attitude of an agent, one cannot blame anyone for this situation. Nevertheless, the situation may still be considered unfair (Smith et al., 1994). We often envy beautiful people or those born with natural gifts. In feeling envious toward these people, we do not accuse them of behaving immorally, but rather consider ourselves to occupy an undeserved inferior position. The situations perceived to be unfair by envious people are often not perceived to be unfair by others.

The issue of equality has occupied a central place in moral discussions. Two major issues are more relevant to our discussion: (a) the nature of equal treatment, and (b) the realms and extent of the desired equality.

At the basis of the first issue is the question of whether inequality necessarily implies inequity. It seems that, in some realms, inequality does imply inequity, but in others, it does not. Mechanistic equality that involves giving an identical and equal amount to each person, irrespective of individual differences, is obviously unsatisfactory. Since people have different needs, it will be unfair to treat them as if they are identical. Indeed, the basic socialist ideal of "*From each according to his ability, to each according to his needs*" assumes a non-mechanistic treatment. At the essence of identical equal distribution is an ongoing comparison down to the last detail; therefore, it is likely to lead to frequent feelings of undeserved inferiority and hence to envy. A situation that ensures that both partners get enough, in the sense of having a sufficient baseline for thriving along with the thriving of the group, seems to be more beneficial for the relationship and for each partner's thriving, and it may reduce envy (Krebs, 2002, Chapters 3–5).

A more complex issue is that of the realm and extent of the desired equality. The egalitarian claim that it is desirable for everyone to have "the same" as other people (in terms of opportunities, money, and other goods) seems to be central to our notion of fairness and justice, though it is disputable. (For criticism, see, e.g., Anderson, 1999; Frankfurt, 1988; Krebs, 2002, Chapters 3–5; Narveson, 1997; Nozick, 1974; Nussbaum,

2013; Parfit, 1998; Raz, 1986.) Despite its obvious value in improving the situation of the poor, the claim that everyone should have the same is clearly wrong in many realms. Can we say that everyone should have the same amount of wisdom or beauty? Morality appears to require that basic needs should be sufficiently provided, but not that they will be distributed in an identical, equal manner.

Turning to the romantic realm, profound love is based on shared activities between two autonomous agents who together pursue the thriving of their group and of their own lives. In order to do this without feeling undeserved inferiority, which often leads to envy, they should have equality of *status*, and in particular ensuring that each partner has the status of a free, autonomous agent (Miller, 1995). Such autonomy and status equality would prevent a discriminatory attitude against the "weaker" partner (usually, the woman) and would impede or reduce the dominance of the "stronger" partner. It would oppose special status as well as special privileges. For example, a young woman dating a young man complained that, whereas he knew the code to her cell phone and computer, she was not allowed to have such information about his devices. Moreover, he continued to meet his ex-lover, but she was not allowed to be in touch with any of her ex-lovers. This is clearly an instance of immoral, unequal status.

Having equal status in the romantic relationship does not mean having a mechanical equality in which each gets and does precisely the same. Thus, Angelika Krebs criticizes egalitarian justice, in which distributive characteristics are comparative and not absolute: "An example for an absolute distributive standard is: no one should suffer from hunger; everyone should have enough to eat. The corresponding comparative standard is: everyone should have equal amounts to eat" (Krebs, 2014b; see also Krebs, 2002).

Krebs (2015) argues that a certain minimal respect for the autonomy of each lover and a certain minimum contribution from each are constitutive of the success of any cooperation, including the romantic one. If one of them does everything while the other sits back and watches, the partnership lacks both reciprocity and interaction. Love, Krebs claims, is thus a symmetrical form of sharing that can overcome differences in class, gender, or race. But symmetry does not imply a strict parity of give-and-take. If one partner loves the other more, he will want to give more, and there is nothing immoral about that. Such strict symmetry is not applicable in parental love. In a romantic relationship, each lover has to contribute, but not necessarily equally and not necessarily in the same way. Krebs further asserts that, whereas mutual support is to be expected in love, you cannot force everyone to love at the same depth, nor to express their love in the same way. However, no lover likes to be neglected (Krebs, 2015). I further discuss below the issue of romantic reciprocity.

Envy in Close Relationships

Envy Within the Family

I have shown the importance of closeness in envy, while indicating that significant psychological closeness may reduce, rather than increase, envy. The issue, however, is complex, as it depends on various contextual and personal factors. Thus, Tesser's (1988) Self-Evaluation Maintenance Model of social behavior suggests that one's self-evaluation may be raised when a close other performs very well on some activity; i.e., one can bask in the reflected glory of the close other's good performance. However, the outstanding performance of a close other can also cause one's own performance to pale by comparison and decrease one's self-evaluation.

In accordance with this model, parents do not usually envy their children's success since they typically consider them as part of their own success and not as something separate that threatens their self-image. However, when those close to us have succeeded in something essential to our own self-image, or when our ties with these people are not very close, envy may replace pride. Parents will usually not aspire to damage their child's position in order to reduce the inequality between them. If such malicious envy occurs, the parent–child relationship is probably not very close and might be malfunctioning. It is interesting to note here that envy is more likely to emerge in the attitudes of children toward their parents than vice versa. A major reason for this difference is that parents create their children and invest a lot in rearing them, whereas the parents are in a sense given to the children. Hence, it is more natural to be proud of your children's achievements than of your parents' achievements, most of which you have not contributed to, and some of which even took place before your birth.

Jealousy in Romantic Relationships

The emotion of jealousy, rather than envy, seems to be more frequent in the romantic realm. The two emotions are often confused, as both involve a negative evaluation of the good fortune of others. Indeed, in some languages, such as Hebrew, there is a single term for both these emotions;

in other languages, such as English, the meanings of the terms "envy" and "jealousy" often overlap, mainly because the word *jealousy* is used in the senses of both romantic jealousy and envy, while *envy* is used in one sense alone, as a social-comparison-based emotion (Smith, Kim, & Parrott, 1988). However, whereas at the basis of envy there is a negative evaluation of our undeserved inferiority, jealousy involves a negative evaluation of the possibility of losing something—typically, a favorable human relationship—to someone else. In envy, we wish for something that someone else has, while in jealousy, we fear that someone else will take something away from us. In contrast to envy, which is essentially a two-party relationship, jealousy is basically a three-party relationship (Parrott & Smith, 1993). The threat in jealousy may be either of completely losing our relationship with the partner, or of losing qualities of that relationship, even though the relationship itself may endure (Ben-Ze'ev, 2010).

Jealousy is typically associated with exclusive human relationships, whereas envy has no such restrictions. Jealousy is more personal and generates greater vulnerability than envy; it is more likely to cause profound injury to our self-esteem since it touches on far more significant aspects of our lives. The threat it carries is posed by a person with intimate and reliable information about us. The severity of that threat may explain why jealousy is so intense, despite the prevalence of sexual infidelity. The intense pain generated by jealousy is not because something extraordinary has happened, but because we may lose something of crucial importance to us. Similarly, although death is common and is expected, it nevertheless generates profound grief.

To illustrate the difference between envy and jealousy, consider the difference between the emotional attitudes of the husband and the lover. The husband's common emotion is jealousy, as he fears losing his wife to the lover. The lover's attitude is not typically one of jealousy, since the wife has not clearly chosen the husband over him; hence, the lover does not experience a loss to someone else. The wife's original choice was made long before she knew the lover, and there are typically objective difficulties in the current situation—related, for instance, to the couple's way of living, children, or financial matters—that hinder canceling her original decision. Accordingly, the lover may believe that the wife does not really prefer her husband to him. The lover's attitude is typically that of envy—being envious of the husband who has the superior situation of being with this woman more frequently. The lover may also feel that the situation is unfair to him, as the woman actually prefers him in terms of love. The husband is the primary partner time-wise and in other matters concerning their daily life together. However, the lover may consider himself to be the primary romantic partner. The lover's inferiority concerning living and spending time together may generate a feeling of inequity and hence of envy. (It seems, then, that contrary to the common assumption, lovers of married people do not always feel like they are living in paradise.) Envy and jealousy may not arise if both the husband and the lover are aware of their uniqueness and that their situations are incommensurate. From this point of view, neither of them is inferior, and neither is in an undeserved situation.

In jealousy, the way to maintain our self-esteem is by proving the suspicions groundless. Improving our situation in envy depends greatly on us; in jealousy, the partner's attitude is more significant. Thus, in the Bible, God is sometimes described as being jealous but not as being envious (in Hebrew, the same word is used for both); this is because God cannot be described as inferior. However, when God is said to be jealous of the people of Israel, this does not imply any flaw in God's behavior; the flaw is in the people of Israel, who, unable to distinguish between good and bad, preferred the false gods. Therefore, I assume that the motivation to improve ourselves is more salient for envy than for jealousy: whereas in jealousy there is often nothing to improve, in envy we can always improve our situation and decrease our inferiority. Moreover, in jealousy there is nothing accidental about what has been lost; rather, it is the result of the other's clear preference. This suggests that many jealous people do not treat their partners as inanimate objects that belong to them, but as free, responsible people who are able to make reasonable choices that are often impossible for us to change (Neu, 2000).

The cognitive element is usually more veridical in envy than in jealousy, as the threat in jealousy can be imaginary. Jealousy often involves fantasy. Marcel Proust compares jealousy to a historian without documents. Frequently, our jealousy does not die when we realize our error; any pretext whatsoever is sufficient to revive this emotion. Indeed, the most frequent event eliciting jealousy among married people is not actual infidelity, but involves the partner paying attention, or giving time and support, to a member of the opposite sex, and in particular to the partner's ex-spouse (Fitness & Fletcher, 1993).

Envy and jealousy involve unpleasant feelings. Jealousy is a more negative personal attitude, expressed in more intense desires and feelings and in being more aggressive than envy. Jealousy is usually more painful than envy because of its more personal nature, and because it is more difficult to bear the loss of something you have than not to gain something you never had. This means that the stakes in jealousy are higher, and the pain becomes worse.

Envy and Overall Status Inequality

Close relationships, such as friendship and romantic love—the ideal characterization of which includes disinterested care for the other who has his or her own intrinsic value—seem to be incompatible with the presence of envy. Nevertheless, the existence of the comparative and the inequity concerns in close relationships may generate envy.

In this regard, I suggest distinguishing between two major circumstances in which romantic envy may occur: (a) the partner is perceived to be *superior* to the subject, and the subject's envy concerns his inferiority to his *partner*, or (b) the partner is perceived to be *inferior* to the subject, or to other possible partners, and the subject's envy concerns *other people* who have a superior partner.

The two types of envy are illustrated in the following story that Robert Frank (2006) recounted about a woman who asked her colleague the following question: "Why is it that the people I fall in love with are never interested in me, whereas the ones who do fall in love with me are never the ones I care about?" Her colleague replied: "You're an 8 constantly chasing after 10s, and constantly being chased by 6s." Someone who is evaluated as "a 10" is superior overall to a person evaluated as "an 8," and if they are in a romantic relationship, the 10 will enjoy higher status.

The above two types of inequality give rise to envy. Concerning the first type, being in love with someone we admire, and even assuming her comparative superiority, gives us the good feeling of being close to such a person and sharing her virtues. We love to admire, be admired, and be in the company of those we admire. In this case, as we bask in the reflected glory of the other, our own self-worth may rise, too, as it is validated by the other's selecting us. Hence admiration, rather than envy, is generated. However, the beloved's superiority may generate envy if the superiority is in domains relevant to our self-esteem and if the close relationship constantly reminds us of our (perceived undeserved) inferiority. Indeed, various studies have revealed that satisfaction in close relationships is influenced by the global perception of doing as well as one's partner (Buunk & van Yperen, 1991; Rusbult & Buunk, 1993). Wishing to do as well as one's partner enhances the generation of envy.

The second case of envy in romantic relationships is when the partner is inferior to the subject and the subject is envious of her friend who has a better partner. Here the issue of undeservingness and the sadness for the road not taken are particularly evident. The fact that we see our partner as inferior to us or to another possible partner typically implies that we deserve a better partner and are actually in a situation of overall undeserved inferiority; this often invokes resentment toward the partner. This type of envy is expressed in the significant role that available alternatives play in close relationships. The presence of such accessible alternatives decreases the satisfaction from and commitment to your current relationship. Accordingly, one way to cope with this type of envy is to use the mechanism of derogating attractive and threatening alternatives (Drigotas & Rusbult, 1992; Johnson & Rusbult, 1989; Rusbult & Buunk, 1993).

The issue of undeserved inferiority in romantic relationships is illustrated in a study indicating that being in an undeserved position in your marriage may encourage extramarital affairs (Prins et al., 1993). This is the case for both the "superior" person, who feels that she could do better, and for the "inferior" one, who feels indignant at being unappreciated by the partner. Involvement in extramarital relationships is more likely for these "superior" and "inferior" people than for those who are considered equal to their partner. The superior person may perceive extramarital relationships as something she deserves because she is getting "less" than she would in other circumstances. The inferior person tends to be involved in extramarital relationships in order to (a) escape the unpleasant state of inequity and (b) prove to herself and to her partner that she actually is equal to the partner and is regarded as attractive and desirable by other possible partners (Prins et al., 1993). It should be noted that, although both the over-benefited and the under-benefited are less content than the equitably treated, the under-benefited are far less content than the over-benefited (Hatfield, Rapson, & Aumer-Ryan, 2008).

In a similar vein, it has been found that the person who stands to lose the most is apt to be the least likely to risk ending the relationship by having another sexual partner. Accordingly, if the woman has a higher level of education than her partner, she is more likely to risk the relationship by having a secondary sexual partner than if both members of the couple have equal levels of education (Forste & Tanfer, 1996). Furthermore, research indicates that feeling inferior (as well as superior) to one's partner is associated with less commitment, less satisfaction, and less love for the partner. The willingness to sacrifice for the partner is lower when reciprocity is absent (Murry et al., 2005; Impett & Gordon, 2008).

These considerations are compatible with Thibaut and Kelley's distinction between Comparison Level (CL) and Comparison Level for

Alternative (CLAlt) (Thibaut & Kelley, 1959). The first level refers to the way people feel they should receive in their given situation; the second level refers to the lowest level of relational rewards people are willing to accept, given their available alternatives. While CL mainly predicts the agent's satisfaction, CLAlt predicts the relationship's stability. The two types of comparison are related; thus, greater availability of alternatives may reduce the level of satisfaction. To the issues of satisfaction and stability, Rusbult (1983) added the idea of "investment that enhances commitment"; this addition takes into account situations in which, despite better alternatives, people choose to remain in a relationship because of great commitment.

The above claims are also relevant for organizations; for instance, in issues of turnover. In their discussion of job turnover, Rusbult and Farrell (1983) argue that

> the most important process of change in influencing turnover decisions is the process of declining commitment, although changes in rewards, costs, alternatives, and investments are all significantly related to stay or leave decisions, and although changes in each of these factors affects changes in job commitment, decline in job commitment appears to most directly and powerfully affect such decisions. (1983, p. 437; see also Farrell & Rusbult, 1981)

Similar conclusions pertain to the romantic realm (e.g., Rusbult, 1983; Rusbult & Buunk, 1993; see also Thibaut & Kelley, 1959).

A relevant issue in this regard is that of romantic compromises, in which we give up a romantic value, such as intense, passionate desire, in exchange for a non-romantic value, like living comfortably without financial concerns. The main issue in these compromises is not merely, or even mainly, whether one is superior to the other, but whether you can get a better deal somewhere else. Romantic compromises are mainly about giving up pursuing more alluring and accessible alternatives. In being with those who you feel are equal to you, you prevent the feeling of inferiority toward your partner as well as toward those who have a higher-level partner (Ben-Ze'ev, 2011).

Generally, inequality might give rise to great admiration in the short term; hence, it may increase the initial love and sexual desire. However, in the long term, significant inequalities become a problem for both sides, whereupon superficial short-term goals (such as being in a relationship with a famous person) become less important. For example, the "higher status" person may begin to show a lack of reciprocity, which will eventually damage the "lower status" person's love and may generate envy, jealousy, resentment, and anger.

The situation is made more complicated by the fact that the extent of the gap and the overall comparative value of each partner also play a part. Feeling bad about an inequality in a certain domain, such as wisdom, can disappear if the overall comparative value is perceived to be similar. In these circumstances, the partner's inferiority in one domain is compensated for by superiority in another. Thus, when people are certain of their worth, they may prefer a partner who is a bit superior to them in one domain and hence will be more beneficial for them. In this case, admiration may be the relevant emotion. For example, in one study, 89% of high-achieving men report that they'd like to marry or have already married a woman who is as intelligent as they are, or who is more so (Whelan, 2006). These men believe that in marrying such a woman they have made the better deal. Inequality in a certain field, such as intellectual capacity, can be compensated for by profound quality in other area; for instance, kindness and caring.

The presence of envy in romantic relationships is destructive to the bond between the partners. Thus, in a comprehensive study of envy, Smith and Kim (2007) argue that envy, which is associated with feelings of inferiority, hostility, and resentment, is correlated with poor physical and mental health. Envy is destructive to one's well-being: it is "negatively correlated with self-esteem and various measures of life satisfaction and positively correlated with depression, neuroticism, hostility, and resentment." The harmful effects of envy extend to physical health: "Low status can reduce people's ability to control and cope with chronic stressors, which then takes its toll on physical health through a variety of possible processes" (Smith & Kim, 2007).

Inequality in Romantic Involvement

"If equal affection cannot be, Let the more loving one be me."

—*W. H. Auden*

So far, I have mainly referred to overall and status inequality; i.e., to the perceived status of each person, and, accordingly, to the role of each partner in the decision-making process. I have shown that this inequality is destructive to romantic relationships. Another type of inequality that I discussed is a distributive inequality, in which the received benefits are unequal. This inequality is a greater problem in society at large than in the small organization of the family, where the ideal of "From each according to his ability, to each according to his needs" can be fulfilled to a greater extent. This also implies that if one partner is currently very busy at work, she may within the family organization be given more (e.g., free time) contribute less (e.g., having a smaller share in the household work).

I will now turn to examine in more detail another type of inequality—one that is unique to romantic relationships: inequality in romantic involvement. This can occur, for example, when one partner loves the other more and invests more in the relationship than the other does.

An explanation of the seemingly surprising presence of envy in close relationships, such as in friendship and romantic love, should refer first and foremost to features related to the two major concerns underlying envy: the inferiority and the inequity concerns. In explaining the presence of resentment in such relationships, the inequity concern is more central. These concerns are mostly manifested in the issues of inequality and reciprocal equity.

Many scholars have emphasized the role of equality in friendship. Thus, for Aristotle and many others in ancient Greek society, friendship was ideally a relationship between equals. Aristotle even quotes a popular saying that "friendship is equality." Aristotle also discusses friendship between people of unequal status, but maintains that in this kind of asymmetrical friendship, there must be some proportional exchange of benefits, which bestows a distributive equality upon the relationship (Konstan, 1998).

The presence of equality in status, as well as in background, enables the presence of another essential feature of close relationships; that is, reciprocity. Aristotle argues that the central problem of exchange is that those who are "different and not equal" must somehow "be made equal" (Aristotle, *Nichomacean Ethics,* 1133a16–19). This is a central problem in reciprocal justice: things that are unequal can never be made equal, and things that are incommensurable can never be made strictly commensurable (Gallagher, 2012). This problem is evident in all organizations in which people interact; it is also central in friendship and more so in romantic love.

It is obvious that reciprocal equity is different from mechanistic reciprocity. Mechanistic reciprocity, which is typical of superficial close relationships, involves simple calculations about what one gives and what one gets in a given relationship. It involves the "tit for tat" mentality. People quantify what they do for each other, and decisions about future activities stem from this calculation. Reciprocal equity becomes more complex when taking into account the nature and circumstances of each partner.

Profound love is incompatible with cases in which only one partner sends loving messages and gives presents, while the other completely refrains from reciprocating. It is not the quantity of messages and presents that counts but the symbolic act of sending and giving them. One may be less prone to writing and giving presents, but still express one's love in other ways. A complete absence of profound reciprocity is contrary to profound romantic love. Profound love does not mean giving the partner exactly the same as the partner gives you, but it does mean the presence of love and reciprocity in both partners.

The equity theory clearly demonstrates the significance of reciprocal equity in romantic relationships. Many studies on close relationships in light of this theory have found the following: The more socially desirable that people are (the more attractive, personable, famous, rich, or considerate they are), the more socially desirable they will expect their mate to be; dating couples are more likely to fall in love if they perceive their relationships to be equitable; couples are likely to end up with someone fairly close to themselves in social desirability; couples who perceive their relationships to be equitable are more likely to get sexually involved; equitable relationships are satisfying and comfortable relationships; inequity is associated with distress, guilt, anger, and anxiety; those in equitable relationships are less likely to risk extramarital affairs than those who are not; equitable relationships are more stable than inequitable relationships (Hatfield, Rapson, & Aumer-Ryan, 2008).

It is clear that the nature and the extent of each partner's romantic involvement cannot and should not be identical; but some measure of profound reciprocity should exist in order for neither partner to consider the difference to be unfair, which would give rise to lack of reciprocal equity and hence to resentment. This often has a negative impact upon marital satisfaction and increases the likelihood of a breakup. The consequences of this inequality have been described as an example of the "principle of least interest." The least interested partner is less committed and has more control over the continuation of the relationship. Accordingly, this partner is often (but not always) the one who terminates the relationship (Sprecher et al., 2006; Waller, 1938). The unequal romantic involvement can also be described along the lines of the investment model of relationship commitment. This model posits that satisfaction with, poor quality of alternatives to, and high investment in the current relationship are necessary to foster commitment to an intimate romantic relationship. The causal sequences among these factors go in multiple directions. Thus, commitment may follow from investments in and from the quality of the relationship, and the good quality of alternatives may reduce satisfaction and investment. People with significant satisfaction and poor-quality alternatives are likely to invest more in their current relationship (Lennon et al., 2013; Rusbult, 1983). A relationship involving significant unequal romantic involvement is often a compromise for both partners, as both of them will experience a low level of satisfaction.

Baumeister and Leary (1995) maintain that mutual belongingness is essential if romantic love is to produce bliss. People prefer relationships in which both parties give and receive care; indeed, mutuality strengthens the romantic relationship. Unequal involvement is a strong predictor of romantic breakup. Studies that compared people who received love without giving it and people who gave love without receiving it found that both groups tended to describe the experience as adverse. Baumeister and Leary conclude that, apparently, "Love is highly satisfying and desirable only if it is mutual." Hence, when love "arises without belongingness, as in unrequited love, the result is typically distress and disappointment." Belongingness provides a sense of meaningful quality, rather than of meaningless quantity. The sense of belonging is indeed significant to a meaningful life (Lambert et al., 2013).

Evaluating the parameters of unequal romantic involvements is complex, given the differences in people's personalities and in the manner and pace that they form loving relationships. Equality in status is essential to profound love in which each partner is considered to be autonomous and to deserve to flourish personally. The lack of such equality is likely to reduce satisfaction. However, the presence of equality in status does not imply the necessity of distributive equality, such as an identical share in domestic chores or identical emotional involvement.

Although in profound love romantic involvement can differ in its nature and degree, the gap between the two partners cannot be so significant that one lover will consider her own attitude as one-sided or unrequited love. Partners can invest differently in their loving relationship, but this can be done only if each partner is fully autonomous and the differences in investment do not stem from distorted traditional norms (such as those related to gender), and they indeed reflect significant differences in each partner's personality and unique circumstances. Thus, a study of the division of child-care has found that egalitarianism is associated with more intimate and higher quality relationships than are in traditional gender arrangements. This was expressed in more satisfaction with the division of child-care, higher-quality sexual relationships, lower levels of couple conflict, and higher overall relationship satisfaction (Carlson, Hanson, & Fitzroy, 2016).

Reducing Envy in Romantic Relationships

I have characterized the focus of concern in envy as referring to our undeserved inferiority. Reducing envy in the romantic group (as well as in organizations) should then refer first and foremost to this concern. In this regard, I will discuss two major ways to achieve this: (a) emphasizing the uniqueness of each partner, and (b) being satisfied with having enough (including a good-enough partner), rather than chasing after "the best." Both ways reduce the comparative concern, which is expressed in feeling inferior, and the equity concern, which is manifested in one partner feeling in an undeserved position.

The Importance of Uniqueness

I believe that a central way of dealing with envy in romantic relationships is to emphasize the unique, rather than the exclusive, place of the subject in the romantic group. Such uniqueness considerably reduces the comparative concern and hence the perception of being in a position of undeserved inferiority (Ben-Ze'ev & Goussinsky, 2008; Ben-Ze'ev & Krebs, 2016).

In their discussion of the value of differentiated selves within groups (or organizations), Baumeister and colleagues (2016) argue that "acquiring a unique role within the group can promote belongingness by making oneself irreplaceable." Such a unique role can be attained by realizing the role of differentiated selves within the given group. While the first step in establishing the group emphasizes "shared common identity and promotes emotional bonds," in a later step, "group members take increasingly differentiated roles that improve performance through specialization, moral responsibility, and efficiency" (Baumeister et al., 2016; see also Beach & Tesser, 1993; Beach et al., 1996).

When applying the above view to the small romantic "group" of two lovers, we may say that in the first stage of romantic relationship, attraction is central for promoting emotional bonds and especially romantic intensity. The second stage seeks to enhance the complementary aspects of the two lovers, thereby increasing differentiated roles that improve their overall thriving; this step is an ongoing process that augments romantic profundity. Similarly, organizations might maximize the dimensions that all can feel they contribute to organizational goals.

The following are two major useful ways in which people can enhance the uniqueness of their beloved and thereby make the beloved less replaceable: (a) perceiving the center of the relationship's framework as the *connection* between the two lovers, rather than each lover separately, and (b) evaluating the other person according to her qualities as a worthy *partner*, rather than as a worthy *individual*.

The Romantic Connection. Profound love cannot develop when envy prevails and satisfaction is low, and when hostility, depression, resentment, and the feeling of being romantically compromised are high. Like in other groups and social organizations, a major way of reducing envy in the romantic group is to emphasize the value of the connection for increasing each individual's chance to thrive.

A relevant model of love in this regard is the dialogue model, which has its origins in Aristotle and has been recently significantly developed by Angelika Krebs (Krebs, 2009, 2014a, 2015). In this model, love is not about each partner's having the other as his or her object; rather, love is about what happens between the partners. It is dialogical. Lovers share what is important in their emotional and practical lives. In loving somebody, you enlarge yourself through closely interacting with and responding to the other person. We do not flourish in isolation; our nature is social. In shared activities, the parties are integrated into a (psychological) whole, which is more than the sum total of two individual actions. In optimally shared activities, both participants contribute (though not necessarily in the same way or to the same extent), and their contributions fit together to actualize the common good (Krebs, 2015). As Rusbult and Buunk nicely put it, "Over time partners may come to think as a unit; they may come to experience the world in cognitive concert" (1993, p. 185; see also Kelley & Thibaut, 1978).

The dialogue model considers the connection between the two lovers to be at the focus of love, and the basic features of the connection are shared emotional states and joint activities; the connection amplifies the thriving of each lover as well as the flourishing of their relationship. If each partner is a necessary factor in contributing to the flourishing of their togetherness, their reciprocal interaction is at the heart of the relationship, and the comparative issue is of lesser concern. Accordingly, envy is less likely to emerge.

Worthy Partner Rather Than Worthy Person. When the romantic connection is at the heart of profound love, the search for such love should not focus on the qualities of a perfect (or at least worthy) *person*, but rather on the perfect (or at least worthy) *partner* who is suitable and compatible for building a flourishing relationship with the subject. The major flaw in the search for a perfect person is that it fails to take account of the type of connection between the would-be couple—which is constitutive of profound love. There are, of course, other people "who are objectively better" and whom you may adore more; however, these people may not love you the way your equal does, and accordingly, they are likely to be less satisfying romantic partners for you. Yearning for them is futile and destructive and generates romantic compromises (Ben-Ze'ev, 2011).

When the person's characteristic as a partner is at the focus of lovers' concern, and each partner is unique and necessary for their common flourishing (which also includes the personal flourishing of each), comparison is harder to do and is of lesser significance; in such circumstances, the issue of undeserved inferiority; hence, envy is hardly of any relevance.

Conclusion

I have suggested that envy is mainly concerned with our undeserved inferiority. Both the comparative and equity concerns are significant in envy and can refer to the subject's comparison with the partner and with other possible romantic partners. Coping with envy within the romantic group should address these two concerns. I have argued that emphasizing the subjects' uniqueness in the romantic group, and in particular their joint thriving, is crucial in this regard. A few useful attitudes that enhance the recognition of the agent's uniqueness are: viewing the connection as the focus of love, evaluating the other person mainly as a partner rather than as a separate individual, and aiming at a sufficient level of baseline reciprocity rather than aiming at mechanistic equality. Envy may be present in various romantic relationships, but its emergence and intensity depend, among other things, upon the nature of the love that we develop. Thus, envy is typically absent in profound love.

Acknowledgments

I am grateful to Angelika Krebs for her major contribution to shaping central ideas in this chapter. I also thank David Heyd for discussions concerning the nature of deservingness in envy. I am indebted to Richard Smith for his many wise comments in our conversations and correspondence. I also thank the other two editors, Michelle Duffy and Ugo Merlone, for their most valuable comments, which have considerably improved the text.

References

Anderson, E. S. (1999). What is the point of equality? *Ethics, 109*, 287–337.

Aristotle (1984). *The Complete Works of Aristotle: The Revised Oxford translation.* (J. Barnes, Ed.). Princeton, NJ: Princeton University Press.

Baumeister, R. F., Ainsworth, S. E., & Vohs, K. D. (2016). Are groups more or less than the sum of their members? The moderating role of individual identification. *Behavioral and Brain Sciences, 39.*

Baumeister R. F., & Leary M. R. (1995). The need to belong: Desire for interpersonal attachments as a fundamental human motivation. *Psychological Bulletin, 117,* 497–529.

Beach, S. R. H., & Tesser, A. (1993). Decision making power and marital satisfaction: A self-evaluation maintenance perspective. *Journal of Social and Clinical Psychology, 12,* 471–494.

Beach, S. R. H., Tesser, A., Mendolia, M., Anderson, P., Crelia, R., Whitaker, D. G., Fincham, F. D.. (1996). Self-evaluation maintenance in marriage: Toward a performance ecology of the marital relationship. *Journal of Family Psychology, 10,* 379–396.

Ben-Ze'ev, A. (1992). Envy and inequality. *Journal of Philosophy, 89,* 551–581.

Ben-Ze'ev, A. (2000). *The Subtlety of Emotions.* Cambridge, MA: MIT Press.

Ben-Ze'ev, A. (2010). Jealousy and romantic love. In S. Hart and M. Legerstee, Eds., *Handbook of Jealousy: Theories, Principles, and Multidisciplinary Approaches* (pp. 40–54). Chichester, UK: Wiley-Blackwell.

Ben-Ze'ev, A. (2011). The nature and morality of romantic compromises. In C. Bagnoli, Ed., *Morality and the Emotions* (pp. 95–114). Oxford, UK: Oxford University Press.

Ben-Ze'ev, A., & Goussinsky, R. (2008). *In the Name of Love: Romantic Ideology and Its Victims.* Oxford, UK: Oxford University Press.

Ben-Ze'ev, A., & Krebs, A. (2016). The unique role of the agent within the romantic group. *Behavioral and Brain Sciences, 39.*

Buunk, D., & Van Yperen, N. W. (1991). Referential comparisons, relational comparisons, and exchange orientation: Their relation to marital satisfaction. *Personality and Social Psychology Bulletin, 17,* 709–717.

Carlson, D. L., Hanson, S., & Fitzroy, A. (2016). The division of childcare, sexual intimacy, and relationship quality in couples. *Gender & Society, 30,* 442–466.

Cialdini, R. B., Borden, R. J., Thorne, A., & Sloan, L. R. (1976). Basking in reflected glory: Three (football) field studies. *Journal of Personality and Social Psychology, 34,* 366–375.

Crosby, F. (1976). A model of egoistical relative deprivation. *Psychological Review, 83,* 85–113.

Crusius, J., & Lange, J., (2014). What catches the envious eye? Attentional biases within malicious and benign envy. *Journal of Experimental Social Psychology, 55,* 1–11.

Descartes, R. (1649/1984). The passions of the soul. In J. Cottingham, R. Stoothoff, & D. Murdoch (Trans.), *The Philosophical Writings of Descartes*. Cambridge, UK: Cambridge University Press.

Drigotas, S. M., & Rusbult, C. E. (1992). Should I stay or should I go? A dependence model of breakups. *Journal of Personality and Social Psychology*, *62*, 62–87.

Duffy, M. K., Scott, K. L., Shaw, J. D., Tepper, B. J., & Aquino, K. (2012). A social context model of envy and social undermining. *Academy of Management Journal*, *55*, 643–666.

Elster, J. (1991). Envy in social life. In R. Seckhauser, Ed., *Strategy and Choices* (pp. 49–82). Cambridge, MA: MIT Press.

Evelyn-White, H. G. (1914). *Hesiod, the Homeric Hymns, and Homerica*. London: Loeb Classical Library.

Farrell, D., & Rusbult, C. E. (1981). Exchange variables as predictors of job satisfaction, job commitment, and turnover: The impact of rewards, costs, alternatives, and investments. *Organizational Behavior and Human Performance*, *27*, 78–95.

Fitness, J., & Fletcher, G. J. O. (1993). Love, hate, anger and jealousy in close relationships: A prototype and cognitive appraisal analysis. *Journal of Personality and Social Psychology*, *65*, 942–958.

Folger, R., & Cropanzano, R. (2001). Fairness theory: Justice as accountability. In J. Greenberg & R. Cropanzano, Eds., *Advances in Organizational Justice, 1*, 1–55. Palo Alto, CA: Stanford University Press.

Forste, R., & Tanfer, K. (1996). Sexual exclusivity among dating, cohabiting, and married women. *Journal of Marriage and the Family*, *56*, 33–47.

Frank, R. H. (2006). When it comes to a search for a spouse, supply and demand is only the start. *New York Times*, Buisness Section, Dec. 21, 2006.

Frankfurt, H. G. (1988). Equality as a moral ideal. In *The Importance of What We Care About*. Cambridge, UK: Cambridge University Press.

Gallagher, R. L. (2012). Incommensurability in Aristotle's theory of reciprocal justice. *British Journal for the History of Philosophy*, *20*, 667–701.

Hatfield, E., Rapson, R. L., & Aumer-Ryan, K. (2008). Social justice in love relationships: Recent developments. *Social Justice Research*, *21*, 413–431.

Hatfield, E., Traupmann, J., Sprecher, S., Utne, M., & Hay, J. (1985). Equity and intimate relationships: Recent research. In W. Ickes, Ed., *Compatible and Incompatible Relationships* (pp. 91–117). New York: Springer.

Hatfield, E., Walster, G. W., & Berscheid, E. (1978). *Equity: Theory and Research*. Boston, MA: Allyn and Bacon.

Impett, E. A., & Gordon, A. (2008). For the good of others: Toward a positive psychology of sacrifice. In S. J. Lopez, Ed., *Positive Psychology: Exploring the Best in People* (pp. 79–100). Westport, CT: Greenwood.

Johnson, D. J., & Rusbult, C. E. (1989). Resisting temptation: Devaluation of alternative partners as a means of maintaining commitment in close relationships. *Journal of Personality and Social Psychology*, *57*, 967–980.

Kelley, H. H., & Thibaut, J. W. (1978). *Interpersonal Relations: A Theory of Interdependence*. New York: Wiley.

Konstan, D. (1998). Reciprocity and friendship. In C. Gill, N. Postlethwaite, & R. Seaford Eds., *Reciprocity in Ancient Greece* (pp. 279–301). Oxford, UK: Clarendon Press.

Krebs, A. (2002). *Arbeit und Liebe. Die philosophischen Grundlagen sozialer Gerechtigkeit [The philosophical foundations of social justice]*. Frankfurt, Germany: Suhrkamp.

Krebs, A. (2009). Wie ein Bogenstrich, der aus zwei Saiten eine Stimme zieht. Eine dialogische Philosophie der Liebe [Like a single bow, drawing out from two strings but one voice. A dialogical philosophy of love]. *Deutsche Zeitschrift für Philosophie, 57*, 729–743.

Krebs, A. (2014a). Between I and Thou—On the dialogical nature of love. In C. Maurer, T. Milligan, & K. Pacovská, Eds., *Love and Its Objects*. London: Palgrave Macmillan.

Krebs, A. (2014b). Why landscape beauty matters. *Land, 3*, 1251–1269.

Krebs, A. (2015). *Zwischen Ich und Du. Eine dialogische Philosophie der Liebe [Between I and Thou. A dialogical philosophy of love]*. Frankfurt, Germany: Suhrkamp.

Lange, J., & Crusius, J. (2015). Dispositional envy revisited: Unraveling the motivational dynamics of benign and malicious envy. *Personality and Social Psychology Bulletin, 41*, 284–294.

Lambert, N., Stillman, T. F., Hicks, J. A., Kamble, S., Baumeiter, R. F., & Fincham, F. D. (2013). Belong is to matter: Sense of belonging enhances meaning in life. *Personality and Social Psychology Bulletin, 39*, 1418–1427.

Lennon, C. A., Stewart, A. L., & Ledermann, T. (2013). The role of power in intimate relationships. *Journal of Social and Personal Relationships, 30*, 95–114.

Miller, D. (1995): Complex equality. In D. Miller & M. Walzer, Eds., *Pluralism, justice and equality* (pp. 197–225). Oxford, UK: Oxford University Press.

Murray, S. L., Rose, P., Holmes, J. G., Derrick, J., Podchaski, E. J., Bellavia, G., & Griffin, D. W. (2005). Putting the partner within reach: A dyadic perspective on felt security in close relationships. *Journal of Personality and Social Psychology, 88*, 327–347.

Narveson, J. (1997). Egalitarianism: Partial, counterproductive and baseless. *Ratio, 10*, 280–295.

Neu, J. (2000). Jealous thoughts. In J. Neu, *A Tear Is an Intellectual Thing* (pp. 41–67). Oxford, UK: Oxford University Press.

Nozick, R. (1974). *Anarchy, State and Utopia*. Oxford, UK: Blackwell.

Nussbaum, M. (2013). *Political Emotions: Why Love Matters for Justice*. Cambridge, MA: Harvard University Press.

Oz, A. (2013). *Between Friends*. London: Chatto & Windus.

Parfit, D. (1998). Equality and priority. In A. Mason, Ed., *Ideals of Equality*. Oxford, UK: Blackwell.

Parrott, W. G., & Smith, R. H. (1993). Distinguishing the experiences of envy and jealousy. *Journal of Personality and Social Psychology, 64*, 906–920.

Pepper, A., Gosling, T., Gore, J. (2015). Fairness, envy, guilt and greed: Building equity considerations into agency theory. *Human Relations, 68*, 1291–1314.

Prins, K. S., Buunk, B. P., & Van Yperen, N. W. (1993). Equity, normative disapproval and extramarital relationships. *Journal of Social and Personal Relationships, 10*, 39–53.

Raz, J. (1986). *The Morality of Freedom*. Oxford, UK: Oxford University Press.

Rusbult, C. E. (1983). A longitudinal test of the Investment Model: The development (and deterioration) of satisfaction and commitment in heterosexual involvements. *Journal of Personality and Social Psychology, 45*, 101–117.

Rusbult, C. E., Buunk, B. P. (1993). Commitment processes in close relationships: An interdependence analysis. *Journal of Social and Personal Relationships*, *10*, 175–204.

Rusbult, C. E., & Farrell, D. (1983). A longitudinal test of the investment model: The impact on job satisfaction, job commitment, and turnover of variations in rewards, costs, alternatives, and investments. *Journal of Applied Psychology*, *68*, 429–438.

Salovey, P., & Rodin, J. (1991). Provoking jealousy and envy: Domain relevance and self-esteem threat. *Journal of Social and Clinical Psychology*, *10*, 395–413.

Smith, A. (1759). *The Theory of Moral Sentiments*. Indianapolis, IN: Liberty Classics.

Smith, R. H., & Kim, S. H. (2007). Comprehending envy. *Psychological Bulletin*, *133*, 46–64.

Smith, R. H., Kim, S. H., & Parrott, W. G. (1988). Envy and jealousy: Semantic problems and experiential distinctions. *Personality and Social Psychology Bulletin*, *14*, 401–409.

Smith, R. H., Parrott, W. G., Ozer, D., & Moniz, A. (1994). Subjective injustice and inferiority as predictors of hostile and depressive feelings in envy. *Personality and Social Psychology Bulletin*, *20*, 705–711.

Spinoza, B. (1677). Ethics. In E. Curley, Ed., *The Collected Works of Spinoza* (408–617). Princeton, NJ: Princeton University Press.

Sprecher, S., Schmeeckle, M., & Felmlee, D. (2006). The principle of least interest: Inequality in emotional involvement. *Journal of Family Issues*, *27*, 1255–1280.

Stouffer, S. A., Suchman, E. A., DeVinney, L. C., Starr, S. A., & Williams, R. M. (1949a). *The American Soldier: Adjustment to Army Life. Vol. II*. Princeton, NJ: Princeton University Press.

Stouffer, S. A., Lumsdaine, A. A., Lumsdaine, M. H., Williams, R. M., Williams, Jr., R. M., Smith, B., et al. (1949b). *The American Soldier: Combat and Its Aftermath. Vol. II*. Princeton, NJ: Princeton University Press.

Taris, T. W., Peeters, M. C. W., Le Blanc, P. M., Schreurs, P. J. G., & Schaufeli, W. B. (2001). From inequity to burnout: The role of job stress. *Journal of Occupational Health Psychology*, *6*, 303–323.

Tesser, A. (1988). Toward a self-evaluation maintenance model of social behavior. In L. Berkowitz, Ed., *Advances in Experimental Social Psychology* (pp. 181–227). New York: Academic Press.

Thibaut, J. W., & Kelley, H. H. (1959). *The Social Psychology of Groups*. New York: Wiley.

van de Ven, N., Zeelenberg, M., & Pieters, R. (2009). Leveling up and down: The experience of benign and malicious envy. *Emotion*, *3*, 419–429.

van de Ven, N., Zeelenberg, M., & Pieters, R. (2011). Why envy outperforms admiration. *Personality and Social Psychology Bulletin*, *37*, 784–795.

Waller, W. (1938). *The Family: A Dynamic Interpretation*. New York: Gordon.

Whelan, C. B. (2006). *Why Smart Men Marry Smart Women*. New York: Simon & Schuster.

19 | The Benefits and Threats from Being Envied in Organizations

W. GERROD PARROTT

Introduction

If envy's effects were contained within a single envious person, there would be little reason for the present volume about envy in organizations. It is envy's influence on interpersonal dyads and groups that makes it relevant to organizations and the workplace. Although it certainly makes sense to analyze the perspective of the envious individual, envy's social aspects are evident even at the individual level of analysis: its appraisal involves social comparison; its action tendencies include emulation, social avoidance, and hostility. Envy involves interactions and relationships, and thus organizations. The present chapter focuses on a particularly interesting subset of those who are affected by envy; namely, on the person who is the target of the envy. Envy, even the mere possibility of envy, places the enviable person in a complex and delicate social situation that brings both costs and benefits (Parrott & Rodriguez Mosquera, 2008).

It is a relatively common experience to feel that one is the target of envy. Even small discrepancies can be enviable, and the reasons for being envied are nearly limitless. Within the organization, invidious social comparisons can be based on countless dimensions. Promotions and salaries certainly can attract envy, as can awards, compliments, and other forms of favorable recognition. But there is a multitude of other ways that a person can be perceived as enjoying advantages. Offices can be bigger or brighter and can have better windows or nicer furnishings; travel can be more pleasant or more generously subsidized; workloads can be less onerous or more prestigious. Supervisors can appear to favor certain workers. Newer members may envy the established status and institutional knowledge of longer-term members, who may in turn envy the special treatment accorded to newer members. Those with young children may envy how those less encumbered can take on special projects or travel, while those without family obligations may envy the leniency granted to those whose departures from work have the unselfish excuse of child-care. Because envy can be intensified when social comparisons are otherwise equal, the enviable are not restricted to those at the top of the organization; envy can be even more intense when directed horizontally within organizational levels than it is when directed from lower to higher levels. Finally, the grounds for envy are not restricted to organization-specific circumstances. Personality, happiness, skills, appearance, wealth, health, leisure—all the traits, experiences, and possessions that elicit envy outside the organization may also attract it within. Thus, far from being limited to a few extreme outperformers, the majority of people in any organization are susceptible to being the targets of envy.

This chapter explores how envy affects those who are envied. The first section presents theories and issues that frame this topic. The following three sections address the pleasurable aspects of being envied, the social difficulties that it causes, the ways it threatens the envied person, and the strategies for coping with other persons' envy. Each of these sections will consider recent research that addresses the social and emotional consequences of being the target of envy, with an emphasis on research that considers envy in organizations.

The Perspective of the Envied Person

Envy, from the perspective of the envied person, has both positive and negative implications. Being the target of envy can be a good thing in the sense that it means that another person perceives the envied person as being superior with respect to a characteristic that is desirable enough to care about. Envy therefore delivers good news by communicating or confirming that one is superior in some way; it brings an acknowledgement that one's good qualities are recognized by others; it suggests that one has achieved a degree of status or good reputation.

At the same time, being the target of envy can have negative implications. Superiority can disrupt relationships that were grounded on equality. Envious people can be unhappy, dissatisfied, resentful, or hostile, and the target of envy may not only feel bad about being responsible for those effects but may also feel threatened by them. Advantages that are perceived as being unfair may elicit additional discontent and hostility.

In an exploratory study, my colleagues and I asked university students in the United States and Spain to remember and describe a time when they believed that another person may have envied them. We asked them to specify what was envied, who was envious, what signs of envy were noticed, how they reacted to the envy, and whether there were any positive or negative implications (Rodriguez Mosquera, Parrott, & Hurtado de Mendoza, 2010). Examination of these accounts provides an informative picture of the range of experiences that follow from being the target of envy. There was considerable overlap between the accounts from the two cultures (although some differences did emerge, which will be discussed later in this chapter). Given that the reports came from students, it is unsurprising that the most frequent reason for being envied was academic achievement. More surprising was the next-most-common reason, which was to be envied for having multiple advantages that together seemed to constitute a better life that is filled with more fun and fewer worries. Other common causes of envy included having a noteworthy talent, being recognized for an impressive accomplishment, having a better love life, and being more attractive. There did not appear to be any necessity for the causes of envy to have a zero-sum quality; some did (such as winning a particular award, or getting the lead role in a play), but there were plenty of others that had a non-zero-sum nature (such as having many friends, or getting a high score on an exam).

Envy typically was directed toward a person who was similar to the envious person: in almost all cases, the envious person was someone who was known by the target of the envy, such as a friend, fellow student, or roommate, and usually the envious person and the target of the envy were of the same sex (Rodriguez Mosquera et al., 2010). The targets of envy were able to describe why they perceived envy; it was usually a deviation from the behavior that would be expected. Most common was a decrease in friendliness (such as social withdrawal or decreased generosity) or a bitter, critical, or sarcastic remark (either directly or in the form of hostile gossip). In other cases, it was a change in talkativeness that seemed to betray envy, either by falling silent or becoming excessively talky. Sometimes the envious person flat out said, "I envy you." Respondents were not usually able to identify a particular facial expression or nonverbal gesture that signaled envy, although they did sometimes report that they detected an envious expression without specifying what it was.

The most common reaction to being envied was appeasement. Our respondents reported being extra nice to the envious person, giving him or her encouragement, and downplaying their advantage. Another strategy was to repair any damage to the relationship by apologizing, showing sympathy, or conversing. Deflecting attention from the advantage by changing the subject or telling a joke was sometimes tried. In some cases the target of envy distanced themselves from the envious person. It was rare (but not unheard of) for the target of envy to try to increase the envy by drawing attention to their advantage, and gloating.

Respondents in this exploratory study described both positive and negative implications of being the target of envy. The desirable effect that was mentioned most often was increased self-confidence. The most commonly mentioned undesirable effects were interpersonal; respondents worried about damage to the relationship, possibly leading to social isolation and rejection. In sum, these accounts suggest that being the target of envy in everyday life is an ambivalent experience, with the potential for both positive and negative consequences (Rodriguez Mosquera et al., 2010).

Useful frameworks for understanding this array of ambivalent experiences have been provided by research in anthropology, social psychology, and the psychology of emotion. In a classic essay on envy, anthropologist George Foster (1972) characterized envy's positive and negative consequences as falling along two axes. One, the *competitive axis*, involves increased status for the envied person and increased motivation for the envious person. The other, the *fear axis*, involves threats and ill-will that tend to be denied by the envious person but nevertheless motivate the envied person to seek protection. Foster's scheme is relevant to the present chapter in that he considers the target of envy as well as the envious person and points out the mixture of positive and negative implications that face the person who is the target.

The ambivalent position of an envied person has also been addressed in the social psychological literature on social comparison. Exline and Lobel (1999) developed a framework for understanding the range of emotions and motivations that are aroused by being the target of upward social comparisons, which includes not only those being envied but more generally those being perceived as having superior status. Those who compare well to others make downward comparisons that elicit positive affect by satisfying competitive and self-enhancement desires and by relieving anxieties about status and adequacy. Pleasure, reassurance, and pride are among the emotions experienced by outperformers. These positive responses are validated and strengthened by signs (such as envy) indicating that other people also perceive the outperformer's superiority. Yet, positive affect is not the only outcome of downward social comparisons. Exline and Lobel (1999) argued that distress arises when a person is the target of an upward comparison: the superior person may feel sorry for the inferior person's unhappiness, and may feel guilty about being the cause; there can be awkwardness and embarrassment surrounding the relationship with the inferior person; and there can be genuine concern about losing the other's sympathy and cooperation, as well as worry about becoming resented or disliked, and fear of being subjected to hostility and retaliation.

Being the target of envy thus has the potential to elicit a wide range of reactions. Of the many factors that influence which of these reactions will occur on any particular occasion, the most fundamental is the nature of the envy itself. In everyday language, the term *envy* is applied to a variety of reactions. In several studies, I solicited autobiographical accounts of naturally occurring experiences of envy from several hundred American undergraduate students (Parrott & Smith, 1993; Smith, Parrott, Ozer, & Moniz, 1994). Although certain situational features were consistently present— the students always described a situation in which the respondent focused on another person who was superior in a respect that was important—the emotions experienced clearly varied. Certain common emotional components can be identified (Parrott, 1991). Often the students reported longing for what another person had; the longing sometimes seemed wistful, and other times frustrating. In some reports, the envy seemed to spring from a focus on the envious person's sense of inferiority, which led to emotions such as sadness (about lacking what another person so conspicuously enjoyed), anxiety (about insecure social status), and despair (about the hopelessness of ever possessing what the envied person possessed). Some reports included significant elements of hostility. The target of envy might be resented for their superiority, which might be perceived as unfair. This resentment might result only in reduced sympathy for the target, but it could take on more serious forms, ranging from cooling a friendship to active dislike or hatred of the target. Some accounts indicated that the envious person tried to resist such hostility; the person might try to direct their frustration away from the target of envy and instead blame the unfairness of circumstances and events; some people reported feeling guilty about their feelings of ill-will.

In a minority of reports, what people described as *envy* actually had a hopeful quality in which the target of envy provided an example of how to achieve a desirable result and inspired motivation to do likewise. No account of envy consisted solely of this reaction—an episode that did would probably be better labeled as admiration—but these hopeful, admiring feelings were occasionally reported as part of an episode of envy that included one or more of the other responses described above.

In sum, people report a variety of distinguishable emotions when asked to report an experience of envy. It is not uncommon for a report to include more than one of these emotions, so it therefore is helpful to think of envy as an episode having a narrative structure (Parrott, 1991).

The variety of reactions subsumed by the term *envy* means that the everyday concept allows for a troublesome degree of ambiguity, which scholars have long attempted to clarify by imposing some distinctions. Moral philosophers frequently distinguish envy that is immoral from envy that is morally acceptable. Rawls (1971) therefore distinguished morally acceptable *benign envy* from immoral *envy proper*, whereas Neu (1980) distinguished *admiring envy* from *malicious envy*, and Taylor (1988) distinguished *admiring* and *emulating* forms of envy from *malicious* envy. Psychologists, more concerned with emotional distinctions than with moral ones, have distinguished types of envy on that basis. Smith et al. (1994), for example, found that envious hostility (including anger, dislike, and hatred) was strongly linked to beliefs that the target's envy-producing advantage was unfair, whereas envious sadness (including feeling depressed, lacking energy, and low) was strongly linked to beliefs that the target's superiority gave rise to a sense of personal inferiority. It is noteworthy that forms of envy in which psychologically hostile elements predominate have some correspondence to what philosophers deem malicious and immoral, whereas forms in which inferiority predominate more resemble what philosophers deem benign and moral.

In recent years psychologists have demonstrated that these distinctions are recognized in everyday life and are even given distinct labels in some natural languages. Van de Ven, Zeelenberg, and Pieters (2009) demonstrated reliable differences in Dutch undergraduates' reports of *afgunst* (a Dutch word meaning "malicious envy") and *benijden* (meaning "benign envy"): reports of *afgunst* averaged higher belief that injustice had been done; higher feelings of frustration; stronger urges to harm, degrade, speak negatively of, and take from others; and greater hope that the target of envy would meet with some failure. In contrast, reports of *benijden* on average involved more admiration of the target, stronger motivation to engage in self-improvement, stronger urges to compliment and be near the target, and greater hope that the target would do well and be a friend. These researchers then demonstrated that people whose languages do not make this distinction nevertheless describe their experiences of envy in ways consistent with the Dutch distinction between *benijden* and *afgunst*. Latent class analysis was applied to ratings of actual experiences of *envy* in the United States and of *envidia* in Spain to demonstrate that similar distinctions could be made even in cultures where the language did not supply separate labels.

From the perspective of the person who is the target of envy, it should make a big difference whether the envy is of a malicious or benign form. The interpersonal consequences of winning a desirable assignment or being singled out for praise are very different if one's colleagues wish one harm than if they wish to become one's friend! The remainder of this chapter will review research on the effects of envy on the target, with an emphasis on envy in organizations. This survey will show that that there is evidence for both enjoyment and discomfort at being the target of envy. In some cases it will be clear that the type of envy being expressed helps determine the relative balance between the desirability and threat that are presented. But in many cases researchers have not clearly specified whether benign or malignant envy is being studied, and it is worth noting that this ambiguity does not necessarily decrease the value of the research—it is not necessarily clear to the target of envy which form of envy is occurring. It is true that in recent years the existence of two or more forms of envy has been increasingly accepted by researchers, and that things will be learned by making this distinction in future research. Nevertheless, the target of envy is not always in a position to know whether their superiority will elicit benign or malicious envy. Sometimes envy is anticipated, not observed. Sometimes the expression of envy will not disambiguate which form is occurring. Sometimes there are multiple envious individuals, and the presence of benign envy in one cannot rule out the occurrence of malicious envy in others. Finally, nothing about the research demonstrating the existence of two types of envy precludes the possibility that a single envious person cannot vacillate between one form of envy and another. For these reasons, research that examines envy without specifying whether it is benign or malicious may well accurately capture the perspective of a person who is the target of envy.

The Pleasurable Aspects of Being Envied

A large body of research shows that downward social comparisons are pleasurable (Smith, 2000). The question is whether that pleasure persists when the downward comparison is made toward a person who is envying upward. Evidence suggests that the pleasure can remain, that it may even be reinforced by the addition of envy, but that it often is reduced by envy. The effect of envy on the pleasure of downward comparisons depends on many variables: circumstances, psychological and cultural characteristics of the target of envy, the relationship between the envier and the target, and the way that envy is expressed.

In one study, European-American university students in the United States and Spanish university students in Spain were asked to read vignettes describing common envy scenarios written from the point of view of the person being envied (Rodriguez Mosquera et al., 2010). One vignette involved winning a prestigious internship, while the other involved living a fulfilling, friendship-filled life at a prestigious university; in both vignettes there was another character who desired the advantage and at the end of the vignette watched the envied person enjoying it. Neither vignette used the word "envy" or described the thoughts and feelings of either character; instead, participants in the study were asked to imagine the situation vividly and then report the thoughts and feelings that each character would probably have and the coping strategies they would be likely to employ.

The results showed that the targets of envy would be expected to experience an element of pleasure. Both vignettes were evaluated as producing substantial levels of pride and self-confidence in the enviable person, as well as moderate levels of feeling good due to having something that someone else desires.

This study explored some of the variables that influence the pleasantness of being envied. Culture is one. In the vignette study just described, the American respondents, when compared to respondents in Spain, expected the target of envy to feel pleasant responses more intensely: more pride, more self-confidence, and more self-affirmation from having something that someone else covets. Intriguingly, however, the Americans also expected the target of envy to feel negative emotions more strongly: they expected the target of envy to feel more guilt and to worry more about being disliked. In short, the Americans expected the experience of being the target of envy to be more intensely ambivalent than did the Spaniards.

This cultural difference makes sense in light of other beliefs reported in this study. Americans anticipated more negative responses from the envious person than the Spaniards did; on average, the Americans expected the envious person to direct more anger and ill will toward them, as well as to feel more inferior. The Spaniards, in contrast, had greater expectation than the Americans that the envious person would feel happy for them. One interpretation of these findings is that one might characterize the Spaniards